THI
NAVY LIST

1996

Corrected to 31st March 1996
(See Notes on page iii)

LONDON; THE STATIONERY OFFICE

ISBN: 0 11 772825 X

The Navy List is compiled and published by order of the Defence Council for the convenience of the Naval Service, but as errors may occasionally occur the Council must expressly reserve the right to determine the status of any Officer according to the actual circumstances of the case, independently of any entry in the Navy List

By Command of the Defence Council,

RICHARD MOTTRAM

Printed in the United Kingdom for The Stationery Office
Dd302955 10/96 C28 G3397 10170

PREFACE

The Navy List is on sale to the public and is published annually in July or as soon as possible thereafter. The Navy List of Retired Officers, also on sale to the public, is published separately and biennially in August

The sections containing largely static data will be published in the next (2000) edition of the Navy List and every subsequent fifth year. The last edition to contain this information was the 1995 edition of the Navy List.

Although not due for update until the year 2000, Information concerning "The Admiralty and Commercial Court of England and Wales and Legal Advisers to The Admiralty Board" has been updated within this edition from the 1995 issue.

This edition of the Navy List has been produced largely from the information held in the Naval Manpower Management Information System and is corrected to include those promotions, appointments etc. promulgated on or before 31 March 1996 as becoming effective on or before 30 June 1996. Section 1 is corrected as far as possible, up to the date of going to press.

Serving officers who notice errors or omissions in Sections 2 and 3 of the List should advise their Appointer. Other errors or omissions should be brought to the attention of the Editor of the Navy List. Any other reader who notices errors or omissions is invited to write to:

The Editor of the Navy List
2SL/CNH
Room **3061**
Centurion Building
Grange Road
Gosport
Hampshire
PO13 9XA

quoting the page(s) in question. Every effort will be made to include corrections and omissions received by the Editor before 28 March. Regrettably, letters cannot be acknowledged.

Officers who succeed to peerages, baronetcies or courtesy titles should notify their appointer so that their computer records can be updated and the changes reflected in the Navy List. The degrees shown after Active Service Officers' names are not necessarily a complete list of those held, but are generally confined to degrees of an honorary nature conferred specially upon an Officer, and those that are so related to the professional duties of an Officer as to give some indication of his professional qualifications.

iv

The master Allowance List for the free distribution of the Navy List is controlled by the Editor. CSE 1e at Llangennech is responsible for the issue of this publication strictly according to the Allowance List. Units are asked to ensure that the Editor and CSE1e are informed of any reduction in requirement. Requests for additional copies and amendment to the master Allowance List should be addressed to CSE1e at Llangennech (using RN Form 53001(Demand for Naval Books)). Firmly attached to this demand should be a letter addressed to the Editor with a clear supporting case.

CONTENTS

CONTENTS

The Queen

LORD HIGH ADMIRAL OF THE UNITED KINGDOM
___

MEMBERS OF THE ROYAL FAMILY

HIS ROYAL HIGHNESS THE PRINCE PHILIP DUKE OF EDINBURGH KG, KT, OM, GBE, AC, QSO

Admiral of the Fleet . . . . 15 Jan 53
Captain General Royal Marines . . . . 1 Jun 53
Admiral of the Fleet Royal Australian Navy . . . . 1 Apr 54
Admiral of the Fleet Royal New Zealand Navy . . . . 15 Jan 53
Admiral of the Royal Canadian Sea Cadets . . . . 15 Jan 53

HER MAJESTY QUEEN ELIZABETH THE QUEEN MOTHER

Commandant in Chief for Women in the Royal Navy . . . . 1 Aug 39

HIS ROYAL HIGHNESS THE PRINCE OF WALES KG, KT, GCB, AK, QSO, ADC

Captain, Royal Navy . . . . 14 Nov 88

HIS ROYAL HIGHNESS THE DUKE OF YORK, CVO, ADC

Lieutenant Commander, Royal Navy . . . . 1 Feb 92
Admiral of the Sea Cadet Corps . . . . 11 May 92

HER ROYAL HIGHNESS THE PRINCESS ROYAL KG, GCVO

Rear Admiral Chief Commandant for Women in the Royal Navy . . . . 1 Jul 74

HIS ROYAL HIGHNESS PRINCE MICHAEL OF KENT KCVO

Honorary Commodore Royal Naval Reserve . . . . 1 Apr 94

HER ROYAL HIGHNESS PRINCESS ALEXANDRA, THE HON LADY OGILVY GCVO

Patron, Queen Alexandra's Royal Naval Nursing Service . . . . 12 Nov 55

___

VICE ADMIRAL OF THE UNITED KINGDOM AND LIEUTENANT OF
THE ADMIRALTY
Admiral Sir James Eberle, GCB

REAR ADMIRAL OF THE UNITED KINGDOM
Admiral Sir Nicholas Hunt, GCB, LVO

PERSONAL AIDES-DE-CAMP TO THE QUEEN
Captain His Royal Highness The Prince of Wales KG, KT, GCB, AK, QSO

Lieutenant Commander His Royal Highness The Duke of York, CVO

FIRST AND PRINCIPAL NAVAL AIDE-DE-CAMP TO THE QUEEN

Admiral Sir Jock Slater, GCB, LVO . . . . 10 Jul 95

FLAG AIDE-DE-CAMP TO THE QUEEN

Admiral Sir Michael Boyce, KCB, OBE . . . . 25 May 95

NAVAL AIDES-DE-CAMP TO THE QUEEN

Captain S. E. Saunders (Commodore)	Appointed 11 Nov 95	Seniority	31 Dec 88
Captain A. P. Masterton-Smith (Commodore)	Appointed 27 Oct 95	Seniority	31 Dec 88
Captain A. E. Slater	Appointed 21 Apr 94	Seniority	30 Jun 87
Captain I. R. Henderson CBE (Commodore)	Appointed 06 Mar 96	Seniority	31 Dec 89
Captain J. A. Beynon (Commodore)	Appointed 04 Feb 95	Seniority	30 Jun 88
Captain J. Band	Appointed 09 Apr 95	Seniority	30 Jun 88
Captain H. W. Rickard CBE (Commodore)	Appointed 11 Oct 95	Seniority	30 Jun 89
Captain J. A. Burch CBE (Commodore)	Appointed 01 Jun 96	Seniority	30 Jun 89

ROYAL MARINE AIDE-DE-CAMP TO THE QUEEN

Brigadier R. E. Dillon . . . . Appointed 6 Dec 94   *Seniority* 31 Dec 92

EXTRA NAVAL EQUERRIES TO THE QUEEN

Vice Admiral Sir Peter Ashmore, KCB, KCVO, DSC
Rear Admiral Sir Richard Trowbridge, KCVO
Rear Admiral Sir Paul Greening, GCVO
Rear Admiral Sir John Garnier, KCVO, CBE
Rear Admiral Sir Robert Woodard. KCVO

ROYAL NAVAL RESERVE AIDES-DE-CAMP TO THE QUEEN

Captain G. D. MacDonald RD* (Commodore) . . . Appointed 1 Jan 96   *Seniority* 1 May 91
Captain M. E. Hocking RD* . . . . Appointed 1 Jan 95   *Seniority* 30 Sep 92

ROYAL MARINE RESERVE AIDE-DE-CAMP TO THE QUEEN

Colonel T. H. Lang RD* . . . . Appointed 1 Mar 95   *Seniority* 28 Sep 91

HONORARY CHAPLAINS TO THE QUEEN

The Ven. M. W. Bucks, BD, AKC
Dr C. E. Stewart B Sc Bd
The Right Rev Monsignor J R N Mullin VG

HONORARY PHYSICIAN TO THE QUEEN

Surgeon Rear Admiral A. Craig MB, ChB, ndc
Surgeon Captain A. R. Marsh FRCP
Surgeon Captain D. L. Swain, LVO, MB, ChB, DObstRCOG, DA, FRCA

HONORARY SURGEONS TO THE QUEEN

Surgeon Vice Admiral A. L. Revell, MB, ChB, DA, FRCA, rcds, ndc
Surgeon Commodore M. P. W. H. Paine, MB, BS, FRCS
Surgeon Commodore I. L. Jenkins, MB, BCh, FRCS

HONORARY DENTAL SURGEON TO THE QUEEN

Surgeon Commodore (D) E. J. Grant, MSc, BDS, LDS RCS (Eng)

ROYAL NAVAL RESERVE
HONORARY PHYSICIAN TO THE QUEEN

Surgeon Captain J Maitland RD*

HONORARY NURSING SISTER TO THE QUEEN

Principal Nursing Officer C. M. Taylor, RRC

HONORARY OFFICERS IN HER MAJESTY'S FLEET

ADMIRALS

His Majesty The King of Sweden, KG . . . . 25 Jun 75

HONORARY OFFICERS IN HER MAJESTY'S ROYAL MARINES

COLONEL

His Majesty The King of Norway GCVO . . . . 18 Mar 81

THE DEFENCE COUNCIL

Chairman

THE RIGHT HONOURABLE MICHAEL PORTILLO, MP
(Secretary of State for Defence)

THE HONOURABLE NICHOLAS SOAMES, MP
(Minister of State for the Armed Forces)

THE RIGHT HONOURABLE JAMES ARBUTHNOT, MP
(Minister of State for Defence Procurement)

THE LORD HOWE
(Parliamentary Under-Secretary of State for Defence)

FIELD MARSHAL SIR PETER INGE, GCB,
(Chief of Defence Staff)

ADMIRAL SIR JOCK SLATER, GCB, LVO, ADC
(Chief of the Naval Staff and First Sea Lord)

RICHARD MOTTRAM Esq.
(Permanent Under-Secretary of State)

GENERAL SIR CHARLES GUTHRIE, GCB, LVO, OBE, ADC, Gen
(Chief of the General Staff)

AIR CHIEF MARSHAL SIR MICHAEL GRAYDON, GCB, CBE, ADC, RAF
(Chief of the Air Staff)

AIR CHIEF MARSHAL SIR JOHN WILLIS, KCB CBE, RAF
(Vice Chief of the Defence Staff)

SIR ROBERT WALMSLEY KCB
(Chief of Defence Procurement)

PROFESSOR SIR DAVID DAVIES, CBE
(Chief Scientific Adviser)

SIR MORAY STEWART KCB, DLITT
(Second Permanent Under-Secretary of State)

THE ADMIRALTY BOARD

Chairman

THE RIGHT HONOURABLE MICHAEL PORTILLO, MP

(Secretary of State for Defence)
(Chairman of the Defence Council and Chairman of the
Admiralty Board of the Defence Council)

THE HONOURABLE NICHOLAS SOAMES, MP

(Minister of State for the Armed Forces)

THE RIGHT HONOURABLE JAMES ARBUTHNOT, MP

(Minister of State for Defence Procurement)

THE LORD HOWE

(Parliamentary Under-Secretary of State for Defence)

Members

ADMIRAL SIR JOCK SLATER, GCB, LVO, ADC

(Chief of the Naval Staff and First Sea Lord)

ADMIRAL SIR PETER ABBOTT KCB

(Commander in Chief Fleet)

ADMIRAL SIR MICHAEL BOYCE, KCB, OBE, ADC

(Second Sea Lord and Commander in Chief Naval Home Command)

SIR MORRAY STEWART KCB, DLITT

(Second Permanent Under-Secretary of State and Secretary of the Admiralty Board)

VICE ADMIRAL SIR TOBY FRERE, KCB

(Chief of Fleet Support)

REAR ADMIRAL F P SCOURSE MBE

(Controller of the Navy)

REAR ADMIRAL J J BLACKHAM

(Assistant Chief of Naval Staff)

Name   *Rank Spec Sub-spec Seniority Where serving*

OFFICERS ON THE ACTIVE LIST
OF THE
ROYAL NAVY, THE ROYAL MARINES,
THE QUEEN ALEXANDRA'S ROYAL
NAVAL NURSING SERVICE; AND
RETIRED AND EMERGENCY OFFICERS
SERVING AND
LIST OF RFA OFFICERS' NAMES

OFFICERS - ACTIVE LIST

Name	Rank	Spec	Sub-spec	Seniority	Where serving
A					
Abbey, Michael Keith , MIMarE	LT CDR	E	MESM	16.05.92	DRAKE CFM
Abbey, Michael Peter, pcea	LT CDR(SL)	X	P	01.10.88	845 SQN
Abbott, Charles Peregrine George, OBE, psc	CDR	S		30.06.84	2SL/CNH
Abbott, David Anthony, BTech	LT(SD)	E	WE	24.02.95	CARDIFF
Abbott, Jonathan James, BEng	LT(SL)	X	MW	01.06.92	MONMOUTH
Abbott, Jeremy Whitwell	LT(SL)	X	FC	01.10.91	899 SQN HERON
Abbott, Louise, BEng	LT(SL)	E	ME	01.06.95	INVINCIBLE
Abbott, Sir Peter (Charles), KCB, MA, rcds, pce	ADM	-	C	03.10.95	CINCFLEET
Abbott, Simon Saintclair	LT CDR	X	PWO(U)	01.06.92	JMOTS TURNHOUSE
Abel, Nigel	SLT(SL)	X	P	01.03.93	848 SQN HERON
Abernethy, Graeme	LT(SL)	X	P	01.07.89	819 SQN
Abernethy, James Richard Gordon	LT	X	PWO(A)	01.02.89	EDINBURGH
Abernethy, Lee John Francis	LT	X	PWO(C)	01.07.90	LONDON
Ablett, Simon David	SLT	E	WE	01.09.95	DARTMOUTH BRNC
Abraham, Paul, pce(sm)	LT CDR	X	SM	01.04.92	CSST SEA
Abson, Ian Tyas	LT(SL)	X	O	01.06.91	815 FLT 201
Ackerley, Richard St John	MID(SL)	X		01.01.95	DARTMOUTH BRNC
Ackland, Heber Kemble, MA	LT	S		01.05.92	MOD (BATH)
Acland, David Daniel , pce, pcea	LT CDR	X	P	01.10.93	EXCHANGE USA
Acland, David James Dyke , jsdc, psc	CDR	X	P	30.06.92	NS OBERAMMERGAU
Acton, James Shermer	LT CDR	X	MCD	01.08.93	MANCHESTER
Adair, Allan Alexander Shafto , pce, psc(a)	CDR	X	PWO	31.12.88	BATTLEAXE
Adam, Ian Kennedy , pce, I(2)Sp	LT	X		01.01.89	NELSON
Adams, Alistair John , BA, BSc, pce	LT CDR	X	PWO(C)	01.03.94	2SL/CNH
Adams, Andrew Mark , BSc, BEng, MIMarE	LT	E	MESM	01.08.88	MOD (BATH)
Adams, Benjamin M	LT(SL)	X	P	16.05.91	UNOMIG
Adams, George	SLT(SL)	E	ME	01.05.93	DARTMOUTH BRNC
Adams, Geoffrey Hugh , BEng	LT	E	ME	01.04.93	FEARLESS
Adams, Ian , BA	LT(SL)	X	P	01.11.90	849 SQN A FLT
Adams, John Eustace , pcea	LT CDR(SL)	X	P	01.09.87	HERON FLIGHT
Adams, Peter , BSc	LT CDR	I		01.01.94	HQRM
Adams, Peter Nigel Elliott	SLT(SL)	X		01.01.93	NEWCASTLE
Adams, Richard Anthony Skelton , BSc	CDR	E	MESM	30.06.92	NBC ROSYTH
Adams, Raymond John , MA, pce	LT CDR	X	PWO(C)	01.08.88	COLLINGWOOD
Adams, Richard Joseph , BEng	LT	E	MESM	01.03.95	VANGUARD(PORT)
Adamson, Darryl	LT(SL)	X	P	16.11.91	815 FLT 228
Adcock, Brian	LT RM	RM	RMP2	01.09.92	847 SQN
Adlam, Gail Margaret , BA	LT	S		01.10.92	COMUKTG/CASWSF

Name	Rank	Spec	Sub-spec	Seniority	Where serving
Adshead, Craig Robert	SLT(SL)	X	O	01.01.94	FONA SULTAN
Ager, Robin Gordon , BSc, CEng, MIMarE, MIMechE, psc	LT CDR	E	ME	01.08.82	LOAN RSS BMATT
Ahern, Daniel James	LT CDR(SL)	X		01.10.95	DRYAD
Ahlgren, Edward Graham	LT	X	SM	01.09.94	REPULSE(PORT)
Ahling-Smith, Helena Edith Maria	SURG LT	-		01.08.95	EXETER
Aiken, James Stuart , pce	CDR	X	AWO(U)	31.12.87	DRYAD
Aiken, Stephen Ronald , pce(sm)	LT CDR	X	SM	01.07.93	SCEPTRE
Ainsley, Roger Stewart , MA, jsdc, pce	CAPT	X	AWO(A)	31.12.94	LIVERPOOL
Ainslie, Arthur Andrew , MBIM	CDR	S	SM	30.06.89	CENTURION
Airey, Simon Edward , MA, jsdc, I(1)Fr, I(1)Ge, I(1)Ru, I(2)Ru	CDR	S		31.12.94	FOSF
Aitchison, Ian James , BSc	LT(SL)	X	O	16.03.94	810 SQN SEAHAWK
Aitken, Andrew , BA	LT	X		01.09.94	SCEPTRE
Aitken, Frederick James , BSc, PGCE, jsdc	CDR	I	METOC	31.12.92	ILLUSTRIOUS
Aitken, Kenneth Matthew	LT(SD)	S	S	27.07.90	RNAS YEOVILTON
Aitkenhead, Gillian Glassford	LT CDR	W		01.10.86	SEA CADET CORPS
Ajala, Ahmedrufai Abiodun , BEng	LT(SL)	E	WE	01.09.94	YORK
Alabaster, Martin Brian , MA, MSc, psc	CDR	E	WE	30.06.92	DARTMOUTH BRNC
Albery, Richard John , pce, psc(a)	CDR	X	PWO	30.06.87	EXCELLENT
Albon, Mark , Cert Ed	LT(SL)	I	METOC	01.09.90	CAPT F2(SEA)
Albon, Ross , BSc (Barrister)	CDR	S	BAR	30.06.93	SEAHAWK
Alcock, Christopher , pcea, psc	LT CDR	X	O	16.12.92	SUTHERLAND
Aldred, Ian Sidney , BSc, CEng, MIEE	CDR	E	WE	30.06.85	MOD (BATH)
Aldridge, Michael	SLT(SL)	X		01.05.96	BOXER
Aldwinckle, Diana Vivienne	LT CDR	Q	FP	31.12.94	FONA
Aldwinckle, Terence	LT(QM)	Q		23.06.91	RH HASLAR
Alexander, Geofrey Ernest	LT CDR	X	C	15.02.86	2SL/CNH FOTR
Alexander, Oliver Douglas Dudley	SLT(SL)	X		01.05.94	BATTLEAXE
Alexander, Robert Stuart , MA, pce, pcea, psc	LT CDR	X	P	01.01.91	CINCFLEET
Alexander, Stephen James	CDR(SD)	E	WESM	01.10.93	NEPTUNE SM1
Alexander, Stuart John	LT(SL)	X	SM	01.04.95	SCEPTRE
Alison, Lynn Alexander	LT CDR(SL)	E	WE	01.10.94	CFM PORTSMOUTH
Allan, David James , QGM	LT(SD)	E	MESM	16.10.92	NEPTUNE NT
Allan, Louis James Walter , BSc, CEng, MRAeS	LT CDR	E	AE	16.04.80	MOD (LONDON)
Allen, Anthony David	LT	X		01.02.90	DRYAD
Allen, Charles William	LT	S		01.08.95	NEPTUNE SM1
Allen, Douglas James Keith , BEng	LT(SL)	X	P	01.08.94	848 SQN HERON
Allen, David Peter	LT(SD)	E	WE	15.06.90	COLLINGWOOD
Allen, David Robert , BEng, AMIEE	LT CDR	E	WE	01.11.95	SHEFFIELD
Allen, Leslie Bernard	LT(SL)	X	MW	01.10.92	BROCKLESBY
Allen, Michael John , pce, psc	LT CDR	X	MCD	01.12.87	SUPT OF DIVING
Allen, Michael John	T/LT(SDT)	E	WESM	10.06.94	CLYDE MIXMAN2
Allen, Patrick Lyons	LT	X	O	01.06.91	849 SQN A FLT
Allen, Paul Miles	LT(SL)	X	O	01.05.91	OSPREY
Allen, Richard	LT(SL)	X	SM	01.07.94	DOLPHIN SM SCHL
Allen, Robert John	CAPT RM	RM		01.09.93	RM POOLE
Allen, Richard Mark	LT CDR	X	SM	01.07.94	TALENT
Allen, Stephen Michael	LT	X	O	01.12.89	820 SQN
Allfree, Joseph , BA	LT	X		01.05.95	MANCHESTER
Allibon, Mark Christopher , pce	LT CDR	X	PWO(A)	01.07.95	CAPT F6 (SEA)
Allison, Aubrey Stuart Crawford , MB, BS, MRCGP, MRCS, LRCP, psc	SURG CDR	-	GMPP	30.06.91	2SL/CNH
Allison, Glenn	LT(SL)	X	P	16.11.94	845 SQN
Allison, Guy John	SLT	X		01.09.95	BRECON
Allison, Kenneth Richard (Loc Maj)	LT RM	RM		25.04.89	RM POOLE
Allkins, Helen Louise , BSc	LT	Q	ACC/EM	08.02.87	UKSU IBERLANT
Allsop, Alistair	SURG SLT	-		20.01.95	DARTMOUTH BRNC
Allwood, Christopher , BSc, PGCE, adp	CDR	I		31.12.93	DNPS
Almond, David Edwin Magor , BA, psc	LT CDR	S		01.07.89	RNSC GREENWICH
Alsop, Sweyn	MID(SL)	X	P U/T	01.07.94	DARTMOUTH BRNC
Alwyn, Joanna Stacey (Act Lt Cdr)	LT(SL)	X	CE	09.01.87	HQ BF HK
Ambler, Kerry Kirsten	LT(SL)	W	X	04.04.91	COLLINGWOOD
Ambrose, Peter David , pce	CDR	X	AWO(A)	30.06.80	2SL/CNH

Name	Rank	Spec	Sub-spec	Seniority	Where serving
Ambrose, Rachael Elizabeth Frakes , BSc	SLT(SL)	X	P U/T	01.01.95	DARTMOUTH BRNC
Ames, Jeremy Peter , BD, AKC	CHAPLAIN	CE		19.06.75	NELSON
Ameye, Christopher Robin , pce	LT CDR	X	MCD	01.08.92	CENTURION
Amos, Julian Harvey James (Loc Capt Rm)	LT RM	RM		01.09.91	UNTAT WARMINSTER
Amphlett, Nigel Gavin , BSc, pcea	LT CDR	X	O	01.05.95	DRYAD
Ancona, Simon James , MA, pce, pcea, psc	LT CDR	X	O	01.02.93	DRYAD
Anderson, Adrian Richard	LT(SL)	X	P	16.05.90	848 SQN HERON
Anderson, Fraser Boyd , BSc	LT CDR(SL)	X	O	01.10.93	PRESTWICK
Anderson, Garry	SLT(SL)	X		01.01.96	DARTMOUTH BRNC
Anderson, Hugh Alastair , LLB	LT	S		16.12.89	2SL/CNH
Anderson, Jeremy John , BA, IEng, MIEEIE	LT(SD)	E	WE	13.06.86	FOSM NWOOD OPS
Anderson, Mark , BSc, pce(sm)	CDR	X	SM	31.12.92	MOD (LONDON)
Anderson, Melvin John	LT CDR(SD)	S	S	01.10.88	2SL/CNH
Anderson, Russell Edward Robert	SLT	X		01.01.94	CAPT D5 SEA
Anderson, Robert Gordon , MSc, AMIEE	CDR	E	WE	31.12.95	RNSC GREENWICH
Anderson, Richard Garnet	LT(SL)	X	P	01.09.91	OSPREY
Anderson, Stuart Christopher , pcea	LT(SL)	X	P	01.09.89	RAF SHAWBURY
Anderson, Stanley Ralph	CAPT RM(SD)	RM		01.10.90	42 CDO RM
Anderson, Steven Thomas	LT RM(SD)	RM		01.01.90	RMR MERSEYSIDE
Andrew, William George , psc	CDR	X	PWO(A)	30.06.93	RALEIGH
Andrews, Ian	LT CDR(SD)	E	MESM	01.10.95	MOD (BATH)
Andrews, Paul Nicholas , pce	LT CDR	X	PWO(A)	01.06.94	DRYAD
Andrews, Stephen Gary	LT	S		01.07.88	NOTTINGHAM
Aniyi, Christopher Bamidele Jost , BEng	LT	E	ME	01.06.93	MOD (BATH)
Ankah, Gregory	SLT	E	ME	01.05.94	DARTMOUTH BRNC
Annett, Ian Gordon , BEng, CEng, MIEE	LT	E	WE	01.05.89	FOSF
Anstey, Robert James	LT	X	SM	01.11.90	TRAFALGAR
Anstis, Penelope Ann (Act Surg Lt)	SURG SLT	-		01.09.92	DARTMOUTH BRNC
Antcliffe, Graham Albert , BSc, CEng, MIEE	CDR	E	WESM	31.12.89	DRAKE CBP
Anthony, Derek James , MBE, jsdc, pce, pce(sm) (Commodore)	CAPT	X	SM	30.06.91	FOSM NWOOD HQ
Anthony, Nicholas Mark Kenwood	CAPT RM	RM	LC	01.09.94	COMACCHIO GP RM
Aplin, Adrian Trevor	LT	S		01.11.91	MOD (LONDON)
Appelquist, Paul	LT	E	WESM	01.10.91	SPARTAN
Appleyard, Graham Stuart	LT CDR(SD)	X	tas	01.04.87	NELSON BRISTOL
Appleyard, Timothy Paul , MA, MRIN, AMNI, psc	LT CDR	X	FC	05.06.88	HERON
Apps, Jonathan Gill , BSc, psc, I(2)Ge	CDR	E	AE	30.06.95	RNAY FLEETLANDS
Archdale, Peter Mervyn	LT CDR	X	PWO(U)	16.03.85	MOD DGUW PTLAND
Archer, Graham William	LT CDR	E	AE	01.04.94	SULTAN
Archer, John Christopher , MBE	LT CDR	X	PWO(U)	08.12.81	ARK ROYAL
Archibald, Brian Robert , BSc, pce	CDR	X	PWO(A)	30.06.94	FOST MPV(SEA)
Arden, Victoria Grace	SLT	X		01.09.94	INVERNESS
Arding, Nicholas Miles Bennett , BSc, psc	CAPT RM	RM		01.09.90	COMUKTG/CASWSF
Argent-Hall, Dominic , BSc, psc	LT CDR	E	WE	01.02.92	MOD (LONDON)
Armes, Carolyn Jane	LT(SL)	S		28.04.95	OSPREY
Armitage, Martin St Clair , BSc, pce, psc	CDR	X	PWO(U)	30.06.92	EXCHANGE USA
Armour, Graeme Alexander	LT RM	RM	PT	27.04.92	HQRM
Armstrong, Charles Albert , pce, psc(a)	CDR	X	PWO(U)	31.12.91	COMSTRIKFORSTH
Armstrong, Evan (Act Surg Lt)	SURG SLT	-		28.12.94	DARTMOUTH BRNC
Armstrong, Ian Geoffrey	LT(SL)	X	P	16.10.91	706 SQN SEAHAWK
Armstrong, John Herbert Arthur James , MA, rcds (Barrister)	RADM	-	BAR	03.01.96	RCDS
Armstrong, Nicholas Peter Bruce , pcea	LT(SL)	X	O	01.07.87	MOD PE ASC
Armstrong, Neil	SLT(SL)	X	P	01.01.94	810 SQN SEAHAWK
Armstrong, Philip William	LT(CS)	-		13.12.88	MOD DNR OUTPORTS
Armstrong, Roger Ian , psc(m) (Loc Lt Col)	MAJ	RM		31.12.92	ACE CENTRAL RGN
Armstrong, Scott Thomas	LT(SL)	X	P	16.08.95	814 SQN
Arnall-Culliford, Nigel David , AFC, psc, tp	CDR(SL)	X	P	01.10.92	GANNET
Arnell, Stephen John	LT(SD)	E	WE	05.06.92	MOD (BATH)
Arnold, Andrew Stewart	LT(SD)	S	W	17.12.93	DRYAD
Arnold, Bruce William Henry , MEng, MSc, CEng, MIMechE	CDR	E	MESM	31.12.92	MOD (BATH)
Arnold, Christopher John , MSc	LT(SL)	I		01.01.92	COLLINGWOOD
Arnold, Kathryn Jane , BSc	LT(SL)	I		21.10.92	SEAHAWK
Arnold, Mark Edward , TEng, MITE (Act Lt Cdr)	LT(SD)	E	WESM	03.11.83	MOD DGSWS BARROW

Name	Rank	Spec	Sub-spec	Seniority	Where serving
Arnold, Nicholas Charles	LT RM	RM		01.09.94	CTCRM
Arnold, Spenser	LT	X		01.10.90	NORTHUMBERLAND
Arrow, John William , BSc, MNI, pce	CDR	X	MCD	31.12.92	SUPT OF DIVING
Arthur, Iain Davidson , pce(sm)	CDR	X	SM	30.06.94	VANGUARD(PORT)
Arthur, John Christopher White	CDR	E	MESM	30.06.90	SACLANT USA
Arthur, Ronald James	LT CDR(SD)	E	ME	01.10.94	DRAKE CFM
Arthy, Simon Edward , BSc	LT RM	RM		26.04.90	HQRM
Artingstall, Bronwen Louise	LT(SL)	S		01.12.94	SEAHAWK
Asbridge, Jonathan Ian	LT	S	SM	16.11.89	SPARTAN
Ash, John Stewart , BA	LT CDR	I	SM	15.07.88	MOD (BATH)
Ash, Timothy	LT(SL)	X	MW	08.07.91	DARTMOUTH BRNC
Ashby, Keith John	SLT(SL)	E	WE	01.05.94	DARTMOUTH BRNC
Ashby, Maxine Kim	SLT(SL)	S		01.05.94	JMOTS TURNHOUSE
Ashby, Philip James Conyers	LT RM	RM		01.09.92	HQ 3 CDO BDE RM
Ashcroft, Adam Charles , MA	LT CDR	X	P	01.12.94	BERKELEY
Ashcroft, Christopher	LT CDR	X	MW	01.08.93	LIVERPOOL
Ashman, Rodney Guy	LT	S		28.02.92	CFLT COMMAND SEC
Ashmore, Sir Edward (Beckwith), GCB, DSC, IRs. jssc, psc	ADM OF FLEET			09.02.77	
Ashton, Christopher Nicholas , BA	2LT(GRAD)	RM		01.09.94	COMACCHIO GP RM
Ashton, Roy David (Act Lt Cdr)	LT(SD)	E	WE	10.06.88	RNEWOSU
Ashton, Richard Eric , MA, MB, BCh, MD, MRCP	SURG CDR	-	CK	31.12.85	RH HASLAR
Ashton Jones, Geraint Ashton , BSc, PGCE	LT(SL)	I		01.03.87	DNPS
Aspden, Andrew Mark , BA, pcea	LT CDR	X	O	01.12.95	810 SQN A FLIGHT
Aspden, Mark Charles	LT	X		01.10.95	ALDERNEY
Aspinall, Robert	LT CDR(SD)	X	REG	01.10.91	NELSON
Asquith, Simon Phillip	LT(SL)	X		01.06.95	TALENT
Astle, Dawn Sandra	MID(SL)	S		01.09.94	GLOUCESTER
Aston, Mark William , BDS, MSc	SGLTCDR(D)	-		19.12.90	HERON
Atherton, Bruce William	2LT(GRAD)	RM		01.09.95	CTCRM LYMPSTONE
Atherton, Gary , BA(OU)	LT(SD)	E	WESM	05.06.92	VANGUARD(PORT)
Atherton, Jason (Act Lt Rm)	2LT	RM		01.09.93	AACC MID WALLOP
Atherton, Martin John	LT CDR	S		20.08.93	HQ 3 CDO BDE RM
Atkins, Ian , BEng	LT	E	ME	01.01.93	CAMPBELTOWN
Atkinson, Charlotte , BSc	LT(SL)	X		01.04.95	DUMBARTON CASTLE
Atkinson, Edwin Cedric , AMINucE, pce, psc	CAPT	X	TAS	31.12.92	MOD (LONDON)
Atkinson, Eden John , BSc	LT(SL)	X	O	16.05.88	849 SQN HQ
Atkinson, Edward John , BSc	LT	X		01.01.92	NEPTUNE BASE OPS
Atkinson, Garth Carson , BSc	LT(SL)	X		01.02.92	MONTROSE
Atkinson, Ian Neville	LT(SL)	S		01.04.91	NAVSOUTH ITALY
Atkinson, John Clarke	CAPT RM(SD)	RM		01.10.95	HQ CDO AVN
Atkinson, Mark	LT CDR	X	MCD	01.02.96	CHATHAM
Atkinson, Richard Jonathan	SLT(SL)	X		01.09.93	HERON
Atkinson, Simon Reay , BSc, (Eur Ing), CEng, MIEE, MRIN, AMIMechE	LT CDR	E	WE	01.01.92	COLLINGWOOD
Atter, John Richard , psc (Loc Col)	LT COL	RM	WTO	31.12.90	COMSTRIKFORSTH
Attrill, Alexander Anthony	LT(SL)	X	P	16.02.87	800 SQN
Attwood, Paul	LT RM	RM		01.09.92	CTCRM
Aubrey-Rees, Adam William , BSc	LT CDR	E	WE	16.04.84	DRAKE CBP
Auld, Andrew Donaldson , DSC, pce, psc, psc(a)	CDR	X	P	31.12.83	SA PRETORIA
Auld, Douglas Martin	SLT(SL)	E	MESM	01.09.94	DARTMOUTH BRNC
Austen, Richard Mark	LT(SD)	S	W	08.04.94	HERON
Austin, Christopher John	SLT(SL)	E	ME	19.06.95	SULTAN
Austin, Ian	T/LT(SDT)	X	H1	18.06.93	RN HYDROG SCHL
Austin, John Damien , BTech	LT CDR(SL)	X		01.10.92	CINCFLEET
Austin, Stewart John , MA, psc (Act Cdr)	LT CDR	S	CMA	16.12.82	CFLT COMMAND SEC
Auty, Stephen John , BSc, ARCS, FRMS, MInstP, psc, jsdc	CAPT	I	METOC	30.06.95	MOD (LONDON)
Avery, Malcolm Byrne , BSc, MRINA, pce, pce(sm), psc	CDR	X	SM	30.06.90	MOD (LONDON)
Avison, Matthew James	LT(SL)	X	O	01.02.91	849 SQN A FLT
Axon, David Brian	LT	X		01.07.90	RICHMOND
Axten, Bruce Andrew , BSc, pce, pcea	LT CDR	X	P	01.01.94	815 SQN HQ
Aydon, Cyril George	LT CDR(SD)	E	WE	01.10.89	2SL/CNH
Ayers, Dominic Edwin Bodkin , BA	SURG LT	-		03.08.95	YORK

Name	Rank	Spec	Sub-spec	Seniority	Where serving
Ayers, Richard Peter Beedom , BSc, CEng, MIEE, psc	CDR	E	WE	31.12.92	CAPT D3 SEA
Ayers, Timothy Paul , BA	LT	X		01.04.95	CHIDDINGFOLD
Aylott, Peter Richard Frank Dobson , BA, n	LT(SL)	X		01.05.92	BRAZEN
Ayres, Christopher Paul , BSc, pce, psc	CDR	X	PWO(U)	30.06.96	PJHQ

B

Name	Rank	Spec	Sub-spec	Seniority	Where serving
Babbington, Katharine Louise Murray , BSc	SLT	X		01.01.95	DARTMOUTH BRNC
Babbington, Peter Murray , MC, nadc, psc (Loc Lt Col)	MAJ	RM	MOR	30.06.86	HQ NORTH
Backhouse, Anthony Wynter , BSc, psc	CDR	S	SM	31.12.90	EXCHANGE AUSTLIA
Backhouse, Jonathan Roland , BA, pce, pcea	LT CDR	X	O	01.03.91	OSPREY
Backus, Alexander Kirkwood , OBE, jsdc, pce (Commodore)	CAPT	X	AWO(A)	31.12.90	BFFI
Backus, Robert Ian Kirkwood , BEng	SLT	X		01.01.94	DARTMOUTH BRNC
Badami, Anish Ashok , BDS, MSc	SGLTCDR(D)	-		01.01.96	RALEIGH
Baddams, David Thomas	LT CDR(SL)	X	P	01.10.92	899 SQN HERON
Badger, Andrew John	LT(SD)	E	WE	30.10.81	COMCEN SOUTHWICK
Badham, David Peter , MB, BSc, BS	SURG LT	-		11.01.92	RH HASLAR
Badrock, Bruce , n	LT	X	H2	05.07.90	HERALD
Baggaley, Jason Antony Lloyd , BSc	LT(SL)	I		01.09.92	SULTAN
Bagwell, Peter , BEng, AMIEE	LT(SL)	E	WESM	01.08.95	CAPTAIN SM2
Bagworth, Joanna Frances , BSc	SLT(SL)	S		01.05.94	SHEFFIELD
Baileff, Roger Ian , pce	LT CDR	X	PWO(U)	01.12.89	EDINBURGH
Bailey, Anthony Mark Savile , psc(m) (Loc Maj)	CAPT RM	RM		01.08.82	SEA CADET CORPS
Bailey, Daniel Standfast	LT RM	RM		01.09.95	HQ 3 CDO BDE RM
Bailey, Howard Jonathan , n	LT(SL)	X		01.04.94	BRITANNIA
Bailey, John , pce	CDR	X	PWO(U)	30.06.89	SEAHAWK
Bailey, Jeremy	SLT	E	ME	01.01.94	NELSON
Bailey, Jonathan James , BSc	LT RM	RM		01.09.93	HQ 3 CDO BDE RM
Bailey, James Walter , AMIMarE	CDR	E	ME	31.12.91	DG SHIPS ROSYTH
Bailey, Kenneth Roy George , MSc (Commodore)	CAPT	E	WE	31.12.88	DNPS
Bailey, Peter , BA, TEng, MRINA, AMRINA, psc	LT CDR(SD)	E	HULL	01.10.85	SULTAN
Bailey, Trudi Samantha , BSc	LT(SL)	I		01.01.94	DEF SCH OF LANG
Bailie, Dennis James , MSc, CEng, MRAeS, jsdc, gw	CDR	E	AE	31.12.87	ACE SRGN ITALY
Baillie, Andrew Robert	LT(SL)	X	P	01.01.91	706 SQN SEAHAWK
Bain, David Iain (Loc Capt Rm)	LT RM(SD)	RM		01.01.91	RM POOLE
Bainbridge, Stuart	LT(SL)	X	P	01.03.95	819 SQN
Baines, Andrew Richard , BSc	SLT(SL)	X	P U/T	01.01.95	DARTMOUTH BRNC
Baines, David Michael Llewellyn , BSc	LT(SL)	I		01.01.92	SULTAN
Baines, Mark Derek , BSc, MA, pcea, psc	LT CDR	X	P	01.02.93	COMAW SEA
Baird, Stuart , BTech	LT(SD)	E	WE	24.02.95	YORK
Baitson, Jayne Amanda , BA	LT(SL)	X		01.11.93	ORKNEY
Baker, Adrian Bruce , MB, BCh, ChB	SURG CDR	-	GMPP	30.06.94	FEARLESS
Baker, Allan Peter	LT CDR	E	ME	26.04.86	LOAN OMAN
Baker, Adrian Paul , BEng	LT	X	O	01.11.91	815 FLT 241
Baker, Grant Charles	LT	E	AE	01.12.89	FONA
Baker, Graham Reginald	LT CDR	E	ME	15.01.88	FOSF
Baker, Kenneth , MSc	LT CDR(SD)	MS	RGN	01.10.91	NAVAL DRAFTING
Baker, Michael Antony , TEng, MIMarE	CDR(SD)	E	ME	01.10.94	FOSF ROSYTH
Baker, Michael John	LT	E	WE	01.06.90	SOMERSET
Baker, Paul Charles Michael , pce (Act Cdr)	LT CDR	X	AWO(U)	01.11.81	NP 1002 DIEGOGA
Baker, Peter Guest , BSc, (Eur Ing), CEng, MIEE	LT CDR	E	WE	01.02.92	EXCHANGE CANADA
Baker, Robert Sam (Act Cdr)	LT CDR	X	PWO(A)	10.09.82	SEA CADET CORPS
Baker, Simon Victor	LT CDR	E	MESM	21.01.93	VANGUARD(PORT)
Bakewell, Timothy (Loc Capt Rm)	LT RM	RM		01.09.93	NP 1061
Balchin, David Jonathan	LT CDR(SL)	X	ATC	01.10.88	HQMATO UXBRIDGE
Balcombe, Jeremy Stephen , BEng	LT(SL)	E	AE	01.09.94	810 SQN SEAHAWK
Baldock, Nicholas Edwin , MB, BCh, ChB, DipAvMed, LRCP, MFOM, MRCS, MRCP (Commodore)	SURG CAPT	-	CO/M	31.12.92	2SL/CNH
Baldwin, Christopher Martin , BA	LT CDR	X	MCD	01.03.95	SUPT OF DIVING
Baldwin, Philip Ivor , BEng, CEng, MIMarE	LT CDR	E	ME	30.08.94	BEAVER
Baldwin, Simon Frederic , BSc, psc	CDR	E	AE	30.06.94	MOD (BATH)
Balfour, Patrick James , BA, pce	LT CDR	X	PWO	16.01.81	NBC PORTSMOUTH
Balhetchet, Adrian Stephen , BEng	LT	E	AE	01.03.92	DARTMOUTH BRNC

Name	Rank	Spec	Sub-spec	Seniority	Where serving
Ball, Andrew	SLT(SL)	X		01.01.95	DRYAD
Ball, David Kenneth Lawrence , BSc	LT CDR	E	ME	01.03.81	MOD DNR OUTPORTS
Ball, Michael Peter , BSc	LT CDR	E	WESM	01.09.91	COLLINGWOOD
Ball, Richard James	LT CDR(SL)	X	H CH	01.09.87	MOD (LONDON)
Ball, Stephen Geoffrey , BSc	LT CDR(SL)	I		01.10.90	DARTMOUTH BRNC
Ball, Stephen James	LT(SD)	E	ME	13.02.92	RALEIGH
Ballance, Theo Baxter	LT CDR(SL)	X	O	01.03.83	FONA
Ballantyne, Ian (Loc Lt Col)	MAJ	RM	C	31.12.85	RMR SCOTLAND
Ballantyne, Malcolm Charles , IEng	LT CDR(SD)	E	AE(L)	01.10.91	DGA(N)ASE MASU
Ballard, Mark Lewis , BEng, AMIEE	LT	E	WESM	01.12.92	MWC GOSPORT
Ballard, Stephen Alexis	2LT(GRAD)	RM		01.09.94	42 CDO RM
Baller, Charles Rupert , BSc	LT	E	ME	01.06.93	BOXER
Balletta, Rene James	SLT	X		01.01.94	SOUTHAMPTON
Balm, Stephen Victor , psc(a)	MAJ	RM	LC	30.06.92	42 CDO RM
Balmain, Stephen Service , MA	LT(SL)	X		01.07.94	YORK
Balmer, Anthony Victor , MB, BS, BSc, MRCGP, DA	SURG CDR	-	GMPP	31.12.93	CTCRM
Balmer, Guy Austin (Loc Capt Rm)	LT RM	RM		24.04.95	UNOMIG
Balston, David Charles William , BA, pce, pce(sm)	LT CDR	X	SM	08.03.89	RNSC GREENWICH
Bamborough, Michael John , MBE, MHCIMA, MILDM	CDR	S		30.06.90	NP 1061
Bamforth, Barry Roy , TEng, AMRINA	LT CDR(SD)	E	HULL	01.10.91	EXCELLENT
Bamforth, Christian John Milton	SLT	E	WESM	01.09.95	DARTMOUTH BRNC
Bance, Nicholas David , BSc	LT(SL)	X	P	16.02.89	702 SQN OSPREY
Bancroft, Paul Leslie , pcea, psc(m) (Loc Col)	LT COL	RM	PH	31.12.89	RMB STONEHOUSE
Band, Jonathon , ADC, BA, jsdc, pce, hcsc	CAPT	X	PWO	30.06.88	ILLUSTRIOUS
Band, James Wright , BEng	LT	E	AE	01.09.90	MOD (BATH)
Banham, Alexander , BEng	SLT(SL)	E	AE	01.01.95	DARTMOUTH BRNC
Bankier, Stewart	LT CDR	X		19.02.96	EXCHANGE RAF UK
Banks, Iain Edward	LT(SL)	X	P	01.06.91	815 FLT 212
Banks, Richard George	CDR	E	AE	30.06.90	2SL/CNH
Banks, Williamlewin	LT(SL)	X	P	16.01.96	815 FLT 210
Bannister, Alan John , psc (Commodore)	CAPT	X	TAS	31.12.87	MOD (LONDON)
Bannister, Andrew Neil	LT(SD)	E	WE	19.02.93	COLLINGWOOD
Banting, Quentin Charles Lindsay , pce, pcea, psc	CDR	X	O	30.06.88	CALEDONIA
Barber, Andrew McLachlan	LT CDR(SD)	E	WE	01.10.90	LOAN DTEO PTSMTH
Barber, Andrew Stephen	LT	X	O	01.12.89	815 FLT 219
Barber, Christopher James Harrison	LT(SL)	X	O U/T	01.10.95	SEAHAWK
Barber, Paul Anthony , BSc, MIEE, pcea, psc(m)	LT CDR	X	P	01.12.85	LOAN CDA NAVY
Barber, Ralph , BA	SLT	S		01.09.93	DARTMOUTH BRNC
Barber, Stephen , BSc, PGCE	LT CDR(SL)	I	METOC	01.09.87	DNPS
Barber, Thomas Anthony , BSc, CEng, MIMechE, psc	LT CDR	E	ME	16.09.81	EXCELLENT
Barclay, John Harrison Buchanan , BSc, CEng	LT CDR	E	AE	01.05.91	RNAY FLEETLANDS
Bardolf-Smith, James Lincoln , LVO, MRIN, pce, psc	CDR	X	PWO(N)	31.12.82	CINCIBERLANT
Barge, Michael Anthony , BA, jsdc	CDR	S		30.06.87	HQRM
Bark, Alexander Martyn , BSc, n	LT	X		01.11.91	BEAVER
Bark, James Spencer	LT	X	SM	01.09.88	CSST SHORE FSLN
Barker, Charles Philip Geoffrey , MB, BS, MCh, FRCS	SURG CDR	-	CGS	31.12.89	RH HASLAR
Barker, David Charles Kingston , pcea	LT CDR	X	O	28.02.96	WESTMINSTER
Barker, John	LT(CS)	X	-	03.01.93	MOD DNR OUTPORTS
Barker, John Wilson	LT(SL)	X	O	16.09.90	702 SQN OSPREY
Barker, Kenneth Arthur , TEng	LT CDR(SD)	E	ME	05.03.93	CARDIFF
Barker, Nicholas James , MA, pce, pcea, psc	LT CDR	X	P	01.05.90	FOST SEA
Barker, Piers Thomas , BSc	LT	X	SM	01.04.89	CSST SHORE FSLN
Barker, Richard Demetrious John , pce, pce(sm)	LT CDR	X	SM	01.12.91	EXCHANGE AUSTLIA
Barling, Nicholas Reid	LT(SL)	X	ATC	01.07.89	INVINCIBLE
Barlow, David , BA	CHAPLAIN	CE		04.04.78	RH HASLAR
Barlow, Martin John	SLT(SL)	X	O	01.01.94	849 SQN B FLT
Barltrop, John Anthony , MA, MSc, CEng, MIEE	CDR	E	WE	31.12.86	SA RIYADH
Barnacle, Christopher Allan , BSc, psc	CDR	E	WE	30.06.88	MOD (LONDON)
Barnbrook, Jeremy Charles	LT	X	P	16.12.88	DRYAD
Barnden, Michael John	LT CDR(SD)	E	WE	01.10.94	STMA
Barneby, Veryan Jon , pce, psc	LT CDR	X	PWO(U)	16.04.81	DRAKE CBP
Barnes, James Richard	LT	X	FC	01.02.92	URNU HULL

Name	Rank	Spec	Sub-spec	Seniority	Where serving
Barnes, Patrick Alan Lambeth , BSc	LT(SL)	X	P U/T	01.04.94	899 SQN HERON
Barnes, Rex Warwick	CAPT RM	RM	LC	01.05.92	RNSC GREENWICH
Barnes, Stewart Michael John , psc	MAJ(SD)	RM		01.10.94	HQRM
Barnes-Yallowley, Jonathan James Hugh , pce, pcea	LT CDR	X	P	16.07.92	810 SQN SEAHAWK
Barnett, Alan Clive , BA	LT	E	AE	01.02.94	801 SQN
Barnett, Matthew	SLT	E	WE	01.09.93	DARTMOUTH BRNC
Barnwell, Keith Leigh	LT CDR	S		23.04.91	NAVSOUTH ITALY
Barraclough, Carole Denise (Act Lt)	SLT(SD)	X	REG	24.07.94	2SL/CNH
Barrand, Stuart Martin , pce	LT CDR	X	PWO(A)	01.02.94	DRYAD
Barratt, John Desmond Bridgeman , MSc	LT CDR	E	MESM	01.06.92	SULTAN
Barratt, Stephen Mitchell (Act Lt)	SLT(SD)	S	W	03.04.94	DRAKE BSO(F)
Barrett, David Leonard	LT(SD)	E	AE(M)	15.10.93	ILLUSTRIOUS
Barrett, Mark Graham	LT(SL)	X	P	01.08.90	HQ CDO AVN
Barrett, Stephen James	LT(SD)	E	WE	09.06.89	CINCIBERLANT
Barrick, Paul Vincent	LT(SD)	X	EW	27.07.90	RNU CHELTENHAM
Barritt, Michael Kenneth , MA, MNI, jsdc	CAPT	X	H CH	30.06.96	MOD (LONDON)
Barron, Patrick Joseph	LT(SD)	X	C	02.04.93	COLLINGWOOD
Barrows, David , BEng	LT(SL)	E		01.08.95	COLLINGWOOD
Barrs, Hugh Alexander , BSc	LT(SD)	E	MESM	19.10.90	MOD (BATH)
Barry, John Peter	SLT	X		01.01.94	RICHMOND
Bartholomew, Ian Munro , ARICS, psc	CDR	X	H CH	31.12.92	HERALD
Bartlett, David Stephen George , BSc	LT	E	AE(P)	01.03.89	NELSON (PAY)
Bartlett, Ian David	LT	E	MESM	01.01.90	RNC DPT NS&TECH
Bartlett, Mark John	SLT	E	WE	01.09.95	DARTMOUTH BRNC
Bartlett, Paul Andrew , BSc	LT(SD)	I		01.01.92	COLLINGWOOD
Barton, Anne Jennifer , BSc	LT(SL)	S		01.06.92	FOSNNI/NBC CLYDE
Barton, Mark Alfred , BEng, CEng, MIMechE	LT	E	ME	01.07.92	MOD DNR OUTPORTS
Barton, Peter Glenn , MSc	LT CDR	E	WE	01.01.94	MARLBOROUGH
Barton, Robert Peter , pce, pcea	CAPT	X	P	31.12.94	FONA
Barton, Sarah	SURG SLT	-		04.10.95	DARTMOUTH BRNC
Barton, Timothy John , pce, psc	CAPT	X	AWO(U)	30.06.94	2SL/CNH FOTR
Bass, John Derek , MSc, gw	CAPT	E	WE	30.06.88	CINCFLEET
Bassett, Dean Anthony	LT	X		01.11.95	NORTHUMBERLAND
Bassett, Neil Edward	LT(SD)	E	WE	19.02.93	COLLINGWOOD
Basson, Andrew Paul , BSc	LT CDR	I		01.01.92	RNSC GREENWICH
Batchelor, Noel James	LT(SL)	X		01.01.96	DOLPHIN SM SCHL
Bate, Christopher	LT CDR(SD)	X	PT	01.10.93	TEMERAIRE
Bate, David Ian George	LT CDR	X	MCD	01.10.95	DRYAD
Bateman, Graham , pce, psc(a)	CDR	X	AWO(A)	31.12.86	2SL/CNH
Bateman, Robert Dudley , BA, MSc, MIMechE	CDR	E	AE	30.06.93	MOD DHSA
Bateman, Stephen John Francis	CDR	X	PWO(A)	30.06.93	HQ NORTH
Bates, John William , MBIM	LT CDR(SL)	X	ATC	01.03.80	MOD (LONDON)
Bates, Michael Geoffrey , psc	CDR	S	SM	31.12.85	NAVAL DRAFTING
Bath, Edward George	LT	X	PWO(A)	01.07.88	BIRMINGHAM
Bath, Michael Anthony William , BSc	LT CDR	S	SM	01.11.95	WESTMINSTER
Batho, William Nicholas Pakenham , pce, psc	CAPT	X	AWO(A)	31.12.95	CNOCS GROUP
Bathurst, Sir (David) Benjamin , GCB, ADC, rcds	ADM OF FLEET			10.07.95	
Batten, Andrew John	LT(SD)	E	WE	19.02.93	COLLINGWOOD
Battrick, Richard Robert	SLT	X		01.01.94	DRYAD
Batty, Michael John , psc	LT CDR	S		01.11.93	DARTMOUTH BRNC
Baudains, David Percival , pce, psc	CDR	X	O	30.06.87	EXCHANGE RAF UK
Baudains, Terence John , BSc, pce	LT CDR	X	P	01.04.89	BRILLIANT
Baum, Stuart Richard , BSc, pce(sm)	LT CDR	X	SM	01.05.91	2SL/CNH
Baxendale, Rodney Douglas , BA, DipTh	CHAPLAIN	CE		14.07.83	ILLUSTRIOUS
Baxendale, Robert Fred , BSc (Loc Capt Rm)	LT RM	RM		01.09.92	NP 1061
Baxter, Graham Francis , pce	CDR	X	PWO(A)	30.06.88	CINCFLEET
Baxter, Iain Menzies , BEng	LT	E	AE	01.01.92	EXCHANGE ARMY UK
Baxter, John Charles	LT(SD)	X	C	27.09.95	RNSC GREENWICH
Baxter, Julian Simon , psc (Loc Lt Col)	MAJ	RM	LC	30.06.92	WARRIOR
Baxter, Kevin Christopher	LT CDR(SD)	E	MESM	01.10.95	DRAKE CBS
Baylis, Clive William	LT CDR(SL)	X	P	01.10.90	801 SQN
Bazley, John Charles , pce (Act Lt Cdr)	LT	X	PWO(A)	28.09.89	FOST SEA

Name	Rank	Spec	Sub-spec	Seniority	Where serving
Beach, James Michael , BA (Loc Capt Rm)	LT RM	RM		01.09.92	PJHQ
Beacham, Philip , BA	LT	X		01.07.95	BEAVER
Beadle, John	CHAPLAIN	SF		30.03.95	EXCELLENT
Beadnell, Nicholas , pce(sm)	CDR	X	SM	30.06.92	CSST SEA
Beadnell, Robert M , MSc	LT(SL)	I		01.01.92	SULTAN
Beadon, Colin John Alexander , MBE, psc(a)	MAJ	RM		30.06.94	HQRM
Beadsmoore, Emma	SURG SLT	-		01.11.93	DARTMOUTH BRNC
Beadsmoore, Jonathan Edgar , n	LT	X	FC	01.02.90	MONMOUTH
Beagley, Christopher Richard , pce, psc, psc(a) (Commodore)	CAPT	X	PWO(N)	30.06.90	MOD (LONDON)
Beale, Michael	SLT(SD)	X	MCD	23.07.95	DRYAD
Beale, Toby	SLT(SL)	X	O U/T	01.01.95	750 SQN OBS SCH
Bean, Maurice Stewart	LT CDR	X	PWO(A)	27.10.91	DGSS BRISTOL
Beard, Geoffrey Sidney , psc	CDR	E	WE	30.06.84	BDS WASHINGTON
Beard, Graham Thomas Charles , BA, psc	LT CDR	S		01.05.91	INVINCIBLE
Beard, Hugh Dominic	LT	X	SM	01.09.91	2SL/CNH
Beard, Richard Geoffrey	SLT(SD)	X	C	10.12.95	DRYAD
Beardall, John , MA, psc	LT CDR(SD)	X	REG	01.10.90	2SL/CNH
Beardall, Michael John Doodson	LT CDR	X	PWO(A)	01.09.95	BIRMINGHAM
Bearne, Jeremy Peter , psc	CDR	X	PWO(U)	31.12.90	MOD (LONDON)
Beaton, Eric John	LT(SD)	X	REG	17.12.93	CINCFLEET
Beaton, Frank Douglas Stewart	LT(CS)	-		16.04.89	MOD DNR OUTPORTS
Beats, Kevan Ashley , pce	LT CDR	X	PWO(U)	16.02.90	CINCFLEET
Beattie, Paul Spencer , n	LT	X		01.10.93	NOTTINGHAM
Beaumont, Ian Hirst , pce, pcea	CDR	X	O	31.12.95	PJHQ
Beaumont, Steven John	LT(SD)	X	C	16.12.94	MARLBOROUGH
Beautyman, Andrew John , BEng	LT(SL)	E	MESM	01.09.94	VANGUARD(STBD)
Beavis, John William	LT CDR	X	PWO(U)	18.11.81	2SL/CNH FOTR
Beazley, Phillip	LT RM(SD)	RM		01.01.93	CTCRM
Bebbington, Simon Peter , pce(sm)	LT CDR	X	SM	01.05.85	SHERWOOD
Beck, Simon Kingsley	LT	X	MW	01.04.91	ATHERSTONE
Beckett, Keith Andrew , BSc	LT CDR	E	MESM	01.03.94	TRIUMPH
Bedding, Simon William Edward , BEng	LT	E	WE	01.04.92	DNPS
Beddoe, Alexis George Titus , BSc	LT(SL)	X		01.01.90	EXCHANGE GERMANY
Bedelle, Stephen James	LT(SD)	E	WE	19.02.93	COLLINGWOOD
Bee, Michael John	CDR(SD)	X	C	01.10.91	ELANT/NAVNW
Bee, Mark Thomas , BA	LT(SL)	I		01.09.92	COLLINGWOOD
Beeby, Michael Joseph	MID(NE)(SL)	X		01.01.96	DARTMOUTH BRNC
Beech, Christopher Martin	LT(SL)	X	SM	01.07.90	VANGUARD(STBD)
Beeley, William Tyas	2LT(GRAD)	RM		01.09.94	CTCRM
Beeson, Guy Frederick	LT RM	RM	PH	30.04.91	845 SQN
Beesting, Alan , BA	SLT(SL)	X		01.05.94	BRAVE
Behets, Brian Timothy James , MBA, FBIM, pce, psc, psc(a)	CDR	X	AWO(C)	31.12.85	MOD (LONDON)
Beirne, Stephen	LT(SL)	X	O	01.06.91	819 SQN
Belding, Paul Stuart , AFC	LT CDR(SL)	X	P	01.03.79	RNAS YEOVILTON
Belgeonne, Damian Peter James , MA, pce, pcea, psc	LT CDR	X	O	01.02.91	MONTROSE
Bell, Andrew Dawson , BSc	CDR	E	AE(P)	31.12.89	FONA
Bell, Adrian Scott , pce	LT CDR	X	PWO(U)	01.06.92	RNSC GREENWICH
Bell, Darrel Patrick James	LT(SD)	E	AE(L)	15.10.93	FONA
Bell, Douglas William Alexander	LT RM	RM	MLDR	26.04.90	CTCRM
Bell, Jeffrey	SLT	E	AE	01.09.93	DARTMOUTH BRNC
Bell, Mark	LT(SL)	S		01.10.92	CFM PORTSMOUTH
Bell, Robert Douglas	LT	X	MCD	01.03.89	DRYAD
Bell, Reginald Paul William	LT CDR	X	PWO(A)	01.10.90	MWC GOSPORT
Bell-Davies, Richard William , BSc, pce, psc	CDR	X	PWO(U)	30.06.93	MOD (LONDON)
Bellfield, Robert James Astley , pce	LT	X	PWO(U)	01.07.88	DRYAD
Bellingham, David Bruce	LT	X		01.09.90	DRYAD
Bellingham, Ian Keith	SLT(SD)	X	EW	24.07.94	NP 1061
Bellis, Brendan Martin , BSc	LT	X		01.03.95	SEAHAWK
Benbow, Warren Kenneth , pce, psc	CAPT	X	P	30.06.93	SA ATHENS
Bence, David Elliott	LT	X	MCD	01.02.90	CATTISTOCK
Benham, Richard Lionel , MNI, pce	LT CDR	X	PWO	01.01.79	ILLUSTRIOUS
Benn, Stephen William , BEng	LT	E	AE	01.02.95	SULTAN

Name	Rank	Spec	Sub-spec	Seniority	Where serving
Bennett, Anthony John	LT(SD)	S	W	14.12.90	45 CDO RM
Bennett, Alan Reginald Courtenay , DSC, jsdc, pce, pcea, psc	CDR	X	P	30.06.90	ILLUSTRIOUS
Bennett, Graham Lingley Nepean	LT CDR	X	PWO(U)	01.07.93	DRYAD
Bennett, Michael John	LT(SD)	E	ME	15.02.91	SULTAN
Bennett, Norman Kenneth , pcea, psc	CDR(SL)	X	P	01.10.94	FONA
Bennett, Neil Malcolm , BA (Loc Capt Rm)	LT RM	RM		01.09.89	HQ 3 CDO BDE RM
Bennett, Paul Martin , BA, pce	LT CDR	X	PWO(A)	01.05.94	WESTMINSTER
Bennett, Robert Webster	LT RM	RM		25.04.94	EXCELLENT
Bennett, Stephen Harry Guy , psc	CDR	X	H CH	31.12.86	LOAN OMAN
Bennett, Steven Robert	LT(SL)	X	P	01.10.89	820 SQN
Bennett, William Dean	LT(SD)	X	SM	25.07.91	NAVSOUTH ITALY
Bennetts, Michael	LT(CS)	-		16.04.89	MOD DNR OUTPORTS
Bennetts, Neil	SLT(SD)	X	C	03.04.94	COLLINGWOOD
Bennion, Paul Bruce	LT(SL)	X	H2	01.03.95	BEAGLE
Benstead, Neil William John	SLT	E	ME	01.09.95	DARTMOUTH BRNC
Bent, George Robert , pce, psc	LT CDR	X	PWO(C)	01.11.82	COLLINGWOOD
Bentham-Green, Nicholas Richard Heriot	CAPT RM	RM	LC	01.09.92	RNSC GREENWICH
Bentley, David Alan	LT(SD)	X	g	06.09.85	CAMBRIDGE
Benton, Angus Michael , BSc	LT	X	MCD	01.09.88	NORTH DIVING GRP
Benton, Peter John , MB, BCh, AFOM	SURG CDR	-	CO/M	31.12.93	INM ALVERSTOKE
Beresford-Green, Paul Maxwell	LT(SL)	S		16.12.92	DRYAD MWC
Berey, Ian David	LT(SL)	X		01.03.94	ORWELL
Berisford, Andrew William	SLT	X		01.09.93	DARTMOUTH BRNC
Bernard, Alain Raymond , BA	SLT(SL)	X		01.09.94	ATHERSTONE
Bernau, Jeremy Charles	LT CDR	X	SM	01.11.91	LOAN CDA ADAC
Bernier, Nicholas Louis Patrick , BSc, CEng, MIEE, psc	CDR	E	WE	31.12.88	MOD (LONDON)
Berry, Allan James , osc(us) (Loc Lt Col)	MAJ	RM		30.06.85	MOD (LONDON)
Berry, Paul	LT(SD)	E	ME	15.06.95	SULTAN
Berryman, Charles Bliss , BEng	LT	E	MESM	01.08.88	NEPTUNE NT
Bessell, David Alexander , BA	LT	X	SM	01.06.93	DOLPHIN SM SCHL
Best, Peter	ACT LT RM(SD)	RM		01.01.96	RM SCHOOL MUSIC
Best, Russell Richard , BA, pce, psc	CDR	X	PWO(U)	31.12.95	CINCFLEET
Bestwick, Michael Charles	LT RM	RM		25.04.94	CTCRM
Betteridge, Jeremy Trevor , pce, pcea, psc	CDR	X	P	30.06.96	2SL/CNH
Betton, Andrew	LT	X	O	01.02.91	815 FLT 202
Bevan, Noel Stuart , MB, BS, LRCP, MRCGP, MRCS	SURG CDR	-	GMPP	30.06.87	JSMU HK
Bevan, Simon , BSc, MBA	CDR	I	METOC	31.12.93	JSDC GREENWICH
Beveridge, Robert Christopher , BSc, CEng, MIEE, AMIEE	LT CDR(SL)	E	WE	01.10.92	HQ DFTS
Beveridge, Simon	CHAPLAIN	CE		28.04.93	HQRM
Beverstock, Mark Alistair , BSc	CDR	E	WESM	30.06.96	MOD DGSWS BATH
Bevis, Timothy John (Loc Maj)	CAPT RM	RM		01.09.93	RNSC GREENWICH
Bewick, David John	LT	X		01.07.90	MARLBOROUGH
Bewley, Nicholas	MID	X		01.09.94	DARTMOUTH BRNC
Beynon, John Alan , ADC, BSc, CEng, MIEE, rcds (Commodore)	CAPT	E	AE(P)	30.06.88	MOD (BATH)
Beyts, Nicholas Geoffrey Bruno , psc (Loc Lt Col)	MAJ	RM	AE	30.06.84	DCTA
Bhattacharya, Debdash , BSc	LT(SL)	X	P	16.06.90	810 SQN SEA
Bibbey, Mark William , BA, psc(m) (Loc Lt Col)	MAJ	RM	WTO	30.06.92	RNSC GREENWICH
Bickerton, Richard Edward , BSc	LT(SL)	X	O	01.04.86	LOAN DRA FARN
Biggs, Colin Richard	LT(SD)	E	MESM	14.10.88	CFM PORTSMOUTH
Biggs, David Michael	LT(SL)	X	O	16.12.86	849 SQN B FLT
Biggs, Peter	LT CDR(SD)	X	SM	01.10.93	FOSM NWOOD OPS
Biggs, William Patrick Lowther , BEng, AMIEE	LT	E	WE	01.04.91	RMC OF SCIENCE
Bignell, Stephen , BEng	LT	E	WE	01.04.92	DG SHIPS CAM HSE
Billcliff, Niels , BSc	LT(SL)	X	O	01.11.94	810 SQN SEAHAWK
Billingsley, Peter , MB, BCh, ChB	SURG LT	-		01.08.91	RNDHU DERRIFORD
Billington, Nigel Stephen , BA, psc	LT CDR	S	SM	01.02.88	FOSF
Billington, Tony John	LT(SD)	X	EW	02.04.93	PJHQ
Billson, Geoffrey Kendrick , MNI, jsdc, pce	CAPT	X	AWO(A)	31.12.89	CORNWALL
Bilson, John Michael Frederick , pce	LT CDR	X	PWO(A)	01.01.93	SOUTHAMPTON
Bing, Neil Adrian , BSc	LT(SL)	X	P	01.08.94	FONA VALLEY
Bingham, David Spencer	LT	X	FC	01.03.91	EXCHANGE RAF UK
Binks, Jonathan Patrick , BA	LT	X		01.05.94	ALDERNEY

Name	Rank	Spec	Sub-spec	Seniority	Where serving
Binns, Jonathan Brian , MSc, CEng, MIMarE	CDR	E	MESM	30.06.87	MOD (BATH)
Binns, John Brendon Harold , OBE, MSc, FIMarE, MINucE, jsdc	CDR	E	MESM	31.12.88	FOSM NWOOD OPS
Binstead, Kenneth Nigel	LT(SL)	X	P	01.02.93	EXCHANGE RAF UK
Birbeck, Keith	LT(SD)	E	WESM	05.06.92	DG SHIPS PTLAND
Birch, Richard John (Act Surg Lt)	SURG SLT	-		01.11.92	DARTMOUTH BRNC
Birchall, Stephen John , BSc, CEng, MIMarE	LT CDR	E	MESM	21.10.91	TRENCHANT
Bird, David Edward	LT CDR(SL)	X	P	01.10.93	849 SQN HQ
Bird, Jonathan , BEng	LT(SL)	X	O	01.05.92	819 SQN
Bird, Matthew Graham James , BEng	LT	E	AE	01.11.94	849 SQN HQ
Bird, Richard Alexander James , n	LT	X	H1	01.07.90	ROEBUCK
Birdman, Paul Mark	LT CDR	X	PWO(C)	01.07.94	MOD (LONDON)
Birkett, Claire Louise	SLT	X		01.09.94	DARTMOUTH BRNC
Birley, Jonathan Hugh , pce	LT CDR	X	PWO(U)	01.05.95	LONDON
Birmingham, Tony	LT(SL)	X	P U/T	16.09.94	705 SQN SEAHAWK
Birrell, Stuart Martin , BA (Loc Capt Rm)	LT RM	RM		01.09.89	42 CDO RM
Birse, Gregor James , BA, MSc	LT(SL)	I		01.05.92	PRESTWICK
Birt, David Jonathan , MB, BS, FRCA	SURG LTCDR	-		25.08.94	INVINCIBLE
Bishop, David John , BA	LT(SL)	X		01.01.95	SANDOWN
Bishop, George Charles	LT(SD)	X	AV	27.07.95	RNAS YEOVILTON
Bishop, Keith Alfred , BSc	LT(SL)	X	P	16.06.85	810 SQN OEU
Bishop, Paul Richard , BSc, MIMechE, AMRAeS	CDR	E	AE	30.06.93	MOD (BATH)
Bishop, Robert Johnstone , MNI, pce, psc	CDR	X	PWO(U)	31.12.91	SACLANT BELGIUM
Bishop, Roger St John Stanley , pce, pcea, I(2)Ge	CAPT	X	P	31.12.91	RCDS
Bishop-Bailey, Michael , MBE, BSc, pce	LT CDR	X	O	16.10.79	FONA
Bissell, Angus David	LT(SL)	X	SM	01.02.94	VICTORIOUS(STBD)
Bissett, Ian Michael	LT(SD)	E	AE(L)	17.10.91	RNAS YEOVILTON
Bissett, Phillip Keith	LT(SD)	E	AE(L)	17.10.91	ILLUSTRIOUS
Bissett, Roger William	LT(SD)	E	AE(L)	17.10.91	EXCHANGE RAF UK
Bisson, Jean Jean Paul , MSc	LT CDR	E	WE	01.02.92	RNSC GREENWICH
Bithell, Ian Stephen	LT(SL)	X	ATC	01.11.89	EXCHANGE RAF UK
Bittles, David John , BSc, MBIM, psc	CDR	I		31.12.83	2SL/CNH
Black, Alastair Graham Crawford , I(2)Ge	LT CDR	X	AWO(U)	01.11.80	SEA CADET CORPS
Black, Heather Elizabeth , BA	LT(SL)	I		07.04.88	NELSON RNSETT
Black, Jeremy James McLaren , BA	LT	X		01.02.93	705 SQN SEAHAWK
Black, Simon Andrew	SLT	X		01.09.94	HURWORTH
Blackaller, Wendy Joy , BA	LT	I	METOC	04.04.90	CINCFLEET
Blackburn, David Anthony James , LVO, pce, psc(a)	RADM	-	PWO	16.03.94	BDS WASHINGTON
Blackburn, Paul Reza	LT(SL)	X	P	01.12.93	800 SQN
Blackburn, Stephen Anthony , BSc	LT	E	ME	01.03.90	BIRMINGHAM
Blackburn, Stuart James	LT(SL)	X	SM	01.05.94	FOSM NWOOD OPS
Blackburn Jones, Michael , BSc	LT(SL)	I		01.05.91	DOLPHIN SM SCHL
Blackett, Jeffrey , LLB (Barrister)	CDR	S	BAR	30.06.91	COLLINGWOOD
Blackett, Kay Joanne , BA	LT(SL)	W		14.12.89	MOD DNR OUTPORTS
Blackham, Jeremy Joe , BA, rcds, pce, psc, I(2)Sp	RADM	-	D	18.05.93	MOD (LONDON)
Blackman, Nicholas Trevor , BSc, CEng, MIEE	LT CDR	E	AE	01.01.94	MOD (LONDON)
Blackmore, Mark Stuart	LT	X	O	01.05.95	DRYAD
Blackwell, Jason Mark	SLT(SL)	X	ATCU/T	01.09.95	RNAS YEOVILTON
Blackwell, Richard Edward	LT	S	SM	01.12.88	FOST DPORT SHORE
Blacow, Carl , BEng	LT(SL)	E	ME	01.05.95	BOXER
Blain, Roderick Graham , BA (Barrister)	LT CDR	S	BAR	01.04.92	FOST DPORT SHORE
Blair, Duncan Guy Sanderman , MB, BCh	SURG LT	-		01.08.92	NELSON (PAY)
Blair, Graeme	SLT	E	MESM	01.09.93	DARTMOUTH BRNC
Blair, Samuel Raymond , BSc, pce	LT CDR	X	N	01.05.86	FOSF SEA PTSMTH
Blake, Gary Edmund , BSc	LT CDR	E	WESM	01.07.90	DTR BATH
Blake, Keven Barry	LT CDR(SD)	X	REG	01.10.94	DRAKE CBP
Blake, Michael James , BSc, CEng, FIMarE, MIMechE, AMIMechE	LT CDR	E	MESM	01.10.88	NEPTUNE NT
Blake, Robert Michael , BSc, CEng, MIEE	CDR	E	WE	30.06.84	DRYAD
Blakeley, Trevor , BSc, CEng, MIMarE, MIMechE, psc(a)	CDR	E	ME	31.12.82	WARRIOR
Blakey, Adrian Lawrence	LT CDR	X	MCD	01.03.92	EXCHANGE USA
Blanchford, Daniel , BEng	2LT(GRAD)	RM		01.09.94	CTCRM
Bland, Steven (Act Surg Lt)	SURG SLT	-		01.01.94	DARTMOUTH BRNC

Name	Rank	Spec	Sub-spec	Seniority	Where serving
Blaydes, Mark Hugh	LT CDR(SL)	X	PWO(A)	01.09.85	COCHRANE
Blazeby, Nigel James , BSc, pce	LT CDR	X	PWO(N)	01.06.92	EXCHANGE USA
Blight, Christopher John , MIMgt	LT CDR(SL)	X	P	01.03.82	FAAIT MAN ORG VL
Block, Andrew William George , BA	LT	E	WE	01.07.94	NOTTINGHAM
Blocke, Andrew David	LT(SD)	MS	AD	04.04.96	CDO LOG REGT RM
Blott, Richard John , BSc, CEng, MIEE, psc	CDR	E	WE	31.12.81	LOAN DRA FARN
Blount, Derek Raymond , BSc	LT CDR	E	MESM	01.04.94	RNC DPT NS&TECH
Blount, Keith Edward	LT	X	P	01.02.89	DRYAD
Blowers, Michael David , psc(a), pcea	LT CDR	X	O	01.09.92	815 SQN HQ
Blunden, Jeremy Jonathan Frank , BSc, pce	CDR	X	PWO(N)	30.06.96	BRITANNIA
Blyth, Michael (Act Lt Rm)	2LT	RM		27.04.94	COMACCHIO GP RM
Blythe, Paul Christopher	LT	X	SM	01.10.91	VICTORIOUS(PORT)
Blythe, Tom Stewart	LT RM	RM	LC	01.09.93	539 ASLT SQN RM
Boag, Kyle Ian	LT(SL)	X		01.09.95	SHETLAND
Boag, Robert David	CDR(SL)	X	P	01.10.90	NELSON (PAY)
Board, Michael John	2LT(GRAD)	RM		01.09.94	42 CDO RM
Boast, Mark Thomas , pcea, tp	LT CDR	X	P	01.09.89	899 SQN HERON
Boddington, Jeremy Denis Leonard , BSc	LT CDR	X	P	16.12.95	815 FLT 234
Body, Howard Joseph , BA	LT CDR	I		01.12.91	HQRM
Boggust, David Ian , MSc, CEng, MIMechE	CDR	E	ME	30.06.89	MOD (BATH)
Boissier, Robin Paul , MA, pce, pce(sm), psc	CAPT	X	PWO(N)	30.06.94	MOD (LONDON)
Bolam, Andrew Guy , BSc, MIMarE	LT CDR	E	ME	01.06.94	NOTTINGHAM
Boland, Michael	LT CDR(SL)	X	P	01.03.81	FOST FLT TGT GRP
Bollen, Johanna Michelle	LT(SL)	S		01.01.96	INVINCIBLE
Bolt, Julia Carolyn	LT(SL)	W	S	04.01.92	FOSF
Bolton, Jonathan Praed , BEng	LT	E	ME	01.09.91	SULTAN
Bolton, Matthew Thomas William , BEng, CEng, MIMarE, MIMechE	LT	E	ME	01.08.92	SULTAN
Bolton, Stephen Jack	LT(SL)	X	P	16.10.93	702 SQN OSPREY
Bond, Alan James , BEng	LT	E	AE	09.06.92	814 SQN
Bond, Nigel David	LT CDR	S		01.05.93	FOSF
Bone, Christopher John	LT CDR	E	AE	01.05.92	2SL/CNH FOTR
Bone, Darren Nigel , pce	LT CDR	X	PWO(A)	01.09.95	DRYAD
Bone, James	SLT	X		01.09.94	DARTMOUTH BRNC
Bone, Richard , BSc	LT(SL)	I	SM	13.10.88	NEPTUNE SM1
Bonnar, John Andrew , BEng, AMIEE	LT	E	WE	01.06.93	BEAVER
Bonner, Neil , BEng	LT	E	WESM	01.08.94	MOD DGSWS BATH
Bonnett, Jonathan Mark , BSc, AMInstP, AMIEE	LT(SL)	I		01.10.90	SULTAN
Bonnett, Nicholas John , TEng, MinstAM, AMRINA	LT(SD)	E	HULL	18.02.83	MOD (BATH)
Bonsey, Bernard John Maurice , LMHCIMA, AMBIM	LT CDR(SD)	S	CAT	01.10.95	RALEIGH
Booker, Glenn Raymond	LT CDR(SL)	X	ATC	01.10.89	RNAS YEOVILTON
Booker, Scott Richard	LT(SL)	X	P	16.06.90	820 SQN
Boorman, Justin Keith Page , BSc	LT(SL)	X		01.10.92	BRAVE
Booth, Michael Dennison , DSC, pce, psc	CAPT	X	P	30.06.95	SA BONN
Booth, Peter Scott , pce, psc	CDR	X	N	30.06.83	NBC PORTSMOUTH
Bootland, Erich Gustav , psc	CDR(SD)	MS	AD	01.10.95	2SL/CNH
Boraston, Peter John , BSc, CEng, MIEE	LT CDR	E	WE	01.04.90	DGSS BRISTOL
Borbone, Nicholas	SLT	X		01.01.95	CROMER
Boreham, Nicholas Edward , BSc	LT CDR	E	MESM	01.04.89	CSST SEA
Borland, Stuart Andrew , BSc, CEng, MIEE	LT CDR	E	WE	01.07.94	YORK
Borley, Kim John , MA, CEng, MIEE, jsdc	CAPT	E	WESM	31.12.95	NEPTUNE NT
Bosley, Benjamin Daniel	LT	X		01.10.95	EXCHANGE BELGIUM
Bosshardt, Robert George , BSc	CDR	X	PWO(A)	31.12.93	CDRE MFP
Bostock, Colin Edward	LT CDR	S		09.09.90	SULTAN
Boston, Justin , BA	LT(SL)	I		01.01.93	COLLINGWOOD
Bosustow, Antony Michael	LT	E	WE	01.06.90	MERCURY
Bosustow, Benjamin Francis , BEng	LT(SL)	E	WESM	01.02.91	MOD (LONDON)
Bottomley, Robert John , BSc	LT CDR	E	WE	01.01.81	BDS WASHINGTON
Bottomley, Steven	SLT(SD)	E	AE(L)	06.09.93	848 SQN HERON
Bouch, Sharon Kay , BA	LT(SL)	X		01.01.94	DARTMOUTH BRNC
Bougourd, Mark Anthony	LT	E	AE	01.10.91	FAAIT MAN ORG VL
Boulton, Neil Andrew , BSc	LT(SL)	I		20.11.86	DADPTC SHRIVNHAM
Boulton, Timothy John	LT CDR(SL)	X	AWO(C)	01.09.81	DRYAD

Name	Rank	Spec	Sub-spec	Seniority	Where serving
Bourchier, Sara Anne , BEd	LT(SL)	X		01.09.94	RNAS CULDROSE
Bourn, Kelvin Edward , BSc, psc(a)	LT CDR	X	PWO(N)	09.05.85	CNOCS GROUP
Bourne, Christopher Michael	LT	X	O	16.08.89	DRYAD
Bourne, Donald Sidney	LT(SD)	E	AE(L)	13.10.89	RNAS YEOVILTON
Bourne, Philip John	LT RM(SD)	RM	MTO	01.01.94	HQ CDO AVN
Bourne, Richard Leslie , MIMgt, pce, pcea	CDR	X	P	31.12.95	BFFI
Bowbrick, Richard Charles	LT	X	PWO(A)	01.04.89	BEAVER
Bowden, Matthew Neil , BSc	LT(SL)	I		01.10.86	SULTAN
Bowden, Matthew Thomas Edward , BEng	LT	E	WE	01.01.95	COLLINGWOOD
Bowen, Geoffrey Philip	LT CDR(SD)	X	PWO(A)	01.10.91	DRYAD
Bowen, Michael , BA	LT CDR(QM)	Q	RNT	01.10.91	RN MSS HASLAR
Bowen, Nigel Timothy , pcea	LT	X	O	01.11.88	702 SQN OSPREY
Bower, Andrew John , BSc	LT	X		01.08.93	TALENT
Bower, John William (Act Lt)	SLT(SD)	S	S	24.07.94	EXCHANGE DGST(N)
Bower, Nigel Scott	LT	X	SM	01.04.89	VIGILANT(PORT)
Bowers, John	LT(SL)	X	O	01.03.91	815 SQN HQ
Bowhay, Simon	LT	E	WESM	01.05.91	RNSC GREENWICH
Bowie, Alan , MB, BCh	SURG LT	-		11.03.94	NEPTUNE
Bowker, Eric Arthur , psc	CDR	E	ME	31.12.91	MOD (BATH)
Bowker, Geoffrey Neil	LT CDR(SL)	X	ATC	01.10.93	RNAS YEOVILTON
Bowker, Iain Cameron , BEng	LT	E	MESM	13.02.93	RNC DPT NS&TECH
Bowker, Michael Andrew , MSc, MIMechE, jsdc	CDR	E	MESM	30.06.91	NEPTUNE SM1
Bowkett, Robert Murray , BSc, AMBIM, psc(m)	MAJ	RM		30.06.91	40 CDO RM
Bowley, Jonathan James , BEng, AMIEE	LT	E	WE	01.05.90	RMC OF SCIENCE
Bowman, Robert James , BEng	LT	E	AE	01.05.95	SULTAN
Bowness, Paul	LT(SD)	E	AE(M)	15.10.93	DGA(N)ASE MASU
Bowra, Mark Andrew	2LT(GRAD)	RM		01.09.95	CTCRM LYMPSTONE
Bowyer, Peter John , BEng	LT(SL)	E	AE	01.05.93	846 SQN
Bowyer, Richard John	2LT	RM		01.05.95	CTCRM LYMPSTONE
Boxall, Pauline	SLT	E	ME	01.09.94	DARTMOUTH BRNC
Boxall-Hunt, Brian Paul , AMNI, pce	CDR	X	PWO(A)	30.06.91	NAVSOUTH ITALY
Boyce, Sir Michael (Cecil) , KCB, OBE, ADC, rcds, psc	ADM	-	SM	25.05.95	2SL/CNH
Boyd, James Alexander , jsdc, pce(sm)	CAPT	X	SM	30.06.96	CSST SHORE FSLN
Boyd, Nicholas , MSc, MIMechE	LT CDR	E	ME	01.03.95	RNSC GREENWICH
Boyes, Gareth	SLT	E	ME	01.01.94	DARTMOUTH BRNC
Boyes, Martyn Richard , BEng	LT	E	MESM	01.02.95	SOVEREIGN
Boyes, Norman	LT CDR	E	ME	11.08.88	SULTAN
Boyes, Richard Austen	LT(SL)	X	P	01.03.89	814 SQN
Boyle, Jonathan Bartley , BEng	LT	E	MESM	01.10.94	SPLENDID
Boynton, Stephen Justin , BSc	LT	X		01.12.91	706 SQN SEAHAWK
Brabyn, Adrian Alexander Benjamin , MA	2LT(GRAD)	RM		01.09.95	CTCRM LYMPSTONE
Bracher, Hugh	LT(SD)	E	WESM	10.06.88	MOD DGUW PTLAND
Bradburn, Stephen Joseph , pcea	LT CDR(SL)	X	P	01.10.93	INVINCIBLE
Bradford, Terrance Horace Colin	LT(SD)	MS	AD	04.04.96	D RAD PROT SVCE
Bradley, Matthew Thomas , n	LT(SL)	X		01.05.94	LANCASTER
Bradley, Patrick Martin , BEng	LT	E	WE	01.06.92	MOD DNR OUTPORTS
Bradley, Rupert , LLB	SLT(SL)	X	P U/T	01.05.94	DARTMOUTH BRNC
Brads, Wayne , BSc	LT CDR	I	SM	14.01.94	2SL/CNH
Bradshaw, Kevin Thomas	LT(SD)	E	WE	18.02.94	COLLINGWOOD
Bradshaw, Robert Julian , MA, pce(sm)	CAPT	X	SM	31.12.89	LOAN HYDROG
Brady, Mark Rowland , BSc, pce	LT CDR	X		16.01.81	PJHQ
Brady, Sean Edward	LT	X	SM	01.09.88	MANCHESTER
Brady, Sean , BSc (Com 2lt)	SLT	X		01.01.94	RE ENTRY
Braham, Stephen Wyn , MSc	LT CDR	E	ME	01.10.92	RNSC GREENWICH
Brailey, Ian Stewart	LT(SD)	X	AV	04.04.96	RNAS PORTLAND
Braisher, John Lesley	LT(SD)	X	C	28.07.89	COLLINGWOOD
Braithwaite, Anthony Charles Gerald , MSc, AMRAeS	LT CDR	E	AE	01.08.88	MOD (BATH)
Braithwaite, Jeremy Sean	LT	X		01.01.95	BICESTER
Bramble, Kevin Roy	LT(SL)	X	O	16.07.89	702 SQN OSPREY
Bramley, Stephen , pce, pcea, psc	CDR	X	P	31.12.91	MOD (LONDON)
Bramwell, John Gerald	LT(SL)	X	O	01.04.93	820 SQN
Branch-Evans, Simon Jonathon , MBE, BSc, MDA, CEng, MRAeS	CDR	E	AE	31.12.92	2SL/CNH

Name	Rank	Spec	Sub-spec	Seniority	Where serving
Brand, Simon Martin , BSc, pce, pcea	LT CDR	X	P	01.12.91	EXCHANGE CANADA
Brandon, James , BDS	SGLTCDR(D)	-		13.01.96	42 CDO RM
Branscombe, Paul , OBE, MNI, pce (Commodore)	CAPT	X	SMTAS	31.12.87	MOD (BATH)
Bratby, Alexandra , BEd	LT(SL)	I		01.01.89	2SL/CNH FOTR
Bratby, Simon Paul	LT(SL)	X	P	16.11.94	815 FLT 202
Bratt, Adrian , BSc	SLT	X		01.09.93	DRYAD
Bravery, Martin Anthony Edward	LT	X	P	01.05.91	820 SQN
Brawn, Allan James	LT CDR(SD)	X	AWO(U)	01.10.84	DRYAD
Bray, John David , MSc, CEng, MIEE, MSE	CDR	E	WE	31.12.89	PJHQ
Bray, Matthew Robert	LT RM	RM		25.04.94	40 CDO RM
Bray, Nigel Godfrey Hensman , pce, I(2)Fr	CAPT	X	AWO(C)	30.06.95	MOD (LONDON)
Brayson, Mark	LT(SL)	X	P	16.10.94	702 SQN OSPREY
Brazendale, Colin , MBE	LT CDR(SD)	E	AE(L)	01.10.95	LOAN DTEO BSC DN
Brazier, Francis William Thomas , IEng, FIEIE	LT CDR(SD)	E	WE	01.10.93	OCEAN
Brecken, David George	LT CDR(SD)	E	WE	01.10.94	BF GIBRALTAR(NE)
Breckenridge, Iain Galloway	LT	X	SM	01.07.89	TRENCHANT
Brecknell, Jeremy John , psc (Commodore)	CAPT	S		31.12.89	MOD (LONDON)
Bree, Stephen Edward Peter , MB, BCh	SURG LTCDR	-		01.08.93	RNDHU DERRIFORD
Brember, Peter Bruce	SLT(SD)	X	AV	25.07.93	RNAS PORTLAND
Bremner, David Alexander , BA, AMIEE	LT	E	WE	15.06.90	CAMBRIDGE
Brenchley, Nigel Gerard	LT(SD)	S	W	04.04.96	BF GIBRALTAR(NE)
Brennan, Andrew John	LT(SL)	X		01.09.95	CINCFLEET
Brent, Robert Charles , BA	LT	X		01.02.94	TALENT
Breslin, Michael John , BEM	LT(CS)	-		07.01.90	MOD DNR OUTPORTS
Brett, Patricia	LT	Q		07.05.94	CTCRM
Brian, Neil	LT(SL)	X	O	01.08.92	SEAHAWK
Brice, David John , BA, pce, pcea, psc (Commodore)	CAPT	X	O	30.06.89	MOD (LONDON)
Bridge, Benedict Lenthall	SLT(SL)	X	P	01.03.94	LANG TRNG(UK)
Bridgeman, Jeffrey William Treverton	LT(SD)	S	W	09.01.87	NELSON
Bridger, David William (Act Cdr)	CDR	I	SM	30.06.96	2SL/CNH
Bridger, Richard John , pcea	LT CDR	X	O	01.06.92	FONA
Bridges, Steven Vivian , pce	LT CDR(SL)	X	AWO(A)	01.03.81	HERON
Brier, Christopher Anthony Clive , AMIAM	LT(SD)	S	W	27.07.90	EXCELLENT
Briers, Matthew Peter	LT	X	P	01.11.88	849 SQN B FLT
Brigden, Kevin Wesley , pce, pcea	LT CDR	X	O	16.04.92	RNAS CULDROSE
Briggs, Mark David	SLT(SL)	E	WE	01.09.93	DARTMOUTH BRNC
Briggs, Stephen Leslie	LT(SL)	I	METOC	01.01.87	SULTAN
Brigham, Joanna Margaret	LT(SL)	W	I	10.12.87	CINCFLEET
Brighouse, Neil George	LT RM	RM		24.04.95	MOD DNR OUTPORTS
Bright, David Alan , BSc	LT CDR(SL)	I		01.10.92	EXCHANGE USA
Brightling, Colin	LT(SL)	X	P	01.09.89	810 SQN SEA
Brigstocke, John Richard , rcds, pce, psc	VADM	-	G	19.04.95	FOSF SEA PTSMTH
Brimley, Keith Stuart , BSc, pce	LT CDR	X	AWO(C)	01.12.80	NAVSOUTH ITALY
Brims, Fraser	SURG SLT	-		13.10.94	DARTMOUTH BRNC
Brind, Vincent James	LT(SL)	X	P	01.05.92	750 SQN OBS SCH
Brindley, Kimberlain , pce	LT CDR	X	PWO(A)	04.05.83	CNOCS GROUP
Brinsden, Mark Dudley	SURG LT	-		15.07.93	40 CDO RM
Bristow, Geoffrey David	LT CDR(SL)	X	SM	01.10.88	2SL/CNH FOTR
Bristowe, Paul Andrew , BSc	LT	X		01.03.93	RNU CRANWELL
Britton, Barbara Norma Elisabeth	LT	Q	FP	06.03.86	RH HASLAR
Britton, Nicholas John , BSc	LT CDR	X		01.04.90	SHAPE BELGIUM
Broad, Robert Andrew	LT CDR(SD)	E	AE(M)	01.10.92	MOD (BATH)
Broad, Robert Oliver , BSc, CEng, MIMechE, psc	CDR	E	ME	30.06.90	MOD (BATH)
Broadbent, Anthony , BSc	LT CDR	E	WE	29.11.81	MOD (BATH)
Broadbent, Andrew Craig , BEng	LT	E	WESM	01.08.93	TURBULENT
Broadbent, James Howard , BSc, CEng, MIMarE, MIMechE	CDR	E	MESM	31.12.84	RNC DPT NS&TECH
Broadhurst, Michael John , BSc, psc, ocds(Can)	CAPT	E	ME	31.12.92	BDLS CANADA
Broadhurst, Michael Robert , BA	LT	X	FC	01.12.92	ILLUSTRIOUS
Broadley, Andrew John McKenzie , MB, BMedSc, BCh, ChB	SURG LT	-		01.08.93	42 CDO RM
Broadley, Kevin James , BSc, pce, pcea, psc	LT CDR	X	P	01.01.92	HQ BF HK
Brock, Raymond Frederick	SLT(SD)	S	S	23.07.95	RNAS YEOVILTON
Brockington, Gordon Colin , BSc	SLT	X		01.01.95	DARTMOUTH BRNC

Name	Rank	Spec	Sub-spec	Seniority	Where serving
Brocklebank, Guy Philip , BSc, FRSA, AMBIM, pce	CDR	X	PWO(C)	31.12.92	NWOOD CIS
Brockwell, Paul Edward Norman , MBE, BSc, CEng, MIMarE	CDR	E	MESM	30.06.94	SULTAN
Brodie, Ross William James	LT	X		01.12.94	ANGLESEY
Brodier, Mark Ian	SLT(SD)	E	AE(L)	04.09.95	RNSC GREENWICH
Brokenshire, Laurence Phillip , BSc, BA, Cert Ed, AFIMA, MBCS, jsdc	CAPT	I	SM	30.06.94	2SL/CNH FOTR
Bromage, Kenneth	CHAPLAIN	CE		02.08.92	RALEIGH
Bromige, Timothy Robert James	LT CDR	X	PWO(A)	19.05.92	HQAFNORTHWEST
Brook, John Gordon , BSc, CEng, MIEE, psc	LT CDR	E	WE	21.03.87	MOD (LONDON)
Brooking, Stephen John	LT CDR	E	AE	11.05.87	RNAS CULDROSE
Brooks, Alan Steven , MBE, BSc, BTech, pce, pcea, psc	CDR	X	O	31.12.92	LONDON
Brooks, Barry Philip Stewart , BSc, psc	CAPT	E	WESM	31.12.92	MOD (LONDON)
Brooks, Graeme Christian Gibbon	SLT	X		01.09.94	DULVERTON
Brooks, Gary Lee	LT	X	H2	01.04.91	BULLDOG
Brooks, Mervyn Leigh	LT(SD)	X	AV	16.12.88	INVINCIBLE
Brooksbank, Richard James , BSc, pce, pcea	LT CDR	X	P	01.05.90	FONA NORTHWOOD
Broom, Neil John	LT(QM)	Q	OTSPEC	22.12.86	RNDHU DERRIFORD
Broom, Roger John , pcea	LT CDR	X	P	16.10.88	RNAS YEOVILTON
Brooman, Martin John	LT(SL)	X	P	16.08.95	820 SQN
Broome, Jonathan Richard , BM, BS, DIH, MRCP, AFOM	SURG CDR	-	CO/M	31.12.92	INM ALVERSTOKE
Brosnan, Mark Anthony	LT(SL)	X	O	16.07.93	820 SQN
Broster, Patrick Thomas (Act Lt Cdr)	LT(SL)	X	O	16.01.87	JARIC
Brothers, Anthony Herbert George	LT(SD)	E	WE	18.02.94	RALEIGH
Brotherton, John Darren	LT(SL)	X	P	16.04.90	705 SQN SEAHAWK
Brotherton, Michael , MBE, BD	CHAPLAIN	CE		04.09.84	COLLINGWOOD
Brothwell, Sarah Elizabeth , BA	LT(SL)	X		01.01.93	BRAZEN
Brothwood, Michael Kirk	LT	X	P	01.11.90	820 SQN
Brotton, Peter James	SLT(UCE)	X		01.09.95	NOTTINGHAM
Brough, Geoffrey Alan	CDR	E	WESM	31.12.94	NEPTUNE NT
Brougham, Michael John Douglas , MBE, BSc, CEng, MRAeS, jsdc	CAPT	E	AE(P)	09.12.92	DGA(N) ASE
Broughton, Michael George	LT CDR	X	P	01.10.94	815 FLT 207
Brown, Andrew Allan	LT(SL)	X	P	16.01.90	849 SQN HQ
Brown, Anthony Graham , BSc, pce	LT CDR	X	PWO(N)	01.10.88	LIVERPOOL
Brown, Andrew Martyn , BA, BEng	SLT	E	WE	01.09.94	PLOVER
Brown, Andrew Paul	LT(SL)	X	ATC	01.02.92	RNAS YEOVILTON
Brown, Amanda Patricia Susan	SLT(SL)	X	ATC	01.03.93	RNAS YEOVILTON
Brown, Barry Martin	LT CDR(SD)	S	CAT	01.10.91	HERON
Brown, Colin	LT(SL)	X	ATC	16.08.85	RNAS YEOVILTON
Brown, Christopher Dennis , pcea	LT CDR(SL)	X	P	01.09.87	845 SQN
Brown, Clare , BSc	SLT(SL)	X		01.09.93	DRYAD
Brown, David Campbell , MB, BCh, ChB, MSc, LRCP, MRCS	SURG CDR	-	CO/M	31.12.91	MOD (LONDON)
Brown, David John , BSc	LT CDR	X	SM	01.04.85	NEPTUNE BASE OPS
Brown, Howard Spencer , MBE, pcea	LT CDR	X	P	01.07.93	801 SQN
Brown, Judith Claire , ARRC, psc	LT CDR	Q	OTSPEC	03.03.84	RNDHU DERRIFORD
Brown, Leonard Anthony	LT RM	RM	RMP2	01.09.93	847 SQN
Brown, Michael Eric	LT CDR(SD)	E	WE	01.10.91	MOD (LONDON)
Brown, Malcolm Edward Clive , FCMA, ADIPM	CDR	S	CMA	31.12.88	NELSON RELEASE
Brown, Malcolm Keith , MBE, BSc, pce	CDR	X	PWO(A)	31.12.94	HQAFNORTHWEST
Brown, Michael Roy William , BSc	LT	X	O U/T	01.01.93	750 SQN OBS SCH
Brown, Neil Logan , LLB (Barrister)	LT	S	BAR	16.06.95	YORK
Brown, Nigel Peter , BSc, psc(m) (Loc Maj)	CAPT RM	RM		01.09.91	EXCHANGE ARMY UK
Brown, Paul Angus	LT(SD)	E	AE(M)	07.09.95	RNAS CULDROSE
Brown, Paul Alexander Everett , BA, n	LT	X		01.08.91	GLOUCESTER
Brown, Peter Jonathan , BSc	LT(SL)	X	P	16.02.89	ILLUSTRIOUS
Brown, Peter Richard , pce, psc	LT CDR	X	PWO(A)	16.03.85	FOST DPORT SHORE
Brown, Peter St John , BEng, MIMarE	LT CDR	E	MESM	01.06.95	TIRELESS
Brown, Robert Andrew Mark , pce	CDR	X	PWO(A)	31.12.94	SHAPE BELGIUM
Brown, Robert Colin	CAPT RM(SD)	RM	MTO	01.10.91	RM POOLE
Brown, Robert John	CAPT RM(SD)	RM		01.10.92	CTCRM
Brown, Simon David	LT	X		01.11.94	COVENTRY
Brown, Stephen	LT	X	MW	15.01.93	BERKELEY
Brown, Spencer James	LT(SL)	X	MW	01.10.95	CFP SHORE
Brown, Scott	CHAPLAIN	SF		20.04.93	RALEIGH

Name	Rank	Spec	Sub-spec	Seniority	Where serving
Brown, Simon John Joseph , pce	LT CDR	X	PWO(U)	16.06.87	FOSF
Brown, Steven Michael , BA	LT RM	RM		27.04.95	45 CDO RM
Brown, William Clarke	LT CDR	X	PWO(A)	01.01.94	EDINBURGH
Browne, Gregory Wade , BSc, psc	CDR	E	AE(P)	30.06.88	FAAIT MAN ORG VL
Browning, Martin Lawrence Corbet	LT CDR	X	SM	21.09.86	NBC PORTSMOUTH
Browning, Rowan Susannah , BSc	LT(SL)	I		01.01.90	MOD (LONDON)
Bruce, John , BSc, CEng, MIEE, MINucE, MIERE, psc	CDR	E	WESM	30.06.89	MOD CSSE USA
Bruce, Jonathon Fraser , MBA	LT CDR	S		01.06.90	2SL/CNH FOTR
Bruce, Steven Leonard , BA(OU), MA, psc	MAJ	RM	WTO	30.06.96	LOAN RSS BMATT
Bruce-Jones, Nicholas William , BA, psc(a)	CAPT RM	RM		01.09.92	42 CDO RM
Bruford, Robert Michael Charles	LT	X	FC	01.04.92	RNSC GREENWICH
Bruggenwirth, Stephen Jan Anthony , MA, pce, psc	LT CDR	X	O	01.08.90	FOSF SEA PTSMTH
Brundle, Paul Robert	LT CDR(SL)	X	ATC	01.10.95	FOST DPORT SHORE
Brunink, James William	LT CDR(SD)	E	WE	01.10.92	COLLINGWOOD
Brunsden-Brown, Sebastian Edward	LT(SL)	X	P	16.05.92	NP 1061
Brunskill, John Edmund Tanner	LT(SL)	X	P	01.06.91	750 SQN OBS SCH
Brunswick, Robert Edward , BSc	LT(SL)	X	P	16.10.90	801 SQN
Brunton, Lynn Marie , MB, BSc, BS	SURG LT	-		01.08.93	RH HASLAR
Brunton, Steven Buchanan , MSc, AMIEE, mdtc	CDR	E	WESM	31.12.95	MOD (LONDON)
Brutton, Joseph Henry , BEng	SLT(SD)	E	ME	01.01.95	DARTMOUTH BRNC
Bryan, Rory John Lockton , BA	LT	X		01.01.92	EXCHANGE GERMANY
Bryant, Barry William , pce, pcea, psc	CAPT	X	PWO	08.12.92	ENDURANCE
Bryant, David John	LT CDR(SD)	X	PWO(U)	01.10.94	DEF SCH OF LANG
Bryant, Daniel John Grenfell	LT(SL)	S		01.10.94	REPULSE(PORT)
Bryant, Graham David	LT(SD)	S	CA	12.12.91	RNSC GREENWICH
Bryant, Kevin Graham	SLT(SL)	X	P	01.11.93	SEAHAWK
Bryant, Peter	LT(SD)	E	ME	15.02.85	DRAKE CFM
Bryce, Colin Gerard , BSc, PGCE	LT CDR(SL)	I		01.10.94	CENTURION
Bryce, David Crawford , BSc	LT CDR	X	H CH	01.04.82	CAPTPORT CLYDE
Bryce, James Francis , BA, I(1)Ch	2LT(GRAD)	RM		01.09.94	CTCRM
Bryce, Neville Anthony	LT(SD)	E	MESM	14.10.94	RENOWN(PORT)
Bryning, Christopher John , BSc, jsdc, pce, pcea	CDR	X	P	31.12.90	IRON DUKE
Bryson, Paul Richard	LT CDR	S	SM	16.01.85	SCU LEYDENE ACNS
Bryson, Susan Ainee , BA	LT(SL)	X		01.03.94	WESTMINSTER
Buchan-Steele, Mark Anthony , BSc	LT CDR	S	SM	05.01.94	EXCHANGE USA
Buchanan, Alison Jane , MA	LT CDR(SL)	W	S	01.10.95	MOD (LONDON)
Buchanan, John Robert	LT CDR(SD)	X	REG	01.10.91	SULTAN
Buck, James Edward , n	LT	X		01.04.92	DRYAD
Buckeridge, Vincent Wellsley	LT(SD)	E	WESM	18.02.94	TRAFALGAR
Buckett, Edward Joseph	LT CDR(SL)	X	P	01.10.90	RAF SHAWBURY
Buckingham, Guy	LT	X	SM	01.12.93	TRAFALGAR
Buckingham, Paul	SLT(SD)	S	S	03.04.94	NEPTUNE CFS
Buckland, Richard John Francis , pce, pcea	LT CDR	X	O	01.08.90	MONMOUTH
Buckle, Iain Lawrence , BEng, MBA, CEng, MIMarE (Act Lt Cdr)	LT	E	WE	01.07.88	EXCHANGE USA
Buckley, Dominic David George , BA	LT(SL)	X		01.02.94	RNAS CULDROSE
Buckley, Martin John , BA	LT CDR	X	SM	16.05.85	URNU NEWCASTLE
Buckley, Paul , pce	LT CDR	X	PWO(A)	01.05.84	EXCELLENT
Buckley, Phillip James Anthony , pce, pce(sm)	LT CDR	X	SM	01.04.91	CSST SEA
Buckley, Richard Francis	CHAPLAIN	CE		04.09.79	FOSF
Bucklow, Stephen Paul	LT(SL)	X	P	01.06.91	819 SQN
Bucknall, Robin James Woolcott	LT RM	RM	MOR	26.04.93	ASC CAMBERLEY
Bucknell, David Ian (Act Lt Cdr)	LT	X	PWO(U)	01.07.88	COCHRANE
Bucks, Michael William , QHC, BD, AKC	CHAPLAIN-FLT	CE		18.11.69	2SL/CNH
Budd, Philip Richard , BA, pce	LT CDR	X	AWO(A)	16.12.80	MWC GOSPORT
Budge, Russell George , BSc, psc	LT CDR	E	WE	01.11.81	DGSS BRISTOL
Bugg, Kevin John	SLT(SD)	E	AE(M)	04.09.95	RNSC GREENWICH
Buggy, Michael William , BA, AMIEE	LT CDR	E	WE	01.11.79	MOD (BATH)
Bulcock, Lindsay , BSc	LT(SL)	I		01.11.89	NELSON
Bulcock, Michael	LT(SL)	E	MESM	01.01.96	RNC DPT NS&TECH
Bull, Andrew John , pcea, psc	CDR(SL)	X	O	01.10.95	JACIG
Bull, Christopher Martin Sefton	LT	E	WESM	01.09.89	MOD (BATH)
Bull, Geoffrey Charles , BEng	LT CDR	E	MESM	01.11.94	SCEPTRE

Name	Rank	Spec	Sub-spec	Seniority	Where serving
Bull, Michael Antony John , BSc	SLT(SL)	X		01.09.94	DUMBARTON CASTLE
Bullen, Michael Peter , BA	LT(SL)	X	P	16.08.91	814 SQN
Bullock, Michael Peter , MBE	CDR	S	SM	31.12.95	ELANT/NAVNW
Bullock, SusanMary	LT(SL)	W		04.01.92	LOAN CDA ADAC
Bulmer, Renny John	LT RM(SD)	RM	MTO	01.01.92	COMACCHIO GP RM
Bumby, Kevin James , BSc, CEng, MIEE	LT CDR	E	WE	16.04.80	MOD (LONDON)
Bunn, Elizabeth Mary , BEng	LT	E	AE	01.07.92	DGA(N) ASE
Bunn, Malcolm Edward	LT CDR(SL)	X	P	01.10.91	750 SQN OBS SCH
Bunney, Graham John , BSc	LT(SL)	X	P	01.08.94	706 SQN SEAHAWK
Bunt, Kevin John	LT(SD)	S	S	06.04.95	RNAS CULDROSE
Burbidge, Kay	SLT(SL)	X	O U/T	01.05.96	DARTMOUTH BRNC
Burbidge, Anthony James Hunter , BSc, CEng, MINucE, rcds, jsdc (Commodore)	CAPT	E	MESM	31.12.88	MOD (BATH)
Burbridge, Dominic James , BEng	LT	E	WESM	01.12.94	DOLPHIN SM SCHL
Burch, Jonathan Alexander , CBE, BSc, CEng, FIMgt, rcds, odc(Aus) (Commodore)	CAPT	E	MESM	30.06.89	DRAKE NBC(CFS)
Burden, John Charles	LT CDR	X	MCD	01.11.91	DEF DIVING SCHL
Burdett, Richard Wyndham , BSc, CEng, MIMechE	LT CDR	E	MESM	01.06.92	MOD DGSM DNREAY
Burge, Roger George	LT(SD)	E	WESM	19.02.93	DOLPHIN SM SCHL
Burgess, Andrew James , MB, BSc, BCh, ChB	SURG CDR	-	SA	30.06.96	RNH GIB
Burgess, Brian Coleman	LT CDR(SD)	E	WESM	01.10.87	CENTURION
Burgess, Gary Thomas Myles , BEng	LT	E	MESM	01.02.92	VANGUARD(PORT)
Burgess, Jonathan David Allen , BSc	LT CDR(SL)	X	P	01.10.93	847 SQN
Burgess, Stanley , pcea	LT CDR(SL)	X	P	01.10.90	32(THE ROYAL)SQN
Burgess, William Charles , BSc	LT CDR(SL)	E	AE	01.03.86	MOD (BATH)
Burgoine, Penelope Anne (Act Lt Cdr)	LT(SL)	W	S	05.04.86	SEA CADET CORPS
Burke, David , BA	SLT(SL)	X		01.01.94	DARTMOUTH BRNC
Burke, Michael Christopher , BSc	LT CDR	X	SM	01.09.95	TRAFALGAR
Burke, Paul Dominic , BA	LT CDR	X	SM	01.03.96	VICTORIOUS(STBD)
Burley, Matthew Richard	SLT	E	MESM	01.01.95	DARTMOUTH BRNC
Burlingham, Brett Limmer , BSc, CEng, MIMarE	LT CDR	E	ME	01.11.95	MOD (BATH)
Burlow, Gregory	LT(SL)	X	P	01.03.91	FONA VALLEY
Burne, Timothy George Lancaster , MNI, jsdc, pce	LT CDR	X	PWO	31.12.85	CDRPORT PORTLAND
Burnell, Jeremy Richard Jenner , fsc	CAPT RM	RM		01.09.91	HQRM
Burnell-Nugent, James Michael , MA, jsdc, pce, pce(sm) (Commodore)	CAPT	X	SM	30.06.90	MOD (LONDON)
Burnett, Gilbert Arthur	LT(SD)	E	ME	15.02.91	CFM PORTSMOUTH
Burnham, James Alistair Irby , MA	SLT(SL)	S		01.01.95	DARTMOUTH BRNC
Burningham, Michael Robert , BA	LT	S	SM	01.01.90	RALEIGH
Burnip, John Matthew , BSc	LT CDR	E	ME	01.08.93	IRON DUKE
Burns, Adrian Conleth	SLT(SL)	S		01.01.94	CAPTAIN SM2
Burns, Andrew Paul , BA	LT	X	FC	01.04.93	EXETER
Burns, Bryan , CBE (Commodore)	CAPT	X	C	30.06.83	2SL/CNH
Burns, David Ian , BSc, ARCS	LT	X		01.05.90	DRYAD
Burns, David John , BA, CEng, FIMechE, MINucE, rcds (Commodore)	CAPT	E	MESM	31.12.89	MOD (BATH)
Burns, James Edward	SLT	E	WE	01.01.95	DARTMOUTH BRNC
Burns, Rachel Charlotte , BA	LT	S		01.06.92	DGSS BRISTOL
Burns, Robin Douglas James , BSc	LT(SL)	I	METOC	06.01.91	CAPT F1(SEA)
Burns, Thomas	CHAPLAIN	RC		04.01.94	AFCC
Burrell, Aleck Micheal George (Act Lt Rm)	2LT	RM		28.04.93	45 CDO RM
Burrell, Philip Mark , BSc, psc	CDR	I	MCD	30.06.95	LOAN OMAN
Burrows, John Anthony	LT CDR(SD)	E	WE	01.10.93	CNSA PORTLAND
Burrows, John Campbell	LT(SD)	E	MESM	15.10.93	TRENCHANT
Burrows, Michael John	LT CDR(SL)	X	P	01.10.94	LOAN DTEO BSC DN
Burrows, Michael John , pce	CDR	X	PWO(A)	31.12.94	CINCFLEET
Burrows, Robert Gerwyn	CDR(SL)	X	O	01.10.90	LOAN DTEO BSC DN
Burston, Richard , pce(sm)	CDR	X	SM	30.06.92	MOD (BATH)
Burstow, Richard Stanley	LT(SL)	X	MW	01.05.91	BERKELEY
Burt, Paul Ronald	LT CDR(SD)	S	S	01.10.93	FONA
Burton, Alexander James , BSc, pce	LT CDR	X	PWO(U)	01.09.95	ARGYLL
Burton, Christopher James	LT CDR(SD)	S	S	01.10.89	CFM PORTSMOUTH
Burton, Christopher John , BSc	LT	X	FC	01.01.93	LIVERPOOL
Burton, David Stephen , MSc	CDR	I		31.12.95	2SL/CNH

Name	Rank	Spec	Sub-spec	Seniority	Where serving
Burton, Nicholas Jeremy	LT CDR	S		16.06.89	MOD (LONDON)
Burvill, Justin Paul , BEng	LT	E	MESM	01.03.95	TRAFALGAR
Burwin, Harvey Lee , BEng	LT	E	WE	01.11.88	DGSS BRISTOL
Bush, Alexander John Taylor	LT	X	MCD	01.06.91	BRECON
Bush, Stephen John Duyland , psc	MAJ	RM		31.12.86	CTCRM
Bushell, Gary Robert	LT(SD)	X	PT	15.12.89	SHAPE BELGIUM
Bussey, Emma Louise	SLT(UCE)	X		01.09.95	DARTMOUTH BRNC
Butcher, Linda Joan , ARRC, MEng	LT CDR	Q	RNT	08.01.88	RN MSS HASLAR
Butcher, Martin Charles , pce	LT CDR	X	PWO(C)	16.11.85	CINCFLEET
Butcher, Martin William , MBE, pce, psc	CDR	X	P	30.06.91	RNAS CULDROSE
Butler, Brian Paul , BSc, psc	LT CDR	E	ME	01.09.87	FOST SEA
Butler, David , BSc	LT RM	RM		01.09.93	AACC MID WALLOP
Butler, Ian Anthony	SLT(SD)	E	AE(L)	12.09.94	899 SQN HERON
Butler, Lee Peter	LT(SD)	E	AE(L)	15.10.93	815 OEU OSPREY
Butler, Nicholas Abraham Marsh , pce, pcea	CDR	X	P	30.06.91	FOSF SEA PTSMTH
Butler, Robert John , BSc, (Eur Ing), CEng, MRAeS, jsdc	CDR	E	AE	31.12.88	HQ NORTH
Butterfield, Neil Philip , MB, BS, DA, DipAvMed	SURG CDR	-	GMPP	31.12.92	LOAN BRUNEI
Butterworth, Nigel Gregory , BA	LT	X	FC	01.04.93	GLASGOW
Butterworth, Paul Gerard	SLT	X		01.09.94	DARTMOUTH BRNC
Buxton, Mark John	LT(SD)	E	WESM	09.06.89	CWTA PTSMTH
Buxton, Peter John , BM, BCh, MA, FRCR	SURG CDR	-	CX	31.12.95	RH HASLAR
Buzza, Simon George Livingstone Parry , BSc, psc	MAJ	RM		30.06.93	42 CDO RM
Bye, Marc David , BEng	LT	E	ME	01.05.92	CFM PORTSMOUTH
Byrne, Adrian Charles , IEng, MIPlantE	LT(SD)	E	ME	18.06.93	RALEIGH
Byrne, Thomas , BEng	SLT	X		01.01.94	NORTHUMBERLAND
Byrne, Terence Michael	LT(SD)	X	REG	13.12.95	DOLPHIN
Byron, James David	LT(SL)	X	MW	01.05.95	COTTESMORE
Bywater, Richard Lewis , BEng	LT	E	WE	01.09.91	DRYAD

C

Name	Rank	Spec	Sub-spec	Seniority	Where serving
Cadogan, Brendan Henry , BEng	LT CDR	E	WESM	30.03.93	FOSM FASLANE
Cahill, Christopher John , MB, BS, FRCSEd	SURG CDR	-	CA/E	30.06.91	RH HASLAR
Cahill, Karen , BA	LT	X		01.03.96	ORWELL
Cailes, Michael John (Loc Maj)	CAPT RM	RM	WTO	10.02.81	CTCRM
Cain, Christopher William	SLT(SD)	E	WESM	07.02.94	NEPTUNE SM1
Cain, Neal Edward	LT(SL)	X	P	17.10.91	848 SQN HERON
Caldicott-Barr, Victoria Anne	SLT(SL)	X		01.01.93	SULTAN
Calkin, Douglas Alan , BSc	LT(SL)	X	H2	01.03.93	NP 1008 OFS SVY
Callaghan, Paul Fraser , BSc	LT(SL)	X	P	01.04.89	706 SQN SEAHAWK
Callister, David Roy , pcea	LT CDR(SL)	X	O	01.10.95	FONA OSPREY
Callon, Andrew	CHAPLAIN	CE		05.06.90	NEPTUNE
Calvert, Graham , BSc	LT CDR	E	AE	01.08.92	DGA(N) ASE
Cameron, Andrew John Brunt , pce	CDR	X	PWO(U)	31.12.89	WESTMINSTER
Cameron, Iain	LT	X	P	01.09.91	846 SQN
Cameron, Mark John , BEng	LT(SL)	E	WE	01.04.92	COLLINGWOOD
Cameron, Peter Stuart , BA	CAPT RM	RM		01.09.95	ASC CAMBERLEY
Campbell, David John , MB, BS	SURG LTCDR	-	GMPP	01.05.90	LOAN BRUNEI
Campbell, IainAngus	LT(SL)	X	P	16.04.96	820 SQN
Campbell, James Colin	LT(SL)	I		01.09.89	SULTAN
Campbell, James Kininmonth , MB, BS, LRCP, FRCSEd, MRCS	SURG CDR	-	CGS	30.06.92	RNDHU DERRIFORD
Campbell, Katrina Louise	LT(SL)	W	X	12.09.89	MOD (LONDON)
Campbell, Lawrie Gordon , BA	2LT(GRAD)	RM		01.09.94	COMACCHIO GP RM
Campbell, Leslie Michael , BA	LT	X	MW	01.07.92	BRIDPORT
Campbell, Malcolm Alexander , BEd	LT(SL)	I		01.01.88	DRYAD
Campbell, Mark , BEng	SLT(SL)	X	P U/T	01.05.94	DARTMOUTH BRNC
Campbell, Peter Robert	LT(SL)	X	O	01.01.94	750 SQN OBS SCH
Campbell, Robin David Hastings , BSc, BEng	LT CDR	E	WESM	01.02.95	MOD (BATH)
Campbell-Balcombe, Andre Alexander , BEng	LT(SL)	E	WE	01.07.94	INVINCIBLE
Canning, Christopher , BSc	LT(SL)	X	O	01.03.92	810 SQN A FLIGHT
Canning, Sarah , BSc	LT(SL)	X	P U/T	01.12.95	FONA LINTON/OUSE
Canning, William Andrew , psc(m)	MAJ	RM		30.06.93	CTCRM

Name	Rank	Spec	Sub-spec	Seniority	Where serving
Cannon, Leslie Brian , MB, BSc, BS	SURG LT	-		01.08.92	RH HASLAR
Cantello, David John	LT CDR	X	PWO(U)	01.11.84	NEPTUNE NT
Canter, Paul Charles Beeching , CBE, jsdc, pce, psc (Commodore)	CAPT	X	G	31.12.87	COMAW SEA
Canty, Nigel Robert , BSc	LT CDR	E	MESM	01.09.91	BF GIBRALTAR(NE)
Capes, Stuart George	SLT	X		01.09.93	TORBAY
Capewell, David Andrew , psc(m), fsc	MAJ	RM	WTO	12.12.94	DRYAD MWC
Carden, Peter David , pce	LT CDR	X	O	01.12.92	LINDISFARNE
Carey, Adrian Gilbert	LT RM	RM	LC	25.04.94	RM POOLE
Cargen, Malcolm Robert , BSc	LT CDR	E	AE	01.02.93	RNSC GREENWICH
Cariss, Paul , BSc, CEng, MIMarE, MIMechE	CDR	E	MESM	30.06.90	MOD DGSM DNREAY
Carleton, Christopher Michael , MBE, MNI	LT CDR	X	H CH	01.11.78	LOAN HYDROG
Carlisle, Christopher Richard , BEng	LT	E	ME	01.05.95	LIVERPOOL
Carlton, Ian Philip	LT CDR(SD)	X	g	01.10.89	BF GIBRALTAR(NE)
Carne, John Richard Camin , MB, BA, BCh, BAO	SURG CAPT	-	GMPP	30.06.93	DRAKE CBP
Carne, Richard James Power	LT(SL)	X	O	16.05.87	SEAHAWK
Carnell, Gregory James	LT(SL)	X	O	01.09.91	810 SQN SEAHAWK
Carnt, Stephen Paul , MSc, MIEE, psc, gw	CDR	E	WE	31.12.89	2SL/CNH FOTR
Carpenter, Christopher John , BSc	LT CDR	E	WESM	01.09.90	MOD (BATH)
Carpenter, Philip John , BA	LT(SL)	X	P	01.08.94	848 SQN HERON
Carr, Adam Garry	LT(SL)	X	P	01.07.94	819 SQN
Carr, David Leslie , pcea	LT CDR(SD)	X	O	01.10.89	OSPREY
Carr, Geoffrey , MSc, (Eur Ing), CEng, FIMarE, MIMechE	LT CDR	E	ME	06.03.86	CAPTAIN RNP TEAM
Carr, Kevin	LT RM	RM		29.04.96	45 CDO RM
Carr, Matthew Charles	LT(SL)	X		01.04.96	HERON
Carr, Martin Paul	LT(SD)	E	WE	10.06.88	MCM2 SEA
Carr, Robert Grenville , BEng	LT(SL)	E	WESM	01.10.92	SPLENDID
Carretta, Mark Vincent , BSc	LT CDR(SL)	X	P	01.10.95	845 SQN
Carrick, Richard James , BEng	LT	E	MESM	01.05.89	RNC DPT NS&TECH
Carrigan, Jonathan Andrew	SLT	S		01.09.95	FOST DPORT SHORE
Carrington-Wood, Clive Gordon	LT CDR	X	PWO(A)	01.10.91	COMUKTG/CASWSF
Carroll, Benjamin John , BA, n	LT	X		01.02.90	URNU CARDIFF
Carroll, Paul Christopher , BEng	LT	E	ME	01.03.94	MANCHESTER
Carroll, Philip John , BSc	LT(SL)	X	H1	01.01.86	BEAGLE
Carroll, Peter William Mark , pce(sm)	LT CDR	X	SM	01.10.89	CSST SHORE FSLN
Carson, Michael John , BSc, pce, I(2)Fr	LT CDR	X	PWO(C)	01.12.95	BRITANNIA
Carson, Neil Douglas Ernest , BSc	LT	X	SM	01.01.89	SPLENDID
Carter, Ashley Francis Rees , BSc, CEng, MIEE	LT CDR	E	WE	01.05.93	BRAVE
Carter, Bruce Gordon , CEng, MIERE, psc	CDR	E	WESM	31.12.87	LOAN DTEO BHMAS
Carter, David Alistair Paul , MSc, CEng, MIEE	CDR	E	WE	31.12.84	DGSS BRISTOL
Carter, Ian Paul , pce	LT CDR	X	PWO(A)	01.05.94	EDINBURGH
Carter, John David , BSc	LT CDR	E	WESM	01.06.86	MOD (LONDON)
Carter, John Jervis	LT CDR	X	O	01.03.78	SEAHAWK
Carter, Jonathon Mark , BSc	LT	E	WESM	01.06.88	MOD (LONDON)
Carter, Kendall , BSc, pce	CDR	X	PWO(N)	30.06.95	HQAFNORTHWEST
Carter, Kevin Stanley	LT(SD)	X	PT	29.07.94	SEAHAWK
Carter, Robert Ian	LT CDR(SL)	X	ATC	01.10.95	ILLUSTRIOUS
Carter, Stephen Frank , FFA, psc	CDR	X	SM	31.12.89	DRYAD
Carter, Simon Neil	LT CDR	S		01.02.96	HQ CDO AVN
Carter, Simon Peter	LT(SD)	S	CA	04.04.96	ILLUSTRIOUS
Carter, Thomas Leighton , BSc	LT CDR	X		16.05.82	CDRE MFP
Cartlidge, David , jsdc, psc	CDR	X	MCDPWO	31.12.85	CAPTPORT CLYDE
Cartwright, Darren	LT	X	O	01.09.90	DRYAD
Cartwright, James Andrew	SLT	E	MESM	01.09.95	DARTMOUTH BRNC
Cartwright, John Rollo , pce, psc (Commodore)	CAPT	X	AWO(A)	30.06.86	FOSF
Cartwright, Richard Alan , BSc, MA, CEng, MIMarE, psc	LT CDR	E	ME	01.04.89	DG SHIPS PTSMTH
Carty, Jonathan	SURG SLT	-		01.07.94	DARTMOUTH BRNC
Carver, Anthony Graham , BSc	LT CDR	E	WESM	01.05.89	MOD (BATH)
Case, Alexander Charles , BSc (Loc Capt Rm)	LT RM	RM		24.04.92	EXCHANGE ARMY UK
Case, Paul	LT(SD)	S	S	11.12.92	RNAS YEOVILTON
Cass, Paul Stuart	LT CDR	S		11.02.89	LIVERPOOL
Cassar, Adrian Peter Felix , BA, pce	LT CDR	X	MCD	01.04.91	INVERNESS
Casson, Neil Philip , BSc	LT(SL)	I	SM	01.01.90	DOLPHIN SM SCHL

Name	Rank	Spec	Sub-spec	Seniority	Where serving
Casson, Paul Richard , BEng, MBA	LT CDR	E	ME	01.02.96	NORFOLK
Castle, Alastair Stuart , BSc	LT(SL)	X	P	01.12.89	820 SQN
Cattroll, David	SLT(SD)	E	MESM	13.06.94	SPARTAN
Cattroll, Iain Murdo , BSc	LT CDR	E	WE	01.03.94	ILLUSTRIOUS
Cave, Patricia	LT CDR	Q	ONC	16.10.82	2SL/CNH FOTR
Cawthorne, Matthew William Southworth , psc(m) (Loc Maj)	CAPT RM	RM	MLDR	01.09.93	CINCFLEET
Chadfield, Laurence James , BA	LT(SL)	X		01.03.94	CAMPBELTOWN
Chadwick, Geoffrey Edward , BSc	LT CDR	E	WESM	01.04.82	MOD DGSWS BATH
Chadwick, John , CEng, MIEE, jsdc (Commodore)	CAPT	E	WESM	31.12.89	COLLINGWOOD
Challands, Guy David , BSc, MPhil, CEng, MIEE	CAPT	E	WESM	30.06.92	MOD (LONDON)
Challinor, Ryan Anthony , BSc	LT	S		01.02.92	MAS BRUSSELS
Chalmers, Donald Peter , pce	LT CDR	X	PWO(U)	01.10.91	LONDON
Chalmers, Paul , BSc	LT	X	FC	01.10.91	EDINBURGH
Chaloner, Andrew	LT(SL)	X	P	01.07.94	810 SQN OEU
Chaloner, Robert Patrick	LT CDR(SL)	X	P	01.10.94	HERON FLIGHT
Chamberlain, Henry James , BEng	LT RM	RM		28.04.94	NP 1002 DIEGOGA
Chamberlain, Nicholas Richard Lawrence , BEng	LT	E	WE	01.11.93	BEAVER
Chamberlain, Trevor Ian	LT(SD)	E	ME	18.02.88	COLLINGWOOD
Chambers, David	LT(CS)RM	-		18.10.87	MOD DNR OUTPORTS
Chambers, Ian Richard , BEng	LT	E	WESM	01.05.92	VIGILANT(PORT)
Chambers, Nigel Maurice Christopher , BSc, pce	CDR	X	PWO(U)	30.06.91	MOD (LONDON)
Chambers, Paul	LT(SD)	E	WE	18.02.94	MOD (LONDON)
Chambers, Paul	SLT(SL)	E	WE	01.05.96	GLASGOW
Chambers, Thomas George	LT CDR(SL)	X	MCD	01.10.88	EXCHANGE USA
Chambers, William John , pce	CDR	X	PWO(A)	30.06.93	LOAN OMAN
Chan-A-Sue, Stephen Sangster	LT(SL)	X	P	16.01.92	EXCHANGE RAF UK
Chance, David Malcolm Rowland , MSc	LT CDR	E	WE	01.03.96	COLLINGWOOD
Chandler, Michael , FISM (Act Cdr)	LT CDR(SD)	MS	AD	01.10.88	MOD (LONDON)
Chandler, Marcus Ffrench Hamilton	LT RM	RM	P	30.04.91	846 SQN
Chandler, Nigel James	LT	X	PWO(C)	01.03.89	SHEFFIELD
Chandler, Stephen Arthur	LT CDR	X	PWO(U)	01.01.87	CNOCS GROUP
Channer, Daniel Ian , BSc	LT(SL)	I		01.05.89	SULTAN
Channon, Michael John , BSc	CDR(SL)	I	METOC	01.09.86	SACLANT USA
Chapell, Andrew	LT	S	SM	01.03.89	RALEIGH
Chapman, Charles Leslie , BEng	LT(SL)	E	WESM	01.11.94	DOLPHIN SM SCHL
Chapman, Darren Andrew	LT(SL)	X	P	16.03.90	848 SQN HERON
Chapman, Douglas Brian John , pcea	LT CDR	X	P	01.11.93	845 SQN
Chapman, Geoffrey John Douglas , BSc	LT CDR(SL)	I		01.10.95	EXCHANGE ARMY UK
Chapman, Gareth Lawrence (Act Capt Rm)	LT RM	RM	RMP2	01.09.90	CTCRM
Chapman, Leslie Arthur , pce(sm)	LT CDR	X	SM	01.09.87	VICTORIOUS(PORT)
Chapman, Nicholas John , BA, pce(sm)	LT CDR	X	SM	01.05.90	MOD (LONDON)
Chapman, Nolan Phillip	LT CDR(SD)	S	W	01.10.92	EXETER
Chapman, Peter , BEng	LT	E	WE	01.09.93	NORTHUMBERLAND
Chapman, Robert William Thomas , BA	LT CDR(SL)	I		16.09.74	HERON
Chapman, Simon , BA, BSc	LT RM	RM		01.09.91	MOD DNR OUTPORTS
Chapman, Simon John	LT	X	FC	01.04.90	RNSC GREENWICH
Chapman-Andrews, Peter Charles , LVO, pce, psc	CDR	X	PWO(N)	30.06.89	MOD (LONDON)
Chapple, Colin Peter , BSc, PGCE	LT CDR	I	METOC	01.05.90	CINCFLEET
Chapple, Jonathan Charles Bennett , LLB	LT CDR	X	MCD	01.06.90	RNSC GREENWICH
Charlesworth, Graham Keith , MSc, AMIEE	LT CDR	E	WESM	01.02.94	DOLPHIN SM SCHL
Charlier, Simon Boyce , pce, pcea, psc	CDR	X	P	30.06.95	NORTHUMBERLAND
Charlton, Christopher Robin Arthur MacGaw , BA	LT CDR	S		01.03.89	FOST SEA
Charlton, David Rhoderick , FBIM, MNI, pce, pce(sm), psc	CDR	X	SM	30.06.89	MWC GOSPORT
Charlton, Noel	SLT	X		01.01.95	CROMER
Charnock, Alison	LT	Q		01.09.95	RH HASLAR
Chaston, Stephen Paul	LT	X	SM	01.03.93	TRIUMPH
Chattin, Antony Paul , BEng	LT RM	RM		29.04.93	HQ 3 CDO BDE RM
Chatwin, Nicholas John , BSc, pce, pcea	LT CDR	X	P	01.07.90	DRYAD
Chawira, Denis , BSc	SLT(SL)	X		01.05.94	EXETER
Cheadle, Richard Frank , MSc, CEng, MIMechE, jsdc	CAPT	E	MESM	30.06.93	2SL/CNH
Cheesman, Christopher John , BEng	LT CDR	E	AE	28.06.92	848 SQN HERON
Cheesman, Daniel	2LT(UCE)	RM		01.09.93	CTCRM LYMPSTONE

Name	Rank	Spec	Sub-spec	Seniority	Where serving
Cheesman, David James Maynard	LT	X		01.09.95	SPLENDID
Cheesman, Philip Maynard , MSc, CEng, MIEE, psc	CAPT	E	WE	31.12.93	DNPS
Chelton, Simon Roger Lewis , BA, MIL, I(2)Ja, OCDS(JAP)	CDR	S	SM	30.06.94	2SL/CNH
Cheseldine, David	LT(SD)	E	AE(M)	16.10.92	706 SQN SEAHAWK
Cheshire, Michael , pce	LT CDR	X	PWO(C)	27.06.81	VICTORY
Cheshire, Thomas Edward , BEng	LT(SL)	E	MESM	01.02.94	TRAFALGAR
Chesterman, Graham John , pcea	LT CDR	X	O	01.02.93	FOST SEA
Chestnutt, James Muir	SLT(UCE)	E		01.09.95	DARTMOUTH BRNC
Cheyne, Steven , BSc	LT CDR(SL)	X	P	01.10.93	EXCHANGE USA
Chibnall, Anthony Crichton Stuart , psc(m) (Loc Lt Col)	MAJ	RM		30.06.85	SHAPE BELGIUM
Chichester, Mark Arlington Raleigh , BSc, pce(sm)	LT CDR	X	SM	01.10.90	CAPTAIN SM2
Chick, Nicholas Stevens	LT(SL)	X	P	16.11.95	814 SQN
Chick, Stephen John , BSc, pce	CDR	X	PWO(A)	30.06.96	MOD (LONDON)
Chicken, Simon Timothy , MBE, MA, psc	MAJ	RM	LC	31.12.95	HQRM
Chidley, Timothy James , BSc, CEng, MIMarE	LT CDR	E	ME	01.09.92	MONTROSE
Chilcott, Peter Leslie Herbert	LT(SD)	MS	SM	02.04.93	NEPTUNE NT
Childs, Dianne , BEng	LT	E	WE	01.11.92	CAPTAIN RNP TEAM
Childs, David Geoffrey , BSc	LT CDR	E	AE(P)	01.05.96	RNAS CULDROSE
Childs, John Richard	LT(SL)	X	FC	01.04.94	INVINCIBLE
Chiles, Jennifer Marian , BA	SLT(SL)	S		01.09.94	GLOUCESTER
Chilman, Peter William Howard	LT CDR	S	SM	01.03.93	NAVSOUTH ITALY
Chilton, Antony Lovel , LVO, OBE, jsdc, pce, psc, FIMgt (Commodore)	CAPT	X	N	31.12.91	RNSC GREENWICH
Chilton, Jerard	MID(SL)	E	WE	01.05.94	EDINBURGH
Chilvers, Martyn Iain	2LT(GRAD)	RM		01.09.95	CTCRM LYMPSTONE
Chippindale, Neil	SLT(SL)	X		01.05.95	FEARLESS
Chisnall, David Alan , BEM	CAPT RM(SD)	RM		01.10.91	RM NORTON MANOR
Chittenden, Timothy Clive , MA, MSc, CEng, MIMechE, MINucE, jsdc	CAPT	E	MESM	31.12.94	MOD CSSE LONDON
Chittick, William	SG SLT(D)	-		01.04.95	DARTMOUTH BRNC
Chivers, Paul Austin , pce, pcea	LT CDR	X	O	16.05.94	ILLUSTRIOUS
Choat, Jeffery Hugh	LT(SL)	X	O	16.08.93	750 SQN OBS SCH
Choules, Barrie , MEng	LT	E	MESM	01.09.90	NEPTUNE NT
Chrishop, Timothy Ian , pcea	LT CDR	X	O	01.04.96	DRYAD
Christian, David	LT(SD)	E	ME	10.06.94	DRAKE CFM
Christie, Campbell Stuart , BEd, psc	CDR	I		30.06.94	RNSC GREENWICH
Christmas, Stephen Peter	LT(SL)	X	P	16.08.91	771 SK5 SAR
Christopher, Antony , BEng	SURG SLT	-		01.07.95	DARTMOUTH BRNC
Chubb, John James , BEng, CEng, MIEE	LT	E	WE	01.07.88	MOD (LONDON)
Church, Alan David	LT CDR	S		28.12.89	2SL/CNH
Church, Carl Robert	LT(SL)	S		01.09.90	FOST DPORT SHORE
Church, Stephen Cofield	SLT(SL)	X	P	01.01.93	810 SQN OEU
Churcher, Jeremy Edward , n	LT	X	H2	01.08.91	RN HYDROG SCHL
Churcher-Brown, Christopher John , DPM, LRCP, MRCPsych, MRCS	SURG CDR	-	CN/P	30.06.84	RH HASLAR
Churchill, Timothy Charles , pce	CDR	X	PWO(N)	31.12.93	MOD (LONDON)
Churchill, William John	LT CDR(SD)	E	HULL	01.10.86	FOSF
Churton, Graham , MNI	LT CDR	X	PWO(C)	01.09.80	SCU LEYDENE ACNS
Cirin, Wladislaw Roman Joseph , BSc, psc	CDR	E	MESM	30.06.88	DRAKE CFM
Citrine, Johanna , BEng	LT(SL)	I		01.01.93	SULTAN
Clague, John Joseph , BEng, MEng	SLT(SL)	X		01.09.94	LINDISFARNE
Clancy, Raphael Joseph	CHAPLAIN	RC		02.07.79	CALEDONIA
Clapham, Ian , BSc	CDR	E	MESM	30.06.82	SHAPE BELGIUM
Clapp, Richard Julian , BSc, jsdc, pce, pcea	CAPT	X	P	30.06.95	MOD (LONDON)
Clapson, Keith , osc	CAPT RM	RM		01.07.85	RMB STONEHOUSE
Clare, Roy Alexander George , rcds, pce, psc	CAPT	X	AWO(A)	31.12.90	DRYAD
Clark, Angela Catherine , BSc	LT(SL)	W		01.09.92	RH HASLAR
Clark, Anthony Ivo Harvey , BSc, CEng, MIEE, psc	CAPT	E	WE	31.12.94	SACLANT USA
Clark, Andrew Nelham , BSc	LT CDR	E	MESM	01.09.91	RNC DPT NS&TECH
Clark, Alan Sutherland	SLT(SD)	X	SM	03.04.94	COLLINGWOOD
Clark, Alastair William Charles , psc	LT CDR	X	O	01.03.91	STARLING
Clark, Donald Kennedy , BSc, AMIMarE	LT CDR	E	MESM	01.08.89	NEPTUNE SM1
Clark, Dennis Michael James , MA, psc	CAPT RM(SD)	RM		01.10.94	CDO LOG REGT RM
Clark, Hugh Sinclair , DSC, MNI, pce, psc(a)	CDR	X	P	31.12.83	SA MUSCAT

Name	Rank	Spec	Sub-spec	Seniority	Where serving
Clark, Ian David , BSc	LT CDR	E	MESM	01.11.94	SPLENDID
Clark, James Lea , n	LT	X		01.06.94	WESTMINSTER
Clark, Jessica Margaret , BEng	SLT(SL)	X		01.05.94	LONDON
Clark, Kevin Charles , BEng, MSc	LT CDR	E	ME	01.11.94	LOAN DTEO PYSTCK
Clark, Kenneth Ian MacDonald , pce(sm)	CDR	X	SM	31.12.94	SPLENDID
Clark, Michael Alwyn Stephen	LT CDR(SL)	X	O	01.10.88	INVINCIBLE
Clark, Michael Howard	SLT	X		01.09.93	YORK
Clark, Matthew Thomas	LT(SL)	S	SM	01.11.90	FOSF
Clark, Paul Anthony	LT RM(SD)	RM		01.01.95	HQ 3 CDO BDE RM
Clark, Paul Michael Colin	LT CDR(SL)	X	ATC	01.10.93	OSPREY
Clark, Russell	MID	X		01.01.95	DARTMOUTH BRNC
Clark, Robin John , MB, BS, LRCP, psc	SURG CDR	-	SM	31.12.88	RH HASLAR
Clark, Robert William	LT CDR	S		01.07.88	BEAVER
Clark, Simon Mansfield	LT	S		01.12.90	2SL/CNH
Clark, Simon Richard , BEng	LT	E	WESM	01.05.89	MOD DGSWS BATH
Clark, Timothy Hubert Vian , MA, pce, psc	CDR	X	AWO(U)	30.06.91	RALEIGH
Clarke, Adrian , BSc, AMIEE	LT CDR	E	WE	01.02.94	CNOCS GROUP
Clarke, Andrew Patrick	LT(SL)	X	P	16.05.90	846 SQN
Clarke, Andrew Richard	LT(SL)	E	AE(L)	01.04.96	SULTAN
Clarke, Bernard Ronald	CHAPLAIN	CE		30.06.81	INVINCIBLE
Clarke, Charles Maxwell Lorne , pce	CDR	X	PWO(U)	30.06.95	CINCFLEET
Clarke, Daniel	LT(SL)	X	O	16.03.94	815 FLT 215
Clarke, Daniel	SLT	X		01.01.96	DRYAD
Clarke, Graham Kenneth , psc	CDR	S		30.06.94	DARTMOUTH BRNC
Clarke, Ian Bruce , n	LT(SL)	X		01.07.95	PEACOCK
Clarke, James	LT(SD)	E	WE	13.06.91	COLLINGWOOD
Clarke, Jonathan Clive , BSc	SLT(SL)	X	O U/T	01.01.95	DARTMOUTH BRNC
Clarke, Justin James , BEng	LT	E	WESM	01.12.91	VANGUARD(STBD)
Clarke, John Patrick , CB, LVO, MBE, pce	RADM	-	SM(N)	14.03.94	HYDROG TAUNTON
Clarke, Matthew Dickon , MB, BS	SURG LT	-		04.08.94	BRAVE
Clarke, Nicholas John , pce	LT CDR	X	P	28.07.91	DARTMOUTH BRNC
Clarke, Philip Andrew	LT(SL)	X		01.08.94	BFFI
Clarke, Peter John	LT	X	P	01.02.91	819 SQN
Clarke, Richard , BA	LT(SL)	I		01.12.87	DARTMOUTH BRNC
Clarke, Roger Donald , BSc	LT CDR	E	WE	27.05.92	DG SHIPS CAM HSE
Clarke, Robert	SLT(SL)	X	P	01.03.93	814 SQN
Clarke, RichardWilliam , BEng	LT	E	AE	01.03.94	706 SQN SEAHAWK
Clarke, Timothy John	LT(SL)	I		01.01.87	DADPTC SHRIVNHAM
Clarkson, Suzanne Jane (Act Surg Lt)	SURG SLT	-		01.12.92	DARTMOUTH BRNC
Claxton, Martin Geoffrey	LT CDR	E	MESM	18.02.93	VICTORIOUS(STBD)
Clay, Christopher James , OBE, pce, psc	CDR	X	P	31.12.83	2SL/CNH
Clay, Jason , BSc	SLT	X		01.09.93	DARTMOUTH BRNC
Clay, Samuel Charles	LT(SL)	X		01.06.85	CFP SEA
Clayden, John William Anthony , BSc, CEng, MIMechE, jsdc	CAPT	E	MESM	31.12.91	FOSM NWOOD HQ
Clayton, Christopher Hugh Trevor , pce, psc	CAPT	X	P	31.12.95	CHATHAM
Clayton, Michael James , BA	2LT(GRAD)	RM		01.09.95	CTCRM LYMPSTONE
Clayton, Richard John , BA	LT CDR	X	PWO(A)	01.10.90	MOD (LONDON)
Cleary, Stephen Peter , pce	CDR	X	PWO(A)	31.12.93	2SL/CNH FOTR
Clegg, Martin Leslie , BSc	LT CDR	X	H CH	01.06.90	NP 1016 IN SURV
Clelland, Graham	SLT(SD)	X	REG	23.07.93	ILLUSTRIOUS
Clement, Colin James , BSc	LT CDR(SL)	E	ME	01.10.89	GLASGOW
Clements, Elizabeth Joanne	SLT(SL)	X	ATCU/T	01.05.96	RAF SHAWBURY
Clements, Susan Alfreda , ARRC	LT CDR	Q	RSCNO	07.08.82	RH HASLAR
Clements, Stephen James	LT(SD)	X	g	02.04.93	FOST MPV(SEA)
Cleminson, Mark David , BEng	LT(SL)	E	MESM	16.05.93	RNC DPT NS&TECH
Clemson, Anthony James , BSc	SLT(SL)	X		01.01.95	DARTMOUTH BRNC
Clifford, Clive	SLT(SD)	X	EW	25.07.93	INVINCIBLE
Clifford, Martin Roy , BSc	LT CDR(SL)	X	P	01.10.95	EXCHANGE DENMARK
Clifford, Richard Cormac , MBE (Loc Maj)	CAPT RM	RM		01.07.75	HQRM
Clifford, Timothy John , BEng, MSc	LT CDR	E	AE	01.10.95	MOD (LONDON)
Clink, Adam Duncan , BSc	LT(SL)	X	P U/T	01.12.94	HERON
Clink, John Robert Hamilton , pce	LT CDR	X	PWO(A)	01.09.94	STANAVFORLANT

Name	Rank	Spec	Sub-spec	Seniority	Where serving
Clinton, Lesley Ann , BSc	LT(SL)	X		01.12.92	JARIC
Clinton, Philip Ross	LT CDR	S	SM	11.08.81	NELSON RELEASE
Clough, Christopher Ralph , BSc, CEng, MIEE	LT CDR	E	WE	01.05.96	BEAVER
Clucas, Malcolm Richard	LT(SL)	X	P	01.04.88	706 SQN SEAHAWK
Clucas, Paul Richard	LT(SD)	X	PT	04.04.91	NELSON
Coaker, Stewart Andrew	SLT(SL)	S		01.05.94	DRYAD
Coates, Robert	CHAPLAIN	CE		06.06.95	CAPT F6 (SEA)
Cobb, David Robert	LT CDR	X	PWO(A)	01.11.93	CAMBRIDGE
Cobb, Jill Elizabeth	LT(SL)	W	S	10.12.87	MOD DFS(CIS) GOS
Cobbett, James Frank	LT(SL)	X	P	16.05.90	705 SQN SEAHAWK
Cochrane, The Hon Michael (Charles Nicholas) , pce	LT CDR	X	PWO(N)	01.04.90	NOTTINGHAM
Cochrane, Malcolm David	LT CDR	E	AE	09.08.91	771 SK5 SAR
Cocker, Matthew James , BSc, n	LT	X		01.12.91	MANCHESTER
Cockfield, Francis Bernard , pce, psc	LT CDR	X	AWO(A)	01.05.77	DRAKE CFM
Cocks, Michael Kenneth Falconer , MIERE	CDR	E	AE	31.12.86	MOD (BATH)
Cockshott, Camilla , BA	LT(SL)	I		01.09.94	RALEIGH
Cockton, Peter , QGM	ACT LT RM(SD)	RM	P	01.01.96	42 CDO RM
Codd, Justin , BSc	SLT(SL)	X		01.05.94	YORK
Codling, David , BSc	LT	X		01.05.95	SOVEREIGN
Coffey, Stewart James , BSc	LT(SL)	E	ME	01.06.89	JARIC
Cogan, Robert Edward Charles , BSc	LT(SL)	X	ATCU/T	16.03.93	RNAS CULDROSE
Cogdell, Phillip Charles	LT(SL)	I		01.01.89	SULTAN
Coldrick, Simon Alexander	LT RM	RM	WTO	01.05.90	CTCRM
Cole, Alan Charles , BA	LT	S		01.02.92	SPLENDID
Cole, Christopher Michael , psc	CDR	S		31.12.88	MOD (LONDON)
Cole, David Charles	CAPT RM(SD)	RM		01.10.88	RM BAND PTSMTH
Cole, David John , BA	SLT(SL)	X	O U/T	01.01.95	DARTMOUTH BRNC
Cole, John , n	LT(SL)	X		01.08.95	HECLA
Cole, Margaret Winstone , psc	CDR	W	SEC	01.10.89	2SL/CNH
Cole, Richard Iain	2LT	RM		01.05.95	CTCRM LYMPSTONE
Cole, Simon Philip	LT(SD)	E	WE	15.06.90	MOD DGSS PTSMTH
Cole, Simon Richard	2LT(GRAD)	RM		01.05.95	CTCRM LYMPSTONE
Coleman, Andrew Aitchison	LT(QM)	Q		18.06.93	RH HASLAR
Coles, Andrew Laurence	LT	X	SM	01.08.88	VICTORIOUS(PORT)
Coles, Christopher John , BEng	LT	E	MESM	01.03.89	FOSM GOSPORT
Coles, David Adlard	LT(SL)	X	P	16.09.84	750 SQN OBS SCH
Coles, Gordon John Victor	LT CDR(SD)	E	WESM	01.10.90	ORDNANCE BOARD
Coles, Geoffrey William Grenville , MSc	CDR	E	ME	30.06.90	MOD (BATH)
Coles, Stuart Charles , BA, MEng	SLT	X		01.01.95	DARTMOUTH BRNC
Coles, William Gavin	LT RM	RM		24.04.95	CTCRM
Coley, Anthony Richard , MRIN, pce, psc	LT CDR	X	PWO(A)	16.04.84	LOAN CDA NAG
Coley, Simon John	LT(SL)	X	P	01.07.94	819 SQN
Colley, Charles Jonathan Bennett , BSc	LT	X	MW	01.02.93	BRECON
Collicutt, Barry Frederick , BSc, MBA, MIMechE	CDR	E	AE	30.06.83	DGA(N)ASE MASU
Collicutt, John Michael	LT(SL)	X	P	16.06.94	771 SK5 SAR
Collier, Andrew Sheldon , BA	LT CDR	X		01.06.93	HQAFNORTHWEST
Collier, Steven Richard	LT CDR(SL)	X	P	01.09.85	HERON FLIGHT
Collighan, Giles Thomas	LT	X	FC	01.04.91	ILLUSTRIOUS
Collin, Martin (Act Lt Rm)	2LT	RM		28.04.93	RM POOLE
Collins, Anthony Christopher	LT CDR(SD)	E	WE	01.10.84	NELSON
Collins, David Anthony , BSc, PGCE	LT CDR(SL)	I	METOC	01.10.95	CENTURION
Collins, Graham John Simon	LT CDR	X	MCD	07.04.96	CUMBERLAND
Collins, Mark	SLT(SD)	X	tas	24.07.94	EDINBURGH
Collins, Paul Nicholas , pce, pcea, psc	CDR	X	P	31.12.92	2SL/CNH
Collins, Paul Reginald , BSc	LT CDR	E	WESM	01.09.95	MOD DGSWS BATH
Collins, Peter Ronald	LT RM(SD)	RM		01.01.90	RM POOLE
Collins, Peter	SLT(SD)	X	EW	24.07.94	NP1044
Collins, Richard John	LT CDR(SD)	E	AE(M)	01.10.92	FONA
Collins, Stephen Anthony	SLT(SD)	E	WESM	07.02.94	DOLPHIN SM SCHL
Collins, Sarah Jane , BSc	LT(SL)	I		01.05.88	SULTAN
Collis, Martin John , BEng	LT	E	ME	01.08.91	SULTAN
Colmer, Alan Arhtur , OBE, MITD	CDR(SD)	X	C	01.10.88	MOD DGSW PTSMTH

Name	Rank	Spec	Sub-spec	Seniority	Where serving
Colquhoun, Rodger Thompson	LT(SL)	X	P	01.06.89	FONA
Coltman, Timothy Patrick	SURG LT	-		01.08.95	STANAVFORCHAN
Colvin, Andrew , BSc	LT(SL)	I		01.09.88	RALEIGH
Colwell, Matthew Adrian	LT(SL)	X	P	16.03.91	845 SQN
Colyer, Michael Andrew James , MA	LT(SL)	X		01.05.90	MOD DNR OUTPORTS
Combe, Gavin Robert , BEng	LT	E	WE	01.08.94	BRAVE
Combe, Stephen Anthony Nicholson , BSc	2LT(GRAD)	RM		01.09.95	CTCRM LYMPSTONE
Comrie, Andrew Abbott Cameron , BSc	LT(SL)	I		01.01.91	DNPS
Concannon, John Leslie	LT CDR(SD)	E	WE	01.10.90	MOD DGSW PTSMTH
Condy, Sallie Louise , BSc	LT(SL)	I		25.10.88	NELSON
Congreve, Steven Chistopher	LT RM	RM		29.04.93	ASC CAMBERLEY
Conley, Daniel , OBE, MBA, pce(sm)	CAPT	X	SM	31.12.90	MOD (LONDON)
Connell, John Andrew , MBE, psc	CDR(SD)	X	EW	01.10.93	PJHQ
Connell, John Desmond	LT CDR(SL)	X	P	01.10.91	814 SQN
Connell, Martin John	LT	X	O	16.01.92	815 FLT 216
Connolly, Christopher John , BSc, pce, I(2)Ru	LT CDR	X	PWO(A)	01.03.92	MOD (LONDON)
Connor, Daniel James , MB, BS	SURG LT	-		01.08.92	RH HASLAR
Connor, Michael	SLT(SD)	E	WESM	04.09.95	COLLINGWOOD
Conway, Carl Edward	LT(SL)	X	P	01.06.91	848 SQN HERON
Conway, Julian John	LT CDR	X	PWO(C)	01.11.93	BFFI
Conway, Michael John	SLT(SD)	X	EW	03.04.94	GLOUCESTER
Conway, Stephen Andrew , jsdc	CAPT RM	RM	C	01.09.87	2SL/CNH
Conway, Timothy Alexander , BSc, pcea	LT(SL)	X	O	16.03.85	MOD PE ASC
Cook, Christopher Buchan , BSc	LT(SL)	I		01.05.91	NELSON RNSETT
Cook, Christian Michael	LT	X	SM	01.02.96	FOSM NWOOD OPS
Cook, David John	LT(SL)	X	O	01.03.89	RNSC GREENWICH
Cook, Frederick Colnett	CAPT RM(SD)	RM	MTO	01.10.89	MOD DFS(CIS) GOS
Cook, Gordon Edward	LT(SL)	X	O	16.09.89	815 SQN HQ
Cook, Harry	LT CDR	X	PWO(N)	10.08.83	DRYAD
Cook, Myles Fitzpatrick	LT RM	RM	C	29.04.93	40 CDO RM
Cook, Paul Roger , pce	LT CDR	X	PWO(A)	01.08.93	LIVERPOOL
Cook, Peter William John	CAPT RM	RM		01.05.92	45 CDO RM
Cook, Rupert George Nielsen	LT	X	FC	01.03.91	DRYAD
Cook, Timothy Arnold , BA	LT RM	RM		01.09.90	CDO LOG REGT RM
Cooke, David John , MBE, pce, pce(sm)	CAPT	X	SM	31.12.95	MOD (LONDON)
Cooke, David Marshall	LT CDR(SD)	X	PWO(U)	01.10.92	LOAN BVI
Cooke, Graham John	LT(SD)	X	PT	15.12.89	DRYAD
Cooke, Graham Spencer , BA	LT	X		01.10.93	CFP SEA
Cooke, Jonathan Edward	SLT(SL)	X		01.05.93	BICESTER
Cooke, Michael John	LT(SD)	E	AE(M)	16.10.92	SULTAN
Cooke, Martin Yeats , BA(OU), psc(m), osc	MAJ	RM		30.06.91	COMAW SEA
Cooke, Richard Glanville , TEng, MIMarE, AMIMarE	LT CDR(SD)	E	ME	01.10.88	CFM PORTSMOUTH
Cooke, Simon Stuart , MB, BCh	SURG LTCDR	-		01.08.94	NELSON (PAY)
Cooke-Priest, Nicholas	LT(SL)	X	O	01.05.95	815 FLT 244
Cooling, Robert George , BA, jsdc, pce	CDR	X	PWO(N)	31.12.91	MOD (LONDON)
Coomber, Jonathan Martin , BA	LT RM	RM		01.09.94	COMACCHIO GP RM
Coomber, Mark Andrew	LT CDR	X	FC	18.07.95	INVINCIBLE
Coombes, Derek	CDR	E	WE	31.12.93	HQ DFTS
Coope, Philip James , BEng	LT	E	WE	01.02.95	COLLINGWOOD
Cooper, Alan , MSc, CEng, FIMarE, MINucE, rcds	CAPT	E	MESM	30.06.91	MOD (BATH)
Cooper, Andrew , BEng	LT(SL)	E	ME	01.04.95	FEARLESS
Cooper, Christopher John	LT(SL)	I	METOC	01.06.87	CAPT F6 (SEA)
Cooper, David	LT CDR(SD)	E	ME	01.10.93	SULTAN
Cooper, Gerald Charles	LT(SD)	E	ME	17.02.89	DEF DIVING SCHL
Cooper, John Arnold , BSc, MINucE	CDR	E	MESM	31.12.92	MOD (BATH)
Cooper, John Anthony , MBE	LT CDR(SL)	X	PWO(A)	01.10.88	PJHQ
Cooper, Keith Alan Henry	LT CDR(SD)	X	O	01.10.93	SEAHAWK
Cooper, Kevin Philip , BSc	LT(SD)	E	WE	13.06.91	RALEIGH
Cooper, Kevin Simon	LT	S	BAR	01.01.91	2SL/CNH
Cooper, Mark Andrew (Act Lt Cdr)	LT	X	SM	01.04.88	SOVEREIGN
Cooper, Matthew Christopher , BSc	2LT(GRAD)	RM		01.09.95	CTCRM LYMPSTONE
Cooper, Neil James	LT(SD)	X	AV	03.01.86	FONA COLLINGWOOD

Name	Rank	Spec	Sub-spec	Seniority	Where serving
Cooper, Neil Philip (Act Lt Cdr)	LT(SD)	E	ME	18.02.88	FEARLESS
Cooper, Peter Frank , MSc, CEng, MIMechE	LT CDR	E	MESM	21.04.89	CSST SEA
Cooper, Robert Terence (Act Capt Rm)	LT RM(SD)	RM		01.01.88	RM POOLE
Cooper, Simon John , psc	LT CDR	X	O	01.12.93	814 SQN
Cooper, Simon Nicholas , BA (Barrister)	CDR	S	BAR	30.06.94	2SL/CNH
Cooper, Simon Stanway , BEng, AMIEE	LT	E	WESM	01.05.91	FOSM FASLANE
Cooper-Simpson, Roger John	LT RM	RM		26.04.93	45 CDO RM
Cooter, Mark Pierson , BA, BSc	LT CDR	S		16.03.93	SHAPE BELGIUM
Copeland, Stephen Nicholas	LT	E	AE	01.02.91	EXCHANGE CANADA
Copeland-Davis, Terence William , MSc	LT(SL)	I	METOC	01.05.88	ENDURANCE
Copinger-Symes, Rory Sandham	CAPT RM	RM		01.09.94	FOSF
Coppin, Paul David	LT CDR(SD)	E	AE(L)	01.10.92	DGA(N)ASE MASU
Corbett, Andrew Scott	LT	X	SM	01.06.88	CSST SHORE FSLN
Corbett, Gerard John	LT(SL)	X	ATC	16.01.85	RNAS YEOVILTON
Corbett, Thomas James	LT(SL)	X	FC	01.04.94	HERON
Corbett, William Roger , BSc	LT CDR	I	METOC	01.10.91	CAPT F6 (SEA)
Corbidge, Stephen John	LT RM(SD)	RM		01.01.91	RMR SCOTLAND
Corden, Matthew	MID(SL)	X		01.09.94	MIDDLETON
Corder, Ian Fergus , BA, jsdc, pce, pce(sm)	CDR	X	SM	31.12.93	MOD (LONDON)
Corderoy, John Roger	LT	E	MESM	01.01.90	MOD (BATH)
Corderoy, Richard	MID(UCE)	E		01.09.94	DARTMOUTH BRNC
Cordner, Kenneth , MBIM, psc	CDR	S	SM	31.12.87	TEMERAIRE
Corkett, Kerry (Act Lt)	SLT(SD)	X	REG	24.07.94	2SL/CNH
Cormack, Andrew	SURG SLT	-		09.07.95	DARTMOUTH BRNC
Corn, Russell Andrew Foster	LT RM	RM		01.09.92	RM POOLE
Cornberg, Malcolm Arthur , MBA	CDR	S	CMA	30.06.92	HERON
Cornell, Patricia	LT	Q	ONC	23.03.90	RH HASLAR
Corner, Gordon Charles , pce	LT CDR	X	PWO(C)	01.12.90	BIRMINGHAM
Corner, Ian Lindsey Ferguson , osc	CAPT RM	RM	PH	01.11.83	MOD (LONDON)
Cornes, John Ross	LT(SL)	X		01.04.91	MOD DNR OUTPORTS
Corney, Adam David	LT	X	SM	01.09.93	FOSM NWOOD OPS
Cornick, Robin Michael	LT(SL)	X	MCD	01.07.89	EXCHANGE USA
Cornish, Michael Christopher	LT CDR	X	PWO(A)	01.07.95	BRAZEN
Corrigan, Niall Richard , BSc, pce	CDR	X	PWO(A)	30.06.96	DRYAD
Corrin, Colby St John , LLB	CAPT RM	RM	MLDR	01.09.92	MOD (LONDON)
Corry, Simon Myles , BSc	LT CDR	E	WE	01.02.94	MOD (LONDON)
Coryton, Gervais Richard Arthur , pcea	LT CDR(SL)	X	P	01.09.80	NP1044
Cosby, R A(Richard Ashworth de Sausmarez) , LVO, jsdc, pce	CAPT	X	PWO	30.06.94	NAVSOUTH ITALY
Cossins, Elizabeth Sally	MID(NE)(SL)	X		01.01.96	DARTMOUTH BRNC
Costello, Gerard Thomas , BSc	CDR	E	WESM	31.12.93	VIGILANT(PORT)
Cottee, Benjamin Richard John	LT(SL)	X	ATC	01.09.94	RNAS CULDROSE
Cotterill, Bruce Maxwell , BEng	LT	E	WESM	01.03.92	SST SHORE DEVPT
Cottingham, Neill Peter Stephen	LT(SD)	X	AV	25.07.91	SEAHAWK
Cottis, Mathew Charles	LT(SL)	S	SM	16.11.90	RALEIGH
Cotton, Richard Allan , BSc, MRIN, jsdc, psc	CAPT	X	H CH	31.12.90	MOD (LONDON)
Cotton, Susan	SLT(SL)	X	ATC	01.01.93	RNAS PORTLAND
Couch, Paul	CHAPLAIN	RC		05.05.92	DARTMOUTH BRNC
Couch, Paul Jonathan , MSc, CEng, MRAeS	CDR	E	AE	31.12.94	MOD (LONDON)
Coulson, Jeremy Richard , BEng, PGCE	LT CDR	I		08.12.85	SACLANT USA
Coulson, Peter , BEng	LT	E	WE	01.12.90	COLLINGWOOD
Coulthard, Adrian John , BSc	LT(SL)	I		01.05.90	COLLINGWOOD
Coulthard, John Kinnear , MSc, MIMechE	CDR	E	MESM	31.12.93	MOD (BATH)
Coulton, Ian Christopher	LT(SD)	MS		28.07.89	RH HASLAR
Coulton, Jamie	LT(SL)	X	P	16.06.95	814 SQN
Counter, Paul Richard , MB, BS	SURG LT	-		01.08.94	CDO LOG REGT RM
Coupe, Richard Desmond , psc	CDR	S		30.06.93	2SL/CNH
Coupland, Mark Barry	LT(SL)	X	P	01.03.89	705 SQN SEAHAWK
Course, Andrew James , MSc, AMIEE (Act Lt Cdr)	LT	E	WE	01.02.90	RNSC GREENWICH
Courtenay, Kenneth Andres , pce, pcea, psc	CAPT	X	O	31.12.90	IMS BRUSSELS
Coutts, Warren Alexander	SLT(SL)	X		01.05.94	SPARTAN
Coverdale, Anthony , MSc, psc	CDR	E	MESM	31.12.93	MOD (BATH)
Covington, William MacArtney , pce, pcea, psc	CDR	X	P	30.06.89	MOD (LONDON)

Name	Rank	Spec	Sub-spec	Seniority	Where serving
Cowan, Christopher John , LLB	LT	S		01.07.95	NBC PORTSMOUTH
Cowdrey, Mervyn Charles	CDR	S		30.06.93	2SL/CNH
Cowie, Kevin Michael	LT(SD)	X	C	14.12.90	FLEET COMMS PLYM
Cowley, Nigel Jonathan , pcea, psc	CDR	X	P	31.12.89	FONA
Cowley, Richard Merlin , BSc	LT	X	MCD	01.04.89	DRYAD
Cowper, Ian Robert	LT(SD)	E	ME	10.06.94	DRAKE CFM
Cowton, Elliott Neil , BEd, adp	LT CDR(SL)	I		01.10.91	EXCHANGE USA
Cox, David John , BEng	LT	E	WE	01.06.94	ILLUSTRIOUS
Cox, Hugh Jeremy , MB, BS, FRCS	SURG CDR	-	CE	30.06.93	RH HASLAR
Cox, Jonathan Peter	LT CDR(SD)	X	MCD	01.10.95	FOST DPORT SHORE
Cox, Mark Bamber	SLT(SL)	S		01.05.96	CORNWALL
Cox, Pieter William Studley , BSc	CDR	E	WESM	30.06.93	MOD (LONDON)
Cox, Rex John	LT	X		01.03.93	NELSON (PAY)
Cox, Sean Adrian Joel	LT(SL)	X	P	16.08.93	846 SQN
Cox, Stephen John , psc(m) (Loc Lt Col)	MAJ	RM	MOR	30.06.91	JFOS WILTON
Coyle, Gavin James , BSc	LT	X		01.08.93	NOTTINGHAM
Coyne, Christopher John , BA	LT(SL)	S		01.06.92	FOSM NWOOD OPS
Coyne, John Derek	LT(SD)	X	AV	17.12.93	ILLUSTRIOUS
Crabb, Anthony , BSc	SLT(SL)	X		01.01.94	DARTMOUTH BRNC
Crabtree, Ian Michael , BSc, pce	CDR	X	PWO(A)	31.12.90	DRYAD MWC
Crabtree, Peter Dixon , BA (Barrister)	CDR	S	BAR	31.12.93	FOSNNI/NBC CLYDE
Cragg, Richard Darryl , BEng	LT(SL)	E	MESM	01.12.94	RNC DPT NS&TECH
Craggs, Stuart , BEng	LT(SL)	E	AE	01.02.94	849 SQN HQ
Crago, Philip Thomas , BSc	LT CDR	E	ME	01.04.93	CUMBERLAND
Craib, Alfred George	LT(SD)	E	WE	05.06.92	DG SHIPS CAM HSE
Craig, Alexander , QHP, MB, BCh, ChB, ndc	SURG RADM	-		27.04.93	2SL/CNH
Craig, Douglas Murray	CDR	E	AE	31.12.90	SULTAN
Craig, Gordon William , MBE, BD, MA, PGCE	CHAPLAIN	SF		05.05.81	42 CDO RM
Craig, John Antony	LT(SL)	X	MW	01.05.94	DRYAD
Craig, Kenneth Mitchell , BSc (Loc Capt Rm)	LT RM	RM		28.04.94	NP 1061
Craig, Peter Daniel , BEng	LT CDR	X	PWO(A)	01.02.96	MANCHESTER
Craig, Rodney William Wilson , MNI, jsdc, pce	CDR	X	PWO(A)	30.06.90	COMAW SEA
Cramp, Anthony Michael	LT CDR	X	P	01.01.96	815 FLT 200
Cran, Barrie Charles , BEng	LT	E	MESM	01.12.88	NEPTUNE NT
Craner, Matthew John , MB, BCh	SURG LT	-		01.08.93	45 CDO RM
Cranmer, Alistair , BA	LT(SL)	X	P	01.01.92	DRYAD MWC
Crascall, Stephen John	LT(SD)	X	AV	23.07.93	SEAHAWK
Craven, John Arthur Graham , MIL, MIMgt, I(2)Fr	LT CDR	S		01.09.85	UKSU AFSOUTH
Craven-Phillips, Thomas Charles Dale	CAPT RM	RM	PT	01.02.79	CTCRM
Crawford, John Verschoyle , BSc, CEng, MIMarE	LT CDR	E	ME	01.05.79	DRAKE CFM
Crawford, Leslie	LT(SD)	E	WE	05.12.93	CFM PORTSMOUTH
Crawford, Paul Ian , MB, BS	SURG LTCDR	-	SM	01.08.89	DOLPHIN
Crawford, Ronald Lindsay , psc (Loc Lt Col)	MAJ	RM	PH	30.06.91	SHAPE BELGIUM
Crawley, James Edward	SLT	X		01.09.93	VICTORIOUS(STBD)
Creates, Keith Ian , BA, pce	LT CDR	X	PWO(U)	01.04.87	MWC GOSPORT
Cree, Andrew Martin , BEng	LT(SL)	I		01.09.89	COLLINGWOOD
Cree, Malcolm Charles , BA, pce	LT CDR	X	PWO(A)	01.07.92	CENTURION
Creech, Richard David	LT(SL)	X	O	16.07.85	LOAN DTEO BSC DN
Crews, Nicholas James Kevern , MNI, pce(sm)	CDR	X	SM(N)	31.12.82	DRAKE NBC(CFS)
Crick, Robert John	CDR	S	SM	30.06.95	MOD (BATH)
Criddle, Gary	SLT(SL)	X	O	01.11.93	815 FLT 206
Crimmen, David John	LT(SL)	X	P	01.03.91	RAF SHAWBURY
Cringle, David John , MBE	LT CDR(SD)	X	EW	01.10.88	DGSS BRISTOL
Cripps, Neil Philip James , MB, BCh, FRCS, FRCSEd	SURG CDR	-	SM	31.12.94	NELSON (PAY)
Crispin, Toby Alexander Baldwin , BSc	LT CDR	X	O	01.04.94	HERON
Critchley, Hannah , BA	LT(SL)	S		01.04.95	DNPS
Critchley, Harold John , CEng, MIMarE, MIMechE	CAPT	E	MESM	31.12.90	SULTAN AIB
Critchley, Matthew Stephen , BSc	LT(SL)	I		01.09.90	COLLINGWOOD
Crockatt, Stephen Richard James	LT(SL)	X	P	01.09.90	820 SQN
Croft, Martin	LT CDR(SD)	X	SM	01.10.93	RNSC GREENWICH
Crofts, David Jeffrey , BEng	LT	E	WE	01.02.92	DGSS BRISTOL
Croke, Anthony , pce, pcea, psc, ocds(Can)	CDR	X	P	31.12.91	EXCHANGE USA

Name	Rank	Spec	Sub-spec	Seniority	Where serving
Croker, Richard William , BSc	LT(SL)	I		01.09.85	SULTAN
Crombie, Nicholas , BSc	LT(SL)	X	O	01.02.93	815 FLT 211
Cronin, Alan Robert	LT CDR(SD)	X	AV	01.10.91	SULTAN
Crook, Andrea Susan , BA	LT CDR	S		01.05.92	MARLBOROUGH
Crookes, Waveney Alan	SLT	X		01.01.95	SOMERSET
Croome-Carroll, Michael Patrick John , MBE	LT CDR	X	MCD	27.01.90	SDG PLYMOUTH
Cropley, Andrew , BSc	LT CDR	I	METOC	01.09.94	DARTMOUTH BRNC
Cropper, Fraser	SLT(SL)	E	AE	01.05.93	DARTMOUTH BRNC
Cropper, Martin Andrew Keith , BA	LT CDR	S	SM	16.05.90	DRAKE NBC(CFS)
Crosbie, Donald Ernest Frederick	LT	X	MCD	01.02.92	INVERNESS
Crosbie, David Walker , AMIMarE	LT CDR(SD)	E	ME	01.10.91	FOSNNI
Crosby, John Paul , psc	MAJ	RM	A/TK	30.06.93	MOD (LONDON)
Cross, Alexander Leigh	SLT(UCE)	E	WESM	01.09.95	DARTMOUTH BRNC
Cross, Ian	LT(SL)	S		01.12.95	GANNET
Cross, Martin George , BSc, psc	LT CDR	E	MESM	01.04.88	MOD (BATH)
Crossley, Charles Crispin , BSc	LT CDR	E	ME	01.07.91	BRAZEN
Crossley, Guy Antony	LT(SL)	X	P	16.05.93	846 SQN
Crossley, Kirstin	LT(SL)	X	ATC	01.05.96	RNAS YEOVILTON
Crothers, David Montague , BSc, AMIEE	CDR	E	WESM	30.06.85	MOD (LONDON)
Crouch, John Gerard , BSc	LT(SL)	I		01.05.90	RNC DPT NS&TECH
Crouch, Roger Thomas , OBE, BSc, MIEE, psc	CDR	E	WE	30.06.84	MOD (BATH)
Crouden, Stephen Frederick (Act Capt Rm)	LT RM(SD)	RM		01.01.92	RM POOLE
Croughan, Susan	LT CDR	Q		06.09.88	NELSON
Crowe, David	MID	X		01.01.95	DARTMOUTH BRNC
Crowther, Kevin Wayne , BSc, pce	LT CDR	X	PWO(A)	29.03.91	INVINCIBLE
Crozier, Stuart Ross McDonald , BA (Barrister)	LT CDR	S	BAR	01.04.94	NEPTUNE
Crudgington, Paul , AFC, pcea	LT CDR(SL)	X	F	01.09.87	LOAN DTEO BSC DN
Crumplin, Carolyn Anne	LT CDR(SL)	W	X	01.10.92	MOD (LONDON)
Crundell, Richard John , BEng	LT	E	WE	01.07.92	DG SHIPS CAM HSE
Crutchfield, Aaron , BComm	SLT(SL)	X		01.01.94	BATTLEAXE
Cryar, Timothy Martin Craven , n	LT	X		01.08.90	DRYAD
Cubbage, Jamie , BEng	LT	E	WE	01.04.94	INVINCIBLE
Cullen, Nicola , BSc	LT(SL)	X		01.09.95	FEARLESS
Cullen-Jones, Haydn , FNI, pce	LT CDR	X	AWO(U)	01.09.79	WARRIOR
Cullis, Christopher John	CAPT RM	RM	LC	25.04.96	45 CDO RM
Culwick, Peter Francis , BDS	SGLTCDR(D)	-		01.01.87	DRYAD
Cuming, Brian Hugh Douglas , pce, psc(m)	LT CDR	X	PWO(U)	16.03.81	DGSS BRISTOL
Cummin, Michael Antony , BSc	CDR	E	MESM	31.12.95	FOSM FASLANE
Cumming, Gregor Gordon Ashley , MA, MSc, CEng, MIEE, AIL, fsc, I(2)Sp	CDR	E	WE	30.06.85	DG SHIPS CAM HSE
Cumming, Robert Angus	SLT(SL)	E	MESM	01.01.94	DARTMOUTH BRNC
Cummings, Alan Thomas , pcea	LT	X	O	01.03.89	DRYAD
Cummings, David John , BEng	LT	E	WE	01.11.94	EXETER
Cunane, John Richard	LT(SL)	S	SM	16.02.90	VANGUARD(PORT)
Cundy, Robert Graham (Loc Capt Rm)	LT RM	RM		01.09.89	42 CDO RM
Cunnane, Keith John , BEng	LT	E	WESM	01.03.94	CAPTAIN SM2
Cunningham, Andrew Nicholas	2LT(GRAD)	RM		01.09.94	CDO LOG REGT RM
Cunningham, Craig	LT CDR(SL)	I	SM	01.10.95	NEPTUNE SM1
Cunningham, David Andrew , MB, BS, LRCP, MRCS	SURG CAPT	-	GMPP	30.06.94	NELSON
Cunningham, David Andrew , pcea	LT CDR	X	O	15.12.95	MWC GOSPORT
Cunningham, John Gavin , BA, pce	LT CDR	X	O	01.12.93	URNU LONDON
Cunningham, John Stewart	LT RM(SD)	RM		01.01.91	45 CDO RM
Cunningham, Justin Thomas	LT RM	RM		24.04.92	CTCRM
Cunningham, Nigel John Whitworth	LT(SD)	X	O	27.07.95	815 OEU OSPREY
Cunningham, Paul	LT CDR	S		01.12.91	MOD (BATH)
Cunningham, Richard Alister , pce, pcea, psc	LT CDR	X	P	01.11.91	FONA SEAGOING
Cunningham, Thomas Anthony , pce, pcea, psc	CDR	X	O	30.06.95	GLOUCESTER
Cunnison, Jonathan Bruce , MA, MSc, CEng, jsdc	CDR	E	WE	31.12.90	MOD (LONDON)
Curd, Timothy Allan , pce, psc	CDR	X	PWO(U)	31.12.93	BDS WASHINGTON
Curlewis, Andrew John , BEng	LT(SL)	E	ME	01.04.92	NORFOLK
Curnow, Ian Francis , BSc	LT CDR	E	AE	01.04.93	814 SQN
Curnow, Michael David , BSc, psc	LT CDR	E	ME	01.09.90	FOSF ENG DEVPT

Name	Rank	Spec	Sub-spec	Seniority	Where serving
Curr, Ralph Donaldson , MB, BS, DObstRCOG, LRCP, ... SURG CAPT MRCGP, AKC	SURG CAPT	-	GMPP	30.06.92	2SL/CNH
Curran, Michael Geoffrey Saxon , BSc, CEng, MIMarE	CDR	E	ME	31.12.84	CINCFLEET
Currass, Timothy David , BEng	LT	E	WE	01.03.91	RNU CHELTENHAM
Currie, Duncan Gordon	LT(SL)	X	P	16.12.89	706 SQN SEAHAWK
Currie, David William , BSc, pce	LT CDR	X	PWO(A)	01.04.90	EXETER
Currie, Ian , BEng, CEng, MIMarE	LT(SL)	E	ME	01.04.87	INTREPID
Currie, Stuart McGregor	LT	E	MESM	01.08.91	SUPERB
Curry, Alexander , BA	LT	S		01.05.96	RALEIGH
Curry, Benedict Rodney	CAPT RM	RM		25.04.96	HQ 3 CDO BDE RM
Curry, Robert Edward , BSc	LT	X		01.11.93	PEACOCK
Curtis, Baden James	CAPT RM(SD)	RM		01.10.88	RM POOLE
Curtis, David	SLT(SD)	E	WESM	04.09.95	COLLINGWOOD
Curtis, Paul Anthony	LT(SD)	E	WE	18.10.85	FOSF
Curtis, Robert John	LT(SD)	X	PWO(A)	19.10.92	YORK
Curtis, Roger Stafford	LT	X		01.12.90	DRYAD
Cusack, Nicholas James , BSc, jsdc (Act Maj)	CAPT RM	RM		01.09.89	MOD (LONDON)
Cushen, Andrew Emlyn , MInstAM, AIMgt, psc	LT CDR	S		16.04.89	MOD (LONDON)
Cust, David Robert , pce(sm)	CAPT	X	SM	30.06.94	HQAFNORTHWEST
Cutler, Andrew Rodney	SLT	X		01.09.94	DARTMOUTH BRNC
Cutler, Roger	CHAPLAIN	CE		28.01.91	CALEDONIA
Cutt, John James Douglas , pce(sm), psc	CDR	X	SM	30.06.94	TRIUMPH

D

Name	Rank	Spec	Sub-spec	Seniority	Where serving
D'Arcy, Paul Andrew	LT(SL)	X	O	16.08.90	702 SQN OSPREY
Da Gama, Darryl Douglas	LT	S		01.04.90	FONA
Da Gama, Joseph Anthony Jude , BSc, CEng, MIEE, ... CDR MRAeS, psc	CDR	E	AE	30.06.96	DGA(N) ASE
Dabell, Guy Lester , BSc	LT CDR	E	MESM	01.07.94	VICTORIOUS(STBD)
Daglish, Hugh Blyth ,LVO, pce, psc	CDR	X	FC	30.06.87	BRITANNIA
Dailey, Paul George Johnson , BSc	LT	E	WESM	01.04.89	FOSM NWOOD HQ
Dainton, Steven , n	LT	X		01.03.91	QUORN
Dale, David Graham , BA (Act Lt Cdr)	LT(SL)	X	O	01.11.82	DRYAD
Dale, Michael John , pce, psc	CDR	X	PWO(C)	30.06.93	BDS WASHINGTON
Dale, Nigel (Act Lt)	SLT(SD)	X	SM	25.07.93	ELANT/NAVNW
Dale, Richard Foley , MB, BS, FRCS	SURG CDR	-	CGS	31.12.91	RH HASLAR
Dale-Smith, Guy , BA	LT	X		01.12.89	BRAZEN
Dalgleish, John Richard , MBE, BA, MSc, PhD, MSRP, psc	LT CDR(SD)	MS	SM	01.10.90	CINCFLEET
Dalrymple-Smith, Richard , BSc, CEng, MIEE	CDR	E	WE	30.06.86	ORDNANCE BOARD
Dalton, David John	LT CDR(SD)	E	AE(L)	01.10.92	706 SQN SEAHAWK
Dalton, Fearghal John , BEng	LT(SL)	E		01.07.95	NEPTUNE SM1
Daly, John Edmund , BSc, MBA, CEng, MICE	LT CDR	I		01.05.81	2SL/CNH
Daly, Paul	MID(SL)	X		01.01.95	DARTMOUTH BRNC
Daly-Rayner, Andrew , BEng	LT	E	WE	01.12.92	COVENTRY
Danbury, Ian Gerald , BSc, AMIEE	LT CDR	E	WE	01.12.93	MONTROSE
Dando, Jonathon Neil , n	LT	X		01.08.92	EXETER
Dane, Richard Martin Henry	LT CDR(SL)	X	P	01.10.94	FONA SEAHAWK
Daniel, Andrew Gordon	LT CDR(SD)	X	SM	01.10.95	DGCIS BRISTOL
Daniel, Ian	ACT LT RM(SD)	RM		01.01.96	40 CDO RM
Daniell, Christopher John	LT CDR(SL)	X	O	01.10.95	750 SQN OBS SCH
Daniels, Ian James Russel , BSc	LT CDR(SL)	X	O	01.10.95	849 SQN A FLT
Daniels, Stephen Anthony , pcea, psc, tp	LT CDR(SL)	X	P	01.10.88	848 SQN HERON
Daniels, Trevor Clive , MSc, CEng, MIMarE	LT CDR	E	ME	01.03.89	GLOUCESTER
Daniels, Timothy Nicholas , BA	CAPT RM	RM		01.09.93	HQRM
Dann, Adrian Stuart	LT(SD)	X	MCD	27.07.90	NORTH DIVING GRP
Dannatt, Timothy Mark , MSc, CEng, MIMarE, jsdc	CDR	E	ME	30.06.93	MOD (BATH)
Darbin, Mark Royston , BSc	LT(SL)	E	ME	01.01.86	2SL/CNH
Darch, Brian Nicholas , BSc, CEng, MIMechE, MDA, CDipAF, psc	CDR	E	ME	31.12.83	MOD (BATH)
Darling, James Ian	LT(SD)	E	WE	09.06.89	MCM1 SEA
Darlington, Mark Robinson , BSc	LT CDR	X	PWO(A)	01.07.94	INVINCIBLE
Darlow, PaulRaymond (Act Lt)	SLT(SD)	S	CA	03.04.94	COLLINGWOOD
Darwent, Andrew , BSc	LT CDR	E	WE	01.03.91	CARDIFF

Name	Rank	Spec	Sub-spec	Seniority	Where serving
Darwent, Sean Anthony , BSc	LT(SL)	X	O	01.03.93	820 SQN
Dashfield, Adrian Kenneth , MB, BCh, FRCA, I(2)Ge	SURG LTCDR	-	SM	01.08.94	NP 1061
Dathan, James Hartley Matthew , BA	LT	S		16.08.91	2SL/CNH
Dathan, Timothy James , BEng, MSc	LT CDR	E	ME	01.03.95	EXCHANGE CANADA
Daukes, Nicholas Michael , BSc	LT RM	RM		01.09.94	COMACCHIO GP RM
Daveney, David Alan , BA, BSc	SLT	X		01.09.94	BERKELEY
Davenport, Graham Montague , BSc, pce, psc	LT CDR	X	PWO(C)	01.03.87	MOD (LONDON)
Davenport, Nigel Jefferson , BDS	SG LT(D)	-		14.02.92	OSPREY
Davey, Gary Stuart , BEng	LT	E	AE	01.05.91	DGA(N) ASE
Davey, Paul Francis	LT CDR	X	MCD	04.07.92	LOAN CDA NAG
Davey, Paul John , BSc, CEng, MIMarE	LT CDR	E	ME	01.06.89	DG SHIPS DEVONPT
David, Simon Evan James , BA	LT CDR	S		16.10.94	HERON
David, Timothy William , BSc	LT RM	RM		01.09.92	45 CDO RM
Davidson, Allan Miller	LT	X	P	01.06.90	814 SQN
Davidson, Gordon Douglas Scott	LT RM	RM	P	01.09.90	847 SQN
Davidson, Keith John , psc	CDR	E	AE	30.06.89	MOD DHSA
Davidson, Martin , BEng	LT	E	WESM	01.11.94	DOLPHIN SM SCHL
Davidson, Neil Richard	LT(SL)	X	P	01.04.91	AACC MID WALLOP
Davies, Alan	CAPT RM(SD)	RM		01.10.94	HQ 3 CDO BDE RM
Davies, Andrew James Albert	LT(SL)	X	O	01.08.90	HERON
Davies, Anthony Robin , BA, psc, I(1)Ru, I(2)Du	CDR	X	PWO(A)	31.12.94	DRYAD MWC
Davies, Bryan	SLT(SL)	E	WE	01.01.94	DARTMOUTH BRNC
Davies, Christopher John , pce	LT CDR	X	MCD	01.10.93	CDRE MFP NWOOD
Davies, Christopher Stanley , MA	LT CDR	I	METOC	01.09.90	DARTMOUTH BRNC
Davies, Eleanor Jane , BA	LT(SL)	X	ATC	01.09.93	ILLUSTRIOUS
Davies, Edward Roger	LT CDR(SD)	X	MCD	01.10.90	KING ALFRED
Davies, George Christopher	LT(SL)	I	METOC	01.07.91	RFANSU
Davies, Gareth Ian	LT CDR(SL)	X	ATC	01.03.86	MOD (LONDON)
Davies, Geraint William Tudor	SLT(SL)	X		01.01.95	TRENCHANT
Davies, Huan Charles Ayrton	LT RM	RM		01.09.93	HQ 3 CDO BDE RM
Davies, Henry	SLT(SL)	X	P	01.11.93	814 SQN
Davies, Ian Ellis , n	LT	X	H1	01.12.90	GLEANER
Davies, Ian Hugh , BSc	LT CDR	X	SM	16.10.83	LOAN SAUDI ARAB
Davies, Janette , BChD (Act Sgltcdr(D))	SG LT(D)	-		01.01.92	DOLPHIN
Davies, John Huw , BA	LT CDR	I	METOC	01.09.93	EXCHANGE USA
Davies, Jonathan Peter , BA, BSc	LT CDR	S		01.10.92	BALTAP
Davies, John Robert (Loc Maj)	CAPT RM	RM		01.05.91	45 CDO RM
Davies, Justin Wayne , BEng	LT(SL)	E	ME	01.12.93	IRON DUKE
Davies, Lee , BEng	LT	E	AE	01.01.94	HERON
Davies, Lucinda Emma , BSc	SLT	X		01.09.94	CORNWALL
Davies, Lyndon James	LT(SD)	E	ME	17.02.89	CAPT(H) DEVPT
Davies, Mark Bryan , pcea	LT	X	O	24.01.89	815 FLT 227
Davies, Michael John	LT(SD)	X	PT	24.07.92	OSPREY
Davies, Paul Nicholas Michael , pce, psc	CDR	X	PWO(A)	30.06.92	2SL/CNH
Davies, Peter Roland , CBE, MSc, CEng, MIEE, nadc, gw	CAPT	E	WESM	30.06.93	MOD DGUW PTLAND
Davies, Robert Stephen Brian , jsdc, pce	CDR	X	AWO(A)	31.12.86	MOD (LONDON)
Davies, Sidney John Raymond , MSc	LT CDR	E	MESM	01.02.86	DRAKE CBS
Davies, Stephen Philip	LT(SD)	E	WESM	05.06.92	DOLPHIN SM SCHL
Davies, Stephen Russell	SLT	X		01.09.94	ORKNEY
Davies, Susan (Act Surg Lt)	SURG SLT	-		08.11.94	DARTMOUTH BRNC
Davies, Timothy Gordon , BSc, MRAeS, odc(Fr)	LT CDR	E	AE(P)	01.12.89	845 SQN
Davies, Trevor Martin , BEng	LT	E	WE	01.10.89	LOAN DRA FRT HAL
Davies, William George	SLT(SL)	X	O	01.05.95	706 SQN SEAHAWK
Davis, Andrew Richard	LT CDR(SL)	X	P	01.09.94	801 SQN
Davis, Bryan Charles , BSc	LT CDR	I	SM	01.05.92	FOSM NWOOD OPS
Davis, Bernard James , LLB (Barrister)	CDR	S	BAR	31.12.90	SULTAN
Davis, Christopher John	LT RM(SD)	RM		01.01.93	RM BAND SCOTLAND
Davis, Edward Grant Martin ,MBE (Loc Maj)	CAPT RM	RM		01.09.92	ASC CAMBERLEY
Davis, Francis James	LT CDR	X	PWO	28.11.82	DRYAD
Davis, John Quintin , BSc, jsdc, psc(m), psc (Loc Col)	LT COL	RM		30.06.92	HQRM
Davis, Martin Philip , BSc, pce, pcea, psc	LT CDR	X	O	01.07.88	815 SQN HQ
Davis, Nicholas Howard , jsdc	CDR	S		31.12.84	2SL/CNH FOTR

Name	Rank	Spec	Sub-spec	Seniority	Where serving
Davis, Paul Barry , l(2)Ge	LT CDR(SL)	X	P	01.10.94	705 SQN SEAHAWK
Davis, Rodney David , MSc	LT CDR	I	METOC	09.09.72	ELANT/NAVNW
Davis, Sarah Barbara	LT CDR(SL)	W	S	01.10.95	COLLINGWOOD
Davis, Stephen	SLT(SL)	E	WESM	01.05.93	DARTMOUTH BRNC
Davis-Marks, Michael Leigh , BSc, pce, pce(sm), psc	CDR	X	SM	31.12.95	WARRIOR
Davison, Andrew Paul , BSc, PGCE	LT CDR(SL)	I	METOC	01.10.94	HQ NORTH
Davison, Gregory James	LT(SL)	X	P	01.04.91	702 SQN OSPREY
Davison, James Charles	LT	X		01.11.90	URNU BRISTOL
Davison, Jeffrey Edward	LT	X	PWO(A)	06.04.89	NOTTINGHAM
Davison, Terence John	LT(SD)	E	WE	13.06.86	NELSON
Daw, Simon James	LT(SL)	X	O	16.10.87	750 SQN OBS SCH
Dawkins, Martin William , BSc, MRAeS	LT(SL)	X	P	01.03.89	LOAN DTEO BSC DN
Daws, Petrina Dawn	LT(SL)	W	I	03.04.92	RALEIGH
Daws, Richard Patrick Anthony , BSc, MIEE	LT CDR	E	WESM	01.06.94	TRIUMPH
Dawson, Alan James , BTech	LT(SD)	E	WESM	24.02.95	MOD DGSM PTLAND
Dawson, Edward William , MSc, CEng, MIEE, jsdc, gw	CAPT	E	AE	31.12.95	MOD PE USA
Dawson, John Edwin , MSc, AMIEE, gw	CDR	E	WE	31.12.89	EXCHANGE AUSTLIA
Dawson, Nigel Julian Frederick , BSc	LT(SL)	I		01.09.91	RALEIGH
Dawson, Peter John	LT CDR(SL)	X	ATC	01.10.89	FONA
Dawson, Stewart Hume , BA, MPhil	LT	X		01.10.94	SCEPTRE
Dawson, Stephen Lee , BSc, MA, PGCE, psc	LT CDR	I		12.09.90	2SL/CNH FOTR
Dawson, Stewart Neville	LT(SL)	E	WE	01.01.90	NEPTUNE NT
Dawson, William	LT	X		01.11.90	DRYAD
Day, Kenneth John Coryton , CEng, FIEE, MINucE	CAPT	E	MESM	30.06.91	2SL/CNH
Day, Michael , BSc	LT(SL)	X	P U/T	01.12.95	705 SQN SEAHAWK
Day, Nigel Richard , psc	CDR	S		31.12.91	RALEIGH
Day, Simon Nicholas , BA, BEng	SLT	X		01.09.94	STARLING
Day, Timothy Mark , BSc	LT CDR(SL)	I		01.10.94	INM ALVERSTOKE
Day, Trevor Steven	LT CDR(SD)	E	WE	01.10.95	DGSS BRISTOL
Daykin, Paul Martin	LT CDR	X	PWO(C)	09.09.86	HQAFNORTHWEST
De Burgh, Campbell Donald , BSc, CEng, MIEE, psc	CDR	E	WE	31.12.83	MOD (LONDON)
de Halpert, Jeremy Michael , MRIN, jsdc, pce (Commodore)	CAPT	X	PWO(N)	30.06.90	MOD (LONDON)
de Halpert, Simon David , jsdc, pce	CDR	X	AWO(U)	31.12.84	NS OBERAMMERGAU
de Jager, Hendrikus , psc (Loc Lt Col)	MAJ	RM		31.12.91	JACIG
De Jonghe, Paul Trevor , IEng	LT CDR(SD)	E	WE	01.10.94	EDINBURGH
De La Mare, Richard Michael	LT CDR	S		01.10.94	CDRE MFP
de la Perrelle, John Philip , pce	LT CDR	X	AWO(A)	01.01.78	2SL/CNH FOTR
De Reya, Anthony Luciano	LT RM	RM		01.09.94	40 CDO RM
De Sa, Philip John , pce, psc	CDR	X	PWO(A)	31.12.91	RNSC GREENWICH
de Val, Kevin Leslie , psc (Loc Lt Col)	MAJ	RM	MTO	31.12.86	CTCRM
de Winton, Michael Robert , pcea	LT CDR(SL)	X	P	01.10.91	846 SQN
Deacon, Stephen	LT	X	O	01.06.90	EXCHANGE USA
Deam, Paul	SLT(SD)	X	C	23.07.95	DRYAD
Dean, James Robert	LT	S		01.01.96	LONDON
Dean, Michael Robin , MB, BCh, DObstRCOG, MRCGP	SURG CDR	-	SM	30.06.93	NEPTUNE
Dean, Robert , BSc, jsdc, pce, pce(sm)	CDR	X	SM	31.12.89	MOD (LONDON)
Dean, William Michael Henry , BSc	LT CDR(SL)	X	P	01.10.95	HERON
Deaney, Mark Nicholas , BSc, CEng, MRAeS	LT CDR	E	AE	01.05.92	899 SQN HERON
Dearden, Steven Roy , MSc, CEng, MIMechE	LT CDR	E	MESM	01.10.90	CAPTAIN SM2
Dearling, Peter Charles	LT(SD)	X	MW	29.07.88	FOSF
Deavin, Matthew James	LT(SL)	X	O	01.07.95	849 SQN B FLT
Debenham, Leslie Allen , BEng, CEng, MRAeS, CGIA, mdtc	LT CDR	E	AE	20.10.82	MOD (BATH)
Dechow, William Ernest , BSc	CAPT RM	RM		27.07.92	JSDC GREENWICH
Dedman, Nigel John Keith , pce, pcea, fsc, l(2)Sp	CDR	X	O	31.12.90	MOD (LONDON)
Deeks, Peter James , BEng	LT(SL)	E	MESM	01.01.96	RNC DPT NS&TECH
Deeney, Stephen Jude	LT(SL)	X	ATC	01.05.90	PRESTWICK
Deighton, Derek Simpson , pce	LT CDR	X	PWO(A)	01.05.92	COMAW SEA
Dekker, Barrie James , MB, BS	SURG LT	-		01.08.94	DOLPHIN
Dell, Iain Martin	LT(SD)	MS	AD	23.07.93	NEPTUNE DSQ
Deller, Mark Gareth , psc	LT CDR	X	P	01.03.94	820 SQN
Dembrey, Mark Nicholas Scott , BSc	LT(SL)	X	O	01.07.95	702 SQN OSPREY
Dempsey, Sean	SLT(SL)	X		01.01.96	DARTMOUTH BRNC

Name	Rank	Spec	Sub-spec	Seniority	Where serving
Denes, Christopher Martin , MA, CEng, MIEE, psc	CAPT	E	WE	31.12.89	MOD (LONDON)
Denham, Daniel	SLT(SL)	X	P U/T	01.01.96	705 SQN SEAHAWK
Denham, Nigel John	LT CDR(SD)	X	SM	01.10.94	FOSM NWOOD OPS
Denholm, Iain Glenwright , pce	LT CDR	X	PWO(A)	13.08.94	NOTTINGHAM
Denholm, James Lovell (Act Surg Lt)	SURG SLT	-		01.11.92	DARTMOUTH BRNC
Denison, Alan Rae Van Tiel , MSc, CEng, MIMechE	LT CDR	E	ME	01.02.89	MOD (BATH)
Denning, Michael William Patten	LT RM	RM	P	01.05.90	CTCRM
Denning, Paul Richard , psc(m)	CAPT RM	RM	PH	01.05.91	FONA
Dennis, Matthew John	LT	X	SM	01.10.93	TALENT
Dennis, Philip Edward , BSc	SLT(SL)	X	ATCU/T	01.05.94	RAF SHAWBURY
Dennis-Jones, Michael , BA, CEng, MIEE, psc	CDR	E	WE	30.06.87	HQ DFTS
Denny, Andrew Martin , BDS	SG LT(D)	-		05.01.93	40 CDO RM
Denovan, Paul Andrew , BSc	LT CDR	E	WESM	01.01.94	SOVEREIGN
Dent, Andrew Richard , BSc, jsdc	CDR	E	WE	30.06.84	NELSON (PAY)
Depledge, Ian George , BSc, AMIEE	LT CDR	E	WE	01.04.94	MANCHESTER
Derby, Byron Dylan , BEng	LT	E	WE	01.04.94	CARDIFF
Derby, Peter John	LT(SD)	MS	PD	04.04.91	CINCFLEET
Derrick, Gareth Gwyn James , BSc, CEng, MIEE, AMIEE	LT CDR	E	WESM	01.08.89	FOSM NWOOD HQ
Deuxberry, Hugh Patrick Jeremy , pcea	LT CDR(SL)	X	P	01.09.84	RNAS YEOVILTON
Devereux, Michael Edwin , BA	2LT(GRAD)	RM		01.09.95	CTCRM LYMPSTONE
Deverson, Richard Timothy Mark	LT(SL)	X	P	01.09.90	771 SK5 SAR
Devine, James Graeme , pce, psc	LT CDR	X	AWO(U)	01.07.77	LOAN CDA HLS
Devlin, Hugh Francis Gerard	LT RM(SD)	RM	MTO	01.01.91	DEF SCH OF LANG
Dewar, Duncan Andrew , BSc (Loc Capt Rm)	LT RM	RM		24.04.92	40 CDO RM
Dewhurst, Alexander Timothy , MB, BS	SURG LTCDR	-		01.07.95	RH HASLAR
Dewsnap, Michael David	LT(SD)	E	WE	18.02.94	COLLINGWOOD
Dible, James Hunter	LT	X	P	16.05.89	DRYAD
Dible, Susan Elizabeth	LT(SL)	W		04.01.92	OSPREY
Dickens, David James Rees , pce, psc	CDR	X	PWO(U)	31.12.92	MOD (LONDON)
Dickens, David Stephen , BEng	LT(SL)	E	WE	01.11.92	EXETER
Dickens, Mark Gerald Charles , pce(sm)	LT CDR	X	SM	01.02.87	BDS WASHINGTON
Dickie, Leslie Stewart	LT(SD)	MS	RAD	09.01.87	INM ALVERSTOKE
Dickins, Benjamin Russell , BA	SLT(SL)	X		01.09.94	LEEDS CASTLE
Dickins, Michael David John , BA	LT	S		01.09.95	EDINBURGH
Dickinson, Philip Neville , BA	LT CDR	X	O	01.05.82	LOAN CDA NAG
Dickinson, Richard John , BSc, MA, psc	LT CDR	E	AE	01.04.90	800 SQN
Dickson, Andrew Peat , pce	CAPT	X	PWO(A)	30.06.96	MOD (LONDON)
Dickson, Jameslan , BSc	LT	S		01.05.95	CHATHAM
Dickson, James Peter Edward , BSc	LT(SL)	I	METOC	01.09.86	FOSM NWOOD OPS
Dickson, Stuart James	SURG LT	-		02.08.95	NEPTUNE
Diggle, Wadham Nicholas Neston , BA	LT	X		01.07.92	HE GOV&CINC GIB
Digweed, Kevin Brian	LT CDR(SD)	E	ME	01.10.93	NP 2010
Dillon, Roger Edeveain , ADC, rcds, jsdc, psc (Brigadier)	COL	RM	LC	31.12.92	CTCRM
Dineen, John Micheal George , MA	LT	X		01.04.94	FONA CRANWELL
Dingle, Jonathan Crispin , LLB (Barrister)	CDR	S	BAR	31.12.94	MOD (LONDON)
Dingwall, Mark , BSc	SLT(SL)	X	ATCU/T	01.05.95	RAF SHAWBURY
Dinham, Alan Colin , BSc	LT CDR	I		01.10.88	RNC CEN SUP STF
Dinmore, Alistair John , BA	LT RM	RM		01.09.93	AACC MID WALLOP
Dinsdale, Andrew Malcolm	LT	E	WESM	01.02.92	TORBAY
Disbury, Brian Nicholas	LT RM(SD)	RM		01.01.89	RMR TYNE
Dismore, Oliver Michael Charles , BSc, pce, pcea	LT CDR	X	P	01.01.88	RNAS CULDROSE
Disney, Peter William , pcea	LT CDR	X	O	01.10.94	815 FLT 241
Diver, Paul Harry	LT(SL)	I		01.01.91	SULTAN
Dixon, Raymond Francis , MITE, psc	LT CDR	E	WE	08.06.84	MOD (BATH)
Dobbin, Vincent William (Act Lt Cdr)	LT(SD)	E	WESM	09.06.89	CSST SEA
Dobbins, Stuart James , BA	SLT(SL)	S		01.09.94	WESTMINSTER
Dobie, Fiona Elizabeth	SLT(SL)	W	X	01.09.92	PJHQ
Dobinson, Edwin James	LT CDR(SD)	X	O	01.09.81	CINCFLEET
Dobson, Andrew Boyd	LT(SL)	X	SM	01.08.94	VANGUARD(STBD)
Dobson, Brian John	LT CDR(SD)	S	SM	01.10.95	MOD DFS(CIS) GOS
Dobson, James Kenneth , OBE, BSc, CEng, MIMechE	CDR	E	MESM	30.06.86	NEPTUNE DSQ
Dobson, Michael Francis , BSc, pce	LT CDR	X	PWO(U)	01.01.87	LOAN CDA NAG

Name	Rank	Spec	Sub-spec	Seniority	Where serving
Dobson, Richard Andrew , BSc	LT CDR	X	H1	01.04.91	NP 1016 IN SURV
Docherty, Paul Thomas , BA, pce, psc	CDR	X	PWO(A)	31.12.89	NOTTINGHAM
Docherty, Vincent	CHAPLAIN	RC		03.09.84	EXCHANGE USA
Dodd, James Scott Crossley , BSc, CEng, MIEE	CDR	E	WE	30.06.91	FOST SEA
Dodd, Kevin Michael	LT	X	O	01.04.91	814 SQN
Dodd, Nicholas Charles	LT	S		01.04.91	SCEPTRE
Dodds, Malcolm , jsdc, pce	CDR	X	PWO(N)	31.12.90	MOD (LONDON)
Dodds, Matthew Lewis	SLT(UCE)	X		01.09.95	DARTMOUTH BRNC
Dodds, Ralph Scott , pce, pcea	LT CDR	X	O	01.05.93	DRYAD
Dodgson, Stephen John , BA, MSc	LT CDR	E	WESM	03.10.89	MOD DGUW PTLAND
Doggett, Raymond Arthur , pcea	LT CDR(SL)	X	O	01.03.84	MOD (LONDON)
Doherty, Kenneth	LT CDR(SL)	X	P	01.10.93	815 OEU OSPREY
Doherty, Kiernan Patrick , BEng, AMIMechE, MIMarE	LT	E	MESM	01.03.90	SULTAN
Dolby, Michael John	LT(SD)	E	WE	15.06.90	COLLINGWOOD
Dollin, Andrew John	SLT(SL)	E	AE	01.01.94	DARTMOUTH BRNC
Dolton, Antony , MSc	LT CDR	E	WESM	01.02.92	VICTORIOUS(STBD)
Dominy, David John Douglas , n	LT	X		01.03.92	CORNWALL
Donaldson, James , MBIM, jsdc, pce	CDR	X	PWO(A)	30.06.92	MOD (LONDON)
Donaldson, Stuart Bruce , pce(sm)	LT CDR	X	SM	01.09.91	RICHMOND
Donegan, Claire , LLB	SLT(SL)	X	P U/T	01.05.94	DARTMOUTH BRNC
Doney, Kevin Robert , MBE, BSc, MIMarE, psc	CDR	E	ME	30.06.90	MOD (LONDON)
Donlan, Mark Stephen , BA	LT	S		01.07.90	DRAKE BSO(F)
Donnan, Hugh	LT(SL)	X	O	01.04.96	814 SQN
Donnelly, James Stephen , BEng	LT(SL)	E	AE	01.04.93	LOAN DTEO BSC DN
Donovan, Mark Christopher , BEng	LT(SL)	E	MESM	01.08.92	TRAFALGAR
Donovan, Patrick , BEng	LT(SL)	E	MESM	01.11.91	TRENCHANT
Donovan, Paul Anthony	CHAPLAIN	RC		22.04.85	FOSF SEA DEVNPT
Donovan, Robin John , BA	LT	S		01.01.93	TRENCHANT
Donovan, Sally Jane	SLT(SL)	X	ATCU/T	01.09.93	RAF SHAWBURY
Donworth, Desmond Maurice Joseph	SLT(SL)	X		01.01.94	ENDURANCE
Doolan, Martin , BA	LT CDR	X	PWO(U)	01.02.94	CAPT F4 (SEA)
Doran, Iain Arthur Gustav	LT(SL)	X		01.07.95	ARGYLL
Doran, Shane Edmund , BEng	LT	E	ME	01.07.94	SOUTHAMPTON
Dore, Richard Thomas , BSc, MBA, CEng, MIEE, ndc	CDR	E	AE	30.06.81	NAVAL DRAFTING
Dorey, Paul Hayward , BA, MSc, CEng, MIMechE	LT CDR	E	ME	01.05.92	NORTHUMBERLAND
Dorricott, Alan Joseph	LT CDR(SD)	E	ME	01.10.95	MANCHESTER
Dorset, William , IEng, MIEEIE	LT(SD)	E	WE	03.11.83	FOSF ENG DEVPT
Doubleday, Iain David St John	LT RM	RM		28.04.94	EXCHANGE ARMY UK
Doubleday, Steven	SLT(SL)	X	P U/T	01.05.96	DARTMOUTH BRNC
Doughty, Caroline Mary Alexandra	LT	Q	IC	16.05.90	RN MSS HASLAR
Douglas, Andrew Malcolm , BSc	2LT(GRAD)	RM		01.05.95	CTCRM LYMPSTONE
Douglas, Colin Frederick , pcea	CDR	X	P	31.12.95	FONA
Douglas, Francis Robin , BSc, CEng, MIEE, MIMarE	CDR	E	MESM	31.12.89	DG SHIPS DEVONPT
Douglas, Ian Kenneth Westbrook , psc	CDR	E	WE	31.12.84	DADPTC SHRIVNHAM
Douglas, Paul Gordon	LT(SL)	X	SM	01.06.94	VANGUARD(PORT)
Douglas, Patrick John	LT	X	P	01.06.93	810 SQN SEAHAWK
Douglas-Riley, Timothy Roger , MB, BS, DA, LRCP, MRCGP, MRCS, jsdc	SURG CDR	-	GMPP	31.12.84	CINCFLEET
Douglass, Martin Colin Marc , BEng	LT	E	ME	01.03.91	CFM PORTSMOUTH
Doull, Donald James Murray , BEng	LT	E	MESM	01.11.94	SPARTAN
Dow, Clive Stewart	SLT	S		01.09.94	DARTMOUTH BRNC
Dow, David Campbell , psc(m) (Act Maj)	CAPT RM	RM		01.05.78	NEPTUNE
Dow, William	SURG SLT	-		01.02.94	DARTMOUTH BRNC
Dowd, Jonathan Wyn , BEng	LT RM	RM		01.09.94	45 CDO RM
Dowdell, Robert Edmund John , BSc	LT CDR(SL)	X	P	01.10.94	702 SQN OSPREY
Dowdeswell, Karen Ann , BM	SURG LT	-		01.08.93	COLLINGWOOD
Dowell, Paul Henry Neil , BSc	LT CDR	E	WE	01.08.94	LIVERPOOL
Dowle, Stephen William , MSc, CEng, MIEE, MBCS	CDR	E	WESM	30.06.94	DTR BATH
Downer, Mark John , MEng, MRINA	LT(SL)	E	ME	01.08.93	INVINCIBLE
Downes, Colin , BSc	LT	X		01.09.93	HERON
Downes, Daniel Patrick Joseph , BA, MSc	CAPT RM	RM		01.09.91	DNPS
Downie, Alan John	LT(SD)	E	WE	15.06.90	INTREPID

Name	Rank	Spec	Sub-spec	Seniority	Where serving
Downing, Carl William , BSc	LT CDR	E	AE(P)	01.03.92	815 SQN HQ
Downing, Iain Michael	LT(SL)	X	P	16.09.94	810 SQN A FLIGHT
Downton, John Gerald Murray , MA, jsdc, psc(m), jssc	LT COL	RM	C	31.12.93	COMACCHIO GP RM
Dowsett, Patrick Giles , n	LT	X		01.09.93	STARLING
Doxsey, Roland Arthur , MSc, CEng, MIMechE, jsdc	CDR	E	ME	30.06.89	DRAKE CFM
Doyle, Edward Hugh Michael Birmingham , MB, BA, BCh, ChB	SURG CDR	-	GMPP	30.06.84	BF GIBRALTAR(NE)
Doyle, Gareth Brian , BA	SLT(SL)	X		01.01.95	DARTMOUTH BRNC
Doyle, Gary Lawrence , pce	LT CDR	X	O	01.09.92	FONA NORTHWOOD
Doyle, Nicholas Patrick	LT(SD)	X	g	17.12.93	TAMAR
Doyne-Ditmas, Philip Simon , MBE, pce, pcea, psc	CDR	X	P	31.12.95	EXCHANGE ARMY UK
Drabble, Raymond Charles , BSc	LT CDR	S		16.04.93	EXCHANGE USA
Drake, Edwin Denis	CDR	E	WESM	30.06.96	NEPTUNE SM1
Drake-Wilkes, Nicholas James , BA	LT	X		01.01.95	CENTURION
Draper, Stephen Perry	LT CDR	X	PWO(A)	26.02.96	INVINCIBLE
Dreelan, Michael Joseph	LT(SL)	X		01.08.91	ITCHEN
Dresner, Rupert James	LT RM	RM	RMP2	24.04.95	847 SQN
Drewer, Christopher David , BSc	LT(SL)	E	AE	01.08.89	899 SQN OEU
Drewett, Robin Edward ,MBE, pce, l(2)Ru	LT CDR	X	O	01.03.90	814 SQN
Drodge, Andrew Paul Frank	LT	X	O	01.10.94	810 SQN SEAHAWK
Drummond, Colin James , MEng, AMIMechE	LT	E	MESM	16.11.89	NBC ROSYTH
Drummond, John Richard Geoffrey , MA, pce(sm)	CDR	X	SM	30.06.94	CNOCS GROUP
Drury, Martin Herbert	LT CDR(SD)	X	PT	01.10.93	EXCELLENT
Dryden, Paul Wynne , MB, BCh	SURG LTCDR	-	GMPP	22.01.91	DRAKE CBP
Drylie, Andrew John , BSc	LT CDR	X	SM	01.02.92	DISS ASHFORD
Drysdale, Steven Ronald	LT	X	SM	01.02.89	SPARTAN
Drywood, Tobias , BEng	LT	E	ME	01.04.93	BRILLIANT
Du Port, Antony Neil , pce, psc	CAPT	X	PWO(N)	31.12.92	2SL/CNH FOTR
Dudley, Stephen Mark Terence , MA	LT	S		01.01.91	MOD (LONDON)
Duesbury, Clive Lawrence , BSc	SLT(SL)	E	ME	01.01.95	DARTMOUTH BRNC
Duff, Andrew Patrick	LT	X	SM	01.09.92	VICTORIOUS(STBD)
Duffield, Gary Geddes , MSc, CEng, MRAeS	LT CDR	E	AE	01.02.90	FONA
Duffy, Henry	LT	X		01.05.91	EXCHANGE ARMY UK
Duffy, John Bernard	LT(SL)	X	P	01.07.91	771 SK5 SAR
Duffy, Michael Joseph , MSc, CEng, MIEE, jsdc	CDR	E	WE	31.12.86	DGSS BRISTOL
Duke, Robin Leonard	CDR	E	WE	30.06.91	CAPT D3 SEA
Duke, Ronald Michael	LT(QM)	Q	CPN	24.04.87	DRAKE CBP
Dukes, Nicholas Paul	LT CDR(SL)	X	O	01.10.93	815 FLT 212
Dullage, Bryan , MSc, CEng, MIMarE, MCGI	LT CDR	E	ME	01.03.92	BATTLEAXE
Dumbell, Phillip , BSc, psc	LT CDR	E	WESM	01.09.91	MOD (LONDON)
Duncan, Alan John	LT(CS)	-		16.10.88	MOD DNR OUTPORTS
Duncan, Colin John	LT(SL)	X	P	01.03.94	810 SQN SEAHAWK
Duncan, Giles Stuart	LT(SL)	X	P	16.01.95	814 SQN
Duncan, Ian Stewart , BSc	LT CDR	E	MESM	01.06.94	VICTORIOUS(PORT)
Duncan, Jeremy	LT(SL)	X	P	01.04.91	EXCHANGE USA
Duncan, Kenneth Robert , BSc, PhD	LT(SL)	I		01.01.88	SULTAN
Duncan, Philippa Eve , nadc, psc	CAPT	W	FA	01.04.91	2SL/CNH FOTR
Dundon, John Michael	LT(SL)	X	P	16.04.86	RAF CRANWELL EFS
Dunham, Mark William , BSc, psc(m)	CAPT RM	RM		27.04.90	40 CDO RM
Dunkley, Robert Charles	LT CDR(SD)	X	PT	01.10.89	DRYAD
Dunlop, Christopher Graham Harrison , OBE, rcds, psc(m)	COL	RM		30.06.93	MOD (LONDON)
Dunlop, Michael William Scott	LT	X	PWO(C)	01.01.89	LIVERPOOL
Dunlop, Peter Francis , BSc, pce	LT CDR	X	PWO(U)	01.04.91	CINCFLEET
Dunn, Andrew James Patrick	LT(SD)	E	AE(M)	16.10.92	DGA(N)ASE MASU
Dunn, Christopher John	LT CDR(SL)	X	P	01.10.95	705 SQN SEAHAWK
Dunn, Catherine Louise	LT	X	H2	01.02.95	RNAS CULDROSE
Dunn, Gary Russell	LT	E	WESM	01.05.90	COLLINGWOOD
Dunn, Ian Laurence	CAPT RM	RM	MOR	01.09.86	CAMBRIDGE
Dunn, Nicholas Geoffrey , BSc	LT CDR(SL)	X	P	01.10.92	FONA SEAHAWK
Dunn, Paul Ernest	LT(SD)	X	PT	12.12.91	NEPTUNE
Dunn, Paul Edward	LT	X	SM	01.07.93	SOVEREIGN
Dunn, Roderick Lance Redmond , MB, BS	SURG LTCDR	-		19.02.95	RNDHU DERRIFORD
Dunn, Robert Paul	LT	X	SM	01.03.89	URNU GLASGOW

Name	Rank	Spec	Sub-spec	Seniority	Where serving
Dunne, Michaelgerard , BEM (Act Lt)	SLT(SD)	X	AV	03.04.94	HQ CDO AVN
Dunningham, Stephen	LT(SD)	E	ME	10.06.94	SULTAN
Dunsby, Nicholas Byron	LT(SD)	E	MESM	15.06.95	MOD (BATH)
Dunt, John Hugh , BSc, CEng, FIEE, rcds, psc	VADM	-	WE	21.03.95	MOD (LONDON)
Dunt, Peter Arthur (Commodore)	CAPT	S		30.06.88	2SL/CNH
Dunthorne, Julie Agnes	LT(SL)	S		04.01.92	NEPTUNE CFS
Durbin, Christopher John , pce, psc(m)	LT CDR	X	PWO(A)	01.05.87	CENTURION
Durbin, Christopher Paul Julian , MSc, FRAeS	LT CDR(SL)	I	METOC	03.01.78	LOAN DRA WNFRITH
Durham, Paul Christopher Langton , BEng	LT	X		01.06.93	BIRMINGHAM
Durkin, Mark Thomas Gilchrist	LT CDR	X	MCD	01.06.93	EXCHANGE AUSTLIA
Durnford, Christopher John , MA, pce	LT CDR	X	AWO(U)	01.07.79	2SL/CNH
Durning, William Munro	LT(SD)	MS		02.04.93	RN MSS HASLAR
Durrant, Peter , MBE	LT(SD)	E	WE	29.10.82	DRAKE CFM
Durston, David Howard , pce, pcea, psc, l(2)Ge	CDR	X	P	30.06.92	2SL/CNH
Dustan, Andrew John	LT CDR	E	AE	19.02.93	MOD (BATH)
Duthie, Ruth Mary Mitchell , BSc	LT(SL)	X	H2	01.03.93	RNAS CULDROSE
Dutta, Mahesh , OBE, MSc, CEng, FIEE, nadc	CDR	E	WE	30.06.84	NACISA
Dutton, Andrew Colin	LT	S		01.02.95	BRILLIANT
Dutton, David	LT	X		01.06.89	CHATHAM
Dutton, James Benjamin , BSc, psc(m) (Loc Col)	LT COL	RM	C	31.12.94	MOD (LONDON)
Dutton, Philip John	LT(SD)	E	WESM	05.06.92	VICTORIOUS(PORT)
Dwane, Christopher Malcolm Robin , BSc	LT CDR	S		01.01.89	RALEIGH
Dyche, Trevor	LT(SD)	E	MESM	18.10.85	DRAKE CFM
Dyer, Graham Richard	LT(SD)	E	WE	05.06.92	RNSC GREENWICH
Dyer, Jonathan David Thomas , BSc, BTech	LT(SL)	I		01.09.87	RMC OF SCIENCE
Dyer, Michael David James , BEng	LT CDR	E	WESM	01.04.96	MOD (LONDON)
Dyer, Simon John , BSc, psc	CDR	E	WE	30.06.92	CAPT F6 (SEA)
Dyke, Christopher Leonard , BA	LT CDR	X		01.02.96	CAMPBELTOWN
Dyke, Kenneth Andrew , BEng	LT	E	MESM	01.10.92	VICTORIOUS(STBD)
Dyke, Ralph Charles , MM	CAPT RM(SD)	RM		01.10.93	RM SCHL MUSIC
Dymock, Anthony Knox , BA, pce, psc	CAPT	X	AWO(C)	31.12.91	DRYAD
Dymond, Nicholaus Robert John	LT(SD)	E	WE	18.02.94	COLLINGWOOD
Dyson, Peter Kevin , BSc	LT CDR(SL)	I		01.01.84	DARTMOUTH BRNC

E

Name	Rank	Spec	Sub-spec	Seniority	Where serving
Eagles, Anthony James , AFC, MA, pcea, psc	LT CDR(SL)	X	P	01.03.84	FONA
Eaglestone, Peter Stuart , MIPM, MIMgt, psc	CDR	S		30.06.87	DCTA
Eales, Martin John	LT CDR(SL)	X	P	01.10.93	750 SQN OBS SCH
Eales, Ralph Nicholas , psc(a) (Loc Maj)	CAPT RM	RM	PH	01.12.82	ATTURM
Eardley, John Mark	SLT(SD)	E	WE	07.02.94	SHEFFIELD
Earl, Nicholas Julian Christopher , BEng	LT(SL)	E	AE	01.11.94	SULTAN
Eastaugh, Andrew Charles , BSc, adp	LT CDR(SL)	I		01.10.89	DNPS
Eastaugh, Timothy Colin	LT CDR(SL)	X	P	01.10.93	MWC GOSPORT
Easterbrook, Kevin Ivor Edgar , BEng	LT	E	WE	01.12.91	MOD DGSM PTLAND
Eastley, Barry Roger , BSc, CEng, MIMechE, MRAeS, jsdc	CAPT	E	AE	30.06.96	FAAIT MAN ORG VL
Easton, Candida Elizabeth	LT(SL)	W		12.12.91	RALEIGH
Easton, Darryl Richard William , BEng	LT	E	WE	01.02.95	COLLINGWOOD
Easton, Derek William	LT(SD)	X	PT	04.04.96	HERON
Easton, Robert Nicoll	LT CDR	X	PWO(A)	16.11.84	CDRE MFP
Easton, Richard William	LT CDR(SL)	X	PWO(C)	01.10.90	MOD (LONDON)
Eaton, Christopher Roger	LT CDR(SL)	X	P	01.10.94	SEAHAWK
Eaton, Paul Graham , BSc	LT CDR	I	METOC	01.06.94	FOSM NWOOD OPS
Eatwell, Russell Andrew	LT(SL)	X	P	01.08.89	HERON
Ebbens, Andrew John	CAPT RM	RM		01.09.87	RM POOLE
Ebbutt, Giles John , BA, psc(m)	MAJ	RM	C	30.06.89	MOD (LONDON)
Eberle, Peter James Fuller , pce, psc, l(1)Ge	CDR	X	PWO(C)	31.12.87	EXCHANGE USA
Eccleston, Jamie Mark , BEng	LT	E	MESM	01.03.95	TALENT
Eddie, Alan George Watt , BTech	LT(SD)	E	WE	24.02.95	DRAKE CFM
Edey, Michael John , BSc	LT	X		01.12.93	CHATHAM
Edgar, Jon Anthony	SLT(SL)	S		01.09.94	RALEIGH
Edge, John Howard	LT	S	SM	01.06.89	RICHMOND
Edge, Karla Louise	SLT	X		01.01.94	DARTMOUTH BRNC

Name	Rank	Spec	Sub-spec	Seniority	Where serving
Edge, Philippa Anne , BA	LT(SL)	X		14.12.89	PJHQ
Edgell, John Nicholas , OBE, pce(sm), psc	CDR	X	SM	31.12.93	FOSM NWOOD OPS
Edgley, Andrew David , BA	LT(SL)	I	METOC	16.07.89	CINCFLEET
Edinburgh, His Royal Highness The Prince Philip, Duke of,	ADM OF FLEET			15.01.53	
KG, KT, OM, GBE, AC, QSO					
Appointed					
RAN	ADM OF FLEET			01.04.54	
RNZN	ADM OF FLEET			27.08.58	
Edleston, Hugh Anthony Harold Greswell , jsdc, pce	CAPT	X	AWO(A)	31.12.93	MOD (LONDON)
Edmonds, Anthony John , MSc, psc	LT CDR	E	WESM	01.07.87	CNSA PORTLAND
Edmonds, Gerald	LT CDR	X	C	02.08.85	BALTAP
Edmonds, Graham John Leslie , pce, psc	CDR	X	AWO(A)	31.12.87	MOD (LONDON)
Edmonds, Louisa Ann , BSc	LT	X		01.09.94	RNAS CULDROSE
Edmonds, Ronald Francis , ndc, pce	CDR	X	O	30.06.80	SEA CADET CORPS
Edmonds, Rebecca Mary , BEng	LT(SL)	I		01.05.92	COLLINGWOOD
Edmondson, John Christopher	LT CDR	E	MESM	27.01.91	NEPTUNE DSQ
Edmondstone, William Mark , MB, BS, DIH, LRCP,	SURG CAPT	-	CM	30.06.96	RH HASLAR
MRCS, MRCP, AFOM					
Edmunds, Daryl William	LT(SL)	X	SM	01.07.93	FOSM NWOOD OPS
Edney, Andrew Ralph , MBE, BEng, pce, pcea	LT CDR	X	P	01.04.90	RNSC GREENWICH
Edson, Mark Andrew	LT(SD)	E	WE	22.02.96	CHATHAM
Edward, Gavin James , BEng, AMIEE	LT	E	WE	01.07.95	COLLINGWOOD
Edwardes, Geoffrey Haworth , pce	CAPT	X	G	31.12.91	ELANT/NAVNW
Edwards, Andrew Donald Pryce , MBE, BSc, MIMechE	LT CDR	E	MESM	01.02.88	FOSM NWOOD HQ
Edwards, Andrew George	LT	E	AE(L)	01.10.95	SULTAN
Edwards, Carlos Carew , BSc	LT CDR	S		01.07.85	HQBF GIBRALTAR
Edwards, CharlesJohn Albert , MB, BS, FRCA	SURG LTCDR	-		01.08.90	RH HASLAR
Edwards, Eric George	LT CDR(SD)	X	AV	01.10.92	RFANSU (ARGUS)
Edwards, Ian , BSc, PhD, adp	CDR	I		30.06.87	DNPS
Edwards, John	SLT(SL)	E	AE	01.01.94	DARTMOUTH BRNC
Edwards, Janice Mary	LT CDR(SL)	S		01.04.86	RNC CEN SUP STF
Edwards, John Paul Thomas , BSc, pcea	LT(SL)	X	P	01.03.87	845 SQN
Edwards, Philip Douglas , BChir, MA, FRCSEd	SURG LTCDR	-	SM	21.12.95	NELSON (PAY)
Edwards, Philip John , BSc	LT CDR	I	METOC	01.05.91	COLLINGWOOD
Edwards, Richard	LT(SD)	X	EW	11.12.92	EXCHANGE USA
Edwards, Raymond Allan , MSc, MSRP	LT CDR(SD)	MS	SM	01.10.91	NEPTUNE DSQ
Edwards, Richmond Arthur	LT CDR(SD)	E	WE	01.10.95	LOAN DRA PRTSDWN
Edwards, Steven , BEng	SLT	E	AE	01.09.93	SULTAN
Edwards, Vernon , pce	LT CDR	X	PWO(N)	01.01.82	CINCFLEET
Eedle, Richard John , BA	LT CDR	X	SM	01.03.91	CENTURION
Egeland, Finn Adam	LT CDR	X	PWO(U)	01.04.95	DRYAD
Egerton, Paul Michael , BSc, CEng, MIMarE, MIMechE	CDR	E	ME	31.12.88	CINCFLEET
Egerton, Stephen Brian	SLT(SD)	X	C	10.12.95	DRYAD
Eglin, Ian	CHAPLAIN	CE		27.01.87	HERON
Eitzen, Ruari Paul , MSc, CEng, MRAeS	LT CDR	E	AE	01.11.76	FAAIT MAN ORG VL
Eland, David Arthur	LT(SD)	E	WESM	22.02.96	MOD DFS(CIS) GOS
Elborn, Teresa Kathleen , MHCIMA	LT(SL)	W	S	11.12.92	2SL/CNH
Eldridge, Timothy John	LT(SL)	X	P	01.04.91	819 SQN
Elford, David Graham , MSc, CEng, MRAeS, AMIEE	LT CDR	E	AE	01.05.93	820 SQN
Ellender, Tony John , BSc	LT(SL)	I		01.09.90	INVINCIBLE
Ellerton, Paul	LT(SL)	X	P	16.10.94	702 SQN OSPREY
Ellett, Keith Geoffrey	LT(SL)	X	ATC	01.06.84	FOST DPORT SHORE
Elliman, Simon Mark	LT CDR(SL)	X	MW	01.10.94	DRYAD
Elin, Alexander David Scott , BSc	LT CDR	E	AE	01.04.91	849 SQN HQ
Ellins, Stuart John , BSc, CEng, MIMechE, psc	CDR	E	ME	30.06.91	CAPT D3 SEA
Elliott, Andrew John , BSc	LT CDR(SL)	I	METOC	01.10.94	EXCHANGE AUSTLIA
Elliott, Martin Keith	LT	X	SM	01.07.87	NELSON
Elliott, Michael Peter , BSc, psc, MITD	LT CDR	I		04.01.77	DRYAD
Elliott, Robin , pcea	LT	X	O	01.04.89	702 SQN OSPREY
Elliott, Stephen , BEng	LT(SL)	E	WE	01.07.92	COLLINGWOOD
Elliott, Steven , BEng, AMIEE	LT(SL)	E	WESM	01.07.93	FOSM FASLANE
Elliott, Stephen Ferguson , psc(a)	MAJ	RM		31.12.89	AST(W)

Name	Rank	Spec	Sub-spec	Seniority	Where serving
Elliott, Tobin David , jsdc, pce(sm) (Commodore)	CAPT	X	SMTAS	31.12.87	PJHQ
Elliott, Thomas Fitzgerald , MBE, TEng, IEng, AMIMarE	LT CDR(SD)	E	ME	01.10.90	MOD (BATH)
Ellis, Christopher Thomas , BA	LT(SL)	X		01.03.92	FEARLESS
Ellis, David Francis , BSc	LT(SL)	I		09.07.89	FOSM NWOOD OPS
Ellis, Duncan Ian	LT RM	RM	P	30.04.91	847 SQN
Ellis, Duncan Robert , BEng	LT(SL)	I		01.01.93	COLLINGWOOD
Ellis, James Paul , BEng	LT(SL)	I		01.09.91	COLLINGWOOD
Ellis, Mark Alexandar Harcourt , BSc, osc (Loc Maj)	CAPT RM	RM	MTO	01.09.85	HQ NORTH
Ellis, Matthew Paul , BSc	LT(SL)	I		01.05.93	RNEWOSU
Ellis, Michael Philip	CAPT RM	RM	PH	01.09.89	CENTURION
Ellis, Nicholas Mark	LT(SL)	X		18.07.85	NP 1061
Ellis, Peter John , pce(sm), I(2)Ru	CAPT	X	SM	30.06.92	MOD (LONDON)
Ellis, Richard William , BSc	LT CDR	E	AE	01.10.90	MOD (LONDON)
Ellison, Christopher Vaughan , pce, psc(a) (Commodore)	CAPT	X	PWO(N)	30.06.92	CDRE MFP
Ellison, Toby George	SLT	X		01.01.95	MIDDLETON
Ellman-Brown, Amanda Clare	LT(SL)	W	X	27.07.90	NELSON
Ellwood, Peter George	LT(SD)	X	SM	29.07.94	VANGUARD(PORT)
Elmer, Timothy Brendan , BDS	SGLTCDR(D)	-		16.01.94	SEAHAWK
Elmore, Graeme Martin	CHAPLAIN	CE		30.09.86	FEARLESS
Elsom, Geoffrey Keith	LT(SL)	X	C	27.07.95	FEARLESS
Elsworth, Reginald Keith	LT CDR	E	WESM	24.04.86	MOD DGSWS BATH
Eltringham, Timothy John , OBE, jsdc, pce, pcea	CDR	X	P	30.06.90	MOD (LONDON)
Elvin, Andrew James	LT CDR	X	MCD	06.11.93	NORFOLK
Elward, Michael James	MID(NE)(SL)	X		01.09.95	DULVERTON
Elwell-Deighton, Dean Carl	LT(SL)	X	P	16.09.93	810 SQN SEAHAWK
Elwood, Colin Paul , BSc	LT(SL)	X	P	16.03.90	810 SQN SEAHAWK
Emerton, Mark Simon , MA, MIMgt (Barrister)	LT CDR	S	BAR	01.02.92	NEPTUNE
Emmerson, Graham John	LT CDR	X	PWO(A)	01.06.92	GLASGOW
Emmerson, Stephen Charles	LT(SL)	X		01.03.96	SOUTHAMPTON
Endersby, Roger James Stewart	CDR	S		31.12.86	2SL/CNH FOTR
Enever, Shaun	SLT(SL)	X	O	01.01.94	815 FLT 219
Engeham, Paul Richard , MA, pce	LT CDR	X	AWO(C)	16.01.81	MOD (LONDON)
England, Stephen John , BSc, PGCE	LT(SL)	I	MCD	28.08.85	DEF DIVING SCHL
English, Colin Richard , MSc, CEng, FIMarE, jsdc	CDR	E	ME	30.06.88	CAPT F6 (SEA)
Ennis, Edward , BEM	LT(CS)RM	-		13.10.91	MOD DNR OUTPORTS
Enright, Kevin Dominick , BEng	LT	E	AE	01.09.88	DGA(N) ASE
Enticknap, Kenneth , QGM	LT CDR	E	ME	10.03.89	FOSF
Entwisle, William Nicholas	LT CDR	X	P	01.02.96	815 FLT 226
Entwistle, Stephen Charles , pce	LT CDR	X	PWO(A)	01.12.93	ILLUSTRIOUS
Erskine, Peter Anthony , BA, MSc, MIMechE, MINucE, psc	CDR	E	ME	30.06.96	MOD (LONDON)
Erskine, Robert Noel	LT CDR	S		16.12.86	DOLPHIN
Esaw, Michelle	LT	Q		04.01.92	RH HASLAR
Essenhigh, Angus Nigel Patrick	SLT	X		01.09.94	DARTMOUTH BRNC
Essenhigh, Nigel Richard , rcds, pce, psc	RADM	-	PWO(N)	15.02.94	MOD (LONDON)
Estall, Janet Marion	LT(SD)	I	I	27.07.95	LOAN CDA NAG
Etchells, Stephen Barrie	LT	E	WESM	03.07.92	NEPTUNE SM1
Ethell, David Ross , BEng	LT RM	RM	LC	28.04.94	RM POOLE
Euden, Christopher Peter , BA	LT	X		01.06.95	BOXER
Euridge, Richard Ernest , MBE	CAPT RM(SD)	RM		01.10.90	HQ 3 CDO BDE RM
Evans, Antony , BEng	LT(SL)	E	AE	01.02.94	820 SQN
Evans, Andrew William	LT CDR(SL)	X	SM	01.10.95	MWC GOSPORT
Evans, Barry Roy (Act Lt Cdr)	LT(SD)	E	WE	10.09.86	MOD (BATH)
Evans, Carol , BSc	LT(SL)	X		01.06.91	DRYAD
Evans, Charles , BA	SLT	X		01.09.93	DRYAD
Evans, Craig Hamilton , BSc	LT(SL)	I		01.11.88	2SL/CNH
Evans, Charles William , MB, BS, MPH, DIH, DTM&H, LRCP, MFOM, MRCS, AFOM	SURG CAPT	-	CO/M	30.06.89	RCDS
Evans, David Anthony	LT(SL)	X	ATC	20.12.95	RNAS CULDROSE
Evans, David John , BSc, MIEE, AMRAeS, psc	CDR	E	AE(P)	30.06.95	ILLUSTRIOUS
Evans, Desmond John	LT(SD)	X	AV	28.07.89	RNAS PORTLAND
Evans, David Melville , BSc, pce	CDR	X	PWO(A)	30.06.94	BDS WASHINGTON
Evans, David Mark Mortimer	CAPT RM	RM		01.09.93	ASC CAMBERLEY

Name	Rank	Spec	Sub-spec	Seniority	Where serving
Evans, Edward Michael	LT	S	SM	16.08.89	CINCIBERLANT
Evans, Geraint , AMIEE	LT	E	WE	01.06.90	DGSS BRISTOL
Evans, Gareth	SURG SLT	-		07.07.95	DARTMOUTH BRNC
Evans, Graham Huw , MB, BS, LRCP, FFARCS, MRCS	SURG CDR	-	CA	31.12.92	RNDHU DERRIFORD
Evans, Graham Roy , BSc, pce	LT CDR	X	PWO(U)	01.12.90	DRYAD
Evans, Hugh Russell , BSc	CDR	E	ME	31.12.82	DG SHIPS PTSMTH
Evans, John Richard , BSc, CEng, MIEE, psc	CDR	E	WE	30.06.84	DG SHIPS DEVONPT
Evans, John Walter	LT CDR	X	PWO(C)	06.05.86	2SL/CNH FOTR
Evans, Karl Nicholas Meredith	LT CDR	X	SM	01.05.92	FOSM NWOOD OPS
Evans, Malcolm , MSc	LT(SL)	I		01.05.85	SULTAN
Evans, Mark	LT(SL)	I		01.05.92	SULTAN
Evans, Michael Anthony , BSc	LT CDR	I	METOC	17.05.88	ILLUSTRIOUS
Evans, Martyn Alun , BA	CAPT RM	RM		01.09.93	CDO LOG REGT RM
Evans, Michael Clive , BSc, MIMgt, pce, pcea, psc	CDR	X	P	31.12.94	BIRMINGHAM
Evans, Marc David , MILDM, AMIAM	LT	S		16.05.90	EXCELLENT
Evans, Michael Edward	SLT(SL)	E	MESM	01.05.94	DARTMOUTH BRNC
Evans, Michael John , FFA, MBIM, jsdc	CDR	S		31.12.85	MOD (LONDON)
Evans, Martin Joseph , BSc	LT CDR	X	PWO(U)	01.09.95	NOTTINGHAM
Evans, Marius John Gunning , psc	LT CDR(SL)	X	FC	01.03.86	RNSC GREENWICH
Evans, Nicholas Grant	LT(CS)	-		13.09.88	MOD DNR OUTPORTS
Evans, Phillip Gordon , BSc	LT(SL)	I		01.03.87	RALEIGH
Evans, Peter John (Loc Capt Rm)	LT RM	RM	LC	11.07.94	ENDURANCE
Evans, Robert David , BSc, pce	LT CDR	X	PWO(C)	01.06.88	PJHQ
Evans, Richard Forrest , psc	LT CDR	X	PWO	16.09.81	NELSON (PAY)
Evans, Richard	LT(SL)	X		01.03.93	EXCHANGE NLANDS
Evans, Stephen , BTech	LT(SD)	E	WESM	24.02.95	NEPTUNE SM1
Evans, Sean Desmond , MB, BCh, ChB	SURG CDR	-	GMPP	30.06.93	SULTAN
Evans, Sarah Jane	LT(SL)	-		06.04.86	PJHQ
Evans, William Quennell Frankis , pce	LT CDR	X	PWO(N)	20.10.94	INVINCIBLE
Everett, Edward Jason	LT RM	RM		24.04.95	MOD DNR OUTPORTS
Everritt, Richard (Loc Capt Rm)	LT RM(SD)	RM	MTO	01.01.92	EXCH ARMY SC(G)
Evershed, Marcus Charles , MB, BCh	SURG LTCDR	-		01.08.95	RM POOLE
Every, Mark , BM, BSc	SURG LT	-		03.02.93	ARGYLL
Evison, Toby , BSc	LT(SL)	I		19.09.89	SULTAN
Ewen, Andrew Philip , BEng	LT	E	AE	01.01.93	849 SQN B FLT
Ewen, Raymond John	LT(SD)	S	W	14.12.90	EXCELLENT
Ewence, Martin William , BA, pce, l(2)Du	LT CDR	X	PWO(A)	01.01.91	CORNWALL
Ewers, Alan Martin , BSc	LT CDR	I	METOC	20.08.88	RALEIGH
Ewing, Andrew David , pce, psc	CDR	X	AWO(U)	30.06.91	BDS WASHINGTON
Ewins, Graeme Power , pce	CDR	X	AWO(C)	30.06.89	MOD (LONDON)
Exworthy, Damian , BSc, MA	SLT	S		01.09.94	FEARLESS
Eyre, Kurt Brendan	LT RM	RM		26.04.93	CTCRM

F

Fairbairn, William David Murray , MA, jsdc	CAPT	E	WE	30.06.95	MOD (LONDON)
Fairbank, Brian	CHAPLAIN	CE		03.09.91	DRAKE CBP
Fairbrass, John Emilio , BEng, CEng, MIMechE, l(2)Ru	LT	E	ME	28.04.89	RNSC GREENWICH
Faircloth, Mark	LT(SL)	I	METOC	01.01.91	RFANSU (ARGUS)
Fairgrieve, Lee	LT(SL)	W	X	11.12.92	RNAS YEOVILTON
Fairhead, Samantha	SLT(SL)	X	H2	01.05.94	RNAS CULDROSE
Fairhurst, George Michael , BSc, CEng, MIEE	CDR	E	WE	30.06.87	2SL/CNH FOTR
Falconer, Alistair James	LT(SL)	X	P	01.04.91	819 SQN
Falk, Benedict Hakan Geoffrey , pce	LT CDR	X	PWO(A)	01.04.94	CORNWALL
Fallowfield, Jonathan Paul , BTech	LT(SD)	E	WE	24.02.95	GRAFTON
Fancy, Robert (Act Lt Cdr)	LT	X	SM	01.08.88	SPARTAN
Fanshawe, James Rupert , jsdc, pce, l(2)Fr	CAPT	X	PWO(U)	30.06.96	MOD (LONDON)
Fanshawe, Robert John	CAPT RM	RM		01.01.78	HQRM
Farmer, Jean Louis Vincent , BSc	LT	X		01.03.94	INVINCIBLE
Farmer, John Robert	LT CDR	X	AWO(A)	16.08.82	DRYAD
Farquhar, John William , FRGS, jsdc	CDR	S		30.06.87	NAVSOUTH ITALY
Farquharson-Roberts, Michael Atholl , MB, BS, LRCP, FRCS	SURG CAPT	-	CO/S	30.06.93	RH HASLAR
Farrage, Michael Edward , BSc	LT CDR	I		01.11.92	RNSC GREENWICH

Name	Rank	Spec	Sub-spec	Seniority	Where serving
Farrant, Paul Richard	LT(SL)	X	P	16.08.90	NP 1061
Farrar, Mark William , MB, BS	SURG LTCDR	-	A	01.08.95	NELSON (PAY)
Farrell, Nicholas	LT(SL)	X	SM	01.01.95	TRAFALGAR
Farrell, Sean Michael	LT(SL)	I		01.09.90	DNPS
Farrington, John Lewis , BEng	LT	E	WESM	01.01.94	DRAKE CFM
Farrington, Richard , BA, LLB, pce	CDR	X	PWO(C)	30.06.96	JSDC GREENWICH
Farrington, Stephen Paul , QGM, TEng, IEng, AMIMarE, psc	CDR	X	ME	30.06.96	CAPT D5 SEA
Farrow, Malcolm John Darley , MIMgt, jsdc	CDR	X	C	30.06.83	NBC PORTSMOUTH
Faulconbridge, David , MSc, CEng, MIMarE, AMIEE, psc	CDR	E	MESM	31.12.94	FOSM NWOOD OPS
Faulkner, Daniel William , BEng	LT(SL)	E	AE	01.08.93	899 SQN HERON
Faulkner, Jeffrey James	LT CDR	X	H CH	05.07.91	RN HYDROG SCHL
Faulkner, Richard Ian , BSc	LT CDR	E	ME	01.08.89	FOSF
Faulks, David John	LT CDR	S		01.03.91	DOLPHIN
Faulks, Robert Charles , pce, pcea	LT CDR	X	O	16.11.82	PRESTWICK
Fawcett, Edward Neil	LT CDR(SD)	X	EW	01.10.88	RNU CHELTENHAM
Fawcett, FionaPatrica , BA	LT(SL)	I		01.09.89	ILLUSTRIOUS
Fawcett, Michael Scott	LT	E	WE	01.03.90	COLLINGWOOD
Fear, Richard Keith , BSc	LT CDR	E	WESM	01.12.90	MOD (BATH)
Fearnley, Andrew Thomas	LT(SD)	S	S	13.12.95	INVINCIBLE
Featherstone, Katherine Jane , BDS	SG LT(D)	-		25.04.91	WARRIOR
Febbrraro, Nicholas Robert	CDR	E	MESM	30.06.93	DTR BARROW
Fec, Zbigniew Marian , BA, I(1)Po, I(1)Pl, I(1)Ru, ...	CAPT RM(SD)	RM	MTO	01.10.93	JACIG
I(2)Ru, I(2)Sp (Loc Maj)					
Fedorowicz, Richard	LT(SL)	X	ATC	16.10.88	RNAS CULDROSE
Feeney, Matthew Blake	MID(UCE)	X		01.09.95	DARTMOUTH BRNC
Feeney, Michael Leonard , BEng, CEng, MIMarE	LT	E	ME	01.05.89	SULTAN
Fegan, Paul , BA	LT	S		01.02.93	TRIUMPH
Felgate, Howard , BSc	LT CDR	X		01.05.83	FOSF
Fensome, Raymond George , jsdc	CDR	X	AWO(A)	31.12.83	LOAN CDA HLS
Fenwick, John , OBE, BEng	CDR	E	WESM	30.06.83	MOD DGUW PTLAND
Fenwick, Julie Cheryl , BDS	SGLTCDR(D)	-		03.09.95	MOD (LONDON)
Fenwick, Robin John , BSc	2LT(GRAD)	RM		01.05.95	CTCRM LYMPSTONE
Ferguson, Alan Duncan , CBE, BA, MSc, CEng, MIMarE, ...	CAPT	E	MESM	31.12.87	2SL/CNH FOTR
MIMechE, rcds, jsdc (Commodore)					
Ferguson, Gordon Henry	LT(SD)	E	MESM	16.10.92	TURBULENT
Ferguson, Julian Norman , BA, BSc, pce, pce(sm)	CDR	X	SM	30.06.91	FOSM NWOOD OPS
Ferguson, Robert Grant	LT CDR	X	C	12.12.90	NEPTUNE BASE OPS
Ferguson, Vikki	LT	Q		21.01.95	RNDHU DERRIFORD
Fergusson, Andrew Christopher , BSc (Loc Capt Rm)	LT RM	RM		24.04.92	RM POOLE
Fergusson, Duncan Campbell McGregor , pce, pcea, psc . . .	CDR	X	P	31.12.88	JSDC GREENWICH
Fergusson, Houston James	LT CDR	S	SM	01.03.93	FOSM NWOOD HQ
Fergusson, Nigel Andrew , BSc, AMIEE	LT	E	WE	01.02.91	MOD DGSW PTSMTH
Fergusson, Richard Routledge , MA, adp	LT CDR(SL)	I		01.05.85	NWOOD CIS
Fernihough, Michael Robert , BSc, MIMechE	LT CDR	E	AE	08.12.82	RFANSU
Ferns, Timothy David	LT	S		01.06.91	RALEIGH
Ferrand, Brian Douglas , BEM	LT(CS)	-		22.02.87	2SL/CNH
Ferris, Daniel Peter Sefton , BEng, CEng, AMIEE	LT	E	WE	01.04.91	COLLINGWOOD
Fewtrell, Malcolm , psc	LT CDR	X	PWO(U)	01.09.84	CINCFLEET
Ffrench, David John	LT(SL)	X	P	01.02.90	849 SQN HQ
Fiander, Peter John , BSc, MIMechE	LT CDR	E	MESM	01.02.87	MOD (BATH)
Field, Charles Richard Howard	SLT	E	MESM	01.09.93	RNC DPT NS&TECH
Field, John Dobson , pce	LT CDR	X	PWO(A)	16.04.87	COMAW SEA
Field, Johnathan , BA	SLT(SL)	X		01.05.94	BRAVE
Field, Stephen Nigel Crawford	LT CDR	X	MCD	01.09.86	MOD (LONDON)
Fielder, David , BSc	LT(SL)	I		10.04.91	45 CDO RM
Fields, David Graham , pce, I(1)Ru	LT CDR	X	PWO(A)	01.06.94	CAMBRIDGE
Fieldsend, Mark Andrew , BEng	LT CDR	E	ME	01.03.96	LOAN DRA HASLAR
Fifield, David James , jsdc, pce, ocds(Can)	CAPT	X	P	30.06.96	LOAN CDA HLS
Finch, Bruce Andrew , BA	LT	S		01.08.93	CNH(R)
Finch, Craig Richard	LT(SL)	X	P	16.11.91	705 SQN SEAHAWK
Finch, Iain	MID(SL)	X		01.01.95	DARTMOUTH BRNC
Finch, Paul Andrew , BEng	LT(SL)	X	O	01.06.94	FONA DAEDALUS

Name	Rank	Spec	Sub-spec	Seniority	Where serving
Finch, Robert Leonard , BEng	LT	E	ME	01.05.89	RNSC GREENWICH
Finch, Timothy Stuart Aubrey	LT(SD)	S	CAT	14.12.90	NEPTUNE
Fincham, Barry Edward , BSc, MIMechE	LT CDR	E	MESM	01.01.90	VIGILANT(PORT)
Fincher, Kevin John , pce	LT CDR	X	PWO(C)	01.10.95	MOD (LONDON)
Finlayson, Alasdair Grant , MA, fsc	CDR	S		30.06.96	UKMILREP BRUSS
Finlayson, Ronald Didrik , MA, MBA, CEng, MIEE, psc	CAPT	E	WE	31.12.94	CWTA PTSMTH
Finley, Robert William , BA	LT RM	RM		29.04.93	CTCRM
Finn, David William	SLT(SD)	MS	AD	03.04.94	INM ALVERSTOKE
Finn, Emma Jane	MID(SL)	S		01.09.94	INVINCIBLE
Finn, Graham John	LT(SL)	X	P	01.07.92	848 SQN HERON
Finn, Ivan Richard , BEng	LT	E	AE	01.03.94	800 SQN
Finnemore, Emlyn	LT(CS)	-		24.04.91	MOD DNR OUTPORTS
Finnemore, Richard Andrew , AMBIM, pce	LT CDR	X	PWO(U)	09.07.90	IRON DUKE
Finney, Michael Edwin , pce(sm)	CDR	X	SM	30.06.94	SCEPTRE
Finnie, Harry Morrison	SLT(SD)	E	ME	13.06.94	COVENTRY
Firth, Nigel Richard , pce(sm)	LT CDR	X	SM	01.03.95	REPULSE(PORT)
Firth, Rachel Jane Gardner	LT(SL)	X	ATC	08.04.88	RNAS YEOVILTON
Firth, Stephen Kenneth , MA, MSc, CEng, MIEE	CDR	E	MESM	31.12.90	MOD (LONDON)
Fish, Peter Attwood , pce, psc (Commodore)	CAPT	X	P	31.12.89	FONA
Fisher, Anthony David , pce, psc	CDR	X	D	30.06.85	PJHQ
Fisher, Campbell Edward , MIEE, adp	CDR(SL)	E	WESM	01.10.89	DG SHIPS ROSYTH
Fisher, Clayton Richard Allan	LT	S		06.10.90	MARLBOROUGH
Fisher, Mark Andrew	SURG SLT	-		27.09.93	DARTMOUTH BRNC
Fisher, Morleymor Alfred Leslie , MBE, BSc, CEng, FIMarE, MIMarE, MIMgt	CDR	E	MESM	30.06.94	ROSYTH SOSM(R)
Fisher, Nicholas Gorden , MB, BS	SURG LT	-		01.08.92	RNDHU DERRIFORD
Fisher, Paul , BSc, ARCS, pce, psc	CDR	X	PWO(A)	30.06.90	EDINBURGH
Fisher, Pamela Clare , BEng	LT	E	AE	01.03.95	SULTAN
Fisher, Robert	LT(SD)	E	WE	10.06.88	FOREST MOOR
Fisher, Robert	SLT(SL)	X	P	01.11.93	846 SQN
Fisher, Timon C	SLT(SL)	S		01.01.94	RALEIGH
Fishlock, Geoffrey Norman	LT CDR	S		16.04.86	ADMIN SUP GRP(B)
Fitter, Ian Stuart Thaw , BSc, pcea	LT	X	O	01.05.93	810 SQN SEA
Fitzgerald, Brian (Loc Capt Rm)	LT RM(SD)	RM	MLDR	01.01.89	COMACCHIO GP RM
Fitzgerald, Colin	SLT(SD)	E	AE(M)	12.09.94	815 SQN HQ
Fitzgerald, Eamon , MBE, pce	LT CDR	X	AWO(U)	01.03.80	NELSON
Fitzgerald, Marcus Peter , OBE, BSc, CEng, MIEE	CAPT	E	WESM	30.06.95	MOD (BATH)
Fitzgerald, Nicholas John	LT(SL)	X	P	01.12.92	RAF CRANWELL EFS
Fitzjohn, David , BEng, MSc, CEng, MIEE	LT CDR	E	AE	01.05.96	ILLUSTRIOUS
Fitzpatrick, John Aloysius Joseph	SLT	X		01.09.94	DARTMOUTH BRNC
Fitzsimmons, John Martin , BA	LT RM	RM		24.04.92	847 SQN
Fitzsimmons, Mark Brown	LT CDR	X	PWO(A)	24.09.95	FEARLESS
Fitzsimmons, Susan Mary	SLT	E	WE	01.01.94	COLLINGWOOD
Flack, Alan Austin Walter , BA	LT	X		01.04.95	GLASGOW
Flanagan, John , BA (Barrister)	LT CDR	S	BAR	16.07.92	2SL/CNH FOTR
Flanagan, Martin Eric Anthony , BSc, pce, pcea	LT CDR	X	O	01.02.92	FONA
Flavill, Stephen Michael , BSc	LT(SL)	X	P	01.04.90	815 SQN HQ
Fleisher, Simon Matthew , BSc	LT	E	ME	01.06.92	CFM PORTSMOUTH
Fleming, Ailsa Margaret	LT CDR	S		24.02.90	SEAHAWK
Fleming, Kevin Patrick , BSc	LT(SL)	X	O	01.11.88	LOAN PORTUGAL
Fleming, Stephen Anthony	LT CDR	X		30.09.94	2SL/CNH
Flemwell, Hayley	LT(SL)	X		01.08.95	CUMBERLAND
Fletcher, Bridget Rachel , BA	LT(SL)	S		01.06.92	2SL/CNH
Fletcher, Keith , BSc	LT(SL)	X	O U/T	01.12.95	750 SQN OBS SCH
Fletcher, Nigel	LT	X	MW	01.11.90	DRYAD
Fletcher, Nicholas Edgar , pce, psc	CDR	X	PWO(A)	31.12.94	CNOCS GROUP
Fletcher, Patricia Joyce	LT CDR	W	S	01.04.87	2SL/CNH
Fletcher, Richard John , BA	LT	S		16.03.92	GLASGOW
Fletcher, Robert James	CAPT RM	RM	AE	01.03.78	CTCRM
Fletcher, Suzanne Jane	LT	Q	IC	02.01.96	RH HASLAR
Flint, Helen Anne , BSc	LT(SL)	I		01.05.90	RALEIGH
Flintham, Jason	LT(SL)	X	P	01.05.96	899 SQN HERON

Name	Rank	Spec	Sub-spec	Seniority	Where serving
Float, Roger Andrew , MSc, AMIEE	LT CDR	E	WE	01.05.94	NORFOLK
Flockhart, David Neil , BSc, CEng, MIEE	LT CDR	E	WESM	01.01.83	CAPTAIN SM2
Flower, Richard William , BSc, pce	LT CDR	X	PWO(C)	01.04.88	EXCHANGE CANADA
Flynn, Andrew	SLT	E	AE(L)	01.01.94	SULTAN
Flynn, Liam Peter , BEng	LT(SL)	X	P	01.09.92	814 SQN
Flynn, Michael Thomas	LT CDR	S		01.11.93	RALEIGH
Flynn, Patrick Joseph	LT CDR	X	PWO(A)	31.10.81	CNOCS GROUP
Foale, Simon John , BA	LT CDR	X	O	01.04.89	HQAFNORTHWEST
Fogden, David Richard , BSc, CEng, MIEE	CDR	E	WE	31.12.85	DG SHIPS CAM HSE
Fogden, Peter John	LT CDR(SL)	X	tas	01.09.81	MOD (LONDON)
Fogell, Andrew David	LT(SL)	S	SM	01.11.92	TRENCHANT
Fogg, Duncan Stuart , MA, MSc, CEng, MIEE	LT CDR	E	WE	01.04.93	BRAVE
Follington, Daniel Charles	SLT(SD)	MS		23.07.95	NEPTUNE
Folwell, Mark William	LT	E	WE	01.07.90	DGWES BRISTOL
Forbes, Alexander Riach , BSc	LT	X		01.05.93	DEF DIVING SCHL
Forbes, David Murray , pce, pce(sm)	CDR	X	SM	31.12.89	TRENCHANT
Forbes, Ian Andrew , CBE, rcds, pce, psc(a)	CAPT	X	AWO(A)	30.06.89	INVINCIBLE
Forbes, Paul	SLT(SL)	X	P	01.03.94	810 SQN SEAHAWK
Ford, Anthony	LT(SD)	E	ME	23.02.90	HECLA
Ford, Anthony John	LT(SD)	X	SM	04.04.96	DOLPHIN SM SCHL
Ford, Duncan , MCGI, pce	CDR	X	AWO(A)	30.06.89	PJHQ
Ford, David	LT RM(SD)	RM	MTO	01.01.94	HQ 3 CDO BDE RM
Ford, Gordon Howard (Act Lt Cdr)	LT(SD)	X	AV	16.12.88	MOD (BATH)
Ford, Graham Ronald	LT(SD)	E	MESM	14.10.94	TIRELESS
Ford, James Anthony	LT(SL)	X	P	01.07.90	849 SQN A FLT
Ford, Jonathan Douglas , BEng	LT	E	WE	01.12.93	CAMPBELTOWN
Ford, Martin John	LT	X	O	05.08.90	DRYAD
Ford, Nicholas Paul , TEng	LT CDR(SD)	E	MESM	01.10.93	RALEIGH
Foreman, John Lewis Rutland , pce, I(1)Ru	LT CDR	X	PWO(C)	01.07.95	COMUKTG/CASWSF
Foreman, Simon	SLT	E	WE	01.01.94	DARTMOUTH BRNC
Foreman, Timothy Peter	LT(SL)	X	P	01.05.94	846 SQN
Forer, Duncan Anthony , BSc	LT(SL)	I		01.03.87	2SL/CNH
Forer, Timothy John , BA	LT CDR	S	BAR	01.12.93	CARDIFF
Forester-Bennett, Rupert Michael William	LT(SL)	X	H2	01.01.93	DARTMOUTH BRNC
Forman, Richard Ross	LT(SL)	X	SM	01.07.94	FOST DPORT SHORE
Forrester, Timothy Rae , pcea	LT CDR	X	O	01.12.86	NAVSOUTH ITALY
Forsey, Christopher Roy , MSc, AMIEE	CDR	E	WE	31.12.95	COLLINGWOOD
Forster, Raymond Adrian	LT(SL)	X	ATC	16.04.91	RNAS YEOVILTON
Forster, Robin Makepeace , BA	CAPT RM	RM		01.09.94	HQRM
Forster, Steven	CHAPLAIN	RC		08.08.94	COLLINGWOOD
Forster, Timothy John Alleyne , pce, psc	CDR	X	AWO(A)	31.12.88	FOSF
Forsyth, Andrew Richard , BSc	CDR	S		30.06.94	NELSON
Forsyth, Andrew Westwood , pce, psc	CDR	X	PWO(N)	31.12.87	PJHQ
Forsyth, David Charles	LT(SD)	X	SM	11.12.92	DOLPHIN SM SCHL
Fortescue, Jane Elizabeth	LT CDR(SL)	W		01.10.94	EXCELLENT
Fortescue, Paul Wyatt , BSc	CDR	I	METOC	31.12.91	INVINCIBLE
Fortescue, Robert Christopher , pce, pcea	LT CDR	X	O	01.03.93	DRYAD
Forward, David James	LT(SD)	E	AE(L)	19.10.90	RALEIGH
Foster, Bruce Michael Trevor , BSc	LT(SL)	I		07.12.90	CTCRM
Foster, Crawford Richard Muir , MB, BCh, ChB	SURG LTCDR	-		19.09.93	RH HASLAR
Foster, Duncan Graeme Scott , BSc	LT CDR	X	PWO(A)	01.07.95	CAPT D3 SEA
Foster, David Hugh	LT(SL)	X	MCD	01.05.91	DEF DIVING SCHL
Foster, David Michael , MRIN	LT CDR	X	N	01.05.79	FOSF
Foster, Graham James , BSc	LT	E	MESM	01.10.88	DARTMOUTH BRNC
Foster, Gary John Howard	LT	E	AE	01.04.89	MOD DGA(N)RNHSMP
Foster, Graeme Russell , BSc, psc(m)	CAPT RM	RM	LC	01.09.89	MWC GOSPORT
Foster, Geoffrey Russell Nicholas , psc	CDR	X	P	30.06.91	HQ CDO AVN
Foster, Jeremy Stephen , BA	LT(SL)			01.09.90	DRYAD
Foster, Mark Andrew , MA, CEng, MIMarE, psc	LT CDR	I	SM	01.01.90	DARTMOUTH BRNC
Foster, Nicholas Paul , BSc, MA	SLT(SL)	X		01.09.94	BRIDPORT
Foster, Peter James	LT(SL)	E	MESM	01.09.95	RNC DPT NS&TECH
Foster, Stephen	LT CDR(SD)	E	ME	01.10.91	FOST SEA

Name	Rank	Spec	Sub-spec	Seniority	Where serving
Foster, Simon James Harry , BEng	LT	E	MESM	01.04.91	RNSC GREENWICH
Foster, Toby George , BSc	LT	X		01.04.95	INVERNESS
Foubister, Robert , FIEIE (Act Lt Cdr)	LT(SD)	E	WESM	18.06.87	FOSM FASLANE
Foulger, Robert John , BSc, PGCE	LT CDR	I	METOC	18.09.74	DRYAD
Foulis, Niall David Alexander , BSc	LT	X		01.03.95	SEAHAWK
Fowler, John	LT CDR(SD)	E	WE	01.04.87	CLYDE MIXMAN1
Fowler, Peter James Shakespeare , MSc	LT CDR	E	MESM	01.04.90	VANGUARD(STBD)
Fox, Kevin Andrew , BSc, MIEE	CDR	E	AE(P)	30.06.94	FONA
Fox, Richard George	LT CDR(SL)	X	P	01.10.92	848 SQN HERON
Fox, Trefor Morgan	SLT(SL)	X		01.01.93	DOLPHIN SM SCHL
France, Simon James	LT CDR(SL)	X	MCD	01.10.94	NORTH DIVING GRP
Francis, John	LT CDR(SD)	X	AV	01.10.94	FONA
Francis, Joanne Marie , BDS	SG LT(D)	-		09.01.94	SULTAN
Francis, Simon	SLT(SL)	X	O	01.03.93	RNAS CULDROSE
Francis, Steven John	CAPT RM	RM		25.04.96	EXCHANGE ARMY UK
Francis, Thomas James Roose , MB, BS, MSc, PhD, MFOM	SURG CDR	-	CA/P	31.12.88	INM ALVERSTOKE
Frankham, Peter James , BSc, BEng, CEng, MIMarE	LT CDR	E	WE	01.01.96	GLOUCESTER
Franklin, Benjamin James	LT(SL)	X	O	16.04.90	814 SQN
Franklin, George Durnford , BEng	LT	X		01.02.95	ANGLESEY
Franklin, William Henry , MA	CHAPLAIN	CE		10.01.89	NEPTUNE SM1
Franklyn, Peter Michael , MVO, rcds, pce	RADM	-	PWO(N)	14.11.94	FOST SEA
Franks, Christopher Steven	LT	E	WESM	01.02.90	SCEPTRE
Franks, Donald Ian , adp	LT CDR(SL)	S		01.10.94	DNPS
Franks, Jason Alexander , BA	LT RM	RM		01.09.94	AACC MID WALLOP
Franks, Jeremy Peter , BSc, MIEE, AMRAeS	LT CDR	E	AE	01.12.85	FONA
Franks, Kevin Brian , BSc	LT CDR	X	SM	01.12.87	FOST DPORT SHORE
Franks, Peter Dennis , BSc	LT CDR	I		01.10.93	2SL/CNH FOTR
Fraser, Donald Kennedy	LT CDR	X	PWO(U)	01.07.84	ELANT/NAVNW
Fraser, Eric , BSc, pce, psc	CDR	X	PWO(C)	31.12.94	BOXER
Fraser, Graeme William , MA	LT RM	RM		01.09.94	CTCRM
Fraser, Heather	SLT	E	WE	01.09.93	DARTMOUTH BRNC
Fraser, Ian	LT(SL)	X	P	16.04.96	820 SQN
Fraser, John Anthony	LT(SD)	X	AV	16.12.88	DGA(N) ASE
Fraser, Patrick	SLT(SL)	E	AE(L)	01.01.93	SULTAN
Fraser, Peter Timothy , pcea	LT CDR(SL)	X	O	01.10.94	706 SQN SEAHAWK
Fraser, Robert William , LLB (Barrister)	CDR	S	BAR	31.12.92	MOD (LONDON)
Fraser, Timothy Peter , pce	LT CDR	X	PWO(N)	01.04.93	FOSF SEA PTSMTH
Fraser, Wilson Cameron	LT(SD)	E	WESM	13.06.91	MOD DGSWS BATH
Frazer, Graham William , MNI, pce	LT CDR	X	AWO(U)	01.04.78	NEPTUNE BASE OPS
Frean, James Peter , BA	SLT(SL)	X	P U/T	01.01.95	RE ENTRY
Frederick, David George , BSc	LT RM	RM		01.09.93	CTCRM
Freeborn, Jason Oliver	LT	X		30.06.95	CAMPBELTOWN
Freegard, Ian Paul	LT(SD)	S	W	24.07.92	TAMAR
Freeman, David Andrew Kenneth , LVO, pce	CDR	X	PWO(N)	30.06.90	FOSF NORTHWOOD
Freeman, David Russel	LT	X	O	01.06.88	815 FLT 214
Freeman, Mark Edward	LT RM	RM	PT	01.09.89	MOD DNR OUTPORTS
Freeston, Graham	CDR(SD)	E	WE	01.10.94	MOD (LONDON)
French, Clive Anthony , AKC	CHAPLAIN	CE		28.09.76	RNC CEN SUP STF
French, James Thomas	LT	E	ME	01.07.88	IT S SEA
French, Kevin Lawrence	LT CDR	X	PWO(A)	09.07.93	EXCHANGE USA
French, Stephen Amos , BEng, MSc	LT CDR	E	MESM	10.05.94	VANGUARD(PORT)
Frere, Sir Toby Richard Tobias , KCB, rcds, odc(Aus), jssc	VADM	-	SM	11.12.92	MOD (BATH)
Freshwater, Dennis Andrew , MB, BS	SURG LT	-		09.08.93	RNDHU DERRIFORD
Friendship, Paul Gary (Act Lt Rm)	2LT	RM		28.04.93	CTCRM
Frisken, William David , OBE, MNZIS, jsdc	CDR	X	H CH	31.12.82	HYDROG TAUNTON
Froggatt, Jack Raymond , BSc, CEng, MIEE, psc	LT CDR(SL)	E	WE	01.09.85	CAMBRIDGE
Frost, Jonathan William George	LT CDR(SL)	X	P	01.10.95	705 SQN SEAHAWK
Frost, Mark Adrian , BSc	LT(SL)	I		01.01.91	OSPREY
Froude, Neil William , BEng	LT(SL)	X	O U/T	01.04.94	FONA DAEDALUS
Fry, Jonathan Mark Stewart , MSc	LT CDR	E	ME	01.05.91	RNSC GREENWICH
Fry, Robert Allan , MBE, BSc, MA, psc(m)	LT COL	RM		30.06.93	45 CDO RM
Fryer, Adrian Clifford , BSc	LT(SL)	X		01.02.94	LIVERPOOL

Name	Rank	Spec	Sub-spec	Seniority	Where serving
Fryer, Philip John	LT(SD)	X	AV	02.01.81	SEAHAWK
Fulcher, Jane Louise , BEng	LT(SL)	I		01.03.91	NEPTUNE SM1
Fulford, John Philip Henry , BSc	CDR	E	WESM	31.12.95	MOD DGSWS BARROW
Fulford, Mark Kenneth , BSc, pcea	LT CDR(SL)	X	P	01.10.95	EXCHANGE USA
Fulford, Nicholas James Douglas , BSc	CDR	E	WESM	30.06.83	NACISA
Fulford, Robin Nicholas	SLT(SD)	E	WE	07.02.94	SOUTHAMPTON
Full, Richard	SLT(SL)	X	O U/T	01.11.94	IRON DUKE
Fuller, Charles Edward	SLT(SL)	X	P U/T	01.01.95	705 SQN SEAHAWK
Fuller, Jonathan Peter , BA	LT(SL)	X	H2	01.06.94	HERALD
Fuller, Simon Rowland	LT RM	RM		01.09.94	ASC CAMBERLEY
Fulton, Craig Robert , pce(sm)	LT CDR	X	SM	01.03.95	FOSM NWOOD OPS
Fulton, Robert Henry Gervase , BA, psc(m)	COL	RM	C	30.06.96	RCDS
Funnell, Nicholas Charles , pce, pcea, psc(m)	CDR	X	O	30.06.96	2SL/CNH
Furlong, Claire Alexandra , BA	LT	X		01.05.93	LANCASTER
Furlong, Keith	LT CDR	X	PWO(A)	01.03.96	DRYAD
Furness, Stuart Brian , BSc, AFIMA, pce, pcea	CDR	X	O	30.06.96	CENTURION
Furnish, Kevin Stocks , BTech	LT(SD)	E	AE(M)	14.10.94	MOD PE ASC
Fyfe, Nigel Henry , TEng	LT CDR	E	MESM	11.08.87	CSST SHORE FSLN
Fyfe, Peter Matthew , MNI, psc	CDR	X	AWO(U)	31.12.86	MOD (LONDON)

G

Name	Rank	Spec	Sub-spec	Seniority	Where serving
Gabb, John Harry , MB, BS	SURG CDR	-	GMPP	31.12.87	2SL/CNH
Gabriel, Colin James , BSc	LT CDR	E	WE	01.12.88	FOREST MOOR
Gadie, Philip Anthony (Loc Capt Rm)	LT RM	RM		01.05.90	RM POOLE
Gainford, Paul , BSc	LT(SL)	I		01.01.91	SULTAN
Gair, Simon David Henley , BEng	LT	E	WE	01.02.95	CAMPBELTOWN
Gaitley, Ian , BEng, AMIEE	LT	E	WESM	01.09.89	DOLPHIN SM SCHL
Galbraith, David Scott , BSc	LT(SL)	I		01.09.90	COLLINGWOOD
Gale, Crystal	LT(SL)	S		01.01.95	GLOUCESTER
Gale, Henry Nelson , pce	CDR	X	PWO(U)	30.06.88	SHAPE BELGIUM
Gale, Mark Andrew , BA	LT	E	MESM	01.02.92	VICTORIOUS(STBD)
Gale, Patrick John	CDR	X	MCD	31.12.84	DEF DIVING SCHL
Gale, Sandra Lillian	LT(SL)	W	I	25.04.93	JS SCH OF P I
Gale, Simon Philip (Act Lt Cdr)	LT	X	PWO(U)	01.11.88	NELSON (PAY)
Gall, Michael Robert Carnegie , BDS	SGCDR(D)	-		30.06.95	ILLUSTRIOUS
Gallagher, Anthony	SURG SLT	-		27.07.94	DARTMOUTH BRNC
Galloway, Peter , pcea, psc	CDR	X	O	31.12.86	FOSNNI/NBC CLYDE
Galvin, Catherine	LT	Q	GASTRO	23.01.94	RNDHU DERRIFORD
Galvin, David	LT(SD)	E	WE	15.06.90	MOD (LONDON)
Gamble, John (Act Lt Cdr)	LT(SD)	E	AE(L)	02.11.84	LOAN DTEO BSC DN
Gamble, Malcolm Edward Derrick , BSc, CEng, MIMarE	LT(SL)	I		01.09.87	NEPTUNE SM1
Gamble, Neil	LT(SL)	X	P	01.11.93	810 SQN SEAHAWK
Gamble, Richard	LT(SD)	E	WE	10.06.88	DG SHIPS CAM HSE
Gamble, Stephen Boston , BA, BEng	SLT(SL)	X	P U/T	01.01.95	DARTMOUTH BRNC
Game, Philip Gordon , BEng	LT	E	WE	01.02.94	BOXER
Gardiner, David Anthony	LT	E	ME	01.07.89	INVINCIBLE
Gardiner, Frederick Kenneth John	LT CDR(SL)	I		01.09.84	SULTAN
Gardiner, Ian Ritchie , psc, psc(m)	LT COL	RM		30.06.93	40 CDO RM
Gardiner, Frederick David	LT(SL)	X	ATC	01.09.90	RNAS CULDROSE
Gardner, Brandon Robert James , MA	LT(SL)	X	O	01.05.95	706 SQN SEAHAWK
Gardner, Christopher Reginald Summers , BA, LLB	LT CDR	S	SM	01.01.94	RNSC GREENWICH
Gardner, John Edward , BA	LT	X		01.07.92	LONDON
Gardner, Malcolm	SLT	E	WE	01.09.93	DARTMOUTH BRNC
Gare, Christopher James	MID(NE)(SL)	X		01.09.95	HURWORTH
Garland, Darren Stephen , BEng	LT	E	WESM	01.07.94	DOLPHIN SM SCHL
Garland, John Michael Roy , BSc	CDR	E	WESM	31.12.87	MOD DGUW PTLAND
Garland, Michael Joseph	LT(SL)	X	P	01.08.91	849 SQN B FLT
Garland, Nicholas , BSc	LT CDR	S	CMA	01.11.95	HERALD
Garlick, Edward Christian	LT(SD)	X	AV	25.07.91	MOD (BATH)
Garner, Sean Martin , BA	LT(SL)	X	O U/T	01.08.94	HERON
Garnett, Ian David Graham , psc	VADM	-	P	24.08.95	SACLANT USA
Garratt, John Kenneth , BA, n	LT	X		01.05.91	FOSF SEA PTSMTH

Name	Rank	Spec	Sub-spec	Seniority	Where serving
Garratt, Mark David , pce, pcea	LT CDR	X	P	01.11.92	FONA SEAGOING
Garrett, Stephen Walter , pce(sm)	LT CDR	X	SM	01.12.91	EXCHANGE USA
Gascoyne, David John , BSc	LT CDR	E	ME	01.04.91	RALEIGH
Gaskin, Simon Edward , pce	LT CDR	X		01.11.87	EXCHANGE AUSTLIA
Gass, Colin Joseph , BSc, FRMS, psc, pce	CDR	X	PWO(A)	30.06.90	INVINCIBLE
Gasson, Nicholas Simon Charles , pce	CDR	X	PWO(U)	30.06.95	BDS WASHINGTON
Gatenby, Christopher David , BA	SLT	X		01.09.94	DARTMOUTH BRNC
Gates, Daniel Alexander	SLT(UCE)	X		01.09.95	DARTMOUTH BRNC
Gates, Nigel Sinclair	LT(SL)	X	P	16.03.93	845 SQN
Gauld, Isabella Barclay	CDR	Q	OHNC	14.09.91	2SL/CNH
Gaunt, Neville Raymond , pce, pcea, psc	LT CDR	X	O	16.07.90	FONA
Gavin, Charles Laurence	LT CDR(SD)	X	C	01.10.91	AST(E)
Gay, David	SURG SLT	-		06.07.94	DARTMOUTH BRNC
Gayfer, Mark Ewan , BEng	LT	E	WESM	01.12.92	VANGUARD(PORT)
Gazard, Philip Neil , BEng	LT	E	WE	01.10.91	EXCHANGE RAF UK
Gaze, Richard Norman Glanville	CAPT RM(SD)	RM	MTO	01.10.88	HQRM
Gazzard, Julian Henry	LT	X	PWO(A)	01.06.88	CAMPBELTOWN
Geary, Michael , BSc	LT(SL)	X	O	01.07.93	815 FLT 226
Geary, Timothy William , BEng	LT	E	ME	01.08.88	BRAZEN
Geddes, Colin	CHAPLAIN	RC		15.09.92	CAPT D3 SEA
Geddes, William Bruce	CDR	E	AE	30.06.90	DGA(N) ASE
Geddis, Richard Duncan , BEng	LT	E	WESM	01.09.88	MOD DGUW PTLAND
Geldard, Michael Andrew	LT RM	RM	PT	25.04.94	CTCRM
Gelder, George Arthur , psc	MAJ	RM		31.12.93	HQRM
Gell, Brian Crompton , BA, pce, pcea	LT CDR	X	P	01.04.86	HERON FLIGHT
Gennard, Anthony , BA	LT	S		01.03.95	SHEFFIELD
Gent, Richard Martin	LT CDR	X	H CH	15.04.81	VIVID
Gent, Richard Peter St John , BM, BCh, MA	SURG LTCDR	-	GMPP	01.08.92	EXCHANGE AUSTLIA
Gent, Stephanie Jean	LT(SL)	W		05.04.86	2SL/CNH FOTR
George, Alan Peter , pcea	LT CDR	X	O	16.01.95	FEARLESS
George, David Mark	SLT	X		01.01.93	HERON
George, David Roy , AFC	LT CDR(SL)	X	P	01.09.79	SEAHAWK
George, Jonathan Mark , BEng	LT(SL)	E	WE	01.11.89	WARRIOR
George, Peter	LT	E	ME	01.08.90	SULTAN
George, Patrick David , OBE, BA, psc(m) (Loc Lt Col)	MAJ	RM	WTO	30.06.89	EXCHANGE USA
George, Stephen Augustine , MSc, CEng, MRAeS	CDR	E	AE	31.12.93	MOD PE ASC
Gerrell, Frederick John	LT(SL)	MS		08.04.94	RN MSS HASLAR
Getgood, James Ashley , psc(m), fsc	MAJ	RM		30.06.95	FEARLESS
Gething, Jonathan Blair	LT CDR	X	SM	06.03.94	TRENCHANT
Gibb, Roger Walter , BSc	CDR	E	WESM	31.12.91	MOD (BATH)
Gibbon, Lynne	LT CDR	Q	ONC	05.10.88	RH HASLAR
Gibbons, Nicholas Philip	LT(SL)	X	O	01.10.92	814 SQN
Gibbs, Anthony Maurice	MID(SL)	S		01.06.94	ILLUSTRIOUS
Gibbs, Edward Martyn , BEng, AMIMechE	LT	E	MESM	01.02.90	SULTAN
Gibbs, Neil David , BSc, CEng	LT CDR	E	ME	01.07.95	MOD (BATH)
Gibbs, Philip Norman Charles , BSc	LT CDR	X	PWO(U)	01.02.89	MWC GOSPORT
Gibson, Andrew	LT CDR	E	AE	08.06.91	819 SQN
Gibson, Alastair David , MA	LT	S		16.11.89	MONTROSE
Gibson, Andrew Richard	SURG LT	-		01.08.94	CDO LOG REGT RM
Gibson, David Thomas , BSc	LT CDR	E	AE	01.06.91	RAF WYTON
Gibson, Ernest Alan , psc	MAJ	RM		31.12.90	HQAFNORTHWEST
Gibson, Ian Alexander , pce	CDR	X	PWO(A)	31.12.92	PJHQ
Gibson, Jennifer , BSc	SLT(SL)	X		01.09.93	DRYAD
Gibson, Timothy Andrew , MBE, pce	LT CDR	X	N	16.03.87	URNU SOUTHAMPTON
Gidney, Nigel , osc	CAPT RM	RM		01.09.88	COMACCHIO GP RM
Gilbert, Charles Michael Lloyd , BA (Act Cdr)	LT CDR(SL)	X	P	01.10.88	MOD (LONDON)
Gilbert, Lee Graham , BSc, MBA, AMIMechE	LT CDR	E	AE	01.10.94	810 SQN OEU
Gilbert, Michael Philip , CEng, pce, pce(sm)	CDR	X	SM	31.12.80	MOD (LONDON)
Gilbert, Peter David , BEng, MSc, CEng, MIMarE, MIMechE, MCGI, ACGI	LT CDR	E	ME	01.03.96	DGSS BRISTOL
Gilbert, Stephen Anthony	LT CDR	E	ME	29.04.94	NEWCASTLE
Gilbert, Stephen Kenneth	LT(SD)	S	W	27.07.90	WARRIOR

Name	Rank	Spec	Sub-spec	Seniority	Where serving
Gilchrist, Keith William	LT(SL)	X	O	16.02.91	EXCHANGE RAF UK
Gilding, Douglas Robert , BSc	LT RM	RM		01.09.91	CTCRM
Giles, Andrew Robert	LT CDR	S	S	21.07.92	LANCASTER
Giles, David William , BSc	LT CDR	E	WE	01.07.93	BRAZEN
Giles, Kevin David Lindsay , BSc, pce	LT CDR	X	MCD	01.05.92	CHIDDINGFOLD
Giles, Robert Keith , BEng	LT	X	MCD	01.03.93	DRYAD
Gill, Andrew Russell , BEng	LT	X		01.11.88	INVINCIBLE
Gill, Christopher Michael	LT CDR(SL)	I	METOC	01.10.89	CINCFLEET
Gill, Judith Victoria , ARRC	LT CDR	Q	ONC	09.04.78	RNAS CULDROSE
Gill, Michael	CDR	S		31.12.88	MOD (BATH)
Gill, Mark Hansen , BEng	LT	X		01.07.94	LONDON
Gill, Martin Robert , BEng, MSc	LT CDR	E	MESM	01.04.95	TRENCHANT
Gill, Paul Francis , MSc, MIMechE	LT CDR	E	MESM	01.02.89	MOD (LONDON)
Gill, Steven Clark	LT(SD)	S	S	12.12.91	CFM PORTSMOUTH
Gillam, Richard Leslie , BSc	LT CDR	E	ME	01.12.88	MOD (BATH)
Gillan, Gordon Maxwell , BEng, MSc	LT CDR	E	WE	01.04.95	COLLINGWOOD
Gillanders, Fergus Graeme Roy , pce	CDR	X	PWO(A)	31.12.94	SACLANT USA
Gillard, Victoria	MID	E	ME	01.01.95	NEPTUNE NT
Gillen, Christopher David , MB, BCh, ChB, MRCP	SURG CDR	-	CM	31.12.94	RH HASLAR
Gillespie, Callum David	LT	X	SM	01.08.92	DOLPHIN SM SCHL
Gillespie, Simon Maxwell , BA	CDR	X	PWO(C)	30.06.93	MOD (LONDON)
Gillett, David Alexander	SLT(UCE)	X		01.09.95	DARTMOUTH BRNC
Gillham, Paul Robert	LT(SD)	E	WE	22.02.96	GLOUCESTER
Gillies, Robert Ross , BEng	LT	E	MESM	01.02.89	SULTAN
Gilliland, Samuel Saunderson	LT(SD)	E	WE	13.06.91	CWTA PTSMTH
Gillson, Dennis Malcolm	CAPT RM	RM	AE	01.11.78	RMB STONEHOUSE
Gilmore, Martin	SLT(SL)	X	P	01.11.93	819 SQN
Gilmore, Steven John	MID(UCE)(SL)	E		01.09.95	GLASGOW
Gilmour, Craig James Murray	LT	X		01.12.90	DRYAD
Gilmour, John Ferguson , BA	LT	X		01.07.95	VIGILANT(PORT)
Ginn, Robert Nigel (Loc Capt Rm)	LT RM(SD)	RM		01.01.93	RM POOLE
Ginnever, Mark Stuart Matthew , BSc	LT RM	RM		01.09.94	COMACCHIO GP RM
Gisborne, Walter Charles	LT(SD)	E	WE	19.02.93	CFM PORTSMOUTH
Gittoes, Mark Anthony Warren	CAPT RM	RM		01.09.90	HQ 3 CDO BDE RM
Gladston, Stephen Anderson	LT(SL)	X	P	01.07.91	820 SQN
Gladwell, Trevor John	LT CDR	X	SM	01.12.93	MOD DIS SEA
Glaister, Malcolm Edwin Maynard , BSc	LT	X		01.04.92	FOSF SEA PTSMTH
Glancy, Michael Patrick , OBE, psc	CDR	E	WE	31.12.79	FOSF
Glass, Jonathan Eric , BSc	LT CDR	X		01.09.94	CINCFLEET
Glaze, John William , psc	CAPT RM(SD)	RM		01.10.92	MOD (LONDON)
Glennie, Andrew Michael Gordon , BSc, CEng, MIMarE	LT CDR	E	ME	01.01.94	EXCHANGE NLANDS
Glennie, Brian William	LT(SD)	E	WE	05.06.92	CALEDONIA
Glover, Mark Alec , BM, BA, BCh	SURG LTCDR	-	GMPP	01.08.93	NBC PORTSMOUTH
Glover, Simon Dawson , MB, BCh, ChB, MA, FRCSEd	SURG CDR	-	CO/S	30.06.89	RNDHU DERRIFORD
Gobey, Christopher Graham	LT CDR(SL)	X	SM	01.10.95	NEPTUNE BASE OPS
Gobey, Stephen John	LT CDR(SL)	X	MCD	01.09.80	CNSA PORTLAND
Goble, Ian John	LT CDR(SD)	E	WE	01.10.95	NEWCASTLE
Godber, Steven , BSc	LT CDR	E	AE	24.11.93	MOD DGA(N)RNHSMP
Goddard, Andrew Stephen Nigel , BA	LT	X	WESM	01.02.94	DTR BATH
Goddard, David Jonathan Sinclair , BSc, pce	LT CDR	X	PWO(N)	01.10.87	MIDDLETON
Goddard, Ian Kenneth , pce, psc	CDR	X	PWO(U)	30.06.88	FOSF
Goddard, Josephine , BA	SLT	X		01.09.93	DARTMOUTH BRNC
Goddard, Ronald Alan , AFC, jsdc, pce, pcea	CDR	X	P	31.12.86	NELSON
Godfrey, Kim Richard , BSc	LT CDR	X	MCD	01.09.93	MOD (LONDON)
Godfrey, Malcolm Charles	LT(SD)	S	CA	25.07.91	RNC CEN SUP STF
Godfrey, Stephen Paul , BEng	LT(SL)	X		01.12.92	NEPTUNE BASE OPS
Godwin, Christopher Anthony	LT	X	P U/T	02.09.91	814 SQN
Godwin, Jeffrey Clive	LT CDR(SD)	E	AE(M)	01.10.90	DGA(N) ASE
Godwin, Peter Edward	CDR	S	SM	30.06.88	DRYAD MWC
Gold, John William	LT(SD)	X	EW	06.04.95	ILLUSTRIOUS
Golden, Dominic St Clair	LT	X	FC	01.06.91	INVINCIBLE
Goldie, Keith William , MBE	LT CDR(SD)	E	HULL	01.10.95	CFM PORTSMOUTH

Name	Rank	Spec	Sub-spec	Seniority	Where serving
Golding, Derek John , MSc (Act Cdr)	LT CDR(SD)	MS	SM	01.10.89	MOD (LONDON)
Golding, Simon Jefferies	CHAPLAIN	CE		03.05.77	DRAKE CBP
Goldman, Barry Andrew Louis , MNI, pce, psc	CAPT	X	PWO(N)	30.06.92	FOSF
Goldman, Paul Henry Louis , BEng	LT	E	WE	01.04.91	RMC OF SCIENCE
Goldsmith, Andrew Giles	LT RM	RM		01.09.92	40 CDO RM
Goldsmith, Darran	LT(SL)	X	O	16.08.89	820 SQN
Goldsmith, David Thomas , BEng	LT	E	WE	01.01.94	CUMBERLAND
Goldsmith, Simon Victor William , BSc	LT CDR	X	PWO(U)	01.05.95	NELSON (PAY)
Goldstone, Richard Samuel , BA	LT	X		01.08.94	CROMER
Goldsworthy, Elaine Tania	LT(SL)	S		01.08.95	SOMERSET
Goldsworthy, Peter Jarvie , BEng	LT(SL)	S		01.09.94	FEARLESS
Goldthorpe, Michael	LT(SD)	S	W	06.04.95	ILLUSTRIOUS
Gomm, Kevin , BSc, pce(sm)	LT CDR	X	SM	01.06.91	FOSM NWOOD OPS
Goodacre, Ian Royston	LT	X	SM	01.05.90	VANGUARD(PORT)
Goodale, Helen Joanne	SLT	E	ME	01.09.94	DARTMOUTH BRNC
Goodall, Andrew Mark	LT CDR	X		01.04.93	EXCELLENT
Goodall, David Charles , pce, pcea, psc	CDR	X	P	30.06.89	INVINCIBLE
Goodall, Simon Richard James , BA	CAPT	I		31.12.93	2SL/CNH
Goodbourn, Robert Neil , BEng, AMIEE	LT(SL)	E	WE	01.08.92	CWTA PTSMTH
Goodburn, David Henry	CHAPLAIN	CE		13.09.88	DAEDALUS
Goode, Alun Nicholas	LT	X	FC	01.09.91	ALDERNEY
Goodenough, Neil John , BSc	LT(SL)	X	P	16.02.90	819 SQN
Gooder, Simon Philip , MNI	LT CDR	X	N	01.05.83	DRAKE NBC(CFS)
Goodfellow, Richard Francis , BSc, psc	CDR	E	ME	30.06.86	MOD (BATH)
Goodier, Richard Mark , BA	LT	S		01.08.92	CAMPBELTOWN
Goodings, George James (Act Lt Cdr)	LT(SD)	E	MESM	18.10.83	RENOWN(PORT)
Goodman, Andrew Theodore , BSc	LT	X		01.03.90	CAMPBELTOWN
Goodman, Peter Robert	LT(SL)	S		01.10.94	NAVSOUTH ITALY
Goodman, Trevor Michael	LT(SD)	E	AE(L)	16.10.92	DGA(N) ASE
Goodrich, David Leslie	LT CDR(SD)	E	WE	01.10.93	MOD (LONDON)
Goodrich, Kathryn Ann , BEng	LT(SL)	E	ME	01.06.93	SHEFFIELD
Goodrich, Steven Graham , BSc	LT	X		01.02.93	GLOUCESTER
Goodridge, Terence James	LT RM(SD)	RM		01.01.91	HQRM
Goodsell, Christopher David	LT	X	SM	01.02.91	SCEPTRE
Goodship, Mark Thomas	SLT(SL)	E	ME	01.05.96	YORK
Goodwin, Anna Louise	LT(SL)	S		25.04.92	RNC CEN SUP STF
Goodwin, David	CDR	X	PWO(U)	31.12.93	CNOCS GROUP
Goodwin, Geoffrey , pce	CDR	X	MCD	31.12.89	2SL/CNH
Goodwin, Lincoln Bryan	SLT(SD)	S.	S	03.04.95	NEPTUNE CFS
Gopsill, Brian Richard , MIL, I(1)Ch	LT CDR	S	SM	01.07.85	RALEIGH
Goram, Malcolm	LT(SL)	X	ATC	01.05.87	RNAS CULDROSE
Gordon, David , BA, BSc, psc	LT CDR	I	SM	09.01.92	COLLINGWOOD
Gordon, John Huntly , pce(sm)	CDR	X	SM	30.06.88	VICTORIOUS(PORT)
Gordon, Joseph Patrick Mark , osc, osc(us)	CAPT RM	RM		13.12.81	CTCRM
Gordon, Kenneth Andrew , BDS	SG LT(D)	-		31.08.93	NEPTUNE
Gordon, Mark Winston , MA	2LT(GRAD)	RM		01.09.95	CTCRM LYMPSTONE
Gordon, Neil Leslie , BSc	LT(SL)	E	ME	01.11.92	INVINCIBLE
Gordon, Ronald MacKenzie	LT CDR(SD)	E	WESM	01.10.92	DOLPHIN SM SCHL
Gordon, Stuart Ross , pcea	LT CDR	X	P	01.02.94	RNSC GREENWICH
Gordon-Lennox, Andrew Charles , pce, psc	CDR	X	AWO(U)	30.06.85	MOD (LONDON)
Gorman, Christopher Paul	CAPT RM(SD)	RM		01.10.90	RMB STONEHOUSE
Gorman, Paul Bernard , BEng	LT	E	AE	01.09.95	SULTAN
Gorrod, Peter Charles Alfred	LT(SD)	X	PR	06.09.85	FOST DPORT SHORE
Gorsuch, Paul George , BA	LT CDR	S	SM	16.04.90	2SL/CNH
Gosden, Stephen Richard , MSc, CEng, MIMarE, psc	CDR	E	ME	30.06.94	CAPT F2(SEA)
Goss, Peter George , psc	CDR(SL)	X	ATC	01.10.93	MOD (LONDON)
Gothard, Andrew	SLT(SL)	E	ME	01.05.93	DARTMOUTH BRNC
Gotke, Christopher Torben , BEng	LT(SL)	X	P	01.09.94	FONA VALLEY
Goudge, Simon David Philip , BA	LT	S		01.04.94	JMOTS TURNHOUSE
Gough, Andrew Bankes , FIMgt, MNI, rcds, jsdc, pce, pcea (Commodore)	CAPT	X	O	30.06.88	STANAVFORLANT
Gough, Andrew Charles	LT	X		01.06.95	QUORN

Name	Rank	Spec	Sub-spec	Seniority	Where serving
Gough, Gathorne Lorimer Ward , OBE, pce	CDR	X	G	30.06.79	NELSON (PAY)
Gough, Steven Roy	LT(SD)	X	PT	03.04.92	SULTAN
Gould, James	SLT	X		01.01.96	PEACOCK
Goulding, Jonathan Paul	LT	X		01.03.95	NOTTINGHAM
Gourlay, James Stewart , BSc, psc	CDR	E	AE	30.06.96	MOD (LONDON)
Govan, Richard Thomas , pce, psc	CDR	X	PWO(U)	30.06.92	2SL/CNH FOTR
Gower, John Howard James , BSc, pce(sm)	CDR	X	SM	30.06.94	TRAFALGAR
Gozzard, John , BSc, CEng, MIMarE, MIMechE, jsdc	CAPT	E	MESM	30.06.89	SA MADRID
Grace, David John	LT(SL)	X		01.06.93	DRYAD
Grace, Jonathan Patrick	LT(SL)	X	P	01.05.89	848 SQN HERON
Grace, Trevor Paul	LT(SD)	E	WE	13.06.91	MOD (BATH)
Gracey, Peter Pequignot , BEng, AMIEE	LT	E	WESM	01.07.88	MOD DGSM PTLAND
Gracie, David Lindsay	CAPT RM(SD)	RM		01.10.95	42 CDO RM
Grafton, Martin Nicholas , BSc, MIMechE	LT CDR	E	MESM	01.12.87	NEPTUNE SM1
Graham, Alastair Neil Spencer , BSc	LT	E	WESM	01.08.93	FOSM FASLANE
Graham, David Edward , pce	LT CDR	X	PWO(A)	01.10.91	ILLUSTRIOUS
Graham, David Winston Stuart , BEng	LT	E	MESM	01.08.89	SULTAN
Graham, Gordon Russell , BSc	LT CDR	E	WE	01.04.90	MOD (LONDON)
Graham, Ian Edmund , n	LT	X		01.02.91	URNU SUSSEX
Graham, James , MA, CEng, MIEE	LT	E	WE	01.12.89	RMC OF SCIENCE
Graham, James Edward	LT CDR	S	SM	01.02.91	MOD (BATH)
Graham, Mark Alexander	LT(SL)	X	O	01.10.90	815 SQN HQ
Graham, Penelope Jane , BA	LT(SL)	W	S	03.04.91	DRAKE CBP
Graham, Robert	LT(SD)	E	ME	15.02.91	ILLUSTRIOUS
Graham, Stephen William , OBE, BSc, CEng, MIMarE, jsdc	CAPT	E	ME	31.12.91	FOSF
Graham, Wade Stuart , CEng, MRAeS, MIERE, psc (Act Capt)	CDR	E	AE	31.12.86	RNAY FLEETLANDS
Grainger, Adam Lennox , MA	2LT(GRAD)	RM		01.09.95	CTCRM LYMPSTONE
Grandison, John Alexander Steele	LT CDR(SL)	X	PWO(A)	01.03.86	MWC GOSPORT
Granger, Christopher Ronald	LT(SD)	E	MESM	17.10.86	REPULSE(PORT)
Grant, Alan Kenneth ,OBE, MA, pcea	CDR	X	O	30.06.93	DRYAD
Grant, Brian Gerald	T/LT(SDT)	E	MESM	10.06.94	CLYDE MIXMAN2
Grant, David James	SLT(SD)	E	MESM	14.06.93	SPLENDID
Grant, Edward John , BDS, MSc, DGDP RCS(UK), LDS RCS(Eng) (Commodore)	SGCAPT(D)	-		30.06.87	MOD (LONDON)
Grant, Ian William , psc(m)	MAJ	RM	LC	30.06.91	HQRM
Grant, Roland Stephen , MBE, psc (Loc Lt Col)	MAJ	RM	PT	30.06.90	NS OBERAMMERGAU
Grantham, Stephen Mark , MSc, CEng, MIMechE, MCGI	LT CDR	E	MESM	01.07.93	TRAFALGAR
Grattan-Cooper, Anthony Charles , MNI, pce, pcea, psc	CDR	X	P	30.06.81	LOAN DTEO KYLE
Gratton, Stephen William	LT(SD)	E	WE	18.10.85	CDRE MFP
Graves, Michael Edward Linsan , BSc	CDR	E	WESM	30.06.91	2SL/CNH
Gray, Anthony James , BA	LT CDR	E	AE(P)	01.11.90	810 SQN SEAHAWK
Gray, Anthony John , BSc	LT CDR	E	MESM	01.07.93	VANGUARD(STBD)
Gray, Dennis	LT CDR(SD)	E	ME	01.10.93	CAPT(H) DEVPT
Gray, David Kingston , BEng, AMIEE	LT CDR	E	WE	01.04.95	BATTLEAXE
Gray, David Malcolm , BSc	LT CDR	I	METOC	01.05.85	SEAHAWK
Gray, John Allan , BEng	LT	X	FC	01.06.92	YORK
Gray, James Alan	LT RM	RM		29.04.96	DARTMOUTH BRNC
Gray, James	LT(SL)	X	O	01.04.95	820 SQN
Gray, Martina Emily	LT(SL)	S		24.07.92	DOLPHIN
Gray, Mark Nicholas (Loc Capt Rm)	LT RM	RM		01.09.90	HQ 3 CDO BDE RM
Gray, Paul Reginald	LT(SL)	X	P	01.08.91	820 SQN
Gray, Richard	LT	X	SM	01.03.91	DOLPHIN SM SCHL
Gray, Robert Stanley , BSc (Barrister)	LT CDR	S	BAR	01.01.93	FOSF
Gray, Susan Kathryn	LT CDR(SL)	W	S	01.10.93	2SL/CNH
Gray, Stephen Maxwell	LT CDR(SL)	I		01.10.91	SCOTIA
Gray, Yvonne Michelle , BEd	LT(SL)	X		01.02.93	WALNEY
Grears, Jonathan , BSc	LT(SL)	I		01.09.91	2SL/CNH
Greasley, Michael , BA	SLT	X		01.01.94	DARTMOUTH BRNC
Greatwood, Ian Mark , BEng	LT	E	WESM	01.01.91	MOD (BATH)
Greaves, Christopher John	LT CDR(SL)	X	P	01.10.95	FONA
Greaves, Michael Jonathan , BA, pcea	LT CDR	X	P	01.04.94	702 SQN OSPREY
Greedus, David Arthur	LT RM(SD)	RM		01.01.90	HQ 3 CDO BDE RM

Name	Rank	Spec	Sub-spec	Seniority	Where serving
Green, Andrew John	LT(SL)	I	SM	01.11.88	RNC DPT NS&TECH
Green, Andrew Michael	LT(SD)	E	ME	15.06.95	CFM PORTSMOUTH
Green, Adrian Richard , MSc, MIMechE, AMIMechE	LT CDR	E	MESM	01.05.92	TALENT
Green, Catherine Margaret , BEng	LT(SL)	E	WE	01.06.91	DG SHIPS CAM HSE
Green, Christopher Roger , pcea, psc	CDR	X	P	31.12.81	MOD (LONDON)
Green, David Paul	LT CDR	X	SM	13.08.93	FOSM GOSPORT
Green, David Patrick Savage , BEng	LT CDR	E	WESM	01.05.95	CNOCS GROUP
Green, Gary Edward	LT RM(SD)	RM		01.01.94	42 CDO RM
Green, Gareth Mark , BA (Loc Capt Rm)	LT RM	RM		01.09.91	ENDURANCE
Green, Ian Andrew	SLT(SL)	X	ATC	01.09.94	RNAS YEOVILTON
Green, Jonathan	LT	X		01.06.90	DRYAD
Green, John	CHAPLAIN	CE		04.06.91	CDRE MFP(SEA)
Green, John Anthony , BSc, CEng, MIEE, MinstP, AMInstP, CDipAF	CDR	E	WESM	30.06.89	FOSM NWOOD OPS
Green, Janette Lesley	LT(SL)	W	X	11.12.92	FOSM FASLANE
Green, Michael Gerald Hamilton	CAPT RM	RM	LC	01.09.95	539 ASLT SQN RM
Green, Michael Ronald	LT RM(SD)	RM		01.01.90	CDO LOG REGT RM
Green, Peter James	LT	X	SM	01.07.88	DUMBARTON CASTLE
Green, Peter Louis , BSc	LT(SL)	X	P	01.05.87	814 SQN
Green, Stephen Mark	LT CDR	X	P	01.02.94	RANGER
Green, Stephen Noel , BSc	LT CDR	E	WE	01.05.93	RNSC GREENWICH
Green, Steven Robert	SLT	S		01.09.93	RALEIGH
Green, Trevor Anthony	LT(SD)	X	C	01.10.91	CDRE MFP
Green, Timothy Cooper , BA	LT	X		01.04.94	DOLPHIN SM SCHL
Green, Timothy John , psc(a), I(2)Ru	LT CDR	X	SM	01.05.94	TORBAY
Greenacre, John Francis , BA	LT	X		01.02.93	NEPTUNE BASE OPS
Greenaway, Nicholas Mark	LT CDR	X	PWO(A)	01.08.95	DRYAD
Greenberg, Neil , BSc	SURG LT	-		01.08.94	SPARTAN
Greene, Michael John , BEd, MSc, psc	LT CDR	I		01.01.92	SULTAN
Greener, Carl , MEng	LT	E	WE	01.09.91	DG SHIPS CAM HSE
Greenfield, David Colin , BEng	LT(SL)	X	P	16.11.89	750 SQN OBS SCH
Greenfield, David Peter	LT CDR	X		21.09.92	CNH(R)
Greenfield, Kenneth	LT CDR(SD)	E	ME	01.10.93	MONMOUTH
Greenish, Philip Duncan , BSc, CEng, MIEE, jsdc	CAPT	E	WE	31.12.91	MOD (LONDON)
Greenland, Michael Richard , pcea	LT CDR	X	P	16.04.95	GUERNSEY
Greenlees, Iain Wallace , BSc, pce	CDR	X	PWO(A)	30.06.93	DRYAD
Greenop, Jeremy Peter Spencer , OBE, jsdc, pce, psc	CDR	X	P	31.12.89	NORFOLK
Greenway, Stephen Anthony , BEng	LT	E	ME	01.05.92	FEARLESS
Greenwood, Ian Andrew , MSc	2LT(GRAD)	RM		01.05.95	CTCRM LYMPSTONE
Greenwood, Michael John , BA	LT CDR	I	METOC	01.09.91	PRESTWICK
Greenwood, Nicholas James , BEng	LT	E		01.03.92	NEPTUNE NT
Greenwood, Peter , pce	LT CDR	X	MCD	29.04.93	INVINCIBLE
Greenwood, Peter Adam	MID(SL)	X	P U/T	01.04.95	DARTMOUTH BRNC
Greenwood, Stephen , BSc, CEng, MRAeS	LT CDR	E	AE(P)	01.05.89	MOD (BATH)
Greer, James Patrick , MB, BCh	SURG LT	-	GMPP	31.12.94	RALEIGH
Greetham, Clare , LLB	SLT(SL)	X		01.05.94	MONTROSE
Gregan, David Carl , psc	CDR	X	H CH	30.06.92	RNSC GREENWICH
Gregory, Alexander Michael , OBE, jsdc, pce(sm) (Commodore)	CAPT	X	SM	30.06.88	BDS WASHINGTON
Gregory, Andrew Michael	CDR(SD)	X	PT	01.10.94	MOD PFMP W DOWN
Gregory, Alastair Stuart , BEng	LT	E	ME	01.12.92	TAMAR
Gregory, Errol , BSc	LT(SL)	I		01.09.90	COLLINGWOOD
Gregory, Ian Stuart , pce, pcea, psc	CDR	X	P	30.06.89	MOD (LONDON)
Gregory, Mark , BEng, AMIEE	LT	E	WE	01.01.92	DGSS BRISTOL
Gregory, Paul Clement , MA, MSc	CDR	I	SM	31.12.86	MOD (LONDON)
Gregory, Timothy Maurice , BA, psc(m)	LT COL	RM	C	30.06.96	MOD (LONDON)
Greig, Judith	SLT	E	ME	01.05.96	DARTMOUTH BRNC
Grenfell-Shaw, Christopher , BA, BSc	LT CDR	E	WESM	01.06.95	MOD DIS SEA
Gretton, Michael Peter , MA, rcds, pce, psc	VADM	-	PWO	10.12.94	SACLANT BELGIUM
Grieve, Lynne , BEng	SLT(SL)	X		01.09.94	INVERNESS
Grieve, Steven Harry , BSc, CEng, MRAeS, psc	LT CDR	E	AE	01.11.92	MOD DHSA
Griffin, Helen Elizabeth	LT(SL)	S		01.12.94	COLLINGWOOD
Griffin, Niall Robert	LT(SL)	X	P	01.03.93	848 SQN HERON

Name	Rank	Spec	Sub-spec	Seniority	Where serving
Griffin, William Forrester Griffith , MA, pce, psc(m)	CDR	X	AWO(C)	30.06.81	DRAKE NBC(CNH)
Griffiths, Anthony	LT(SD)	X	MW	03.04.92	CENTURION
Griffiths, Andrew John , MSc	LT CDR	I		26.07.94	EXCELLENT
Griffiths, Alan Richard	LT(SD)	E	WE	09.06.89	CFP SEA
Griffiths, Brian John , BDS	SGCDR(D)	-		31.12.84	NELSON
Griffiths, David Anthony	LT(SD)	MS	SM	24.07.92	2SL/CNH
Griffiths, David Michael , BSc	LT CDR	E	ME	01.06.91	FOSF NORTHWOOD
Griffiths, David Price	SLT(SL)	E	WE	01.05.94	DARTMOUTH BRNC
Griffiths, David Thomas , BSc, pce	LT CDR	X	MCD	01.04.90	GLOUCESTER
Griffiths, Lloyd	SLT(UCE)	E	MESM	01.09.94	DARTMOUTH BRNC
Griffiths, Nicholas Alan	2LT	RM		01.05.95	CTCRM LYMPSTONE
Griffiths, Richard Hywel	SLT(SL)	X		01.03.93	PEACOCK
Griffiths, Sara Louise	LT	Q		30.05.95	RNH GIB
Griffiths, Timothy George	MID(NE)	X		01.09.95	CATTISTOCK
Grimley, Daemon Marcus John , pce, pce(sm)	LT CDR	X	SM	01.11.89	MOD (LONDON)
Grimsey, Roy , BA(OU), pce	LT CDR	X	AWO(C)	05.12.79	PJHQ
Grimsley, Kevin Peter , BSc	LT CDR(SL)	I		01.10.88	DRYAD
Grindel, David John , BEd	LT CDR	I		01.09.94	DRYAD
Grindell, Martin James	LT CDR	S		01.08.91	NELSON
Grindley, Richard John , BA, CEng, MIEE	LT CDR(SL)	E	WE	01.03.83	DGSS BRISTOL
Grindon, Matthew Guy , BEng	LT(SL)	X	P	16.01.91	EXCHANGE ARMY UK
Grixoni, Martin Reynold Roberto	CAPT RM	RM		01.09.90	RM POOLE
Grocott, Peter Clark	LT(SD)	S	W	08.04.94	2SL/CNH
Grogono, Jeremy George Bennett	LT(SL)	X	P	01.12.90	RAF SHAWBURY
Groom, Ian Stuart , BEng	LT	E	ME	01.03.91	SULTAN
Groom, Mark Richard , MB, BCh, ChB, aws	SURG LTCDR	-	P	01.08.92	WARRIOR
Grose, Matthew William , BSc	LT(SL)	X		01.02.93	CAMPBELTOWN
Groves, Christopher Keith	LT	X	SM	01.10.91	DOLPHIN SM SCHL
Grunwell, Andrew John	LT(SL)	X	P	16.09.94	815 FLT 214
Gubbins, Victor Robert , BSc	CDR	E	ME	31.12.93	EXCHANGE USA
Guest, Simon James (Loc Capt Rm)	LT RM	RM		26.04.93	HQ 3 CDO BDE RM
Guild, Nigel Charles Forbes , BA, PhD, MIEE, AFIMA, jsdc (Commodore)	CAPT	E	WE	31.12.90	DGSS BRISTOL
Guiver, Paul , BEM	SLT(SD)	X	MCD	03.04.94	DRYAD
Gullett, Humphrey Richard , MA	SLT(SL)	S		01.09.94	CHATHAM
Gulley, Trevor James , MSc, CEng, MCGI	LT CDR	E	ME	01.08.93	RICHMOND
Gulzar, Nadeem , BA	SLT(SL)	S		01.09.93	FEARLESS
Gunn, Christopher Phillip	LT(SD)	X	REG	11.12.92	EXCELLENT
Gunn, Hugh Iain	LT(SL)	E	WESM	01.12.95	NEPTUNE SM1
Gunn, William John Simpson , BSc	LT CDR	I	METOC	01.11.94	CINCFLEET
Gunther, Paul Thomas	LT(SD)	E	WESM	13.06.91	DOLPHIN SM SCHL
Gurmin, Stephen John Albert	LT CDR	X	PWO(C)	18.05.95	JMOTS TURNHOUSE
Gurr, Andrew William George	LT	X	FC	01.05.92	800 SQN
Gutteridge, Jeffrey David James	LT(SD)	E	WE	20.12.90	CWTA PTSMTH
Guy, Mark Andrew , BEng	LT(SL)	E	WE	01.05.93	COLLINGWOOD
Guy, Philip Stuart , BA	2LT(GRAD)	RM		01.09.95	CTCRM LYMPSTONE
Guy, Richard John , MB, BCh	SURG LTCDR	-		15.08.93	ILLUSTRIOUS
Guy, Robert Lincoln , LVO, MNI, jsdc, pce	CAPT	X	PWO	30.06.91	JSDC GREENWICH
Guy, Terry John , psc	CDR	E	WESM	30.06.93	MOD DGSWS BATH
Guy, Thomas Justin , n	LT	X		01.05.92	BATTLEAXE
Guyatt, Anthony Edward , BA	CDR	S		30.06.86	MOD (LONDON)
Guyer, Simon Thomas Glode , psc(m)	MAJ	RM	LC	30.06.95	45 CDO RM
Gwilliam, Andrew Clive , pce (Act Cdr)	LT CDR	X	PWO(C)	01.09.82	IMS BRUSSELS
Gwilliam, David Meredith	LT(SD)	E	AE(L)	16.10.92	SEAHAWK
Gwillim, Vivian George	CAPT RM	RM	ML2	13.04.93	JSIO ASHFORD

H

Name	Rank	Spec	Sub-spec	Seniority	Where serving
Habershon, David Broadhurst , pce, psc	CDR	X	PWO(U)	30.06.90	CDRE MFP
Habgood, Stella , BSc	SLT	X		01.01.94	WESTMINSTER
Hacon, Philip Eric , BA	LT(SL)	X	P U/T	01.12.94	706 SQN SEAHAWK
Haddacks, Paul Kenneth , rcds, pce, psc	RADM	-	PWO(N)	20.02.94	SHAPE BELGIUM
Hadden, Christopher Sutcliffe , BSc, MBA, MIMgt	CDR	S		31.12.90	2SL/CNH

Name	Rank	Spec	Sub-spec	Seniority	Where serving
Hadden, Peter Gordon , BSc, PhD, CEng, MIM, jsdc, psc	CDR	I		30.06.84	BRNC RNSU SOTON
Haddon, Richard , MB, BS, DipAvMed, LRCP, MRCGP, MRCS, AFOM	SURG LTCDR	-	GMPP	19.10.87	CINCFLEET
Haddow, Fraser , psc (Loc Lt Col)	MAJ	RM	MLDR	31.12.92	MOD (LONDON)
Haddow, Timothy	SLT	E	WE	01.01.94	DARTMOUTH BRNC
Hadfield, David	LT CDR	E	MESM	14.02.90	VICTORIOUS(PORT)
Hadnett, Edmond Robert , pce	LT CDR	X	PWO(A)	01.01.92	RAF BENTLEY PRIY
Haggart, Peter Dewar	LT(SD)	X	C	01.12.91	MOD (LONDON)
Haggerty, Shaun Michael	SLT(SL)	E	AE	01.01.94	DARTMOUTH BRNC
Hague, Susan , BM, FRCSEd (Act Surg Cdr)	SURG LTCDR	-	CO	01.07.88	RH HASLAR
Haigh, Alastair James , BSc	LT(SL)	X	P	01.12.92	820 SQN
Haigh, Julian , BA	SLT(SL)	S		01.01.95	DARTMOUTH BRNC
Haill, Simon John Jackson , pce, psc	CDR	X	PWO(U)	31.12.93	2SL/CNH
Hails, Peter William	LT CDR(SL)	X	P	01.09.78	HERON
Hailstone, Jonathan Henry Steven , BA	LT CDR	X	O	16.05.94	MOD (LONDON)
Haines, Paul Roger	LT	E	WE	01.07.88	DGSS BRISTOL
Haines, Russell	SLT(SL)	S		01.05.96	LANCASTER
Haines, Steven William , MA, PhD, FRGS, MNI, MRIN, MIMgt, psc	CDR	I		30.06.93	MOD (LONDON)
Hains, Justin , BSc	SLT	X		01.01.94	DARTMOUTH BRNC
Hainsworth, Pauline Mary	LT	Q	OPHTH	30.03.94	RH HASLAR
Hale, Ian Brian	LT RM	RM	WTO	01.09.93	RMR MERSEYSIDE
Hale, John Nathan	LT RM	RM		27.04.95	42 CDO RM
Haley, Colin William , pce, psc(a)	LT CDR	X	PWO(A)	01.07.90	DRYAD
Haley, Timothy	LT CDR(SD)	S	CAT	01.10.92	2SL/CNH
Haley, Timothy John , MSc, CEng, MIMarE	CDR	E	ME	30.06.96	LANCASTER
Halford, Phillip , BSc	LT CDR(SL)	X	ATC	01.09.84	RNAS CULDROSE
Hall, Andrew Jeremy , BSc	LT	E	AE	01.08.90	815 SQN HQ
Hall, Alexander Peter , BSc, pcea	LT CDR	X	O	01.03.93	819 SQN
Hall, Barry James	LT	E	MESM	01.11.90	SPARTAN
Hall, Christine	LT	Q		01.03.91	RH HASLAR
Hall, Christopher Nigel , BSc	LT CDR	E	WE	01.05.90	DRAKE CFM
Hall, Carl Stuart	LT(SL)	X	SM	01.11.94	FOST DPORT SHORE
Hall, Darren	SLT(SL)	S	P	01.03.93	845 SQN
Hall, David Allen , MSc, CEng, FIMgt, MIMarE	CAPT	E	MESM	31.12.91	DG SHIPS ROSYTH
Hall, Derek Alexander	LT(SD)	S	W	02.04.93	NELSON
Hall, David , BDS	SGLTCDR(D)	-		04.02.92	LOAN BRUNEI
Hall, David William , BSc	LT CDR(SL)	X	O	01.10.90	MOD PE ASC
Hall, Elizabeth Clair , BSc, PGCE	LT(SL)	S		15.12.88	EXCELLENT
Hall, Eleanor Louise , BA	LT	S		01.05.95	NBC PORTSMOUTH
Hall, Jeremy William Morris , BSc, jsdc	CDR	E	MESM	31.12.92	MOD (LONDON)
Hall, Neil Jeremy	LT CDR	X	PWO(A)	01.03.93	ILLUSTRIOUS
Hall, Nicholas Malet , psc, psc(m), fsc (Loc Col)	LT COL	RM		31.12.88	IMS BRUSSELS
Hall, Robert Langford , BSc, pce	LT CDR	X	PWO(C)	01.05.93	BRIDPORT
Hall, Richard Mark , MA, psc	CAPT RM	RM		01.09.90	RNSC GREENWICH
Hall, Stephen , BEng	LT	E	AE	01.06.91	INVINCIBLE
Hall, Steven Brian , BSc	LT RM	RM		28.04.94	CTCRM
Hall, Simon Jeremy , MSc, psc (Loc Maj)	CAPT RM	RM	MLDR	01.09.92	RM POOLE
Hall, Thane Trent , BEng	LT	E	WESM	01.04.95	DOLPHIN SM SCHL
Hallett, Simon John , BSc	LT	S		01.03.93	RFANSU (ARGUS)
Halliday, David Alistair , BA, pce	CDR	X	PWO(A)	30.06.96	JSDC GREENWICH
Halliwell, David Colin , BEng	LT	E	MESM	01.03.92	RNSC GREENWICH
Halls, Bernard Charles , TEng, IEng, MIEEIE	LT(SD)	E	WE	18.10.85	DG SHIPS CAM HSE
Hally, Philip John , BSc	LT	S		01.11.92	FOST SEA
Halton, Paul Vincent	LT	X	SM	01.06.90	SOVEREIGN
Ham, David William , MSc, CEng, MIEE	CDR	E	WE	30.06.95	MOD (LONDON)
Hambling, Patricia Margaret , ARRC	CDR	Q	GU	09.07.90	RH HASLAR
Hambling, Simon Peter , MB, ChB	SURG LTCDR	-	SM	08.08.94	RH HASLAR
Hambly, Brian John	LT(SL)	E	WESM	01.11.95	COLLINGWOOD
Hambly, Mark	SLT	E	MESM	01.01.94	DARTMOUTH BRNC
Hambly, Patrick Trevan	LT(SL)	X	SM	01.01.93	DOLPHIN SM SCHL
Hambly, Richard Savage , BDS, MSc	SGCAPT(D)	-		31.12.88	MOD (LONDON)
Hambrook, David Edwin , MBE	LT CDR(SD)	E	WE	01.10.91	COLLINGWOOD

Name	Rank	Spec	Sub-spec	Seniority	Where serving
Hamilton, Adrian Gamble , FFA	CDR	S		30.06.87	NELSON RELEASE
Hamilton, Angus John Burnside , BEng	LT	E	P	01.04.90	820 SQN
Hamilton, Colin Fendall Butler , pce, ocds(US)	CAPT	X	C	30.06.91	PJHQ
Hamilton, Gregory Robert	LT CDR	X		01.10.94	EXCHANGE RAF UK
Hamilton, Ivan James	LT(SL)	X	P	16.11.91	705 SQN SEAHAWK
Hamilton, Richard Alexander , BSc	LT CDR(SL)	I		01.10.93	DNPS
Hamilton, Robert William , MBE, BSc, CEng, FIMarE	CDR	E	ME	31.12.84	2SL/CNH FOTR
Hamilton, Susanna , BEng	LT(SL)	E	ME	01.07.94	BATTLEAXE
Hamilton, Stuart William Thomas	LT(SL)	X	FC	01.05.92	ILLUSTRIOUS
Hamilton-Bing, Simon Paul Edward	LT(SL)	X	ATC	01.01.87	EXCHANGE RAF UK
Hammersley, James Michael , MSc	LT CDR(SL)	I		01.10.94	NELSON RNSETT
Hammett, Barry Keith , MA	CHAPLAIN	CE		11.07.77	AFCC
Hammond, David Evan , BSc	2LT(GRAD)	RM		01.09.94	42 CDO RM
Hammond, Mark Christopher (Loc Capt Rm)	LT RM	RM	P	26.04.93	EXCHANGE USA
Hammond, Nicholas John , BTech, PGCE, psc	LT CDR	I	METOC	01.09.85	NAVSOUTH ITALY
Hammond, Paul Adrian , BEng, MSc, MIEE, gw	LT CDR	E	AE	01.07.94	SULTAN
Hammond, Paul John	SLT	X		01.01.93	NORFOLK
Hamp, Colin John , BSc, pce, pcea, psc	LT CDR	X	O	16.04.89	810 SQN SEAHAWK
Hance, John Rowland , pce	CAPT	X	AWO(A)	31.12.90	SACLANT USA
Hancock, Andrew Philip	LT	X		01.01.91	ARUN
Hancock, Robert Thomas Alexander , AMIEE	LT(SL)	E	WE	01.09.95	COLLINGWOOD
Hancox, Michael John , BEng	LT	E	MESM	01.02.91	RENOWN(PORT)
Hand, Christopher John , MB, BS	SURG LTCDR	-		04.01.95	RH HASLAR
Handley, Jonathan Mark , pce	LT CDR	X	PWO(U)	01.12.89	STANAVFORLANT
Hands, Adrian Peter	LT CDR(SL)	X	P	01.10.94	RAF CRANWELL EFS
Hannaford, William Craig , MBE	LT CDR(SD)	E	WE	01.10.90	COLLINGWOOD
Hannah, William Fergusson	LT RM(SD)	RM		01.01.94	HQ 3 CDO BDE RM
Hanneman, Martin , BSc	LT(SL)	X	P U/T	01.04.96	HERON
Hannigan, Paul Francis	LT(SL)	X	P	16.01.91	848 SQN HERON
Hanrahan, Martin	LT(SL)	X	P	08.01.90	845 SQN
Hanslip, Michael Richard	LT CDR(SD)	E	WE	01.10.91	TAMAR
Hanson, Mark Nicholas , BA	SLT	S		01.09.93	FOSNNI/NBC CLYDE
Hanson, Nicholas Anthony , CEng, MIMarE	LT	E	WE	01.06.90	DG SHIPS PTLAND
Harbour, John Robert MacKay , psc	CDR	S		31.12.93	JSDC GREENWICH
Harbour, Roy Larry , BSc, psc	LT CDR	I		16.09.75	IMS BRUSSELS
Harbroe-Bush, Robert Douglas , BSc, CEng, MIEE, psc	CDR	E	WESM	31.12.88	2SL/CNH
Harbun, David Gethin , pce	CDR	X	FC	30.06.91	MOD (LONDON)
Harcourt, Robert James , BSc	LT(SL)	I	METOC	01.01.92	RFANSU
Hardacre, Paul Vincent , BSc	LT CDR	X	SM	01.06.94	FOSM NWOOD OPS
Hardern, Simon Paul , pce	LT	X	PWO(U)	01.11.88	WALNEY
Hardiman, Nicholas Anthony , BEng	LT	E	MESM	01.05.92	TRENCHANT
Harding, Carl Sinclair , BEng	LT(SL)	I		01.09.92	SULTAN
Harding, David John	SLT	S		01.01.94	DOLPHIN SM SCHL
Harding, David Malcolm , BSc, CEng	LT CDR	E	AE	01.05.95	EXCHANGE USA
Harding, Gary Alan , BEng, AMIEE, psc	LT CDR	E	WE	01.12.94	LANCASTER
Harding, Hadrian Robert , BEng	SLT(SL)	E	ME	01.09.94	EDINBURGH
Harding, Roy , pce, psc	CAPT	X	TAS	30.06.88	NEPTUNE
Harding, Roland Arthur , BSc, CEng, MIMarE, AMIEE	CDR	E	MESM	31.12.87	MOD (LONDON)
Harding, Russell George , BSc, pce, pcea	CDR	X	O	31.12.95	DRYAD
Hardwick, Mark	SLT(SL)	S		01.05.95	DARTMOUTH BRNC
Hardy, Duncan Mark	LT RM	RM		24.04.95	CTCRM
Hardy, Leslie Brian	LT(SD)	X	PR	16.12.94	INVINCIBLE
Hardy, Lee Charles , pce	LT CDR	X	PWO(A)	01.12.92	FOSF SEA PTSMTH
Hardy, Simon	LT(SL)	X	H2	01.06.91	NP 1016 IN SURV
Hare, John Herbert , BA	LT(SL)	I	METOC	01.09.85	FEARLESS
Hare, Nigel James	LT CDR	X	PWO(N)	01.01.94	FOST MPV(SEA)
Hare, Timothy William , BSc, CEng, MIEE, jsdc	CAPT	E	WESM	30.06.93	MOD (BATH)
Hargraves, John , BDS, MSc, LDS RCS(Eng), psc	SGCAPT(D)	-		31.12.91	CINCFLEET
Hargreaves, Neale	LT(SL)	X	O	01.09.89	LOAN DTEO BSC DN
Harker, Andrew Robert	LT RM	RM		01.09.95	MOD DNR OUTPORTS
Harkness, Neil , BChD, MSc	SGCDR(D)	-		31.12.79	HONG KONG DENTAL
Harland, Nicholas Jonathan Godfrey , BSc, jsdc, pce	CDR	X	O	30.06.91	LANCASTER

Name	Rank	Spec	Sub-spec	Seniority	Where serving
Harley, Louise Dawn , BSc	LT(SL)	I		01.05.87	2SL/CNH FOTR
Harlow, Simon Richard	LT(SL)	X	P	01.05.93	815 FLT 241
Harman, David John , IEng, FIEIE	LT CDR	E	WE	18.07.89	DG SHIPS PTSMTH
Harman, Michael John	CHAPLAIN	CE		20.09.79	FOST DPORT SHORE
Harmer, Jason Neil Jonathon	LT(SL)	X	P	16.07.89	EXCHANGE N ZLAND
Harms, James	LT(SL)	X	P	01.03.95	FONA VALLEY
Harper, Andrew Charles , BEng	LT	E	WESM	01.07.89	NEPTUNE SM1
Harper, Christopher Hodges , BSc	LT CDR	X	H2	01.09.95	ROEBUCK
Harper, Ian Lorimer	LT(SD)	X	AV	23.07.93	RNAS CULDROSE
Harper, James Andrew	LT(SD)	X	O	27.07.90	815 FLT 235
Harper, Philip Robert	SLT	X		01.09.93	DARTMOUTH BRNC
Harper, Robert Jackson , BSc	LT CDR	I		25.09.91	WARRIOR
Harper, Stuart Anderson , psc	LT CDR	X	MCD	01.02.81	DEF EXP ORD SCHL
Harradine, Paul Anthony	CAPT RM(SD)	RM		01.10.94	40 CDO RM
Harrall, Phillip Anthony Robertson , AFC, MBIM,	LT CDR(SL)	X	O	03.03.85	MOD (LONDON)
MRAeS, MRIN, psc					
Harrap, Nicholas Richard Edmund , pce(sm), jsdc	CDR	X	SM	31.12.95	CINCFLEET
Harries, Jon Michael Henry , BSc, CEng, FIEE, MIEE, jsdc	CAPT	E	WE	31.12.91	ORDNANCE BOARD
Harriman, Claire , BSc	LT(SL)	X	O	01.06.93	815 FLT 207
Harriman, Martin , BSc, MA, pce, psc	LT CDR	X	O	01.10.92	815 SQN HQ
Harrington, Anthony	LT CDR(SD)	MS	RGN	01.10.91	INM ALVERSTOKE
Harrington, Jonathan Barratt , BEng	LT(SL)	E	WE	01.08.95	BRAVE
Harrington, Lee	MID(NE)	E	ME	01.05.95	ILLUSTRIOUS
Harris, Andrew Gordon , BEng, AMIEE	LT(SL)	E	WE	01.05.92	COLLINGWOOD
Harris, Andrew Ian , pcea	LT CDR	X	O	16.12.92	CAPT F4 (SEA)
Harris, Carl	LT RM	RM		01.09.94	AACC MID WALLOP
Harris, John Ronald Joseph , BA	LT	S		01.04.95	BEAGLE
Harris, John William Robert , MNI, jsdc, pce, pce(sm)	CAPT	X	SM	31.12.90	NEPTUNE SM1
Harris, Keri John	LT	X	O	01.04.91	810 SQN SEAHAWK
Harris, Melvin , MITE	CDR	E	WE	30.06.89	CAPT F4 (SEA)
Harris, Mark Edward , BDS	SG LT(D)	-		10.12.93	CINCFLEET
Harris, Maxwell	LT(SL)	X	P	01.08.95	820 SQN
Harris, Michael Trevor	LT(SL)	S	CA	08.04.94	SEAHAWK
Harris, Nicholas Graham Talbot , psc	LT CDR	X	P	01.03.79	CINCIBERLANT
Harris, Nicholas Henry Linton , MBE, pce, pce(sm), ocds(US)	CAPT	X	SM	30.06.95	MOD (LONDON)
Harris, Philip Norman , MPhil, MNI, pce, psc	CDR	X	O	31.12.85	LOAN ABU DHABI
Harris, Richard Paul , BA	SLT(SL)	S		01.05.94	NOTTINGHAM
Harris, Shane Leonard , MSc, pcea	LT CDR	X	P	16.07.93	BATTLEAXE
Harris, Tristan	LT RM	RM		01.09.95	42 CDO RM
Harris, Timothy Ronald , pce	CDR	X	PWO(U)	31.12.90	ILLUSTRIOUS
Harris, William Bissett , BSc, CEng, MIMarE (Commodore)	CAPT	E	ME	30.06.92	MOD (BATH)
Harrison, Adrian , BEng	LT	E	MESM	01.02.93	TRIUMPH
Harrison, Clive Anthony , I(1)Sp	LT CDR	X	PWO(A)	01.03.94	JMOTS TURNHOUSE
Harrison, David	LT(SD)	E	WESM	24.02.95	DOLPHIN SM SCHL
Harrison, Mark Andrew	SLT(SL)	E	WE	01.05.96	CAMPBELTOWN
Harrison, Matthew Sean , BEng, MSc, CEng, MIEE	LT CDR	E	WE	01.01.94	MOD (LONDON)
Harrison, Paul Dominic	LT(SL)	X	O	01.10.90	849 SQN HQ
Harrison, Paul Geoffrey , BTech	LT	E	AE(L)	01.07.90	702 SQN OSPREY
Harrison, Peter Martin	LT CDR	X	O	16.04.90	815 FLT 202
Harrison, Richard Anthony , MSc, CDipAF, psc, gw, I(1)Po	CDR	E	WESM	31.12.89	MOD (LONDON)
Harrison, Richard Frederick	LT CDR	X	PWO(A)	22.03.87	CAMBRIDGE
Harrison, Roger Geoffrey , psc	CDR	X	P	31.12.87	NP1044
Harrison, Richard , BA	LT(SL)	X	P U/T	01.04.96	HERON
Harrop, Ian , BEng	LT CDR	E	MESM	01.05.96	FOSM FASLANE
Harry, Andrew David , BEng	LT CDR	X		01.04.96	FOST DPORT SHORE
Harry, Marc Andrew	LT(SL)	X		01.04.96	VANGUARD(STBD)
Harry, Nicholas John Fairfield Victor , BSc, CEng,	CDR	E	ME	31.12.85	MOD (BATH)
MIMechE, MDA					
Harry, Peter Norman	LT CDR(SD)	S	S	01.10.91	RALEIGH
Hart, Camilla Louise	LT(SL)	S		01.02.96	CUMBERLAND
Hart, Derek John , BSc, CEng, MIEE	CDR	E	WE	30.06.94	SOMERSET
Hart, Daniel Robert , BSc	LT(SL)	I	METOC	01.08.91	CAPT F1(SEA)

Name	Rank	Spec	Sub-spec	Seniority	Where serving
Hart, Jonathan , MSc, CEng, MIEE, psc	CDR	E	WESM	31.12.91	EXCHANGE AUSTLIA
Hart, John James	CAPT	S		30.06.90	FOSF
Hart, John William Sydney , BSc, PhD, rcds, psc	CAPT	I	SM	31.12.88	2SL/CNH
Hart, Mark Alan , BSc, pce	LT CDR	X	PWO(A)	01.12.94	LIVERPOOL
Hart, Neil Lawrence Whynen	LT(SL)	S		01.05.94	VANGUARD(PORT)
Hart, Paul Andrew	LT(SL)	I		01.05.87	EXCELLENT
Hart, Robert	LT CDR(SD)	E	WE	01.10.94	DGSS BRISTOL
Hart, Tobin Giles De Burgh	LT(SL)	X	P	01.07.91	848 SQN HERON
Hart, Willem Cornelis	LT CDR(SD)	E	ME	01.10.92	YORK
Hartley, Andrew Paul , BEng	LT(SL)	E	ME	01.09.94	ILLUSTRIOUS
Hartley, Barrie Howard	LT(SD)	X	AV	03.05.85	EXCHANGE USA
Hartley, David , pce(sm)	LT CDR	X	SM	01.06.91	NEPTUNE BASE OPS
Hartley, John , BSc, FRMS, psc	CDR	I	METOC	31.12.80	SULTAN AIB
Hartley, John Laurence , BSc	LT(SL)	X	P	01.02.89	702 SQN OSPREY
Hartley, Philip Terence , BSc, CEng, MIEE, AMIEE	LT CDR	E	WESM	01.06.88	FOSNNI/NBC CLYDE
Hartley, Stephen William , BSc, PGCE	LT(SL)	I		01.01.86	LOAN BRUNEI
Hartnell, Stephen Thomas , BSc, psc (Loc Lt Col)	MAJ	RM		31.12.91	RM POOLE
Harvey, Barrie	SLT	E	ME	01.01.95	DARTMOUTH BRNC
Harvey, Colin Ashton , BSc	LT CDR	E	MESM	01.03.93	SUPERB
Harvey, Gary	SLT(SD)	E	ME	14.06.93	NEWCASTLE
Harvey, John Bartlett , LVO, pce	CAPT	X	O	30.06.93	OSPREY
Harvey, Jane Scriven	SLT(SL)	X	ATC	01.09.92	INVINCIBLE
Harvey, Keith , pce	CDR	X	MCD	30.06.93	DRYAD
Harvey, Paul Anthony	LT CDR(SL)	X	ATC	01.10.91	RNAS CULDROSE
Harvey, Roger Charles , BSc, CEng, MRAeS, psc	CDR	E	AE	30.06.82	FAAIT MAN ORG VL
Harvey, Robert Matthew Malvern Jolyon	LT	X		01.09.89	DRYAD
Harwood, Christopher George , BTech	LT(SD)	E	WE	24.02.95	LONDON
Harwood, David Byron , MBE	LT CDR(SD)	E	WESM	01.10.94	SUPERB
Harwood, Lee Brian	MID(NE)(SL)	X		01.09.95	LEDBURY
Haseldine, Stephen George	LT(SL)	X	ATC	01.03.86	EXCHANGE RAF GER
Haselock, Simon , psc (Loc Maj)	CAPT RM	RM	WTO	01.11.84	HQ ARRC
Haskell, Eric Thomas	LT CDR(SD)	E	WE	01.10.94	CWTA PTSMTH
Haslam, Philip James	LT	X	FC	01.10.90	DRYAD
Hassall, Harry , MSc	LT CDR(SL)	I		01.10.95	NELSON RNSETT
Hassall, Ian	SLT(SL)	E	ME	01.09.94	DARTMOUTH BRNC
Hastilow, Nicholas , BA	LT(SL)	X	P U/T	01.08.95	702 SQN OSPREY
Hatch, Giles William Hellesdon , pce	LT CDR	X	PWO(A)	01.04.92	NORTHUMBERLAND
Hatchard, Peter John , BSc, jsdc, pce	CDR	X	PWO(C)	30.06.94	MOD (LONDON)
Hatcher, Rhett Slade	LT	X	P	01.03.90	815 FLT 211
Hatcher, Timothy Robert	LT(SD)	E	WESM	19.02.93	CWTA PTSMTH
Hattersley, Jonathan Peter George , LLB (Barrister)	LT CDR	S	BAR	01.02.87	NELSON
Hatton, Hubert Frederick , psc (Act Cdr)	LT CDR	X	P	22.02.77	PJHQ
Hawes, Grace Elaine , psc	LT CDR	W	X	01.01.91	MOD (LONDON)
Hawker-Cole, Robert Charles , MSc	LT(SL)	I		01.12.91	NELSON
Hawkes, Jonathan Derrick	LT(SD)	X	PT	23.07.93	2SL/CNH
Hawkins, Ian	LT CDR	E	AE	12.07.89	RNAS CULDROSE
Hawkins, James Seymour	LT	X	O	16.08.90	815 FLT 217
Hawkins, Katherine Alice	SLT(SL)	S		01.05.94	ROEBUCK
Hawkins, Martin Adam Jeremy	LT CDR	X	O	01.05.95	DARTMOUTH BRNC
Hawkins, Nicholas Simon , BA (Barrister)	CDR	S	BAR	30.06.96	2SL/CNH
Hawkins, Richard Culworth , BA, jsdc, pcea	CDR	X	P	30.06.92	RNAS YEOVILTON
Hawkins, Robert Henry	LT CDR(SL)	X	MCD	01.10.91	FOST MPV(SEA)
Hawkins, Shane Robert	SLT(SL)	E	WE	01.05.94	DARTMOUTH BRNC
Hawkyard, Nicholas Julian Kirvan , pce	LT CDR	X	AWO(A)	01.11.80	CNOCS GROUP
Hawley, Stephen Christopher , BEng	LT	E	ME	01.03.94	BEAVER
Haworth, John , IEng, MIMechIE	LT CDR	E	ME	25.10.91	FOSF
Haworth, Jonathan	SLT	E	WE	01.05.94	DARTMOUTH BRNC
Haworth, Stephen	LT(SD)	E	WE	18.02.94	MOD DGSM PTLAND
Hawthorne, Michael John , pce	LT CDR	X	SM	01.01.93	FOSM NWOOD OPS
Hay, Brian William , BTech	LT CDR(SL)	I	METOC	14.09.79	NELSON
Hay, James Donald , BSc	LT CDR	E	WE	01.06.93	FOST SEA
Hay, Michael	SLT	E	WE	01.09.95	DARTMOUTH BRNC

Name	Rank	Spec	Sub-spec	Seniority	Where serving
Haycock, John Edward , psc(m)	MAJ	RM	C	30.06.83	COMAW SEA
Haycock, Timothy Paul , pcea	LT CDR	X	O	01.06.94	RNSC GREENWICH
Hayde, Phillip John , BSc	LT(SL)	X	P	01.05.89	899 SQN OEU
Hayden, Stephen Clive , BA, ACIS	LT CDR	S	CMA	01.09.93	CFLT COMMAND SEC
Hayden, Timothy , BSc	SLT(SL)	X	P U/T	01.05.94	DARTMOUTH BRNC
Haydon, John Ralph , MSc, DObstRCOG, DIH, LRCP, MFOM, MRCGP, MRCS, AFOM, jsdc	SURG CAPT	-	CO/M	30.06.92	MOD (LONDON)
Hayes, Brian John	SLT(SD)	X	PT	03.04.95	DRAKE CBP
Hayes, David John	LT CDR(SD)	MS	AD	01.10.90	RNDHU DERRIFORD
Hayes, Francis Anthony Murray , pce	LT CDR(SL)	X	PWO	01.09.86	CINCFLEET
Hayes, James Victor Buchanan , BSc	LT CDR	E	WESM	01.04.95	DOLPHIN SM SCHL
Hayes, Nigel Horace	LT CDR	X	PWO	01.11.79	FONA
Hayes, Stuart John	LT CDR	X	MCD	01.06.93	SOUTHAMPTON
Hayhoe, Robert David	LT(SL)	E	ME	01.11.91	MOD (BATH)
Hayle, Elizabeth Anne , BA	LT(SL)	I	PI	16.12.87	MOD (LONDON)
Hayle, James Kenneth	LT CDR	S	SM	01.04.96	IRON DUKE
Hayles, Mark Anthony	LT	X		01.09.93	MOD (BATH)
Hayles, Nicholas Clive	LT CDR(SL)	S	CMA	01.09.87	2SL/CNH
Haynes, John William	LT(SD)	X	PT	16.12.88	FONA
Hayter, Edward George Bazaine , BSc	LT	X		01.01.93	FOSNNI/NBC CLYDE
Hayward, Andrew Leonard	SLT(SL)	X		01.05.94	BIRMINGHAM
Hayward, Clive Edward William , BA	LT	X	SM	01.06.88	VANGUARD(PORT)
Hayward, Geoffrey	LT(SL)	X	O	16.07.91	849 SQN B FLT
Hayward, Leon Richard , OBE, psc	CDR	E	WE	31.12.89	FOSF
Hayward, Peter James	LT CDR	S		01.04.86	EXCELLENT
Haywood, Guy	LT CDR	X	P	01.10.95	SOUTHAMPTON
Haywood, Paul	LT CDR(SD)	X	AV	01.10.91	FONA
Haywood, Peter James , BEng	LT(SL)	X	P	01.07.94	706 SQN SEAHAWK
Haywood, Simon Anthony	LT CDR(SD)	E	WESM	01.10.94	JARIC
Hazell, Marcus John Douglas , BSc	2LT(GRAD)	RM		01.09.95	CTCRM LYMPSTONE
Head, Allen Matthew	LT(SL)	X		01.12.95	RM SCHL MUSIC
Head, Rupert Richmond D Esterre	CDR	S		30.06.89	BRITANNIA
Head, Steven Andrew , BEng	LT	E	WE	01.03.93	GLOUCESTER
Head, Stephen Geoffrey , BA, BEng	SLT(SL)	E	WE	01.09.94	DARTMOUTH BRNC
Heal, Jeremy Phillip Carlton , psc	MAJ	RM		31.12.94	MOD (LONDON)
Healy, Anthony John	LT CDR(SD)	X	EW	01.10.94	RNU RAF EDZELL
Healy, Andrew Marcus Cahir	LT CDR(SD)	X	MCD	01.10.93	DRYAD
Heames, Richard Mark	SURG LT	-		01.08.94	COVENTRY
Heaney, Martin , BSc	SLT(SL)	X	O U/T	01.05.94	DARTMOUTH BRNC
Hearnden, Graham Eric , pce	LT CDR	X	AWO(C)	01.04.79	INVINCIBLE
Heath, Barry Clive , BSc, psc	MAJ	RM		31.12.86	2SL/CNH
Heath, Craig William	SURG LT	-		01.08.94	VANGUARD(PORT)
Heath, Graham Robert	LT CDR(SD)	E	WESM	01.10.90	MOD DGSWS BATH
Heather, Christopher Vernon Stewart , TEng	LT(SD)	E	WE	29.10.82	COLLINGWOOD
Heatly, Robert Johnston , MBE, osc(us)	MAJ	RM		31.12.95	EXCHANGE ARMY UK
Heaver, David Gerard Verney , BA, psc(m)	LT COL	RM		30.06.96	HQAFNORTHWEST
Hedgecox, David Colin	SLT	E	WE	01.01.94	COLLINGWOOD
Hedger, Neil Alexander , MB, BSc, BCh, MRCP, AFOM	SURG LTCDR	-		01.08.88	NELSON (PAY)
Hedges, Justin William , BSc	LT RM	RM		01.09.94	NP 1061
Hedgley, David Nicholas , pce	LT CDR	X	PWO(N)	01.11.87	FOST SEA
Hedworth, Anthony Joseph , BComm	LT(SL)	X	P	01.08.94	706 SQN SEAHAWK
Hefford, Christopher John , BSc	SLT(SL)	X		01.09.94	STARLING
Heil, Catherine	SLT(SL)	X	O U/T	01.09.94	750 SQN OBS SCH
Heir, Juswant Singh	LT(SL)	I		01.05.89	RALEIGH
Helby, Philip Faulder Hasler , MBE, BSc, MBA, AMIEE	LT CDR	E	MESM	16.07.82	DRAKE CFM
Heley, David Nicolas	LT CDR	X	PWO(U)	01.01.95	CORNWALL
Heley, Jonathan Mark , BEng	LT CDR	E	MESM	01.11.94	TORBAY
Helliwell, Michael Andrew	LT	E	AE	01.05.90	SULTAN
Helliwell, Martyn Gregory	LT(SD)	X	AV	17.12.93	SULTAN
Hellyn, David Robert	LT(SD)	E	WE	13.06.91	CWTA PTSMTH
Helps, Adrian Richard , BEng	LT	E	MESM	01.06.92	TIRELESS
Hember, Marcus	MID(NE)(SL)	X		01.01.96	DARTMOUTH BRNC

Name	Rank	Spec	Sub-spec	Seniority	Where serving
Hembrow, Terence	LT RM(SD)	RM		01.01.90	539 ASLT SQN RM
Hempenstall, John Albert , QHC, MA	CHAPLAIN	CE		06.05.70	HQRM
Hempsell, Adrian Michael	LT	X		01.06.94	EXCHANGE FRANCE
Hempsell, Richard Ian , BSc	LT	X		01.06.92	DRYAD
Hemsworth, Kenneth John , BEng	LT(SL)	E	ME	01.08.92	SULTAN
Hemsworth, Michael Kim , BSc	CDR	S		30.06.89	2SL/CNH
Henderson, Andrew David	LT RM(SD)	RM		01.01.91	CTCRM BAND
Henderson, Iain Robert , CBE, ADC, pce, pcea, psc (Commodore)	CAPT	X	P	31.12.89	NBC PORTSMOUTH
Henderson, Peter Philip	LT(SD)	E	WE	24.02.95	CWTA PTSMTH
Henderson, Robert John	SLT(SD)	E	AE(M)	04.09.95	RNSC GREENWICH
Henderson, Stuart Philip , BEng	LT	E	ME	01.03.91	EXCELLENT
Henderson, Thomas Maxwell Philip , BSc, pce	LT CDR	X	PWO(U)	01.04.91	EXCHANGE NLANDS
Hendrick, Jonathan	LT(SL)	S	SM	01.06.86	VIGILANT(PORT)
Hendrickx, Christopher John	LT	E	WE	01.05.96	COLLINGWOOD
Hendry, Philip Alexander	LT(SL)	X		01.10.95	NP1044
Hendy, Laurence Samuel , BEng	LT(SL)	E	WE	01.09.94	ARGYLL
Hendy, Richard	SLT(SL)	S		01.05.95	DARTMOUTH BRNC
Heneghan, John Francis , BEng	LT(SL)	I		01.09.87	MWC GOSPORT
Henley, Simon Michael , MBE, BSc	CDR	E	AE	31.12.91	RNAS PORTLAND
Hennell, Nigel Jeffrey , AFC, pcea	LT CDR(SL)	X	P	01.03.80	SEAHAWK
Hennessey, Timothy Patrick David , BSc, pce, psc	CDR	X	O	30.06.93	MOD (LONDON)
Henry, Dorcas , BSc	LT(SL)	I	METOC	15.05.89	PRESTWICK
Henry, Mark Frederick	SURG SLT	-		01.11.93	DARTMOUTH BRNC
Henry, Phillip	LT CDR(SL)	X	O	01.09.85	LOAN DTEO BSC DN
Henry, Timothy Michael	LT(SL)	X		01.09.93	ARGYLL
Hens, Alexander Roberts , BA	2LT(GRAD)	RM		01.09.95	CTCRM LYMPSTONE
Henty, Iain , BSc, pcea	LT(SL)	X	O	01.08.86	750 SQN OBS SCH
Hepburn, John , BA, LLB, MinstAM, MIMgt	LT CDR	S		01.02.83	CAMBRIDGE
Hepworth, Andrew W D	LT(SL)	I		22.04.90	RNC CEN SUP STF
Herdman, Anthony Claudius , ndc, jsdc, pce	CDR	X	PWO(N)	30.06.81	FOSNNI
Herington, Paul Wilfred , MA, jsdc, pce	CAPT	X	AWO(A)	30.06.92	EXETER
Heritage, Lee James , BSc, CEng, MIMarE, psc	CDR	E	ME	30.06.96	FOSF
Herman, Thomas Rolf , BSc, pce(sm)	CDR	X	SM	30.06.92	NEPTUNE SM1
Hermer, Jeremy Peter (Act Capt Rm)	LT RM	RM		01.09.94	TRAINTEAM BRUNEI
Herridge, Peter Gary , BSc, MA, psc	CDR	E	AE	28.11.95	FAAIT MAN ORG VL
Herriman, John Andrew	LT(SL)	X	MCD	01.04.91	SUPT OF DIVING
Herring, Jonathan James Auriol , BSc, MA, psc (Loc Maj)	CAPT RM	RM		01.09.90	HQ BF HK
Heselton, Branden Lawrence , MA, CEng, MIEE, psc	CAPT	E	WE	30.06.96	HQAFNORTHWEST
Hesling, Gary	SLT	X	H2	01.01.93	BULLDOG
Hett, David Anthony , BSc, DA, LRCP, FFARCS, MRCS	SURG CDR	-	CA	31.12.93	RH HASLAR
Heward, Alan Frank	LT RM(SD)	RM	MTO	01.01.93	RMR LONDON
Hewitt, Antony , BEng	LT CDR	E	MESM	01.06.95	NEPTUNE SM1
Hewitt, David Leslie	LT(SD)	X	PWO(A)	12.12.91	DRYAD
Hewitt, Ian Kerr , MBE, MA, CEng, MIEE, pce	LT CDR	X	WE	01.03.74	FOSF
Hewitt, Ian Rhoderick , OBE, jsdc, pce, pce(sm) , odc(US)	CAPT	X	SM	31.12.93	MOD (LONDON)
Hewitt, Lloyd Russell	SLT(SD)	S	W	03.04.95	RALEIGH
Hibberd, Karen Michelle	SLT	X		01.09.94	DARTMOUTH BRNC
Hibberd, Nicholas James	LT	X	SM	01.11.89	TRIUMPH
Hibbert, Martin Christopher	LT(SL)	X		01.06.85	COCHRANE
Hibbert, Peter Nigel , MNI, pce, pce(sm), jsdc	CDR	X	SM	31.12.90	LOAN CDA ADAC
Hibbert, Richard John Norman , CEng, FIMechE, MIMarE, psc (Commodore)	CAPT	E	ME	31.12.89	2SL/CNH
Hicking, Neil , BSc	LT CDR(SL)	I	METOC	01.10.94	CINCFLEET
Hickman, Simon Michael , BSc	LT RM	RM		01.09.93	42 CDO RM
Hickson, Craig Julian	LT(SL)	X	P	01.04.89	RAF CRANWELL EFS
Hickson, Michael Stuart Harris	LT	E	AE(L)	01.08.95	SULTAN
Higgins, Andrew John	LT(SL)	X		01.08.95	HERON
Higgins, Godfrey Nigel , BEng	LT(SL)	E	AE	01.04.91	DGA(N) ASE
Higgins, Philip , pce, pce(sm)	CDR	X	SM	30.06.83	SEA CADET CORPS
Higgs, Robert James	LT(SD)	X	C	27.07.90	COLLINGWOOD
Higgs, Thomas Arthur , BSc	LT	S		01.02.94	ILLUSTRIOUS
Higham, Anthony , pce, psc	CDR	X	PWO	30.06.89	MOD (LONDON)

Name	Rank	Spec	Sub-spec	Seniority	Where serving
Higham, James Godfrey , BEng, AMIEE	LT	E	WE	01.01.93	DG SHIPS CAM HSE
Highe, Philip , BEng	LT	E	MESM	01.01.95	VICTORIOUS(PORT)
Hildesley, Timothy Ian , OBE, psc	CDR	X	PWO	30.06.86	LOAN RSS BMATT
Hill, Adrian , BSc	SLT(SL)	X	O U/T	01.05.94	DARTMOUTH BRNC
Hill, Barry Leslie , BEng	LT(SL)	E	WE	01.01.87	MOD DFS(CIS) GOS
Hill, Christopher Arthur John , OBE, BSc	CDR	E	MESM	31.12.84	MOD (BATH)
Hill, David , BEng	LT	E	AE	01.03.91	CENTURION
Hill, Elizabeth Carol Anne	LT(SL)	S		12.12.91	UKSU SHAPE
Hill, Graham Alan , MB, BCh, ChB, FRCS	SURG LTCDR	-		01.08.91	NELSON (PAY)
Hill, George Alexander	LT(SD)	E	WESM	15.06.90	DOLPHIN SM SCHL
Hill, Giulian Francis , BEng	LT	E	ME	01.07.90	MOD (BATH)
Hill, John	CHAPLAIN	CE		17.01.94	CAPT F4 (SEA)
Hill, Malcolm Nigel , BSc, AMIEE, psc	CDR	E	WESM	31.12.89	MOD (LONDON)
Hill, Mark Robert , pcea	LT	X	P	22.06.88	DARTMOUTH BRNC
Hill, Nigel George	LT(SD)	X	MCD	28.07.89	CROMER
Hill, Philip John , BEng	LT	E	WESM	01.06.88	DRAKE CFM
Hill, Richard Andrew	LT CDR	X	MW	01.09.95	CDRE MFP
Hill, Roy Keith John	LT	S	CMA	16.02.89	HECLA
Hill, Stuart John Moody , BSc	LT(SL)	X	P	01.11.91	819 SQN
Hill, Simon Patrick , OBE, MPhil, psc(m)	COL	RM		31.12.94	BDS WASHINGTON
Hill-Norton, The Lord, GCB	ADM OF FLEET			12.03.71	
Hilliard, Robert Godfrey , DipTh	CHAPLAIN	CE		01.08.80	EXCELLENT
Hillier, John , LRAM, ARCM, pdm	LT RM(SD)	RM		01.01.88	HQRM
Hillier, Nicholas John , BSc, nadc	CDR	E	WE	30.06.84	MWC GOSPORT
Hills, Anthony Alexander	LT CDR	X	P	01.12.94	GLOUCESTER
Hills, Ian Edward	SLT(SL)	X	P U/T	01.05.95	FONA LINTON/OUSE
Hills, Richard Brian , BA	LT RM	RM		24.04.92	HQ 3 CDO BDE RM
Hilson, Steven Millar	LT(SL)	X	O	01.10.91	702 SQN OSPREY
Hilton, David , MNI	CDR(SD)	X	MCD	01.10.95	RNSC GREENWICH
Hime, Iain Machin , MBIM, MNI, pce	CAPT	X	P	30.06.90	DA BRIDGETOWN
Hinch, David Graham William	LT(SL)	X	P	01.07.91	899 SQN HERON
Hinch, Neil Eric	LT CDR(SD)	X	PT	01.10.93	TEMERAIRE
Hinchcliffe, Alan , BSc	LT(SL)	X	P	01.09.94	810 SQN SEAHAWK
Hinchliffe, Peter Brenton , BSc, MNI, pce(sm), psc	CDR	X	SM	30.06.94	SPARTAN
Hind, Paul , pce, pce(sm), psc (Act Cdr)	LT CDR	X	SM	01.03.79	FOSM NWOOD OPS
Hindmarch, Stephen , BA	SLT(SL)	X	P U/T	01.05.94	DARTMOUTH BRNC
Hindson, Craig Lee , BEng	LT(SL)	E	ME	01.04.94	ILLUSTRIOUS
Hine, Nicholas William	LT CDR	X	SM	01.05.96	TORBAY
Hinks, Karl James , BEng	LT(SL)	E	ME	01.10.93	INVINCIBLE
Hipsey, Stephen Jon , BSc	LT CDR(SL)	I	METOC	01.10.89	LOAN CDA ADAC
Hird, Richard Peter , BSc	LT	X		01.01.95	BIRMINGHAM
Hirst, Richard Augustus , MA, MSc, CEng, FIEE, MBCS, psc	CAPT	E	WE	31.12.88	MOD (BATH)
Hirst, Robert Thomas	LT CDR	X	SM	01.09.88	JACIG
Hiscock, Fabian Henry , OBE, BSc, pce, pce(sm)	CAPT	X	SM	31.12.91	JMOTS TURNHOUSE
Hiscock, Stephen	SLT	E	WE	01.09.92	COLLINGWOOD
Hitchings, Deborah Louise , BA	LT(SL)	X		01.01.94	HERON
Hoare, Peter	LT(SL)	X	O	01.05.94	815 FLT 209
Hoath, Moira Elizabeth Jane , MA, CEng, MBCS, AFIMA	LT CDR(SL)	W	E	01.10.88	DADPTC SHRIVNHAM
Hoather, Martin Stephen	SLT(UCE)	E	WE	01.09.95	DARTMOUTH BRNC
Hobbs, Alan Ronald	LT CDR	X	PWO(A)	01.04.93	EXCHANGE NLANDS
Hobbs, David Andrew , MBE (Act Cdr)	LT CDR	X	P	01.07.77	DCTA
Hobbs, Richard	LT CDR(SD)	E	WE	01.10.95	SOUTHAMPTON
Hobbs, William George	LT CDR(SD)	E	AE(M)	01.10.92	FAAIT MAN ORG VL
Hobson, Charles William Peter , psc	MAJ	RM		31.12.93	HQ 3 CDO BDE RM
Hobson, Ian Stuart , BTech	LT(SD)	E	WESM	18.02.94	VICTORIOUS(PORT)
Hobson, Peter , BA , psc	CDR	X	H CH	31.12.90	CAPT(H) DEVPT
Hockenhull, Sally Iris	SLT(SL)	X	ATCU/T	01.09.92	RNAS CULDROSE
Hockin, William Richard John , MNI, MIMgt, AMNI, jsdc, pce	CDR	X	AWO(A)	31.12.89	2SL/CNH
Hocking, Christopher Bernard , psc	LT	X		01.03.94	ATHERSTONE
Hockley, Christopher John , MEng, MSc, MIMarE, psc	CDR	E	ME	30.06.93	MOD (LONDON)
Hockley, Graham Peter , BSc, CEng, MIMarE, psc	CDR	E	ME	30.06.92	CAPT F1(SEA)
Hodge, Christopher Gordon , MEng, MSc, CEng, MIMarE	CDR	E	MESM	30.06.89	MOD (BATH)

Name	Rank	Spec	Sub-spec	Seniority	Where serving
Hodge, Christopher Michael , BEng	LT(SL)	E	MESM	01.09.94	VICTORIOUS(PORT)
Hodgkins, Jonathan Mark , pce, pcea	LT CDR	X	O	01.12.92	BRITANNIA
Hodgkiss, Leonard , BSc	LT CDR	E	MESM	11.08.91	MOD (BATH)
Hodgson, Benjamin , BSc	LT(SL)	X	O U/T	01.12.95	ITCHEN
Hodgson, Jane Lee , BSc	LT(SL)	W	S	04.04.90	NELSON
Hodgson, Timothy Charles , BSc, MA, CEng, MIMarE, MIMechE, I(1)Ru	LT CDR	E	MESM	01.04.93	SA MOSCOW
Hodkinson, Christopher Brian , BA	LT	X		01.10.88	GRAFTON
Hodkinson, Simon Lloyd , MB, BS, FRCSEd, FRCS(ORTH)	SURG CDR	-	CO/S	30.06.94	RH HASLAR
Hodsdon, Robin Euan , BSc	CDR	I	SM	31.12.90	COLLINGWOOD
Hodson, William Martin	CDR	E	AE	31.12.94	MOD (LONDON)
Hogan, David , BSc, CEng, MIEE	LT CDR	E	WE	19.10.90	FOSF NORTHWOOD
Hogan, Terence (Act Lt Cdr)	LT(SD)	X	AV	15.12.89	FOSF
Hogben, Andrew Lade	LT	X		01.03.92	URNU MANCHESTER
Hogg, Andrew	LT(SL)	X	ATCU/T	16.03.96	RNAS YEOVILTON
Hogg, Anthony John Marsden , AFC, pce	CAPT	X	P	30.06.91	MOD (LONDON)
Hogg, Christopher William , BSc	LT	X	FC	01.03.89	DRYAD
Hogg, Steven John	LT(SD)	E	WESM	10.06.88	DG SHIPS CAM HSE
Holberry, Anthony Paul , psc	CDR	E	WE	31.12.94	SUTHERLAND
Holden, David Michael	LT	X		01.07.95	SHETLAND
Holden, John Thomas , TEng, IEng, AMRINA	LT CDR(SD)	E	HULL	01.10.94	DRAKE CFM
Holden, Neil	LT(SL)	X	MCD	01.04.89	DEF EXP ORD SCHL
Holden, Paul Andrew	LT(SD)	E	AE(L)	07.09.95	SULTAN
Holden, Robert John	LT(SL)	X	O	16.01.90	849 SQN A FLT
Holden, Simon David , BEng	LT	E	AE	24.08.89	RNSC GREENWICH
Holder, John Michael , BA, BSc	SLT(SL)	X	P U/T	01.01.95	DARTMOUTH BRNC
Holder, Richard John	CDR(SD)	S	W	01.10.94	MOD DFS(CIS) GOS
Holder, Shaun Richard , MSc (Act Lt Cdr)	LT(SD)	MS	SM	27.07.90	DRAKE CBS
Holdsworth, Howard William	LT CDR	E	AE	17.02.91	MOD PE ASC
Holgate, Christopher James	CDR	E	ME	31.12.91	CFM PORTSMOUTH
Holihead, Philip Wedgwood , pce, psc(a)	CDR	X	PWO(A)	30.06.93	FOSF
Holland, John Vallis , BDS, LDS, FDS, RCS	SGCAPT(D)	-	COSM	30.06.93	RNH HASLAR
Holland, Nicholas Roy	LT(SD)	S	S	08.04.94	FONA
Holland, Simon Martin Walkington , BSc	LT(SL)	I		01.05.89	SULTAN
Holley, Andrew John , pcea	LT CDR(SL)	X	P	01.10.95	819 SQN
Hollidge, John Howard , BSc, psc, CEng, FIMarE, MBIM	CDR	E	ME	30.06.89	MOD (BATH)
Hollington, Robin Edward Charles , MSc, psc(a) (Loc Maj)	CAPT RM	RM		01.09.90	MOD (LONDON)
Hollins, Rupert Patrick , MA	LT	S	BAR	01.12.88	2SL/CNH
Hollis, Allen , MSc	LT CDR(SD)	E	ME	01.10.93	DNPS
Hollis, Christopher , BEng, AMIEE	LT	E	WE	01.04.89	SUTHERLAND
Hollis, Stephen Paul	SLT(SL)	X	MCD	01.09.93	MCM3 SEA
Holloway, Jonathan Toby , MSc, CEng, MIMechE	CDR	E	MESM	31.12.95	JSDC GREENWICH
Holloway, Martyn Charles Gordon	LT CDR	X	MCD	01.03.80	DEF DIVING SCHL
Holloway, Nicholas , BEM	ACT LT RM(SD)	RM		01.01.96	RM DIV ASMT
Holloway, Steven Andrew	SLT(SL)	X		01.05.94	CHATHAM
Holman, Graeme Charles , pcea	LT CDR	X	O	01.10.91	MWC GOSPORT
Holmes, Christopher John	LT RM	RM	C	30.04.91	42 CDO RM
Holmes, Graham , pce(sm)	LT CDR	X	SM	01.12.87	BF GIBRALTAR(NE)
Holmes, Jonathan	SLT(SD)	X		25.07.93	BEAGLE
Holmes, Michael John , BSc, CEng, MIEE, MBIM, jsdc	CAPT	E	WESM	30.06.94	MOD DGSWS BATH
Holmes, Matthew John , BSc	LT RM	RM		01.09.89	ASC CAMBERLEY
Holmes, Robert , pce, psc(a)	CDR	X	PWO(A)	31.12.95	2SL/CNH
Holmes, Robert Andrew Gordon , BEng	LT	E	AE	01.05.95	SULTAN
Holmes, Rupert Womack , BEng	LT CDR	E	AE	01.04.95	INVINCIBLE
Holmes-Mackie, Nicholas William , BSc	LT CDR	E	AE	01.07.89	MOD (BATH)
Holt, Andrew Frederick , BSc	LT CDR	X	H CH	01.10.88	BULLDOG
Holt, David Christopher Boyd , MB, BCh, ChB, MSc, DIH, MFOM, AFOM	SURG CDR	-	CO/M	31.12.83	MOD (LONDON)
Holt, Justin Sefton (Loc Capt Rm)	LT RM	RM	LC	01.01.93	RM POOLE
Holt, Steven	LT	X	PWO(U)	01.04.89	BRAVE
Holyer, Raymond John , MSc	LT CDR(SD)	MS	P	01.10.93	MOD (LONDON)
Honey, John Philip , BSc, CEng, MIMarE, MIMechE	LT CDR	E	MESM	01.03.88	NEPTUNE DSQ

Name	Rank	Spec	Sub-spec	Seniority	Where serving
Honnoraty, Mark Robert	LT(SD)	X	SM	08.04.94	DOLPHIN SM SCHL
Hood, Cherry Kathleen	LT(SL)	W	S	23.10.92	NAVAL DRAFTING
Hood, Kevin Christopher	LT	S		16.01.90	EXCELLENT
Hood, Kevin Michael	LT	E	MESM	01.04.90	VIGILANT(PORT)
Hood, Matthew John	CAPT RM	RM	WTO	25.04.96	HQRM
Hook, David Arnold , psc(m)	CAPT RM	RM		01.05.92	45 CDO RM
Hooker, Christopher James , pce	LT CDR	X	AWO(A)	16.05.80	DRYAD
Hookway, Brian Charles , BSc, PGCE (Act Cdr)	LT CDR(SL)	I		12.09.79	JSCSCPT
Hoole, Robert John	LT CDR(SL)	X	MCD	01.03.84	DG SHIPS PTLAND
Hooley, Roland George , MSc	LT CDR	E	ME	01.10.93	WESTMINSTER
Hooper, Gary Peter	LT(SD)	E	WE	18.02.94	DRAKE CFM
Hooper, Johanna	MID	S		01.01.96	DARTMOUTH BRNC
Hooton, Daniel Alexander Spangler Homer	SLT(SL)	X		01.09.93	IRON DUKE
Hooton, David Richard , BA	SLT(SL)	X	P U/T	01.01.95	DARTMOUTH BRNC
Hope, Guy Richard	LT	E	ME	01.11.89	MOD (BATH)
Hope, Karl , BSc	LT(SL)	I		01.09.84	COLLINGWOOD
Hope, Mark	SLT	E	AE(L)	01.09.93	SULTAN
Hoper, Paul Roger	LT(SL)	X	O	01.11.86	RNSC GREENWICH
Hoper, Philip Steven , MBE, I(2)Ru	LT CDR(SD)	X	EW	01.10.94	RNU CHELTENHAM
Hopkins, Laurence Charles , pce, psc, psc(m)	CAPT	X	P	30.06.91	MOD (LONDON)
Hopkins, Richard Michael Edward	2LT	RM		01.09.94	COMACCHIO GP RM
Hopkins, Steven David	LT(SL)	X	P	16.07.94	846 SQN
Hopley, David Alan , OBE, psc (Loc Lt Col)	MAJ	RM		31.12.91	JSDC GREENWICH
Hopper, Ian Michael	SLT	X		01.05.94	CORNWALL
Hopper, Simon Mallam , BA	LT	X		01.02.93	NOTTINGHAM
Hopper, Stephen Owen	LT CDR	X	PWO(N)	01.07.93	FEARLESS
Hore, Peter Geoffrey , LRPS, MHCIMA, AIL, psc, I(2)Sp, I(2)Sw	CAPT	S		31.12.90	DRAKE CBP
Hore, Robert Charles , psc	CDR	E	ME	31.12.93	2SL/CNH
Horn, Peter Barrick	LT CDR	X	PWO(A)	01.05.93	COMUKTG/CASWSF
Horne, Archibald	LT(SD)	X	C	17.12.93	MOD (LONDON)
Horne, Jason Richard	LT	X	SM	01.10.95	SPLENDID
Horne, Timothy George , MA, MSc, pce	LT CDR	X	PWO(A)	01.04.88	RNSC GREENWICH
Horne, Trevor Kingsley , MRIN, psc	CDR	X	H CH	31.12.94	RN HYDROG SCHL
Horner, Patrick Andrew	LT CDR	X	PWO(A)	01.08.94	MANCHESTER
Hornung, Christopher	LT RM	RM		24.04.92	RMR BRISTOL
Horrell, Michael Ian ,OBE, BSc, psc	CDR	E	ME	31.12.90	FOST SEA
Horrocks, Christopher Carl	LT(SD)	X	EW	23.07.93	RNU CHELTENHAM
Horsley, Alan Malcolm Ronald , pce	LT CDR	X	PWO(N)	01.07.94	ILLUSTRIOUS
Horsted, Peter James , MEng, MSc, CEng, MIMarE, MIMechE, MINucE, psc	CDR	E	ME	30.06.89	2SL/CNH
Horswill, Mark Nicholas	LT	S		01.08.89	RALEIGH
Horton, Alistair Scott James , BA	LT	X		01.05.94	HERON
Horton, Peter Adam , BSc, MBA	LT CDR	E	WE	01.01.94	BIRMINGHAM
Horton, Robert Ian , AFC, MRAeS, pcea, tp	CDR	X	P	30.06.94	LOAN DTEO BSC DN
Horton, Simon William , BA	LT	X		01.10.92	NOTTINGHAM
Horwell, Brian Bernard	LT(SD)	E	WE	13.06.91	COLLINGWOOD
Hosker, Timothy James , BSc, MA, psc	CDR	S		30.06.92	CINCFLEET
Hosking, David Blaise , MBE, MA, pce, psc	CDR	X	PWO(U)	31.12.94	LOAN OMAN
Hosking, David Lawrence , BSc	LT CDR	I	METOC	18.09.75	CINCFLEET
Hoskins, Alan Bruce , BSc, CEng, MIEE, psc	CDR	E	WESM	31.12.88	RNSC GREENWICH
Hough, Clive Charles	LT RM	RM		29.04.93	HQ CDO AVN
Houghton, Andrew Warren , MA, PGCE	LT CDR(SL)	I		01.10.88	DARTMOUTH BRNC
Houghton, Philip John , MA, pce	LT CDR	X	PWO(U)	01.07.94	DRYAD
Houlberg, Kristian Anthony Niels	SURG LT	-		01.08.94	CHATHAM
Houlberg, Kenneth Mark Torben , n	LT	X		01.11.90	FOSF
Hounsom, Timothy Rogers	SLT	X		01.09.94	DARTMOUTH BRNC
Hourigan, Mark Peter	SLT(SL)	X	P	01.01.93	846 SQN
House, Nigel Patrick Joseph , psc, jssc	MAJ	RM	PT	31.12.91	HQRM
House, Robin Edward Douglas , FBIM, MNI, jsdc, pce	CDR	X	PWO	30.06.85	MOD (LONDON)
Houston, Darren John McCaw	LT	X		01.10.93	DRYAD
Houvenaghel, Ian Michael (Act Lt Rm)	2LT	RM		01.09.93	RM POOLE
Howard, Charles William Wykeham	CHAPLAIN	CE		28.09.82	BF GIBRALTAR(NE)

Name	Rank	Spec	Sub-spec	Seniority	Where serving
Howard, Daniel Gordon	LT(SL)	X	ATC	01.06.89	EXCHANGE GERMANY
Howard, Henry Colin Francis , MBE (Loc Lt Col)	CAPT RM	RM		01.07.79	LOAN ABU DHABI
Howard, Jeremy John , MBE, MNI, ndc, pce, psc, psc(m), ocds(Can)	CAPT	X	TAS	31.12.87	NATO MEWSG VL
Howard, Keith Anthony , MSc	LT CDR	E	ME	01.07.90	MOD (BATH)
Howard, Neil	LT(SL)	E	AE	01.03.90	DGA(N) ASE
Howard, Nicholas Henry , BSc	LT	E	AE	01.06.92	RNAS PORTLAND
Howard, Oliver Melbourne , MB, ChB, MRCP	SURG CAPT	-	CM	31.12.94	MOD (LONDON)
Howard, Peter MacArthy	LT	X	P	16.08.88	SOUTHAMPTON
Howard, Roderick Graeme , TEng, AMIMarE	LT CDR(SD)	E	ME	01.10.91	2SL/CNH
Howard, Simon Charles , BSc, pce, psc	CDR	X	PWO(A)	31.12.92	MANCHESTER
Howard-Williams, Ralph Blin , nadc, psc	MAJ	RM	WTO	01.01.85	RM POOLE
Howarth, Dillon Wharton , MSc, pce, pcea	LT CDR	X	O	01.06.90	BATTLEAXE
Howarth, Stephen Joseph	2LT	RM		01.09.94	CTCRM
Howat, William Kim , pce, psc	CDR	X	AWO(U)	30.06.82	SHAPE BELGIUM
Howden, Allan James , pcea, tp	LT CDR(SL)	X	P	01.10.89	MOD PE ASC
Howden, Norman	CDR(SD)	S	W	01.10.93	2SL/CNH
Howden, Paul Elliott , MB, BS	SURG LT	-		01.08.91	RNAS PORTLAND
Howe, Douglas Lawrence	LT CDR	E	WE	23.11.81	FEARLESS
Howe, Julian Peter , BA	LT	X		01.05.94	HERON
Howe, Michael James	LT(SD)	X	g	06.01.78	RALEIGH
Howe, Paul Alfred , BSc	CAPT RM	RM	MLDR	01.05.94	HQ 3 CDO BDE RM
Howe, Sarah Elizabeth , BDS	SGLTCDR(D)	-		27.01.88	INVINCIBLE
Howe, Virginia Helen , BSc	LT(SL)	I	METOC	01.09.89	FOSM NWOOD OPS
Howell, Gwynne Evan Daniel , MB, BS	SURG LTCDR	-		01.08.89	CENTURION
Howell, Henry , MSc	LT(SL)	I	METOC	25.09.91	CAPT F4 (SEA)
Howell, Kevin	CDR(SD)	E	WESM	01.10.91	MOD DGSWS BATH
Howell, Leigh Curtis	LT(SL)	X	P	16.08.92	MOD DNR OUTPORTS
Howell, Michael	LT CDR(SD)	S	W	01.10.93	CAMPBELTOWN
Howell, Michael Alfred , MB, BS, MA, FRCS	SURG LTCDR	-	A/E	01.08.92	NELSON (PAY)
Howell, Robert , pce (Commodore)	CAPT	X	C	31.12.89	MOD (LONDON)
Howell, Simon Brooke	LT CDR	X	PWO(A)	01.11.93	DRYAD
Howells, David Lewis , BA, BA(OU), MSc, CEng, MIMarE, MINucE	LT CDR	E	MESM	30.06.86	FOSM NWOOD OPS
Howells, Gary Russell , BSc	LT CDR(SL)	I		01.10.90	CENTURION
Howells, John , BSc	LT CDR	I		01.01.93	HQRM
Howells, Martin John	LT(SD)	MS	SM	29.07.94	NEPTUNE DSQ
Howells, Sian	LT(SL)	E	ME	01.05.96	DARTMOUTH BRNC
Howes, Francis Hedley Roberton , BSc, MA, psc	MAJ	RM	MLDR	30.06.96	40 CDO RM
Howes, Nicholas James	LT(QM)	Q	ACC/EM	28.03.86	RNH GIB
Howgill, Michael Colin	LT	X	MCD	01.03.93	WALNEY
Howick, Stephen William , MSc, CEng, MIEE	CDR	E	WE	30.06.87	MOD (LONDON)
Howorth, Keith , BSc, pce, pcea	LT CDR	X	O	01.12.92	OSPREY
Howse, Robert David , pce, psc	LT CDR	X	P	01.05.79	JWS POOLE
Howse, Robert James , BA	LT	E	WESM	01.12.93	FOSM NWOOD OPS
Hoyle, Geoffrey Robert , pce, psc(a)	LT CDR	X	AWO(U)	01.05.79	DRYAD
Hoyle, John Jefferson	LT(SD)	E	AE(M)	17.10.91	DGA(N)ASE MASU
Hoyle, Stephen Antony	LT(SL)	X	SM	01.03.95	NEPTUNE BASE OPS
Hubble, Robert Sydney Edgar	LT(SL)	X	P	16.12.87	OSPREY
Hudson, Jeremy David , BA	CAPT RM	RM	MLDR	01.09.93	42 CDO RM
Hudson, Michael John , MBE	LT CDR	X		14.06.86	FEARLESS
Hudson, Nicholas Graeme , jsdc, pce	CDR	X	PWO(U)	30.06.91	MOD (LONDON)
Hudson, Peter Derek , pce	CDR	X	PWO(N)	31.12.95	NP1044
Hudson, Philip Trevor	LT(SD)	X	AV	01.08.88	SULTAN
Hudson, Ralph Palliser Milbanke , MSc, MIMechE, psc	LT CDR	E	MESM	01.04.88	MOD (BATH)
Huggins, Geoffrey Edward , BSc, CEng, MIEE	LT CDR	E	WE	15.09.82	MOD (LONDON)
Hughes, Andrew Simon , MB, BCh, MRCGP	SURG CDR	-	GMPP	31.12.95	HQ 3 CDO BDE RM
Hughes, David Brian Reginald , BSc, CEng, FIMarE, FIMechE, jsdc	CAPT	E	ME	30.06.89	2SL/CNH
Hughes, Daniel Colin , BA	2LT(GRAD)	RM		01.09.95	CTCRM LYMPSTONE
Hughes, Desmond Joseph , MBE	CDR(SL)	X	O	01.10.91	SACLANT USA
Hughes, David James	SURG LT	-	SM	01.08.94	VANGUARD(STBD)
Hughes, David Pirie	LT(SL)	X	P	16.07.85	771 SK5 SAR
Hughes, Gary George Henry	LT(SD)	X	C	02.04.93	DGCIS BRISTOL
Hughes, Gareth Llewelyn	LT CDR	S		01.05.92	RNSC GREENWICH

Name	Rank	Spec	Sub-spec	Seniority	Where serving
Hughes, John Glyn	LT(SL)	X	SM	01.01.95	REPULSE(PORT)
Hughes, Jon-Paul Hudson (Loc Capt Rm)	LT RM	RM		01.09.90	EXCHANGE ARMY UK
Hughes, Marco Anwyl Stephen , BEng	LT	X	O U/T	01.01.93	750 SQN OBS SCH
Hughes, Mark Jonathan	LT RM	RM		01.09.94	45 CDO RM
Hughes, Nicholas	SLT	E	ME	01.09.93	DARTMOUTH BRNC
Hughes, Nicholas Justin , pce(sm)	LT CDR	X	SM	01.09.90	GUERNSEY
Hughes, Paul Antony , MB, BS, DObstRCOG, MRCGP	SURG LTCDR	-	GMPP	01.08.91	UKSU AFSOUTH
Hughes, Peter Charles	LT CDR(SL)	S		01.10.95	DNPS
Hughes, Peter John , LVO, pce, psc	CDR	X	PWO(N)	31.12.87	2SL/CNH
Hughes, Robin David , BEng, CEng, MIMarE	LT	E	ME	01.02.89	MOD (BATH)
Hughes, Robert Ian , BSc	CDR	E	WESM	31.12.92	MOD (LONDON)
Hughes, Stephen John , psc(m)	MAJ	RM		30.06.94	2SL/CNH FOTR
Hughes, Scott Maurice , BSc	SLT(SL)	X	P U/T	01.01.95	DARTMOUTH BRNC
Hughes, William	MID	E	ME	01.09.94	SOUTHAMPTON
Hughesdon, Mark Douglas , BEng, MSc, AMIEE	LT	E	WE	01.02.90	DGSS BRISTOL
Hugo, Ian David , pce, pce(sm)	LT CDR	X	SM	01.12.91	BRECON
Hulland, Nigel William , MB, BCh, ChB	SURG LTCDR	-	GMPP	16.08.87	NEPTUNE
Hulme, Laon Stuart Grant , MBIM, jsdc, pce	CDR	X	D	31.12.83	MOD (LONDON)
Hulme, Timothy Mark , BA, pcea	LT	X	O	01.03.89	815 FLT 229
Hume, Charles Bertram , BSc	CDR	E	MESM	31.12.91	DTR BATH
Humphrey, David Alexander , BA, jsdc, pce(sm)	CDR	X	SM	31.12.93	TRENCHANT
Humphrey, David Roger (Barrister)	CAPT	S	BAR	30.06.92	2SL/CNH
Humphrey, Ivor James	SLT(SD)	E	WE	07.02.94	EDINBURGH
Humphreys, John Illingworth , pce(sm)	CDR	X	SM	30.06.94	NEPTUNE BASE OPS
Humphreys, Robert James , pce	LT CDR	X	PWO(A)	01.01.94	GLASGOW
Humphries, John Edward	LT CDR(SL)	X	P	01.10.92	HERON FLIGHT
Humphries, Jason Eric	LT(SL)	X		01.04.95	NORTHUMBERLAND
Humphries, Susan Mary , BSc	SLT(SL)	X		01.01.95	DARTMOUTH BRNC
Humphrys, James Alan , BSc, MA, pce, psc	CDR	X	PWO(U)	31.12.93	DRYAD MWC
Humphrys, Nicholas Barclay , BA	LT CDR	X	AWO(C)	16.02.78	CNOCS GROUP
Hunkin, David John	LT	X	MCD	01.06.92	SDG PLYMOUTH
Hunt, Anthony John	CDR	E	WE	30.06.87	SHAPE BELGIUM
Hunt, Charles James , BEng	LT(SL)	I	METOC	01.09.89	DRYAD
Hunt, Emma Louise	LT(SL)	S		01.06.91	FONA
Hunt, Fraser Brain George	LT(SL)	X	P	01.03.96	814 SQN
Hunt, Gerald Clive , pce	CDR	X	O	30.06.85	PJHQ
Hunt, Jeremy Simon Paul , BSc	LT CDR	I	METOC	05.02.95	RNAS YEOVILTON
Hunt, Patrick Edward Robin David	LT(SD)	E	WE	05.06.92	COLLINGWOOD
Hunt, Philip Vivian , MSc, CEng, MIMechE, MRAeS, jsdc	CDR	E	AE	31.12.88	BDS WASHINGTON
Hunt, Stephen Christopher	LT(SL)	X	FC	01.07.94	INVINCIBLE
Hunt, Stephen Neil	LT(SL)	X	P	16.10.90	849 SQN HQ
Hunter, Bruce John , BSc	LT CDR	E	MESM	01.07.90	DRAKE CBS
Hunter, Jeremy Grant	2LT(GRAD)	RM		01.09.94	40 CDO RM
Hunter, Kevin Patrick , BSc	LT CDR	E	ME	01.08.87	COMAW SEA
Hunter, Neil Mitchell , BSc, pcea	LT CDR	X	P	01.01.94	CROMER
Hunter, Peter Alexander , MSc	LT(SL)	I		01.01.86	NEPTUNE SM1
Hunter, Paul Robert	LT(SL)	X	P	01.10.93	819 SQN
Hunter, Toby Charles Graeme , psc(m)	MAJ	RM	A/TK	30.06.90	CTCRM
Huntington, Simon Peter , BSc, n	LT	X		01.10.91	URNU NEWCASTLE
Huntley, Ian Philip , BA, psc(m) (Loc Maj)	CAPT RM	RM		01.09.90	CINCFLEET
Hunwicks, Sarah Elizabeth , BEng	SLT(SL)	E	AE	01.09.94	BEAVER
Hurford, Edward	SLT(SL)	X	P U/T	01.09.93	DARTMOUTH BRNC
Hurford, Peter Giles , BSc, FIMechE, MIMechE	CAPT	E	MESM	31.12.94	DRAKE CBS
Hurley, Christopher , BSc	LT	X		01.06.94	SHEFFIELD
Hurrell, Piers Richard	LT	X		01.07.91	ORWELL
Hurry, Andrew Patridge	LT CDR	X	P	01.11.94	815 FLT 211
Hussain, Amjad Mazhar , MSc, CEng, MIEE, jsdc	CDR	E	WE	31.12.92	INVINCIBLE
Hussain, Shayne , BSc, PhD	LT(SL)	I	METOC	01.01.91	RNAS PORTLAND
Hussey, Stephen John , pce(sm)	LT CDR	X	SM(G)	15.07.93	EXCHANGE AUSTLIA
Hussey, Steven John , BSc	LT RM	RM	RMP2	01.09.92	847 SQN
Hutchings, Charles Roger , BSc, CEng, FIEE, FBIM, psc	CAPT	E	WE	31.12.89	NELSON
Hutchings, James Stewart	LT(SD)	E	AE(M)	16.10.92	HQ CDO AVN

Name	Rank	Spec	Sub-spec	Seniority	Where serving
Hutchings, Peter William , BSc	LT CDR	E	WE	01.04.89	CDRE MFP
Hutchings, Richard , DSC, psc (Loc Lt Col)	MAJ	RM	PH	30.06.90	CINCFLEET
Hutchings, Sam David	SURG SLT	-		18.10.93	DARTMOUTH BRNC
Hutchins, Iain	SLT	X		01.01.96	DRYAD
Hutchins, Richard Frank , BEng	LT	E	MESM	01.06.93	TRIUMPH
Hutchins, Timothy Paul , BSc	LT	E	AE(P)	01.06.88	RNAS YEOVILTON
Hutchins, Timothy , BSc	SLT(SL)	X	O U/T	01.01.94	RNAS CULDROSE
Hutchinson, Alisdair John	LT(SL)	I		01.01.89	MOD (LONDON)
Hutchinson, Christopher John , BSc	LT(SL)	I	METOC	01.09.88	FOSM NWOOD OPS
Hutchinson, Oliver James Procter	LT	X	FC	01.09.89	SOMERSET
Hutchinson, Peter , IEng, AMIMarE	SLT(SL)	E	ME	14.06.93	FEARLESS
Hutchinson, Philip Ian (Act Lt Rm)	2LT	RM		01.09.93	COCHRANE
Hutchinson, Timothy James , BSc, CEng, MIMarE, MINucE	CDR	E	MESM	30.06.91	NEPTUNE DSQ
Hutchinson, Thomas Stanley	LT CDR	S	SM	01.07.83	ACE CENTRAL RGN
Hutchison, George Bruce , pcea	LT CDR	X	O	01.02.95	JMOTS TURNHOUSE
Hutchison, Neil David Paton , BA	LT	X		01.09.94	ITCHEN
Hutchison, Paul Gordon , MIMarE	LT	E	MESM	01.05.90	RNC DPT NS&TECH
Hutchison, William Keith , pce, pcea, psc, I(2)Ge (Commodore)	CAPT	X	P	30.06.86	CINCFLEET
Hutton, Graham	LT(SL)	X	O	01.11.91	849 SQN HQ
Hutton, James Kyle , psc(m) (Loc Maj)	CAPT RM	RM		01.05.91	HQ 3 CDO BDE RM
Hutton, Katherine , BEd	LT(SL)	I		01.09.90	SEAHAWK
Hutton, Karen Louise	LT(SL)	W	X	12.12.91	DRYAD
Hutton, Simon John	LT CDR	X	SM	01.11.95	VICTORIOUS(PORT)
Huxtable, Nigel , MA	LT CDR(SL)	I		01.09.87	2SL/CNH
Hyde, Clifford David	LT CDR(SD)	E	WESM	01.10.91	DOLPHIN SM SCHL
Hyde, Trevor	LT CDR(SD)	E	WESM	01.10.94	BDS WASHINGTON
Hygate, Alison Margaret , BEng	LT	X		01.05.94	MOD (LONDON)
Hyland, Roger Alan	LT(SD)	E	WE	22.02.96	GLASGOW
Hyldon, Christopher John , BSc, MIEE, jsdc	CDR	E	AE	30.06.91	FONA
Hynett, William Anthony	LT(SL)	X	P	16.06.95	800 SQN
Hyslop, David Ross , BSc, CEng, MIEE, psc	CDR	E	WE	30.06.91	MOD (LONDON)

I

Name	Rank	Spec	Sub-spec	Seniority	Where serving
Ibbotson, Richard Jeffery , DSC, MSc, CGIA, pce	CDR	X	PWO(U)	31.12.90	COMUKTG/CASWSF
Iles, Terence Derek Stanton	LT CDR	X	MCD	16.03.82	DRYAD
Imrie, Peter Blain , DSM	LT(SD)	X	AV	14.12.90	INVINCIBLE
Ince, David Peter	LT	X	MCD	01.12.89	BICESTER
Inge, Daniel	LT(SL)	X	ATCU/T	01.05.95	RNAS YEOVILTON
Ingham, Ivan Michael	LT	X	FC	01.05.91	DRYAD
Ingham, Phillip Clayton , pce, psc	CDR	X	PWO(N)	30.06.92	SACLANT USA
Ingram, Gareth John , BSc	SLT	X		01.09.93	LINDISFARNE
Ingram, Richard Gordon , pce	LT CDR	X	PWO(A)	01.06.92	RAF BRACKNELL
Inskip, Ian , pce, psc	CDR	X	PWO(N)	31.12.83	2SL/CNH
Ireland, Alasdair Robbie , pce	LT CDR	X	PWO(A)	01.04.93	COTTESMORE
Ireland, Diana Mary , BA	LT(SL)	W		27.07.85	RNAS PORTLAND
Ireland, John Mitchell	LT(SD)	E	MESM	15.10.93	VALIANT
Ireland, Philip Charles	LT	X	MCD	01.03.89	DRYAD
Ireland, Roger Charles , MBE, MILDM	CDR	S	SM	31.12.95	MOD CSSE LONDON
Irons, Paul Andrew	LT	X		01.07.89	DRYAD
Irons, Rupert , BSc	LT	X		01.05.96	ORWELL
Irvine, Paul Douglas Thomas , OBE, osc (Loc Lt Col)	MAJ	RM	C	31.12.89	SA OSLO
Irwin, Mark Andrew , BEng	LT(SL)	E	ME	01.03.92	DRAKE CBP
Isaac, Philip	LT CDR	S		10.06.91	BF GIBRALTAR(NE)
Issitt, David James , BA, BSc, jsdc	CDR	E	AE(P)	30.06.90	RNAS CULDROSE

J

Name	Rank	Spec	Sub-spec	Seniority	Where serving
Jack, Peter John , adp	LT(SL)	S		16.09.89	DNPS
Jacklin, John Paul	LT CDR(SD)	X	REG	01.10.87	FOSF
Jackman, Andrew Warren , pce	LT CDR	X	PWO(C)	01.07.90	COMUKTG/CASWSF
Jackman, Richard William , BSc, psc	CDR	E	WE	30.06.92	DSSC BATH
Jackson, Alan Roger	CDR	S	SM	31.12.91	MAS BRUSSELS
Jackson, Andrew Stephen , BSc	LT	E	MESM	01.01.89	MOD (BATH)

Name	Rank	Spec	Sub-spec	Seniority	Where serving
Jackson, David John , BEng	LT	E	AE	01.03.92	RMC OF SCIENCE
Jackson, Gary Kevin	LT(SD)	X	REG	15.12.89	COLLINGWOOD
Jackson, Ian	SLT(SL)	X		01.09.94	SPLENDID
Jackson, Ian Anthony , BSc	LT CDR	E	ME	01.04.96	GRAFTON
Jackson, Michael Anthony , BEd, FRMS, psc	LT CDR	I	METOC	25.07.84	CINCFLEET
Jackson, Mark Harding	CHAPLAIN	CE		19.04.83	SEAHAWK
Jackson, Matthew John Andrew , BA	2LT(GRAD)	RM		01.09.94	40 CDO RM
Jackson, Norman Cullen , BSc, CEng, MIEE, psc	CDR	E	WE	31.12.87	BDS WASHINGTON
Jackson, Peter , FBIM, MRIN, pce, pcea, ocds(Pak), psc	CAPT	X	O	31.12.93	SA ISLAMABAD
Jackson, Paul Anthony	LT(SD)	S	W	13.12.95	DNPS
Jackson, Peter	LT	E	AE	01.02.91	DGA(N) ASE
Jackson, Simon , pce, psc(a)	LT CDR	X	AWO(A)	01.01.79	EXCELLENT
Jackson, Stuart Harry , BSc, MBA, MRAeS	LT CDR	E	AE	01.07.89	FONA
Jackson, Stevan Kenneth	LT CDR(SD)	MS		01.10.93	INM ALVERSTOKE
Jackson, Stephen Michael	LT CDR	E	ME	09.02.89	MOD (BATH)
Jacques, Marcus James	LT(SL)	X	FC	01.07.94	DRYAD
Jacques, Nicholas Adrian	LT(SL)	X	O	01.06.93	706 SQN SEAHAWK
Jagger, Charles Edward , BSc, pcea, psc	LT CDR	X	P	16.04.83	HERON
Jagger, Paul Richard Albert , MSc, AMIEE	CDR	E	WESM	30.06.95	VICTORIOUS(PORT)
Jaggers, Gary George	LT(SD)	X	O	16.12.94	814 SQN
Jaini, Andrew	SLT(SL)	X		01.01.94	CAMPBELTOWN
James, Adam Jon	LT(SL)	X	H1	01.06.88	BULLDOG
James, Alexander	MID(UCE)	X		01.09.94	CHIDDINGFOLD
James, Christopher , BSc, CEng, MIMarE, MIMechE	LT CDR	E	MESM	01.06.91	VIGILANT(PORT)
James, Colin Francis , MIERE	CDR	E	WE	31.12.86	NAVAL DRAFTING
James, Carolyn Shane	A/LT(FS)	FS		01.05.95	NELSON
James, Christopher William , pce	LT CDR	X	PWO(A)	27.10.93	CINCFLEET
James, David Russell , pce, pcea, psc	CDR	X	O	31.12.94	MOD (LONDON)
James, Ian , BDS	SG LT(D)	-		09.01.94	CINCFLEET
James, Julian Stephen Hilary	SLT(SL)	X	P	01.05.95	705 SQN SEAHAWK
James, Michael Ashton , pce, psc	CDR	X	AWO(C)	31.12.84	MOD (LONDON)
James, Paul Edward	LT(SD)	E	AE(M)	13.10.89	FONA SEAGOING
James, Paul Melvyn	LT RM	RM		01.09.94	RMR SCOTLAND
James, Robert Martin , MBE, MBA	LT CDR(SL)	I		21.09.91	DARTMOUTH BRNC
James, Stuart Alain (Act Capt Rm)	LT RM	RM		01.09.89	CTCRM
James, Trevor Charles	LT CDR(SL)	E	WE	01.10.91	COLLINGWOOD
James, Timothy Edward , BEng	LT(SL)	E	ME	01.05.94	ARGYLL
Jameson, Andrew Charles , LLB	LT CDR	S	BAR	01.11.94	MANCHESTER
Jameson, Barbara Gail Lilian , BDS	SGLTCDR(D)	-		20.12.94	COLLINGWOOD
Jameson, Roger Mark , BSc	LT(SL)	X	P	16.01.93	705 SQN SEAHAWK
Jamieson, Roger Euan , BSc	SLT	X		01.01.93	DRYAD
Janaway, Paul , BSc, CEng, MIEE	LT CDR(SL)	E	WE	01.10.93	ARK ROYAL
Janzen, Alexander Nicholas , BA	2LT(GRAD)	RM		01.09.95	CTCRM LYMPSTONE
Jappy, Gavin William George , BA	SLT(SL)	X		01.09.94	CROMER
Jaques, Dominic Andrew	LT	X	SM	01.01.88	TIRELESS
Jaques, David Anthony	LT(SL)	X	O	16.08.92	750 SQN OBS SCH
Jardine, Darren Scott , n	LT(SL)	X		01.11.95	INVINCIBLE
Jardine, Graham Andrew , pcea	LT CDR	X	O	16.09.89	FOST SEA
Jarrett, Michael Howard	LT CDR(SD)	S	S	01.04.86	MOD (LONDON)
Jarrett, Michael Thomas John	LT	X		01.06.95	SPEY
Jarrett, Owen	LT CDR	X	PWO(A)	22.05.85	DRYAD
Jarvis, David Henry , MB, BCh, ChB	SURG LTCDR	-		01.08.95	RM SCHL MUSIC
Jarvis, David John , BSc, CEng, MIEE, psc	CDR	E	WESM	31.12.90	MOD (LONDON)
Jarvis, Ian Lawrence , BSc, psc	CDR	E	WE	30.06.88	MOD (LONDON)
Jarvis, Lionel John , MB, BS, LRCP, FRCR, MRCS	SURG CDR	-	CX	30.06.90	RH HASLAR
Jarvis, Laurence Richard , BSc	LT(SL)	E	ME	01.04.88	FEARLESS
Jasper, Mark , BSc	LT	X		01.07.95	BRIDPORT
Jay, Kenneth George , MA	CDR	E	AE(P)	31.12.86	BDS WASHINGTON
Jaynes, Peter Robert William , BSc, CEng, MIMarE, psc	CDR	E	ME	31.12.90	FOSF
Jeffcoat, Stewart Murray , BA, GradIMA	CDR	E	ME	31.12.93	SUTHERLAND
Jefferis, Ian Michael , MA, pce, pcea, psc	LT CDR	X	P	01.03.89	RNAS PORTLAND
Jefferson, Peter Mark	LT(SL)	X	O	16.10.85	EXCHANGE USA

Name	Rank	Spec	Sub-spec	Seniority	Where serving
Jefferson, Toby	SLT	E	AE	01.05.94	DARTMOUTH BRNC
Jeffery, Peter Hamilton , jsdc, pce, tp, I(2)Ge	CAPT	X	AWO(U)	30.06.92	MOD (LONDON)
Jeffrey, Ian , BSc, BA, CEng, MIEE, MIL, psc, I(2)Fr	CDR	E	WE	30.06.85	ACE SRGN ITALY
Jelbart, Keith	LT(SL)	X	O	01.02.94	750 SQN OBS SCH
Jellyman, Paul Anthony , BSc, psc	CDR	I	METOC	30.06.89	FOSF
Jenkin, Alastair Michael Hugh , BSc	LT CDR	E	WE	01.02.92	ASC CAMBERLEY
Jenkin, James Richard Saint Lawrence	LT CDR	X	SM	01.05.92	PJHQ
Jenkins, Edward James (Act Lt Rm)	2LT	RM		27.04.94	40 CDO RM
Jenkins, Gwyn	LT RM	RM		01.09.94	RM POOLE
Jenkins, Gari Wyn , BEng	LT CDR	E	WE	01.09.95	LONDON
Jenkins, Ian Francis , BSc, CEng, MIEE, psc	CDR	E	WE	30.06.89	MOD (LONDON)
Jenkins, Ian Lawrence , QHS, MB, BCh, FRCS (Commodore)	SURG CAPT	-	CU	31.12.88	MOD (LONDON)
Jenkins, Simon Spencer , BEng	LT(SL)	I	METOC	01.09.89	CAPT F1(SEA)
Jenkins, William Richard Scott , BSc, CEng, FIEE, psc, gw	LT CDR	E	WE	31.12.84	2SL/CNH
Jenks, Anthony William Jervis	LT CDR	X	H CH	16.04.87	MOD (LONDON)
Jennings, Matthew Paul , BTech, MA, MRAeS, pcea, psc	LT CDR(SL)	X	P	01.10.89	705 SQN SEAHAWK
Jennings, Paul James	LT CDR	X	PWO(U)	01.08.88	HQAFNORTHWEST
Jennings, Paul Scott , BSc	LT	X		01.02.93	ALDERNEY
Jennings, William , BEng	LT	E	ME	01.03.95	NOTTINGHAM
Jenrick, Martin Frederick	LT CDR(SD)	X	MCD	01.10.95	SDG PORTSMOUTH
Jepson, Nicholas Henry Martin (Act Lt Rm)	2LT	RM		01.09.92	CTCRM
Jeram-Croft, Lawrence Mayvore , BSc	CDR	E	AE(P)	30.06.92	JSDC GREENWICH
Jermy, Stephen Charles , BSc, pce	CDR	X	O	30.06.90	FOST SEA
Jermyn, Nicholas Charles , BA	LT RM	RM	LC	01.09.93	FEARLESS
Jervis, Neil David , pce(sm)	LT CDR	X	SM	01.07.92	JMOTS TURNHOUSE
Jess, Ian Michael , MA, MSc, CEng, MIMarE, psc	CDR	E	ME	31.12.94	INVINCIBLE
Jessop, Paul Edward , BEng, MSc, CEng, MIMechE	LT CDR	E	MESM	01.03.95	TALENT
Jewitt, Charles James Bagot	LT	S		01.07.88	MONMOUTH
John, Gareth David , BSc, CEng, MIEE	LT CDR	E	WE	01.09.92	MOD (BATH)
John, Michael Leyshon	CDR	E	WESM	30.06.91	MOD (LONDON)
Johns, Adrian James , BSc, pce, pcea, psc	CAPT	X	P	31.12.94	CAMPBELTOWN
Johns, Andrew William	SLT	X		01.09.95	DOLPHIN SM SCHL
Johns, James Andrew , BSc	LT	X		01.02.94	BRIDPORT
Johns, Leslie Ernest	SLT(SD)	X	REG	23.07.95	FEARLESS
Johns, Michael Glynn , pcea	LT(SL)	X	O	01.11.88	SEAHAWK
Johns, Robin Francis , CEng, MIMarE	CAPT	E	ME	31.12.90	SA SANTIAGO
Johns, Tony , MSc, psc	CDR	E	MESM	31.12.95	VENGEANCE(PORT)
Johnson, Alan Douglas , psc, psc(m)	CDR	S		30.06.86	FOST DPORT SHORE
Johnson, Anthony Robert	LT(SL)	X	O	16.02.95	815 FLT 239
Johnson, Andrew Stephen , pce	LT CDR	X	PWO(A)	01.02.92	FOST SEA
Johnson, Bryan , BSc, pce	LT CDR	X	PWO(U)	01.05.88	CNOCS GROUP
Johnson, Chad Colin Burnett , BEng	LT	E	AE	01.04.94	FONA CRANWELL
Johnson, Graham Andrew Halsted , MB, BSc, BS	SURG LT	-		01.08.91	RNDHU DERRIFORD
Johnson, Grenville Philip , MBE, pce, jsdc	CDR	X	MCD	31.12.91	MOD (LONDON)
Johnson, Graham Robert , BA	CDR	X	AWO(C)	30.06.87	BDS WASHINGTON
Johnson, James Charles , BEng	LT CDR	E	WESM	23.01.94	MOD DGSM PTLAND
Johnson, Lee Samuel , n	LT	X		01.03.92	DRYAD
Johnson, Michael Anthony , pce	CAPT	X	G	31.12.91	DNPS
Johnson, Martin Douglas	LT(SD)	S	W	02.04.93	FOREST MOOR
Johnson, Michael David	LT(SD)	S	W	17.12.93	WARRIOR
Johnson, Michael John	LT(SD)	E	WE	19.02.93	NOTTINGHAM
Johnson, Mark Ralph Edward	SLT(UCE)	X		01.09.95	NOTTINGHAM
Johnson, Peter Richard , FFA, MBIM	LT CDR	S		01.11.83	UKSU IBERLANT
Johnson, Symon	SLT(SL)	X	P	01.01.93	845 SQN
Johnson, William Charles	LT CDR	E	WESM	30.09.90	MOD (LONDON)
Johnston, Charles Gardner , MB, BCh, BAO, ChB, FFARCS, FFARCSI	SURG CDR	-	CA	31.12.87	RNDHU DERRIFORD
Johnston, James Angus , BEng	SLT	X		01.09.93	DOLPHIN SM SCHL
Johnston, Richard Patrick , MB, BS, DipAvMed	SURG LTCDR	-	O/M	01.08.89	INM ALVERSTOKE
Johnston, Timothy Alan	LT CDR	X	P	01.06.95	BOXER
Johnstone, Clive Charles Carruthers , BA, BSc	LT CDR	X	PWO(A)	01.12.94	BRITANNIA
Johnstone, Ian Stuart , BSc, CEng, MRAeS	LT CDR	E	AE	01.04.89	MOD DHSA

Name	Rank	Spec	Sub-spec	Seniority	Where serving
Johnstone, James Oliver , BA	SLT	X		01.01.93	DARTMOUTH BRNC
Johnstone-Burt, Charles Anthony , BA, pce, pcea	CDR	X	P	30.06.92	BRAVE
Joll, Simon Mark , BA	LT	S		01.10.93	SOVEREIGN
Jolliffe, Graham Edward , BSc	LT CDR	E	AE	01.08.90	846 SQN
Jolliffe, James George , pcea	LT CDR(SL)	X	O	01.09.83	OSPREY
Jolly, John Edward Ian	LT CDR	X	HCH	16.12.84	LOAN OMAN
Jones, Anthony , psc	CDR	S		31.12.91	OSPREY
Jones, Alan , BEM	CAPT RM(SL)	RM		01.10.93	RMB STONEHOUSE
Jones, Alun David , BA	LT	X	P	01.11.89	810 SQN B FLIGHT
Jones, Adam Edward , BEng	LT	X		01.12.94	MIDDLETON
Jones, Alan Frank	LT(SL)	I		01.09.91	COLLINGWOOD
Jones, Alan John , MITE	LT CDR(SL)	E	WE	01.10.92	MOD DGSW PTSMTH
Jones, Adrian Rolf Timothy , MSc	LT CDR	E	WE	01.03.93	ARGYLL
Jones, Anthony William , BSc	LT CDR	E	WE	01.07.77	DG SHIPS CAM HSE
Jones, Barry Andrew , BSc	LT CDR(SL)	X	P	01.10.91	705 SQN SEAHAWK
Jones, Bryn Sherwood , BSc	LT CDR	X	PWO(U)	16.11.81	MWC GOSPORT
Jones, Craig Anthony , n	LT	X		01.11.91	ILLUSTRIOUS
Jones, David Allen	LT(SD)	E	MESM	15.10.93	NEPTUNE NT
Jones, David Bryan	LT	E	MESM	01.07.91	SUPERB
Jones, David Clement , BSc	LT CDR	E	MESM	01.06.91	MOD (BATH)
Jones, Daniel , BSc.	SLT(SL)	X		01.05.94	BOXER
Jones, David Lloyd , BTech	LT(SD)	E	WE	24.02.95	LIVERPOOL
Jones, David Leonard , BEM	LT(CS)RM	-		16.10.88	2SL/CNH
Jones, David Michael , MSc, TEng, IEng, AMIMarE	LT CDR(SD)	E	ME	01.10.88	SULTAN
Jones, David , BEng	SLT	E	WE	01.09.93	COLLINGWOOD
Jones, Ernest John	LT(SD)	X	AV	07.01.88	OSPREY
Jones, Ernest Thomas	LT CDR(SD)	X	PR	01.10.90	DRYAD
Jones, Edward Wynne , OBE, LLB	CHAPLAIN	CE		02.02.78	CTCRM
Jones, Gareth David , BSc	LT(SL)	I		01.09.91	COLLINGWOOD
Jones, Gary James	LT RM(SD)	RM		01.01.95	45 CDO RM
Jones, Glyn Robert , BA	LT CDR	I	METOC	01.09.95	CSST SEA
Jones, Gary , BSc	SLT(SL)	X	P U/T	01.01.94	FONA CRANWELL
Jones, Huw Ashton , MSc	LT CDR	E	MESM	01.03.94	SPARTAN
Jones, Jenny , BA	SLT(SL)	X		01.01.95	DARTMOUTH BRNC
Jones, John Alexander	LT(CS)	-		12.08.85	MOD DNR OUTPORTS
Jones, John Kempton Phillips , MBE, BEM, TEng	LT CDR(SD)	E	MESM	01.10.91	VALIANT
Jones, Kenneth , BSc, jsdc, psc	CDR	I		30.06.86	SULTAN AIB
Jones, Leslie , BA, l(2)Ru	LT CDR	X	PWO(C)	01.07.92	DARTMOUTH BRNC
Jones, Lynn	LT	Q	REGM	11.11.90	RNDHU DERRIFORD
Jones, Michael	LT CDR	X	PWO(A)	01.03.95	BIRMINGHAM
Jones, Mark Andrew	SLT(SD)	S	W	10.12.95	CINCFLEET
Jones, Martin Clifford , BSc, n	LT CDR	X	H1	01.10.93	CAPT(H) DEVPT
Jones, Martin David , BA	LT	X		01.01.95	ORKNEY
Jones, Mark Douglas , BEng	LT(SL)	X	O	01.08.95	702 SQN OSPREY
Jones, Martin Ross , BSc, CEng, MIMechE	LT CDR	E	MESM	01.07.91	RNC DPT NS&TECH
Jones, Matthew Russell , BSc (Act Capt Rm)	LT RM	RM		01.09.91	NP 1002 DIEGOGA
Jones, Nigel Patrick	LT	X	SM	01.02.91	VANGUARD(STBD)
Jones, Paul	LT CDR	X	MCD	01.07.92	MCM1 SEA
Jones, Philip Andrew , MA, pce	CDR	X	PWO(C)	31.12.93	JSDC GREENWICH
Jones, Paul David	LT(SL)	X		01.11.95	DOLPHIN SM SCHL
Jones, Peter Haydn, jsdc	CDR	X	H CH	30.06.89	2SL/CNH
Jones, Paul	LT(SL)	X	P	01.09.94	702 SQN OSPREY
Jones, Peter William , psc	LT CDR	S		01.07.85	PJHQ
Jones, Richard Brian , pce	LT CDR	X	P	16.06.80	MWC GOSPORT
Jones, Russell	SLT(SD)	E	MESM	19.06.95	RNC DPT NS&TECH
Jones, Richard Llewelyn Philipps , MBE, pce(sm), psc	CDR	X	SM	31.12.83	SHAPE BELGIUM
Jones, Richard Mostyn	LT(SL)	X	MW	01.05.94	DRYAD
Jones, Roderick Vernon	SLT(SD)	E	ME	14.06.93	YORK
Jones, Richard William , MSc, CEng, MIMarE	LT CDR	E	ME	01.03.93	CORNWALL
Jones, Stephen Martin	LT(SL)	X	ATC	01.08.93	RAF SHAWBURY
Jones, William Edward Paul	CDR	S	SM	31.12.85	NEPTUNE
Jordan, Andrew Aidan , BA	LT	X		01.09.93	BRITANNIA

Name	Rank	Spec	Sub-spec	Seniority	Where serving
Jordan, Anna Frances	SLT(UCE)	X		01.09.95	DARTMOUTH BRNC
Jordan, Adrian Mark , BDS, LDS RCS(Eng)	SGLTCDR(D)	-		07.12.90	LOAN BRUNEI
Jordan, Christopher Worrall	LT CDR(SD)	X	g	01.10.91	DRYAD
Jordan, Louis	LT(SD)	E	ME	18.06.93	SULTAN
Jordan, Nicholas Stuart	LT(SD)	E	WE	13.06.91	MCM3 SEA
Jordan, Peter David , BEng	LT CDR	E	MESM	01.12.95	MOD (BATH)
Jose, Steven , BA	LT	E	AE	01.03.94	FONA CRANWELL
Joyce, David Andrew , BEng, AMIEE	LT	E	WE	01.12.92	LANCASTER
Joyce, Philip , BSc (Loc Capt Rm)	LT RM	RM		25.04.91	COMACCHIO GP RM
Joyce, Thomas Jeremy	LT	X	P U/T	01.11.91	820 SQN
Joyner, Adam , pce, pcea	LT CDR	X	P	01.05.89	BEAVER
Juckes, Martin Anthony (Act Lt)	SLT(SD)	E	AE(L)	06.09.93	SULTAN
Judd, Simon Alexander	LT(SL)	X	P	01.09.87	FONA
Julian, Timothy Mark	LT(SL)	X	P	16.11.92	771 SK5 SAR
Jury, James Anthony , CEng, MIEE	LT CDR(SL)	E	WE	01.03.78	LOAN DTEO ABRPTH

K

Name	Rank	Spec	Sub-spec	Seniority	Where serving
Karsten, Thomas Michael , BA	CDR	X	PWO(U)	31.12.94	SHEFFIELD
Kassapian, David Lee , BA	LT RM	RM		01.09.90	ASC CAMBERLEY
Kearney, James Richard	LT(SL)	X	FC	01.09.91	HERON
Kearney, Paul Leonard	LT RM	RM		27.04.95	COMACCHIO GP RM
Keay, Howard , FIMgt, pce, pce(sm), psc	CAPT	X	SM	30.06.94	IMS BRUSSELS
Keble, Kenneth Wayne Latimer , pce, pcea	CDR	X	O	31.12.95	JSDC GREENWICH
Keefe, Patrick Charles , BSc	CDR	S		31.12.95	2SL/CNH
Keefe, Sally-Anne , BA, l(2)Fr	LT CDR(SL)	W	S	30.04.92	2SL/CNH
Keegan, William John , BSc, CEng, MIEE, psc	CDR	E	WE	31.12.93	MOD (LONDON)
Keeley, Stephen Peter	LT(SD)	E	MESM	15.06.95	CLYDE MIXMAN1
Keeling, Frank Graham , MBE	LT CDR(SD)	S	S	01.10.91	ARK ROYAL
Keen, Neil , BEng, AMIEE	LT	E	WE	01.06.93	GLASGOW
Keith, Donald , BD, MA	CHAPLAIN	SF		15.05.84	DARTMOUTH BRNC
Keith, John Alexander , BA	SLT(SL)	X		01.01.95	DARTMOUTH BRNC
Kelbie, Ewan , BA, pcea	LT CDR	X	P	01.11.93	800 SQN
Kelk, Stephen John	LT	X	SM	01.07.89	REPULSE(PORT)
Kellett, Andrew , BEng	LT(SL)	E	ME	01.02.95	BATTLEAXE
Kellow, Stephen John	LT(SD)	E	WESM	15.06.90	DG SHIPS CAM HSE
Kelly, Aidan Brendan , BSc	LT(SL)	I		01.11.90	SULTAN
Kelly, Anthony Paul	LT RM(SD)	RM	MTO	01.01.94	COMACCHIO GP RM
Kelly, David Barry , BSc, CEng, MIMarE, MIMechE	LT CDR	E	ME	01.01.81	LOAN DRA HASLAR
Kelly, Howard Clifton , BEng	LT	E	MESM	01.04.94	SCEPTRE
Kelly, John Anson , BEng	LT(SL)	E	ME	01.02.92	EDINBURGH
Kelly, James William , BA	CAPT RM	RM		01.09.89	DARTMOUTH BRNC
Kelly, Martin , BDS	SG LT(D)	-		01.01.92	BF GIBRALTAR(NE)
Kelly, Martin Dominic Richard	LT CDR	S		01.04.85	COLLINGWOOD
Kelly, Nigel	CHAPLAIN	CE		26.05.92	NELSON
Kelly, Philip Michael	2LT(GRAD)	RM		01.09.94	40 CDO RM
Kelly, Richard , pce(sm)	LT CDR	X	SM	03.04.91	NEPTUNE SM1
Kelly, Thomas	LT(SD)	X	MCD	16.12.94	COTTESMORE
Kelly, Timothy Joseph	LT CDR(SD)	X	AV	01.10.93	HQ CDO AVN
Kelly, William Henry , BSc, psc	CAPT	I		31.12.90	SHAPE BELGIUM
Kelynack, Mark	LT(SL)	X	O	16.04.95	810 SQN B FLIGHT
Kemp, Bruce Ian	LT(SL)	X	ATC	01.09.81	RNAS YEOVILTON
Kemp, Michael Stanley	LT CDR(SD)	E	AE(M)	01.10.95	NAVAL DRAFTING
Kemp, Peter John	LT RM	RM	MLDR	01.09.91	RMR TYNE
Kempsell, Ian Douglas , BSc, CEng, MIMarE	LT CDR(SL)	E	ME	01.10.93	DRAKE CBP
Kendrick, Alexander Michael , BA, BEng	SLT	E	WE	01.09.94	CHATHAM
Kendrick, Richard , BA, PGCE	LT(SL)	I		01.03.90	NEPTUNE
Kenealy, Timothy Michael	LT CDR(SD)	X	PT	01.10.92	TEMERAIRE
Kennaugh, Alastair John , BSc, PGCE, psc	CDR	I	SM	31.12.88	2SL/CNH
Kennedy, Angelina , LLB	SLT(SL)	S		01.09.94	CORNWALL
Kennedy, David John , BSc, MIEE	LT CDR(SL)	E	WE	01.03.83	NACISA
Kennedy, Ian	SLT	E	WESM	01.01.95	DARTMOUTH BRNC
Kennedy, Ian James Andrew , BEng	LT CDR	E	ME	01.08.95	MOD (BATH)

Name	Rank	Spec	Sub-spec	Seniority	Where serving
Kennedy, Nigel Henry , BSc, MIMarE, psc	LT CDR	E	ME	01.05.92	LONDON
Kenney, Ronald Paul	LT(SD)	MS		27.07.90	HQ 3 CDO BDE RM
Kennington, Lee Alexander , BSc	LT(SL)	X	O	01.10.94	810 SQN SEAHAWK
Kenny, Stephen James , pce	LT CDR	X	PWO(A)	01.12.93	FOST SEA
Kent, Alan James , BA	LT(SL)	X	O	01.10.94	702 SQN OSPREY
Kent, Mark Arthur	LT	X	PWO(C)	01.08.89	CORNWALL
Kent, Martin David , pce	LT CDR	X	PWO(N)	01.05.89	DRYAD
Kenward, Peter David , BSc, MA, CEng, MRAeS, psc	CDR	E	AE(P)	30.06.95	MOD PE ASC
Kenworthy, Richard Alan (Act Capt Rm)	LT RM	RM		30.04.91	HQ 3 CDO BDE RM
Kerchey, Stephen John Victor , BSc	LT CDR	E	WE	20.01.91	FOST SEA
Kern, Alastair Seymour	LT RM	RM		01.09.93	RM POOLE
Kerr, Adrian Nicholas , BEng	LT	E	WESM	01.01.93	TALENT
Kerr, Alan Thomas Frederick	LT(SD)	X	MW	06.04.95	INVERNESS
Kerr, Deborah Jean , MB, BSc, BMedSc, BCh, ChB	SURG LT	-		01.08.92	RNDHU DERRIFORD
Kerr, Jack	LT(SD)	X	PR	17.12.93	BRITANNIA
Kerr, Jennifer	MID(SL)	S		01.01.95	DARTMOUTH BRNC
Kerr, Mark William Graham , BA, pce, psc	CAPT	X	PWO	31.12.93	CAPTAIN RNP TEAM
Kerr, Robert Gifford , BA, MSc, CEng, FIEE, rcds, jsdc, gw	CAPT	E	WE	30.06.88	MOD (LONDON)
Kerr, Sarah Virginia , BSc	LT(SL)	X		01.02.94	BATTLEAXE
Kerr, William Malcolm McTaggart	LT CDR	X	MCD	09.03.90	DRYAD
Kerridge, Timothy Paul , BSc, pcea	LT(SL)	X	O	16.08.84	EXCHANGE AUSTLIA
Kerry, James Trevor , pce	LT CDR	X	PWO(A)	01.06.86	LOAN BRUNEI
Kershaw, Christopher Robert , MB, BCh, ChB, MA, DCH, LRCP, FRCP, MRCS	SURG CDR	-	CC	30.06.85	RH HASLAR
Kershaw, Damian	SURG SLT	-		27.10.95	DARTMOUTH BRNC
Kershaw, Steven	LT	E	WESM	01.11.89	MOD DIS SEA
Kerslake, Richard William	LT	X	P	01.02.91	815 FLT 206
Kerslake, Stephen Charles	LT CDR(SD)	X	C	01.10.92	2SL/CNH
Kerwood, Richard John	LT(SD)	S	CA	25.07.91	NELSON
Kessler, Mark Lance	LT(SL)	X	MCD	01.11.86	DEF DIVING SCHL
Ketteridge, Brian Peter , psc (Loc)	MAJ(SD)	RM		19.02.93	MOD (LONDON)
Ketteringham, Michael John , BA	LT	X		01.03.94	MANCHESTER
Kettle, Richard Andrew , BA	LT RM	RM		24.04.92	HQRM
Key, Benjamin John	LT CDR	X	O	01.04.96	815 FLT 210
Key, David Frank , pce, pcea	LT CDR	X	P	01.11.91	SOUTHAMPTON
Keyworth, Anthony John	LT	X	P	01.04.89	846 SQN
Kidd, Clive John Charles , BSc, (Eur Ing), CEng, MIEE	LT CDR	E	WE	01.12.82	SCU LEYDENE ACNS
Kidd, James Christian , MSc, psc, gw	CDR	E	WE	31.12.89	COLLINGWOOD
Kidd, Joanna , BA	SLT	X		01.09.93	SHEFFIELD
Kidner, Peter Jonathan , BSc, CEng, FRAeS, psc, psc(m)	CAPT	E	AE	31.12.93	MOD DHSA
Kies, Lawrence Norman , BSc	LT(SL)	I		01.01.94	SULTAN
Kilby, Stewart Edward , pcea	LT CDR	X	O	01.04.96	815 FLT 203
Kilgour, Niall Stuart Roderick , pce, pce(sm), psc	CAPT	X	SM	30.06.92	MONTROSE
Kilmartin, Steven Norman	LT RM	RM		01.09.94	MOD DNR OUTPORTS
Kimball-Smith, Patrick	SLT	E	WE	01.01.94	CORNWALL
Kimberley, Robert , BSc, n	LT(SL)	X		01.07.90	MOD DNR OUTPORTS
Kimmons, Michael , BA	CDR	S		31.12.90	ILLUSTRIOUS
King, Anthony Michael , BSc, MDA, CEng, MRAeS	CDR	E	AE(P)	31.12.91	CINCFLEET
King, Antony Richard	LT(SL)	X	O	01.03.92	849 SQN A FLT
King, Charles Edward William , BA, MILDM	CDR	S		30.06.96	JSDC GREENWICH
King, Craig John	SLT(SL)	X	O	01.06.93	FONA SULTAN
King, David Christopher Michael , BSc (Loc Capt Rm)	LT RM	RM	A/TK	01.09.89	DARTMOUTH BRNC
King, Dean Stewart	LT(SD)	E	WE	22.02.96	COLLINGWOOD
King, Edward Michael , MSc, CEng, MIEE	LT CDR	E	WE	01.06.93	CHATHAM
King, Gordon Charles	SLT(SD)	E	MESM	14.06.93	SCEPTRE
King, John Nicholas Gaunt , BSc, pce	LT CDR	X	PWO(U)	01.07.93	2SL/CNH
King, Nigel Alan , pcea, psc(m)	LT CDR	X	P	01.12.84	FONA

Name	Rank	Spec	Sub-spec	Seniority	Where serving
King, Nicholas William , BEng . . . . LT	E	MESM		01.05.89	NEPTUNE DSQ
King, Paul Christopher , MSc . . . . LT CDR	E	ME		01.09.92	MARLBOROUGH
King, Richard James , BSc . . . . LT(SL)	X	P		01.11.88	849 SQN B FLT
King, Richard John , BSc . . . . LT RM	RM			28.04.94	HQ 3 CDO BDE RM
King, Richard William , BSc, pce, pcea . . . . LT CDR	X	P		16.09.92	CUMBERLAND
King, Steven John . . . . LT(SL)	X	P		16.06.92	849 SQN A FLT
Kingdom, Mark Andrew , BEng . . . . SLT(SL)	X	AE		01.09.94	INVINCIBLE
Kings, Simon John Nicholson , pce, pcea . . . . LT CDR	X	O		01.01.93	DULVERTON
Kingsbury, James Arthur Timothy , BSc (Barrister) . . . LT CDR	S	BAR		01.02.91	FONA
Kingsbury, Simon Hugh , BEng, AMIEE . . . . LT CDR	E	WE		01.04.96	DSSC PTSMTH
Kingston, Ian James . . . . LT(SL)	X	P		01.04.88	846 SQN
Kingwell, John Matthew Leonard , BA, pce . . . . LT CDR	X	PWO(U)		01.05.96	DRYAD
Kinsey, Simon Lowther . . . . SLT(SL)	X			01.09.95	QUORN
Kirby, Christopher John . . . . LT(SD)	X	C		13.12.95	NELSON (PAY)
Kirby, Nicholas Breakspear , BSc, CEng, MIEE, jsdc, psc . . . . CAPT	E	WESM		31.12.87	SULTAN AIB
Kirby, Stephen Redvers , BSc, pce, pcea, psc, ocds(USN) . . . . CDR	X	O		30.06.89	MOD (LONDON)
Kirk, Adrian Christopher . . . . SLT	E	AE		01.01.95	DARTMOUTH BRNC
Kirk, John , TEng, psc . . . . CDR(SD)	E	ME		01.10.95	NAVAL DRAFTING
Kirk, Trevor Leslie , BSc, psc . . . . LT CDR	E	WE		01.06.87	DRAKE CFM
Kirkbright, Keith Leslie Mellor . . . . LT(CS)	-			17.02.91	MOD DNR OUTPORTS
Kirkham, Simon Philip . . . . LT(SL)	X	P		16.08.94	810 SQN OEU
Kirkpatrick, Alison Jane . . . . LT CDR(SL)	W	S		01.10.91	MOD (LONDON)
Kirkpatrick, John , OBE, BSc, AMIEE, jsdc . . . . . . CAPT	E	WESM		31.12.95	DTR BATH
Kirkup, John Paul , BSc . . . . LT CDR	I			01.03.94	CFP SHORE
Kirkwood, James Alistair Delange , LLB, pce . . . . LT CDR	X	PWO(A)		01.04.90	CAMPBELTOWN
Kirkwood, Nicholas Charles , BA . . . . LT CDR	I			01.09.88	NWOOD CIS
Kirkwood, Tristram Andrew Harry , BSc . . . . LT	X			01.11.94	BEAVER
Kissane, Robert Edward Thomas , BEng . . . . LT	E	WE		01.04.89	DGSS BRISTOL
Kistruck, David John . . . . LT(SL)	X	P		01.06.89	899 SQN HERON
Kitchen, Stephen Anthony . . . . LT	E	P		01.01.90	845 SQN
Kite, Robert George Harvey , TEng, AMIMarE . . . . . . LT CDR(SD)	E	ME		01.10.92	EXCELLENT
Knapp, Martin Geoffrey Arthur , pce, psc . . . . CDR	X	C		30.06.84	MOD (LONDON)
Knibbs, Mark , BA, pce . . . . LT CDR	X	PWO(U)		19.06.92	FOST SEA
Knight, Alastair Cameron Fergus , BSc . . . . LT(SL)	X	P		01.08.94	706 SQN SEAHAWK
Knight, Andrew Robert . . . . LT(SL)	X	P		01.10.90	810 SQN SEAHAWK
Knight, Anthony William , BSc, pce . . . . LT CDR	X	PWO(C)		01.02.90	ILLUSTRIOUS
Knight, Damon Ashley , pce . . . . LT CDR	X	PWO(A)		01.04.92	FOSF SEA PTSMTH
Knight, David John , psc . . . . CDR	S			31.12.89	DARTMOUTH BRNC
Knight, Diane Joy . . . . LT	Q			18.01.94	RNDHU DERRIFORD
Knight, Daniel Simon . . . . MID(UCE)	X			01.09.95	GLASGOW
Knight, David William , BSc . . . . LT	X	FC		01.06.93	INVINCIBLE
Knight, Emma . . . . SURG SLT	-			31.10.94	DARTMOUTH BRNC
Knight, Jeremy Denis . . . . LT(SD)	X	EW		13.12.95	EXCHANGE USA
Knight, Keith John , BTech . . . . LT(SD)	E	WESM		24.02.95	CON DCN
Knight, Matthew Sangster . . . . LT(SL)	X			08.08.94	SOMERSET
Knight, Paul James . . . . LT	E	AE		01.05.89	MOD (LONDON)
Knight, Paul Richard , BSc . . . . LT CDR	E	MESM		01.09.93	RNSC GREENWICH
Knight, Robert Harry . . . . LT(SD)	E	MESM		15.06.95	RENOWN(PORT)
Knight, Stephen David . . . . SLT(UCE)(SL)	X	P U/T		01.09.95	DARTMOUTH BRNC
Knights, Robin . . . . LT(SD)	X	PWO(U)		17.12.93	ILLUSTRIOUS
Knill, Robin Lloyd . . . . LT(SD)	S	S		24.07.92	DGA(N) ASE
Knock, Gareth Paul . . . . LT	S			01.10.93	VANGUARD(STBD)
Knott, Michael Bruce . . . . LT(SL)	X			01.02.93	RNSC GREENWICH
Knowles, John Michael , pce, pcea, psc . . . . CDR	X	P		31.12.89	MOD (LONDON)
Knowles, Michael Mark . . . . LT(SD)	S	W		24.07.92	DNPS
Knowling, Philip John , MSc, CEng, MIEE, jsdc . . . . . . CDR	E	AE		31.12.91	MOD (BATH)
Knox, Margaret Mary . . . . LT(FS)	FS			17.04.89	HQRM
Knox, Nicolas OliverGunning , BSc, CEng, MIMarE, pce, psc . . . . CDR	E	MESM		30.06.86	D WORKS (SS)
Kohler, Andrew Philip . . . . LT	X	FC		01.04.94	BIRMINGHAM
Kongialis, James Allyn , BSc . . . . CDR	E	WESM		30.06.89	MOD (LONDON)
Krosnar-Clarke, Steven , MSc . . . . LT(SL)	I			01.06.89	OSPREY
Krykunivsky, Nikolaus Valeric . . . . SLT(SL)	X	ATCU/T		01.05.96	RAF SHAWBURY

Name	Rank	Spec	Sub-spec	Seniority	Where serving
Kurth, Rolf Peter Ernst	LT(SL)	X		01.12.94	DRYAD
Kyd, Jeremy Paul , n	LT	X		01.02.90	RNSC GREENWICH
Kyte, Andrew Jeffrey , BA	LT	S		16.12.88	CHATHAM

L

Name	Rank	Spec	Sub-spec	Seniority	Where serving
Labone, Richard David	LT CDR	X	H1	01.05.90	HECLA
Lacey, Ian Nigel , MSc, PhD	LT CDR	I		16.06.91	NWOOD CIS
Lacey, Stephen Patrick , pcea	LT CDR	X	O	16.05.93	INVINCIBLE
Lacy, David Anthony	CHAPLAIN	RC		04.08.81	DRAKE CBP
Lade, Christopher John , BSc, pce	LT CDR	X	MCD	01.01.90	PJHQ
Lages, Anthony Ernest , BA, BSc	LT CDR(SL)	I		01.10.89	SHAPE BELGIUM
Laggan, Peter John	LT(SD)	S	W	11.12.92	NAVSOUTH ITALY
Laing, Iain	LT	E	WE	01.09.93	SOUTHAMPTON
Laird, Colin Rory , pce, pcea, psc	CDR	X	O	31.12.85	MOD DNR OUTPORTS
Lake, Peter Howard	LT(SD)	E	ME	15.02.91	CENTURION
Lake, Richard Victor , MA (Act Capt)	CDR	X	O	31.12.86	2SL/CNH
Lamb, Andrew Gordon	LT	X		01.12.94	DRYAD
Lamb, Christopher Francis , BSc	LT	X	SM	01.03.92	FOSM NWOOD OPS
Lamb, Kathryn Georgina , BDS, DGDP RCS(UK)	SGLTCDR(D)	-		18.01.95	DRAKE CBP
Lamb, Robert , jsdc, pce, pcea, psc	CDR	X	P	31.12.90	MOD (LONDON)
Lamb, Selina Katherine , BA	LT(SL)	X		01.02.94	ENDURANCE
Lamb-Hughes, Grenville , BSc, CEng, FRAeS, psc (Commodore)	CAPT	E	AE	30.06.89	MOD PE ASC
Lambert, Allison	LT(SL)	X	X	09.08.92	FOST DPORT SHORE
Lambert, Anthony Wayne , MB, BS, FRCS	SURG LTCDR	-	GS	01.08.91	NELSON (PAY)
Lambert, Brian , pce	LT CDR	X	PWO(A)	02.06.88	CHATHAM
Lambert, Ian Robert	SLT(SL)	X	P U/T	01.05.93	HERON
Lambert, Kevin John , pcea, psc	LT CDR	X	P	16.11.88	MWC GOSPORT
Lambert, Nicholas Richard , BSc, pce	CDR	X	PWO(A)	31.12.95	BRAZEN
Lambert, Paul , BSc, MPhil, pce, pce(sm)	CAPT	X	SM	30.06.96	DRYAD
Lambert, Patrick Bernard , TEng, AMIMarE	LT CDR(SD)	E	ME	01.10.90	NELSON
Lambert-Humble, Stephen , BDS, MSc	SGCAPT(D)	-		31.12.95	MOD (LONDON)
Lambie, Timothy James	LT(SL)	X	MCD	01.09.91	EXCHANGE FRANCE
Lambourn, Peter Neil , pce, pcea, psc	LT CDR	X	O	01.12.89	ATHERSTONE
Lambourne, David John , BSc	LT(SL)	X	P	01.02.88	706 SQN SEAHAWK
Lamont, Neil John	LT	X	SM	01.07.91	VIGILANT(PORT)
Lancashire, Antony Craig , MA	2LT(GRAD)	RM		01.09.95	CTCRM LYMPSTONE
Lancaster, Andrew Nigel	LT(SL)	X	O	01.09.91	750 SQN OBS SCH
Lancaster, Craig	2LT(GRAD)	RM		01.09.94	42 CDO RM
Lancaster, Neil	SLT(SL)	X		01.05.94	LIVERPOOL
Lander, Martin Christopher , pce, pcea, psc	CDR	X	O	30.06.95	MOD (LONDON)
Landrock, Graham John	LT CDR	X	MCD	01.09.93	YORK
Lane, Arthur William Spencer	LT	X	SM	01.04.90	TIRELESS
Lane, David Fredrick	CDR	S		30.06.92	FONA
Lane, Gavin Barry Douglas , pce(sm)	CAPT	X	SM	30.06.90	DRYAD MWC
Lane, Geoffrey Thomas , TEng, AMIMarE	CDR(SD)	E	ME	01.10.91	SULTAN
Lane, Michael George , BSc, psc	CAPT	S		31.12.95	2SL/CNH
Lane, Roger Guy Tyson , OBE, jsdc, psc(m), fsc	LT COL	RM	WTO	30.06.95	42 CDO RM
Lane, Robert Michael	LT(SD)	E	ME	18.02.88	NBC PORTSMOUTH
Lane, Richard Norton	LT	X		01.04.89	DRYAD
Lang, Andrew James Nicholas , BEng	LT(SL)	E	AE	01.04.89	RNSC GREENWICH
Langbridge, David Charles , MSc	CDR	E	MESM	30.06.93	JSDC GREENWICH
Langhorn, Nigel	CDR	X	PWO(A)	30.06.96	CINCFLEET
Langley, Eric Steven , pce	LT CDR	X	PWO(A)	01.02.93	EXCHANGE CANADA
Langmead, Michael Anthony	LT(SD)	E	AE(M)	14.10.88	FIELD GUN FAA
Langrill, Mark Philip , BEng, MA	LT(SL)	I		01.09.92	SULTAN
Langrill, Tracey Jane , MA	LT(SL)	X		01.02.95	RICHMOND
Langrish, Gary James	LT(SL)	X	P	01.10.92	899 SQN OEU
Langrishe, James Hoadly , pce	LT CDR	X	PWO(U)	16.04.81	MOD (LONDON)
Lankester, Peter , BTech, pce, pcea, psc	CDR	X	P	30.06.92	BDS WASHINGTON
Lankester, Timothy John , BSc, psc	CDR	E	ME	30.06.92	MOD (BATH)
Lanni, Martin Nicholas	LT(SL)	X	P	01.09.95	819 SQN
Lansdell, Richard John , BSc, psc(a)	CDR	E	AE	31.12.89	MOD DHSA

Name	Rank	Spec	Sub-spec	Seniority	Where serving
Large, John Lawrence	LT CDR	S	SM	17.01.90	FOSM NWOOD HQ
Large, Stephen Andrew , BEng	LT	E	ME	01.03.95	CHATHAM
Larkins, Philip Douglas	LT(SL)	X	P	01.10.93	815 SQN HQ
Larmour, David Rutherford , pce	CDR	X	O	31.12.89	2SL/CNH
Larmuth, James David Downes	LT(SL)	X	SM	01.08.95	FOSM NWOOD OPS
Lashbrooke, David Piers , BSc, CEng, MRAeS, MBIM, psc	CAPT	E	AE	30.06.90	RCDS
Latham, Neil Degge , MSc, CEng, MIMechE, jsdc	CAPT	E	ME	30.06.96	MOD (LONDON)
Lauchlan, Robert Alexander , BSc	LT	E	WESM	01.08.92	VIGILANT(PORT)
Laughton, Fiona Ann	LT(SL)	W	I	04.01.92	PJHQ
Laughton, Peter	SLT	X		01.01.94	DARTMOUTH BRNC
Launchbury, Stephen Joseph	CAPT RM(SL)	RM		01.10.95	45 CDO RM
Laurence, Timothy James Hamilton , MVO, BSc, pce	CAPT	X	PWO(U)	30.06.95	CUMBERLAND
Lauretani, Andrew Stephen David	LT(SL)	X	P	16.10.89	705 SQN SEAHAWK
Laurie, James Richard , IEng, FIEIE	LT CDR(SD)	E	WE	01.10.87	DG SHIPS CAM HSE
Lauste, William Emile , BA	LT(SL)	I		01.03.87	DGA(N) ASE
Laverty, Robert Edwin , ARICS, jsdc	CDR	X	H CH	30.06.81	MOD (LONDON)
Laverty, Robert Edwin , BA	LT	X		01.02.95	SOVEREIGN
Lavery, John Patrick	LT CDR	S		16.05.95	MOD (LONDON)
Lavin, Gerard Joseph , BEng	LT(SL)	E	ME	01.09.93	SULTAN
Law, Alistair Neil , OBE, pce, psc, ocds(Can)	CDR	X	O	30.06.80	SHAPE BELGIUM
Law, John	LT CDR	X	MCD	27.03.95	DRYAD
Lawler, Jon Andrew	LT CDR(SL)	X	P	01.10.95	899 SQN HERON
Lawler, John Daniel	LT CDR(SD)	X	C	01.10.88	DGCIS BRISTOL
Lawrance, Gregory Michael	LT(SL)	X	P	16.05.92	849 SQN B FLT
Lawrence, Michael John , pcea	LT CDR(SL)	X	P	01.09.79	FONA SEAHAWK
Lawrence, Stephen Paul , n	LT CDR(SL)	X	H CH	01.10.93	LOAN HYDROG
Lawrence, Steven Raymond	LT(SD)	E	ME	17.02.89	FOSTSEA NBCDDVPT
Laws, Philip Eric Arthur , LLB	LT CDR	S		16.02.93	2SL/CNH
Lawson, Geoffrey John	LT(SD)	X	tas	13.12.95	ILLUSTRIOUS
Lawson, Louise Linda	SURG LT	-		01.08.94	RFANSU (ARGUS)
Lawson, Robin Ian , n	LT CDR	X	H1	02.08.93	CDRE MFP
Lawson, Richard Keith	LT(SL)	X	O	16.03.96	814 SQN
Lawson, Suzanne	SLT(SL)	X		01.05.93	DRYAD
Lawson, Stephen Jonathan , pce(sm)	LT CDR	X	SM	01.09.91	ACE SRGN GIBLTAR
Lawton, Andrew Charles Richard , BSc	LT CDR	E	ME	01.11.85	FOSF
Lawton, Gary Spencer	LT(SL)	X	SM	01.01.93	NEPTUNE BASE OPS
Laycock, Antony , BSc	LT(SL)	X	O	01.03.95	702 SQN OSPREY
Laycock, Patrick James	LT CDR(SD)	S	W	01.10.91	DRYAD
Layland, Stephen	LT CDR	X	PWO(N)	01.03.92	INVINCIBLE
Le Manquais, Terence William David , BSc, MRIN, psc	CDR	I		30.06.86	NELSON RELEASE
Lea, John	LT	X	O	01.01.90	849 SQN HQ
Lea, Jeffrey Henry Arthur , BSc, CEng, MIMarE, psc	CDR	E	ME	31.12.94	CDRE MFP
Lea, Sebastian Augustine Pollard , n	LT(SL)	X		01.11.91	SHEFFIELD
Leach, Sir Henry (Conyers), GCB, psc	ADM OF FLEET			01.12.82	
Leach, Simon	LT(SL)	X	P	01.04.92	845 SQN
Leach, Sarah	SLT	E	ME	01.09.93	DARTMOUTH BRNC
Leaman, Richard Derek , OBE, pce	CDR	X	PWO(A)	30.06.91	MOD (LONDON)
Leaney, Michael John , BSc	LT CDR	X	MCD	01.03.90	CDRE MFP
Leaning, David John	LT(SD)	E	MESM	15.10.93	DRAKE CFM
Leaning, Mark Vincent , MA, pcea, psc	LT CDR	X	P	01.09.91	819 SQN
Lear, Jonathan James Bailey , OBE, psc	MAJ	RM	MOR	30.06.89	CTCRM
Leatherby, James Hawton	CDR	S	SM	31.12.90	FOSM NWOOD HQ
Leaver, Charmian Elizabeth Lucy , MA, MSc	LT(SL)	I	METOC	01.07.91	RNAS YEOVILTON
Leavey, Brian Michael , MA, MSc, FBIM	CAPT	I		30.06.89	NELSON
Leavey, John William	T/LT(SDT)	X	SM	18.06.93	MWC GOSPORT
Ledingham, Herbert John , pcea, psc(m)	CDR	X	P	30.06.90	PJHQ
Lee, Daniel John , pce, psc	LT CDR	X	PWO(A)	01.08.87	FOSF SEA PTSMTH
Lee, Jonathan Coling	LT CDR(SL)	X	MW	01.10.94	DRYAD
Lee, Matthew Martin	LT CDR(SL)	X	ATC	01.10.91	RNAS PORTLAND
Lee, Nigel David	SLT(SL)	X		01.09.94	MARLBOROUGH
Lee, Nicholas Foden , BEng, MIMechE, pcea	LT(SL)	X	P	01.04.85	706 SQN SEAHAWK
Lee, Oliver Andrew (P/2lt)	2LT(SSLC)	RM		28.10.91	RE ENTRY

Name	Rank	Spec	Sub-spec	Seniority	Where serving
Lee, Peter Alan , BEng, AMIMechE	LT	E	ME	01.08.91	NP1044
Lee, Philip Marsden , BSc	LT(SL)	X	P U/T	01.10.94	705 SQN SEAHAWK
Lee, Robert	LT(SL)	X	P	01.10.91	848 SQN HERON
Lee, Steven Patrick	LT RM	RM		27.04.95	42 CDO RM
Lee, Steven Yiu Lam , BEng	LT(SL)	E	WE	01.01.96	COLLINGWOOD
Lee, Warren	SLT	E	WE	01.09.94	DARTMOUTH BRNC
Leech, Kevin Peter Hollister	LT(SL)	I	METOC	01.01.91	HECLA
Leeder, Roger John	LT(CS)	-		17.02.91	MOD DNR OUTPORTS
Leedham, Howard Norman , MBE	LT CDR	X	P	16.07.92	MOD (LONDON)
Leeming, Robert John , BSc	CDR	E	ME	30.06.91	MOD (BATH)
Lees, Edward Charles , n	LT	X		01.02.91	ILLUSTRIOUS
Lees, Rodney Burnett (Barrister)	RADM	-	BAR	21.02.95	2SL/CNH
Lees, Simon Neville	LT(SL)	I		02.09.93	SEAHAWK
Legg, Malcolm Robert , pcea, psc(a)	CDR	X	O	30.06.90	DRYAD MWC
Leggett, Christopher Charles , TEng, AMINucE	LT CDR(SD)	E	MESM	01.10.89	NEPTUNE DSQ
Leggett, Stephen Edward	LT CDR	E	AE	13.01.88	RNAS PORTLAND
Leigh, John , osc(us)	CAPT RM	RM	MLDR	01.09.89	HQRM
Leigh, Mark Andrew , BSc	LT	X		01.02.93	SHEFFIELD
Leigh, Siobhan	LT(SL)	W		25.07.91	DOLPHIN SM SCHL
Leigh-Smith, Simon John , BM, BCh	SURG LT	-		01.08.91	RNDHU DERRIFORD
Leighton, Barry , FRSA	CAPT	S		31.12.89	2SL/CNH
Leighton, Matthew Richard , BA	SLT(SL)	X	P U/T	01.01.95	DARTMOUTH BRNC
Leitch, Iain Robertson , BSc	LT	X	PWO(A)	01.10.88	DRYAD
Lemkes, Paul Douglas , pce	LT CDR	X	PWO(A)	01.03.93	EXETER
Lemon, Robert Gordon Arthur , BSc	LT CDR	E	WESM	01.09.84	DGSS BRISTOL
Lemon, Robin William George	LT RM	RM		01.09.93	HQRM
Lennon, John	LT CDR(SD)	X	C	01.04.84	MOD (LONDON)
Lensh, Russell MacKenzie , BSc	LT(SL)	I		01.06.90	MOD DGSWS BATH
Leonard, Mark	LT(SL)	E	WE	01.09.89	HQ DFTS
Lett, Jonathan David	LT	X		01.07.93	WESTMINSTER
Letts, AndrewJohn , BEng, AMIEE	LT	E	WE	01.07.95	COLLINGWOOD
Levine, Andrew John	LT RM	RM		29.04.96	CTCRM
Lew-Gor, Simione Tomasi Warren	SURG LT	-		05.09.95	CTCRM
Lewin, The Lord, KG, GCB, LVO, DSC, idc, psc	ADM OF FLEET			06.07.79	
Lewins, Grant	LT(SD)	S	W	08.04.94	HERON
Lewis, Andrew James , BA, BEng	SLT	E	ME	01.09.94	BEAVER
Lewis, Benjamin Charles , BSc	SLT(SL)	X	P U/T	01.01.95	DARTMOUTH BRNC
Lewis, Catherine Anne	SURG LT	-		31.08.93	BRAZEN
Lewis, David Arthur , pce, psc	CAPT	X	AWO(A)	30.06.93	BEAVER
Lewis, David James	LT(SL)	X	O	01.07.90	848 SQN HERON
Lewis, David John , BEng	LT	E	WE	01.09.93	BIRMINGHAM
Lewis, David Malcolm John , MBE	LT CDR	E	ME	26.04.90	FOSF NORTHWOOD
Lewis, Douglas Raymond Snell , CBE, FBIM, FRSA, FIMgt, psc (Commodore)	CAPT	S		30.06.89	MOD (LONDON)
Lewis, Gary David	LT CDR	S		01.09.89	DRAKE BSO(W)
Lewis, Guy David , BEng	LT(SL)	E	ME	01.11.93	LONDON
Lewis, John Keene , BSc, BEng	LT CDR	E	WESM	01.11.93	TRAFALGAR
Lewis, Keith	SLT(SD)	X		03.04.94	CATTISTOCK
Lewis, Neil Melwyn , BSc	LT CDR	I	SM	27.10.91	NELSON RNSETT
Lewis, Peter Reginald , pce	LT CDR	X	PWO(U)	21.11.86	IT S SEA
Lewis, Richard	LT(SL)	X	O	01.05.86	EXCHANGE USA
Lewis, Robbie James , BSc	LT RM	RM		28.04.94	40 CDO RM
Lewis, Shaun , MIL, psc, I(1)Ch	LT CDR	S	SM	16.02.90	FOSNNI/NBC CLYDE
Lewis, Stephen Bernard , pce, psc	LT CDR	X	PWO(U)	01.01.87	COMAW SEA
Lewis, Simon John , BSc	LT(SL)	I		01.01.93	DRYAD
Lewis, Sara Jane , LLB	SLT	S		01.09.94	INVINCIBLE
Lewis, Timothy John	LT CDR	X	MCD	05.02.95	DRYAD
Lewis, Timothy John	CHAPLAIN	CE		28.11.89	FOSF SEA DEVNPT
Ley, Alastair Blevins	LT	X	SM	01.11.95	VICTORIOUS(PORT)
Ley, Jonathan Ashley	LT	X		01.08.92	GLOUCESTER
Leyden, Tristan Neil	2LT	RM		01.09.94	COMACCHIO GP RM
Leyshon, Brian Stuart , pce, pcea	LT CDR	X	P	16.03.83	PJHQ

Name	Rank	Spec	Sub-spec	Seniority	Where serving
Leyshon, Robert John , BDS	SG LT(D)	-		09.01.94	CINCFLEET
Leyshon, Timothy David	LT	S		16.09.90	LIVERPOOL
Lias, Carl David , BEng	LT(SL)	E	MESM	01.05.88	MOD (BATH)
Lidbetter, Scott , pce (Commodore)	CAPT	X	P	31.12.92	HERON
Liddle, Stephen Johnstone	LT RM	RM		01.09.94	2LI PADERBORN
Liggins, Michael Philip , BSc	LT(SL)	X	P	01.03.90	HERON
Liggins, Steven John , MB, BSc, BDS, BCh, FDS, FDS RCSEdin	SGLTCDR(D)	-	SOSM	01.03.89	CENTURION
Light, Alexander John	LT(SL)	X	P	16.03.92	NP 1061
Lightbody, Craig Stewart , BA	LT RM	RM		01.09.93	CTCRM
Lightfoot, Charles David , BSc, pce(sm)	LT CDR	X	SM	01.07.90	FOSM FASLANE
Lightfoot, Christopher Morrison , pce, psc	CDR	X	PWO(N)	30.06.89	CFP SHORE
Lightfoot, Robert Andrew , BSc	LT CDR	X	ATC	16.06.90	RNAS CULDROSE
Lilburn, Lawrence Kevin , BSc	LT(SL)	X	P	01.12.92	845 SQN
Lilley, David John , BSc, pce	LT CDR	X	O	01.07.91	DARTMOUTH BRNC
Lincoln, Keith James	LT	E	WE	01.07.95	COLLINGWOOD
Linderman, Ian Ronald	LT(SL)	I		01.01.91	42 CDO RM
Lindley, Nicholas Paul , BSc	CAPT RM	RM		01.09.93	ASC CAMBERLEY
Lindley, Richard Anthony , MIEE, MBIM, psc	CDR	E	WE	30.06.88	CFM PORTSMOUTH
Lindsay, David , BEng	LT(SL)	X	P U/T	01.09.91	800 SQN
Lindsay, Gordon	LT(SD)	E	WESM	09.06.89	CSST SHORE FSLN
Lindsay, Ian Barry	SLT(SL)	X	O	21.01.95	849 SQN HQ
Lindsay, Irvine Graham	LT CDR	X	SM	01.04.96	TRIUMPH
Lindsey, Richard	LT(SL)	X	SM	01.06.95	DOLPHIN SM SCHL
Lineker, Robert John , BSc, CEng, MIEE	CDR	E	WESM	30.06.93	MOD CSSE USA
Lines, James Micheal	LT CDR	S		16.11.95	BRAZEN
Ling, Christopher , BSc	SLT	E	AE	01.09.93	SULTAN
Ling, John William Legrys , BEng	LT(SL)	X	O	01.04.95	SEAHAWK
Lingard, David Malcolm Hood , BSc, CEng, FIEE, MISecM	CDR	E	WE	30.06.82	SA ANKARA
Linscott, Philip Anthony	LT(SL)	X	P	16.08.89	819 SQN
Linstead-Smith, Peter John , BSc, MBA, MIEE	CDR	I	SM	31.12.81	2SL/CNH FOTR
Lintern, Robert David	LT	X	H2	01.10.94	RNAS CULDROSE
Lippiett, Richard John , MBE, rcds, jsdc, pce, psc (Commodore)	CAPT	X	PWO	12.12.88	DRYAD
Lipscomb, Paul , BSc	LT CDR	E	MESM	01.11.95	DTR BARROW
Lison, Andrew Christopher , BEng	LT	E	AE	01.05.92	800 SQN
Lister, Andrew	LT(SL)	X	P	16.06.93	845 SQN
Lister, John Andrew , pce	CDR	X	O	31.12.88	RAF AWC
Lister, John Saille	LT CDR	S		16.11.84	MOD DNR OUTPORTS
Lister, Mark	LT	X	SM	01.01.89	DOLPHIN SM SCHL
Lister, Simon	LT(SD)	X	SM	08.04.94	DOLPHIN SM SCHL
Lister, Simon Robert , MSc, AMIMechE, I(1)Ru	CDR	E	MESM	31.12.93	MOD (BATH)
Lister, Stephen Richard	LT CDR	S	SM	01.04.93	CINCFLEET
Litchfield, Julian Felix	LT CDR	S		16.07.93	2SL/CNH
Litster, Alan (Loc Capt Rm)	LT RM	RM	LC	01.09.91	COCHRANE
Little, Charles Stewart Anderson , BSc, pce, pce(sm)	LT CDR	X	SM	01.02.90	MOD (BATH)
Little, Graeme Terence , BEng	LT CDR	E	ME	01.01.96	MOD (BATH)
Little, Nicholas Richmond , BSc, pce	LT CDR	X	PWO(U)	01.06.88	2SL/CNH
Little, Rhoderick McKeand , BSc, CDipAF, CEng, MIEE, psc	CDR	E	WESM	30.06.90	MOD (LONDON)
Little, Simon Gregory , BSc	LT	X		01.03.95	BLACKWATER
Littleboy, Martin Nelson , MPhil, pce, psc, I(2)Ru	CAPT	X	AWO(A)	31.12.94	MOD (LONDON)
Livesey, John Edward	SLT(SL)	X		01.12.94	VANGUARD(STBD)
Livesey, Paul , BSc, PGCE	LT CDR(SL)	I		01.10.88	NEPTUNE
Livett, Michael William , BSc, ACMA	LT CDR	S	CMA	16.05.83	2SL/CNH FOTR
Livingstone, Alan James	LT RM	RM		01.09.90	ASC CAMBERLEY
Livingstone, Charles Edward , BSc	LT CDR	E	WE	01.10.86	ORDNANCE BOARD
Livingstone, David Lionel Harold , DSC, pcea	LT CDR	X	P	01.12.89	MOD (LONDON)
Livingstone, Ian	CHAPLAIN	SF		13.08.90	SEAHAWK
Llewelyn, Barry	LT CDR(SD)	S	CAT	01.10.95	BRITANNIA
Llewelyn, Kevin	LT(SL)	X	ATC	16.10.85	RNAS CULDROSE
Lloyd, Christopher John (Act Lt Cdr)	LT(SD)	MS		02.08.88	CDO LOG REGT RM
Lloyd, David Philip John	LT CDR	S		01.09.91	MOD (BATH)
Lloyd, Geraint Wyn , BEng	LT(SL)	E	ME	01.04.92	CUMBERLAND

Name	Rank	Spec	Sub-spec	Seniority	Where serving
Lloyd, Paul Robert , pce	LT CDR	X	PWO(N)	01.05.92	FOST SEA
Lloyd, Paul Stephen	LT CDR(SL)	X	PWO(A)	01.10.94	HERON
Lloyd, Stephen John , MSc, CEng, MIMarE, psc	CDR	E	MESM	30.06.94	MOD (BATH)
Lloyd, Susan , BSc	LT(SL)	I		01.09.90	JSIO ASHFORD SEA
Loane, Michael MacAire	LT(SL)	X	MCD	01.06.93	DRYAD
Lobley, Richard Arthur , BEng	LT CDR	E	MESM	01.09.95	NEPTUNE DSQ
Lochrane, Alexandre Edmond Ross	LT CDR	X	SM	01.07.95	DRYAD
Lock, Andrew Glen David (Loc Capt Rm)	2LT	RM		28.04.93	NP 1061
Lock, Willam Robert , BDS, MSc, DGDP RCS(UK), LDS RCS(Eng)	SGCDR(D)	-		30.06.83	NELSON
Locke, Simon Alastair , BSc, MIEE, psc	CAPT	E	AE	30.06.93	EXCHANGE AUSTLIA
Lockett, David John	LT	X		01.04.96	ARGYLL
Lockwood, Ian Terry , psc	LT CDR	S		08.07.92	NELSON
Lockwood, Roger Graham , BA, rcds, jsdc	CAPT	S		31.12.91	2SL/CNH
Lockwood, Richard John Stanley , MSc, CEng, MIMarE, AMINucE	LT CDR	E	MESM	19.04.84	2SL/CNH FOTR
Lockyer, Roger William , jsdc, pce	CAPT	X	PWO(N)	30.06.90	2SL/CNH
Lodge, Christopher Norman , BEng	LT(SL)	I		01.02.93	SULTAN
Lodge, Stephen Gary , BDS	SG LT(D)	-		29.03.92	45 CDO RM
Lofthouse, Ian , MA	LT CDR	E	MESM	01.12.88	2SL/CNH
Logan, Joseph Majella	LT(SL)	X	FC	01.10.91	EXCHANGE RAF UK
Logan, Robert	LT(SL)	I		21.06.91	SULTAN
Lomax, Debra	SLT(SL)	X	O	01.01.95	706 SQN SEAHAWK
Lombard, Didier , pce, pce(sm), odc(Fr)	CDR	X	SM	31.12.91	MOD CSSE LONDON
London, Martin Richard	LT(SL)	X	P	01.05.82	800 SQN
Loneragan, Michael John , MSc, psc, gw	CDR	E	WE	30.06.95	NWOOD CIS
Long, Anthony Donald	LT	X	O	16.05.90	DRYAD
Long, Adrian Montague , BEng, AMIEE	LT	E	WE	01.04.92	RNSC GREENWICH
Long, Derek Ray	LT CDR	X	PWO(A)	17.02.83	NAVAL DRAFTING
Long, Michael Selden	LT(SL)	X	MW	01.04.96	CATTISTOCK
Long, Nicholas Andrew , MSc, CEng, MIEE	LT CDR	E	WE	01.05.91	MOD (LONDON)
Long, Philip John , MBE, jsdc, pce	CDR	X	PWO(U)	30.06.94	MOD (LONDON)
Long, Stuart Gemmell , BSc	LT(SL)	X		01.11.94	BEAVER
Long, William Gerald Hanslip	LT(SL)	X	P	01.12.93	2SL/CNH
Longbottom, Christopher John , MEng, MSc, CEng, MIMarE, MIMechE, psc	CDR	E	MESM	30.06.95	SSC DGSM BATH
Longstaff, Richard , MSRP	LT(SD)	E	WE	13.06.86	COLLINGWOOD
Loosley, David Peter , BSc	LT	X		01.03.93	CORNWALL
Lord, Andrew Stephen , BA, MEng, PGCE	LT CDR(SL)	I		01.09.87	NEPTUNE
Lord, David Anthony , MBE, MA, MBIM, pcea	LT CDR(SL)	X	P	01.09.86	ASC CAMBERLEY
Lord, Martin	LT(SD)	E	WE	15.06.90	CWTA PTSMTH
Lord, Richard John , MSc, jsdc	CAPT	E	WE	30.06.92	BF GIBRALTAR(NE)
Lord, Richard James	LT(SL)	X	P	01.10.94	FONA VALLEY
Loring, Andrew , BSc	LT CDR	E	ME	01.03.93	BOXER
Lort, Timothy Esmond	LT CDR(SL)	X	P	01.10.95	845 SQN
Lott, John , psc(m), fsc (Loc Lt Col)	MAJ	RM	A/TK	30.06.86	SACLANT USA
Louden, Carl	SLT(SD)	X	C	23.07.95	DRYAD
Loughran, David William	LT(SL)	X	O	01.03.89	EXCHANGE RAF UK
Loughran, Terence William , pcea, psc, ocds(Can)	RADM	-	P	01.06.95	FONA
Lovatt, Graham John	LT(SL)	X	FC	01.04.95	MANCHESTER
Lovatt, Iain William Muir , BEng	LT	E	WE	01.09.95	COLLINGWOOD
Love, Richard	SLT(SL)	E	AE	01.05.95	DARTMOUTH BRNC
Love, Robert Thomas , BSc, CEng, FIMarE, psc	CDR	E	ME	30.06.90	MOD (LONDON)
Love, Tristram Simon Nicholas , BEng	LT	E	WESM	01.07.93	MWC GOSPORT
Lovegrove, Raymond Anthony , MSc, CEng, MIEE	LT	E	WE	01.10.88	LOAN DRA FARN
Lovegrove, Tracie Evelym , BSc	LT	X		01.12.93	EXETER
Lovell, David John , pce(sm)	LT CDR	X	SM	16.11.91	MOD (LONDON)
Lovell, Richard John , BSc	LT	X		01.01.95	BOXER
Lovelock, Richard Benjamin , psc(m)	MAJ	RM		30.06.94	HQRM
Lovelock, Roger Francis , BSc	LT CDR	E	WE	01.09.74	MOD DGSW PTSMTH
Lovett, Michael John , BSc (Act Cdr)	CDR	E	WE	30.06.96	DG SHIPS CAM HSE
Lovett, Richard Frederick , MSc, DipEd, nadc	CDR	I	METOC	30.06.80	NELSON

Name	Rank	Spec	Sub-spec	Seniority	Where serving
Low, Christopher David Tullis , MB, BCh, ChB, FRCSEd	SURG LTCDR	-		01.08.91	NELSON (PAY)
Low, Iain Alistair Duncan , MA, pce, pcea	LT CDR	X	P	01.07.88	FONA
Low, Mark Edward	LT(SD)	E	WESM	13.06.91	CWTA PTSMTH
Lowe, Julian Charles , BEng, BTech	LT	E	ME	01.08.91	SULTAN
Lowe, Stanley Alan	LT CDR(SD)	S	CAT	01.10.94	COVENTRY
Lowe, Stuart Michael , BEng	LT	E	WE	01.12.92	WESTMINSTER
Lowe, Timothy Miles , pce	CDR	X	PWO(N)	31.12.95	DRYAD
Lower, Iain Stuart , BSc, n	LT	X		01.10.91	LIVERPOOL
Lowes, Christopher	LT(SD)	E	WE	05.06.92	FOSF
Lowson, Roderick Mark	LT	X	PWO(A)	01.04.89	ILLUSTRIOUS
Lowther, Andrew Damon , BSc	2LT(GRAD)	RM		01.09.95	CTCRM LYMPSTONE
Lowther, James Marcus , BA, n	LT(SL)	X		01.07.90	RICHMOND
Loxdale, Patrick Henry , MB, BS, FRCS	SURG LTCDR	-		01.08.90	NELSON (PAY)
Loxdale, Susan Jane , MB, BS	SURG LTCDR	-		01.08.95	NELSON
Loynes, Philip Ronald , LLB, psc(m)	MAJ	RM		31.12.94	HQRM
Luard, James Richard , BSc, CEng, MRAeS, psc	CAPT	E	AE	30.06.90	FONA
Lucey, Richard Noel , pce	CDR	X	PWO(C)	30.06.89	MOD (LONDON)
Luckraft, Christopher John , BD, AKC	CHAPLAIN	CE		05.08.87	HQ CDO AVN
Lucocq, Nicholas , BSc	LT(SL)	X		01.08.95	ATHERSTONE
Lugg, John	ACT LT RM(SD)	RM		01.01.96	RM DIV ASMT
Luker, Geoffrey Peter	LT CDR	X	PWO(A)	01.03.83	CWTA PTSMTH
Lumsden, Peter , BEng	SLT	X		01.09.94	DARTMOUTH BRNC
Lunn, Adam Christopher , pce, pcea	LT CDR	X	P	01.06.94	GLASGOW
Lunn, David Vaughan , MB, BCh, ChB, DA, FFARCS	SURG CDR	-	CA	30.06.91	RNDHU DERRIFORD
Lunn, James Francis Clive , BSc, CEng, MIMarE, MIMechE, psc	CDR	E	MESM	31.12.93	MOD (LONDON)
Lunn, Mark Henry Bernard , BSc	LT	E	MESM	01.07.92	SPLENDID
Lunn, Robert , BSc.............................	LT RM	RM		01.09.92	CTCRM
Lunn, Thomas Ramsay	LT	X		01.01.95	GUERNSEY
Luscombe, Michael David , pcea	LT(SL)	X	P	16.07.88	EXCHANGE AUSTLIA
Lusted, Roy Peter	LT(SD)	E	AE(L)	13.10.89	819 SQN
Lustman, Arnold Marc	LT	S	SM	25.09.90	TALENT
Lyall, Alistair Jonathan , MBE, jsdc, pce(sm)	CAPT	X	SM	30.06.92	CAPTAIN SM2
Lycett, Brian Lewis , IEng, MIEEIE	LT CDR(SD)	E	WE	01.10.87	FOSF
Lyddon, Anthony Charles , jsdc, pce	CAPT	X	AWO(C)	30.06.90	MOD (LONDON)
Lydiate, Gary , pce	LT CDR	X	PWO(A)	01.01.95	MANCHESTER
Lye, David James , psc	CDR	X	H CH	31.12.92	HECLA
Lygo, Martin Howard , MB, BS, MA	SURG LTCDR	-	SM	28.08.91	NELSON (PAY)
Lynch, Derek John Martin , pce	LT CDR	X	AWO(C)	01.07.79	LOAN CDA NAG
Lynch, Geoffrey Philip	T/LT(SDT)	X	EW	10.06.94	DRYAD
Lynch, Michael , MA, psc	LT CDR	S	SM	24.03.91	RALEIGH
Lynch, Patrick Anthony	LT CDR(SD)	E	AE(M)	01.10.92	FONA
Lynch, Rory Denis Fenton , BA, I(1)Sp	LT(SL)	X	P	16.04.90	849 SQN HQ
Lynch, Stephen	LT(SL)	X	O	01.08.91	EXCHANGE RAF UK
Lynn, Ian Herbert	SLT	X		01.01.93	FOSF
Lynn, Robert Alan	LT CDR(SD)	S	W	01.10.89	RH HASLAR
Lynn, Steven Robert	LT	E	WE	01.04.90	DGSS BRISTOL
Lyons, Alan	SLT(SL)	E	WE	01.05.95	DARTMOUTH BRNC
Lyons, Michael	SLT	E	MESM	01.01.94	FOSM NWOOD OPS

M

MacArthur, Malcolm James	LT(SL)	X	O	01.02.92	750 SQN OBS SCH
MacAskill, Colin Hugh	LT(SD)	S	CA	11.12.92	CALEDONIA
MacAulay, Neil	LT CDR(SD)	E	WE	01.10.95	FOSF
MacAulay, Natalie May Abigail , BSc	LT	X		01.12.94	SHEFFIELD
MacBean, Christopher Ciaran	LT CDR(SL)	X	P	01.10.93	771 SK5 SAR
MacColl, Andrew	LT(SL)	X	ATC	01.05.96	RNAS CULDROSE
MacCormick, Alexander Wright , psc	LT COL	RM	C	31.12.95	HQRM
MacDonald, Alasdair Iain , BSc, MDA, CEng, MIEE, MBIM	LT CDR	E	WE	01.01.91	COLLINGWOOD
MacDonald, Alastair James , BEng	LT	E	WE	01.09.94	INVINCIBLE
MacDonald, Douglas Hugh Lawson , BSc, pce	CDR	X	MCD	30.06.91	MCM2 SEA
MacDonald, Glen Dey , BA	LT CDR	X		01.05.91	MOD DNR OUTPORTS
MacDonald, George Ewen , LLB	CDR	S		30.06.92	INVINCIBLE

Name	Rank	Spec	Sub-spec	Seniority	Where serving
MacDonald, Ian Robert	CAPT RM	RM		08.02.93	HQRM
MacDonald, John Robert	LT	E	WESM	01.01.90	2SL/CNH
MacDonald Watson, Alastair Ian , BSc, CEng, MIEE, MIExpE, psc	CDR	E	WE	31.12.83	MOD (BATH)
MacDougall, Gavin Ross	LT(SL)	S		01.10.90	HQ 3 CDO BDE RM
MacDougall, Stewart John	LT(SD)	E	WESM	19.02.93	TIRELESS
Mace, Stephen Barry	LT CDR	E	WE	01.02.96	MOD DGUW PTLAND
MacFarlane, Ian Scott , jsdc	CDR	S	SM	31.12.83	FOSNNI
MacFarlane, Iain Stuart David , BSc	LT(SL)	X	P	01.04.94	810 SQN SEAHAWK
MacGillivray, Ian , BEng	LT	E	WE	01.10.90	RNSC GREENWICH
MacGregor, Peter Charles	LT(CS)	-		08.05.89	MOD DNR OUTPORTS
MacIver, George , BSc	LT	X	SM	01.02.90	SOVEREIGN
MacKay, Andrew Colin , BA	SLT	S		01.09.93	SULTAN
MacKay, Colin Alexander	SLT(SL)	X		01.01.93	TRIUMPH
MacKay, Colin Ross , BSc	LT CDR	I		01.09.91	MOD (LONDON)
MacKay, David Hugh	LT CDR(SL)	X	P	01.10.93	EXCHANGE USA
MacKay, Graeme Angus , pce, pcea	LT CDR	X	O	01.02.91	ARGYLL
MacKay, Peter , BEng	LT	E	WE	01.12.90	LOAN DRA PRTSDWN
MacKay, Roderick , BEng, AMIEE	LT(SL)	E	WE	01.06.89	MOD DGSW PTSMTH
MacKay, Stephen Victor , pce, psc	CDR	X	AWO(U)	30.06.86	JT PLAN STAFF
MacKay, William John Carl , BSc	LT(SL)	X	P	01.01.95	706 SQN SEAHAWK
MacKenzie, Kenneth Donald , psc	CDR	X	O	30.06.83	RH HASLAR
MacKenzie, Michael David , BSc	LT CDR	X	SM	01.11.95	URNU CAMBRIDGE
MacKett, Duncan Geoffrey , pce	LT CDR	X	PWO(A)	01.05.88	SHEFFIELD
Mackey, Martin Christopher	LT	X	MCD	01.06.91	BRIDPORT
Mackie, David Francis Sarsfield , BEng	LT	E	WE	01.03.91	RMC OF SCIENCE
Mackie, Simon (Act Surg Lt)	SURG SLT	-		01.02.94	DARTMOUTH BRNC
MacKinlay, Garry Andrew , BSc (Loc Capt Rm)	LT RM	RM		01.09.91	HQRM
MacKinnon, Donald James , BEng	LT	X		01.01.92	BATTLEAXE
MacLean, Cameron Lachlan , BEng	LT(SL)	E	WESM	01.10.92	FOSM FASLANE
MacLean, David James , BTech, MSc, MRINA, jsdc	CAPT	E	ME	30.06.94	MOD (LONDON)
MacLennan, Iain Ross , MB, BCh	SURG LTCDR	-	GMPP	01.07.89	COLLINGWOOD
MacLennan, William Ross , psc, psc(m)	MAJ	RM		30.06.93	MOD (BATH)
Macleod, David Brett , MB, BS	SURG LTCDR	-		01.02.93	NELSON (PAY)
Macleod, James Norman , BEng, AMIEE	LT	E	WE	01.03.93	BRILLIANT
Macleod, Mark Stuart , BEng	LT	E	AE	01.02.94	FONA CRANWELL
MacMahon, Timothy John , pcea, odc(Fr), I(1)Fr	CDR(SL)	X	P	01.10.91	MWC GOSPORT
MacMillan, Gordon	LT(SL)	X	P	16.09.90	819 SQN
MacNaughton, Francis George , BA, pce	LT CDR	X	PWO(A)	01.05.87	FOST FLT TGT GRP
MacNeil, Stephen William	LT(SL)	X	P	01.03.93	706 SQN SEAHAWK
MacPherson, Martin Douglas , OBE, pce (Commodore)	CAPT	X	SM(N)	31.12.88	MOD (LONDON)
MacTaggart, Alexander John Lorne	LT	E	ME	01.03.90	SUTHERLAND
Madders, Brian Richard , MBE	CHAPLAIN	RC		09.09.85	RALEIGH
Madders, Robin Mark	LT(SD)	E	MESM	15.10.93	SUPERB
Maddick, Mark Jeremy	CAPT RM	RM	LC	25.04.96	EXCHANGE NLANDS
Maddison, John	ACT LT RM(SD)	RM		01.01.96	CDO LOG REGT RM
Maddison, Simon	LT(SL)	X		01.07.95	SMOPS NELSON
Madge, Anthony Willian John	LT CDR(SD)	X	PR	01.10.94	CNOCS GROUP
Madge, Richard , BSc, jsdc	CDR	E	WE	31.12.88	MOD (LONDON)
Madgwick, Edward Charles Cowtan	SG SLT(D)	-		01.01.94	DARTMOUTH BRNC
Madgwick, John Edward Vicary , FIMgt, MNI, pce, psc(m), psc(a)	CDR	X	O	30.06.86	SHAPE BELGIUM
Maese, Philip Andrew (Loc Capt Rm)	LT RM(SD)	RM		01.01.90	ASC CAMBERLEY
Magan, Michael James Christopher , BEng, MSc, AMIEE	LT CDR	E	WE	01.03.95	COLLINGWOOD
Magill, Thomas Eugene (Act Lt)	SLT(SD)	X	AV	24.07.94	HQ CDO AVN
Magill, William John , BSc, CEng, MIEE	CDR	E	WE	30.06.89	MOD DGSM PTLAND
Maginn, Felix Gerard	LT(SL)	X		01.11.93	COCHRANE
Magowan, Robert Andrew , BSc (Act Capt Rm)	LT RM	RM		01.09.90	COMACCHIO GP RM
Magrath, Alan Richard	SLT(SD)	S	S	01.05.95	SULTAN
Maguire, Anton Paul Duncan	LT CDR	S		01.11.81	DRAKE BSO(F)
Maher, Anthony Michael (Act Capt Rm)	LT RM(SD)	RM	MTO	01.01.90	HQRM
Maher, Michael Patrick	LT CDR	X	PWO(A)	16.05.96	GLOUCESTER
Mahony, Christopher David Copineer	LT CDR	X	P	12.04.96	815 SQN HQ
Mahony, David Grehan	LT CDR	X	O	16.04.96	BEAVER

Name	Rank	Spec	Sub-spec	Seniority	Where serving
Maidment, Keith Charles , MSc, CEng, MIMarE	LT CDR	E	ME	01.03.87	DG SHIPS DEVONPT
Maidment, Phillip Charles	LT CDR(SD)	E	WE	01.10.95	NOTTINGHAM
Maidwell, Nicholas Charles	LT(SL)	X	P	01.01.90	706 SQN SEAHAWK
Mailes, Ian Robert Arthur	LT(SL)	X	O	16.04.94	706 SQN SEAHAWK
Main, Edward Stafford , BSc, CEng, MIMarE	LT CDR	E	ME	01.10.90	FOST SEA
Main, Jamie Robert Campbell , BA (Act Capt Rm)	LT RM	RM		01.09.89	HQRM
Mair, Brian	LT CDR	X	MCD	05.03.93	MCM3 SEA
Makepeace, Philip Andrew , BEng, AMIEE	LT	E	WE	24.12.90	MOD DGSS PTSMTH
Malbon, Fabian Michael , rcds, pce, psc	RADM	-	PWO(N)	15.01.96	2SL/CNH
Malcolm, Stephen Robert , pce	LT CDR	X	H CH	01.06.91	BICESTER
Malcolmson, Alan Douglas	LT CDR(SD)	E	AE(M)	01.10.91	2SL/CNH
Maley, Catherine Elizabeth	SLT(UCE)(SL)	X	O U/T	01.09.95	DARTMOUTH BRNC
Malin, Michael John	LT CDR	X	H CH	01.04.88	BEAGLE
Malins, Damian Joseph Holland , BSc	LT	S		01.05.95	COLLINGWOOD
Malkin, Sharon Louise , BA	LT(SL)	E		01.07.95	SULTAN
Mallalieu, Adam John	CAPT RM	RM		01.09.92	RNSC GREENWICH
Mallen, David John	LT(SL)	E	AE(L)	01.01.96	SULTAN
Malley, David Spencer	CDR	E	WE	30.06.86	MOD DGSW PTSMTH
Malley, Mark Paul , BEng	LT	E	WESM	01.01.93	VICTORIOUS(STBD)
Mallinson, Robert , BEng	LT	E	AE(O)	01.03.89	815 OEU OSPREY
Mallows, Tamsin	LT	Q		09.12.93	RH HASLAR
Maltby, Michael Robert James , BSc	LT CDR	E	ME	01.06.91	MOD (BATH)
Maltby, Richard James	LT RM	RM		29.04.96	CTCRM
Manchanda, Keith Sajir , MBE, pce, pcea	LT CDR	X	O	01.03.84	MOD DNR OUTPORTS
Mandley, Philip John , BSc	LT(SL)	I		01.05.90	EXCHANGE RAF UK
Manfield, Michael David	LT	X	SM	01.01.91	VICTORIOUS(STBD)
Manger, Garth Stuart Cunningham	CAPT RM	RM		25.04.96	RM POOLE
Mann, Barbara Louise , BD	LT	X		01.03.93	RALEIGH
Mann, Gary Digby , BA	LT(SL)	I	SM	01.07.86	CSST SHORE DEVPT
Mann, Simon Alexander , BSc	LT	X	MW	01.03.93	PSYOPS TEAM
Mannering, Peter David , pce	CDR	X	AWO(U)	31.12.86	SACLANT USA
Manning, Duncan	2LT(GRAD)	RM		01.09.94	45 CDO RM
Manning, Garth Alfred , pce, psc	CDR	X	AWO(U)	31.12.88	NAVAL DRAFTING
Manning, Martin Graham Bickley , AFC, pce, pcea, psc	CAPT	X	O	31.12.95	RNSC GREENWICH
Mannion, Robert Victor	LT CDR	X	SM	01.06.95	FEARLESS
Mannion, Timothy Shaun	LT CDR(SL)	X	P	01.09.86	FONA
Mansbridge, Brian James , MBE, psc	CDR(SL)	X	MCD	01.10.92	RNLO GULF
Mansell, Paul Robert , psc(m)	CAPT RM	RM		01.09.91	42 CDO RM
Manser, Clare Theresa	LT(SL)	S		25.04.93	FONA
Manser, Darren	LT(SL)	X	P	01.04.94	846 SQN
Mansergh, Michael Peter , BA, pce, I(2)Fr	CDR	X	PWO(C)	30.06.94	ROCLANT PORTUGAL
Mansergh, Robert James , LLB, pce, pce(sm)	CDR	X	SM	30.06.91	CSST SEA
Mansfield, Raymond Andrew George	LT CDR(SD)	E	AE(M)	01.10.93	FONA
Manson, Colin Robert , BSc	LT(SL)	I	METOC	01.01.88	CAPT F1(SEA)
Manson, Paul David	LT(SL)	X	ATC	01.05.94	RNAS CULDROSE
Manson, Peter Duncan	LT RM	RM	P	01.09.92	847 SQN
Manson, Thomas Edward	LT	E	AE(P)	01.10.90	815 FLT 203
Mant, James Nicholas , BSc	LT CDR	E	WE	01.10.89	MWC GOSPORT
Manton, Lisa Marie , BEng	LT(SL)	E	ME	01.01.95	MONTROSE
Marandola, Stefan John	LT(SL)	X	O	01.09.94	849 SQN HQ
March, Cameron John (Loc Maj)	CAPT RM(SD)	RM		01.10.90	WARRIOR
March, Duncan Roger (Act Lt Rm)	2LT	RM		28.04.93	FEARLESS
Marchant, Timothy Alan Cardew , pce	LT CDR	X	PWO(U)	01.02.91	COVENTRY
Mardlin, Stephen Andrew	LT	S		01.04.91	NEPTUNE
Mardon, Karl Fraser	LT CDR	X	PWO(U)	02.09.92	ELANT/NAVNW
Marino, David Jones , MBE	CAPT RM(SD)	RM		01.10.93	RNSC GREENWICH
Marjoram, Gareth Keri	LT(SL)	E	WESM	01.05.96	CAPTAIN SM2
Mark, Robert Alan , BSc	CDR	X	H CH	30.06.90	MOD (LONDON)
Markey, Adrian Philip , BEng	LT	X	O U/T	01.08.93	750 SQN OBS SCH
Markham, Philippa Mary , BEd	LT	S		01.02.92	RH HASLAR
Markowski, Isabel Maria , BEd	LT(SL)	W	X	10.12.87	2SL/CNH
Marks, Martin Roger , BSc, CEng, FIMarE, FIMechE, MHSM	CDR	E	ME	31.12.80	RH HASLAR

Name	Rank	Spec	Sub-spec	Seniority	Where serving
Marks, Nicholas , BSc, CEng, MRAeS, MDA	CDR	E	AE	31.12.89	RNAS YEOVILTON
Marley, Edward Christopher Philip , n	LT	X		01.03.92	IRON DUKE
Marley, Peter Shaun , BSc, MA, jsdc, pcea, psc(m)	CDR	I		31.12.87	EXCELLENT
Marmont, Kerry Lewis , BSc	LT CDR	E	WESM	01.05.92	MOD (BATH)
Marney, Justin , BDS	SG LT(D)	-		12.07.91	NELSON
Marok, Jani , BSc	CAPT RM	RM		30.04.95	CTCRM
Marquis, Adrian Colin , BEng	LT(SL)	X	P	01.08.94	706 SQN SEAHAWK
Marr, David Charles Worth , pcea	LT CDR(SL)	X	P	01.10.94	848 SQN HERON
Marr, James	SLT	E	MESM	01.05.94	DARTMOUTH BRNC
Marratt, Richard James , BSc	LT(SL)	I		01.09.90	HQRM
Marriott, Mark Nicholas , BEng, MSc	LT	E	AE	01.04.91	MOD DGA(N)RNHSMP
Marriott, Neil Kenneth	LT(SL)	X		01.12.95	DRYAD
Marsh, Alan Roger , MB, BS, FRCP, ndc	SURG CAPT	-	CM	30.06.87	RH HASLAR
Marsh, Brian Henry ,MBE, BSc	LT(SL)	X	O	01.12.88	702 SQN OSPREY
Marsh, David Julian , BSc	CDR	S		31.12.93	DOLPHIN
Marsh, David Thomas	LT CDR(SD)	S	W	01.10.94	MOD (LONDON)
Marsh, Michael Peter Alan	LT(SD)	X	PR	13.12.95	PJHQ
Marsh, Roger John Lewis	LT CDR(SL)	X	ATC	01.10.92	MOD (LONDON)
Marsh, Thomas Vivian , MA, MSc, CEng, MIMarE	LT CDR	E	ME	01.04.88	FOSF
Marshall, Fleur Tiffany (Act Surg Lt)	SURG SLT	-		01.10.92	DARTMOUTH BRNC
Marshall, Geoffrey	CDR(SD)	MS	AD	01.10.91	RN MSS HASLAR
Marshall, John Nicholas , BSc	LT CDR	E	MESM	01.06.89	FOSM NWOOD HQ
Marshall, Jonathan Paul , psc	LT CDR	S		01.01.83	MOD DNR OUTPORTS
Marshall, Paul , BEng	LT	E	ME	01.03.93	RICHMOND
Marshall, Peter Ernest , MSc	LT CDR(SL)	I		01.01.83	DNPS
Marshall, Richard Anthony , pce, psc(m)	CDR	X	MCD	31.12.92	MOD (LONDON)
Marshall, Richard George Carter	LT CDR	X	PWO(C)	01.05.95	INVINCIBLE
Marson, Gary Michael	SLT(SD)	E	WE	04.09.95	COLLINGWOOD
Marston, Peter Alan , BA	LT CDR	S		16.04.96	GLASGOW
Marston, Sarah Alice Bedford , BSc	LT(SL)	I		27.07.86	DRYAD
Marten, Andrew	LT(SL)	X	ATC	01.04.95	RNAS YEOVILTON
Martin, Anthony John	SLT(SD)	X	C	10.12.95	DRYAD
Martin, Bruce Anthony , BSc	LT	E	MESM	01.05.89	SULTAN
Martin, Colin John , pce, pcea	LT CDR	X	O	16.06.92	702 SQN OSPREY
Martin, Darren Hinna , BSc	LT	X		01.03.90	LEEDS CASTLE
Martin, Elizabeth Janet , BSc	LT CDR(SL)	I	PI	01.04.91	PJHQ
Martin, John Henry	T/LT(SDT)	S	S	18.06.93	DOLPHIN
Martin, Kathleen Margaret , psc	CDR	W	PI	01.04.88	MOD (LONDON)
Martin, Michael Peter	LT CDR(SD)	E	AE(L)	01.10.93	RNAS CULDROSE
Martin, Michael Terence , BEng	LT CDR	E	ME	12.05.92	RNSC GREENWICH
Martin, Nathan Alan	2LT	RM		01.09.94	42 CDO RM
Martin, Neil Douglas , BSc, pcea, psc	LT CDR	X	O	01.06.87	HERON
Martin, Nicholas	SURG SLT	-		01.01.96	DARTMOUTH BRNC
Martin, Paul John , BSc, psc(m)	MAJ	RM		31.12.93	HQRM
Martin, Roger Graham	LT CDR	X	PWO(A)	01.09.95	NELSON (PAY)
Martin, Simon Charles , pce, pce(sm), psc	CDR	X	SM	31.12.88	BRITANNIA
Martin, Simon James , BEng	LT	E	WESM	01.02.92	TRIUMPH
Martin, Timothy Frederick Wilkins , LLB (Barrister)	CDR	S	BAR	30.06.92	2SL/CNH
Martin, Toby Kenneth , psc, I(2)Fr	CAPT	S		31.12.90	MOD (LONDON)
Martin, Victor George	LT CDR(SD)	E	AE(L)	01.10.90	MOD PE ASC
Martinson, Isabel Jane Alexandra	LT CDR(SL)	S		01.10.92	DRAKE BSO(F)
Martyn, Alan Wallace , MSc	LT CDR	E	AE	01.07.93	LOAN DRA BEDFORD
Maskell, John Malcolm , adp	LT(SD)	E	MESM	16.02.84	2SL/CNH FOTR
Mason, Andrew Harold , BSc	LT CDR	E	AE	01.12.91	FONA
Mason, Alexander Malcolm , OBE, ocds(No), fsc	COL	RM	RL	30.06.94	MOD (LONDON)
Mason, Colin Edward , ACMA	LT CDR	S	CMA	16.11.83	2SL/CNH
Mason, Caroline Mary , BEng	LT	E	ME	01.03.94	FEARLESS
Mason, Darren Jon , BA, BEng	SLT(SL)	X		01.09.94	PEACOCK
Mason, Hugh Oliver Dudley	LT(SL)	X	P	16.04.93	EXCHANGE CANADA
Mason, Jeffrey Sinclair , psc	MAJ	RM	LC	31.12.95	SULTAN AIB
Mason, Martin	LT(SD)	E	AE(M)	19.10.90	SULTAN
Mason, Michael Miles David , BSc, pce, pcea	CDR	X	O	30.06.93	ACE SRGN ITALY

Name	Rank	Spec	Sub-spec	Seniority	Where serving
Mason, Nicholas Hugh , BSc	LT CDR	I		28.08.90	2SL/CNH FOTR
Mason, Richard William , BSc, MA, CEng, MIEE, psc	CDR	E	WE	30.06.93	MOD (LONDON)
Massey, Alan Michael , BA, pce, psc, I(1)Ge	CAPT	X	PWO(A)	30.06.96	DRYAD
Massey, Paul	LT(SD)	X	AV	23.07.93	RNAS YEOVILTON
Massey, Steven	LT(SL)	X	P	01.02.91	845 SQN
Massie-Taylor, Christopher Gerald , OBE, pce, psc	CAPT	X	MCD/MW	31.12.93	SAUDI AFPS SAUDI
Masters, James Christopher	LT CDR	X	PWO(A)	01.05.96	SHEFFIELD
Masters, Richard Hilary , BTech, MITD	LT CDR	I		01.01.92	FOSF
Masterton-Smith, Anthony Philip , ADC, CEng, MIEE, jsdc (Commodore)	CAPT	E	WE	31.12.88	DARTMOUTH BRNC
Mather, Graeme Philip	LT	E	ME	01.07.90	RM POOLE
Mather, Richard (Act Surg Lt)	SURG SLT	-		01.08.94	DARTMOUTH BRNC
Mather, Stephen , MBE, pce, pcea	CDR	X	O	30.06.95	MOD (LONDON)
Mathews, Andrew David Hugh , MSc, CEng, MIMarE, MIMechE, psc	CDR	E	MESM	30.06.92	2SL/CNH
Mathews, Len , pcea	LT CDR(SL)	X	P	01.09.83	RNAS CULDROSE
Mathias, Philip Bentley , MBE, pce(sm), psc	CDR	X	SM	31.12.92	2SL/CNH
Mathias-Jones, Peter David , pce	LT CDR	X	PWO(U)	01.09.90	EXCHANGE USA
Mathieson, Kevin Richard	LT CDR(SL)	X	P	01.10.95	SEAHAWK
Matters, Andrew Charles , BSc, CEng, MIMechE	CDR	E	ME	30.06.92	MOD (BATH)
Matthews, Duncan Neil , BSc, pce, pcea	LT CDR	X	P	01.10.91	SHETLAND
Matthews, David William	LT	E	WESM	01.01.90	RMC OF SCIENCE
Matthews, George , psc	CAPT RM(SD)	RM	MLDR	01.10.95	HQRM
Matthews, Gary Anthony , MB, BCh	SURG LT	-		01.08.93	CTCRM
Matthews, Graham Gavin , BA	LT(SL)	X	P	01.03.86	702 SQN OSPREY
Matthews, Justin	LT(SL)	X	O	16.05.94	849 SQN B FLT
Matthews, Jonathan James (Act Surg Lt)	SURG SLT	-		01.03.93	DARTMOUTH BRNC
Matthews, Peter , BSc, pce	CDR	X	AWO(A)	30.06.89	MWC GOSPORT
Matthews, Paul Brian , BEng	LT(SL)	I		01.01.91	2SL/CNH
Matthews, Paul Kinley	LT(SL)	S		01.10.95	2SL/CNH FOTR
Matthews, Quentin Stacey	LT	X		01.08.93	ARGYLL
Matthews, Russell James , BEng, CEng, MIEE	LT	E	WE	01.07.89	DGSS BRISTOL
Matthews, Stuart Grendon	LT CDR	X	PWO(N)	01.06.95	EXCHANGE CANADA
Matthews, William	CHAPLAIN	SF		12.08.91	COLLINGWOOD
Mattick, David James , BSc, CEng, MIEE, MINucE	CDR	E	MESM	30.06.84	MOD (BATH)
Mattin, Paul Roger	LT RM	RM	MLDR	26.04.93	CTCRM
Mattless, Terence William	LT CDR(SD)	X	g	01.10.90	SEA CADET CORPS
Mattock, Damian Brian	SLT	X		01.09.95	DOLPHIN SM SCHL
Maude, Christopher Philip , pcea	LT CDR(SL)	X	P	01.10.92	LOAN DTEO BSC DN
Maude, David Howard	LT(SD)	E	AE(L)	16.10.92	RNFSAIC
Maughan, Jonathan Mortimer Collingwood ,LVO, MRIN, MNI, pce	CDR	X	PWO(N)	31.12.92	BRITANNIA
Maw, Martyn John , BSc	LT CDR	E	WESM	01.12.90	CWTA PTSMTH
Mawby, Peter James	LT CDR(SD)	E	WESM	01.10.94	MOD (BATH)
Mawhood, Christopher Scott	CAPT RM	RM	MLDR	01.09.87	2SL/CNH
Mawson, Anthony Joseph , BSc	LT CDR	E	WESM	02.06.88	MOD (BATH)
Maxwell, Alan Brian Crawford , BDS	SGLTCDR(D)	-		13.07.87	CENTURION
Maxwell, Rachel , BA	LT	X		01.05.94	LEEDS CASTLE
Maxwell-Cox, Michael James , IEng, AMIMarE	LT(SD)	E	ME	15.02.91	FOST MPV(SEA)
Maxwell-Heron, Glen David , BA	LT	E	ME	01.04.91	FEARLESS
May, Colin	SLT	X		01.01.94	ITCHEN
May, Dominic Peter (Loc Capt Rm)	LT RM	RM	MLDR	26.04.93	EXCHANGE ARMY UK
May, Hugh Preston , psc	CAPT	X	H CH	31.12.92	CAPT(H) DEVPT
May, John William	LT(SL)	X	P	01.07.95	819 SQN
May, Nigel Peter	LT	X	P	01.09.90	849 SQN A FLT
May, Phillip (Act Lt Rm)	2LT	RM		01.09.92	40 CDO RM
May, Peter James	LT(SD)	X	C	27.07.95	SHAPE BELGIUM
May, Steven Charles , BEng	LT	E	ME	01.09.95	INVINCIBLE
May-Clingo, Martin Stephen	LT(SD)	X	AV	04.04.91	JS PHOT SCHOOL
Mayall, Christopher Stuart	T/LT(SDT)	X	C	10.06.94	DGSS BRISTOL
Maybery, James Edward (Loc Capt Rm)	LT RM	RM		01.05.90	EXCHANGE ARMY UK
Mayell, Julie Ann , BA	LT(SL)	W		14.07.92	RNAS CULDROSE
Mayhew, Nicholas Morvaren , pce, pcea, psc	LT CDR	X	P	16.08.90	RNSC GREENWICH
Maynard, Andrew Thomas Westenborg (Act Capt Rm)	LT RM	RM		01.09.90	NELSON (PAY)
Maynard, Charles Ian , BA	LT	X		01.02.95	BERKELEY

Name	Rank	Spec	Sub-spec	Seniority	Where serving
Maynard, Lisa , BA	LT(SL)	W	X	03.04.91	CENTURION
Mayne, Alison , BA	LT(SL)	W		14.12.89	RALEIGH
Mayne, Charles William Erskine , BEng	2LT(GRAD)	RM		01.09.94	CDO LOG REGT RM
Mayoh, Christine , BA	LT(SL)	W	S	24.07.91	DNPS
Mazdon, Timothy , BA	LT(SL)	X	P U/T	01.04.96	HERON
Maze, Andrew Terence , BSc	CHAPLAIN	SF		11.09.79	EXCELLENT
Mc Laren, James Patrick (Loc Capt Rm)	LT RM	RM		30.04.91	COCHRANE
McAleese, George , TEng, MITE	CDR(SD)	E	WESM	01.10.90	CWTA PTSMTH
McAllister, Duncan	SURG SLT	-		01.02.94	DARTMOUTH BRNC
McAllister, Ian Frank , pcea	LT CDR(SL)	X	O	01.09.83	RNAS YEOVILTON
McAlpine, Paul Anthony	LT CDR	X	MCD	01.08.94	ARGYLL
McAnally, John Henry Stuart , LVO, MNI, MRIN, rcds, pce, psc, hcsc	RADM	-	N	11.01.96	2SL/CNH FOTR
McArdell, Steven James Ronald	LT(SL)	X	P	01.04.90	RNAS CULDROSE
McArdle, Richard	LT(SL)	X	SM	01.08.95	VANGUARD(PORT)
McArthur, Calum James Gibb , BM, BS, BAO, DObstRCOG, LRCP, MRCGP	SURG CDR	-	GMPP	30.06.92	WARRIOR
McAuslin, Thomas McDonald , MSc	LT(SD)	MS	SM	04.04.91	NEPTUNE NT
McAvoy, Simon Peter	SLT(SL)	X	P	01.01.94	EXCELLENT
McBain, Mandy Sheila	LT(SL)	W	S	11.12.92	FOSF
McBarnet, Thomas Francis , BSc, pce	LT CDR	X	PWO(U)	01.07.91	CAPT F1(SEA)
McBratney, James Alexander Grant	SLT	X		01.01.94	DARTMOUTH BRNC
McBride, Peter Joseph	CHAPLAIN	RC		15.08.91	NEPTUNE
McCabe, Daniel Stewart	LT(SD)	E	WE	19.02.93	NEPTUNE BASE OPS
McCabe, Garry Patrick , BA	2LT(GRAD)	RM		01.09.95	CTCRM LYMPSTONE
McCabe, Joseph , BA, psc	MAJ	RM	MOR	31.12.92	HQRM
McCabe, Shane Edward Thomas , BSc	SURG LT	-		01.08.95	HQ 3 CDO BDE RM
McCafferty, Michael James	LT(SL)	X	H2	01.06.95	CAPT(H) DEVPT
McCaffery, George Frederick	LT(SD)	E	AE(M)	16.10.90	INVINCIBLE
McCall, Iain Robert	LT	X		01.07.88	DRYAD
McCall, Malcolm John , MA, DPhil, PGCE	CHAPLAIN	SF		27.08.80	NELSON
McCallum, Neil Ritchie	SLT	E	ME	01.09.94	DARTMOUTH BRNC
McCartain, Michael Brendon William , BSc, pce, pcea, psc	LT CDR	X	O	01.05.93	NEWCASTLE
McCarthy, Patrick John	CDR	S		31.12.91	COLLINGWOOD
McCarthy, Steven James , BEng	LT	E	ME	01.01.95	MARLBOROUGH
McCartney, Clive	LT	E	ME	01.05.90	LOAN DTEO PYSTCK
McCaughey, Vincent Joseph , BComm	LT(SL)	I		01.03.93	SULTAN
McClarty, Martin	LT(SD)	E	WESM	22.02.96	SUPERB
McClay, William Jason , BEng	2LT(GRAD)	RM		01.09.95	CTCRM LYMPSTONE
McCleary, Simon Paul	SLT(SL)	E	WESM	01.05.94	DARTMOUTH BRNC
McClement, Duncan	MID	E	MESM	01.09.94	DARTMOUTH BRNC
McClement, Timothy Pentreath , OBE, jsdc, pce, pce(sm)	CAPT	X	SM	30.06.92	PJHQ
McClintock, David Victor Perry , BSc, CEng, MIEE, psc	CAPT	E	WE	31.12.93	DG SHIPS CAM HSE
McCloskey, Ian	SLT(SL)	E	ME	01.01.94	YORK
McCombe, John	SLT	E	ME	01.09.93	CORNWALL
McConochie, Andrew David , BSc	LT CDR	S		16.04.96	ARGYLL
McCorkindale, Peter Robin , BDS	SGLTCDR(D)	-		13.06.96	CINCFLEET
McCormack, Conor Patrick	LT RM	RM	LC	30.04.91	COMAW SEA
McCormick, John Patrick , BEng	LT CDR	E	AE	20.09.93	RNAS YEOVILTON
McCowan, David James	LT(SL)	X	P	16.06.95	845 SQN
McCoy, Mark	SLT(SL)	E	AE	01.05.96	FEARLESS
McCready, Geoffrey Alan Roy , MBE, FBIM, AIL, pce, pce(sm), I(2)Ru	CDR	X	SM	31.12.90	CAPTAIN SM2
McCreesh, Paul Michael	LT(SL)	X	P	01.02.90	810 SQN SEAHAWK
McCue, Duncan , BA	LT	E	ME	01.10.90	SULTAN
McCulloch, Alistair Michael Broadbent , BSc	LT(SL)	X	P	16.05.92	845 SQN
McCulloch, Isla , BSc	SLT(SL)	X		01.01.94	DARTMOUTH BRNC
McCullough, Ian Neil (Loc Capt Rm)	LT RM	RM	MLDR	01.09.90	EXCHANGE ARMY UK
McCutcheon, Graeme	LT(SL)	X	P	01.02.95	815 FLT 216
McDermott, Mark	LT(SL)	X	P	01.01.90	819 SQN
McDermott, Owen David , BEng	LT	E	WE	01.10.91	DG SHIPS ROSYTH
McDermott, Paul Andrew	SLT(SD)	X	MCD	24.07.94	GLOUCESTER

Name	Rank	Spec	Sub-spec	Seniority	Where serving
McDermott, William Martin , OBE, psc	LT COL	RM	MOR	31.12.95	CTCRM
McDonald, Anthony John	LT	X	MW	01.07.91	RNSC GREENWICH
McDonald, Ian Gordon	LT(SL)	X	O	01.05.91	814 SQN
McDonald, James	A/LT(CS)	-		06.02.94	MOD DNR OUTPORTS
McDonald, John James Bruce	LT CDR	X	P	01.05.84	FONA
McDonald, Norman	LT(SL)	X	P	01.09.94	849 SQN HQ
McDonnell, David	LT(SL)	I	METOC	24.01.91	CAPT F4 (SEA)
McDonnell, Peter William , pce(sm)	LT CDR	X	SM	01.04.92	ANGLESEY
McDonough, Ambrose Gerrard , BSc	LT	X	MCD	01.07.88	SHEFFIELD
McDougall, David William , BSc	SLT(SL)	S		01.01.94	EDINBURGH
McElwaine, Richard Ian , BSc	CDR	E	AE(P)	31.12.94	INVINCIBLE
McEvoy, Graeme Edward Brian , BA	LT	X	SM	01.12.91	LOAN CDA ADAC
McEvoy, Lee Patrick	SLT(SD)	X	EW	24.07.94	PJHQ
McEwan, Andrea , BA	SLT(SL)	X		01.01.94	DARTMOUTH BRNC
McFadyen, Howard , OBE, BSc, CEng, MIMechE	CDR	E	MESM	31.12.87	MOD (BATH)
McFarlane, Andrew Lennox , BSc, CEng, MIMechE	CDR	E	MESM	30.06.93	VIGILANT(PORT)
McGarel, David Francis	LT(SD)	S	CA	25.07.91	MOD (BATH)
McGhee, Craig	2LT(GRAD)	RM		01.09.94	45 CDO RM
McGhie, Ian Andrew	LT	X	SM	01.07.89	CSST SHORE FSLN
McGinley, Mark Patrick , BSc	LT(SL)	I		25.01.91	SULTAN
McGinty, Michael James	LT	X	SM	01.04.91	DRYAD
McGlory, Stephen Joseph , BA, I(1)Sp	LT	X		01.06.94	LINDISFARNE
McGrane, Richard	SLT(SD)	X	C	03.04.94	COLLINGWOOD
McGrenary, Andrew	LT CDR	X		01.01.94	FOSF SEA PTSMTH
McGuire, James	SLT(SL)	X		01.01.93	TRAFALGAR
McGuire, Michael Joseph , n	LT	X		31.08.90	DRYAD
McGunigall, Roy	SLT(SD)	MS	AD	03.04.94	DRAKE CBS
McHale, Gareth John , BSc, pce, pcea	LT CDR	X	O	01.12.91	820 SQN
McHale, Kevan	LT(SD)	E	AE(M)	17.10.91	FONA HERON
McHugh, Martin John	LT CDR(SL)	X	ATC	01.09.87	RNAS CULDROSE
McHugh, Richard Henry	SLT	E	ME	01.09.94	DARTMOUTH BRNC
McHugh, Terence Patrick , BSc	LT(SL)	X		01.08.89	LOAN SAUDI ARAB
McInerney, Andrew Jonathon	LT RM	RM		01.09.92	HQ 3 CDO BDE RM
McInnes, James Gerald Kenneth , BSc	LT CDR	E	WESM	01.06.95	MOD CSSE USA
McIntosh, James	SURG SLT	-		15.10.94	DARTMOUTH BRNC
McIntosh, Keith David	LT CDR(SD)	E	HULL	01.10.94	TEMERAIRE
McIntyre, Alastair William	LT(SD)	X	tas	25.07.91	RNU ST MAWGN SEA
McJarrow, Duncan James , BDS, LDS RCS(Eng)	SGLTCDR(D)	-		01.01.91	HERON
McKay, Paul Anthony , pcea	LT CDR	X	O	16.08.85	LOAN OMAN
McKeating, John Brendan , BM, BCh, MSc, Dip FFP, DipIMC RCSED, MRCGP, JCPTGP	SURG LTCDR	-	GMPP	01.02.94	BF GIBRALTAR(NE)
McKee, Hamish McLeod , BA, BComm	SLT(SL)	X	O U/T	01.01.95	DARTMOUTH BRNC
McKee, Robert Lloyd , BSc	LT(SL)	X	P	16.10.87	HERON FLIGHT
McKellar, Robert Archibald , pcea, psc	LT CDR	X	O	01.06.81	SEA CADET CORPS
McKendrick, Andrew Michael , pce	LT CDR	X	SM	01.07.92	TRAFALGAR
McKenzie, David , BSc, CEng, MIMarE	LT CDR	E	ME	31.10.90	FOST SEA
McKenzie, Hastings Wolfe , BSc	LT	E	ME	01.01.93	SULTAN
McKenzie, Ian Scott , MBE, jsdc, pce	CDR	X	P	31.12.87	MOD (LONDON)
McKenzie, Kenneth John , BSc, CEng, MIMarE, psc	CDR	E	ME	30.06.87	FOST SEA
McKenzie, Malcolm	LT(SL)	X	O	16.04.93	GLOUCESTER
McKeown, Francis Edward	LT(SD)	E	WESM	13.06.91	CLYDE MIXMAN1
McKeown, Justin Reaney	LT RM	RM		23.09.90	CTCRM
McKernan, James	LT(SD)	X	C	27.07.95	MOD (LONDON)
McKie, Andrew , MA, pcea, psc	LT CDR(SL)	X	P	01.10.89	820 SQN
McKillop, Helenora Elisabeth Lang	LT	Q	OTSPEC	14.02.86	RH HASLAR
McKinlay, Stewart	LT(SL)	X	P	01.04.87	RAF CRANWELL EFS
McKinlay, Stuart , BEM, MSc	LT CDR(SD)	MS	LT	01.10.93	2SL/CNH
McKinney, Damian Graydon Dennis , MBE, BSc, MA, psc	MAJ	RM		30.06.96	HQ 3 CDO BDE RM
McKinney, Mark Douglas	LT RM	RM	MLDR	01.05.90	MOD DNR OUTPORTS
McKnight, Derek	LT(SL)	X	MCD	01.07.91	BROCKLESBY
McKnight, Nicholas William	LT CDR(SL)	S		01.10.93	DNPS
McLachlan, Jennifer	SURG LT	-		17.08.95	NORTHUMBERLAND

Name	Rank	Spec	Sub-spec	Seniority	Where serving
McLachlan, Michael Paul	LT(SD)	E	ME	18.06.93	SUPT OF DIVING
McLaren, Ian ,MBE, pce, psc	LT CDR	X	PWO(A)	16.03.88	MOD (LONDON)
McLarnon, Christopher Patrick Charles , BSc	LT(SL)	I		01.09.91	DOLPHIN
McLaughlan, Charles John	LT(SD)	MS	PD	08.04.94	RN MSS HASLAR
McLaughlan, Claire Louise	LT	Q	IC	21.08.89	RN MSS HASLAR
McLaughlin, Dermot Patrick	SLT(SL)	E	MESM	01.01.94	DARTMOUTH BRNC
McLean, Colin John Roberts	LT CDR(SD)	E	ME	01.10.92	RM POOLE
McLean, Helen Mary	LT(SL)	W	X	11.12.92	MOD DNR OUTPORTS
McLean, Rory Alistair Ian , OBE, pce	CAPT	X	P	30.06.92	FEARLESS
McLees, John , pce(sm), ocds(Ind)	CAPT	X	SMTAS	30.06.89	BDLS INDIA
McLellan, John Bruce , OBE, pce	CDR	X	AWO(U)	31.12.84	MOD (BATH)
McLennan, Andrew	LT(SL)	X	O U/T	01.10.95	702 SQN OSPREY
McLennan, Richard Glenn , BSc, I(1)Sp	LT CDR	E	AE	01.01.90	SULTAN
McLeod, Christiaan John (Loc Capt Rm)	2LT	RM		29.04.92	RMB STONEHOUSE
McLewee, Colin James	LT(SD)	E	ME	18.06.93	DG SHIPS PTSMTH
McLintock, Mark William , MA	LT(SL)	X		01.05.94	YORK
McManus, Peter	LT CDR(SL)	X	P	01.10.89	706 SQN SEAHAWK
McMichael-Phillips, Scott James , BSc	LT CDR	X	H CH	01.08.93	LOAN HYDROG
McMillan, George Harrison Grant , BCh, MSc, MD, FRCP, FFOM, FRCPGlas, MRCP, AFOM, jsdc (Commodore)	SURG CAPT	-	CO/M	31.12.92	2SL/CNH
McMullan, Neil Leslie , BA	LT(SL)	I		01.01.93	RALEIGH
McNair, Euan Alan , AFC, pce, pcea, psc	CDR	X	P	30.06.95	PJHQ
McNally, Neville James	LT	S		01.11.90	INVINCIBLE
McNamara, Ian	SLT	E	WESM	01.09.93	COLLINGWOOD
McNaughton, John Alistair	LT CDR	X	SM	01.07.93	CNOCS GROUP
McNeile, Rory Hugh , BA	LT CDR	X	P	16.05.93	URNU OXFORD
McNeill, Ian , BA, psc(m) (Loc Col)	LT COL	RM		31.12.92	2SL/CNH
McNeill Love, The Hon Robin (Michael Cox) , MB, BS, DObstRCOG	SURG CDR	-	GMPP	30.06.96	ILLUSTRIOUS
McQuaker, Stuart Ross	LT CDR	X	PWO(A)	01.08.94	CAPT F1(SEA)
McQueen, Jason Bedwell , BSc	LT	X		01.07.93	DUMBARTON CASTLE
McRae, Philip Compton , BEng	LT	E	WESM	01.12.91	REPULSE(PORT)
McRae, William , psc	MAJ(SD)	RM		26.03.93	COMACCHIO GP RM
McTaggart, Douglas Alexander	SLT(SL)	E	WE	07.02.94	BIRMINGHAM
McTear, Nigel James	LT(SD)	X	AV	11.12.92	ILLUSTRIOUS
McWilliams, Adrian	SLT(SL)	X	O U/T	01.01.95	DARTMOUTH BRNC
McWilliams, Jacqueline , BA	LT(SL)	X		01.03.96	WALNEY
Meadows, Brian	LT(SD)	X	PT	03.04.92	COLLINGWOOD
Meaken, John , BSc, CEng, MIEE, psc	CDR	E	MESM	31.12.89	DRAKE CBS
Meakin, Brian Richard , BSc	LT(SL)	X	O	01.04.85	MWC GOSPORT
Mealing, David William	SLT	E	AE	01.09.94	DARTMOUTH BRNC
Mealing, Steven	SLT(SL)	E	ME	01.05.96	CAMPBELTOWN
Meardon, Martin John , psc(a) (Brigadier)	COL	RM	PH	13.12.91	2SL/CNH
Mearns, Craig McDonald , MA	LT	S		01.05.89	BF GIBRALTAR(NE)
Meatyard, Christopher George Brandon , psc	CDR	X	MCD	31.12.88	MOD (LONDON)
Meazza, Vivian Michael , psc	CDR	X	AWO(A)	30.06.84	WARRIOR
Medland, Owen John , BA	LT	X		01.10.94	CUMBERLAND
Mee, Geoffrey	LT(SD)	E	AE(M)	17.10.91	SULTAN
Meechan, William (Act Lt)	SLT(SD)	MS	AD	03.04.94	2SL/CNH
Meeds, Kevin	LT CDR	X	O	16.12.95	815 FLT 218
Meek, Camilla Simpson , BEng	LT(SL)	E	ME	01.03.94	GLASGOW
Meeking, Christopher George	LT	X	FC	09.01.92	NOTTINGHAM
Mehta, Raj Philip , BEng	LT(SL)	E	WE	01.12.93	CUMBERLAND
Mellor, Adrian John , MB, BCh	SURG LT	-	SM	06.09.91	RNDHU DERRIFORD
Mellor, Barry John	LT CDR	S		16.05.93	HERON
Melly, Richard Graham , MSc, CEng, MIMarE, psc	CAPT	E	ME	31.12.95	DG SHIPS PTSMTH
Melrose, John , BSc, adp	LT CDR	I	METOC	27.10.83	DNPS
Melson, Peter John , CBE, FNI, jsdc, pce	CAPT	X	AWO(U)	30.06.89	HQ BF HK
Melton, Colin , BEng	LT	E	WE	01.11.91	DGSS BRISTOL
Melville-Brown, Martin Giles	LT(SD)	S	CA	08.04.94	DRAKE BSO(F)
Melville-Brown, Penelope Gillian , BA, PGCE (Barrister) (Act Cdr)	CDR	W	S	30.06.96	FOSF
Menheneott, Christopher John , OBE, nadc, psc (Loc Lt Col)	MAJ	RM	LC	31.12.84	MOD (BATH)

Name	Rank	Spec	Sub-spec	Seniority	Where serving
Menlove-Platt, Christopher John , BSc, CEng, MIMarE	CDR	E	ME	31.12.93	MOD (BATH)
Menzies, Angus , MBIM	CDR	S	SM	30.06.90	MOD (LONDON)
Menzies, Anthony John , BSc	LT CDR	E	AE(P)	01.05.90	FONA
Mercer, David Crispin	LT(SL)	X	P	16.01.93	750 SQN OBS SCH
Mercer, Ian Stuart	MID(NE)(SL)	X	O U/T	01.01.96	DARTMOUTH BRNC
Mercer, Keith Roger	LT(SL)	X	P	16.10.94	819 SQN
Mercer, Paul John	LT(SL)	X	O	01.04.96	814 SQN
Mercer, Stuart James	SURG LT	-		03.08.95	CAPTAIN SM2
Merchant, Ian Charles	LT CDR	S		05.01.94	MOD (LONDON)
Merchant, Jeremy	ACT LT RM(SD)	RM		01.01.96	CTCRM
Meredith, Nicholas , BSc	LT CDR	X	SM	01.04.94	VICTORIOUS(STBD)
Merewether, Henry Alworth Hamilton , pcea	LT	X	O	01.05.90	FOST SEA
Merrett, Gordon James , LLB, pce, psc, psc(m)	CDR	X	AWO(A)	30.06.88	PJHQ
Merrick, Leigh Courtney Phillips , I(2)Ru	CAPT	S		30.06.92	DA KIEV
Merriman, Malcolm Roy , BA	LT(SD)	E	MESM	14.10.88	DRAKE CBS
Merriman, Peter Orrill , BSc, MIMechE	LT CDR	E	MESM	01.01.90	TURBULENT
Merritt, Jonathan James , BEng, MSc, CEng, MIMarE	LT CDR	E	ME	01.05.96	SULTAN
Mervik, Christopher Fields , pce, pcea, ocds(Can)	CDR	X	P	31.12.91	CINCFLEET
Meryon, Richard John Kingsmill , MSc, CEng, MIMechE, jsdc	CAPT	E	ME	31.12.92	MOD (BATH)
Messenger, Gordon Kenneth , BSc, psc (Loc Maj)	CAPT RM	RM	MLDR	01.09.91	MOD (LONDON)
Metcalf, Harvey Nevill , AMBIM	LT CDR	X		01.01.79	NWOOD CIS
Metcalf, Robin	LT(SD)	E	ME	10.06.94	SULTAN
Metcalfe, Anthony Paul Warren , BA, pce	LT CDR	X	PWO(U)	01.12.91	DRYAD
Metcalfe, Michael Peter , BEM (Act Lt)	SLT(SD)	X	EW	25.07.93	FOST SEA
Metcalfe, Philip Geoffrey , BEng, MSc, MIEE	LT CDR	E	WESM	01.02.96	LOAN CDA ADAC
Metcalfe, Philip Ian , BEng	LT	E	WE	01.07.93	CORNWALL
Metcalfe, Richard John	SLT(SD)	E	WE	04.09.95	COLLINGWOOD
Methven, Paul , BEng	LT	E	MESM	01.05.92	TORBAY
Metters, Anthony John Francis , AKC	CHAPLAIN	CE		27.02.79	SULTAN
Meyer, Stephen Richard , pce, psc (Commodore)	CAPT	X	PWO(N)	31.12.89	MOD (LONDON)
Michie, Anthony Richard , BSc	LT CDR	E	WE	26.08.92	IRON DUKE
Mickleburgh, Allan	LT(SD)	X	REG	07.01.88	2SL/CNH
Middlebrook, Mark Simon , pce	LT CDR	X	PWO(U)	30.03.93	FOST DPORT SHORE
Middlemas, Simon Robert , BSc, MIMechE	CDR	E	MESM	30.06.96	MOD DGSM DERBY
Middleton, David Jeremy , n	LT	X		01.03.91	BRAVE
Middleton, Toby Patrick Windsor , BSc	CAPT RM	RM	LC	01.05.94	ASC CAMBERLEY
Midgley, Julian Trowan John	SLT(UCE)	E	WE	01.09.95	DARTMOUTH BRNC
Midmore, Martin Jonathan	LT(SD)	E	AE(M)	14.10.94	FOST FLT TGT GRP
Midwinter, Mark John , MB, BSc, BS, FRCS	SURG LTCDR	-	GS	10.09.90	RNDHU DERRIFORD
Miklinski, Anthony Stanley , BSc, DipEd, psc	CDR	I		31.12.89	MOD (LONDON)
Milburn, Philip Kenneth , pce	LT CDR	X	PWO(A)	01.01.95	DRYAD
Miles, Graham John , BSc, BEng	LT(SL)	E	AE	01.07.93	849 SQN A FLT
Miles, Richard , MB, BS, MRCP	SURG LT	-		01.08.91	RH HASLAR
Miles, Rebecca Lewis , BSc	SLT	X		01.09.94	BATTLEAXE
Miles, Sean Andrew	LT	X		01.06.95	EDINBURGH
Miles, Stuart Douglas	LT CDR(SD)	S	CAT	01.10.92	NELSON
Miles, Trevor Michael	LT CDR(SD)	S	S	01.10.93	GANNET
Millar, Gordon Craig , BEng	LT(SL)	E	AE	01.06.93	819 SQN
Millar, Sean Jason	LT	X	MCD	01.09.94	DULVERTON
Millar, Stuart William Sinclair , MB, BS	SURG LT	-		01.08.91	BF GIBRALTAR(NE)
Millard, Andrew Robert	LT	X		01.01.91	DULVERTON
Millard, Colin Geoffrey , BSc, CEng, MIMarE	LT CDR	E	ME	16.04.81	NAVAL DRAFTING
Millen, Ian Stuart	LT(SD)	X	EW	29.07.94	PJHQ
Millen, Stuart Charles William	LT(SL)	X	P	01.04.93	849 SQN HQ
Miller, Andrew	SURG SLT	-		24.09.95	DARTMOUTH BRNC
Miller, Andrew James Gildard , pce, I(2)Sp	CAPT	X	PWO(A)	31.12.94	MOD (LONDON)
Miller, Colin Robert	LT(SL)	X	O	16.05.91	MOD PE ASC
Miller, David Edward	SLT(SD)	MS	AD	25.07.93	DRAKE CBS
Miller, David Sutherland	LT CDR	X	P	01.04.95	815 FLT 221
Miller, Gary	LT(SD)	X	AV	17.12.93	INVINCIBLE
Miller, John Charles , IEng, MIMarE	LT(SD)	E	MESM	17.10.86	NELSON
Miller, Julian Mark	LT	X		01.04.90	DRYAD

Name	Rank	Spec	Sub-spec	Seniority	Where serving
Miller, Mandy Catherine	SLT	E	WE	01.09.94	DARTMOUTH BRNC
Miller, Nicholas William Henry , BSc	SLT	X		01.09.93	DUMBARTON CASTLE
Miller, Paul David	LT	X	FC	01.02.93	HERON
Miller, Richard Hugh	LT	E	WESM	01.03.90	REPULSE(PORT)
Miller, Roger James	LT CDR(SD)	E	WESM	01.10.89	NEPTUNE NT
Milligan, Robert James Charles	LT(SL)	X	O	16.04.92	815 SQN HQ
Millin, Alexander James	LT(CS)RM	-		12.06.88	MOD DNR OUTPORTS
Milliner, Christopher Liam , BSc	LT RM	RM		01.09.94	CDO LOG REGT RM
Millington, John Henry	LT CDR(SD)	X	REG	01.10.92	2SL/CNH FOTR
Millman, Dominic John , BSc	LT(SL)	I	METOC	01.01.92	RNAS CULDROSE
Mills, Andrew , BEng	LT CDR	E	WESM	01.05.95	CSST SHORE DEVPT
Mills, Andrew	SLT(SL)	X	O U/T	01.03.94	FONA SULTAN
Mills, Barrie , BMus	LT RM(SD)	RM		01.01.90	RNSC GREENWICH
Mills, Gordon William	LT(SD)	E	WE	09.06.89	EXCELLENT
Mills, Ian , BEng	LT(SL)	E	WE	01.08.92	MOD (LONDON)
Mills, Keith Paul , DSC	CAPT RM	RM		01.09.89	CTCRM
Mills, Stuart David , BSc, MIMarE	LT CDR	E	MESM	01.05.95	MOD DGSM DNREAY
Mills, Sydney	LT(SL)	X	P	01.01.95	810 SQN SEAHAWK
Mills, Thomas Clark , BSc	LT CDR	I		01.10.93	COLLINGWOOD
Millward, Jonathan , MRIN, AMNI, pce, pce(sm), psc	LT CDR	X	SM	01.09.91	CUMBERLAND
Millward, Jeremy	LT CDR(SL)	X	P	07.04.89	800 SQN
Milne, Andrew Richard , BA	CAPT RM	RM	MLDR	01.09.88	2SL/CNH
Milne, David Murray Ferguson , BSc, AMIEE	LT CDR	E	WE	16.08.79	MOD (BATH)
Milne, Ivor George	CDR(SL)	X	O	01.10.93	FOSNNI
Milne, James William	LT CDR(SD)	E	WE	01.10.92	DG SHIPS CAM HSE
Milne, Peter Barkes , BEng	LT(SL)	X	P	16.09.91	819 SQN
Milne, Simon Stephen , MBE, BSc, psc	MAJ	RM		31.12.93	45 CDO RM
Milner, Hugh Christopher	CAPT RM	RM		01.09.89	CENTURION
Milner, Henry James Rennie , BSc, ARCS, pce	LT CDR	X	PWO(U)	16.04.81	FO PLYMOUTH OPS
Milner, Robert (Act Surg Lt)	SURG SLT	-		06.04.94	DARTMOUTH BRNC
Milnes, John Lee , pce, pce(sm)	CAPT	X	SM	31.12.93	MOD (BATH)
Milsom, Jonathan	LT(SL)	E	AE	01.10.91	SULTAN
Milton, Anthony Arthur , OBE, MPhil, rcds, jsdc, psc(m) (Brigadier)	COL	RM	C	31.12.95	HQ 3 CDO BDE RM
Milton, Graham Boyd McCullough , pcea	LT CDR(SL)	X	P	01.10.89	771 SK5 SAR
Milton, George James Gordon , BSc, CEng, MIEE, psc	CDR	E	WESM	31.12.90	MOD (LONDON)
Milton, Gary Peter	LT(SL)	X	O	01.05.93	706 SQN SEAHAWK
Mimpriss, Graham Donald , n	LT	X	H2	01.04.91	FEARLESS
Mincher, David Joseph Francis , BEng	LT	E	MESM	01.07.94	VIGILANT(PORT)
Minns, Peter Frank , MA	LT CDR	X	PWO(U)	01.11.91	COMUKTG/CASWSF
Minter, James Hugh Howard , BA	LT	X		01.10.93	CHATHAM
Mitchell, Arthur James , BEng	LT(SL)	E	AE	01.06.90	MOD DHSA
Mitchell, Bernard Anthony , BSc	LT CDR	E	WESM	01.11.79	MOD (BATH)
Mitchell, Christopher David	SLT	X		01.01.94	CHIDDINGFOLD
Mitchell, Colin Roderick	LT(SL)	X	P	01.09.92	819 SQN
Mitchell, Clive William	LT	E	WESM	01.04.90	RENOWN(PORT)
Mitchell, Henry George Murray	LT CDR	X	P	16.10.93	FONA
Mitchell, James , BA	LT(SL)	X	P U/T	01.12.95	705 SQN SEAHAWK
Mitchell, Michael	LT(SD)	X	AV	11.12.92	FOSF PHOT UNIT
Mitchell, Philip	T/LT(SDT)	X	ATC	18.04.91	RNAS PORTLAND
Mitchell, Patrick	LT(SD)	E	MESM	05.06.92	NEPTUNE SM1
Mitchell, Richard Hannay , pce	CDR	X	FC	31.12.88	PJHQ
Mitchell, Stephen Derek , IEng, MIMechIE	LT(SD)	E	MESM	15.06.95	TRIUMPH
Mitchinson, Leslie	LT(SD)	X	C	27.07.90	COLLINGWOOD
Mitton, Andrea Louise , BA	LT(SL)	S		01.09.92	RALEIGH
Mizen, Anthony Edward , BPh, psc	CDR	I		30.06.87	NELSON RNSETT
Mizen, Martin William , BA, LLB, psc	CDR	S		31.12.92	DNPS
Moberly, Nigel George Hamilton , BSc, MIEE, AMIEE, psc	CDR	E	WE	30.06.91	MOD (BATH)
Mockford, James Arthur (Act Lt Cdr)	LT(SD)	E	AE(M)	19.10.94	2SL/CNH FOTR
Moffatt, Neil Robert , BSc	LT CDR	E	MESM	01.11.93	TIRELESS
Moffatt, Roger , pcea	LT CDR(SL)	X	P	01.10.95	MOD PE ASC
Moir, Simon , BSc, CEng, MIEE, jsdc	CDR	E	WESM	30.06.87	CAPTAIN SM2
Moll, Andrew Gerald , jsdc, pce	CDR	X	PWO(A)	31.12.94	YORK

Name	Rank	Spec	Sub-spec	Seniority	Where serving
Mollard, Michael Joseph , BSc	LT(SL)	X	P	01.01.95	706 SQN SEAHAWK
Molyneaux, Dean George , BSc, AMIEE, psc	CDR	E	WE	30.06.94	MOD (LONDON)
Molyneux, Simon Derek , pce	LT CDR	X	AWO(A)	01.02.79	LOAN DRA PRTSDWN
Monaghan, Michael , BA	LT CDR(SL)	I		22.09.90	COLLINGWOOD
Moncrieff, Ian , BA, pce	CDR	X	PWO(C)	30.06.92	CINCFLEET
Moncur, James Webster	LT RM	RM	MLDR	24.04.95	42 CDO RM
Money, Christopher Millar	LT(SL)	X	P	01.03.94	849 SQN A FLT
Money, Robert Irving , MNI, jsdc, pce, pcea, psc	CDR	X	O	30.06.84	MOD (LONDON)
Monger, Paul David , BSc	LT CDR(SL)	I	METOC	01.10.94	RNAS CULDROSE
Monger, Ronald Charles , MIEE	LT CDR(SL)	I		11.05.76	SULTAN
Monk, Christopher David , BSc	LT(SL)	I		01.02.89	CTCRM
Monk, Christopher Edward , BSc	LT(SL)	I		01.08.85	NWOOD CIS
Monk, Colin , BSc	SLT	X		01.01.94	DARTMOUTH BRNC
Monk, Stephen Richard	LT(SL)	X		01.06.95	LIVERPOOL
Monkcom, Keith Melvyn , pce, psc	LT CDR	X	PWO	01.05.78	SULTAN AIB
Montgomery, Charles Percival Ross , BEng, pce, psc	CDR	X	PWO(U)	31.12.90	MOD (LONDON)
Montgomery, Michael Henry	LT	X	SM	01.12.89	NEPTUNE SM1
Moodie, Graeme Russell , jsdc, pce, pcea	CDR	X	O	31.12.87	MOD (LONDON)
Moodie, John Preston McNaught	LT CDR	X	AWO(U)	01.05.79	FLYING FOX
Moody, David Christopher , BEng, AMIEE	LT(SL)	E	WE	01.07.92	DRYAD
Moore, Christian Benedict	LT RM	RM		01.09.89	RM POOLE
Moore, Christopher Ian	LT CDR	X	PWO(A)	01.10.93	FOST SEA
Moore, Christopher Richard , BA	LT(SL)	I		01.05.87	SEAHAWK
Moore, David Duncan Vincent	LT(SD)	S	W	25.07.91	UKNMR SHAPE
Moore, Geoffrey James , BTech	LT CDR	I		01.09.82	NELSON RNSETT
Moore, Martin , BA	LT(SL)	X		01.06.92	COCHRANE
Moore, Michael Anthony Claes , LVO, pce, psc, I(1)Sw	VADM	-	N	26.01.94	NAVSOUTH ITALY
Moore, Maurice John , BSc	LT CDR(SL)	I		01.10.92	DARTMOUTH BRNC
Moore, Martin Nicholas	LT CDR(SD)	E	WESM	01.10.95	DOLPHIN SM SCHL
Moore, Michael Ronald	LT(SD)	E	WE	29.10.82	COLLINGWOOD
Moore, Paul Grenville , BDS	SG LT(D)	-		31.12.93	CDO LOG REGT RM
Moore, Piers Henry George	LT	X	SM	01.06.88	SCEPTRE
Moore, Simon , pce, psc (Commodore)	CAPT	X	PWO	31.12.88	MOD (LONDON)
Moore, Sean Barry , BA	LT(SL)	S		01.09.95	FOSM NWOOD OPS
Moore, Suzanne Kathryn , BEd	LT(SL)	X		01.11.93	DRYAD
Moore, Simon Paul , BA	LT(SL)	X		01.10.95	LEEDS CASTLE
Moores, Colin Peter , BEng	LT(SL)	E	ME	01.09.91	SULTAN
Moores, John (Act Lt)	SLT(SD)	S	S	03.04.94	RNAS PORTLAND
Moores, John Keith , BSc, pce, pce(sm)	LT CDR	X	SM	01.09.89	DARTMOUTH BRNC
Moores, Leslie , AMIEE	LT CDR	E	WE	01.12.81	LOAN OMAN
Moorey, Christopher George , pce	LT CDR	X	PWO(A)	01.03.94	DRYAD
Moorhouse, Dominic , BSc	LT RM	RM		01.09.93	COMACCHIO GP RM
Moorhouse, Edward James	LT RM	RM		24.04.95	45 CDO RM
Moorhouse, Stephen , BSc	SLT(SL)	X	O U/T	01.09.93	750 SQN OBS SCH
Moran, Julian (Act Lt Rm)	2LT	RM		27.04.94	CTCRM
Moran, Russell	MID(SL)	X		01.01.95	DARTMOUTH BRNC
Moran, Simon David	LT(SL)	X	P	01.08.94	846 SQN
Moreby, Martin Francis	LT(SD)	X	AV	02.04.93	INVINCIBLE
Moreland, Michael John , BSc, psc(m)	LT CDR	E	MESM	01.12.90	SPARTAN
Morgan, Andrew Kevin Glyn , MSc, Cert Ed	LT CDR	I		06.02.92	MOD (LONDON)
Morgan, David , BSc, CEng, MRAeS, jsdc	CDR	E	AE	30.06.90	JSDC GREENWICH
Morgan, David Henry , BSc	LT(SL)	X		01.10.94	DULVERTON
Morgan, David Richard , jsdc, pce(sm)	CDR	X	SM	31.12.84	SHAPE BELGIUM
Morgan, Forbes Scott	LT	E	ME	01.12.89	MOD (BATH)
Morgan, John Hutchinson , jsdc, pce	CAPT	X	AWO(A)	30.06.93	MOD (BATH)
Morgan, Luke Alexander	LT(SL)	X	P	16.09.92	705 SQN SEAHAWK
Morgan, Nicholas Vaughan , MB, BS, FRCS, FRCSEd	SURG CDR	-	GMPP	31.12.86	JSDC GREENWICH
Morgan, Peter , MIMarE	SLT(SD)	E	ME	19.06.95	SULTAN
Morgan, Peter Thomas , DSC, pce, psc	LT CDR	X	PWO(A)	01.08.90	PJHQ
Morgan, Stephen Alexander (Act Lt Cdr)	LT(SD)	E	WE	10.06.88	DGSS BRISTOL
Morgan-Hosey, John Noel , BEng	LT(SL)	E	MESM	01.01.92	REPULSE(PORT)
Morgon, Richard Henry , BA	LT	X		01.08.93	DOLPHIN SM SCHL

Name	Rank	Spec	Sub-spec	Seniority	Where serving
Morisetti, Neil , BSc, jsdc, pce	CDR	X	PWO(A)	31.12.92	MOD (LONDON)
Morland, Robert Michael	LT CDR(SD)	X	C	01.10.95	NWOOD CIS
Morley, Adrian	LT RM	RM		29.04.96	DARTMOUTH BRNC
Morley, Anthony Derek , MSc	LT CDR(SL)	I		01.10.89	PJHQ
Morley, Dominic Stuart , LLB	SLT(SL)	X		01.01.95	DARTMOUTH BRNC
Morley, John	LT(CS)	-		17.02.91	MOD DNR OUTPORTS
Morley, James David	LT	X	FC	01.08.92	STARLING
Morley-Smith, Nigel Humphrey , MA	LT CDR	E	WE	01.02.78	MOD (LONDON)
Morrell, Andrew John	LT(SD)	X	SM	25.07.91	ELANT/NAVNW
Morris, Andrew Julian , BSc	LT CDR	E	WESM	01.08.93	RMC OF SCIENCE
Morris, Anthony Martin	LT(SL)	X	P	01.07.93	815 FLT 227
Morris, Alan Philip	LT CDR(SD)	S	W	01.10.95	NEPTUNE SM1
Morris, David Alexander James	SLT(SL)	X		01.09.92	RNSC GREENWICH
Morris, David Simon , pce(sm)	CDR	X	SM	30.06.91	MOD (LONDON)
Morris, Frank	CDR(SD)	X	EW	01.10.90	RNEWOSU
Morris, James Andrew John , BSc	LT RM	RM		01.09.91	ASC CAMBERLEY
Morris, John	CHAPLAIN	CE		06.10.92	FOSF SEA DEVNPT
Morris, Kevin Ian	SLT(SD)	S	CA	24.07.94	RALEIGH
Morris, Nigel Jonathan , BSc, CEng, MIEE	LT CDR	E	WE	01.09.92	MOD (BATH)
Morris, Paul , BSc	LT(SL)	I		01.06.89	NELSON RNSETT
Morris, Paul Edward Mannering (Loc Capt Rm)	LT RM	RM	PH	01.05.90	ASC CAMBERLEY
Morris, Peter John , BEng, AMIEE	LT CDR	E	WESM	10.06.92	TIRELESS
Morris, Philip John	LT(SD)	X	C	14.12.90	COMCEN SOUTHWICK
Morris, Paul Nigel , MSc	CDR	I	SM	31.12.90	RNC DPT NS&TECH
Morris, Richard John	LT	X		01.04.89	TRUMPETER
Morris, Roderick Rowan , BSc, jsdc	CDR	S		30.06.90	2SL/CNH
Morris, Simon Timothy , BEng	LT(SL)	E	WESM	01.05.88	DRAKE CFM
Morrison, Bruce	LT(SL)	X	P	01.12.90	820 SQN
Morrison, Christopher John Neill , nadc, pce, psc	CAPT	X	PWO(N)	31.12.91	NATO DEF COL
Morrison, Calum Petter	LT RM	RM		29.04.93	40 CDO RM
Morrison, Graham Lindsay , BDS, MBA, DRD, FDS RCSEdin, jsdc	SGCDR(D)	-	OSM	30.06.86	2SL/CNH
Morrison, George Ross	LT CDR(SD)	E	AE(M)	01.10.95	DGA(N)ASE MASU
Morrison, Gordon William	LT(SL)	X	P	01.10.91	JATEBRIZENORTON
Morrison, Kenneth William	LT CDR(SD)	E	ME	01.10.92	RNSC GREENWICH
Morrison, Kenneth William John , BSc, CEng, FIEE	CAPT	E	WE	30.06.91	DGSS BRISTOL
Morrison, Paul	LT(SD)	X	O	13.12.95	820 SQN
Morrison, Robert William	LT(SD)	E	ME	13.02.92	HERALD
Morrissey, Steven John	LT RM	RM	PT	01.09.94	DOLPHIN
Morritt, Dain Cameron , BEng, psc	LT CDR	E	WE	01.08.94	CUMBERLAND
Morrow, Anthony John Clare , ndc, pce (Commodore)	CAPT	X	C	30.06.88	BRITANNIA
Morse, Andrew Charles , pcea	LT CDR	X	O	01.01.92	FONA
Morse, James Anthony , BSc, pce	LT CDR	X	PWO(N)	01.01.93	CAPT F4 (SEA)
Morshead, Christopher Hurle , BEng, CEng, MRAeS	LT CDR	E	AE	01.05.95	DGA(N) ASE
Mortimer, Richard Peter , BEd	LT	X		01.08.94	NOTTINGHAM
Mortlock, Lisa Eleanor	LT	Q		23.05.95	RH HASLAR
Morton, Crispin Paul , BA	LT CDR	X	P	01.08.90	815 SQN HQ
Morton, Ian	LT(SD)	X	MCD	02.01.81	MOD (LONDON)
Morton, Matthew Christopher	LT	X	FC	01.06.93	SOUTHAMPTON
Morton, Nigel Peter Bradshaw , BSc	LT CDR	S		01.07.93	RNSC GREENWICH
Morton, Thomas , nadc, pce	CAPT	X	AWO(C)	31.12.91	FOSF
Moss, Alexander David	LT CDR	E	ME	06.10.91	MOD (BATH)
Moss, Jason Richard	LT	X		01.06.94	DRYAD
Moss, Peter	LT CDR	X	O	18.02.92	ILLUSTRIOUS
Moss, Patrick John	LT(SD)	E	WESM	13.06.91	VANGUARD(STBD)
Moss, Richard Ashley	LT	X	O	01.03.91	810 SQN SEAHAWK
Moss, Timothy Edward	LT(SD)	E	ME(L)	15.02.91	FEARLESS
Moughton, John Robert	LT(SD)	E	WE	03.11.83	STMA
Mould, Philip	LT(SL)	X	P	01.05.93	RAF CRANWELL EFS
Mould, Timothy Paul	SLT(SD)	E	WE	04.09.95	COLLINGWOOD
Moules, Matthew , BSc	SLT(SL)	X		01.05.94	ARGYLL
Moult, Richard Michael , BSc, psc	LT CDR	I	METOC	09.01.80	SEAHAWK

Name	Rank	Spec	Sub-spec	Seniority	Where serving
Moulton, Simon , BSc	LT(SL)	X	O	01.01.92	819 SQN
Mount, James Bruce	MID(NE)(SL)	X	P U/T	01.01.96	DARTMOUTH BRNC
Mountford, Penny Claire	SLT(UCE)	E		01.09.95	DARTMOUTH BRNC
Mountjoy, Brian John	LT(SD)	E	WESM	05.06.92	NEPTUNE NT
Mowatt, Patrick	SLT	X		01.01.94	DARTMOUTH BRNC
Mowlam, David John Mark , pce, psc	CAPT	X	AWO(C)	31.12.93	NAVSOUTH ITALY
Moxey, David Erskine	LT CDR	S	SM	01.04.91	DRYAD
Moys, Andrew John	LT(SL)	I	METOC	01.09.88	820 SQN
Moyse, Robert Edward , BSc (Loc Maj)	CAPT RM	RM		01.09.86	EXCHANGE AUSTLIA
Muddiman, Andrew , BA (Com 2lt)	2LT(SSLC)	RM		28.10.91	CTCRM
Mudford, Hugh Christopher , psc	CAPT RM	RM		01.09.89	HQRM
Mudge, Adrian Michael , BSc	LT(SL)	X	O	01.07.93	849 SQN A FLT
Muggeridge, Michael Alfred David , MITD	LT CDR(SD)	X	C	01.04.85	CNOCS GROUP
Mugridge, Anthony Robert , MB, BCh, ChB, FRCSEd	SURG CDR	-	CGS	30.06.84	NELSON (PAY)
Mugridge, David Robert , BA	LT	X		01.02.90	IRON DUKE
Mugridge, Terence James George	LT CDR(SD)	MS	P	01.10.94	INM ALVERSTOKE
Muir, Keith , pcea	LT CDR	X	O	01.03.93	849 SQN A FLT
Mules, Anthony John , n	LT	X		01.03.90	BOXER
Mules, Sarah Anne	LT(SL)	W		11.12.92	DRAKE RELEASE
Mullane, Michael James , pce, psc	CDR	X	P	31.12.85	MOD (LONDON)
Mullen, Andrew John , psc	CDR	S	SM	30.06.95	FOST DPORT SHORE
Mullen, Jason John , BA	LT(SL)	X		01.10.94	DRYAD
Mulligan, Iain Douglas , psc, l(2)Fr	LT CDR	S		01.06.79	ELANT/NAVNW
Mullin, John Raymond Noel , QHC	PR CHAPLAIN	RC		04.09.78	2SL/CNH
Mullin, Peter Neil , BSc, MIMechE	LT CDR	E	MESM	01.11.88	MOD (LONDON)
Mullins, Andrew	SLT	E	MESM	01.01.93	DARTMOUTH BRNC
Mullins, Julie	LT(FS)	FS		04.01.94	NEPTUNE
Mulvaney, Paul Andrew , BSc	LT(SL)	E	AE	01.06.92	846 SQN
Munday, Ian Vernon , pce, pcea, psc	LT CDR	X	O	01.04.85	SEAHAWK
Mundin, Adrian John , BSc, CEng, MIMechE	LT CDR	E	ME	01.04.92	ILLUSTRIOUS
Mundy, Joseph Charles	CDR(SD)	X	AWO(C)	01.10.89	CNOCS GROUP
Mungo, Francis Byrne , MSc, rcds, jsdc, psc (Commodore)	CAPT	E	MESM	31.12.88	MOD (BATH)
Munns, Adrian , OBE, rcds	CAPT	S		31.12.92	FOSF
Munns, Andrew Robert , BEng	LT CDR	E	ME	01.01.96	SOMERSET
Munns, Christopher Ronald , jsdc	CDR	X	SM	31.12.89	MOD (LONDON)
Munro, Ian Robert , TEng, AMIMarE, psc	CDR	E	ME	30.06.92	FOSF NORTHWOOD
Munro, Kenneth , BEng, CEng, MIMarE	LT CDR	E	ME	01.04.95	DNPS
Munro, Stuart Ross , MSc, Cert Ed	CDR(SL)	I		01.10.90	DNPS
Munro-Lott, Peter Robert John , BA, pcea	LT(SL)	X	O	16.09.86	750 SQN OBS SCH
Munroe, Jacqueline Ann , BA	LT(SL)	I		01.09.90	NWOOD CIS
Muntz, Howard Arnold Johnston	LT(SL)	X	SM	01.07.94	NEPTUNE BASE OPS
Murch, Julian David , MSc, MIEE, psc	CDR	E	WE	30.06.90	2SL/CNH
Murchie, Alistair Duncan	SLT	E	ME	01.01.95	DARTMOUTH BRNC
Murchison, Ewen Alexander , BSc	LT RM	RM		01.09.93	42 CDO RM
Murdoch, Andrew Peter , BSc	LT	S		01.09.95	FOST DPORT SHORE
Murdoch, Andrew William , BSc, AMIEE	LT CDR	E	WESM	01.06.93	VANGUARD(STBD)
Murdoch, Christopher	LT	X		01.08.94	CHATHAM
Murdoch, Stephen John	LT CDR	S		16.03.93	MOD (LONDON)
Murgatroyd, Andrew Clive , MBE, pce, BSc	CDR	X	PWO(A)	31.12.94	JSDC GREENWICH
Murison, Lisa , MA	LT	X		01.05.95	NORFOLK
Murnane, Paul Martin , pce	LT CDR(SL)	X	PWO(A)	01.03.85	FOSF SEA PTSMTH
Murns, Nicolas Peter , BSc	LT RM	RM	LC	28.04.94	539 ASLT SQN RM
Murphie, John Dermot Douglas , pce	CDR	X	MCD	31.12.95	MOD (LONDON)
Murphy, Anthony (Act Lt Cdr)	LT(SD)	MS		29.07.88	HQRM
Murphy, Brian Joseph , BSc, pce, pcea, l(2)Fr	LT CDR	X	O	16.02.82	EAGLET
Murphy, Diccon , BSc	LT(SL)	X	P	01.04.92	819 SQN
Murphy, Fergal Daniel	LT(SL)	E	WE	01.11.91	WARRIOR
Murphy, James , BSc	LT CDR	S	SM	01.06.92	CAMBRIDGE
Murphy, Nicholas , MNI	LT CDR	X	PWO(U)	01.09.90	LINDISFARNE
Murphy, Paul Anthony , BA	LT	S		01.03.92	DOLPHIN SM SCHL
Murphy, Peter John , BA, PGCE	LT CDR(SL)	I		01.10.91	EXCHANGE AUSTLIA
Murphy, Paul , BSc	LT(SL)	I		01.03.87	DRAKE NBSM(CNH)

Name	Rank	Spec	Sub-spec	Seniority	Where serving
Murphy, Peter William , BEng	LT CDR	E	MESM	01.09.95	VANGUARD(STBD)
Murphy, Stephen	SLT	E	ME	01.01.94	RNC DPT NS&TECH
Murphy, Steven Robert Anthony , BA	LT	X	SM	01.09.90	TRENCHANT
Murray, Alexander Bruce	LT RM	RM		26.04.93	CDO LOG REGT RM
Murray, Andrew Sidney	LT(SL)	X	P	16.03.91	706 SQN SEAHAWK
Murray, Colin Alexander , BDS	SG LT(D)	-		23.09.91	RNH HASLAR
Murray, David	LT(SD)	X	PT	07.01.88	SULTAN
Murray, David Cairns , MA, DipEd, psc	CAPT	I	METOC	30.06.88	NAAFI HQ & REPS
Murray, Grant McNiven	LT	E	WESM	01.06.90	DOLPHIN SM SCHL
Murray, Robert Henry , MBE, BSc, MIMechE	LT CDR	E	MESM	01.01.82	DRAKE CBS
Murray, Stephen	LT(SD)	E	MESM	15.10.93	SULTAN
Murray, Stephen John	LT CDR(SL)	X	O	01.10.89	810 SQN SEAHAWK
Murray, Sarah Joanne , MB, BCh	SURG LTCDR	-	GMPP	01.08.92	CTCRM
Murray, William Richard Charles , BA	LT RM	RM		01.09.94	EXCHANGE ARMY UK
Murrison, Andrew William , MB, BCh, ChB	SURG LTCDR	-	GMPP	01.08.90	NBC PORTSMOUTH
Murrison, Richard Anthony	LT	S		01.03.89	NEWCASTLE
Murton, William Maurice , BSc	LT CDR(SL)	X	P	01.10.92	705 SQN SEAHAWK
Muscroft, Paul James Victor	LT CDR(SD)	E	WE	01.10.93	CFM PORTSMOUTH
Musters, John Basil Auchmuty , osc, l(2)lt	CAPT	S		30.06.93	2SL/CNH
Musto, Edward Charles , BA	CAPT RM	RM		01.09.90	ASC CAMBERLEY
Mutch, Jonathan Rocliffe , BSc	LT(SL)	X	P	01.09.94	FONA VALLEY
Muxworthy, Angela Mary Blythe , psc	CDR	W	I	31.12.95	NWOOD CIS
Myers, Geoffrey William , OBE, BChD, MSc, DGDP RCS(UK), LDS RCS(Eng), jsdc	SGCAPT(D)	-		31.12.94	MOD (LONDON)
Myerscough, Andrew Paul	LT	E	AE	01.10.88	814 SQN
Myres, Peter John Lukis	LT	X	O	01.01.91	815 FLT 228

N

Name	Rank	Spec	Sub-spec	Seniority	Where serving
Naden, Andrew Charles Keith , BSc, CEng, MIMarE	LT CDR	E	ME	01.09.92	SHEFFIELD
Naden, James Ralph , BA	LT CDR(SL)	I		01.10.94	SHAPE BELGIUM
Nadin, Robert Bernard	LT CDR	X	P	01.09.95	EXCHANGE USA
Naidoo, Deborah Jane , BA	LT(SL)	S		01.01.94	GANNET
Nail, Vaughan Anthony , psc	LT CDR	X	H CH	16.09.88	SCOTT
Nailor, Andrew	LT CDR(SD)	E	ME	01.10.95	BIRMINGHAM
Nairn, Alan Barclay , BSc	LT	S		01.02.91	2SL/CNH FOTR
Nairn, Robert , psc	LT CDR	S		25.04.88	MOD (LONDON)
Naish, Anthony John Waddington , psc	LT CDR	S		16.08.77	NEPTUNE
Naismith, David Hamilton , BSc, pcea	LT CDR	X	O	01.05.91	MOD PE ASC
Nance, Adrian Ralph , OBE, BSc, pce	CDR	X	PWO(A)	31.12.89	MOD (LONDON)
Napier, Graham Andrew	SLT(SD)	E	AE(M)	06.09.93	DGA(N) ASE
Napier, Kenneth MacLean , MBE	LT CDR	S		01.08.77	PJHQ
Nash, Philip , BSc	LT(SL)	X	O U/T	01.04.96	RNAS CULDROSE
Nathanson, Helen , BA	SLT	X		01.09.94	BATTLEAXE
Naylor, Andrew James	LT(SL)	X	P	16.06.94	814 SQN
Naylor, Ian Frederick , BA, AKC	CHAPLAIN	CE		16.09.86	CAPT D5 SEA
Naylor, Keith Ernest Edmond	LT CDR(SD)	X	AV	01.10.92	SEAHAWK
Neal, Alistair John Duncan , MB, BCh, DipAvMed	SURG CDR	-	GMPP	30.06.96	BRITANNIA
Neal, Simon Matthew	LT(SL)	X	O	16.01.92	706 SQN SEAHAWK
Neave, Andrew Michael	LT(SL)	X	ATC	08.08.89	RAF WEST DRAYTON
Neave, Christopher Bryan , BSc, pcea	CDR	E	AE(P)	31.12.94	MOD (LONDON)
Necker, Carl Dominic	LT	X		01.11.91	SHETLAND
Needham, Phillip David , DSC	LT CDR(SL)	X	O	01.10.92	LOAN DTEO BSC DN
Neil, Simon John , pce	LT CDR	X	MCD	01.01.91	HURWORTH
Neild, Timothy	LT	X		01.11.95	COTTESMORE
Nelms, Malcolm John , BSc	LT CDR	I	METOC	01.09.88	FOSF
Nelson, Andrew	LT CDR(SD)	E	WESM	01.10.95	NEPTUNE SM1
Nelson, Christopher Stuart , BSc	LT	X		01.03.93	ORKNEY
Nelson, Dominic Edward , BSc	LT CDR	X	PWO(A)	01.04.88	CAMBRIDGE
Nelson, David Lawrence	LT CDR(SL)	X	P	01.10.92	NELSON RNSETT
Nelson, Digby Theodore , BSc, psc	CDR	S		30.06.94	RALEIGH
Nelson, Michael	LT(SL)	X		01.01.94	SPEY
Nelson, Matthew	SLT(SL)	X	P U/T	01.05.96	DARTMOUTH BRNC

Name	Rank	Spec	Sub-spec	Seniority	Where serving
Nelson, Timothy Brian , pce	LT CDR	X	PWO(A)	16.06.83	DRYAD
Nelstrop, Andrew	SURG SLT	-		07.08.95	DARTMOUTH BRNC
Netherclift, Andrew William , OBE, BSc, CEng, MIMarE, psc	CAPT	E	ME	31.12.89	NBC PORTSMOUTH
Nethercott, Lyndon Raymond	LT CDR(SD)	E	AE(L)	01.10.94	LOAN DTEO BSC DN
Nettleton, Philip James	LT(SL)	X	P	24.03.87	MOD DNR OUTPORTS
Neve, Piers Charles	LT CDR	X	SM	11.02.94	VIGILANT(PORT)
New, Christopher Maxwell , BEng	LT	E	ME	01.04.89	LOAN DTEO PYSTCK
Newall, Jeremy Andrew	LT(SL)	X	ATC	01.03.82	RNAS YEOVILTON
Newcombe, Philip James , BA(OU)	LT CDR(SD)	MS	PD	01.10.91	INM ALVERSTOKE
Newell, Gary Douglas , BA	LT(SL)	I		01.08.87	COLLINGWOOD
Newell, Jonathan Michael , MSc, CEng, MIMarE, MIL, fsc, I(1)Fr, I(2)Fr	LT CDR	E	ME	01.03.91	2SL/CNH
Newell, Phillip Russell , BEng	LT(SL)	X	H2	01.06.93	HECLA
Newing, Anthony Gordon , I(2)Ru	CAPT RM	RM	PADJT	01.07.75	HQRM
Newing, Stephen Geoffrey , psc (Loc Maj)	CAPT RM	RM	WTO	01.05.92	EXCHANGE ARMY UK
Newland, Mark Ian	LT	X	PWO(U)	01.10.88	EXCHANGE FRANCE
Newlands, George Alexander , pce, pcea, psc	LT CDR	X	O	01.02.89	RNAS CULDROSE
Newling, Nigel Francis Lancelot , BSc	LT CDR	E	WE	01.06.82	MOD (BATH)
Newman, David	SLT(SL)	E		01.05.96	SOUTHAMPTON
Newman, Paul Henry , BSc	LT CDR	I	METOC	01.05.89	ILLUSTRIOUS
Newsom, Simon John Bowden , MSc, CEng, FIEE, jsdc, psc (Commodore)	CAPT	E	WE	30.06.89	MOD (LONDON)
Newson-Smith, Mark Stephen , MB, BCh, MFOM, FRGS, MRAeS, MIOSH (Act Surg Cdr)	SURG LTCDR	-	CO/M	01.08.89	INM ALVERSTOKE
Newton, Bryan James , BSc, CEng, MIMechE	LT CDR	I	SM	01.05.91	DOLPHIN SM SCHL
Newton, David John , psc	LT CDR	X	P	01.06.90	PJHQ
Newton, Garry Arnold , pce(sm), I(1)Ru, I(2)Ru	LT CDR	X	SM	01.04.91	VANGUARD(PORT)
Newton, James	LT(SL)	X	P	16.09.95	846 SQN
Newton, Mark John	LT(SL)	X	P	01.08.91	848 SQN HERON
Newton, Michael Ronald , FIEIE	LT CDR	E	WE	22.09.87	BRNC RNSU SOTON
Nice, Paul Richard Arthur	LT(SL)	X		01.10.95	BLACKWATER
Nicholas, Bryan John , BSc	LT(SL)	X	P	16.05.90	771 SK5 SAR
Nicholas, Stephen Paul , BEng	LT(SL)	E	MESM	01.04.94	VICTORIOUS(STBD)
Nicholas, Timothy William	LT CDR(SL)	X	P	01.10.91	RAF SHAWBURY
Nicholl, Stuart (Act Surg Lt)	SURG LT	-		07.01.95	DARTMOUTH BRNC
Nicholls, Barry Austin	LT RM(SD)	RM		01.01.93	RMB STONEHOUSE
Nicholls, David Vernon , psc(m)	COL	RM	MLDR	30.06.95	NP1044
Nicholls, Guy Anthony	LT(SD)	E	WE	13.06.91	CFM PORTSMOUTH
Nichols, Elizabeth Anne , MB, BS	SURG LT	-		01.08.91	JSMU HK
Nicholson, David Jeremy	LT(SL)	X	P	16.06.89	MOD PE ASC
Nicholson, David Peter	2LT(UCE)	RM		01.09.94	CTCRM LYMPSTONE
Nicholson, Graeme , MB, BCh	SURG LTCDR	-	GMPP	01.08.92	RNAS CULDROSE
Nicholson, Heather , BSc	LT	S		06.04.89	RALEIGH
Nicholson, Kristin James , BA	LT	S		01.08.94	NP 2010
Nicholson, Paul James	LT(SD)	E	WE	10.06.88	CAPT(H) DEVPT
Nicholson, Simon Charles Lawrence , pce	CDR	X	MCD	30.06.96	CWTA PTSMTH
Nicholson, Shaun Raymond	LT	X		22.11.94	HURWORTH
Nicklas, Colin James , BEng, AMIEE	LT	E	WE	01.06.92	DARTMOUTH BRNC
Nickolls, Kevin Paul , BEng	LT	E	AE	01.01.92	EXCHANGE GERMANY
Nicol, Peter James Stewart , MB, BS, LRCP, MRCS	SURG CDR	-	GMPP	30.06.94	NELSON
Nicoll, Andrew John	SLT	E	WESM	01.09.94	DARTMOUTH BRNC
Nicoll, Anthony John Keay , pce, pce(sm)	CDR	X	SM	30.06.87	CSST SHORE FSLN
Nicoll, Steve Kenneth (Loc Capt Rm)	LT RM(SD)	RM	MTO	01.01.94	FONA SUPPORT
Nimmons, Paul	SLT(SL)	E	MESM	01.01.93	CARDIFF
Nisbet, James Henry Thomas	LT CDR	X	MCD	01.07.95	GLASGOW
Niven, Graham David	LT CDR	X	AWO(A)	01.03.81	DARTMOUTH BRNC
Nixon, Michael Charles , OBE, jsdc, pcea	CDR	X	P	30.06.90	INVINCIBLE
Nixon, Paul William , BSc, CEng, MIMechE	CDR	E	MESM	30.06.96	NEPTUNE SM1
Noakes, Kevin Massie , BEng	LT	E	WE	01.05.94	EDINBURGH
Noble, Geoffrey David , BA, psc, I(1)Sw	CDR	S	SM	31.12.89	2SL/CNH
Noble, Mark Jonathan Dean , psc	MAJ	RM	PH	31.12.94	2SL/CNH
Noble, Phillip Peter , MSc	LT CDR(SD)	MS	SM	01.10.92	FOSM NWOOD OPS

Name	Rank	Spec	Sub-spec	Seniority	Where serving
Noblett, Peter Gordon Arthur	LT(SL)	X	SM	01.11.91	TRENCHANT
Nolan, Anthony Laurence	LT CDR(SD)	X	C	01.10.95	ELANT/NAVNW
Nolton, James Raymond , BSc	LT CDR	E	ME	01.02.86	NEPTUNE NT
Noon, David	SLT(SD)	S	CA	23.07.95	DOLPHIN
Noon, Paul	SLT(SL)	X	P U/T	01.01.96	705 SQN SEAHAWK
Norford, Michael	SLT(SD)	X	PT	03.04.94	HERALD
Norgan, David James , BA	LT	X		01.07.93	COVENTRY
Norgate, Perry Raymond Edward	SLT(SD)	E	ME	19.06.95	SULTAN
Norman, Alison Esther Phyllis	CHAPLAIN	SF		01.10.92	CAPT F1(SEA)
Norman, Jonathan Richard Aston , BSc	LT RM	RM		01.09.91	2SL/CNH
Norman, Phillip Douglas	LT(SD)	E	WE	18.02.94	COLLINGWOOD
Norman, Peter Gilford	CAPT RM	RM	LC	01.09.92	RNSC GREENWICH
Norman, Simon John	LT(SL)	X	P	16.06.83	750 SQN OBS SCH
Norman, Shaun Lindsay , BEng	LT(SL)	E	AE	01.06.89	SULTAN
Norman-Walker, Belinda Sophie , BA	LT(SL)	S		01.05.95	FOSM NWOOD OPS
Normanshire, David Jess , BSc	SLT(SL)	X	O U/T	01.01.95	DARTMOUTH BRNC
Norris, Andrew Michael , BSc	LT(SL)	I		01.03.87	SULTAN
Norris, Guy Patrick	LT(SL)	X	O	16.07.93	820 SQN
Norris, James Garnet , BA	LT	E	AE	01.11.92	899 SQN HERON
Norris, Richard Edward , BDS, LDS RCS(Eng)	SGCDR(D)	-		30.06.96	EXCHANGE USA
Norris, Robert John , pce	CDR	X	PWO(A)	30.06.95	DA SINGAPORE
Norris, William	SURG SLT	-		01.07.94	DARTMOUTH BRNC
Norsworthy, Claire Victoria	LT(SL)	S		04.04.91	CINCFLEET
North, Nigel John , DSC, pcea	LT CDR(SL)	X	P	01.03.85	RNAS PORTLAND
Northcote, Kevin Hendon	LT(SD)	X	PT	04.01.85	DRAKE CBP
Northcott, Michael Kevin	SLT(SL)	E	WE	01.05.95	DARTMOUTH BRNC
Northcott, Martin Richard , CEng, MIMarE	LT CDR(SD)	E	ME	01.10.90	DG SHIPS PTSMTH
Northover, Adam Frederick , BSc	SLT	X		01.09.94	PEACOCK
Northwood, Gerard Rodney , pce	LT CDR	X	PWO(A)	01.01.93	ALDERNEY
Norton, Andrew Jonathan , BSc, CEng, MIEE, psc	CDR	E	WE	30.06.87	2SL/CNH
Notley, Louis Paul	LT CDR	S	SM	01.03.96	NORTHUMBERLAND
Nowell, Jonathan Simon	LT(SL)	X	O	01.10.90	820 SQN
Nowosielski, Frank	LT CDR(SD)	X	AV	01.10.93	SULTAN
Noyce, Nigel Roderick	LT	X		15.01.89	BFFI
Noyce, Roger Grenville , MRINA	LT(SL)	X		01.06.95	SHETLAND
Noyce, Vincent Robert Amos	LT	X	FC	01.11.93	801 SQN
Noye, Charles Lovell , MBE, AMINucE	LT CDR	E	MESM	21.02.84	CAPTAIN SM2
Noyes, Andrew John Frederick , jsdc, psc, psc(m)　(Loc Lt Col)	MAJ	RM		31.12.84	HQRM
Noyes, David James	LT	S		01.12.89	ILLUSTRIOUS
Nugent, Colin James	LT(SD)	X	EW	29.07.94	DRYAD
Nunn, Christopher John , OBE, nadc, psc(a)　(Loc Lt Col)	MAJ	RM	PH	30.06.88	HQ ARRC
Nunn, Gerald Eric , BSc, PGCE	LT CDR(SL)	I		01.10.95	SULTAN
Nurse, Michael Talbot , BSc, I(2)Ge	LT CDR	E	AE	01.06.88	2SL/CNH
Nurser, John Arthur , BA	LT CDR(SD)	E	WE	01.10.92	FOSF
Nurton, Katherine , BDS	SG LT(D)	-		08.08.95	HONG KONG DENTAL
Nurton, Robert , B, A, BA	CHAPLAIN	CE		27.09.77	WARRIOR

O

Name	Rank	Spec	Sub-spec	Seniority	Where serving
O'Brien, John Dermot	CDR(SD)	X	AV	01.10.94	FONA
O'Brien, Kieran John , BEng	LT	E	AE	01.02.92	RNSC GREENWICH
O'Brien, Peter Charles , BSc, PGCE, adp	LT CDR	I	METOC	23.04.88	DNPS
O'Brien, Patrick Michael Christopher , BEng, MIEE	LT(SL)	I		01.01.87	RNSC GREENWICH
O'Brien, William Christopher , DFM	CAPT RM(SD)	RM	PH	01.10.93	CTCRM
O'Byrne, Patrick Barry Mary	LT	X	SM	01.11.92	DOLPHIN SM SCHL
O'Callaghan, Sean Tiernan	LT(SD)	MS		03.04.92	INM ALVERSTOKE
O'Connell, Morgan Ross , MB, BCh, BAO, DPM, FRC.Psych	SURG CAPT	-	CN/P	31.12.93	RH HASLAR
O'Connell-Davidson, John Brian	LT CDR(SD)	E	MESM	01.10.92	DRAKE CBS
O'Connor, Rodney Charles , aws	CDR	X	O	31.12.83	ACE SRGN TURKEY
O'Donnell, Ian Mark　(Loc Capt Rm)	LT RM(SD)	RM	MTO	01.01.91	RNSC GREENWICH
O'Flaherty, Christopher Patrick John	LT	X	MCD	01.03.91	FOST MPV(SEA)
O'Grady, Matthew James	LT CDR	S	SM	16.11.92	UN NEW YORK
O'Hara, Gerard Connor　(Act Lt Rm)	2LT	RM		01.09.92	42 CDO RM

Name	Rank	Spec	Sub-spec	Seniority	Where serving
O'Leary, Adrian Michael	LT(SL)	X	O U/T	01.10.95	HERON
O'Leary, Simon Richard , BSc, n	LT(SL)	X		01.01.92	CHATHAM
O'Neill, Patrick John , MA, MSc	LT CDR	E	WESM	01.05.92	MOD (BATH)
O'Neill, Paul	LT	E	MESM	01.10.95	RNC DPT NS&TECH
O'Neill, Richard Kim , pce, psc	CDR	X	O	31.12.89	FEARLESS
O'Neill, Steven	LT RM	RM		29.04.96	CTCRM
O'Nyons, Yorick Ian , BA	LT	X		01.07.94	DOLPHIN SM SCHL
O'Reilly, Sean Anthony , pce, psc	CDR	X	MCD	31.12.95	CDRE MFP
O'Reilly, Terence Michael	LT CDR	E	AE	27.05.90	702 SQN OSPREY
O'Shaughnessy, David John	SLT	E	ME	01.01.95	DARTMOUTH BRNC
O'Shaughnessy, Francis William Gurney , fsc, I(1)Sp, I(2)Sp	LT CDR	X	PWO	08.10.80	INTREPID
O'Shaughnessy, Patrick Joseph	LT(SD)	E	WE	15.06.90	DG SHIPS CAM HSE
O'Shea, Eamon Patrick	LT	E	AE	01.07.90	DGA(N) ASE SHAWK
O'Sullivan, Aidan Marian	LT CDR(SD)	X	O	01.10.92	849 SQN HQ
O'Sullivan, Barrie Oliver	LT(SL)	X	P	16.11.90	EXCHANGE USA
O'Sullivan, Michael Louis James , BSc	LT	X	H2	01.08.93	RNSC GREENWICH
O'Toole, Mathew Charles	SLT	E	MESM	01.09.94	DARTMOUTH BRNC
Oakes, Ian	LT(SL)	X	P	16.06.94	846 SQN
Oakes, Raymond Leslie	LT CDR(SD)	X	C	01.10.94	FONA
Oakey, John Derek	LT CDR	X	PWO(U)	30.01.83	DRYAD
Oakey, Kathryn	LT(SL)	W	S	25.04.92	FONA
Oakley, Nicholas George , MSc, AMIEE	LT CDR	E	WESM	01.08.93	TRENCHANT
Oakley, Sarah Ellen , BA	SLT	X		01.09.94	SHEFFIELD
Oatley, Timothy	LT(SL)	X	O	16.07.94	810 SQN OEU
Obrien, Ian Patrick , BTech	LT(SD)	E	WE	24.02.95	FEARLESS
Obrien, Paul Terence , BSc, PhD	SLT(SL)	X		01.01.95	DARTMOUTH BRNC
Oddy, David Mark	LT(SL)	X	P	16.08.90	HQ CDO AVN
Offen, Suzanne Marion	LT	Q		18.01.94	RNDHU DERRIFORD
Officer, Robert Lennie	LT(SL)	X		01.02.96	DRYAD
Offord, Matthew Ronald	LT	X	SM	01.04.94	VIGILANT(PORT)
Oflaherty, John Stephen , BEng	LT(SL)	E	ME	01.01.94	CARDIFF
Ogden, Braddan	LT(SL)	X	O	01.04.95	702 SQN OSPREY
Ogden, George Herbert , MB, BCh	SURG LTCDR	-	SM	01.02.96	RH HASLAR
Ogilvie, Mark Anthony	LT(SL)	X	P	01.10.94	846 SQN
Ogle, Nicholas	SLT(SL)	X		01.01.94	ENDURANCE
Oherlihy, Simon Ian , MA	2LT(GRAD)	RM		01.09.94	COMACCHIO GP RM
Okukenu, Dele	LT(SL)	X	P	01.01.96	845 SQN
Oldfield, Paul Henry , MSc, MBCS	LT CDR(SL)	I		01.10.95	NWOOD CIS
Oliphant, William	LT	S		01.10.90	HQBF CYPRUS
Olive, Peter Nicholas , n	LT	X		01.11.90	LONDON
Oliver, Graham	LT(SL)	I	METOC	01.05.91	RFANSU
Oliver, Kevin Brian , BEng	LT RM	RM	MLDR	01.09.90	HQ 3 CDO BDE RM
Ollerton, Justin	SLT(SL)	X	P	01.05.93	810 SQN SEAHAWK
Olliver, Adrian John	LT(SL)	S	SM	16.09.88	MOD (BATH)
Onions, Judith Mary , ARRC	LT CDR	Q	IC	11.02.91	UKSU AFSOUTH
Onyike, Chinyere Eme , BEng, MSc, AMIEE	LT	E	WE	01.01.94	MANCHESTER
Orchard, Adrian Paul	LT(SL)	X	P	16.01.91	899 SQN HERON
Ord, Michael	SLT(SL)	E	AE	01.01.94	DARTMOUTH BRNC
Ordway, Christopher Norman Maurice Patrick	2LT	RM		01.09.94	COMACCHIO GP RM
Organ, Peter John , CEng, FIMarE, nadc, ndc, psc	CAPT	E	ME	30.06.90	SA THE HAGUE
O'riordan, Michael Patrick , BSc, pce, pcea	LT CDR	X	P	01.04.89	CATTISTOCK
Ormshaw, Richard John , pcea, tp	LT CDR(SL)	X	P	01.10.90	815 OEU OSPREY
Orridge, Stephen Kenneth , BSc, CEng, MIMechE	LT CDR	E	MESM	01.07.90	MOD (BATH)
Orton, David Michael , BSc	LT(SL)	I		01.05.91	SULTAN
Osbaldestin, Richard	SLT(SL)	X		01.01.95	DRYAD
Osborn, Colvin Graeme , BSc	LT	X		01.06.94	SCEPTRE
Osborn, Richard Marcus	LT	X		01.02.91	DRYAD
Osbourn, Simon Edwin John , pce	LT CDR	X	PWO(U)	01.04.93	EDINBURGH
Osman, Mark Ronald , pcea, psc	LT CDR(SL)	X	P	01.09.86	705 SQN SEAHAWK
Oswald, Sir (John) Julian (Robertson), GCB, rcds,psc	ADM OF FLEET			02.03.92	
Osmond, Justin Bruce , BEng	LT	E	AE	01.02.91	LOAN DRA FARN
Ottewell, Paul Steven	SLT	X		01.09.94	DARTMOUTH BRNC

Name	Rank	Spec	Sub-spec	Seniority	Where serving
Oulds, Keith Anthony , BEng	LT	X	MW	01.09.92	CROMER
Oura, Adrian Nicholas	2LT(UCE)	RM		01.09.95	CTCRM LYMPSTONE
Ovenden, Keith	LT(SD)	E	AE(M)	15.10.93	RNAS YEOVILTON
Ovenden, Neil Stephen Paul	LT CDR	X	PWO(U)	01.02.95	EXETER
Ovens, Jeremy John , BSc, pce, pcea	LT CDR	X	O	01.01.91	RNSC GREENWICH
Ovens, Michael James	LT	X	PWO(U)	01.07.90	EXCHANGE AUSTLIA
Overington, Nigel , BSc, pce	CDR	X	PWO(U)	31.12.90	MOD (LONDON)
Owen, Elaine Beverly	LT CDR	S		10.12.90	WARRIOR
Owen, Gerard , BSc	LT(SL)	X		01.01.93	DRYAD
Owen, Glyn	SLT(SL)	X	O	01.09.94	702 SQN OSPREY
Owen, Nigel Richard , jsdc, pce	CAPT	X	AWO(U)	30.06.93	ACE SRGN ITALY
Owen, Peter Clive , pcea	LT CDR(SL)	X	P	01.10.91	MOD PE ASC
Owen, Philip Dennis	LT CDR(SL)	X	ATC	01.10.93	RAF SHAWBURY
Owen, William Andrew , BSc, PGCE	LT(SL)	I		01.11.88	EXCELLENT
Owens, Daniel Tudor , BEng	LT	E	ME	01.08.91	SULTAN

P

Name	Rank	Spec	Sub-spec	Seniority	Where serving
Pace, Steven	LT(SD)	E	MESM	16.10.92	MOD (BATH)
Pacey, Peter John , MA, MSc, nadc	CAPT	E	WE	31.12.91	MOD (LONDON)
Pack, Simon James , CBE, psc(m)	MAJ GEN	RM		04.12.94	HQBF GIBRALTAR
Packham, Craig Nicholas Ronald	LT(SL)	X	P	01.03.96	820 SQN
Paddock, Lee David	LT(SL)	X	SM	01.03.94	SCEPTRE
Page, Christopher Leslie William , CEng, MIMechE	CAPT	E	ME	31.12.91	MOD (LONDON)
Page, Durward Charles Miller , BSc	LT RM	RM		01.09.94	COMACCHIO GP RM
Page, David Michael , BSc, CEng, MIEE	LT CDR	E	WE	01.04.90	2SL/CNH
Page, Lewis , BA	LT(SL)	X		01.04.94	DRYAD
Page, Michael Christian , MA, psc (Loc Maj)	CAPT RM	RM	LC	01.09.89	BALTAP
Page, Mark	MID(SL)	X	O U/T	01.05.95	DARTMOUTH BRNC
Page, Simon Peter , BSc	LT CDR	X	PWO(A)	01.05.89	DRYAD
Page, Simon Peter , BEd	LT	I	SM	01.09.89	CSST SHORE FSLN
Page, Trevor Andrew	LT(SD)	E	ME	10.06.94	EXCELLENT
Paice, Simon David , BA	LT	X	H2	01.04.94	BULLDOG
Paine, Michael Patrick William Halden , QHS, MB, BS, FRCS (Commodore)	SURG CAPT	-	CO/S	31.12.88	CINCFLEET
Painter, Christopher John , BSc, AMBCS	LT CDR	S		23.02.87	MOD (BATH)
Pakes, Danyel Tobias	LT	E	WESM	01.01.96	NEPTUNE SM1
Paley, Ian Peter , BSc	LT CDR	E	MESM	01.09.91	TORBAY
Palfrey, Lindsay Jane , BSc	LT(SL)	I	FA	01.09.89	MOD DNR OUTPORTS
Pallister, Richard John Thornton OBE,	CDR(SL)	X	ATC	01.10.91	FONA
Pallot, Marcus Louis Alexander , LLB	LT	S		01.03.92	DARTMOUTH BRNC
Palmer, Alan Charles , MB, BS	SURG LT	-		01.03.92	HERALD
Palmer, Corin Brian (Loc Capt Rm)	LT RM	RM	WTO	01.09.90	HQRM
Palmer, Christopher Laurence , BSc, pce, pcea, psc	CDR	X	O	30.06.91	DARTMOUTH BRNC
Palmer, David Leonard , OBE	CDR(SD)	X	EW	01.10.87	MOD (LONDON)
Palmer, Geoffrey David	LT CDR(SD)	X	PR	01.10.88	NAVAL DRAFTING
Palmer, John , BA, BEng	SLT(SL)	E	WE	01.06.93	DARTMOUTH BRNC
Palmer, James Ernest , BSc	LT CDR	E	WE	01.10.87	PJHQ
Palmer, Michael Edward , BEng	LT	E	WE	01.11.93	RICHMOND
Palmer, Michael Robert , MBE, TEng, AMRINA, psc	LT CDR(SD)	E	HULL	01.04.83	NEPTUNE NT
Palmer, Phillip Alan , BA	LT CDR	X	SM	01.07.89	FOSM NWOOD OPS
Palmer, Rhoderick Adrian Nigel , BSc, ACGI, psc	CDR	E	AE	30.06.90	MOD (LONDON)
Palmer, Richard John , BEng, AMRAeS, AMIEE	LT	E	AE	01.11.90	EXCHANGE USA
Pamphilon, Michael John , pcea, psc	LT CDR	X	P	01.03.88	FONA
Pancott, Brian Michael , BSc, psc, mdtc	CDR	E	WE	31.12.91	MOD (LONDON)
Pannett, Leonard William , BSc	SLT(SL)	E	WESM	01.02.94	DARTMOUTH BRNC
Panteli, John Michael , BEng	LT(SL)	E	AE	01.04.91	MOD DGA(N)RNHSMP
Panther, Andrew Mark , BEng	LT	E	WE	01.07.92	DSSC PTSMTH
Pardoe, Elton Ramsey	LT(SL)	X		01.12.94	DRYAD
Paris, William , BEng	LT(SL)	E	WE	01.05.93	MOD DNR OUTPORTS
Park, Brian Campbell , BA	LT(SL)	S		01.06.94	NBC PORTSMOUTH
Parker, Brian Charles	CDR(SD)	E	AE(M)	01.10.92	RNAW PERTH
Parker, George Patrick , BEd, jsdc	CDR	I		31.12.90	CENTURION

Name	Rank	Spec	Sub-spec	Seniority	Where serving
Parker, Henry Hardyman , MA	LT CDR	E	WESM	01.01.94	RNSC GREENWICH
Parker, Ian Robert , BSc, MIMechE	CDR	E	MESM	31.12.93	MOD (BATH)
Parker, Jeremy Vernham , BSc, psc(m), osc (Loc Lt Col)	MAJ	RM		30.06.92	CINCFLEET
Parker, Jeremy William , pce, ocds(USN)	CAPT	X	AWO(A)	31.12.94	SACLANT USA
Parker, Mark Neal , BEng, MSc, CEng, MIMarE, MCGI	LT CDR	E	ME	01.03.91	EXETER
Parker, Robert John	SLT	X		01.01.94	BRAZEN
Parker, Roger Metson , MA, MSc, CEng, FIEE, rcds, ndc, psc	CAPT	E	WE	31.12.87	EXCELLENT
Parker, Stephen John , MB, BSc, BS, FRCS, FRCSEd	SURG LTCDR	-	SM	01.08.94	RH HASLAR
Parker, Timothy , BSc	LT(SL)	I		01.11.95	COLLINGWOOD
Parkes, Roger John , pce, psc	CDR	X	AWO(A)	30.06.84	2SL/CNH FOTR
Parkin, Malcolm Ian , BEng	LT	E	ME	01.07.91	SULTAN
Parkinson, Andrew	SLT(SD)	X	AV	23.07.95	RFANSU
Parkinson, James Michael , BSc, CEng, MIEE, nadc, jsdc (Commodore)	CAPT	E	WESM	30.06.90	MOD (LONDON)
Parkinson, Richard Ian , BA	LT	E	AE	01.01.92	DGA(N) ASE
Parks, Edward Patrick , jsdc (Loc Maj)	CAPT RM	RM		01.09.90	RNSC GREENWICH
Parnell, Adam David , BEng	LT	E	WE	01.04.93	DRYAD
Parr, Gavin Nicholas	LT RM	RM		01.09.95	DEF SCH OF LANG
Parr, Matthew John , BSc, pce, pce(sm)	LT CDR	X	SM	01.10.92	FOSM NWOOD OPS
Parr, Michael John Edward	SLT	X		01.01.94	EDINBURGH
Parr, Nicola Karen	SLT(SL)	X		01.09.94	CUMBERLAND
Parrett, Andrew	SLT(SD)	X	C	25.07.93	COLLINGWOOD
Parrett, John William	LT(SD)	E	MESM	16.10.92	NEPTUNE NT
Parris, Kevin John , BSc, jsdc, pce	CDR	X	PWO(U)	31.12.88	MOD (LONDON)
Parrish, Cedric Arthur Myers , OBE, MA, MPhil, I(2)Ru (Act Capt)	CDR	E	WESM	31.12.80	SA MOSCOW
Parrock, Neil Graham	LT(SL)	X	P	01.07.95	819 SQN
Parrott, James Philip	SLT	X		01.09.93	GLOUCESTER
Parry, Alexander Keith Illiam , BSc	LT(SL)	S		01.02.90	COMAW SEA
Parry, Christopher Adrian , BSc, PhD	SURG LT	-		12.08.94	RNAS YEOVILTON
Parry, Christopher John , MA, pce, pcea, psc	CDR	X	O	30.06.89	DRYAD MWC
Parry, David Reginald	LT(SD)	X	EW	03.04.92	CENTURION
Parry, Jonathan	LT RM	RM		27.04.95	45 CDO RM
Parry, Jonathan David Frank	LT	X	P	01.05.92	820 SQN
Parry, Mark	SLT	E	AE	01.09.93	DARTMOUTH BRNC
Parry, Nicholas Thomas , BSc, AMIEE, CGIA, psc, mdtc	CDR	E	WESM	31.12.94	CSST SEA
Parry, Roger John	LT(SD)	E	AE(M)	16.10.92	DGA(N) ASE
Parry, Robin Wyn , BSc, CEng, MIMechE, psc	CDR	E	ME	31.12.93	SULTAN
Parsonage, Robert James	LT CDR	E	MESM	07.10.89	VICTORIOUS(STBD)
Parsons, Andrew David , BSc	LT	X		01.01.92	DRYAD
Parsons, Brian Robert , BSc	LT CDR	E	AE	01.02.93	801 SQN
Parsons, Christopher Graham , BSc, MDA, CEng, MIEE	LT CDR	E	WE	01.03.92	COLLINGWOOD
Parsons, Geoffrey , MSc, CEng, MIEE, MBIM, gw	CDR	E	WE	30.06.93	PAAMS PARIS
Parsons, Patrick Hugh , osc(us)	MAJ	RM	MLDR	31.12.92	CDO LOG REGT RM
Parsons, Philip Kelvin Charles , MSc	LT CDR	I		29.07.85	DNPS
Parsons, Simon Christopher , MA, CEng, MIEE, AMIEE	LT CDR	E	WE	01.04.92	MOD DFS(CIS) GOS
Partington, John , MRIN, MIMgt	LT CDR	X	H CH	01.09.84	MOD (LONDON)
Parton, Stephen Lewis	LT	S		01.07.89	BRAVE
Partridge, Carl	SLT(SL)	X	O	01.01.93	FONA DAEDALUS
Parvin, Philip Stanley , BEng, MSc, CEng, MIMarE, MIMechE	LT	E	MESM	01.02.89	MOD (BATH)
Parvin, Richard Alan	2LT(GRAD)	RM		01.05.95	CTCRM LYMPSTONE
Pask, Raymond George , AMIMarE	LT CDR	E	ME	07.01.88	CFM PORTSMOUTH
Pass, David , BSc	LT(SL)	X	O U/T	01.12.95	RNAS CULDROSE
Passingham, Rodney Edris , MSc, CEng, MIEE	CDR	E	WE	31.12.89	MOD (BATH)
Paterson, Fergus James Blair	LT	X		01.08.91	DRYAD
Paterson, Michael Paul , n	LT	X		01.06.93	CUMBERLAND
Paton, Alan John Malcolm	SLT(SD)	E	ME	19.06.95	SULTAN
Paton, Christopher Mark	2LT(GRAD)	RM		01.09.94	COMACCHIO GP RM
Paton, John , jsdc, pce	CDR	X	PWO(U)	31.12.88	2SL/CNH
Patrick, James , MSc, psc	CDR	I		30.06.89	RM POOLE
Patterson, Andrew , BSc	LT(SL)	X	P	16.03.93	706 SQN SEAHAWK
Patterson, David , BEng	LT	E	WE	01.12.94	IRON DUKE
Patterson, John , BSc	SLT	X		01.01.94	DARTMOUTH BRNC
Patterson, Michael Colin	LT(CS)RM	-		17.04.88	MOD DNR OUTPORTS

Name	Rank	Spec	Sub-spec	Seniority	Where serving
Patterson, Scott Douglas	SLT	E	WE	01.01.95	DARTMOUTH BRNC
Patterson, Stephen Robert , BSc	LT RM	RM		01.09.93	NP 1061
Pattinson, Ian Howard , BSc	LT CDR	S		01.05.91	2SL/CNH
Pattison, Kelvin , BA(OU), MA(Ed)	LT CDR(SL)	I	METOC	01.10.89	2SL/CNH
Paul, Russell William Fordyce , psc	CAPT RM	RM	LC	01.09.90	COMACCHIO GP RM
Paul, Timothy John , BEng, MIMechE	LT(SL)	E	ME	01.08.92	CDRE MFP
Paulson, Richard Brian , AMIEE	LT	E	WE	01.05.96	COLLINGWOOD
Pavey, Emma Lesley , LLB	SLT(SL)	X		01.01.95	DARTMOUTH BRNC
Payling, Robert Stuart , BSc	LT(SL)	X	P	16.04.89	RAF SHAWBURY
Payne, Daniel	LT(SD)	E	ME	13.02.92	ENDURANCE
Payne, Diane	SURG SLT	-		01.07.94	DARTMOUTH BRNC
Payne, John Durley , BSc, n	LT	X		01.06.90	DRYAD
Payne, Matthew John	LT(SL)	X		01.05.93	BLACKWATER
Payne, Malcolm Selby	T/LT(SDT)	X	C	10.06.94	DGCIS BRISTOL
Payne, Philip John , BA	LT	X	H2	01.07.94	ROEBUCK
Payne, Richard Charles	LT CDR	X	P	16.04.93	LEEDS CASTLE
Payne, Richard William , BA	LT	X		01.12.94	DOLPHIN SM SCHL
Payne, Terry , BEng	LT(SL)	E	WE	01.12.93	LIVERPOOL
Payne-Hanlon, Peter Norman , FIEIE, MIMgt	CDR	E	WESM	31.12.90	2SL/CNH FOTR
Peace, Richard William	SLT(SD)	E	MESM	13.06.94	TRIUMPH
Peach, Christopher Charles , pce	CDR	X	O	30.06.88	MOD (LONDON)
Peach, Graham Leslie , BSc, MIEE, psc	CDR	E	WE	30.06.95	2SL/CNH
Peachey, Richard , BSc	LT(SL)	X	P U/T	01.03.95	705 SQN SEAHAWK
Peachment, Beverly Lynn , BSc	LT(SL)	I		01.01.93	COLLINGWOOD
Peacock, Alan Selwyn , pce	LT CDR	X	PWO(N)	19.11.79	NBC PORTSMOUTH
Peacock, John Gordon	LT CDR(SL)	I		22.09.90	DNPS
Peacock, Michael Robert	LT(SD)	E	MESM	14.10.88	DG SHIPS DEVONPT
Peacock, Stephen , BSc, AMIEE	LT CDR	E	WESM	01.06.92	TURBULENT
Peacock, Timothy James , BA	LT	X	P	01.01.90	810 SQN A FLIGHT
Peak, Martyn	SLT(SD)	X	g	03.04.95	COLLINGWOOD
Pear, Ian Keith , BSc, MIMarE	LT CDR	E	MESM	01.04.96	MOD (BATH)
Pearce, Andrew	SLT	E	WE	01.09.93	DARTMOUTH BRNC
Pearce, Alan William	LT CDR(SL)	I		22.09.90	COLLINGWOOD
Pearce, Barry Seward , CEng, MIERE	LT CDR(SL)	E	WE	01.03.81	CFM PORTSMOUTH
Pearce, Damianjason , BSc	LT RM	RM		29.04.93	45 CDO RM
Pearce, Jonathan Kenneth Charles , BA, I(1)Ab	CDR	S		31.12.91	DRAKE BSO(F)
Pearce, Karen , BSc, I(1)Ru	LT CDR	I		01.05.93	2SL/CNH
Pearce, Lucy	SURG SLT	-		27.07.94	DARTMOUTH BRNC
Pearce, Michael John , psc (Act Cdr)	LT CDR	S		01.02.82	2SL/CNH FOTR
Pearce, Mark Lawrence	LT CDR	S		16.05.91	2SL/CNH
Pearce, Rebecca Anne	SLT(SL)	S		01.05.94	CSST SHORE FSLN
Pearce, Suzanne Ellen	LT(SL)	W	I	04.04.91	SULTAN AIB
Pearce, Timothy Ross , MA, psc (Loc Maj)	CAPT RM	RM		01.09.90	MOD (LONDON)
Pearey, Michael Scott , DSC, BSc, pcea	LT CDR	X	O	01.07.90	FOSF
Pears, Ian James , BSc	LT(SL)	X		01.01.91	SULTAN
Pearson, Benjamin James , BDS	SGLTCDR(D)	-		05.01.94	CINCFLEET
Pearson, Charles Peter Bellamy , BEng	LT(SL)	E	ME	01.08.93	BRAVE
Pearson, Christopher Robert , MB, BCh, BChir, MA, DLO	SURG LTCDR	-	GMPP	15.05.89	NELSON (PAY)
Pearson, George Sneddon , OBE, rcds	CDR	X	N	31.12.78	NELSON (PAY)
Pearson, John Jeremy , pce, psc, psc(a), odc(US)	CAPT	X	O	31.12.87	MOD DFCT
Pearson, Jon Richard	LT(SD)	E	WE	05.06.92	2SL/CNH
Pearson, Michael Edward	LT CDR(SD)	S	CAT	01.10.89	SAUDI AFPS SAUDI
Pearson, Michael Forbes	LT	X	O U/T	01.03.93	819 SQN
Pearson, Neil , BEng, CEng, MIMarE	LT	E	ME	01.08.89	CORNWALL
Pearson, Nigel John , MSc, CEng, MRAeS, jsdc	CAPT	E	AE	30.06.94	SULTAN AIB
Pearson, Stephen John	LT CDR	X	O	01.02.95	NOTTINGHAM
Peck, Ian John , BSc, CEng, MRAeS	LT CDR	E	AE	01.03.90	RNAS YEOVILTON
Peckham, David Reginald , BSc, (Eur Ing), CEng, MIEE, psc	LT CDR	E	WE	31.12.94	CAPT D5 SEA
Pedler, Mark David , BEng	SLT(SL)	X	P U/T	01.01.95	DARTMOUTH BRNC
Peel, Giles Robert , BSc, ACIS	LT CDR	S		01.11.93	MOD (BATH)
Peerman, Stephen John	LT CDR(SD)	E	WE	01.10.95	NWOOD CIS
Pegden, Clive , MSc	LT CDR	E	AE	16.02.81	SULTAN

Name	Rank	Spec	Sub-spec	Seniority	Where serving
Pegg, Russell Montfort , pce	CDR	X	PWO(U)	31.12.95	BDS WASHINGTON
Pegg, Stephen Michael , pce, psc	CDR	X	AWO(A)	30.06.88	SACLANT USA
Pegrum, Terrence Allen	LT(SL)	X	P	01.11.90	848 SQN HERON
Peilow, Benjamin Francis , BA, MILDM, psc	CDR	S		31.12.92	MOD (BATH)
Pell, Geoffrey Charles	LT CDR	X	AWO(A)	01.05.80	DAEDALUS
Pellow, Andrew John , BEng	LT(SL)	I		01.07.88	NEPTUNE SM1
Pelly, Gilbert Ralph	CAPT RM	RM		25.04.96	CTCRM
Pelly, Richard Cecil , MA, MSc, CEng, FIMarE, MIMechE	CAPT	E	ME	31.12.93	MOD (BATH)
Pemble, Matthew William Arthur	LT	E	WESM	01.05.91	REPULSE(PORT)
Pendle, Martin Erle John , BSc, jsdc	CDR	E	ME	30.06.95	PJHQ
Penfold, Michael Jamie	LT(SD)	E	WE	18.02.94	COLLINGWOOD
Pengelly, Simon Andrew Bruce	SLT(SL)	X	P U/T	01.01.94	EXCELLENT
Pennefather, David Anthony Somerset ,CB, OBE, rcds, psc(m), hcsc	MAJ GEN	RM	C	07.07.95	HQRM
Pennefather, William Jonathan Richard , jsdc	CDR	S		30.06.87	NELSON
Penniston, John Raymond , BSc	LT CDR	E	MESM	01.09.89	MOD (BATH)
Penny, Anthony David , MSc, AMIEE	CDR	E	WE	31.12.95	CAPT F6 (SEA)
Penprase, Jason Michael	LT(SL)	X		01.10.94	SEAHAWK
Penrice, Ian William	LT(SL)	X	P	01.08.94	846 SQN
Pentreath, Jonathan Patrick , BSc	LT CDR	X	P	01.12.95	815 FLT 246
Peppe, Alasdair George	LT	X		01.06.95	STARLING
Pepper, Martin Richard , BSc, pce, pcea, psc	CDR	X	O	31.12.92	RNAS PORTLAND
Percey, Steven John , BA	LT RM	RM		01.09.93	HQ 3 CDO BDE RM
Percharde, Michael Robert , BSc, pce	LT CDR	X	PWO(A)	16.08.90	LEDBURY
Percival, Andrew William , BA	LT	X		01.03.95	BRIDPORT
Percival, Fiona	SLT	X		01.05.94	YORK
Percival, Michael Christopher	LT	S		01.07.91	HQ CDO AVN
Perfect, David Maxwell , jsdc, pce(sm)	CDR	X	SM	31.12.86	ELANT/NAVNW
Perkins, John Robert , LRAM, LGSM, ARCM, pdm	CAPT RM(SD)	RM		01.10.93	RM BAND PLYMOUTH
Perkins, Michael Jonathan , BA, pce	CDR	X	PWO(A)	30.06.96	MOD (LONDON)
Perkins, Ross John	SLT	E		01.09.93	FEARLESS
Perks, James Le Seelleur	LT	X	SM	01.03.90	SPARTAN
Perowne, Benjamin Brian , rcds, pce, psc (Commodore)	CAPT	X	AWO(C)	31.12.87	CINCFLEET
Perowne, James Francis , OBE, pce(sm)	RADM	-	SM	04.01.95	FOSM NWOOD OPS
Perry, Andrew James	LT	S		16.07.91	CAPTAIN SM2
Perry, Guy Alan	LT(SL)	X	P	16.06.91	846 SQN
Perry, Jonathan Neil , MB, BCh (Act Surg Cdr)	SURG LTCDR	-	CX	01.08.90	RNDHU DERRIFORD
Perry, Richard , BSc, psc	LT CDR	E	MESM	01.11.90	SPLENDID
Perry, Russell John	LT(SL)	X	MW	01.11.93	QUORN
Perry, Robert William	LT RM(SD)	RM	MTO	01.01.92	HQ 3 CDO BDE RM
Perry-Evans, Sean Patrick Alfred , BSc, CEng, MIMarE, psc	LT CDR	E	ME	01.06.90	SULTAN
Peters, Adam John Urlin , BSc	LT CDR	X	SM	01.08.87	ENDURANCE
Peters, William Richard , BA	SLT	X		01.09.92	DRYAD
Petheram, Anthony John (Act Lt Cdr)	LT	X	PWO(C)	01.09.89	COLLINGWOOD
Petheram, Michael John , pce	LT CDR	X	PWO(U)	29.06.92	SANDOWN
Petherick, Jason Stewart	LT	X	FC	01.04.90	BOXER
Pethybridge, Richard Alan	LT	X		01.05.89	EXETER
Petitt, Simon Richard	LT	E	WE	01.02.90	COLLINGWOOD
Petrie, Melville James , MA, MIL, psc, l(2)Ch	LT CDR	S		16.07.84	TAMAR
Pett, Jeremy Graham , BSc	LT CDR	I		03.05.91	COLLINGWOOD
Pettitt, Gary William , pce	LT CDR	X	PWO(U)	01.01.94	FOST SEA
Petzer, Garth	CHAPLAIN	CE		09.01.96	DARTMOUTH BRNC
Pharoah, Richard John	LT CDR	X	P	01.08.80	SA MALAYSIA
Pheasant, John Christian Stephen , BSc	LT	S		01.10.93	2SL/CNH
Phelps, Guy , BSc	LT(SL)	X	P U/T	01.12.95	EXCELLENT
Phelps, Michael Anthony , BSc	CDR	E	ME	30.06.84	EXCELLENT
Phenna, Andrew , BEng	LT CDR	E	WE	01.03.96	MOD DGSW PTSMTH
Phesse, John Paul Lloyd	LT(SD)	E	AE(M)	15.10.93	ARK ROYAL
Philebrown, Stephen Robert , IEng, FIEIE	LT CDR	E	WE	23.04.90	DG SHIPS CAM HSE
Philip, Alistair David , BA, BSc	SLT(SL)	X		01.09.94	CHATHAM
Philip, Michael William , BSc	LT(SL)	I		01.09.88	NP 1061
Phillips, Andrew Ralph , MIMechIE	LT(SD)	E	AE(M)	07.09.95	SULTAN
Phillips, David Alan , pce, psc	CAPT	X	AWO(U)	30.06.93	RCDS

Name	Rank	Spec	Sub-spec	Seniority	Where serving
Phillips, David George , pce(sm)	CDR	X	SM	30.06.95	REPULSE(STBD)
Phillips, Gavin Peter	LT(SL)	X	P	16.12.92	801 SQN
Phillips, Ian Michael	LT(SD)	MS		29.07.94	RNH GIB
Phillips, James Nicholas , BEng	LT	E	WE	01.03.95	BOXER
Phillips, Jason	LT(SL)	X	O	01.03.91	810 SQN SEA
Phillips, Jeffrey Raymond	LT CDR	X	PWO(A)	09.07.89	DRYAD
Phillips, Matthew , BSc	LT(SL)	X	P U/T	01.04.96	HERON
Phillips, Michael Frederick	CDR	E	AE	30.06.85	LOAN DRA FARN
Phillips, Mark Jeremy , pce, pcea	LT CDR	X	P	01.07.92	FOST SEA
Phillips, Richard Thomas Ryder , MNI, pce, odc(Aus)	RADM	X	PWO	21.05.96	MOD (LONDON)
Phillips, Stephen Brian	LT CDR(SL)	X	O	01.03.79	FONA SULTAN
Phillips, Stephen John , MA, psc (Loc Maj)	CAPT RM	RM		01.09.90	PJHQ
Phillips, Timothy John , MSc, psc, gw	CDR	E	WE	30.06.92	ILLUSTRIOUS
Phillis, Ian Richard , MRAeS	LT(SL)	X	P	16.09.90	SEAHAWK
Philo, Julian Quentin	LT	E	ME	01.06.90	BRITANNIA
Philpot, David John , BEng	LT(SL)	E	WESM	01.06.95	CAPTAIN SM2
Philpott, Ashley Michael	SLT	X		01.09.93	DOLPHIN SM SCHL
Philpott, Geoffrey Richard , BA	CDR	S		30.06.90	BDS WASHINGTON
Philpott, Nigel Edward	LT	S		01.05.89	GLOUCESTER
Philpott, Trevor Acton , OBE, psc (Loc Lt Col)	MAJ	RM	PADJT	31.12.83	COMSTRIKFORSTH
Phipps, Tracey Anne , BA	LT(SL)	X	H2	01.02.94	GLEANER
Pickbourne, Martin , IEng, AMIMarE	LT CDR(SD)	E	ME	01.10.95	INVINCIBLE
Picken, Jeffrey David	LT CDR(SD)	E	MESM	01.10.90	CSST SHORE DEVPT
Pickering, Ian Jeffery	LT(SL)	X		01.03.96	DARTMOUTH BRNC
Pickering, Martin John , BA	CDR(SL)	I	METOC	01.10.92	SEAHAWK
Pickles, Ian Seaton , pce(sm)	LT CDR	X	SM	01.05.91	ORKNEY
Picksley, Michael Raymond	LT(SD)	E	WE	15.06.90	FLEET COMMS PLYM
Pickstone, Phillip Charles	LT CDR	E	MESM	20.08.93	TURBULENT
Pickthall, David Nicholas , BSc	LT CDR	E	WE	01.02.92	2SL/CNH FOTR
Pickup, Richard Allan , BSc, psc(m) (Loc Maj)	CAPT RM	RM		01.05.91	EXCHANGE ARMY UK
Picton, Annette Mary , psc	CAPT	W	SEC	30.06.96	MOD (LONDON)
Pierce, Adrian Kevern Maxwell , n	LT	X		01.02.92	BIRMINGHAM
Piercy, Peter Arthur Hacklett	LT CDR(SD)	X	PT	01.10.94	NELSON
Pierson, Matthew Fraser	LT RM	RM		01.09.92	40 CDO RM
Piggott, Graham David , MNI, pce, psc (Act Capt)	CDR	X	AWO(C)	30.06.86	NWOOD CIS
Pike, Martin Stephen , BSc	LT CDR	S		01.03.91	MOD (LONDON)
Pike, Richard	SLT(SL)	X	ATCU/T	01.03.94	RNAS CULDROSE
Pike, Sally	LT	Q	ONC	13.04.92	JSMU HK
Pike, Stuart	LT(SL)	X	P	16.02.95	814 SQN
Pile, Ian , TEng, AMIMarE	LT CDR(SD)	E	ME	01.10.89	SULTAN
Pile, Kenneth James , IEng, MIEEIE	LT CDR(SD)	E	WE	01.10.91	MOD DGSW PTSMTH
Pilkington, Alexander Gregory Howarth , BSc	LT RM	RM		01.09.94	CDO LOG REGT RM
Pillar, Andrew Robert , OBE, psc(a)	LT COL	RM		30.06.93	42 CDO RM
Pillar, Christopher David	LT CDR	X	PWO(U)	01.03.95	CAPT F2(SEA)
Pilley, Michael Anthony , pce	LT CDR	X	PWO(U)	16.09.84	LOAN OMAN
Pilsworth, Dermod Scott , MSc, CGIA	LT CDR	E	WE	01.06.85	CWTA PTSMTH
Pink, Simon Edward , n	LT	X		01.01.94	NORFOLK
Piper, Clare Jeanette	LT	Q		06.03.94	RNDHU DERRIFORD
Piper, Neale Derek	LT(QM)	Q		23.11.95	RNH GIB
Pipkin, Christopher , MB, BS, MRCPath	SURG CDR	-	CL	30.06.94	RH HASLAR
Pipkin, Peter John	MID(NE)	E	WE	01.05.95	NOTTINGHAM
Pipkin, Simon Christian	LT CDR(SL)	X	P	01.10.95	771 SK5 SAR
Pitcher, Caroline Dorothy	LT(SL)	W	S	04.01.92	CINCFLEET
Pitcher, James	LT CDR(SD)	E	AE(L)	01.10.93	RNAS CULDROSE
Pitcher, Paul , BA	LT	X		01.11.94	SPEY
Pitcher, Stephen John	LT	X	P	01.03.89	DEF SCH OF LANG
Pitchford, Ian Charles , BEng	LT	E	AE	01.08.95	SULTAN
Pitt, Johnathan Mark	LT(SL)	X	SM	01.06.94	EXCHANGE NLANDS
Pittard, Peter Michael , TEng, IEng, MITE, MIEEIE	LT CDR(SD)	E	WE	01.10.91	COLLINGWOOD
Pittaway, Christopher William , MVO, BA, pcea	LT CDR(SL)	X	P	01.03.85	LOAN DTEO BSC DN
Plackett, Andrew John , MA	LT(SL)	I		01.05.92	COLLINGWOOD
Plaice, Graham Conyers	LT(SD)	S	SM	12.12.91	VICTORIOUS(STBD)

Name	Rank	Spec	Sub-spec	Seniority	Where serving
Plant, Ian Robert , BSc	LT CDR	E	AE	01.07.90	MOD (LONDON)
Plant, Jeremy Neil Melrose , BSc	LT CDR	E	AE	01.05.92	DMCA BRISTOL
Plant, Martin Gary	LT CDR	E	WE	13.06.91	DSSC GLASGOW
Platt, Jonathan Howard , BSc	SLT(SL)	X	P U/T	01.01.94	HERON
Platt, Nicola	SLT(SD)	S	S	03.04.95	NELSON
Platt, Timothy Samuel , BSc	LT	X	MCD	01.04.92	MIDDLETON
Player, Hugh	MAJ	RM		26.06.90	CDO LOG REGT RM
Player, Rodney Charles	LT(SL)	X	P	16.02.88	899 SQN HERON
Pledger, David	LT(SD)	X	AV	16.12.94	SULTAN
Plewes, Andrew Burns	LT RM	RM		27.04.95	42 CDO RM
Plummer, John David , jsdc, pce	CDR	X	PWO	31.12.84	ELANT/NAVNW
Plumridge, Paul (Act Lt Cdr)	LT(SD)	E	ME	18.02.83	FORWARD
Pocock, David	LT(SL)	S		16.10.88	UKNSE AFNORTH NY
Podger, Kevin Gordon Ray , BSc, psc	CDR	E	MESM	30.06.95	CSST SEA
Podmore, Anthony , BSc	LT CDR	I		01.09.94	GANNET
Podmore, Colin Frederick , BSc, CEng, MIMarE, psc	CDR	E	ME	30.06.90	LOAN DRA HASLAR
Polding, Martin , BA	LT(SL)	X	P	01.05.94	848 SQN HERON
Poll, Martin	CHAPLAIN	CE		14.06.90	DARTMOUTH BRNC
Pollitt, David Nigel Anthony , pce(sm), psc	LT CDR	X	SM	01.04.89	FOSM NWOOD OPS
Pollock, David John	LT CDR	X	SM	01.01.95	TRIUMPH
Pollock, Malcolm Philip , pcea	LT CDR	X	O	01.07.95	URNU ABERDEEN
Pollock, Sir Michael, (Patrick), GCB, LVO, DSC, psc	ADM OF FLEET			01.03.74	
Pomeroy, Mark Anthony	LT(SD)	E	ME	18.06.93	BRITANNIA
Pomfrett, Nicholas John , BSc, pce, pce(sm)	LT CDR	X	SM	01.02.90	FOSM NWOOD OPS
Pond, David William , BEd, MIMgt, psc	CDR	I	METOC	30.06.91	SULTAN
Ponsford, Philip	LT(SL)	X	SM	01.07.91	DOLPHIN SM SCHL
Ponting, Lorraine	LT	Q	REGM	11.01.91	WARRIOR
Poole, Andrew James , BEd	LT(SL)	X	MCD	01.06.92	CHIDDINGFOLD
Poole, David , BA	LT CDR(SD)	E	ME	01.10.94	CAMPBELTOWN
Poole, Jason Lee , pce	LT CDR	X	MCD	01.04.94	MCM2 SEA
Poole, Timothy , BSc	LT(SL)	X	O	16.01.92	810 SQN SEAHAWK
Pooley, Steven William , BSc	LT	E	WESM	01.07.88	CWTA PTSMTH
Pope, Catherine Manuela , MSc	LT CDR	I	METOC	16.09.92	RNSC GREENWICH
Porrett, Johnathan Anthony	LT	S	SM	01.07.90	NELSON
Port, Leslie Alan , MBE	LT CDR	X	P	15.04.83	HQ CDO AVN
Porter, Andrew James , BEM	LT(SD)	E	WE	05.06.92	FOST SEA
Porter, Christopher William	LT CDR(SL)	X	O	01.10.94	MOD DGA(N)RNHSMP
Porter, Derek Lowry , BA	SLT(SL)	S		01.01.95	DARTMOUTH BRNC
Porter, Matthew Edward , BSc (Loc Capt Rm)	LT RM	RM		25.04.91	RM POOLE
Porter, Peter Alexander	LT RM	RM		27.04.95	45 CDO RM
Porter, Suzanne (Act Surg Lt)	SURG SLT	-		01.07.94	DARTMOUTH BRNC
Porter, Simon Paul	LT CDR	X	PWO(A)	01.09.94	EXETER
Porter, Timothy Benedict , BA	LT	S		01.05.94	SEAHAWK
Pothecary, Richard Edward , AMNI, pce	CDR	X	PWO(A)	31.12.93	ELANT/NAVNW
Potiphar, Darren Wayne	SURG LT	-		01.08.94	DRAKE CBP
Pott, Christopher Dutton , pce, psc(m), osc(Nig)	CDR	X	PWO	31.12.87	SHAPE BELGIUM
Potter, Andrew Michael , CDipAF	LT CDR	S		16.04.80	NELSON
Potter, David George	T/LT(SDT)	S	CA	02.09.94	SULTAN
Potter, David John	SLT(SD)	X	O	24.07.94	706 SQN SEAHAWK
Potter, Michael John , MA, MSc, CEng, MIMarE, MINucE, MinstP, psc	CDR	I	SM	31.12.89	2SL/CNH
Potter, Stephen (Loc Capt Rm)	LT RM(SD)	RM		01.01.91	RM POOLE
Potts, Duncan Laurence , BSc, pce	CDR	X	PWO(U)	30.06.96	BRILLIANT
Potts, Gary	SLT(SL)	E	WESM	01.05.93	DARTMOUTH BRNC
Potts, Jonathan Martyn , BSc	LT(SL)	I		01.03.88	SULTAN
Potts, Kevin Maxwell	LT CDR	X	P	01.02.92	815 SQN HQ
Poulter, Anthony Mervyn , OBE, pce, pce(sm)	CAPT	X	SM	30.06.92	WARRIOR
Pounder, Adam Guy Piers , pce	CDR(SL)	X	PWO(U)	01.10.93	SACLANT USA
Pounder, Michael	LT(SD)	X	H2	23.07.93	ENDURANCE
Pounds, Nicholas Ernest , psc(m)	LT COL	RM	A/TK	30.06.94	CDO LOG REGT RM
Powell, David Charles , MSc	CDR	E	ME	31.12.95	MOD (BATH)
Powell, Edward , BSc	SLT(SL)	X	P U/T	01.01.94	FONA CRANWELL

Name	Rank	Spec	Sub-spec	Seniority	Where serving
Powell, Jacqueline , LLB	LT(SL)	S		24.02.91	2SL/CNH
Powell, James Nicholas , BA	LT(SL)	X	P	01.09.91	819 SQN
Powell, Keith Andrew Thomas John , BSc (Loc Maj)	CAPT RM	RM		04.02.78	JACIG
Powell, Mark Andrew , BSc	LT	E	WESM	01.03.90	MOD (BATH)
Powell, Michael Justin	LT	S		01.07.91	CORNWALL
Powell, Richard Laurence , pce, pcea	LT CDR	X	P	01.11.92	IRON DUKE
Powell, Roger Norman , BA, BSc, psc	CDR	E	AE	31.12.94	MOD (LONDON)
Powell, Steven , pce, pcea, psc(a)	LT CDR	X	O	16.04.92	COMUKTG/CASWSF
Powell, Stephen John	LT CDR(SL)	X	P	01.10.93	LOAN DTEO BSC DN
Powell, Steven Richard	LT	X	MW	01.07.90	HURWORTH
Powell, William Glyn	LT	X	O	16.12.90	DRYAD
Power, Mark Davyd	LT	X		01.07.88	CFP SEA
Powis, Jonathan , pce, pce(sm)	CDR	X	SM	31.12.92	VICTORIOUS(STBD)
Powles, Derek	SLT	E	ME	01.09.92	SULTAN
Pratt, Angela Susan	LT	Q		29.08.90	RH HASLAR
Pratt, Ian Heggie , BSc, CEng, MIEE	LT CDR	E	WE	01.03.93	EXETER
Preece, David Graeme	LT	S		01.08.93	NEPTUNE SM1
Preece, David Wyndham , BEng, AMRAeS	LT(SD)	E	AE(L)	15.10.93	RNSC GREENWICH
Preece, Richard Mark , BM, BCh, ChB	SURG LTCDR	-	GMPP	01.08.93	MOD (LONDON)
Prendergast, Matthew	SURG SLT	-		01.07.95	DARTMOUTH BRNC
Prendergast, Sally-Ann , BSc	LT(SL)	I		26.02.90	CTCRM
Prentice, David Charles	LT	X	EW	22.12.89	DRYAD
Prescott, John , BSc, adp	LT CDR	E	WE	01.06.83	HQ DFTS
Prescott, Shaun , BEng, CEng, MIEE	LT	E	WE	01.11.88	MOD DGUW PTLAND
Prescott-Pickup, Marie Louise , BSc	LT(SL)	I		01.09.89	NWOOD CIS
Pressdee, Simon	SLT(SL)	X		01.01.96	DRYAD
Pressly, James Winchester , BSc	LT RM	RM		25.04.91	CDO LOG REGT RM
Preston, Mark Richard	LT(SL)	E	ME	01.01.90	DRAKE CFM
Preston, Ross Walker	2LT(GRAD)	RM		01.09.94	45 CDO RM
Preston-Jones, Noel Clisby	CAPT	S		31.12.94	MOD C OF N
Pretty, Darren	SLT	X		01.01.96	DARTMOUTH BRNC
Price, Andrew Michael	LT RM	RM		01.05.90	HQ 3 CDO BDE RM
Price, David John , pce	LT CDR	X	PWO(A)	01.04.93	PJHQ
Price, Dallas John Alistair , MB, BS, MRCP	SURG LTCDR	-		09.08.93	RNDHU DERRIFORD
Price, David William	LT(SD)	X	REG	14.12.90	MCTC
Price, Dominic William , BA	LT	X	H2	01.07.94	HERALD
Price, Frederick Earle Francis , MBE, MA, PhD, psc	CDR	I		30.06.95	CINCFLEET
Price, Graham	LT CDR(SD)	S	S	01.10.94	BIRMINGHAM
Price, Graham Paul , BEng	LT	E	MESM	01.12.91	REPULSE(PORT)
Price, John Philip , psc	CDR	E	ME	30.06.96	MOD (BATH)
Price, Julian	LT(SL)	X	O	16.11.94	819 SQN
Price, Martin John , BA, psc (Loc Maj)	CAPT RM	RM	MLDR	01.09.91	PJHQ
Price, Timothy Andrew , n	LT	X		01.07.90	RNSC GREENWICH
Price, Tania Lucille	LT CDR(SL)	W	I	01.10.92	CENTURION
Price, Terence Martin	LT(SD)	X	SM	24.07.92	PJHQ
Price, Terence Peter	LT(SD)	E	WE	09.06.89	DG SHIPS CAM HSE
Price, Trevor William , BSc	LT CDR	I	METOC	01.01.92	2SL/CNH FOTR
Price, Victoria	SURG SLT	-		29.08.95	DARTMOUTH BRNC
Prichard, John Leslie Lloyd , CEng, MIMarE, MIL, psc, l(2)Fr	LT	E	ME	30.06.94	MOD (LONDON)
Prideaux, David Martin	LT CDR(SD)	E	WE	01.10.87	MOD DGSW PTSMTH
Priestland, Colin Richard , BDS, MSc, MGDS RCS	SGCDR(D)	-		30.06.94	NELSON DTS
Priestley, Michael John , jsdc, pce	CDR	X	O	30.06.87	SHAPE BELGIUM
Prime, John Roger Martin , pce, psc, psc(a)	CDR	X	PWO(N)	30.06.88	DOLPHIN
Prince, Andrew Charles Vaughan , pce, pcea	LT CDR	X	O	16.02.88	DRYAD
Prince, Mark Edward , BEng	LT	E	MESM	01.07.93	VANGUARD(STBD)
Pring, Stuart James , BA	SLT(SL)	S		01.05.94	BOXER
Pringle, Anthony , pcea	LT CDR	X	P	01.07.90	FEARLESS
Prinsep, Timothy John , BEng	LT	E	WE	01.06.92	DG SHIPS CAM HSE
Prior, Grant Michael	LT	E	WE	01.07.89	CWTA PTSMTH
Prior, Kate Rebecca Edna Jane	SURG SLT	-		15.09.93	DARTMOUTH BRNC
Prior, Michael Francis	CDR	S		30.06.89	FEARLESS
Pritchard, David George , TEng	LT CDR(SD)	E	MESM	01.10.91	SULTAN

Name	Rank	Spec	Sub-spec	Seniority	Where serving
Pritchard, Gavin Scrimgeour	LT CDR	X	SM	01.01.95	DRYAD
Pritchard, Rayson Cann	CAPT RM	RM		01.08.85	CTCRM
Pritchard, Simon Andrew	CAPT RM	RM		18.04.94	RNSC GREENWICH
Pritchard, Trevor Glyn , BSc, CEng, MRAeS, MDA	CDR	E	AE	31.12.92	RNAY FLEETLANDS
Procter, Jamie Edward , BEng, MA	LT(SL)	I		01.09.92	SULTAN
Proctor, Simon John Lewis , BEng	LT	X	O	01.01.90	815 FLT 234
Proctor, William John Gibbon , BEng	LT	E	WE	01.03.94	CHATHAM
Prosser, Alan John , BSc, psc	CDR	I		31.12.85	IMS BRUSSELS
Proud, Andrew Douglas , BEng	LT(SL)	E	AE	01.05.94	814 SQN
Proudlock, John Kelso , BSc	CAPT RM	RM		01.09.94	HQRM
Pryde, Colin Swinton , BEng	LT CDR	E	AE	01.07.94	MOD (LONDON)
Prynn, Robert Michael , CEng, MIERE, I(2)Ge	CDR	E	WE	31.12.85	MOD DGSW PTSMTH
Puddicombe, Charles Alexander	2LT(UCE)	RM		01.09.94	CTCRM LYMPSTONE
Puffett, Nigel William , MEng	LT(SL)	X	O	01.08.94	FOSF
Pugh, Jonathan , BEng	LT(SL)	E	WE	01.10.94	NEWCASTLE
Pugh, Joseph Robert	2LT(GRAD)	RM		01.09.94	CDO LOG REGT RM
Pugh, Martin Reginald	LT(SD)	X	C	08.04.94	MOD (LONDON)
Pugsley, David Alan	LT CDR	S		01.04.92	NAVAL DRAFTING
Pullan, Keith James	LT(SL)	X	H2	01.07.95	HECLA
Pullman, Caroline	CHAPLAIN	SF		10.09.90	HERON
Pullyblank, Roger John	LT CDR(SD)	MS	AD	01.10.89	DRAKE CBP
Pulvertaft, Rupert James (Loc Capt Rm)	LT RM	RM	MOR	01.05.90	HQ 3 CDO BDE RM
Punch, Gerard Kevin , BA, BEng	SLT(SL)	E	ME	01.09.93	BOXER
Punton, Ian Matthew , BEng	LT	E	AE	01.03.92	DGA(N) ASE
Purdie, Christine Frances Anne , BDS	SG LT(D)	-		26.09.93	CINCFLEET
Purvis, David	SLT	E	AE(L)	01.09.93	DARTMOUTH BRNC
Puxley, Michael	SLT	E	WESM	01.05.94	DARTMOUTH BRNC
Pye, Michael Francis , BA	LT CDR	I		01.03.87	DNPS
Pye, Philip Martin	LT(SD)	S	CA	11.12.92	MOD (BATH)
Pyne, Robert	CHAPLAIN	CE		23.01.90	DRYAD

Q

Name	Rank	Spec	Sub-spec	Seniority	Where serving
Quade, Nicolas Alexander Clive	SLT	E	MESM	01.09.94	DARTMOUTH BRNC
Quantrill, Steven William , BSc	SLT(SL)	S		01.09.94	DARTMOUTH BRNC
Quaye, Duncan Thomas George , BSc	LT CDR	E	ME	01.05.91	FOSF
Quekett, Ian Peter Scott , BEng	LT	E	WE	01.08.91	CFM PORTSMOUTH
Quick, Neville Hellins , BSc, CEng, MIEE	LT CDR	E	WE	01.05.91	DGSS BRISTOL
Quine, Nicholas John , MA, psc	LT CDR	E	WE	01.12.88	BOXER
Quinlan, Patrick Hugh	CAPT RM	RM		17.03.85	45 CDO RM
Quinn, Martin Edward	LT(SL)	S	SM	01.02.94	MOD DNR OUTPORTS
Quinn, Paul Anthony , BA, MBIM, MHCIMA, jsdc	CDR	S	SM	30.06.91	FOSF
Quinn, Shaun Andrew	LT(SL)	X	O	16.05.92	810 SQN SEAHAWK
Quinnell, Kenneth Robert Arthur	LT CDR(SD)	X	C	01.10.92	MOD (LONDON)

R

Name	Rank	Spec	Sub-spec	Seniority	Where serving
Raby, Nigel John Francis , MSc, jsdc	CAPT	E	WE	30.06.95	MOD (LONDON)
Race, Nigel James	LT CDR	X	PWO(C)	01.04.93	FEARLESS
Rackham, Anthony , BSc	SLT(SL)	X		01.09.93	DRYAD
Radakin, Antony David	LT	X		01.11.89	DRYAD
Radbourne, Neville Ian	LT(SD)	E	WE	05.06.92	DG SHIPS CAM HSE
Radcliffe, Frederick Glyn , psc	LT CDR(SD)	S	CAT	01.10.90	SEAHAWK
Radcliffe, Nicholas , LLB	LT CDR	S		16.02.91	MOD (BATH)
Radford, Andrew , BEng	LT(SL)	X	P	01.06.92	820 SQN
Radmore, Keith Vernon	LT CDR	X	SM	23.09.91	INVINCIBLE
Rae, Anthony James William , BSc	LT(SL)	X	P	16.06.89	801 SQN
Rae, Alistair	SLT	E	WE	01.05.93	DARTMOUTH BRNC
Rae, Derek , BSc	SLT	X		01.09.93	DRYAD
Rae, Paul , BSc	LT(SL)	I		01.06.92	COLLINGWOOD
Rae, Stephen Gordon , AGSM	LT	S		01.02.92	NEPTUNE NT
Rae, Scott MacKenzie , MBE, BD	CHAPLAIN	SF		02.02.81	NEPTUNE
Raeburn, Craig , BSc	SLT(SL)	X		01.05.94	ARGYLL
Raeburn, Mark , n	LT	X		01.07.94	CAMPBELTOWN

Name	Rank	Spec	Sub-spec	Seniority	Where serving
Raeburn, Timothy Jon , BSc	2LT(GRAD)	RM		01.05.95	CTCRM LYMPSTONE
Raffaelli, Philip lain , MB, BA, BCh, MSc, MFOM, MRCGP, AFOM	SURG CDR	-	CO/M	31.12.90	MOD (LONDON)
Raffle, Anthony John	LT CDR(SD)	E	WE	01.10.92	DG SHIPS CAM HSE
Raggett, Andrew , MVO, pcea	LT CDR(SL)	X	P	01.09.87	ILLUSTRIOUS
Rahman, Junia	SURG SLT	-		04.08.94	DARTMOUTH BRNC
Rainbow, John , MRIN, MIM	LT CDR	X		14.09.81	AST(N)
Raine, Paul Anthony Walllace (Act Cdr)	LT CDR	X	FC	01.09.78	SEA CADET CORPS
Raisbeck, Paul Temple , pce	LT CDR	X	MCD	01.11.93	CDRE MFP
Raitt, James Edwin , BSc	2LT(GRAD)	RM		01.09.95	CTCRM
Ralph, Andrew Philip	LT(SL)	X	FC	01.04.96	EDINBURGH
Ralphson, Mark David , BEng	LT	E	WE	01.06.93	COLLINGWOOD
Ramm, Steven Charles , pce(sm), psc	CDR	X	SM	30.06.91	BDS WASHINGTON
Rampton, William George	LT CDR	E	AE	17.02.80	MOD (BATH)
Ramsay, Graham Patrick , pce	CDR	X	PWO(N)	30.06.92	BDS WASHINGTON
Ramsdale, Timothy John , BSc	LT(SL)	X	P	16.04.89	848 SQN HERON
Ramsey, Jeremy Stephen , BSc	LT CDR	S		16.04.89	COLLINGWOOD
Ramsey, Ryan Trevor	LT	X		01.11.92	SPARTAN
Ramshaw, George William Lilwall , BSc, CEng, MIEE	LT CDR	E	WE	01.01.93	GLASGOW
Rance, Maxwell George William	LT CDR	S		16.08.95	SOUTHAMPTON
Rand, Marc James , BEng	LT	E	ME	01.05.93	MOD (BATH)
Randall, David Frederick , BA	LT CDR	S		16.01.94	DNPS
Randall, Lisa Sarah , BM	SURG LT	-		14.08.92	RH HASLAR
Randall, Nicholas John , BSc	LT	X	PWO(U)	01.11.89	YORK
Randall, Richard David , BSc	LT CDR	E	MESM	01.08.92	BRITANNIA
Randell, Guy	LT(SL)	X	P	01.12.90	750 SQN OBS SCH
Ranger, John Leonard (Act Lt Cdr)	LT(SD)	E	WE	18.10.85	LOAN OMAN
Rankin, Ian Gordon , MSc, CEng, MIEE, CGIA, mdtc	CDR	E	WESM	30.06.91	MOD (BATH)
Rankin, Neil Erskine , CB, CBE, pcea, psc	RADM	-	P	10.08.92	NELSON
Rankine, Ivor Matthew	SLT(SD)	E	MESM	19.06.95	RNC DPT NS&TECH
Ranson, Christopher David , MSc	LT CDR	E	WE	01.02.91	FOST SEA
Rapp, James Campsie , pce, psc	CAPT	X	O	31.12.92	MOD (LONDON)
Rasor, Andrew Martin	LT(SL)	X	P	01.07.92	EXCH ARMY SC(G)
Ratcliffe, John Paul , BSc	CDR	I		30.06.92	DRYAD
Ratcliffe, Kevin Francis , BSc	CDR	E	AE(P)	30.06.96	DGA(N) ASE
Rawal, Krishna Mark	SURG LT	-		31.01.93	WESTMINSTER
Rawles, Julian	SLT(SD)	X	ATCU/T	01.01.96	RAF SHAWBURY
Rawlings, David Matthew	LT CDR(SD)	E	AE(M)	01.10.89	SULTAN
Rawlings, Damian Paul , BEng, CEng, MIMarE	LT CDR	E	ME	01.08.95	DARTMOUTH BRNC
Rawlings, Francis David	LT(SD)	S	W	03.09.87	OSPREY
Rawlings, Gary Charles	LT CDR(SD)	I		01.10.89	SEAHAWK
Rawlinson, David	LT(SL)	X	P	16.03.95	848 SQN HERON
Rawlinson, Stephen James , BEng	LT	E	MESM	01.03.91	RESOLUTION(PORT)
Rawson, Clive	LT CDR(SL)	X	O	01.10.94	FONA SEAHAWK
Rawson, Scott Michael	LT	E	MESM	01.04.95	TORBAY
Raybould, Adrian Glyn , BSc, CEng, MIEE	LT CDR	E	WESM	01.01.93	SCEPTRE
Rayner, Brett Nicholas , psc, I(1)Ch (Act Capt)	CDR	S		30.06.90	DA PEKING
Rayner, John Martin	LT CDR	X	P	16.04.86	NELSON
Raynham, Matthew Carl , BA	2LT(GRAD)	RM		01.09.95	CTCRM
Raynor, Sean David	SLT(SD)	E	WE	04.09.95	COLLINGWOOD
Read, Alistair , BSc	LT CDR(SL)	I	METOC	01.10.94	EXCHANGE NLANDS
Read, Alun John	LT(SL)	X	P	01.09.84	815 SQN HQ
Read, Clinton Derek	2LT	RM		01.05.95	CTCRM LYMPSTONE
Read, Crispin , BA	LT(SL)	X	P	16.05.92	820 SQN
Read, Jonathan	LT	E	WESM	23.05.89	MWC GOSPORT
Read, Keith Frank , CEng, FIEE, MINucE, rcds, jsdc	CAPT	E	WESM	31.12.87	SA ROME
Read, Matthew	SLT	E	ME	01.09.93	DARTMOUTH BRNC
Read, Paul Steven	SLT(SL)	E	WE	01.01.94	DARTMOUTH BRNC
Read, Richard Harold , BSc, psc	LT CDR	X	H CH	01.09.81	DRAKE NBSM (CFS)
Read, Richard John , BA	2LT(GRAD)	RM		01.09.94	CTCRM
Readwin, Roger Roy	SLT	X		01.09.93	BERKELEY
Reah, Stephen , BEng	LT	E	ME	01.06.92	SULTAN

Name	Rank	Spec	Sub-spec	Seniority	Where serving
Rearden, Richard Joseph	LT RM(SD)	RM		01.01.94	CDO LOG REGT RM
Reason, Ian Malcolm , MSc	LT	E	AE	01.07.89	FONA
Reddish, Christopher Alan	LT	X	PWO(A)	01.06.89	BRILLIANT
Redfearn, Graham	LT CDR	S		01.03.84	FONA
Redfern, Timothy Andrew	LT(SL)	X		01.10.90	PEACOCK
Redford, Duncan Edward MacDonald	SLT	X		01.09.93	DOLPHIN SM SCHL
Redford, Keith McInnes , jsdc, pce	CDR	X	PWO(N)	30.06.83	BF GIBRALTAR(NE)
Redman, Christopher Douglas Jeremy , BDS, LDS, RCS(Eng)	SGLTCDR(D)	-		19.07.93	LOAN BRUNEI
Redman, Charles Jeremy Rufus , n	LT	X		23.11.90	SOMERSET
Redman, Heidi Shelly	LT(SL)	S		01.08.95	2SL/CNH FOTR
Redstone, Colin	LT CDR	S	SM	12.12.91	NEPTUNE CFS
Reece, Nigel David , BEng	LT	E	MESM	01.03.92	MOD (BATH)
Reed, Andrew William , BSc	LT CDR	X	PWO(A)	01.10.94	BRAVE
Reed, Darren Kieth , BA	SLT	X		01.09.94	SOUTHAMPTON
Reed, Frank , BA, MSc, psc	CDR(SD)	MS	P	01.10.93	MOD (LONDON)
Reed, Jonathan Charles	LT(SD)	E	AE(M)	07.09.95	771 SK5 SAR
Reed, James Hamilton , pce, pcea	LT CDR	X	P	01.04.95	DRYAD
Reed, Jeremy Jameson , BA, BSc	LT RM	RM		01.09.91	40 CDO RM
Reed, James William	LT RM(SD)	RM		01.01.93	RMB STONEHOUSE
Reed, Mark , BSc	LT(SL)	I	METOC	01.01.88	PRESTWICK
Reed, Matthew Trevor , n	LT	X		01.10.93	RNSC GREENWICH
Reeder, Robert , OBE, BSc, MIMechE	CDR	E	AE	31.12.91	FAAIT MAN ORG VL
Reen, Stephen Charles	LT(SL)	X	P	01.11.92	845 SQN
Rees, Andrew , MRINA, MRIN	LT CDR	X	O	19.03.81	DRAKE CBP
Rees, John Blain Minto , BSc, jsdc	CDR	I		30.06.90	2SL/CNH
Rees, Justin Harrington , BSc, MILDM, AMIAM	LT CDR	S	SM	16.02.90	CINCFLEET
Rees, John Patrick	LT	S		29.06.91	FOST SEA
Rees, Melanie Suzanne , BSc	LT(SL)	X		01.06.94	BRAVE
Rees, Paul	SURG SLT	-		10.06.94	DARTMOUTH BRNC
Rees, Richard , BEng	SLT	S		01.09.93	DARTMOUTH BRNC
Reese, David Michael , BSc	LT(SL)	X	O	01.03.95	810 SQN SEAHAWK
Reeve, Jonathon , MA, CEng, MIEE, psc	CAPT	E	MESM	30.06.91	MOD (BATH)
Reeve, John Michael	LT(SD)	E	ME	14.02.86	INTREPID
Reeve, Margaret Wendy	LT(SL)	S		12.12.90	CDRE MFP
Reeves, Beresford Victor Charles , LVO, pce	CDR	X	PWO(N)	31.12.85	MOD (LONDON)
Reeves, Christopher James , BSc	LT	X	SM	01.12.92	VIGILANT(PORT)
Reeves, Kurt , BEng	LT(SL)	E	ME	01.09.94	GLOUCESTER
Reid, Alastair Bruce , MA	LT(SL)	X	P	01.01.83	706 SQN SEAHAWK
Reid, Charles Ian , BSc	LT CDR	X	SM	01.02.93	MOD (LONDON)
Reid, Christopher Joseph , MB, BS	SURG LT	-		01.08.93	RM POOLE
Reid, Duncan , MBE, BA, BA(OU)	LT CDR(SD)	E	AE(L)	01.10.91	MOD PE ASC
Reid, Gavin , BEng	LT(SL)	X	O	01.09.95	706 SQN SEAHAWK
Reid, Iain Charles , BA	LT(SL)	X	P	01.06.88	FONA VALLEY
Reid, Jason Charles James , BEng	LT	E	WESM	01.04.93	CWTA PTSMTH
Reid, Jonothan Grant	LT(SL)	X	P	16.04.90	702 SQN OSPREY
Reid, Martyn , pce, pcea, psc	CDR	X	O	30.06.94	DRYAD MWC
Reid, Martyn Richard	LT(SL)	X		01.04.95	MONTROSE
Reid, Paul Frederick	LT(SD)	X	SM	24.07.92	DOLPHIN SM SCHL
Reid, William Andrew , BA	SLT	X		01.09.93	DOLPHIN SM SCHL
Reidy, Paul Alan	LT	X	SM	01.11.90	SPLENDID
Reilly, Thomas Gerald	LT(SD)	X	C	03.06.92	BF GIBRALTAR(NE)
Reindorp, David Peter	LT	X	PWO(A)	01.07.88	GLOUCESTER
Rendell, Derrick John	SLT(SD)	E	MESM	14.06.93	SOVEREIGN
Rendle, Ian	LT(SL)	X	P	01.02.85	848 SQN HERON
Renfrey, Edward Donald John-Baptist , DipTh	CHAPLAIN	CE		02.02.84	RM POOLE
Rennie, Alistair Baillie	LT RM	RM		29.04.96	42 CDO RM
Rennison, William Ross ,OBE, BSc	CDR	I		31.12.86	2SL/CNH
Renwick, John	LT CDR	S	SM	23.08.95	SOMERSET
Resheph, Amelia	MID(UCE)	E		01.09.95	MANCHESTER
Reston, Samuel Craig (Act Surg Lt)	SURG SLT	-		01.10.93	DARTMOUTH BRNC

Name	Rank	Spec	Sub-spec	Seniority	Where serving
Revell, Anthony Leslie , QHS, MB, ChB, FFARCS, DA, ... rcds, ndc	SURG VADM	-	CA	16.08.94	MOD (LONDON)
Revens, Carl Andrew	2LT(GRAD)	RM		01.05.95	CTCRM LYMPSTONE
Reynolds, Andrew Graham	LT	E	ME	01.02.90	MOD (BATH)
Reynolds, Christopher Herbert , BSc, MBIM, pce(sm)	LT CDR	X	SM	01.04.87	MOD (LONDON)
Reynolds, Peter Anthony , BSc, psc	MAJ	RM		31.12.89	2SL/CNH
Reynolds, Stephen Antony	LT RM	RM	RMP1	30.04.91	AACC MID WALLOP
Reynolds, Timothy Edward , BA, BSc	LT CDR	I	METOC	01.05.92	CINCFLEET
Reynolds, Timothy Paul , BSc	LT(SL)	I		01.05.87	DARTMOUTH BRNC
Rhodes, Andrew Gregory , BEng	LT CDR	E	WE	01.07.95	DGSS BRISTOL
Rhodes, Martin	LT(SL)	X	O	01.09.95	819 SQN
Rice, Peter Langford	LT CDR(SL)	X		01.09.83	DEF NBC CENTRE
Rich, Alvin Arnold , pce	CDR	X	O	30.06.90	OSPREY
Rich, David Charles	LT	X	SM	01.04.89	TALENT
Rich, Jonathan George	LT CDR(SL)	X	P	01.10.89	849 SQN B FLT
Rich, Karl James Nicholas Charles , MSc	LT(SD)	MS		03.04.92	INM ALVERSTOKE
Richards, Alan David , pce, pcea	CDR	X	P	31.12.93	JSDC GREENWICH
Richards, Angus , BA	LT(SL)	X	O U/T	01.12.95	SPEY
Richards, Bryan Robert , DEH	LT(SD)	MS	AD	23.07.93	MOD (BATH)
Richards, Christopher Martin , pce, psc	CDR	X	PWO(A)	30.06.95	RNSC GREENWICH
Richards, Fraser	SLT(SD)	X	SM	25.07.93	DOLPHIN SM SCHL
Richards, Guy , BSc	LT(SL)	X		01.08.93	TRENCHANT
Richards, Gregory Bernard , BA	LT	X		01.05.93	ANGLESEY
Richards, Ian Sewart Hanson , jsdc, pce(sm)	CDR	X	SM	31.12.87	SHAPE BELGIUM
Richards, James	SLT	E	WESM	01.01.95	DARTMOUTH BRNC
Richards, Nicola Jane	LT	S		29.07.88	COCHRANE
Richards, Simon Timothy	LT(SL)	X	O	16.06.93	750 SQN OBS SCH
Richards, Stephen William	LT RM(SD)	RM	MTO	01.01.92	HQRM
Richardson, Daniel , BEng	LT	E	WE	01.01.94	MONMOUTH
Richardson, Douglas , BEng	LT	E	MESM	01.10.94	TORBAY
Richardson, Gavin	LT(SL)	X	O	01.04.92	771 SK5 SAR
Richardson, Geoffrey , BSc	LT(SL)	X	P	01.08.91	750 SQN OBS SCH
Richardson, George Nicholas , BA	LT	S		01.07.93	SULTAN
Richardson, Ian James Ward , BSc, CEng, MIEE, psc	CAPT	E	WE	31.12.95	MOD (BATH)
Richardson, James Brian , pce, psc (Act Cdr)	LT CDR	X	AWO(U)	16.07.81	SEA CADET CORPS
Richardson, Mark Anthony , BSc	LT(SL)	I		01.09.85	NAVSOUTH ITALY
Richardson, Michael Collin	LT RM(SD)	RM		01.01.93	HQ 3 CDO BDE RM
Richardson, Michael Peter	LT CDR	S		16.07.91	FOSF
Richardson, Nicholas Mark	LT(SL)	X	P	01.05.88	EXCHANGE RAF UK
Richardson, Peter	LT(SL)	X	P	16.01.92	HERON
Richardson, Peter Stephen Mark , BEng, AMIEE	LT	E	WE	01.08.91	CWTA PTSMTH
Richardson, Stephen Frank	LT(SD)	E	WE	18.06.87	FOSF
Riches, Ian Charles , pce(sm)	LT CDR	X	SM	01.10.90	DOLPHIN SM SCHL
Riches, Keith Martin , BSc, pce, psc (Act Cdr)	LT CDR	X	MCD	01.06.82	DSSC BATH
Richford, Terence Fitzpatrick	LT CDR(SD)	X	C	01.10.92	HQBF GIBRALTAR
Richings, Peter Charles , pcea	LT CDR(SD)	X	P	01.03.87	702 SQN OSPREY
Richman, Philip Jonathan	LT(SD)	E	WESM	13.06.91	MOD DGSM PTLAND
Richmond, Iain James Martin , BA, pce, pcea	LT CDR	X	P	01.05.91	DRYAD
Richmond, Leslie (Act Lt Cdr)	LT(SD)	X	C	29.07.88	NWOOD CIS
Richter, Alwyn Stafford Byron , BEng, AMIEE	LT	E	WE	01.09.92	DGWES CHERTSEY
Rickard, Hugh Wilson , CBE, ADC, BSc, psc, I(2)Du (Commodore)	CAPT	I	METOC	30.06.89	RALEIGH
Rickard, Rory Frederick , MB, BCh, BAO	SURG LT	-		03.08.93	RH HASLAR
Ridd, Dean Alan	LT(SL)	X	P	01.04.91	INVINCIBLE
Riddle, Ian David , BEng	LT(SL)	E	WESM	01.09.95	CAPTAIN SM2
Riden, Donald Keith , BM, BDS, LDS, FDS RCS(Eng)	SGLTCDR(D)			01.08.90	CENTURION
Ridge, Mervyn Henry	SLT(SD)	E	WESM	07.02.94	DOLPHIN SM SCHL
Ridland, Keith	CAPT	S		30.06.94	SA CARACAS
Ridley, William Kenneth , BSc, psc	CDR	E	ME	30.06.87	INTREPID
Ridley Jones, Brian Duncan , BA, MBA, MSc	LT CDR	I		01.05.88	BDS WASHINGTON
Ridout, Simon Scott , MB, BS, MSc, MFOM, AFOM	SURG CDR	-	CO/M	31.12.89	FO PORTSMOUTH
Rigby, Jeremy Conrad , BA, MILDM, I(2)Sw	LT CDR	S		16.01.94	PJHQ
Rigby, Robin	LT(CS)	-		07.01.90	MOD DNR OUTPORTS

Name	Rank	Spec	Sub-spec	Seniority	Where serving
Riggall, Andrew David	LT(SL)	X	P	01.05.96	845 SQN
Riley, Graeme Alexander	SLT(SD)	E	MESM	14.06.93	TURBULENT
Riley, Michael Jaeger , BSc, jsdc, pce	CDR	X	PWO(A)	31.12.93	HQRM
Rimington, Anthony Kingsmill , BA	SLT	X		01.09.93	BROCKLESBY
Rimington, John Anthony , jsdc, pce	CAPT	X	AWO(U)	31.12.92	UKNMR SHAPE
Rimmer, Michael , pce	LT CDR	X	PWO(C)	01.04.90	COMAW SEA
Rimmer, Robin	LT(SD)	E	WE	05.06.92	CFM PORTSMOUTH
Ripley, Benjamin Edward	LT(SL)	X	H2	01.11.94	ROEBUCK
Rippingale, Stuart Nicholas , BSc	LT CDR	I		01.10.95	CAPT IST STAFF
Risdall, Jane Elizabeth , MB, BS, MA, DA	SURG LTCDR	-	SA	10.09.90	NELSON (PAY)
Risley, Jonathan , BSc, adp	LT CDR	I		01.10.92	SACLANT USA
Ritchie, David Michael	LT(SL)	X	P	16.03.90	FONA LINTON/OUSE
Ritchie, John Noble	LT(SL)	X	SM	01.04.90	CSST SHORE FSLN
Ritchie, William James	LT RM(SD)	RM	MTO	01.01.90	HQ CDO AVN
Ritsperis, Athos , MSc	LT(SL)	I		01.01.92	SEAHAWK
Rix, Anthony John , pce, psc	CDR	X	PWO(U)	30.06.92	GLASGOW
Robb, Brian David , MHCIMA	SLT(SD)	S	CA	01.05.95	EXCELLENT
Robb, Matthew Cruickshanks , OBE, BA, CGIA, psc, mdtc	CDR	E	WE	30.06.92	CAPT F2(SEA)
Robbins, Julian Garth	LT CDR	E	AE	01.03.84	FONA
Robbins, Jeremy Matthew Francis , BSc, psc(m)	MAJ	RM	C	31.12.93	45 CDO RM
Robbins, Margaret Joy , psc	CDR	W	X	31.12.92	EXCELLENT
Roberts, Alan Lloyd	LT CDR(SD)	X	AV	01.10.93	HQ MOD FIRE SVCS
Roberts, Antony Paul , MB, BS, DObstRCOG (Act Surg Cdr)	SURG LTCDR	-	GMPP	01.02.89	RNAS YEOVILTON
Roberts, Christopher , BSc	LT(SL)	I		29.09.88	RM POOLE
Roberts, Dean , BEng	LT(SL)	E	WE	01.04.94	MONTROSE
Roberts, David Alan , pce	LT CDR	X	PWO(A)	01.05.92	CNOCS GROUP
Roberts, Douglas Charles Keith , BSc	LT CDR	E	ME	16.06.78	FOSF
Roberts, David Howard Wyn , BA	LT CDR	X	PWO(A)	01.04.91	DRYAD MWC
Roberts, Ellis William	LT CDR(SD)	E	AE(M)	01.10.95	RNAS PORTLAND
Roberts, Grant Michael Frank	SLT(SL)	X	O U/T	01.11.95	702 SQN OSPREY
Roberts, Iain Gordon , BSc, BEng	LT(SL)	E	WESM	01.10.91	MOD (LONDON)
Roberts, Ian Thomas , pce(sm)	LT CDR	X	SM	18.01.93	ACDS(POL&NUC)USA
Roberts, John Lee	LT(SL)	X	P	16.10.94	810 SQN SEAHAWK
Roberts, Kenneth Eric , BEng	LT	E	WE	01.01.92	CWTA PTSMTH
Roberts, Malcolm , BSc	LT CDR(SL)	E	WE	01.10.92	COLLINGWOOD
Roberts, Martyn , BEng	LT(SL)	X	O	01.10.88	706 SQN SEAHAWK
Roberts, Martin Alan	LT(SL)	X	O	01.11.94	819 SQN
Roberts, Michael Nicholas Dinan , BDS, LDS RCS(Eng), jsdc	SGCDR(D)	-		30.06.81	RALEIGH
Roberts, Nigel , BSc	SLT(SL)	X	O U/T	01.05.94	DARTMOUTH BRNC
Roberts, Nigel Lewis	LT CDR(SL)	X		01.09.82	NAVSOUTH ITALY
Roberts, Nicholas Steven , BEng, MSc	LT CDR	E	WE	01.03.95	MONTROSE
Roberts, Peter Stafford	LT	X	FC	01.10.95	INVINCIBLE
Roberts, Stephen	LT(SD)	X	AV	12.12.91	RNAS YEOVILTON
Roberts, Selvin Clive , BEng	LT(SL)	E	MESM	01.03.91	MOD DGSM DNREAY
Roberts, Stephen David , CEng, MIEE	LT	E	WE	01.04.90	RMC OF SCIENCE
Roberts, Stephen James	SLT	X		01.09.94	BLACKWATER
Roberts, Suzanne Marie , BA	LT	S		01.06.94	HERON
Roberts, Stephen Paul , I(2)Ab	LT(SD)	X	EW	02.04.93	FOSF
Roberts, Timothy John , BEng	LT CDR	E	MESM	01.07.95	MOD (BATH)
Robertshaw, Ian	SLT	E	WESM	01.01.94	COLLINGWOOD
Robertson, David Colin , BSc	LT CDR	E	AE	01.10.90	RNAS YEOVILTON
Robertson, David Cameron , n	LT	X	H2	01.06.89	RN HYDROG SCHL
Robertson, Douglas Malcolm , BSc	LT CDR(SL)	X	ATC	01.10.93	FONA OSPREY SEA
Robertson, Frederick William , pcea	LT CDR(SL)	X	P	01.03.86	846 SQN
Robertson, James Thomas , BSc	LT	X		01.10.93	BRECON
Robertson, Kevin Francis , pce	LT CDR	X	PWO(C)	01.07.91	FOSF SEA PTSMTH
Robertson, Keith Raymond , BSc	LT(SL)	I		01.05.91	DNPS
Robertson, Michael George , BSc	LT CDR	X	O	01.04.94	DARTMOUTH BRNC
Robertson, Malcolm Nairn	LT(SD)	E	MESM	19.10.90	SULTAN
Robertson, Neil Bannerman	LT RM	RM		26.04.93	42 CDO RM
Robertson, Neil David Vionnee , MNI, pce, pce(sm), psc	CAPT	X	SM	30.06.91	SA TOKYO
Robertson, Paul Noel	LT(SL)	X	O	01.11.90	819 SQN

Name	Rank	Spec	Sub-spec	Seniority	Where serving
Robertson Gopffarth, Alexander Alistair John	SLT	X		01.09.94	DARTMOUTH BRNC
Robin, Christopher Charles Edward , pcea	LT CDR	X	P	01.09.94	LANG TRG-ABROAD
Robinson, Andrew , BSc	LT CDR	I	METOC	06.05.88	MOD (LONDON)
Robinson, Andrew Mark Edward , BA	LT RM	RM		01.09.92	CTCRM
Robinson, Anthony Robert	LT CDR(SL)	X	PWO(A)	01.03.86	CNOCS GROUP
Robinson, Bruce Douglas , BSc	LT CDR(SL)	I	METOC	01.10.93	FOST SEA
Robinson, Charles Edward Thayne , pce	LT CDR	X	PWO(U)	01.08.93	FOST SEA
Robinson, Christopher Paul , MBE, pce, pcea, psc	CDR	X	O	31.12.87	ACE SRGN GIBLTAR
Robinson, David Ian , MSc, MIEE, psc	LT CDR	E	WE	01.02.84	DGSS BRISTOL
Robinson, Guy Antony	LT	X		01.11.89	DRYAD
Robinson, Graham David Brice , pce, psc	CAPT	X	AWO(A)	31.12.88	TEMERAIRE
Robinson, Ionie Alexandra Louise	LT(SL)	I		01.01.90	DRYAD
Robinson, James Oliver , pce, psc(a)	LT CDR	X	AWO(A)	01.07.80	EXCELLENT
Robinson, Jason Paul	SLT(SL)	X	P	01.01.94	706 SQN SEAHAWK
Robinson, James Stuart , pce	LT CDR	X	PWO(U)	01.10.90	FOSF SEA PTSMTH
Robinson, Lloyd Charles	LT(SL)	X		01.06.93	RM POOLE
Robinson, Mark Alan , BA	LT(SL)	X	ATC	01.06.90	RAF SHAWBURY
Robinson, Melvin Erroll , MBE, pcea	CDR	X	P	30.06.96	RNSC GREENWICH
Robinson, Michael Peter , BSc	LT	E	MESM	01.11.88	MOD (BATH)
Robinson, Michael , BSc	LT(SL)	X	O U/T	01.05.94	RAF SHAWBURY
Robinson, Marcus Wyn , BD	CHAPLAIN	SF		01.11.82	2SL/CNH
Robinson, Nicholas Michael , jsdc, psc(m) (Loc Col)	LT COL	RM	PADJT	30.06.89	MOD (LONDON)
Robinson, Nicholas Ulric Spencer	LT	X		01.04.90	DRYAD
Robinson, Paul Henry , pce, pce(sm)	CDR	X	SM	31.12.91	DRYAD MWC
Robinson, Susan , BSc	LT	X		01.06.94	CORNWALL
Robison, Garry Stuart , psc(m) (Loc Lt Col)	MAJ	RM		30.06.93	EXCHANGE ARMY UK
Robison, Wilfred John	LT CDR	E	MESM	25.11.85	NBC ROSYTH
Robley, William	SLT(SL)	X	P	01.11.92	810 SQN SEAHAWK
Robotham, Trevor , TEng, MIEE, psc	CAPT	E	WE	30.06.92	ORDNANCE BOARD
Roche, Stephen Meyrick , psc (Loc Lt Col)	CAPT RM	RM		01.01.78	BMATT S AFRICA
Roddy, Michael Patrick , BSc	LT RM	RM		27.04.95	42 CDO RM
Rodgers, Darren	LT(SL)	X	P	01.01.94	848 SQN HERON
Rodgers, David Harry , IEng, AMIMarE	LT(SD)	E	ME	18.02.83	MOD (BATH)
Rodgers, Nicholas Parker , MSc, PGCE, psc	CDR	I	METOC	31.12.95	CINCIBERLANT
Rodgers, Steven	LT(SD)	E	WE	15.06.90	MOD DGSW PTSMTH
Rodley, John Frederick , pce, psc	CAPT	X	AWO(U)	31.12.92	MARLBOROUGH
Rodrigues, Martin Tadeu	LT(SD)	S	W	07.01.83	DOLPHIN SM SCHL
Rodwell, Toby Richard James , BSc	LT	E	WESM	01.02.94	FOSM NWOOD OPS
Rogers, Alan	LT(SD)	X	AV	03.04.92	RALEIGH
Rogers, Alastair David Forbes , MA, psc(m)	MAJ	RM	PH	30.06.91	CTCRM
Rogers, Anthony George , AFC	CDR	X	O	31.12.85	RAF AWC
Rogers, Andrew Gavin , AMIEE	LT	E	WE	01.02.90	RNSC GREENWICH
Rogers, Christopher Mark , BEng	LT	E	WE	01.06.92	DARTMOUTH BRNC
Rogers, Ian Arthur , BSc, MEng, CEng, MIMechE	LT CDR	E	MESM	01.01.96	DTR BARROW
Rogers, Julian Charles Everard	LT(SL)	X	SM	01.03.91	CSST SHORE FSLN
Rogers, James , BA	SLT(SL)	X	P U/T	01.05.94	DARTMOUTH BRNC
Rogers, Malcolm Stuart , BSc	CDR	I		30.06.90	ACE SRGN ITALY
Rogers, Philip Malcolm	LT(SL)	I		01.01.89	FONA
Rogers, Roland Jeremy , MSc	LT CDR(SL)	I	METOC	01.10.91	LOAN DRA WNFRITH
Rogers, Simon James Peter , BA	2LT(GRAD)	RM		01.09.95	CTCRM LYMPSTONE
Rogers, Timothy Hugh Goddard	LT	X		04.06.91	BLACKWATER
Rogerson, Clive Stephen James	LT CDR(SL)	X	MCD	01.10.92	CNOCS GROUP
Rogerson, David Morton John , LRAM, ARCM, pdm (Act Maj)	CAPT RM(SD)	RM		01.10.92	MOD (LONDON)
Roll, Kevin Stuart	LT(SL)	X	P	01.06.92	810 SQN SEA
Rollings, Hilary Erica , BSc	LT(SL)	E	ME	01.02.93	ILLUSTRIOUS
Rolph, Andrew Peter Mark	LT	X	PWO(C)	16.11.89	CUMBERLAND
Romney, Emma Victoria , BA	LT	S		01.12.92	INVINCIBLE
Romney, Paul David	LT	X		01.01.90	DRYAD
Ronaldson, Gordon Ian , BEng	LT	E	ME	01.01.95	LANCASTER
Ronaldson, Tanya	SURG LT	-		01.08.93	RNDHU DERRIFORD
Rook, David John (Act Lt Cdr)	LT(SD)	E	WE	10.06.88	INVINCIBLE
Rook, Graeme Inglis , BSc	LT	E	WE	01.04.90	MOD DNR OUTPORTS

Name	Rank	Spec	Sub-spec	Seniority	Where serving
Root, William Richard	CDR(SD)	X	C	01.10.92	CON DCN
Roots, Sally	LT(SL)	E	AE	01.08.90	DGA(N) ASE SHAWK
Roper, Martin	LT CDR	X	O	01.11.90	MOD (LONDON)
Roscoe, Robert David , BEng	LT	E	WE	01.04.91	MOD DGSW PTSMTH
Rose, Daniel Joseph , LRCP, MRCGP, MRCS	SURG CDR	-	GMPP	30.06.85	DOLPHIN
Rose, James Denton , MB, BS	SURG LT	-		01.08.92	RNDHU DERRIFORD
Rose, John Gordon , MBE, psc(m)	LT COL	RM		30.06.96	CINCFLEET
Rose, Michael Frederick , BEng, CEng, MIMechE	LT	E	ME	01.09.92	SULTAN
Rose, Michael Stuart , MSc	LT CDR(SL)	I		01.10.91	CNOCS GROUP
Rosewell, William Anthony	LT(CS)	-		05.01.92	MOD DNR OUTPORTS
Ross, Angus Allan , BA	CDR	S		30.06.91	2SL/CNH
Ross, Alastair Boyd , CBE, rcds, pce, pcea, psc	RADM	X	O	02.08.96	MOD (LONDON)
Ross, Andrew Charles Paterson , BSc	CAPT RM	RM		25.04.96	HQRM
Ross, Angus Kenneth , BSc, pce	CDR	X	PWO(U)	30.06.94	FOSF SEA PTSMTH
Ross, Bruce James	LT CDR	X	PWO(U)	16.11.89	PJHQ
Ross, Ian , BEng	LT	E	ME	01.08.92	SULTAN
Ross, Jonathan Hubert , BSc	CAPT RM	RM		01.09.95	HQRM
Ross, Robert Alasdair , MB, BS	SURG LTCDR	-		01.08.91	DARTMOUTH BRNC
Rossiter, Mark Anthony , BEng	LT(SL)	E	ME	01.02.91	SULTAN
Roster, Shaun	LT(SL)	X	O	16.11.94	815 FLT 200
Rostron, Andrew Frank , BA, PGCE	LT(SL)	I		19.09.90	SULTAN
Rostron, David William , BEng	LT(SL)	E	MESM	01.01.92	TORBAY
Rotheram, Martin , ndc, psc (Commodore)	CAPT	X	O	31.12.87	CINCIBERLANT
Rothwell, John Francis	LT CDR(SL)	X	PWO(A)	01.09.82	DGSS BRISTOL
Rothwell, Mark Kinsey , BSc, MNI, pce	CDR	X	PWO(N)	30.06.94	FOSF
Rouse, Janice Rosalyn Dean , BA, MSc, MBIM, psc	LT CDR	W	E	01.04.83	CWTA PTSMTH
Routh, Nicholas George , BSc	LT(SL)	I		01.01.88	CTCRM
Routledge, William David	SLT(SD)	X	PT	10.12.95	DRYAD
Rowan, Mark	SLT(SD)	X	C	24.07.94	MONTROSE
Rowan, Nicholas Anthony , BEng	LT	E	MESM	01.12.93	VANGUARD(PORT)
Rowbottom, Christopher	LT(SL)	X	O	01.09.89	NAIC NORTHOLT
Rowe, Andrew James	LT(SD)	E	WE	19.02.93	ACE SRGN GIBLTAR
Rowe, Kevin Christopher	LT(SL)	X	O	01.01.93	849 SQN A FLT
Rowe, Paula , MBA	LT(SL)	I		02.09.89	ILLUSTRIOUS
Rowe, Vivian Noel , psc(m) (Loc Lt Col)	MAJ	RM	MLDR	31.12.88	RMR TYNE
Rowell, Graham Edward , MSc	CDR	E	AE	30.06.94	MOD (LONDON)
Rowell, Michael Frederick	LT CDR	X	P	01.06.79	FONA DARTMOUTH
Rowland, Paul Nicholas , BEng	LT	E	MESM	01.01.92	VICTORIOUS(PORT)
Rowlands, Andrew	SLT	E	WE	01.01.94	COLLINGWOOD
Rowlands, Geoffrey Alan , BSc, FRMS	LT CDR(SL)	I	METOC	01.09.85	RNAS PORTLAND
Rowlands, Kevin , BSc	LT(SL)	X		01.03.92	MANCHESTER
Rowles, Howard Alan	LT(SD)	E	WE	29.10.82	DG SHIPS PTSMTH
Rowley, Marc Cameron	LT(SL)	X	P	16.04.89	819 SQN
Rowley, Robert Austin , OBE, BSc, jsdc (Commodore)	CAPT	E	ME	30.06.88	NAVAL DRAFTING
Rowley, Sean	LT(SL)	X	O	16.11.94	815 FLT 246
Rowlstone, David John (Loc Capt Rm)	LT RM	RM		11.06.93	NP 1061
Rowse, Mark Lawrence , BEng, CEng	LT	E	WE	01.07.89	COLLINGWOOD
Roy, Alexander Campbell , osc(us) (Loc Lt Col)	MAJ	RM		31.12.90	ACE SRGN ITALY
Roylance, Jaimie Fraser	2LT(GRAD)	RM		01.09.93	CTCRM
Royle, Sally	LT	Q	BURNS	08.08.90	RH HASLAR
Royston, Stuart James	LT	X		01.05.90	DRYAD
Ruane, John	LT(CS)	-		04.10.88	MOD DNR OUTPORTS
Ruddock, Gordon William David	LT(SL)	X		01.07.95	FOSNNI/NBC CLYDE
Rudge, George Harry Albert , BDS, BA(OU), MScD, FDS, RCS, RCSEd	SGCAPT(D)	-	COSM	30.06.90	RNDHU DERRIFORD
Rudman, Christopher John , BSc	LT CDR	I	SM	15.05.90	SULTAN
Ruglys, Matthew Paul , PhD	LT(SL)	I	METOC	16.11.86	RNAS CULDROSE
Runchman, Phillip Charles , BM, BCh, MA, FRCS	SURG CDR	-	CGS	30.06.85	RH HASLAR
Rundle, Anthony Littlejohns	LT(SD)	E	WE	19.02.93	COLLINGWOOD
Rundle, Robert Mark , BSc, psc(m) (Loc Lt Col)	MAJ	RM	WTO	30.06.87	RMR MERSEYSIDE
Rusbridger, Robert Charles , MSc, psc	CDR	E	ME	30.06.95	MOD (BATH)
Rushworth, Benjamin John	SLT	X		01.09.94	DARTMOUTH BRNC

Name	Rank	Spec	Sub-spec	Seniority	Where serving
Russan, William Richard	LT CDR(SD)	E	MESM	01.10.93	DRAKE CFM
Russell, Andrew	SLT	E	WESM	01.09.94	DARTMOUTH BRNC
Russell, Bruce , BEng, AMIEE	LT	E	WESM	01.05.92	VANGUARD(STBD)
Russell, Colin	MID	E		01.05.95	GLOUCESTER
Russell, David John , rcds, pce, pce(sm)	CAPT	X	SM	31.12.93	MOD (LONDON)
Russell, Nigel	LT(SL)	X	FC	01.12.94	LIVERPOOL
Russell, Paul	LT	X	FC	01.05.93	FOST SEA
Russell, Philip Robert , BTech	LT	E	ME	01.02.90	DG SHIPS DEVONPT
Russell, Rebecca Marijke , BSc	LT(SL)	X		01.07.95	NORTHUMBERLAND
Russell, Rafael Michael Japhet , BA	LT(SL)	X	P	01.03.90	845 SQN
Russell, Simon Jonathon , AMRAeS, psc	LT CDR	E	AE	22.08.90	DARTMOUTH BRNC
Russell, Thomas	LT CDR	X	MCD	01.07.93	EXCHANGE CANADA
Russell, Timothy James , MA, MBA, CEng, FIMarE, MIMechE, jsdc	CDR	E	MESM	30.06.86	JSCSCPT
Russell, Timothy James , BSc	LT(SL)	X	MW	01.07.90	MIDDLETON
Russell Clark, Carole	SLT(SL)	E	WE	01.05.93	DARTMOUTH BRNC
Rutherford, Kevin John , BSc	LT(SL)	X	P	01.04.94	848 SQN HERON
Rutherford, Timothy James , BEng	LT(SL)	E	AE	01.09.93	810 SQN SEA
Rutterford, Peter Joseph , BA, BA(OU), LRAM, ARCM, pdm	LT RM(SD)	RM		28.02.86	RM SCHOOL MUSIC
Ryan, Deborah Frances	LT	Q		20.10.94	RNDHU DERRIFORD
Ryan, Dennis Graham , BSc	LT CDR	E	AE(P)	01.03.93	RNAY FLEETLANDS
Ryan, John Benedict	LT	S		01.06.90	ROSYTH SOSM(R)
Ryan, John Patrick , BSc	LT	X		01.12.91	MONTROSE
Ryan, Nicholas , BEng	LT	E	ME	01.06.95	GLOUCESTER
Ryan, Richard Michael , BSc	LT	X	O	01.04.89	810 SQN SEAHAWK
Ryan, Sean Joseph , BA	LT	X		01.04.93	TORBAY
Rycroft, Alan Edward , MNI, pce, pcea	CDR	X	O	30.06.96	DRYAD
Ryder, Steven John , MB, BCh, FRCS, FRCSEd, AFOM	SURG CDR	-	SO/M	30.06.90	EXCHANGE USA
Ryder, Stephen Maurice , TEng, IEng, AMIMarE	LT CDR(SD)	E	ME	01.10.94	LOAN BRUNEI
Ryder, Timothy John	LT(SD)	MS	AD	23.07.93	DRAKE CBS
Rydiard, David Martin , BSc, AMNI, pce, psc	LT CDR	X	PWO(N)	01.12.81	LOAN RSS BMATT
Rye, John Walter , BSc, MA, psc	CAPT RM	RM	C	01.09.84	HQ CDO AVN
Rymer, Alan Robert , BSc, psc	CDR	E	ME	30.06.92	CAPT F4 (SEA)

S

Name	Rank	Spec	Sub-spec	Seniority	Where serving
Saddleton, Andrew David (Loc Capt Rm)	LT RM	RM	LC	01.09.89	CTCRM
Sadler, Christopher John , pce	LT CDR	X	O	01.02.90	YORK
Sadler, John Barrie , CEng, FIEE, nadc (Commodore)	CAPT	E	WESM	30.06.90	MOD DGSWS BATH
Sage, David Ian , n	LT(SL)	X	H2	01.01.91	HERALD
Salisbury, David Peter	LT CDR	X	P	01.02.96	702 SQN OSPREY
Salley, Robert Keith	LT(SD)	X	AV	09.01.87	FOST FTG SEA
Salmon, Andrew , MA, psc	MAJ	RM		30.06.95	HQRM
Salmon, Michael Alan	LT(SL)	X	O	01.05.88	849 SQN B FLT
Salmon, Robert David	SLT(SD)	X	EW	23.07.95	DRYAD
Salt, Hedley Stephen	LT(SL)	X	P	01.09.93	815 FLT 229
Salt, Jane Elizabeth , psc	CDR	W	SEC	31.12.94	MOD (LONDON)
Salter, Jeffrey Alan , BEng	LT CDR	E	WE	10.02.94	CNSA PORTSDOWN
Salter, Mark David , pcea	CDR(SL)	X	P	01.10.95	FONA CRANWELL
Salzano, Gerard Mark	CAPT RM	RM		30.04.95	RNSC GREENWICH
Samborne, Michael David Palmer , pce, pce(sm)	CDR	X	SM	30.06.87	MOD (LONDON)
Sampson, Philip Henry , psc(m)	CAPT RM	RM		01.09.89	CTCRM
Sams, Colin	LT CDR(SL)	X	ATC	01.09.80	MOD (LONDON)
Samuel, Katja Lilian Hamilton , BA	LT	S		01.08.93	RNSC GREENWICH
Sanders, Andrew William Tyrrell , BSc	LT CDR	E	WE	01.08.80	MOD DGSW PTSMTH
Sanderson, Lee	SLT(SL)	E	WE	01.09.93	DARTMOUTH BRNC
Sanderson, Peter Charles , MSc, CEng, MIEE	CAPT	E	MESM	31.12.92	NEPTUNE DSQ
Sanderson, Robert Christopher , BDS, FDS	SGCDR(D)	-	COSM	30.06.89	RNH HASLAR
Sanderson, Richard Dennis , pce	CDR	X	AWO(C)	30.06.85	MOD (LONDON)
Sandiford, David Braddock , MNI	CDR(SL)	X	MCD	01.10.89	NELSON (PAY)
Sandle, Neil David , BEng	LT	E	ME	01.09.95	MONTROSE
Sandover, Richard John , BSc, pce, pcea, psc	LT CDR	X	O	20.04.87	810 SQN SEAHAWK
Sanguinetti, Hector Robert , l(1)Sp	LT CDR	X	PWO(C)	01.02.95	BEAVER
Sansford, Adrian James , BEng	LT(SL)	E	MESM	01.07.92	SCEPTRE

Name	Rank	Spec	Sub-spec	Seniority	Where serving
Sant, Paul Quentin	LT(SL)	X	P	01.10.90	810 SQN OEU
Santrian, Karl	SLT(SD)	X		01.01.94	FONA CRANWELL
Sargent, Kevin Stephen , MBE	SLT(SD)	E	AE(M)	12.09.94	845 SQN
Sargent, Lindsay Michael , BSc	LT	X		01.10.93	IRON DUKE
Sargent, Nicholas	SLT(SL)	E	AE	01.05.96	NOTTINGHAM
Sargent, Philippa Mary , BA	LT(SL)	X		01.12.92	LINDISFARNE
Satterthwaite, Benjamin John , BA	LT(SL)	X		01.02.95	MARLBOROUGH
Saunders, Christopher Edmund Maurice , BSc	SLT	X		01.01.95	DARTMOUTH BRNC
Saunders, John Neil , MBE	LT CDR(SL)	X	O	01.03.87	849 SQN HQ
Saunders, John Nicholas	LT CDR(SL)	X	N	01.10.90	DRYAD
Saunders, Peter William , BEng	LT	E	AE	01.06.92	RNAS CULDROSE
Saunders, Stephen Evered , ADC, FBIM, rcds, ndc, pce (Commodore)	CAPT	X	AWO(U)	31.12.88	MOD (LONDON)
Saunders, Timothy Mark , BSc	LT CDR	I	SM	01.09.94	SCEPTRE
Sauze, Martin James , BEd	LT CDR(SL)	I	METOC	01.10.88	CINCFLEET
Savage, Alan Paul , BSc	LT(SL)	I		01.07.91	2SL/CNH ASHFORD
Savage, Mark Roger	LT	X	MCD	01.09.90	YORK
Savage, Nigel David	CAPT	S		30.06.95	MOD (BATH)
Savage, Rosemary , ARRC	LT CDR	Q	FP	09.09.86	DRAKE CBP
Savage, Shane , BSc	LT CDR(SL)	X	ATC	01.10.94	RNAS CULDROSE
Saward, Justin Robert Ernest , BEng	SLT(SL)	E		01.01.95	DARTMOUTH BRNC
Sawyer, Trevor James	CAPT RM(SD)	RM		01.10.94	COMACCHIO GP RM
Saxby, Christopher James , BEng, MSc, MIMarE, MCGI	LT CDR	E	ME	01.11.94	DSSC BATH
Saxby, David George	LT(CS)	-		25.04.93	MOD DNR OUTPORTS
Saxby, Keith Alan	LT CDR	X	PWO(A)	24.02.94	DRYAD
Sayer, David Julian , pce, psc	CDR	X	AWO(A)	31.12.88	MOD (BATH)
Sayer, Jamie Michael , BA, BEng	SLT(SL)	E	ME	01.09.94	BIRMINGHAM
Sayer, Peter William , MSc, psc	LT CDR	E	AE	16.12.76	DGA(N) ASE
Sayles, Stephen	CDR	E	ME	31.12.91	NEPTUNE
Saynor, Roger Michael	LT(SD)	X	PT	15.12.89	RALEIGH
Scandling, Peter	SLT	X		01.09.93	NEPTUNE SM1
Scandling, Rachel Jane	LT(SL)	S		01.05.96	RNSC GREENWICH
Scarth, William , BSc, pce	LT CDR	X	MCD	01.03.91	CHIDDINGFOLD
Schillemore, Paul Colin	LT(SD)	E	WE	18.10.85	DG SHIPS CAM HSE
Schmidt, James Frederick Kurt , BSc	LT CDR	E	MESM	01.03.91	SOVEREIGN
Schnadhorst, James Charles	LT CDR	X	PWO(U)	01.05.95	BRAVE
Schofield, Mark Kenneth , BSc	LT(SL)	I		01.01.93	PRESTWICK
Schreier, Paul , MA, MEng, DPhil	SLT	X		01.01.94	DRYAD
Schunmann, Ceri Peter Ingo , BSc	LT(SL)	X		01.12.93	DRYAD
Schwab, Robert Anthony	LT(SL)	X	P	02.10.87	899 SQN HERON
Schwarz, Paul Michael Gunter	LT CDR(SL)	X	ATC	01.10.88	RNAS PORTLAND
Scivier, John Stapleton	LT(SL)	X	ATC	01.02.91	RNAS CULDROSE
Scoles, Jonathon Charles , OBE, pce, psc	CDR	X	PWO(U)	31.12.89	2SL/CNH
Scopes, David , BEng	LT	E	AE	01.01.95	SULTAN
Scorer, Samuel James , pce	CDR	X	PWO(U)	30.06.90	JSDC GREENWICH
Scott, Christopher Ralph , psc	CAPT RM	RM		01.09.92	2SL/CNH
Scott, David Bryan	LT CDR	X		01.04.77	DRAKE CBP
Scott, Jason Andrew	LT	X	MCD	01.04.89	LEDBURY
Scott, James Baxter , BEng	LT CDR	E	MESM	01.05.96	DRAKE CFM
Scott, Michael , BEng	LT	E	WESM	01.05.91	MOD DGSM PTLAND
Scott, Melvyn Anthony George	LT(SD)	E	ME	27.02.87	LOAN DRA PRTSDWN
Scott, Malcolm Mitchell , MB, BS, FRCSEd	SURG CDR	-	SO/S	31.12.93	NELSON (PAY)
Scott, Mark Robert	LT(SL)	X	P	16.12.93	RAF SHAWBURY
Scott, Nigel Leonard James , BEng	LT CDR	E	WESM	01.04.96	UPHLDER TRG TEAM
Scott, Philip Henry , pce	LT CDR	X	PWO(A)	01.09.88	MANCHESTER
Scott, Peter James Douglas Sefton	CHAPLAIN	CE		03.09.91	HQRM
Scott, Richard Antony , BEng	LT(SL)	E	WE	01.08.94	BATTLEAXE
Scott, Roderick Cameron , MB, BSc, BCh, FFARCS (Act Surg Cdr)	SURG LTCDR	-	CA	01.08.89	RH HASLAR
Scott, Robert John	LT	X	O	02.03.90	815 FLT 219
Scott, Richard John	LT CDR	X	PWO(U)	26.01.93	EXCHANGE AUSTLIA
Scott, Robert Munro , psc	LT CDR	S		01.05.84	2SL/CNH FOTR
Scott, Stephen Charles	ACT LT RM(SD)	RM		01.01.96	RM DIV ASMT

Name	Rank	Spec	Sub-spec	Seniority	Where serving
Scott, Simon John (Act Capt Rm)	LT RM	RM	LC	01.09.89	TAMAR
Scott, William Maddin , BSc	LT	S		01.03.93	DOLPHIN
Scott-Dickins, Charles Angus , BSc	LT CDR(SL)	I	METOC	01.10.94	RNAS YEOVILTON
Scourse, Frederick Peter , MBE, MA, CEng, FIEE, ndc	RADM	-	WESM	18.04.94	MOD DGSS BATH
Screaton, Richard	SLT	E	ME	01.09.93	SULTAN
Screech, Michael Courtney , FInstAM, MinstAM	LT CDR	S	SM	01.08.81	CAPTAIN SM2
Scruton, Neil , BSc, psc	LT CDR	X	H CH	16.03.84	PRESIDENT
Seabrook, Ian	LT(SL)	X	P	16.03.91	800 SQN
Seabrooke-Spencer, David John , BA	LT CDR	X	PWO(A)	01.07.94	FOST SEA
Seakins, Patrick Edward	LT	X		01.02.90	LINDISFARNE
Sealey, Nicholas Peter , BSc, CEng, MIMarE, psc	CDR	E	ME	30.06.94	SOMERSET
Sealy, Douglas Edward , pcea	LT CDR(SL)	X	P	01.10.94	RAF SHAWBURY
Seaman, Philip John	LT(SD)	E	WE	19.02.93	MOD (LONDON)
Sear, Jonathan Jasper (Loc Capt Rm)	LT RM	RM		01.09.91	HQ ITC
Searight, Mark Frederick Chamney (Loc Capt Rm)	LT RM	RM	WTO	01.05.90	EXCHANGE USA
Searle, David Michael , BSc, pce, pcea, psc	LT CDR	X	P	01.02.89	819 SQN
Searle, Edward Francis , BSc, CEng, MIEE, MIMarE, psc	CAPT	E	ME	31.12.95	NBC PORTSMOUTH
Searle, Russell John , BSc, pce	CDR	X	PWO(C)	30.06.91	COLLINGWOOD
Seatherton, E F(Elliot Frazer Kingston) , MBE, pce	CDR	X	PWO(N)	31.12.95	DRYAD
Seaward, Robert Colin , OBE, pce, pce(sm), psc	CDR	X	SM	30.06.85	ACE SRGN ITALY
Secretan, Simon James , BEd, n	LT	X		01.08.88	DRYAD
Seddon, John Stephen Maurice	LT CDR	S	SM	16.10.88	ILLUSTRIOUS
Seekings, Andrew Laurence , BSc	LT(SL)	I	METOC	01.06.89	FOSM NWOOD OPS
Segebarth, Robert Andrew	LT(SL)	X	P	16.02.96	845 SQN
Selby, Roger Charles	LT(SD)	E	MESM	14.10.94	TRAFALGAR
Sellar, Trevor Jefferson	LT RM(SD)	RM		01.01.95	HQRM
Sellars, Scott John , BA	LT	X		01.07.94	GUERNSEY
Sellers, Graham Donald , BEng	LT	E	WE	01.02.93	COLLINGWOOD
Selway, Mark Anthony	SLT	E	AE	01.01.95	DARTMOUTH BRNC
Selwyn, Peter David , BSc	LT CDR	E	WESM	01.07.90	SPARTAN
Sennitt, John William , BSc	LT CDR	E	WE	01.08.92	RICHMOND
Sephton, John Richard , BSc, psc	LT CDR	I	METOC	17.06.91	DRYAD
Sergeant, Nicholas Robin	LT(SL)	E	WE	09.06.89	COMCEN SOUTHWICK
Seward, David Robert , pce, psc	LT CDR	X	AWO(U)	16.06.80	RALEIGH
Seward, Stafford Allan	LT(SD)	X	g	06.04.95	FOST DPORT SHORE
Sewed, Michael Antony , BSc	LT CDR(SL)	X	O	01.10.94	815 OEU OSPREY
Sewell, Douglas Eric	LT CDR(SL)	X		19.07.79	NP 1020 NAV TNG
Sewell, Iain Timothy Tait , BSc, psc	CDR	X	H CH	31.12.90	COCHRANE
Sewell, Mark Anthony Philip	SLT(SL)	X	P	01.01.94	810 SQN SEAHAWK
Sewry, Michael Ronald , BSc, CEng, MIEE	CDR	E	AE	31.12.95	RAF BRACKNELL
Sexton, Michael John	LT CDR	E	WE	19.02.89	WESTMINSTER
Sexton, Nicholas , BSc	LT(SL)	I		01.09.94	DARTMOUTH BRNC
Seymour, Kevin William	LT	X	P	01.10.88	899 SQN HERON
Seymour, Richard Paul , AFC, ndc	CDR	X	P	30.06.81	FONA
Shackleton, (Scott)	CHAPLAIN	SF		20.04.93	45 CDO RM
Shadbolt, Simon Edward , MBE, BSc, psc(m) (Loc Lt Col)	MAJ	RM		31.12.93	PJHQ
Shalders, Martin	LT(SL)	X	P	01.02.95	846 SQN
Shallcroft, John Edward	LT(SL)	X	P	01.11.89	814 SQN
Shand, Christopher Michael , BSc	LT CDR	E	WESM	01.11.82	MOD (BATH)
Shapiro, Philip	LT CDR(SD)	X	REG	01.10.92	EXCELLENT
Sharkey, Elton Richard , BEng	LT	E	MESM	01.07.95	RNC DPT NS&TECH
Sharkey, Michael	CHAPLAIN	RC		01.10.90	NELSON
Sharland, Simon Patrick , BA	CAPT RM	RM	LC	01.09.90	HQRM
Sharman, David John Thomas , MSc, AMIEE	LT CDR	E	WE	01.03.94	CAMPBELTOWN
Sharman, Timothy , MSc, mdtc	LT CDR	X	PWO(U)	16.02.85	MWC GOSPORT
Sharp, Colin Carlisle Gwinnett , rcds, psc	CDR	S		31.12.88	NELSON
Sharp, Colin Edward Fraser , BSc	LT CDR	E	ME	01.02.83	MOD (BATH)
Sharp, Gavin Charles	LT(SL)	X	MCD	01.01.94	QUORN
Sharpe, Gary Anthony	LT RM(SD)	RM	MTO	01.01.91	CTCRM
Sharpe, Grantley James , pce	LT CDR	X	PWO(U)	01.02.88	FOST SEA
Sharpe, Thomas Grenville	LT	X		01.10.94	BROCKLESBY
Sharpley, John Guy , MB, BCh, MA	SURG LTCDR	-		08.02.96	NELSON (PAY)

Name	Rank	Spec	Sub-spec	Seniority	Where serving
Sharrocks, Ian	SLT(SL)	X	P U/T	01.01.96	705 SQN SEAHAWK
Shaughnessy, Toby Edward	SLT	X		01.01.95	DUMBARTON CASTLE
Shave, Antony James , BA	LT RM	RM		01.09.93	CTCRM
Shaw, Clare Elizabeth , MB, BCh, Dip FFP	SURG LT	-		01.08.93	RNDHU DERRIFORD
Shaw, Graeme Roberts , BEng, AMIEE	LT	E	WE	01.11.92	CFM PORTSMOUTH
Shaw, Ian Brian , BEng	LT CDR	E	WESM	15.09.91	NEPTUNE NT
Shaw, Kevin Norman Graham , MA, PhD, CEng, MIEE, MRIN	LT CDR	E	WE	01.02.94	NORTHUMBERLAND
Shaw, Michael Leslie , BEng	LT	E	AE	01.05.93	DGA(N) ASE
Shaw, Mark William Barber , MSc, CEng, MIEE, psc	CDR	E	WE	30.06.94	2SL/CNH
Shaw, Philip Anthony , MVO, pce, pcea	CDR(SL)	X	P	01.10.89	FONA
Shaw, Peter Alan	LT(SL)	X	ATC	01.11.83	RNAS PORTLAND
Shaw, Philip Andrew George , BSc, MA, pce, pcea, psc	LT CDR	X	P	01.07.92	2SL/CNH
Shaw, Paul James	LT	S		01.07.90	EXETER
Shaw, Rebekah	LT(SL)	W		01.05.96	MOD DNR OUTPORTS
Shaw, Stuart	SURG SLT	-		01.02.94	DARTMOUTH BRNC
Shaw, Steven Matthew	LT CDR	S		01.03.95	NBC PORTSMOUTH
Shawcross, Jayne Maxine	LT CDR(SL)	W	X	03.01.95	RNAS YEOVILTON
Shawcross, Paul Kenneth , BSc	LT CDR(SL)	X	P	01.10.91	815 FLT 239
Sheard, Simon Charles , MB, BCh, MSc, MRAeS	SURG CDR	-	CO/M	30.06.95	CINCFLEET
Shears, Nicholas Mark Randal , BSc	LT(SL)	X		18.11.94	ILLUSTRIOUS
Sheehan, Mark Andrew , pce, pcea, psc	LT CDR	X	O	01.07.92	GRAFTON
Sheils, Damian Edmund Tyrie	LT(SL)	X	P	16.07.94	814 SQN
Sheldon, Mark Laurence	SLT(SD)	E	WE	07.02.94	MARLBOROUGH
Sheldrake, James , BEng	SLT(SL)	X		01.05.94	BATTLEAXE
Sheldrake, Terence William , BSc, pce, pcea	LT CDR	X	O	29.04.83	RNAS CULDROSE
Shellard, Graeme Iain , BEng	LT(SL)	E	WE	01.03.94	CORNWALL
Shepherd, Alan	LT CDR(SD)	E	WE	01.10.92	LOAN BRUNEI
Shepherd, Charles Scott , BSc	LT	X	SM	01.01.89	TORBAY
Shepherd, David	LT CDR	X	SM	09.11.95	CSST SHORE FSLN
Shepherd, Iain , BSc, pce	CDR	X	PWO(A)	30.06.92	FOSF
Shepherd, Martin Paul	SLT	X		01.09.93	RNU CRANWELL
Shepherd, Paul Rodney , pcea	LT CDR(SL)	X	O	01.10.92	750 SQN OBS SCH
Shepherd, Roger Guy , BEng	LT CDR	E	WESM	01.05.96	MOD CSSE LONDON
Sheppard, David George	LT(SD)	E	WE	15.06.90	RMC OF SCIENCE
Shergold, Paul James	LT RM(SD)	RM		01.01.95	45 CDO RM
Sherlock, Francis Christopher Edwin , MSc, CEng, MIMarE, psc	CDR	E	ME	31.12.92	OCEAN
Sherriff, David Anthony	LT CDR	X	P	01.01.96	NORTHUMBERLAND
Sherriff, Jacqueline , BA	LT(SL)	X		01.12.93	CAPT IST STAFF
Sherwin, Charles Philip , BSc (Act Capt)	CDR	E	WE	31.12.83	LOAN DRA PRTSDWN
Shetler-Jones, Philip Richard (Loc Capt Rm)	LT RM	RM		01.09.95	NP 1061
Shield, Simon James , pce(sm)	LT CDR	X	SM	01.07.93	RNSC GREENWICH
Shields, Carole Tracey	LT(SL)	S		25.07.91	INVINCIBLE
Shinn, David Ernest	LT CDR(SD)	E	AE(M)	01.10.87	2SL/CNH
Shipman, Stephen Alan Christopher , FRICS, BA, MSc	LT CDR	X	H CH	01.04.81	RN HYDROG SCHL
Shipperley, Ian , BSc, CEng, MIMechE	LT CDR	E	ME	01.05.92	SOUTHAMPTON
Shirley, Andrew John	LT(SL)	E	MESM	01.08.89	SULTAN
Shirley, Malcolm Christopher , BSc, CEng, FIMarE,	CAPT	E	ME	30.06.89	SULTAN
psc, I(2)Fr (Commodore)					
Shirley, Wayne Peter	LT CDR	E	WE	12.10.93	CORNWALL
Shone, Derek Edward , psc	CDR(SD)	MS	P	01.10.87	RNH GIB
Shorland Ball, Timothy Daniel , MA, psc	CAPT	S		30.06.89	FONA
Shorland-Ball, Timothy John	SLT(UCE)	X		01.09.95	DARTMOUTH BRNC
Short, Andrew Simon James , BEng, CEng, MIEE, AMIEE	LT	E	WE	01.05.90	RMC OF SCIENCE
Short, Gavin Conrad , BSc, BEng, AMIEE	LT CDR	E	WESM	01.03.92	CAPTAIN SM2
Short, John Jeffrey , BEng	LT	E	MESM	01.06.88	DTR BATH
Shrimpton, Matthew William	LT(SL)	X	P	01.04.92	815 FLT 212
Shrives, Michael Peter , pce, pcea, psc	CDR	X	P	30.06.95	SULTAN AIB
Shrubsole, Steven John , BEng	LT	E	WE	01.12.91	COLLINGWOOD
Shuttleworth, Stephen	SLT(SD)	E	ME	13.06.94	ILLUSTRIOUS
Shutts, David , AMIMechE	LT	E	ME	01.06.90	RNSC GREENWICH
Sibbit, Neil Thomas , pce, pcea	CDR	X	O	30.06.96	RNSC GREENWICH
Sibley, Graeme Paul	LT RM	RM		27.04.95	COMACCHIO GP RM

Name	Rank	Spec	Sub-spec	Seniority	Where serving
Sicker, Luke (P/2lt)	2LT(SSLC)	RM		19.10.92	RE ENTRY
Sidebotham, Michael John	LT(SD)	S	CAT	28.07.89	RNSC GREENWICH
Sidebotham, Richard Stephen , BSc	LT CDR(SL)	I		01.09.86	CTCRM
Sidoli, Giovanni Eugenio , BDS, MSc	SGCDR(D)	-		31.12.95	BF GIBRALTAR(NE)
Sigley, Arthur	MID	X		01.09.94	MONTROSE
Sigournay, Donald Stephen	LT CDR(SL)	X	P	01.10.91	HERON FLIGHT
Silcock, Christopher Anthony James , BA, pce, psc(m)	CAPT	X	PWO(A)	31.12.95	RCDS
Sillars, Malcolm Crawford , pce, psc	CDR	X	PWO(A)	31.12.95	MONMOUTH
Sillers, Barry , BSc	LT	X		01.12.94	VICTORIOUS(PORT)
Silva, Anthony Robert	LT(SD)	X	MW	16.12.88	EXCHANGE AUSTLIA
Silver, Christina Kay	LT CDR(SL)	W	X	01.10.93	HQ DFTS
Sim, Donald Leslie Whyte , MA, pce, pcea, ocds(USN)	CDR	X	O	30.06.90	MOD (LONDON)
Simcock, Julia Louise	SLT	X		01.01.95	WALNEY
Simcox, Paul Alan	LT RM(SD)	RM		01.01.94	42 CDO RM
Simm, Craig	SLT(SL)	E	AE	01.05.95	DARTMOUTH BRNC
Simm, Geoffrey William Grainger , MA	LT CDR	I	METOC	01.05.76	OSPREY
Simmonds, Duncan Charles , pce, psc	LT CDR	X	PWO(C)	11.02.86	RNLO JTF4
Simmonds, Gary Fredrick	LT(SD)	E	AE(L)	19.10.90	SULTAN
Simmonds, Peter Bruce , psc(a)	CAPT RM	RM	MOR	01.08.83	42 CDO RM
Simmonds, Richard Charles Kenneth , LLB	LT(SL)	X	O	16.07.94	815 FLT 229
Simmonds, Richard Michael , pce, psc(a)	CDR	X	MCD	31.12.90	MCM3 SEA
Simmonds-Short, Mathew Richard	LT(SL)	X	P	05.05.91	845 SQN
Simmonite, Gavin Ian	MID(NE)(SL)	X	P U/T	01.01.96	DARTMOUTH BRNC
Simmons, Anthony Lawrence Patrick , BSc	LT(SL)	X		01.11.92	CDRPORT PORTLAND
Simmons, Nigel Douglas , MSc, AMIEE	LT CDR	E	WESM	01.04.93	DOLPHIN SM SCHL
Simmons, Robert James , BSc	LT CDR	E	ME	01.11.79	MOD (BATH)
Simms, David	LT(SL)	X	O	16.03.96	814 SQN
Simons, Andrew Stebbles	LT CDR(SD)	X	PT	01.10.90	CAMBRIA
Simpson, Antonia , LLB	LT(SL)	S		01.05.96	RALEIGH
Simpson, Colin Chisholm	LT(SL)	X	P	01.03.93	815 SQN HQ
Simpson, David Keith	LT(SL)	X	O	16.11.93	820 SQN
Simpson, Emma Jane , BA, I(2)Ru	LT(SL)	W	X	04.04.90	CINCFLEET
Simpson, Ian Heaton	LT CDR	S		01.06.93	FEARLESS
Simpson, Julia Beatrice , ADC, BSc, CEng, MBCS, nadc, psc, adp	CAPT	W	MET	01.04.88	NELSON
Simpson, James Howard Benedict	SLT(SL)	X		01.09.92	DOLPHIN SM SCHL
Simpson, Martin Joseph	LT	X	PWO(U)	01.07.88	BIRMINGHAM
Simpson, Peter	LT(SD)	MS	CDO	04.04.91	RFANSU (ARGUS)
Simpson, Richard Hamilton Charles	CDR	E	WESM	30.06.79	CAPTAIN SM2
Sinclair, Andrew Bruce , odc(Aus)	LT CDR	X	P	01.02.84	LOAN DTEO BSC DN
Sinclair, Angus Hugh , BA, jsdc	CAPT	S	SM	30.06.96	CINCFLEET
Singleton, Mark Donald	SLT(SD)	X	AV	10.12.95	RFANSU
Sitton, John Barry	LT(SL)	E	MESM	01.12.95	RNC DPT NS&TECH
Skeels-Piggins, Talan Stephen	LT	X	FC	01.10.95	YORK
Skeer, Martyn Robert , pcea	LT CDR	X	P	04.04.94	ANGLESEY
Skelding, Roy Harold , pce	LT CDR	X	PWO(U)	01.09.84	MOD DNR OUTPORTS
Skelley, Alasdair Neil Murdoch , MA	LT	X		01.03.95	BRAVE
Skelton, John Steven , BEng	LT(SL)	E	ME	01.07.94	INVINCIBLE
Skelton, Ralph Anthony	LT(SD)	E	WE	05.06.92	COLLINGWOOD
Skidmore, Christopher Mark , BA	LT CDR	S	SM	01.12.93	MOD (LONDON)
Skidmore, Paul James , BSc	SLT	X		01.01.95	DARTMOUTH BRNC
Skidmore, Rodney Peter	LT(SL)	X	P	01.09.92	702 SQN OSPREY
Skiera, Allan Paul	LT CDR(SL)	X	PWO(U)	01.03.82	LOAN CDA ADAC
Skinner, Adrian James	LT(SD)	MS	AD	23.07.93	2SL/CNH
Skinner, Clifford Geoffrey	CAPT RM(SD)	RM		01.10.93	CTCRM
Skinner, John Richard , pce, psc, psc(a)	CDR	X	P	30.06.89	MOD (BATH)
Skinner, Neil Peter Francis	LT CDR(SD)	E	WE	01.10.92	2SL/CNH
Skinns, Gary Michael	CDR	X	PWO(U)	30.06.90	FOSF
Skittrall, Steven	SLT	E	AE	01.01.95	DARTMOUTH BRNC
Skrzypczak, Peter Raymond	LT CDR(SD)	X	C	01.10.95	EXCHANGE CANADA
Skuce, John Leonard	LT(SL)	I		01.10.88	NELSON
Skuse, Matthew , BSc	LT RM	RM		01.09.92	RM POOLE

Name	Rank	Spec	Sub-spec	Seniority	Where serving
Slack, Jeremy Mark (Loc Capt Rm)	LT RM	RM	LC	01.05.90	RM POOLE
Sladden, Richard Douglas , MSc, CEng, MIEE, gw	CDR	E	WE	30.06.87	MOD (LONDON)
Slade, Christopher	LT CDR(SL)	X	P	01.10.90	SEAHAWK
Slade, John Leslie	LT CDR(SD)	X	REG	01.10.91	2SL/CNH
Slater, Andrew Everard , ADC, rcds, psc	CAPT	S		30.06.87	NELSON
Slater, Sir Jock(John Cunningham Kirkwood) ,	ADM	-	N	29.01.91	MOD (LONDON)
GCB, LVO, ADC, rcds, pce					
Slavin, David Eric , MB, BS, MSc, LRCP, MRCS, AFOM	SURG LTCDR	-	GMPP	02.02.87	CAPTAIN SM2
Slawson, James Mark , BSc	LT CDR	E	ME	01.10.90	RNSC GREENWICH
Sloan, Daniel Jan , BEng	LT(SL)	I		01.09.91	SULTAN
Sloan, Mark Usherwood , BSc, pce, psc	CDR	X	PWO(U)	30.06.92	MOD (LONDON)
Sloane, Christopher Mark , jsdc, pce, psc	CAPT	X	TAS	30.06.88	MOD (LONDON)
Slocombe, Christopher Alwyn	LT(SL)	X	P	16.04.88	RNSC GREENWICH
Slocombe, Nicholas Richard	LT(SL)	X	ATC	01.11.91	RNSC GREENWICH
Slowe, Kim David John , pce, psc	CDR	X	P	30.06.93	SACLANT USA
Small, Richard James , BSc	SLT(SL)	E	WE	01.01.95	DARTMOUTH BRNC
Smalley, Graham Thompson	T/LT(SDT)	S	S	18.04.91	NEWCASTLE
Smallman, Laurence Delaney , BSc, pce	LT CDR	X	PWO(U)	01.12.93	MOD (LONDON)
Smallwood, Richard Iain	LT(SL)	X	SM	01.06.94	TORBAY
Smart, Ian	LT CDR	X	PWO(C)	01.01.93	DRYAD
Smart, Steven Joe	LT(SD)	E	ME	23.02.90	BRITANNIA
Smee, Norman Lee , pce, psc	CDR	X	AWO(A)	30.06.92	MOD (LONDON)
Smerdon, Christopher David Edward , BA	LT CDR	S	SM	01.07.94	BATTLEAXE
Smith, Andrew , BSc, psc	CDR	E	WE	30.06.88	DGSS BRISTOL
Smith, Anthony	LT(SL)	X	O U/T	01.10.95	SEAHAWK
Smith, Alan Ben , BSc, psc	CDR	E	WE	31.12.90	DGSS BRISTOL
Smith, Austin Bernard Dudley	LT(SL)	X	P	01.05.96	815 FLT 218
Smith, Adrian Charles , BSc	LT CDR	E	AE	16.03.84	MOD PE ASC
Smith, Anthony (Loc Lt Col)	MAJ	RM		31.12.85	HQRM
Smith, Adrian Gerald	LT	E	WE	01.02.91	MERCURY
Smith, Andrew Paul	LT	X	PWO(A)	01.04.90	NEWCASTLE
Smith, Barbara Carol	LT CDR	Q	SCM	01.10.92	RNDHU DERRIFORD
Smith, Brian Joseph	LT(SL)	X		01.12.91	PLOVER
Smith, Brian , BDS	SGLTCDR(D)	-		13.09.93	CAPTAIN SM2
Smith, Christopher Julian	LT CDR	S		16.03.96	GRAFTON
Smith, Clive Peter	LT	X	MCD	01.07.89	SOUTHAMPTON
Smith, Clive Sherrif , MSc, CEng, MIMarE	CDR	E	MESM	30.06.92	FEARLESS
Smith, David	LT(SL)	X	O	01.11.85	OSPREY
Smith, David Andrew Harry McGregor , FHCIMA	CAPT	S		31.12.92	SACLANT USA
Smith, David John , pce, psc	CDR	X	PWO	30.06.85	DRAKE NBSM (CFS)
Smith, Daniel James , BA	LT(SL)	X	P	01.05.94	848 SQN HERON
Smith, David Leslie	LT(SL)	X	FC	01.03.96	ILLUSTRIOUS
Smith, David Thomas	LT(SL)	X	O	16.06.91	810 SQN SEAHAWK
Smith, Gregory Charles Stanley	LT	X	O	01.01.90	849 SQN B FLT
Smith, Graeme Douglas James , BSc	LT(SL)	X		01.01.93	RICHMOND
Smith, Gordon Hovell	LT(SD)	E	ME	18.06.93	DARTMOUTH BRNC
Smith, Graham	CHAPLAIN	CE		25.05.93	NELSON
Smith, Gregory Kenneth , BSc, MIProdE, adp	LT CDR(SL)	I		01.10.93	DNPS
Smith, Graham Kenneth , BComm (Loc Capt Rm)	LT RM	RM		24.04.92	EXCHANGE ARMY UK
Smith, Gordon Stuart	LT(SD)	X	AV	04.05.84	HQ CDO AVN
Smith, John , ACIS	LT CDR	S	CMA	01.03.79	RALEIGH
Smith, John Charles , BSc, pcea	LT CDR	X	O	06.01.87	810 SQN OEU
Smith, Jason Edward , MB, BS	SURG LT	-		01.08.93	RNDHU DERRIFORD
Smith, Jason James (Act Surg Lt)	SURG SLT	-		01.12.92	DARTMOUTH BRNC
Smith, Kevin Alexander , BSc	LT CDR	E	MESM	01.04.95	MOD (LONDON)
Smith, Kevin Bernard Albert	LT CDR	X	PWO(A)	01.04.96	SOUTHAMPTON
Smith, Keven John	LT CDR(SL)	X	P	01.10.95	848 SQN HERON
Smith, Kenneth Marshall	LT CDR	X	TAS	16.11.88	MOD (LONDON)
Smith, Kirsten Mary Louise	SLT	X		01.05.94	DARTMOUTH BRNC
Smith, Malcolm	CDR	S	SM	30.06.96	FOSM NWOOD HQ
Smith, Melvin Andrew , MSc, mdtc	CDR	E	WE	31.12.95	MOD (LONDON)
Smith, Michael Daren	LT(SL)	X	O	01.02.96	815 FLT 208

Name	Rank	Spec	Sub-spec	Seniority	Where serving
Smith, Michael James	LT(SD)	E	WE	13.06.91	MOD DFS(CIS) GOS
Smith, Michael	SLT	E	WESM	01.09.93	DARTMOUTH BRNC
Smith, Martin Linn , BSc, psc (Loc Maj)	CAPT RM	RM		01.05.92	RM POOLE
Smith, Mark MacFarlane , BEng	LT	E	AE	01.11.90	CINCFLEET
Smith, Mark Richard , BEng	LT CDR	E	ME	14.07.95	SAUDI AFPS SAUDI
Smith, Martin Russell Kingsley , BA	LT CDR	I	METOC	01.09.93	CAPT F6 (SEA)
Smith, Nicholas Derek , psc	CAPT RM	RM	AE	01.03.80	AST(E)
Smith, Nigel John	SLT(SD)	X	tas	25.07.93	ARGYLL
Smith, Nicholas James Dominic	SLT(SL)	X	O U/T	01.11.95	702 SQN OSPREY
Smith, Nigel Paul , BA, pce, psc	CDR	X	PWO(U)	31.12.89	SA CAIRO
Smith, Nigel Peter , BA, pce	LT CDR	X	PWO(U)	01.07.91	FOSF SEA PTSMTH
Smith, Nicholas Peter , BSc	LT(SL)	I		01.05.92	RMB STONEHOUSE
Smith, Nigel Shawcross , BSc, CEng, MIEE	CDR	E	WE	30.06.91	JSDC GREENWICH
Smith, Philip Colin , BA	LT(SL)	I		16.06.89	WARRIOR
Smith, Peter Geoffrey , BSc	LT(SL)	X	O	01.01.90	LOAN DRA MALVERN
Smith, Richard Barry Winston , BSc	LT(SL)	I		26.10.88	COLLINGWOOD
Smith, Robert Charles Vernon	LT(SL)	X	O	16.04.91	702 SQN OSPREY
Smith, Richard David	SLT(SL)	X		01.05.93	BULLDOG
Smith, Robert	SLT(SD)	X	O U/T	10.12.95	750 SQN OBS SCH
Smith, Russell , BSc	SLT(SL)	X	P U/T	01.05.94	DARTMOUTH BRNC
Smith, Robert Sidney	LT CDR(SD)	S	W	01.10.93	RALEIGH
Smith, Richard William , MB, BCh, MRCP	SURG CDR	-	CP/M	30.06.92	RNDHU DERRIFORD
Smith, Richard William Robertson	LT CDR	X	PWO(U)	01.05.93	RICHMOND
Smith, Stewart Allan	CAPT RM	RM	LC	01.09.90	FEARLESS
Smith, Stephen Bower , AMIMechE	LT(SL)	E	MESM	01.05.90	DOLPHIN SM SCHL
Smith, Stuart Frederick	LT CDR(SL)	X	ATC	01.09.82	RNAS YEOVILTON
Smith, Stephen Frank	LT RM(SD)	RM	MTO	01.01.93	CTCRM
Smith, Steven Luigi , pce	LT CDR	X	PWO(A)	01.02.92	DRYAD
Smith, Steven , MB, BCh, ChB	SURG LTCDR	-		01.08.95	RNDHU DERRIFORD
Smith, Tracy Deborah	LT CDR(SL)	W	X	01.04.91	NELSON
Smith-Jaynes, Ernest Royston	CDR(SD)	E	WESM	01.10.94	CNSA PORTLAND
Smithson, John William	LT CDR(SL)	X	ATC	01.09.87	RNAS PORTLAND
Smithson, Peter Edward , MSc, CEng, MRAeS	LT CDR	E	AE	01.07.93	FONA
Smyth, Michael James	LT CDR(SD)	E	WE	01.10.94	COLLINGWOOD
Snaith, David Richard	SLT(SL)	X		01.09.93	EXETER
Sneddon, Russell Neil	LT(SL)	X	P	16.06.92	810 SQN SEAHAWK
Snelling, Paul Douglas , BEng	LT(SL)	E	MESM	01.10.94	VANGUARD(PORT)
Snelson, David George , FIMgt, MNI, pce, psc	CAPT	X	AWO(A)	30.06.94	MOD (LONDON)
Sneyd, Eric Patrick Bartholomew , BEng	LT CDR	I		20.06.93	SCU LEYDENE ACNS
Snoddon, Robert	LT(SD)	X	EW	11.12.92	HQ NORTH
Snook, Raymond Edward , pce, pcea	LT CDR	X	O	01.03.89	MARLBOROUGH
Snow, Christopher Allen , BA, pce	CDR	X	PWO(U)	30.06.93	MOD (LONDON)
Snow, Maxwell Charles Peter , BSc, pce, pcea, psc	CDR	X	P	30.06.93	MOD (LONDON)
Snow, Paul Frederick , BSc	LT CDR	E	ME	01.10.94	SULTAN
Snowball, John Clifford , AFC, MA	LT CDR(SL)	X	P	01.10.93	HQ CDO AVN
Snowball, Simon John , MA, psc	LT CDR	X		01.12.90	NELSON (PAY)
Snowden, Michael Brian Samuel	SURG LT	-		01.08.94	VICTORIOUS(PORT)
Snoxall, Peter John , BSc, CEng, MIEE	LT CDR	E	WESM	01.08.92	TALENT
Soar, Gary	LT(SL)	X	O	16.04.93	706 SQN SEAHAWK
Soar, Trevor Alan , OBE, pce, pce(sm)	CDR	X	SM	31.12.91	MOD (LONDON)
Sodhi, Mohinder Paul Tony , MSc	LT(SL)	I		23.09.90	MOD DNR OUTPORTS
Solleveld, Stephen Robert , pcea	LT	X	P	01.06.88	815 FLT 208
Solly, Matthew MacDonald , BSc	LT(SL)	I		22.05.92	SULTAN
Somervaille, Ian Plomer , CBE, psc (Commodore)	CAPT	S		31.12.87	2SL/CNH FOTR
Somerville, Angus James Dunmore , LLB, pce	CAPT	X	PWO(A)	30.06.94	MOD (LONDON)
Sopinski, Gregory Francis	LT(SL)	X	P	16.09.90	814 SQN
Soul, John Oliver , MB, BS, LRCP, LMSSA, FRCS, MRCS, jsdc	SURG CAPT	-	CGS	31.12.90	RNDHU DERRIFORD
Soul, Nicholas , BEng	LT(SL)	X	P U/T	01.07.95	EXCELLENT
South, David	SLT(SD)	X	PR	10.12.95	DRYAD
Southern, Peter John	LT CDR(SD)	E	MESM	01.10.90	UPHLDER TRG TEAM
Southern, Paul Jonathan	LT(SD)	E	ME	15.06.95	SULTAN

Name	Rank	Spec	Sub-spec	Seniority	Where serving
Southorn, Mark Douglas	LT	X		01.02.91	ARK ROYAL
Southwell, Neil Peter	SLT(SD)	X	C	24.07.94	NORFOLK
Soutter, Laurence Donald Lister , BSc	CDR	E	WESM	30.06.87	CINCFLEET
Sowden, Lesley Margaret	SURG LT	-		02.08.95	CAMPBELTOWN
Sowerby, Andrew Brian	SLT	X		01.09.94	LEDBURY
Spalding, Richard Edmund Howden , BSc, AMIEE	LT CDR	E	WE	01.04.89	COLLINGWOOD
Spalding, Timothy John Wallis , MB, BS, FRCS	SURG CDR	-		30.06.94	RH HASLAR
Spalton, Gary Marcus Sean , BSc, pce	CDR	X	PWO(U)	31.12.92	BDS WASHINGTON
Spanner, Helen Mary	LT(SL)	W	I	02.05.87	DRAKE CBP
Spanner, Paul	LT RM	RM		01.05.94	42 CDO RM
Sparke, Philip Richard William , BA, I(1)Ge	LT	S		01.03.92	UKSU SHAPE
Sparkes, Peter James , BSc, n	LT	X		01.06.91	SOUTHAMPTON
Sparkes, Simon Nicholas	LT(SL)	X	P	01.04.92	RAF SHAWBURY
Spayne, Nicholas John	LT(SD)	X	PWO(U)	11.12.92	GLASGOW
Speake, Jonathan , BEng	LT(SL)	X	O	01.12.90	810 SQN SEA
Speat, Leo William	LT CDR(SL)	I	SM	01.03.81	DARTMOUTH BRNC
Spedding, Harry George William	SLT	E	WE	01.01.95	DARTMOUTH BRNC
Speller, Nicholas Simon Ford , pce(sm)	LT CDR	X	SM	01.05.88	FOSF
Speller, Richard Andrew	LT CDR	X	PWO(N)	01.09.81	2SL/CNH
Spence, Andrei Barry , BSc	LT CDR	S	BAR	16.12.93	FOST DPORT SHORE
Spence, Jeremy Andrew John	LT CDR(SL)	X	P	01.10.92	FONA
Spence, Nicholas Anthony , pce	LT CDR	X	PWO(U)	01.09.90	WESTMINSTER
Spence, Robert Graeme , BA	LT(SL)	X	P	01.08.94	848 SQN HERON
Spencer, Carl Richard , BSc, PGCE	LT(SL)	I		01.09.89	SULTAN
Spencer, Elizabeth Anne , BSc	LT CDR	I	METOC	01.05.92	INVINCIBLE
Spencer, Gary James , BSc, pcea	LT CDR(SL)	X	P	01.10.94	810 SQN SEAHAWK
Spencer, Jonathan Charles Victor , MBE, psc	MAJ(SD)	RM		04.09.92	HQRM
Spencer, Michael	LT CDR	X	P	16.06.79	RAF HANDLING SQN
Spencer, Peter , MA, MSc, jsdc	RADM	-	WE	16.03.95	MOD (BATH)
Spencer, Richard Anthony Winchcombe , BA	CAPT RM	RM		01.09.93	42 CDO RM
Spencer, Steven John	LT(QM)	Q		12.10.91	RNH GIB
Spencer, William Murray , MA	LT CDR	X	H CH	01.04.88	LOAN HYDROG
Spens-Black, Gerard Peter , pce, pcea	LT CDR	X	P	16.01.85	HERON
Spicer, Clive Graham , BSc, CEng, MIMarE	CDR	E	ME	31.12.95	LOAN OMAN
Spicer, Mark Nicholas , BSc, psc (Loc Lt Col)	MAJ	RM		30.06.92	MOD (LONDON)
Spillane, Paul	SLT(SL)	X	O	01.03.93	849 SQN B FLT
Spiller, Michael Francis , BSc, psc	LT CDR	S		01.03.90	2SL/CNH
Spiller, Stephen Nicholas	SLT	E	WE	01.09.94	DARTMOUTH BRNC
Spiller, Vanessa Jane	LT	X	C	28.07.89	DRYAD
Spinks, David William	SLT	X		01.05.94	EXETER
Spires, Trevor Allan , BSc, nadc	CAPT	I	SM	31.12.94	2SL/CNH
Spofforth-Jones, Martyn Aubrey	SLT(SD)	E	ME	13.06.94	NOTTINGHAM
Spooner, Peter David	LT(SD)	E	AE(M)	15.10.87	RNFSAIC
Spooner, Ross	SLT	E	AE(L)	01.01.94	SULTAN
Spooner, Sophie Louise	LT(SL)	E		01.06.95	NORTHUMBERLAND
Spring, Andrew Ralph James , n	LT	X		01.03.90	DARTMOUTH BRNC
Spring, Jeremy Mark , BEng	LT(SL)	E	AE	01.05.93	801 SQN
Springett, Julia Katherine	LT(SL)	W	X	10.12.87	NWOOD CIS
Springett, Simon	CHAPLAIN	CE		10.09.91	40 CDO RM
Spurgeon, Nicola Ann	LT(SL)	W	I	25.04.92	SACLANT USA
Squibb, Clifford John , BSc, pcea, psc	LT CDR	X	P	16.01.84	TAMAR
Squire, Elizabeth , BA	LT(SL)	X	O U/T	01.04.96	FONA SULTAN
Squire, Paul Anthony , BSc, MIEE, adp	LT CDR(SL)	E	WE	01.10.90	MOD (LONDON)
St Aubyn, John David Erskine , BSc	LT CDR	E	WESM	01.12.95	DTR BATH
Stace, Ivan Spencer , BEng, MSc (Act Lt Cdr)	LT	E	WESM	01.01.89	MOD (LONDON)
Stacey, Andrew Michael , BSc	LT	X		01.06.94	BRILLIANT
Stacey, Hugo Alister	LT CDR(SL)	X	P	01.10.93	EXCHANGE USA
Stafford, Benjamin	MID(UCE)	E		01.09.94	DARTMOUTH BRNC
Stafford, Derek Bryan	LT RM	RM		27.04.95	AACC MID WALLOP
Stagg, Antony Robert , BEng	LT	E	AE	01.04.95	SULTAN
Stagg, Kevin Anthony , BSc	LT CDR	E	WE	01.05.80	MOD DGSS PTSMTH
Stait, Benjamin Geoffrey	SLT(SL)	X		01.05.96	COTTESMORE

Name	Rank	Spec	Sub-spec	Seniority	Where serving
Stait, Carolyn Jane , psc	CDR	W	S	30.06.92	2SL/CNH
Staley, Simon Peter Lee	LT	X	O	01.02.91	849 SQN HQ
Stallion, Ian Michael , BA, pce(sm), I(2)No	CDR	X	SM	31.12.94	VANGUARD(STBD)
Stamp, Derek William	T/LT(SDT)	E	ME	10.06.94	CLYDE MIXMAN2
Stamp, Gordon , MA, pce, psc	CDR	X	MCD	30.06.95	SAUDI AFPS SAUDI
Stamper, Jonathan Charles Henry , BSc	LT(SL)	I		01.01.92	SULTAN
Stanesby, David Laurence , BSc, BA(OU), PGCE, psc	CDR	I	METOC	30.06.88	CINCFLEET
Stanford, Christopher David , MA, MNI, rcds, pce, psc (Commodore)	CAPT	X	AWO(C)	30.06.88	MOD (LONDON)
Stanford, Jeremy Hugh , BA, jsdc, pce	CDR	X	P	31.12.94	MOD (LONDON)
Stangroom, Alastair	LT CDR	X	MCD	24.03.95	LONDON
Stanham, Christopher Mark	SLT(SD)	E	AE(M)	06.09.93	820 SQN
Stanhope, Mark , OBE, MA, MNI, pce, pce(sm), psc	CAPT	X	SM	30.06.91	MOD (LONDON)
Stanley, Anne Gillian , BSc	LT CDR	I	METOC	17.03.94	MOD (LONDON)
Stanley, Christopher Edward , pce, psc	CDR	X	PWO(A)	30.06.94	RNSC GREENWICH
Stanley, Ian , DSO, pce, psc	CDR	X	P	30.06.86	FONA
Stanley, Nicholas James	LT(SL)	X	O	16.09.93	815 SQN HQ
Stanley, Nicholas Paul , psc	CDR	X	PWO(U)	30.06.95	GRAFTON
Stanley, Paul , BEd, jsdc	CDR	I	SM	30.06.92	2SL/CNH
Stanley-Whyte, Berkeley John , BSc, IEng, MIMgt, AMIMarE, AMIEE	LT CDR	E	WESM	01.04.91	NEPTUNE SM1
Stannard, Mark Philip	LT	X		01.08.89	MOD (LONDON)
Stanton, David Vernon , pcea	LT CDR(SL)	X	O	01.10.91	706 SQN SEAHAWK
Stanton, Paul Charles Maund , BSc	LT	S		16.02.89	2SL/CNH
Stanton, Richard Francis , BSc, CEng, MIEE, AIL, I(1)Ru, I(2)Ge	LT CDR	E	WESM	01.05.79	ETS GERMANY
Stanton, Roger Tyrrell , BSc, CEng, MIMarE	CDR	E	MESM	31.12.90	MOD (BATH)
Stanton-Brown, Peter James , BSc	LT	X	SM	01.02.93	VICTORIOUS(STBD)
Stapley, Sarah Anne , MB, BCh, ChB	SURG LTCDR	-		01.08.95	RNDHU DERRIFORD
Stark, Trevor Alan , psc	CAPT RM	RM		01.12.82	2SL/CNH
Starks, Michael Robert , BSc, MA, CEng, MRAeS, psc	LT CDR	E	AE	01.12.90	MOD DGA(N)RNHSMP
Staveley, John Richard	LT CDR	X	MCD	01.01.87	SACLANT USA
Staveley, Sir William (Doveton Minet), GCB, DL, rcds, psc	ADM OF FLEET			25.05.89	
Stead, Richard Alexander	LT(SD)	MS	AD	06.04.95	CDO LOG REGT RM
Steadman, Robert , BA	SLT	X		01.01.94	DARTMOUTH BRNC
Stear, Timothy James Fletcher (Act Lt Rm)	2LT	RM		01.09.92	45 CDO RM
Stearns, Rupert Paul , MA, psc	MAJ	RM	LC	30.06.96	CTCRM
Steed, Bernard Eric , OBE, MRINA, psc	CDR	X	O	31.12.81	DRAKE CBP
Steeds, Sean Michael , pce, pcea	LT CDR	X	P	01.01.90	706 SQN SEAHAWK
Steel, Alastair James , BSc, AMIEE	LT CDR	E	WESM	03.11.92	MOD (BATH)
Steel, Christopher Michael Howard , BSc, CEng, MIEE, jsdc	CDR	E	WESM	31.12.92	CAPTAIN SM2
Steel, David George , BA, jsdc (Barrister)	CDR	S	BAR	31.12.94	CINCFLEET
Steel, David Goodwin	LT(SD)	MS	CDO	28.07.89	COMAW SEA
Steel, Peter St Clair , BSc, jsdc	CDR	X	P	30.06.91	MOD (LONDON)
Steel, Robert Ali , BEng	LT(SL)	E	ME	01.09.93	WESTMINSTER
Steel, Rodney James , BSc, CEng, MIMechE	CDR	E	AE(P)	31.12.90	JSDC GREENWICH
Steel, Sara-Jane	SLT(SL)	X		01.01.96	DARTMOUTH BRNC
Steele, Karen Sheila	LT(SL)	S		01.07.92	NAVSOUTH ITALY
Steele, Roger Philip , jsdc, pce	CDR	X	PWO(C)	31.12.88	DRYAD MWC
Steele, Trevor Graeme	LT(SD)	X	O	11.12.92	EXCHANGE RAF UK
Steer, Andrew David	SLT	X		01.01.95	LONDON
Steer, Michael A	LT(SL)	I	METOC	01.05.91	FOSM NWOOD OPS
Stefanie, Neil Bradshaw , jsdc	CDR	E	ME	31.12.91	2SL/CNH
Steil, Cameron Wellesley Rutherford	LT(SL)	X		01.02.93	CFP SHORE
Steinhausen, Julian Lionel Paul, BSc	LT CDR	E	ME	01.0376	DNPS
Stellingworth, Jill Pamela , rcds, psc	CDR	W	SEC	01.04.89	RNSC GREENWICH
Stembridge, Daniel Patrick Trelawney	LT(SL)	X	P	16.04.94	702 SQN OSPREY
Stenhouse, Nicholas John , BSc, MA, CEng, MIEE, AMIEE, psc	CDR	E	WE	31.12.93	DGSS BRISTOL
Stenhouse, Ronald Cowan , MA	LT CDR	X	PWO(A)	01.05.91	FOST SEA
Stenning, Michael William , psc	CDR	X	AWO(C)	30.06.88	SCU LEYDENE ACNS
Stenton, Mark John , MB, BS	SURG LT	-		01.08.93	RH HASLAR
Stephen, Barry Mark , BA	LT	X		01.03.94	BRAZEN
Stephen, John Arnold	LT(SD)	X	C	25.01.92	CON DCN
Stephens, David Robert	LT CDR(SD)	X	EW	01.10.93	LOAN CDA NAG
Stephens, Peter Michael , BSc	LT CDR	E	AE	16.11.79	2SL/CNH

Name	Rank	Spec	Sub-spec	Seniority	Where serving
Stephens, Richard John , BSc	LT(SL)	I	METOC	01.09.90	CAPT F2(SEA)
Stephens, Richard James (Loc Capt Rm)	LT RM	RM		01.05.90	FONA SUPPORT
Stephens, Richard Philip	LT(SD)	X	EW	18.04.93	RNU CHELTENHAM
Stephens, Robert Philip William	LT CDR(SD)	X	AV	01.10.94	845 SQN
Stephens, Simon Edward , PhD	CHAPLAIN	CE		02.09.80	CAPT(H) DEVPT
Stephenson, David , BEng	LT CDR	E	ME	22.11.95	MOD (BATH)
Stephenson, Edward Kenneth	LT(SD)	S	W	17.09.82	DNPS
Stephenson, Frederick , BSc, CEng, MIMechE	LT CDR	E	AE	16.05.80	FONA
Stephenson, Geoffrey Thomas	LT CDR(SL)	X	P	01.03.87	RNAS CULDROSE
Stephenson, Keith James MacFarlane , BA	LT(SL)	X	O	01.05.94	FONA SULTAN
Stephenson, Philip George	SLT(SD)	S	S	23.07.95	DRAKE BSO(W)
Stevens, Andrew Mark Robert	SLT(SL)	X		01.03.94	COTTESMORE
Stevens, Richard Mark	LT	X		10.03.91	SPEY
Stevens, Robert Patrick , pce, pce(sm) (Commodore)	CAPT	X	SM(N)	30.06.89	MOD (LONDON)
Stevenson, Aubrey	LT(SD)	E	ME	23.02.90	ARK ROYAL
Stevenson, Charles Bernard Hilton , BSc, psc	CAPT	I	METOC	31.12.95	2SL/CNH
Stevenson, Julian Patrick , BEng	LT(SL)	E	MESM	01.11.93	TALENT
Stevenson, Lucinda	SG SLT(D)	-		01.01.94	DARTMOUTH BRNC
Stevenson, Robert MacKinnon , BDS, MSc, MGDS RCS	SGCDR(D)	-		31.12.90	DRAKE CBP
Stevenson, Victoria Jane	SURG SLT	-		10.09.93	DARTMOUTH BRNC
Stewart, Annabel Barbara , BSc	LT	X		01.02.95	BOXER
Stewart, Andrew Carnegie , pce	LT CDR	X	PWO(C)	01.12.90	DRYAD
Stewart, Alastair Malcolm , BEng, MIMechE	LT	E	MESM	01.11.90	SULTAN
Stewart, Charles Edward , QHC, BSc, BD, PhD	PR CHAPLAIN	SF		29.02.76	2SL/CNH
Stewart, David James , OBE, MC, BSc, MA, psc	MAJ	RM		02.01.95	CTCRM
Stewart, Gillian	LT(SL)	S		01.01.96	RALEIGH
Stewart, James , psc	CAPT RM(SD)	RM	MLDR	01.10.91	HQ 3 CDO BDE RM
Stewart, John Cameron , BEng, AMIEE	LT CDR	E	WESM	01.11.94	NEPTUNE SM1
Stewart, James Neil , BSc	LT CDR	I	SM	01.09.93	FOSM NWOOD OPS
Stewart, Kenneth Currie , BSc	LT(SL)	I		01.09.90	PJHQ
Stewart, Michael David , MB, BCh, ChB	SURG LTCDR	-		03.08.93	RH HASLAR
Stewart, Peter Charles , BEng	LT	E	MESM	01.02.89	NEPTUNE SM1
Stewart, Robert Gordon , BSc	LT CDR	X	H1	01.02.90	RNSC GREENWICH
Stewart, Robert Murray	CAPT RM	RM		01.03.89	HQRM
Stewart, Rory William , BSc	LT CDR	E	MESM	01.07.91	TRAFALGAR
Stickland, Charles Richard , BSc	LT RM	RM	LC	30.04.91	ASC CAMBERLEY
Sticklee, Andrew Charles , TEng, MITE (Act Lt Cdr)	LT(SD)	X	WE	30.10.81	MOD DFS(CIS) GOS
Stidston, David Bernard	LT CDR(SL)	X	ATC	01.10.94	RNAS PORTLAND
Stidston, Ian James , BSc	LT CDR	I		01.09.91	CTCRM
Stillwell, Andrew James , BEd, adp	LT CDR	I		01.09.87	DRAKE NBSM(CNH)
Stillwell-Cox, Andrew David Robert , LHCIMA, MCFA	LT(SD)	S	CA	17.12.93	DARTMOUTH BRNC
Stinton, Carol	LT	Q	OTSPEC	09.11.89	RNH GIB
Stirling, Douglas , BSc	SLT(SL)	X	P U/T	01.05.94	DARTMOUTH BRNC
Stirzaker, Mark , BSc	LT	E	MESM	01.11.88	SULTAN
Stiven, Timothy , BSc	SLT	E	ME	01.09.93	SULTAN
Stobie, Ian Charles Angus , MBE	LT CDR	X		28.07.88	SEAHAWK
Stobie, Paul Lionel	LT(SD)	E	AE(L)	16.10.92	LOAN DTEO BSC DN
Stock, Christopher Mark	LT(SL)	X	O	01.05.93	819 SQN
Stockbridge, Anthony Julian , MA	SLT(SL)	S		01.09.94	DARTMOUTH BRNC
Stocker, Nicholas John , BSc	LT RM	RM		01.09.93	CTCRM
Stockings, Timothy Mark , BSc, pce	LT CDR	X	P	01.05.94	BOXER
Stockman, Colin David , BA, pce, pce(sm), psc	CDR	X	SM	31.12.90	FOSM NWOOD OPS
Stockton, James Philip , psc	LT CDR(SD)	X	SM	01.10.91	FOSM NWOOD OPS
Stockton, Kevin Geoffrey	LT(SL)	X	MCD	01.03.94	SANDOWN
Stoffell, David Peter	LT(SL)	S		01.07.93	DRAKE CFM
Stokes, Alan William	LT(SD)	E	WESM	05.06.92	DG SHIPS PTLAND
Stokes, Richard , BSc, CEng, MIEE	LT CDR	E	WESM	01.02.94	TORBAY
Stone, Colin Robert Macleod , pce	LT CDR	X	PWO(U)	01.05.85	TAMAR
Stone, Paul Christopher Julian , BSc	LT(SL)	X	P	16.05.89	LOAN DTEO BSC DN
Stone, Paul Douglas , BSc, FIMgt, pce, psc, hcsc (Commodore)	CAPT	X	PWO	31.12.89	2SL/CNH
Stone, Robert Benjamin , BSc, CEng, FIMarE, psc	CDR	E	ME	30.06.81	DG SHIPS DEVONPT
Stone, Richard James	SLT(SD)	E	ME	19.06.95	SULTAN

Name	Rank	Spec	Sub-spec	Seniority	Where serving
Stone, Richard Peter	LT CDR(SL)	X	P	01.10.95	899 SQN HERON
Stoneman, Timothy John , BSc, MA, pce, psc	CDR	X	PWO(A)	31.12.91	PJHQ
Stones, Nicholas Anthony	LT	X	FC	01.04.95	BIRMINGHAM
Stonham, Barry Valentine , FHCIMA	CDR(SD)	S	CAT	01.10.95	MOD (BATH)
Stonor, Philip Francis Andrew , pce, pcea, odc(Fr), I(2)Fr	CDR	X	P	31.12.95	WEU
Stoot, Christopher John , MB, BS, DIH, DipAvMed, AFOM	SURG CDR	-	CO/M	31.12.91	SULTAN
Storey, Ceri Leigh , BEng	LT	E	MESM	01.09.95	RNC DPT NS&TECH
Storey, Michael , BSc, CEng, MIEE, jsdc, I(2)Fr	CDR	E	WESM	31.12.90	MOD (LONDON)
Storrs-Fox, Roderick Noble , BSc	CDR	S		31.12.95	MOD (LONDON)
Stott, John Anthony	LT CDR	E	WESM	26.05.91	SPLENDID
Stovin-Bradford, Matthew	LT RM	RM		01.09.92	CTCRM
Stowe, Elisabeth Jane , BA	SLT	S		01.01.95	DARTMOUTH BRNC
Stowell, Perry Ivan Mottram , n	LT	X		01.04.90	DRYAD
Stowell, Robin Barnaby Mottram	LT	E	ME	01.01.96	EXETER
Strange, Richard Frank , pce, pce(sm)	CAPT	X	SM	31.12.91	DOLPHIN
Strange, Steven Paul	SLT(SL)	E	WESM	01.05.94	DARTMOUTH BRNC
Stratford, Peter John	LT(SL)	X		01.04.95	GLOUCESTER
Strathern, Roderick James	LT	X	MW	01.10.90	WALNEY
Strathie, Gavin Scott	SLT(SL)	X		01.01.93	INVINCIBLE
Stratton, John Denniss , BSc, psc	CDR	E	AE(P)	30.06.93	MOD PE ASC
Stratton-Brown, Robert , BA	LT(SL)	X		01.03.94	VICTORIOUS(PORT)
Straughan, Christopher John , MBE, pce	LT CDR	X	PWO(U)	01.12.90	NORFOLK
Straughan, Harry , BSc, psc	LT CDR	I		01.09.89	FOSF
Straughan, Kerry Elizabeth	LT(SL)	W	X	26.07.86	VICTORY
Straughan, Scott , BEng	SLT(SL)	X	P U/T	01.01.94	DARTMOUTH BRNC
Straw, Andrew Nicholas	LT CDR	S		16.03.96	LONDON
Stredwick, Clare Angelika , BA	LT(SL)	W	I	03.04.91	NELSON RNSETT
Street, Robert William , MBE	CDR(SD)	X	PR	01.10.92	2SL/CNH
Streeten, Christopher Mark , BSc	LT CDR	E	WESM	01.06.95	DOLPHIN SM SCHL
Streets, Christopher George , MB, BSc, BCh	SURG LT	-		01.08.93	RNDHU DERRIFORD
Stretton, Darrell George	SLT(SD)	X	AV	03.04.94	RNAS PORTLAND
Stretton, Peter Michael	LT(SL)	X	O	16.06.87	820 SQN
Strick, Charles Gordon , BSc	LT CDR	E	WESM	01.02.93	VIGILANT(PORT)
Stride, James Alan , BSc	SLT	X		01.09.93	DRYAD
Stride, Jamieson Colin	LT	X		01.04.95	BRECON
Stringer, Karl David Paul	SLT(SL)	X	P	01.09.94	848 SQN HERON
Stringer, Michael Charles , MILDM	CDR	S		31.12.89	PJHQ
Stringer, Roger Andrew	LT(SL)	X	P	01.06.87	INVINCIBLE
Strong, Tobias Charles , BA	LT	X		01.11.94	HERALD
Stroude, Paul Addison , BTech	SLT	X		01.09.93	LEEDS CASTLE
Strudwick, Russell (Act Lt)	SLT(SD)	S	W	24.07.94	NEPTUNE
Strutt, Jason Fearnley , BEng	LT	E	WE	01.05.92	LOAN DRA PRTSDWN
Stuart, Charles William McDonald	LT CDR	S		01.03.83	2SL/CNH
Stuart, Euan Edward Andrew , BA, MEng	SLT(SL)	X		01.09.94	PLOVER
Stubbings, Paul Richard	LT CDR(SD)	E	MESM	01.10.93	DRAKE CBS
Stubbs, Gary	LT(SL)	X	P	16.09.94	846 SQN
Stubbs, Ian	LT(SL)	X		01.10.95	PEACOCK
Stubbs, Martin Andrew	LT(SD)	E	WESM	22.02.96	MOD DGUW PTLAND
Stubbs, Paul Nigel , MA	LT CDR(SL)	I		01.05.81	PJHQ
Studley, Steven Alan	SLT(SL)	X		01.01.95	CAMPBELTOWN
Sturdy, Clive Charles Markus	SLT(SL)	X		01.09.92	MONMOUTH
Sturman, Matthew , psc(m), osc	LT COL	RM		31.12.94	HQRM
Stuttard, Mark Christopher , pce	LT CDR	X	PWO(A)	01.07.94	CAPT F4 (SEA)
Stuttard, Stephen Eric	LT(SL)	X	AV	27.07.90	ILLUSTRIOUS
Style, Charles Rodney , MA, pce	CAPT	X	PWO(U)	30.06.93	FOST SEA
Styles, Stephen Brian	LT(SD)	E	WESM	19.02.93	NEPTUNE NT
Suckling, Paul Morris , BSc	LT CDR(SL)	E	MESM	01.10.94	MOD (BATH)
Suckling, Robin Leslie	LT(SL)	X	O	16.08.90	RNAS CULDROSE
Suddes, Lesley Ann , BA	LT	I	METOC	01.10.92	SEAHAWK
Suddes, Thomas	LT CDR(SD)	X	AV	01.10.94	TEMERAIRE
Sugden, Michael Rodney	LT CDR(SL)	E	ME	01.10.94	COCHRANE
Sugden, Stephen Robert	LT(SD)	E	WE	18.02.94	CFM PORTSMOUTH

Name	Rank	Spec	Sub-spec	Seniority	Where serving
Sullivan, Colin , BA, psc	LT CDR	I	METOC	01.04.88	MOD (LONDON)
Sullivan, Mark	SLT(SD)	E	WE	07.02.94	DARTMOUTH BRNC
Sullivan, Mark Nigel	SLT(SL)	E	ME	01.09.94	DARTMOUTH BRNC
Summerfield, David Edward , osc(us) (Act Maj)	CAPT RM	RM		01.05.91	DRYAD MWC
Summers, James Alexander Edward , BEd	LT(SL)	I		24.05.90	RM POOLE
Summerton, Duncan John , MB, BSc, BCh	SURG LTCDR	-		01.08.93	RH HASLAR
Sumner, Michael Dennis	LT CDR(SD)	E	WESM	01.10.94	VICTORIOUS(PORT)
Sunderland, John Dominic , MSc, CEng, MIEE	LT CDR	E	WESM	01.04.91	2SL/CNH
Sutcliffe, John , pcea	LT CDR	X	O	21.12.94	SOMERSET
Sutcliffe, Marcus Jason	LT(SL)	X	P	16.06.85	750 SQN OBS SCH
Sutcliffe, Mark Richard	SLT	X		01.01.94	LANCASTER
Sutcliffe, Roy William	LT(SD)	E	WESM	15.06.90	NEPTUNE SM1
Sutherland, Gordon Massie	LT(SD)	E	WE	05.06.92	MOD (BATH)
Sutherland, Neil	LT RM	RM		24.04.95	CTCRM
Sutherland, Scott Alexander McLeod	SLT(SL)	X	O U/T	01.05.94	FONA SULTAN
Sutherland, William Murray , MA	CDR	I		30.06.93	2SL/CNH
Sutton, Brian , MSc	LT CDR(SL)	I		07.01.82	EXCHANGE USA
Sutton, Gary Brian , pce	LT CDR	X	PWO(N)	01.09.93	PLOVER
Sutton, Gareth David , BSc, CEng, MIMarE	LT CDR	E	ME	01.06.93	ARGYLL
Sutton, Richard Michael John	LT(SL)	X	P	01.06.93	705 SQN SEAHAWK
Sutton, Robert William	LT CDR(SD)	X	AV	01.10.95	DGA(N) ASE
Sutton, Stephen John	LT RM	RM		29.04.96	BOXER
Sutton-Scott-Tucker, Jonathan James , BSc	LT CDR	S		01.03.96	RALEIGH
Swabey, Brian	CHAPLAIN	CE		14.07.92	DOLPHIN
Swailes, Simon Phillip	SLT(SL)	X		01.01.95	ATHERSTONE
Swain, Andrew Vincent	LT	X	H1	05.03.89	HECLA
Swain, David Leslie , LVO, QHP, MB, ChB, FFARCS, DA, DObstRCOG	SURG CAPT	-	CA	30.06.86	RH HASLAR
Swain, David Michael , BSc, MNI, pce, pcea	CDR	X	O	31.12.91	JMOTS TURNHOUSE
Swain, Timothy Guy , BA, BEng	LT(SL)	E	O	01.02.88	LOAN DTEO BSC DN
Swaine, Robin	LT CDR(SD)	X	C	01.10.91	CINCIBERLANT
Swainson, David John , CEng, MIMechE	CDR	E	MESM	31.12.91	MOD (BATH)
Swales, Steven Michael	LT CDR(SL)	X	P	01.10.94	EXCHANGE USA
Swan, Christopher Paul , BEng	LT	E	WE	01.03.94	LONDON
Swan, Peter William Hewett , pce (Commodore)	CAPT	X	AWO(C)	30.06.93	ACE SRGN ITALY
Swan, Ralph Thomas	LT(CS)	-		18.10.87	2SL/CNH
Swan, Wendy	LT(SL)	W		01.12.95	TEMERAIRE
Swann, John Ivan	LT(SD)	X	EW	28.07.89	SCU LEYDENE ACNS
Swanney, Ian Newton	LT(SD)	E	AE(M)	14.10.88	EXCHANGE AUSTLIA
Swannick, Clare Marie , BA	LT(SL)	W	I	24.07.91	MOD DNR OUTPORTS
Swannick, Derek John , BSc	LT(SL)	I	METOC	01.09.88	ROEBUCK
Swarbrick, Richard James , BA	LT CDR	X	P	01.12.94	810 SQN B FLIGHT
Sweeney, Keith Patrick Michael , BEng	LT	E	ME	01.07.95	YORK
Sweeney, Liam Christopher Kevin , BSc	LT	X	H2	01.12.93	GLEANER
Sweeny, Brian Donald , IEng, AMIMarE	LT CDR(SD)	E	HULL	01.10.93	MOD (BATH)
Sweet, Paul , BSc	LT	X		01.12.94	MANCHESTER
Swift, Ian David	LT(SL)	I		01.01.87	2SL/CNH FOTR
Swift, Jacqueline Anne	LT(SL)	W	X	25.07.91	RFANSU (ARGUS)
Swift, Robin David	LT	X	PWO(U)	01.07.89	LANCASTER
Swigciski, David Phillip	LT	X		01.02.95	LANCASTER
Swinden, Martin Barrie , BSc	LT(SL)	I		01.01.93	2SL/CNH FOTR
Syer, Patrick George , pce, pcea, psc	CDR	X	P	31.12.82	FONA
Sykes, Jeremy James William , MB, BCh, ChB, MSc, FFOM, MFOM (Act Surg Capt)	SURG CDR	-	CO/M	31.12.84	2SL/CNH
Sykes, Malcolm , BEng, MSc, psc	LT CDR	E	MESM	16.11.92	TIRELESS
Sykes, Robert Alan , BA	LT(SL)	X	O	16.08.86	EXCHANGE BRAZIL
Sykes, Steven John , pce(sm)	CDR	X	SM	31.12.94	MOD (LONDON)
Symington, Zena Marie Alexandrea	SLT(SL)	X		01.09.94	LIVERPOOL
Symonds, Peter Hugh , jsdc, pce, psc	LT CDR	X	P	16.05.81	MOD (LONDON)
Syrett, Matthew , BSc	LT	X		01.08.95	LEDBURY
Syvret, Mark Edward Vibert , BSc (Loc Maj)	CAPT RM	RM		01.09.93	PJHQ
Szemerenyi, Paul Nicholas	LT(SL)	X	SM	01.12.91	DOLPHIN SM SCHL

Name	Rank	Spec	Sub-spec	Seniority	Where serving

T

Name	Rank	Spec	Sub-spec	Seniority	Where serving
Tabberer, Ian Craig , BSc	SLT	X		01.01.94	DARTMOUTH BRNC
Tabeart, George William	LT	X	SM	01.11.89	DOLPHIN SM SCHL
Tacey, Richard	LT(SL)	X		01.12.95	IRON DUKE
Tailor, Sudhirkumar , BSc, PGCE	LT(SL)	I		01.05.89	SULTAN
Tait, John Simon , BA	LT(SL)	I		09.10.88	NELSON
Talbot, Christopher Martin	LT(SD)	X	C	12.12.91	MOD (LONDON)
Talbot, George Keith , BSc, PGCE, MA(Ed), MITD	LT CDR(SL)	I		01.09.86	NELSON RNSETT
Talbot, Nigel Adrian , BSc, MEng, PGCE	LT CDR(SL)	I		01.10.93	NELSON RNSETT
Talbot, Richard Jonathan , pce, psc(m) (Act Capt)	CDR	X	AWO(C)	31.12.84	HQ DFTS
Talbot, Richard Paul	LT CDR	X		01.03.96	DRYAD
Talbott, Aidan Hugh	LT	S		01.12.92	CAPT IST STAFF
Tall, David Michael , OBE, jsdc, pce, pce(sm)	CAPT	X	SM	31.12.94	ACDS(POL&NUC)USA
Tamayo, Brando Christian Craig	SURG LT	-		01.08.94	REPULSE(PORT)
Tamblyn, Jonathan Tregair , MBIM, MBCS, rcds, psc, adp (Commodore)	CAPT	E	WE	30.06.90	DGSS BRISTOL
Tanner, Michael John	LT RM	RM		01.09.95	40 CDO RM
Tanner, Richard Carlisle	LT(SL)	X	SM	01.03.95	VICTORIOUS(PORT)
Tanser, Susan Jane , MB, BS	SURG LT	-		01.08.91	RNDHU DERRIFORD
Tant, Martin Charles Otto , MB, BS	SURG LT	-		01.08.91	NELSON (PAY)
Tant, Zoe Margaret , BEd	LT(SL)	W	S	03.04.91	RNSC GREENWICH
Tapp, Roderick Craig , BSc	LT	X		01.10.94	RALEIGH
Tappenden, Edward James	SLT	X		01.05.95	VIGILANT(PORT)
Tapping, Kenneth	LT(SD)	E	AE(M)	19.10.90	DGA(N)ASE MASU
Tarr, Barry Stuart	LT CDR	E	MESM	01.07.92	VICTORIOUS(PORT)
Tarr, Michael Douglas , BSc, pce	CDR	X	PWO(A)	30.06.93	MOD (LONDON)
Tarr, Richard Nicholas Vaughan , BSc	LT CDR	E	MESM	01.08.93	RESOLUTION(PORT)
Tarran, Martin Richard Mitchell , CEng, MIMarE	LT CDR	E	ME	01.06.93	BRAVE
Tarrant, David Charles , pce	LT CDR	X	PWO(C)	01.08.93	COMUKTG/CASWSF
Tarrant, Robert Kenneth , pce(sm)	LT CDR	X	SM	01.02.92	EXCHANGE USA
Tasker, Greg , psc(m)	MAJ	RM		31.12.95	HQRM
Tate, Andrew John , BSc, AMIEE, psc	CDR	E	WESM	31.12.92	MOD (LONDON)
Tate, Christopher	LT(SL)	X	O	01.07.95	815 FLT 221
Tate, Derek Alan	LT CDR(SD)	E	AE(L)	01.10.92	MOD (LONDON)
Tate, Graeme	LT(SL)	X	P	01.02.95	814 SQN
Tate, Simon John , BSc	LT CDR	E	AE	01.01.96	MOD (LONDON)
Tatham, Peter Hugh , BSc, CEng, FCIS, MBCS, MIMgt	CDR	S		31.12.88	MOD (LONDON)
Tatham, Stephen Alan , BSc	LT(SL)	I		01.09.91	DRYAD
Tatlow, Joanne Mary , BA	LT(SL)	I		01.09.95	COLLINGWOOD
Tatman, Alan Keith , MRIN, pce	CDR	X	O	30.06.84	WEU
Tattersall, Philip David	LT	X	SM	01.07.88	LOAN CDA NAVY
Tattersall, Richard Brian	LT(SL)	X	P	01.07.91	801 SQN
Tayler, James Ralph Newton	LT(SL)	X	P	01.05.90	810 SQN SEA
Taylor, Anna	LT(SL)	I		01.09.89	2SL/CNH
Taylor, Anthony Frederick Murray , FBIM, MNI, pce(sm)	CDR	X	SM	31.12.86	SACLANT USA
Taylor, Andrew John , BA	LT CDR(SL)	I	METOC	01.10.89	DADPTC SHRIVNHAM
Taylor, Andrew John	LT	X	SM	23.06.88	2SL/CNH
Taylor, Alastair John Sym , BA, jsdc, pce (Commodore)	CAPT	X	AWO(A)	30.06.90	CINCFLEET
Taylor, Andrew Lyndon , BA	LT(SL)	I		01.05.91	NWOOD CIS
Taylor, Anthony Richard	LT	X	SM	01.11.90	ENDURANCE
Taylor, Brian David	LT	X		01.07.88	CAMBRIDGE
Taylor, Christopher David , BSc, pcea	LT CDR	X	P	01.04.89	LOAN DTEO BSC DN
Taylor, Claire Mavis , RRC, QHNS	CAPT	Q	RNT	09.07.90	MOD (LONDON)
Taylor, Carl Richard	SLT(SL)	S		01.05.94	MANCHESTER
Taylor, Hazel Jane	LT(SL)	E	WE	01.02.96	COLLINGWOOD
Taylor, Ian Kennedy	LT(SD)	S	S	16.12.94	ILLUSTRIOUS
Taylor, John Jeremy , MSc, CEng, MIMarE	CDR	E	MESM	30.06.96	MOD (BATH)
Taylor, Jonathan Paul	SLT(SD)	X	SM	24.07.94	COLLINGWOOD
Taylor, John William , MIPM	LT CDR(SL)	X	ATC	01.09.87	RNAS YEOVILTON
Taylor, Keith , BEng	LT	E	WESM	01.11.89	NEPTUNE SM1
Taylor, Kenneth Alistair , BSc, pce, pcea	LT CDR	X	O	01.11.90	RNSC GREENWICH

Name	Rank	Spec	Sub-spec	Seniority	Where serving
Taylor, Kirsty	SG SLT(D)	-		01.04.95	DARTMOUTH BRNC
Taylor, Kenneth John	LT(SD)	E	WESM	18.02.94	FOSM NWOOD OPS
Taylor, Keith	SLT(SL)	E	WE	01.05.95	DARTMOUTH BRNC
Taylor, Leslie	LT CDR(SL)	X	P	01.10.94	LOAN PORTUGAL
Taylor, Lester Geoffrey	LT CDR	X	SM	15.11.92	RNU ST MAWGN SEA
Taylor, Mark Andrew	LT	X	P	01.02.91	815 FLT 201
Taylor, Marcus Anthony Beckett	LT RM	RM	LC	01.09.94	CAMPBELTOWN
Taylor, Martin Kenneth , osc	MAJ	RM		30.06.94	HQ 3 CDO BDE RM
Taylor, Mark Richard	LT(SD)	X	C	29.07.94	FOST SEA
Taylor, Nicholas Frederick , MA, pce	LT CDR	X	PWO(C)	16.02.87	MOD (LONDON)
Taylor, Neville Graham , BSc, pce(sm)	LT CDR	X	SM	01.04.89	MWC GOSPORT
Taylor, Neil Robert , BEng	LT(SL)	E	ME	01.06.91	FOSF
Taylor, Peter George David , BSc	CAPT RM	RM		25.04.96	HQ 3 CDO BDE RM
Taylor, Paul James , BSc, PGCE, adp	LT CDR(SL)	I		01.10.92	HQAFNORTHWEST
Taylor, Robert , BEng	LT	E	WE	01.09.91	COLLINGWOOD
Taylor, Rodney Hemingfield , BM, BSc, BS, MD, LRCP, FRCP, MRCS, MRCP	SURG CDR	-	CM	31.12.88	RH HASLAR
Taylor, Robert James	LT(SL)	X	O	16.02.94	702 SQN OSPREY
Taylor, Spencer Alan , MSc, CEng, MIEE, AMIEE	LT CDR	I		01.02.91	2SL/CNH FOTR
Taylor, Stephen Bryan , CQSW	A/LT(FS)	FS		01.05.95	DRAKE CBP
Taylor, Stuart David , BSc	2LT(GRAD)	RM		01.09.95	CTCRM LYMPSTONE
Taylor, Stephen John , BEng	LT(SL)	E	WE	01.06.89	LOAN DRA PRTSDWN
Taylor, Stephen John , BA	LT CDR	S	SM	16.04.96	2SL/CNH
Taylor, Simon Jonathan , BEng	SLT(SL)	X		01.01.95	DARTMOUTH BRNC
Taylor, Stephen Mark	LT CDR	S		01.11.93	OSPREY
Taylor, William John , osc, I(2)No (Loc Maj)	CAPT RM	RM		01.09.90	PJHQ
Teague, Fiona Maria , BA	LT	X		01.03.94	ORWELL
Teasdale, Derrick	LT(SD)	E	WESM	15.06.90	NEPTUNE NT
Teasdale, David Andrew , BA	LT	X		01.12.93	DOLPHIN SM SCHL
Teasdale, Keith Stanley	SLT(SD)	S	W	03.04.94	OSPREY
Teasdale, Robert Mark , BA	LT CDR	S		16.01.93	CORNWALL
Tebbet, Paul Nicholas	LT	X		01.09.89	NORFOLK
Teer, David Raymond , OBE, MBIM, pce	CDR	X	AC	30.06.88	CINCFLEET
Teideman, Ian Charles , BEng	LT	E	WE	01.03.92	FOSF
Tellam, Shane Mark , MB, BS	SURG LT	-		01.08.91	RH HASLAR
Tempest, Richard John , BSc, CEng, MIEE, psc	CAPT	E	WESM	30.06.90	SA BRAZIL
Temple, Miles	LT(SL)	X		01.11.94	GLASGOW
Templeton, Thomas Appleyard Molison , IEng, MIEEIE	LT(SD)	E	WE	09.06.89	RNSC GREENWICH
Tench, Mark , BSc	LT(SL)	I	SM	01.09.88	SULTAN AIB
Tennant, Michael Ian	SURG LT			14.09.95	HECLA
Tennant, Malcolm Stuart , MBIM, MRINA, MRIN	LT CDR	X	O	01.03.78	DALRIADA
Tennuci, Robert George	LT	X	FC	01.12.91	NELSON (PAY)
Terrill, Keith William , BA	LT CDR(SL)	X	O	01.03.85	750 SQN OBS SCH
Terry, Adrian John , BSc	LT(SL)	X		01.06.90	HERON
Terry, John Michael , MSc, CEng, MIMarE	LT CDR	E	ME	01.04.88	SULTAN
Terry, Nigel Patrick	SLT(SL)	X	P	01.08.93	820 SQN
Terry-Brown, Peter Charles , BA	LT(SL)	X		01.06.92	DRYAD
Tetley, Mark	LT(SL)	X	O	01.07.91	771 SK5 SAR
Tetlow, Hamish Stuart Guy , BA	LT	X	SM	01.07.88	REPULSE(PORT)
Tew, John Philip , MA	LT	S	BAR	16.04.89	DARTMOUTH BRNC
Thatcher, Louise Frances Victoria	MID(UCE)	X		01.09.95	MANCHESTER
Thatcher, Robert Peter , BSc, CEng, MIEE, psc	CDR	E	WE	30.06.89	NBC PORTSMOUTH
Thicknesse, Philip John , MA, pce, pcea, psc	LT CDR	X	P	01.07.90	LEEDS CASTLE
Thirkettle, Julian Andrew , BEng	LT(SL)	E	AE	01.02.94	845 SQN
Thistlethwaite, Mark Halford , BSc, psc	LT CDR	E	AE(O)	01.03.91	MOD (LONDON)
Thoburn, Ross , OBE	CDR	X	O	30.06.92	TAMAR
Thom, Dean , BSc	SLT(SL)	X	P U/T	01.05.94	DARTMOUTH BRNC
Thomas, Ann Louise , BEng	LT(SL)	I		01.01.91	DARTMOUTH BRNC
Thomas, Arthur Peter William , BSc	LT(SL)	X	P	01.08.86	750 SQN OBS SCH
Thomas, Christopher Charles , MA, pce, psc	LT CDR	X	PWO(A)	01.07.89	BROCKLESBY
Thomas, Christopher David , PhD, CEng, MIMechE	CDR	I	METOC	31.12.85	2SL/CNH FOTR
Thomas, David Glen , BSc	LT CDR	E	MESM	01.03.93	SULTAN

Name	Rank	Spec	Sub-spec	Seniority	Where serving
Thomas, Dan	MID(SL)	X	P U/T	01.01.95	FONA CRANWELL
Thomas, David Jonathan	SLT(SD)	S	S	10.12.95	NELSON
Thomas, David Lynford , BDS, MSc, LDS RCS(Eng), MGDS RCS, MGDS RCSEd	SGCDR(D)	-		30.06.87	NEPTUNE
Thomas, David William Wallace , BA	CHAPLAIN	CE		18.10.88	DRAKE CBP
Thomas, Francis Stephen	LT CDR	S		12.09.92	FOSF
Thomas, Geoffrey Charles , BSc, pce, pce(sm)	CDR	X	SM	30.06.95	TORBAY
Thomas, Glynn Rae	LT(SL)	X	H2	01.10.91	BEAGLE
Thomas, Jeffrey Evans	LT(SD)	X	EW	25.07.91	HQ 3 CDO BDE RM
Thomas, Jeremy Huw	LT	E	WESM	01.02.90	JARIC
Thomas, Jeremy Hywel , psc(m)	MAJ	RM	WTO	31.12.91	HQ 3 CDO BDE RM
Thomas, Kevin Ian , BSc	LT CDR(SL)	I	METOC	01.10.92	BF GIBRALTAR(NE)
Thomas, Leslie	LT(SD)	X	C	02.04.93	CNOCS GROUP
Thomas, Martyn George	LT(SD)	E	ME	17.02.89	CFM PORTSMOUTH
Thomas, Matthew Norman , BA(OU)	LT CDR	X		01.01.89	COLLINGWOOD
Thomas, Neal Raymond	LT(SD)	X	EW	23.07.93	RNU RAF DIGBY
Thomas, Neill Wynell , DSC, jsdc, pce	CAPT	X	P	31.12.92	SA SEOUL
Thomas, Owain Richard , BSc, MIMechE	LT CDR	E	ME	01.12.85	LOAN BRUNEI
Thomas, Paul Anthony Moseley , MSc, CEng, FIMechE, MIMechE	RADM	-	MESM	13.09.95	MOD CSSE LONDON
Thomas, Paul Geraint	LT CDR	X	PWO(U)	01.11.94	IRON DUKE
Thomas, Paul Stuart , TEng, AMIMarE	LT CDR(SD)	E	ME	01.10.94	LIVERPOOL
Thomas, Patrick William	LT RM(SD)	RM		01.01.90	CTCRM
Thomas, Richard Anthony Aubrey	LT	X		01.09.90	DRYAD
Thomas, Richard Charles , MB, BS	SURG LT	-		05.08.92	RNDHU DERRIFORD
Thomas, Richard Kevin , BSc	LT	X	PWO(U)	01.06.88	SHEFFIELD
Thomas, Robert Paul , pce, pcea, psc	CDR	X	O	30.06.95	PJHQ
Thomas, Simon Alan , pce, pcea, psc(a)	CDR	X	P	31.12.93	2SL/CNH
Thomas, Stephen Mark , BEng	LT	E	ME	01.01.93	LOAN DTEO PYSTCK
Thomas, Stephen	LT(SL)	X	P	16.05.96	810 SQN SEAHAWK
Thomas, William Gwynne , BSc, pce, pcea	LT CDR	X	O	16.06.92	BOXER
Thompson, Andrew	LT	E	AE(M)	01.07.88	SULTAN
Thompson, Andrew Joseph , BSc, BEng	LT(SL)	I		01.01.93	COLLINGWOOD
Thompson, Andrew Robert	LT(SL)	X	O	01.02.92	810 SQN OEU
Thompson, Bernard Dominic , BA	LT CDR	X	MCD	01.09.94	MARLBOROUGH
Thompson, Charles Richard	LT CDR	X	MCD	16.07.81	RN HYDROG SCHL
Thompson, David Huw	2LT	RM		01.09.94	40 CDO RM
Thompson, David James , ndc, jsdc, pce, psc	CAPT	X	O	30.06.91	SA PARIS
Thompson, David William	SLT(SL)	E	MESM	01.01.94	DARTMOUTH BRNC
Thompson, Frederick Gladwyn , MBE, MSc, CEng, MIEE, MINucE, jsdc (Commodore)	CAPT	E	WESM	31.12.90	FOSNNI/NBC CLYDE
Thompson, Gary	LT CDR(SD)	X	C	01.10.95	COLLINGWOOD
Thompson, Graham Michael , BEM	LT RM(SD)	RM		01.01.95	40 CDO RM
Thompson, Geoffrey Norman	LT CDR	E	WE	25.01.88	FOST SEA
Thompson, Mark George	LT	X		01.03.95	TRAFALGAR
Thompson, Michael , BEng	SLT	E	ME	01.09.93	SULTAN
Thompson, Miles Oliver	LT	X	SM	01.01.90	MOD DNR OUTPORTS
Thompson, Neil James	LT CDR(SL)	X	P	01.10.94	848 SQN HERON
Thompson, Peter William , pce	LT CDR	X	PWO(U)	01.04.90	SOMERSET
Thompson, Robert Anthony	LT(SL)	X	O	01.08.89	EXCHANGE USA
Thompson, Richard Charles , BEng	LT	E	AE	01.02.89	MOD (LONDON)
Thompson, Robert Joseph , BSc	CDR	E	ME	30.06.95	JSDC GREENWICH
Thompson, Stephen John , MSc, MCGI	LT CDR	E	ME	01.09.92	BRILLIANT
Thomsen, Lavinia Lisa , BSc	SLT(SL)	X		01.09.94	BEAVER
Thomsett, Harry Fergus James	LT RM	RM		01.09.94	40 CDO RM
Thomson, Allan Brown , fsc, osc	MAJ	RM	MLDR	31.12.92	CTCRM
Thomson, Colin Douglas , BSc	LT	X	H2	01.02.93	DRYAD
Thomson, Duncan , pce	LT	X	PWO(U)	01.07.88	EXCHANGE USA
Thomson, Iain Rodger	LT(SL)	E	WESM	01.04.91	2SL/CNH
Thomson, Jonathan James , OBE, QGM, psc(m), hcsc (Brigadier)	COL	RM		31.12.91	PJHQ
Thomson, Keith Morrison , BEng	SLT(SL)	X	P U/T	01.01.95	DARTMOUTH BRNC
Thomson, Robert	LT(SL)	E	WE	01.04.96	DARTMOUTH BRNC

Name	Rank	Spec	Sub-spec	Seniority	Where serving
Thorburn, Andrew	LT(SD)	X	AV	27.07.90	SEAHAWK
Thorburn, Sally Ann , psc	CDR	W	SEC	31.12.91	RNSC GREENWICH
Thorn, Richard George , MSc, CEng, MIERE	CDR	I	METOC	30.06.88	FOSF
Thornback, John Gordon (Act Lt Cdr)	LT(SD)	E	WE	02.11.84	ELANT/NAVNW
Thorne, Dain Jason	SLT	E	AE	01.09.94	DARTMOUTH BRNC
Thorne, Simon Mark , BSc	LT(SL)	X	P	01.04.90	810 SQN OEU
Thornewill, Simon Clive , DSC, MRAeS, tp (Commodore)	CAPT	X	P	30.06.91	SEAHAWK
Thornton, Brian Patrick	SLT(SD)	S	CA	03.04.94	RALEIGH
Thornton, Charles Exley , BA, pcea	LT CDR	X	O	01.02.84	LOAN DTEO BSC DN
Thornton, Michael Crawford , pce, pcea, psc	LT CDR	X	P	08.02.84	815 SQN HQ
Thornton, Philip John , pcea	LT CDR(SL)	X	P	01.10.93	702 SQN OSPREY
Thorp, Benjamin	SLT	E	ME	01.01.94	MOD (BATH)
Thorpe, Conrad Dermot (Act Capt Rm)	LT RM	RM		01.09.91	CDO LOG REGT RM
Thorpe, Christopher Robert , BSc, psc	CDR	E	WE	31.12.92	CAPT F1(SEA)
Thorpe, Ian , pce, pcea, psc	CAPT	X	P	31.12.94	PJHQ
Thrippleton, Mark Graham , BEng	LT(SL)	E	AE	01.03.95	SULTAN
Thurstan, Richard William Farnall	LT RM	RM	LC	01.05.90	539 ASLT SQN RM
Thwaites, Gerard James , BSc, CEng, MIMechE, psc	CDR	E	MESM	30.06.91	GRAFTON
Tibbits, Charles Syson , MRIN, pce, pce(sm), psc	LT CDR	X	SM	16.11.78	EXCHANGE AUSTLIA
Tibbitt, Ian Peter Gordon , MA, CEng, MIEE, jsdc	CDR	E	AE	30.06.90	MOD (LONDON)
Tidball, Ian , BEng	LT(SL)	X	P	01.02.92	846 SQN
Tidbury, Neil , pce(sm) (Act Cdr)	LT CDR	X	SM	05.07.85	FOSM NWOOD OPS
Tighe, Gary , BA, pcea	LT CDR	X	P	01.02.91	815 FLT 209
Tighe, John Geoffrey Hugh , OBE, jsdc, pce	CAPT	X	AWO(A)	31.12.95	NATO DEF COL
Tighe, Simon	SLT(SL)	X		01.05.96	NELSON
Tigwell, Nigel Keith , BSc, CEng, MDA	LT CDR	E	MESM	01.04.92	REPULSE(PORT)
Tilden, Philip James Edward	SLT	X		01.09.94	DARTMOUTH BRNC
Tilley, Duncan Scott Jamieson , pce	LT CDR	X	H1	01.02.91	NP 1008 OFS SVY
Tillion, Andrew Malcolm	LT(SL)	X	P	01.05.90	848 SQN HERON
Tilney, Duncan Edward , BA	SLT(SL)	X		01.09.94	ANGLESEY
Timms, Stephen John , MBA, MSc, CEng, MIMarE, MIMechE, jsdc	CDR	E	MESM	30.06.91	NEPTUNE NT
Tindal, Nicolas Henry Charles , pcea	LT CDR	X	P	01.02.96	DRYAD
Tindall-Jones, Lee Douglas , BSc, CEng, MIEE, psc	LT CDR	E	WESM	01.07.90	MOD (BATH)
Tinkley, Neil Robert	LT CDR(SL)	X	ATC	01.03.83	OSPREY
Tinsley, Glenn Nigel	LT CDR	S		01.10.90	2SL/CNH
Tipper, Michael Royston , BEng	LT	E	WESM	01.06.90	MOD DGSM PTLAND
Tippey, Mark Andrew , BSc	LT(SL)	I		01.05.91	INVINCIBLE
Titcomb, Andrew Charles , BEng	LT	E	WESM	01.06.89	MOD DNR OUTPORTS
Titcomb, Mark Richard , BSc	LT	X	SM	01.02.90	ITCHEN
Titcomb, Richard Stanley Bowman	LT CDR(SD)	E	HULL	01.10.94	2SL/CNH FOTR
Tite, Anthony	LT(SL)	X	O	01.02.94	750 SQN OBS SCH
Titmus, Garry David , pce, psc	CDR	X	PWO(N)	30.06.82	LOAN OMAN
Titmuss, Julian Francis , BA	LT	S		01.12.94	BOXER
Titterton, Phillip James , pce(sm)	LT CDR	X	SM	01.03.94	CSST SHORE DEVPT
Tod, Jonathan James Richard , KCB, CBE, rcds	VADM	-	P	28.06.94	CINCFLEET
Todd, Clare Francesca Jane , BSc	LT(SL)	I		01.09.88	MOD DNR OUTPORTS
Todd, Donald , pce	LT CDR	X	AWO(A)	01.01.82	BF GIBRALTAR(NE)
Todd, Kevin , MBE	LT CDR(SD)	E	WESM	01.10.93	DOLPHIN
Todd, Michael Anthony	LT RM(SD)	RM		01.05.95	40 CDO RM
Toft, Burton Penn , BSc, CEng, FIMechE, jsdc	CAPT	E	ME	31.12.88	MOD (BATH)
Toft, Michael David , BEng	LT CDR	E	WE	01.03.96	MOD DGUW PTLAND
Tolhurst, John Gordon , CB	RADM	-	AWO(A)	29.09.92	FOSNNI/NBC CLYDE
Tolley, Peter Frederick Richmond , MB, BCh	SURG CAPT	-	GMPP	31.12.95	CINCFLEET
Tomes, Adrian Carl	MID(NE)(SL)	X		01.09.95	SHETLAND
Tomkins, Alan Brian	LT(SD)	E	WE	19.02.93	DG SHIPS PTSMTH
Tomlin, Peter Dawson	LT(SD)	X	PT	15.12.89	BF GIBRALTAR(NE)
Tomlinson, David Charles	SLT(SD)	X	AV	03.04.94	RFANSU
Tomlinson, James Henry	LT(SD)	X	PR	27.07.95	PJHQ
Tomlyn, Matthew Thomas Hedley	LT	X	SM	01.04.94	PJHQ
Toms, Robert James , BSc	LT CDR	X	PWO(U)	16.01.83	CINCFLEET
Toms, Trevor Martyn	LT CDR(SL)	X	P	01.10.90	SEAHAWK
Tong, David Keith , BA, rcds, psc(m)	MAJ	RM		31.12.90	HQRM

Name	Rank	Spec	Sub-spec	Seniority	Where serving
Tooley, John Edward Hewetson , MIEE	LT(SL)	I		01.09.87	DOLPHIN SM SCHL
Toomey, Nicholas John , BSc	LT	S		01.11.88	RALEIGH
Toon, John Richard	LT CDR(SD)	E	AE(M)	01.10.92	NELSON (PAY)
Toor, Jeevan Jyoti Singh , BSc	LT(SL)	I	METOC	01.09.90	814 SQN
Toothill, John Samuel	LT	X	SM	01.04.89	VANGUARD(STBD)
Tooze, Lee	LT(SL)	X	P	01.04.94	810 SQN SEAHAWK
Torvell, Matthew David Bingham , BSc, psc	LT CDR	E	WE	01.08.89	FOSF
Toshney, Richard	SLT(SL)	X	O	01.01.95	706 SQN SEAHAWK
Tothill, Nicholas Michael	LT CDR	S		01.12.92	MOD C OF N
Tottenham, John Geoffry , BSc, pce, pce(sm)	CDR	X	SM	31.12.92	VIGILANT(PORT)
Tough, Richard Stuart (Act Lt Cdr)	LT(SD)	S	W	17.09.82	NEPTUNE
Tougher, Raymond	LT CDR(SD)	E	AE(L)	01.10.93	SULTAN
Tovey, Paul Fenwick , BEd, MIPM, CDipAF, adp	LT CDR(SL)	I		12.09.79	HQRM
Towell, Peter James	SLT(SD)	E	ME	19.06.95	SULTAN
Towl, Peter Bramley , BSc	LT CDR	X	AWO(A)	01.05.81	DRAKE NBSM (CFS)
Towler, Alison , BSc	LT	S	BAR	14.12.89	FOSM NWOOD HQ
Towler, Perrin James Bryher	LT CDR	X	PWO(A)	01.06.94	LANCASTER
Townsend, Christopher Neil , BSc, I(2)Ge	LT CDR(SL)	X	P	01.10.91	32(THE ROYAL)SQN
Townsend, David	SLT(SD)	E	WE	01.09.93	DARTMOUTH BRNC
Townsend, Graham	LT(SL)	X	O	01.05.94	706 SQN SEAHAWK
Townsend, John Robert	CDR	E	WE	31.12.88	MOD (LONDON)
Townshend, Jeremy John , BSc	LT CDR	I		03.04.92	MOD (LONDON)
Toy, Malcolm John , BEng, MRAeS	LT CDR	E	AE	01.11.94	SULTAN
Tozer, Colin Vinson	LT CDR(SL)	X	PWO(A)	01.10.88	FOSF
Tracey, Alan David	SLT(SL)	E	AE	01.05.94	DARTMOUTH BRNC
Trasler, Mark Farnham	LT(SD)	MS	LT	03.04.92	CINCFLEET
Trathen, Neil Charles , BSc, pce	LT CDR	X	PWO(N)	01.02.92	2SL/CNH
Traynor, David Francis	LT	E	WE	01.07.90	LOAN DRA PRTSDWN
Treanor, Martin Andrew , BSc	LT CDR	E	AE	01.03.91	RNSC GREENWICH
Tredray, Thomas Patrick , BA	LT	X		01.02.93	GRAFTON
Tregaskis, Nicola , BA	SLT(SL)	X		01.01.93	BRAVE
Tregunna, Gary Andrew	LT(SL)	X		01.04.96	DOLPHIN SM SCHL
Treharne, Julian Jane	LT(SL)	W	C	11.12.92	NEPTUNE BASE OPS
Trelease, Frederick Michael , BA, MSc	LT CDR(SL)	I		01.10.89	DRAKE CBP
Tremelling, Alan John , pce, psc, ocds(Can), fsc (Act Cdr)	LT CDR	X	O	01.06.78	SEA CADET CORPS
Trevarthen, Alan Geoffrey , BSc	LT CDR(SL)	X	MCD	01.10.91	MOD (BATH)
Trevithick, Andrew Richard , BSc, GradIMA	CDR	I	METOC	31.12.93	MOD (LONDON)
Trevor, Mark Gerard	LT CDR	X	PWO(C)	01.04.95	EXETER
Trewby, John Allan , MA, CEng, FIEE, rcds, psc	RADM	-	WE	01.03.94	MOD (BATH)
Trewhella, Graham Gilbey , BSc, psc	LT CDR	I	SM	01.05.91	EXCELLENT
Tribe, Jeremy David , BSc	LT(SL)	X	P	16.10.87	815 OEU OSPREY
Tribe, Philip David	LT	X	FC	01.12.90	DRYAD
Tribe, Peter John , BA, rcds, psc, I(1)Fr	CAPT	S		31.12.90	MOD (LONDON)
Trickett, Conrad Bryan	LT RM	RM		01.09.94	45 CDO RM
Trinder, Stephen John	LT(SD)	S	CA	30.01.96	OSPREY
Tritschler, Edwin Lionel , BEng, BTech	LT	E	AE	01.10.90	SULTAN
Trott, Craig , BEng	LT(SL)	X	P	01.02.93	846 SQN
Trott, Edward Allan , BEng	LT	E	AE	01.12.94	SULTAN
Trott, Peter Alan , BSc, AMIEE	LT CDR	E	WE	19.05.83	COLLINGWOOD
Trotter, Steven , MA, MSc, CEng, MIMarE	LT CDR	E	ME	01.12.87	TAMAR
Trubshaw, Christopher , pcea	LT	X	P	01.11.88	810 SQN A FLIGHT
Trump, Nigel William	LT	S		16.01.90	CINCFLEET
Trundle, David Jonathan William	LT CDR	S	SM	01.01.95	EDINBURGH
Trundle, Nicholas Reginald Edward , pce, pcea	LT CDR	X	O	01.07.89	ILLUSTRIOUS
Tsoi, Andy Cham Man , BDS	SG LT(D)	-		09.01.94	DRAKE CBP
Tucker, Kevin Michael	LT(SL)	S		01.08.91	FEARLESS
Tucker, Robin Simon	LT(SD)	S	CA	17.12.93	DRYAD
Tuffley, Christopher Robin , LVO, pce, osc	CAPT	X	P	30.06.91	MOD (LONDON)
Tulley, James Robert , BSc	LT CDR	S		16.07.91	BRITANNIA
Tulloch, Andrew , BSc, DPhil	LT(SL)	I		01.09.89	RNC DPT NS&TECH
Tulloch, David Neil , MB, BS, FRCSEd	SURG CDR	-	CU	31.12.90	RH HASLAR
Tulloch, Frederik Martin , BSc	LT CDR	E	WE	01.04.93	BRILLIANT

Name	Rank	Spec	Sub-spec	Seniority	Where serving
Tulloch, Stuart William	LT RM(SD)	RM		01.01.95	CDO LOG REGT RM
Tumelty, Gerwyn Charles , BEng, MSc	SLT(SL)	E	ME	01.01.95	DARTMOUTH BRNC
Tunnicliffe, Peter Alan , BEng, PhD	LT CDR(SL)	I	METOC	01.03.87	SEAHAWK
Tupman, Keith Campbell	LT RM(SD)	RM		01.01.92	HQRM
Tuppen, Russell Mark , pce, pcea	LT CDR	X	O	01.01.92	RNSC GREENWICH
Tupper, Robert William	LT(SD)	S	SM	14.12.90	TRAFALGAR
Turle, Paul James	SLT(SD)	E	ME	13.06.94	MONMOUTH
Turnbull, Graham David	LT CDR	X	H1	01.04.94	MOD (LONDON)
Turnbull, John James	T/LT(SDT)	X		10.06.94	NELSON BRISTOL
Turnbull, Nicholas Robin , BSc, BDS, FDS RCSEdin	SG LT(D)	-		02.01.92	FEARLESS
Turnbull, Paul Sands , MB, BS	SURG LTCDR	-	GMPP	01.08.92	NEPTUNE
Turnbull, Rodney Stewart	LT RM	RM		01.09.93	HQBF GIBRALTAR
Turnbull, Simon Jonathan Lawson , pce	LT CDR	X	PWO(U)	01.01.94	CAPT IST STAFF
Turner, Antony Richard	2LT(UCE)	RM		01.09.95	CTCRM LYMPSTONE
Turner, Christopher , LLB	SLT	X		01.01.94	DARTMOUTH BRNC
Turner, David , pce	LT CDR	X	MCD	03.06.91	SAUDI AFPS SAUDI
Turner, Derek Bayard , BSc	LT CDR	X	H CH	01.04.95	ENDURANCE
Turner, David John	LT CDR(SD)	S	W	01.10.91	DNPS
Turner, David	LT(SL)	X	P	01.06.95	820 SQN
Turner, Ian , BSc, psc	CDR	X	H CH	31.12.91	DRYAD
Turner, Jonathan Anthony Edward , BEng (Act Lt Cdr)	LT	E	WE	01.08.88	CNOCS GROUP
Turner, Joseph Seymour Hume , MA, I(2)Fr	LT	S		01.04.91	2SL/CNH
Turner, Kerry Ann , BEng	LT(SL)	I	METOC	01.09.90	RNAS CULDROSE
Turner, Mark Stephen , MB, BCh, ChB, MRCP	SURG LT	-		01.08.91	RNDHU DERRIFORD
Turner, Nicholas Joseph	LT CDR	X	PWO(A)	01.11.89	CINCFLEET
Turner, Roger Bentley , BSc, CEng, FIMarE, I(2)Ru	CAPT	E	MESM	30.06.95	MOD (BATH)
Turner, Robert Brian , BSc	LT(SL)	I		01.05.92	MOD (LONDON)
Turner, Robert Francis , BA(OU)	LT(SD)	S	W	11.12.92	RALEIGH
Turner, Robert Milligan , pce, psc (Commodore)	CAPT	X	P	31.12.90	2SL/CNH
Turner, Simon Alexander , BSc	2LT(GRAD)	RM		01.09.94	45 CDO RM
Turner, Stephen Edward , pce	CDR	X	PWO(U)	31.12.93	MOD (LONDON)
Turner, Shaun Mark , pce(sm), jsdc, pce	CDR	X	SM	30.06.90	DTR BATH
Turner, Timothy Adam Shore	LT RM	RM		27.04.95	45 CDO RM
Turton, Trevor Martyn Howard , MA, psc, psc(m)	LT CDR	S		16.11.79	SULTAN
Tweed, Christopher James , BSc	LT CDR	E	WE	01.02.89	FOSF
Twine, John Harold , BA	LT(SL)	I		01.01.91	COMACCHIO GP RM
Twist, David Charles	LT(SD)	S	W	11.12.92	TAMAR
Twist, Martin Thomas , BSc	LT RM	RM		01.09.94	COMACCHIO GP RM
Twitchen, Richard Christopher , pce, psc, psc(m)	CDR	X	PWO(A)	31.12.90	DRYAD
Tyack, Terence James	LT(SL)	X	P	01.06.89	846 SQN
Tyce, David John	LT RM(SD)	RM	MTO	01.01.94	42 CDO RM
Tyler, Jeremy Charles	SLT	X		01.01.94	DRYAD
Tyler, Peter Leslie	LT	S		01.07.88	ENDURANCE
Tyrrell, Patrick John , OBE, LLB, MA, GradInstPS, jsdc	CAPT	I	SM	31.12.92	RCDS
Tyrrell, Richard Kim	CAPT RM	RM	LC	01.09.86	40 CDO RM

U

Name	Rank	Spec	Sub-spec	Seniority	Where serving
Ubhi, Wayne Gurdial	SLT	E	ME	01.09.93	SHEFFIELD
Udensi, Ernest Andrew Anene Anderson , BEng, MIEE	LT(SL)	E	WE	06.01.91	RNSC GREENWICH
Underdown, Martyn Sinclair , CEng, MIERE, psc	CDR	E	WE	30.06.88	SHAPE BELGIUM
Underwood, Andrew Gavin Howard , BSc, MNI, MIM, pce, pcea	CDR	X	O	31.12.91	RICHMOND
Underwood, Nicholas John , BSc, psc(a)	CAPT RM	RM		01.09.88	CDO LOG REGT RM
Underwood, Paul John	LT RM(SD)	RM	MTO	01.01.93	40 CDO RM
Unsworth, Robert Neil , BSc	LT RM	RM		01.09.93	HQRM
Unwin, Philip John , pce, psc	CDR	X	PWO	30.06.83	2SL/CNH
Upright, Stephen William , BSc, pce(sm)	CDR	X	SM	30.06.93	DOLPHIN SM SCHL
Upton, Iain David , BSc	LT CDR	E	WE	01.02.93	FOSF
Upton, Timothy Charles , BA	LT	X		01.11.94	SHEFFIELD
Usborne, Andre Christopher , BSc, psc	CDR	E	WE	31.12.92	DRAKE NBC(CFS)
Usborne, Christopher Martin , BSc, CEng, MIEE	CDR	E	WE	30.06.94	CAPT F1(SEA)
Utley, Michael Keith , n	LT	X		01.05.93	URNU BIRMINGHAM

Name	Rank	Spec	Sub-spec	Seniority	Where serving
V					
Vale, Peter Douglas , BSc	LT CDR	E	ME	01.03.79	NELSON
Vallis, John , BSc, n	LT	X		01.05.92	YORK
Vallis, Richard William , BSc, CEng, MIMarE	LT CDR	E	MESM	01.05.89	NEPTUNE NT
Vamplew, David	LT CDR(SD)	E	AE(L)	01.10.91	2SL/CNH FOTR
Van Beek, Dirk , BSc, MIEE, psc, psc(m)	CDR	E	WE	30.06.96	MOD DGSW PTSMTH
Van Beek, Luke , BSc, MBA, psc, psc(m)	CDR	E	WE	31.12.91	FOSF
Van Berkel, John Gregory , MSc	LT CDR	E	ME	01.08.91	EXCHANGE CANADA
van der Horst, Richard Evert , BSc	CAPT RM	RM		01.09.95	40 CDO RM
Van-Den-Bergh, William Lionel	LT(SD)	X	FC	27.07.90	899 SQN HERON
Vance, Trayton Oconnor	LT RM	RM		01.09.94	CTCRM
Vanderpump, David John , BSc, BEng	LT CDR	E	ME	01.09.93	COVENTRY
Vandome, Andrew Michael , BSc	LT CDR	E	WE	01.02.92	CON DCN
Varley, Ian Guy , BEng	LT	X		01.01.93	705 SQN SEAHAWK
Vartan, Mark Richard , BSc	LT(SL)	X		01.10.94	GLASGOW
Vasey, Stephen George	LT CDR(SD)	X	PT	01.10.92	2SL/CNH
Vaughan, David Michael , BA, pce, pce(sm)	CDR	X	SM	31.12.90	SOVEREIGN
Veal, Alan Edward	LT	E	WE	01.08.95	COLLINGWOOD
Venables, Adrian Nicholas	LT	X		01.12.89	COMUKTG/CASWSF
Ventura, Don Clark	LT CDR	X	H1	01.01.94	HERALD
Verney, Peter Scott	LT	X	FC	01.08.91	URNU LIVERPOOL
Vickers, John	LT	E	AE	01.11.90	RNAY FLEETLANDS
Vickery, Timothy Kenneth , BSc	LT CDR	X	PWO(U)	01.11.95	BRILLIANT
Victor, Jonathan David , BDS	SGCDR(D)	-		30.06.91	CINCFLEET
Vincent, Adrian	LT(SL)	I		01.09.90	SULTAN
Vincent, Claire Elaine , n	LT(SL)	X		25.04.92	MONTROSE
Viner, Timothy Robin , BSc	2LT(GRAD)	RM		01.05.95	CTCRM LYMPSTONE
Vink, James Dingeman	SLT	X		01.05.93	BOXER
Vitali, Robert Charles	LT	X	PWO(A)	01.02.90	EXCHANGE AUSTLIA
Vogel, Lanning David	SLT	S		01.01.95	GRAFTON
Vollentine, Lucy	SLT	S		01.09.95	NELSON
Von Hoven, Anthony Christopher , BA, pcea	LT(SL)	X	P	01.08.85	EXCHANGE RAF UK
Vorley, Simon , BSc	SLT(SL)	X	P U/T	01.01.94	FONA CRANWELL
Vosper, Iain Attrill , BA, psc(m), I(1)Ab, MPhil	CDR	S		30.06.85	MOD C OF N
Vowles, Mitchell	SLT(SD)	X	PR	24.07.94	HECLA
Vowles, Timothy John	LT(SL)	S		01.09.92	DRAKE CBP
Voyce, John Edington , BEng	LT	E	ME	01.09.94	NORTHUMBERLAND
W					
Waddington, Andrew Kennneth	LT CDR	X	H1	01.12.95	EXCHANGE AUSTLIA
Waddington, John , BSc	LT CDR	E	WESM	01.05.94	REPULSE(PORT)
Wade, Geoffrey Adrian	LT CDR	S		01.02.96	SULTAN
Wade, Nicholas Charles , BSc	LT CDR	X	PWO(C)	01.01.90	FOSF
Wadham, John , psc	CDR	E	ME	30.06.92	ARK ROYAL
Wagstaff, Neil	LT(SD)	MS	AD	10.04.95	DMEDLUDGERSHALL
Wain, Keith David , MA, MSc, CEng, MBCS	LT CDR	E	WE	01.12.81	MOD (LONDON)
Wain, Robin Nicholas , pcea, psc, ocds(Can)	CDR	X	O	31.12.95	RNSC GREENWICH
Wainhouse, Michael James	LT	X		01.07.89	DRYAD
Wainwright, Barnaby George , BA, MNI, pce, pcea	LT CDR	X	P	01.09.89	BRAVE
Wainwright, Paul Albert	LT CDR	X	PWO(A)	16.03.85	2SL/CNH
Waite, Christopher William , pce, psc, psc(m)	CAPT	X	P	30.06.95	DRAKE CBP
Waite, Timothy	LT(SL)	X	P	01.11.94	845 SQN
Wakefield, Anthony Gordon , BSc	LT(SL)	X	P	16.01.90	815 SQN HQ
Wakefield, Gary Malcolm , pcea	LT CDR	X	P	01.03.93	846 SQN
Wakeford, Adrian , BSc, psc (Loc Maj)	CAPT RM	RM		01.07.80	HQRM
Wakeford, Ian Frederick	SLT(UCE)	X		01.09.94	DARTMOUTH BRNC
Wakeling, Jonathan Lee , MA	CDR	I		31.12.94	HQRM
Wakely, Stephen Argent , MC (Loc Maj)	CAPT RM(SD)	RM		01.10.94	RM POOLE
Waldock, Michael Ian , BSc, PGCE	LT(SL)	I		01.01.88	SULTAN
Wales, Benjamin David , BSc	LT	S		01.03.95	DOLPHIN
Walker, Alasdair James , MB, BCh, ChB, FRCS	SURG CDR	-	CGS	30.06.91	RNDHU DERRIFORD

Name	Rank	Spec	Sub-spec	Seniority	Where serving
Walker, Antony James , BSc	LT	X		01.02.95	NOTTINGHAM
Walker, Andrew John	CAPT RM(SD)	RM		01.10.92	CTCRM
Walker, Andrew John	LT RM	RM		28.04.94	CTCRM
Walker, Clive Leslie	LT CDR	S		16.10.93	DARTMOUTH BRNC
Walker, Carl Stephen , psc	CDR	S		30.06.95	FONA
Walker, Donald William Alexander , BA	LT	S		01.05.94	BULLDOG
Walker, Ellis George	LT(SD)	X	REG	17.12.93	RALEIGH
Walker, Gareth , BSc	LT(SL)	X		01.07.93	CHATHAM
Walker, Gavin Stewart Logan	CAPT RM	RM	MTO	01.09.90	NP 1061
Walker, Martin , BEng, MSc	LT CDR	E	WE	31.07.94	COVENTRY
Walker, Mark Christopher , pcea	LT CDR(SL)	X	P	01.10.94	848 SQN HERON
Walker, Mark Justin , BEng	LT(SL)	I		01.01.91	NELSON RNSETT
Walker, Michael John	LT(SD)	X	g	04.04.96	RALEIGH
Walker, Michael William , MSc	LT CDR(SD)	MS	RGN	01.10.94	2SL/CNH
Walker, Nigel Albert	LT(SD)	S	CAT	27.07.90	HQ BF HK
Walker, Nicholas John , BSc	LT CDR	E	MESM	01.07.94	SOVEREIGN
Walker, Nicholas Lee , pce	LT CDR	X	PWO(U)	01.02.93	GRAFTON
Walker, Nicholas MacLaren , BSc	LT	X	P	01.01.92	FONA VALLEY
Walker, Patrick John , MNI, pce, pce(sm)	CAPT	X	SM	31.12.93	2SL/CNH
Walker, Peter Richard , BSc	I			27.11.85	RM POOLE
Walker, Robbie Andrew , BEng, MSc, CEng, MIEE	LT(SL)	I		01.09.90	SULTAN
Walker, Robert Dixon	LT(SD)	E	WESM	05.06.92	MOD (LONDON)
Walker, Richard Eden , MA, psc	CAPT RM	RM		01.09.91	45 CDO RM
Walker, Stephen Paul	LT(SL)	X		01.01.96	TALENT
Wall, David Keith , BSc	LT(SL)	X	O U/T	01.12.93	BROCKLESBY
Wallace, Allan , BSc	LT CDR	X	PWO(U)	01.12.95	CAPT F6 (SEA)
Wallace, David James , BSc	LT(SL)	I		01.03.87	RM POOLE
Wallace, George William Alexander , AFC, BSc, pce, pcea, ocds(Can), osc	CDR	X	P	30.06.94	MOD (LONDON)
Wallace, Kenneth Neil , BDS	SG LT(D)	-		31.01.93	CINCFLEET
Wallace, Michael Rupert Barry , BA, pce, jsdc	CDR	X	PWO(U)	30.06.95	MOD (LONDON)
Wallace, Simon Jonathan	LT(SL)	X	FC	01.03.94	EXETER
Waller, Steven Adrian	LT	X	SM	01.03.91	DOLPHIN SM SCHL
Walliker, Michael John Delane	LT CDR	X	SM	01.05.95	TALENT
Wallis, Andrew (Loc Capt Rm)	LT RM	RM		01.09.93	WARRIOR
Wallis, Adrian John	LT CDR	X	O	16.04.96	DARTMOUTH BRNC
Wallis, Jonathan Spencer	LT(SL)	X	P	01.08.92	HERON
Wallis, Lee Allan	SURG LT	-		01.08.94	MONTROSE
Walls, Kevin Finlay	LT RM	RM	MLDR	26.04.93	45 CDO RM
Walmsley, Diane	LT CDR	Q	FP	04.12.88	DRAKE CBP
Walmsley, Elizabeth Ann	LT CDR	S		08.02.96	SHEFFIELD
Walmsley, Peter Alan , BSc	LT(SL)	I		01.01.93	SULTAN
Walpole, Peter Kenneth , BSc, pce	CDR	X	PWO(C)	31.12.91	SACLANT USA
Walsh, Andrew Stephen James	LT(SL)	X	P	16.05.87	899 SQN HERON
Walsh, Dennis Gerard	LT(SD)	E	AE(L)	07.09.95	RNAS PORTLAND
Walsh, Jane Sabina	LT(SL)	W		11.12.92	DGA(N) ASE
Walsh, Kevin Michael , BSc	SLT	X		01.01.94	EXETER
Walsh, Mark Anthony	LT(SD)	S	CA	06.04.95	INVINCIBLE
Walsh, Sean Christopher	LT(SL)	X	ATC	01.11.91	RNAS YEOVILTON
Walter, Philip Graham , BSc	LT CDR	E	WESM	23.07.93	RENOWN(PORT)
Walters, David Nicholas	CAPT RM	RM	LC	18.04.86	EXCHANGE NLANDS
Walters, Jonathan , BSc	LT(SL)	X	O	16.06.86	810 SQN OEU
Walters, Richard John , BSc	LT	X		01.02.93	LINDISFARNE
Walters, Stephen Geoffrey , MA, MSc, AMIEE, CGIA	LT CDR	E	WESM	01.04.89	CNSA PORTLAND
Walton, Anthony Frederick , BSc, psc	CDR	E	ME	30.06.91	ILLUSTRIOUS
Walton, Andrew Paul	LT(SD)	MS	AD	04.04.96	RH HASLAR
Walton, Colin Peter , BEng	LT	E	WE	01.09.92	CWTA PTSMTH
Walton, Christopher Paul , BEng	LT	E	MESM	01.04.93	TRENCHANT
Walton, David	LT CDR	X	PWO(U)	01.09.84	2SL/CNH FOTR
Walton, Jonathan Charles , MSc, mdtc	LT CDR	E	WE	01.12.90	DG SHIPS CAM HSE
Walton, Stephen David	SLT	X		01.05.94	ARUN
Walton, Stephen Paul	LT(SD)	E	AE(L)	14.10.94	RNAS YEOVILTON

Name	Rank	Spec	Sub-spec	Seniority	Where serving
Walton-Waters, Lyndsay Donald , MBE	LT CDR	X	SM	01.09.84	MOD DIS SEA
Ward, Andrew James	LT(SL)	X	MCD	01.06.95	DRYAD
Ward, Colin David	ACT LT RM(SD)	RM		01.01.96	HQ CDO AVN
Ward, David Steven	LT(SD)	X	PT	12.12.91	PLOVER
Ward, Francis Stanley (Act Cdr)	LT CDR	X	PWO(U)	01.03.85	MOD (LONDON)
Ward, John Emlyn , pce, pcea	CDR	X	O	31.12.94	SEAHAWK
Ward, Jason George (Loc Capt Rm)	LT RM	RM		27.04.92	HQ 3 CDO BDE RM
Ward, Nicholas John	CDR(SL)	X	PWO(A)	01.10.94	JT PLAN STAFF
Ward, Nicholas James , n	LT	X		01.09.91	DARTMOUTH BRNC
Ward, Peter Nicholas , psc (Loc Lt Col)	MAJ	RM		31.12.82	RM POOLE
Ward, Rees Graham John , MA, MSc, CEng, MIEE, jsdc, gw (Commodore)	CAPT	E	WE	30.06.89	MOD (LONDON)
Ward, Simon	SLT	X		01.01.95	SOUTHAMPTON
Ward, Stephen David	LT	E	MESM	01.01.90	CAPTAIN SM2
Ward, Simon Ira	LT	X		01.10.90	DRYAD
Ward, Timothy John , MIMarE	LT	E	MESM	11.01.91	SULTAN
Warden, John Mitchell , BA, BSc	LT CDR	I	SM	01.09.92	RNC DPT NS&TECH
Wardle, Mark	LT(SD)	X	C	17.12.93	COLLINGWOOD
Ware, Samuel Arthur	LT(SL)	X	P	01.01.95	819 SQN
Wareham, Michael Paul , BEng	LT CDR	E	MESM	01.06.94	TRIUMPH
Waring, John , BSc, PhD	LT(SL)	I		01.04.91	RNC DPT NS&TECH
Warlow, Colin Norman , MB, BCh, BAO, DTM&H, MRCGP	SURG CDR	-	GMPP	31.12.75	NELSON
Warlow, Mark Richard Norman	LT CDR	X	MCD	01.05.93	EXCHANGE CANADA
Warn, Christopher John	LT	X	SM	01.07.90	REPULSE(PORT)
Warne, Emma Jane , BSc	LT	S		01.07.93	BRAVE
Warne, Robert Leslie , MSc, CEng, MIEE, psc, gw	CDR	E	WE	31.12.88	2SL/CNH FOTR
Warneken, Andrew Ellery , BEng	LT	X		01.10.94	VANGUARD(PORT)
Warnett, Derek Louis , MSc, CEng, MIEE, MIMarE, jsdc	CAPT	E	MESM	30.06.94	MOD (BATH)
Warnock, Gavin , BSc	LT CDR(SL)	X	P	01.10.95	EXCHANGE GERMANY
Warr, Richard Frank	LT(SD)	E	WESM	19.02.93	TRENCHANT
Warren, Brian Howard , BSc, pce	CDR	X	PWO(U)	30.06.96	2SL/CNH
Warren, Keith Leslie , BSc	LT CDR	E	ME	01.06.82	CINCFLEET
Warren, Martin Kenneth , MSc	LT CDR(SL)	I		01.01.96	CENTURION
Warren, Thomas Stephen Evrall	CAPT RM(SD)	RM		01.10.95	HQRM
Warrender, William Jonathan	LT	X	FC	01.05.92	GLASGOW
Warrington, Paul Thomas , BEng	LT	E	MESM	01.01.91	RESOLUTION(PORT)
Warwick, Philip David	LT CDR	X	PWO(U)	01.04.96	CAPT F6 (SEA)
Washer, Nicholas Barry John , BSc	LT	X	FC	01.01.92	SOUTHAMPTON
Wass, Martin James , BSc	LT CDR	X	PWO(A)	01.08.90	LOAN CDA HLS
Waterer, Richard Alan , LRAM, pdm (Loc)	MAJ(SD)	RM		29.07.94	RM SCHOOL MUSIC
Waterfield, Simon Jon	LT	X	SM	01.06.94	SPARTAN
Waterhouse, Phillip	LT(SL)	S		01.04.93	BEAVER
Waterman, David	LT(SD)	E	ME	10.06.94	SULTAN
Waterman, John Henry , BSc, MA, psc	LT CDR	E	ME	01.07.88	EDINBURGH
Waters, Christopher David , BSc, CEng, MIEE, MBIM, nadc	CDR	E	WESM	31.12.87	MOD CSSE LONDON
Waters, Christopher Martin	LT CDR	X	PWO(U)	01.05.86	MOD DGSM PTLAND
Waters, Nigel Roger , BSc	LT CDR	S	SM	16.04.96	VICTORIOUS(PORT)
Waterworth, Stephen Norman , BEng	LT(SL)	E	WE	01.04.93	ILLUSTRIOUS
Waterworth, Terence Jack	LT(CS)	-		05.09.93	2SL/CNH
Watkins, Andrew Patrick Leonard , BSc	2LT(GRAD)	RM		01.05.95	CTCRM LYMPSTONE
Watkins, Colin Francis Frederick , pce, psc	CDR	X	O	31.12.89	SEA CADET CORPS
Watkins, Kevin John	SLT(SL)	E	ME	01.09.94	DARTMOUTH BRNC
Watkins, Timothy Crispin , BSc	LT(SL)	X	P	16.09.89	RAF CRANWELL EFS
Watkinson, Neil Gareth , BSc	LT RM	RM		01.09.92	RMR LONDON
Watson, Andrew , BEng	LT(SL)	X	O U/T	01.12.95	RNAS CULDROSE
Watson, Christopher Charles , BA, pce, I(2)Ru	LT CDR	X	PWO(A)	16.05.86	DRYAD
Watson, Clive Raymond , BTech	LT(SD)	E	WE	24.02.95	NEWCASTLE
Watson, Charles Robert	LT(SD)	E	WE	22.02.96	ILLUSTRIOUS
Watson, David Robert , MSc, CEng, MIEE	LT CDR	E	WESM	01.12.89	NEPTUNE SM1

Name	Rank	Spec	Sub-spec	Seniority	Where serving
Watson, Ian	LT CDR(SL)	X	P	01.10.92	899 SQN HERON
Watson, Ian	LT	X		01.03.95	BRILLIANT
Watson, Jeffrey	LT(SD)	E	AE(L)	15.10.93	FAAIT MAN ORG VL
Watson, John Keith	CHAPLAIN	SF		28.11.73	DRAKE CBP
Watson, Lloyd James	LT CDR(SL)	X	P	01.10.94	FONA OSPREY
Watson, Malcolm	LT CDR(SD)	E	AE(M)	01.10.91	RNAS PORTLAND
Watson, Philip Frank	LT RM(SD)	RM		01.01.93	BRNC BAND
Watson, Peter Gerald Charles , BEng	LT	E	MESM	25.10.88	SUPERB
Watson, Patrick Halfdan , pce, psc, I(2)Da	CAPT	X	PWO	30.06.96	MOD (LONDON)
Watson, Richard Ian	ACT LT RM(SD)	RM		01.01.96	RM DIV ASMT
Watson, Richard John	LT CDR	X	SM	01.08.89	MOD (LONDON)
Watson, Russell Peter , BSc, CEng, MIMarE	LT CDR	E	MESM	01.09.89	FOSM NWOOD HQ
Watson, Stuart Benedict Cooper	SLT(SD)	S	W	23.07.95	NEPTUNE
Watt, Anthony James Landon	LT	X	MCD	01.05.92	DARTMOUTH BRNC
Watt, Graeme Nigel Dirhem , BA, ACMA	LT CDR	S	CMA	01.04.92	MOD (LONDON)
Watt, Stuart , pce	LT CDR	X	PWO(A)	29.09.88	GLASGOW
Watterson, Keith , MSc, CEng, MIMechE, jsdc	CAPT	E	MESM	31.12.92	MOD (LONDON)
Watts, Alun David	LT CDR	S	SM	01.01.94	CSST SEA
Watts, Alexandra Jane , BA	LT(SL)	S		01.09.95	CDRE MFP
Watts, Andrew Peter	LT CDR	X	O	01.10.93	CAMPBELTOWN
Watts, David John	LT	S	SM	01.10.89	CINCIBERLANT
Watts, Graham Michael , BSc, psc	CDR	E	ME	31.12.95	SULTAN
Watts, Jason , BSc	SLT(SL)	X	P U/T	01.09.93	HERON
Watts, Margaret Dora	LT	Q	CC	23.12.85	BF GIBRALTAR(NE)
Watts, Peter , BSc, CEng, FIMarE, MIMarE, MINucE	CDR	E	MESM	30.06.85	2SL/CNH
Watts, Paul Stuart	LT(SL)	X	P	01.05.92	706 SQN SEAHAWK
Watts, Robert	LT	X	SM	01.07.93	DOLPHIN SM SCHL
Watts, Richard Dennis , psc(m) (Loc Maj)	CAPT RM	RM		07.07.93	40 CDO RM
Watts, Raymond Frederick , BSc	CDR	E	WE	31.12.92	MOD (BATH)
Watts, Sandra Fay	LT(SL)	W	S	01.12.95	DNPS
Waugh, Peter John , MB, BCh, MA, DipAvMed, LRCP, LRCS, AFOM	SURG CDR	-	CO/M	30.06.90	RNAS CULDROSE
Weale, John Stuart , BA	LT CDR	X	SM	01.01.95	SPLENDID
Weall, Elizabeth Mary , ARRC	LT CDR	Q	OTSPEC	06.11.83	RH HASLAR
Wearmouth, Paul William Anthony	CDR(SD)	E	WE	01.10.95	NWOOD CIS
Weaver, Andrea Louise , BEng	LT(SL)	E	WE	01.07.93	BRAZEN
Weaver, Keith Nicholas , BSc	LT CDR(SL)	I	METOC	01.10.90	RNAS YEOVILTON
Weaver, Neil	SLT(SD)	E	MESM	13.06.94	TALENT
Webb, Andrew James , BSc	LT CDR	X	SM	01.05.95	DRYAD
Webb, Christopher McDonald	LT(SL)	X	O	16.12.86	EXCHANGE CANADA
Webb, Ian Francis Roderick	LT(SL)	X	MW	01.11.94	SANDOWN
Webb, John Richard	LT CDR(SD)	S	S	01.10.92	2SL/CNH
Webb, Matthew David	SLT	X		01.09.94	ARUN
Webb, Philip Vivian	LT CDR(SD)	E	WESM	01.10.94	VANGUARD(PORT)
Webb, Robin Edward , BSc, CDipAF, CEng, MIEE, psc	LT CDR	E	WE	01.02.78	DGSS BRISTOL
Webber, Christopher John , BEng	LT(SL)	I	METOC	03.04.86	RNAS PORTLAND
Webber, Joanne Patricia , BA	LT(SL)	X	O	01.02.95	810 SQN SEAHAWK
Webber, Kerry Jane	SLT(SL)	X		01.01.94	BRAZEN
Webber, Richard James	SURG LT	-		01.02.96	DARTMOUTH BRNC
Webber, Shaun Anthony (Loc Capt Rm)	LT RM	RM	PT	01.09.89	45 CDO RM
Webber, Steven John Anthony Maltravers , MA, ACMA, ACIS	LT CDR	S	CMA	01.02.94	BRILLIANT
Weberstadt, Roy Richard , pce(sm)	CDR	X	SM	31.12.93	FOSM NWOOD OPS
Webster, Andrew Philip , BA	LT(SL)	X		01.11.94	HERON
Webster, Graham , pce(sm)	CDR	X	SM	31.12.89	CAPTPORT CLYDE
Webster, Patrick Michael	LT(SL)	X	P	01.09.87	771 SK5 SAR
Webster, Timothy John Cook , psc(m)	CAPT RM	RM		01.05.91	40 CDO RM
Weedon, Kevin Donald	LT CDR	E	ME	19.06.94	MOD (BATH)
Weeks, Callum James , BA	SLT(SL)	X		01.09.94	BIRMINGHAM
Weeks, Richard Royston , TEng	LT(SD)	E	MESM	14.10.88	SULTAN
Weightman, Nicholas Ellison	LT(SL)	X	P	16.02.94	801 SQN

Name	Rank	Spec	Sub-spec	Seniority	Where serving
Weir, Scott Duncan	LT(SL)	E	WESM	01.02.90	NEPTUNE SM1
Welborn, Colin George , pce, psc(m)	CDR	X	PWO(A)	31.12.92	STANAVFORCHAN
Welburn, Ross Coates	LT(SD)	X	EW	04.04.96	PJHQ
Welburn, Roy Stuart , BSc	LT CDR	E	AE	01.03.91	EXCHANGE USA
Welch, Andrew , MBE	LT CDR	X	O	13.10.95	815 SQN HQ
Welch, Anthony John	LT	X	MW	01.05.90	CDRE MFP
Welch, Andrew Timothy , FNI, MNI, pce	CDR	X	AWO(A)	31.12.88	CAMBRIDGE
Welch, Brian Christopher , BSc, AMIEE, psc	CDR	E	WE	30.06.87	CWTA PTSMTH
Welch, David Alexander	SLT	X		01.05.94	MONTROSE
Welch, Jonathan , BSc, MNI, pce	CAPT	X	PWO(U)	31.12.95	SACLANT USA
Welch, James	SURG SLT	-		03.10.94	DARTMOUTH BRNC
Weldon, David	SURG SLT	-		10.01.95	DARTMOUTH BRNC
Weldon, William Ernest , QHC, MA	CHAPLAIN	CE		14.04.71	COCHRANE
Welford, Robert Clive , BEng	LT	X		01.02.91	ARUN
Welland, Christopher Patrick Bache , OBE, ndc	CDR	X	PWO	31.12.81	NAVSOUTH ITALY
Wellesley, Richard Charles Rupert , pce, pcea	CDR	X	O	31.12.94	FONA NORTHWOOD
Wellesley-Harding, Ian Richard , BA, MIPM, jsdc, psc(m)	CDR	S	SM	31.12.89	NELSON
Wellington, Stuart , BEng	LT	E	WE	01.02.90	MOD DGSS PTSMTH
Wells, Alison Jane , BDS	SG LT(D)	-		09.01.94	NEPTUNE
Wells, Barry Charles	LT(SD)	E	WESM	18.02.94	MOD DGSM PTLAND
Wells, Barrie	SLT(SD)	X	C	03.04.95	ANGLESEY
Wells, David Andrew Hester , pcea	LT CDR	X	O	29.11.86	SEAHAWK
Wells, David George	LT(SL)	X		01.09.90	IT S SEA
Wells, Michael Douglas , pcea	LT CDR(SL)	X	P	01.03.85	INVINCIBLE
Wells, Michael Peter , BSc	SLT	S		01.09.94	LANCASTER
Welsh, Andrew , BA	SLT(SL)	X		01.05.94	BIRMINGHAM
Welton, William Brodie Dexter	LT CDR	X	PWO(C)	01.09.94	DRYAD
Werrin, Lee Richard	LT(SL)	S		01.09.86	DNPS
West, Anthony Bernard	LT(SD)	X	REG	29.07.94	BF GIBRALTAR(NE)
West, Andrew William	LT(SD)	S	W	11.12.92	2SL/CNH
West, Alan William John , DSC, rcds, pce, psc, hcsc	RADM	-	AWO(A)	22.02.94	COMUKTG/CASWSF
West, Darren , BSc	LT(SL)	X		01.01.96	MIDDLETON
West, Graham George , BEng	LT(SL)	E	ME	01.08.93	CAPT IST STAFF
West, Geraint Richard , BSc, n	LT CDR	X	H1	01.03.93	EXCHANGE USA
West, Michael Wallace , pce	LT CDR	X	PWO(A)	05.08.92	GLOUCESTER
West, Philip James , BA	LT(SL)	X	O	16.05.93	849 SQN A FLT
West, Ronald James , BA	LT CDR(SD)	X	C	01.10.87	MOD (LONDON)
West, Rory Julian , BSc	LT	X	O U/T	01.06.93	750 SQN OBS SCH
West, Sarah , BSc	SLT(SL)	X		01.09.94	SANDOWN
Westbrook, Jonathan Simon , MBE, pce(sm)	CDR	X	SM	30.06.95	TALENT
Western, William John Harry , BTech, CEng, MIMechE, psc	CDR	E	AE(O)	30.06.89	RNAS YEOVILTON
Westlake, Adrian John , BSc	LT CDR	E	WESM	01.05.93	MOD DGSM PTLAND
Westley, David Richard	LT(SL)	X	P	16.08.91	847 SQN
Westoby, Richard Malcolm	CAPT RM	RM	LC	01.09.90	RM POOLE
Weston, Mark William , BDS, MSc, DGDP RCS(UK)	SGCDR(D)	-		31.12.88	2SL/CNH
Weston, Peter	LT(CS)	-		22.02.88	MOD DNR OUTPORTS
Westwood, Mark Robin Timothy , BEng, MSc	LT CDR	E	MESM	01.07.94	VIGILANT(PORT)
Westwood, Martin William , pce, pcea, psc	CDR	X	P	30.06.95	SOMERSET
Westwood, Nigel Robert , pce	CDR	X	PWO(U)	30.06.94	ELANT/NAVNW
Westwood, Stephen Philip Charles , BSc, CEng, MIMarE	CDR	E	ME	30.06.87	FOSF ENG DEVPT
Whales, Nigel Charles Francis , AMIMarE, psc	CDR	E	ME	31.12.90	LOAN DRA HASLAR
Whalley, Richard James	LT(SL)	S		01.04.93	SEAHAWK
Whalley, Simon David , psc	CDR	S	SM	31.12.94	COMUKTG/CASWSF
Wharrie, Ewan Killen Balnave , BSc	LT(SL)	I		01.09.92	CNOCS GROUP
Whatmough, David Edward , MA, CEng, MIMechE	CAPT	E	ME	30.06.96	MOD (BATH)
Wheal, Adrian Justin , BEng	LT	E	MESM	01.09.92	VANGUARD(STBD)
Wheater, Katharine Jane , BA	LT	E	WE	01.04.94	NORFOLK
Wheatley, Philip Lawrence , pce, psc	LT CDR	X	O	01.12.81	PJHQ
Wheaton, Bowden James Stewart	LT(SL)	X	O	01.06.90	EXCHANGE RAF UK
Wheeldon, Thomas Bertram	LT(SD)	E	ME(L)	15.02.91	CLYDE MIXMAN1
Wheeler, Brian , BSc	CDR	E	WE	31.12.86	MOD DNR OUTPORTS
Wheeler, Nicholas Jules	LT	X		01.10.95	DOLPHIN SM SCHL

Name	Rank	Spec	Sub-spec	Seniority	Where serving
Wheen, David Gandell , osc, osc(us) (Loc Lt Col)	MAJ	RM		31.12.84	RMR LONDON
Wheen, Peter Acworth Charles , pce	CDR	X	C	31.12.79	MOD (BATH)
Whetton, Anthony Graham , AMIMarE	LT CDR(SD)	E	ME	01.10.91	MOD (BATH)
Whetton, Julia Barbara Dawn	LT(SL)	W	S	12.11.87	DRAKE CBP
Whight, Robert Anthony , BEng	LT	E	MESM	01.02.93	SOVEREIGN
Whild, Aaron Alexander	LT(SL)	E	WESM	01.02.90	DRAKE CFM
Whild, Douglas James	SLT(SD)	X	PR	24.07.94	BRILLIANT
Whitaker, Hugh Rudkin , MIPM, jsdc	CAPT	S		31.12.95	FOSM NWOOD HQ
Whitaker, Michael John , BSc, CEng, MIMechE	LT CDR	E	AE	01.04.89	RMC OF SCIENCE
Whitby, Stephen , BSc, PGCE	LT CDR	X	PWO(U)	01.01.92	CALEDONIA
White, Andrew Raymond , BSc, CEng, MIEE, AMIEE	CDR	E	WESM	31.12.94	FOSM NWOOD OPS
White, Douglas Robert , BEng	LT(SL)	I		01.05.88	SULTAN
White, David Simon Haydon , OBE, MNI, MRIN, jsdc, pce(sm)	CDR	X	SM	31.12.89	SACLANT BELGIUM
White, Graham Leonard , BSc, CEng, MIEE	LT CDR	E	WE	16.12.81	MOD (BATH)
White, Haydn John (Loc Capt Rm)	LT RM	RM	LC	01.05.90	CTCRM
White, Sir Hugo (Moresby) , GCB, CBE, pce	ADM	-	SM	15.12.92	HE GOV&CINC GIB
White, Ian Frank	SLT(SD)	X	SM	03.04.95	DOLPHIN SM SCHL
White, Jonathan Andrew Paul	LT	X	SM	01.11.90	TRENCHANT
White, Johnathan Charles Edwin , BSc	SLT(SL)	X	O U/T	01.05.94	RAF SHAWBURY
White, Jonathan Eric , BSc	LT	S		01.05.95	FOSM NWOOD OPS
White, John James	LT RM(SD)	RM	MLDR	01.01.89	RMR BRISTOL
White, Kevin Frederick	SLT(SL)	E	ME	01.05.94	DARTMOUTH BRNC
White, Melvyn Andrew , MBE, BEM	LT CDR(SD)	MS	RGN	01.10.94	RN MSS HASLAR
White, Martin Eugene	LT CDR(SL)	X	ATC	01.10.88	FONA
White, Mark William , BSc, pce, psc	LT CDR	X	PWO(U)	01.07.90	DRYAD
White, Peter	LT CDR	X	PWO(A)	01.02.87	DARTMOUTH BRNC
White, Philip Alan	LT CDR	E	MESM	16.02.92	SCEPTRE
White, Paul Duncan Charles	LT(SL)	X	SM	01.05.95	TRIUMPH
White, Paul John , MSc, CEng, MIEE, MIExpE	LT CDR	E	WE	01.02.91	MONMOUTH
White, Robert Fredrick	LT(SD)	E	WE	05.06.92	DG SHIPS CAM HSE
White, Robert Leonard	LT(SD)	E	AE(L)	14.10.94	RNAS YEOVILTON
White, Simon Henry Wilmot , BA	LT(SL)	X	P	16.06.93	820 SQN
White, Sarah Michelle	SLT(SL)	X		01.09.95	SANDOWN
White, Stephen Noel , BA, I(2)Ch	LT CDR	S		16.03.91	RALEIGH
White, Stephen Paul	LT(SD)	E	WESM	10.06.88	SCU LEYDENE ACNS
Whitehead, Darryl	LT CDR(SL)	X	P	01.10.92	815 FLT 215
Whitehead, Peter	SLT(SL)	X	O U/T	01.05.95	RNAS CULDROSE
Whitehead, Steven John , BEng	LT	E	AE	01.03.92	DGA(N) ASE
Whitehorn, Iain James , BSc, CEng, MIMarE	CDR	E	MESM	30.06.94	RNC DPT NS&TECH
Whitehouse, Mark Justin , BSc	LT CDR	E	WE	01.03.94	NELSON
Whitehouse, Niall Robert	SLT	E	AE	01.09.94	DARTMOUTH BRNC
Whiteley, Christopher Vivian , BSc, psc(m), fsc	CAPT RM	RM		01.05.88	CTCRM
Whiteley, Nicholas Simon , BSc	LT CDR	E	ME	01.02.90	EXCHANGE AUSTLIA
Whitelock, Michael Anthony	LT(SL)	X	P	01.03.93	819 SQN
Whitfield, Joe Alexander	LT(SL)	X	P	16.06.91	848 SQN HERON
Whitfield, Kenneth David , BEng	LT	E	AE	01.03.92	RNAS CULDROSE
Whitfield, Philip Mark , BSc	2LT(GRAD)	RM		01.09.95	CTCRM
Whitfield, Robert Matthew Patrick , BSc	LT	X		01.05.95	WESTMINSTER
Whitlam, John	LT(SD)	X	PR	16.12.94	DRYAD
Whitley, Ian Derek Brake , n	LT	X		01.06.91	EDINBURGH
Whitlum, Andrew , BEng	SLT(SL)	X	P U/T	01.05.94	DARTMOUTH BRNC
Whitmee, Michael	LT(SL)	X		01.08.95	DOLPHIN SM SCHL
Whittaker, Mark Adrian , BM	SURG LT	-		01.08.92	RH HASLAR
Whittaker, Neill James , BSc, BEng	LT CDR	E	WESM	01.07.93	CSST SEA
Whittaker, Peter Allan , jsdc, psc(m) (Loc Lt Col)	MAJ	RM		31.12.80	UKMILREP BRUSS
Whittingham, Debra Jayne	LT(SL)	W	X	28.07.89	FOST DPORT SHORE
Whitworth, Robert Maitland	LT(SL)	X		01.05.88	INVINCIBLE
Whybourn, Lesley	SURG SLT	-		01.07.94	DARTMOUTH BRNC
Whyntie, Adrian , BSc, CEng, MIEE	CDR	E	WE	30.06.94	GRAFTON
Whyte, Andrew Peter	LT	X		13.12.92	BRILLIANT
Whyte, Iain	LT	I		01.04.93	RMB STONEHOUSE
Wickenden, Andrew Roy	LT	X		01.08.91	CFP SEA

Name	Rank	Spec	Sub-spec	Seniority	Where serving
Wicking, Geoffrey	LT(SL)	E	AE	01.05.94	848 SQN HERON
Wiffin, Anthony Francis	LT(SD)	E	AE(M)	13.10.89	EXCHANGE ARMY UK
Wigham, Timothy Walter (Act Lt Rm)	2LT	RM	PT	01.09.92	DARTMOUTH BRNC
Wilcocks, Philip Lawrence , DSC, BSc, AMRINA, pce, psc(a)	CAPT	X	PWO(A)	30.06.95	MOD (LONDON)
Wild, Stephen	LT CDR(SL)	X	MCD	01.10.89	SUPT OF DIVING
Wildin, Andrew	SLT(SL)	E	WE	01.01.94	DARTMOUTH BRNC
Wildin, Victoria , BA	SLT(SL)	S		01.09.93	DARTMOUTH BRNC
Wiles, Stephen John , MSc, CEng, MRAeS	LT CDR	E	AE	01.04.92	MOD DHSA
Wilken, Annelise	SLT(SL)	X	ATCU/T	01.05.95	DAEDALUS
Wilkes, David John , BEng	LT(SL)	I		01.01.90	SULTAN
Wilkie, Andrew Robert (Act Capt Rm)	LT RM(SD)	RM		01.01.92	PROJECT BOWMAN
Wilkins, Richard Ronald , BEng	LT(SL)	E	MESM	01.06.92	VIGILANT(PORT)
Wilkinson, Antonio	LT CDR(SD)	E	AE(M)	01.10.91	MOD DHSA
Wilkinson, Andrew John , BSc	LT CDR	X		16.12.86	SULTAN
Wilkinson, Colin Howard , MEng	LT(SL)	E	AE	01.12.91	LOAN DRA BEDFORD
Wilkinson, David Henry	LT	X		01.06.92	CAPT IST STAFF
Wilkinson, Jane	LT(SD)	X	REG	04.04.96	NEPTUNE
Wilkinson, Julie Margaret	LT(SL)	W	I	04.01.93	ILLUSTRIOUS
Wilkinson, Michael	SLT(SL)	X	P U/T	01.07.93	FONA VALLEY
Wilkinson, Nicholas John , CB, FBIM, rcds, nadc, psc(m), l(2)Fr	RADM	-		02.01.91	JSDC GREENWICH
Wilkinson, Peter John , BA, pce, pce(sm)	CAPT	X	SM	31.12.95	MOD (LONDON)
Wilkinson, Peter McConnell	LT(SL)	X	P	16.02.87	706 SQN SEAHAWK
Wilkinson, Richard Murray , BSc, PGCE, MDA, jsdc	CDR	I		31.12.91	2SL/CNH
Wilkinson, Robin Nicholas	LT(SL)	X	P	16.10.89	810 SQN SEAHAWK
Wilkinson, Simon Roger , jsdc	CDR	S	SM	31.12.83	MOD (LONDON)
Wilks, George Robert Douglas	LT(CS)	-		19.11.85	MOD DNR OUTPORTS
Will, Andrew Watt , BSc	LT CDR	E	WE	01.06.84	MOD (LONDON)
Willcocks, Laurence Arthur , MBE, pce	LT CDR	X	AWO(U)	16.10.78	SEA CADET CORPS
Willcox, Ian	LT CDR	X	MCD	01.03.94	MONTROSE
Willett, Roger John , BA	LT CDR(SL)	I	METOC	04.01.81	CINCIBERLANT
Williams, Andrew Bruce , BSc, MIMechE	LT CDR(SL)	I		01.10.93	MWC GOSPORT
Williams, Andrew David Justin , BSc, psc(a)	MAJ	RM	PH	30.06.96	847 SQN
Williams, Andrew John	LT	E	MESM	01.02.90	SULTAN
Williams, Arthur Jocelyn , BA	LT CDR	X	SM	01.06.95	NEPTUNE SM1
Williams, Anthony Peter , DSC, pce	LT CDR	X	MCD	01.11.93	LIVERPOOL
Williams, Anthony	SLT	X		01.01.96	DRYAD
Williams, Bruce Nicholas Bromley , BSc, pce, psc	CDR	X	PWO(U)	30.06.93	PJHQ
Williams, Clifford Charles , BSc, MIEE, MRAeS, MCGI	LT CDR	E	AE	04.03.82	MOD (LONDON)
Williams, Colin Nicholas Owen , BSc	LT	X		01.06.93	LONDON
Williams, David	LT(SD)	S	S	24.07.92	TURBULENT
Williams, Deborah , BEd	LT(SL)	I		16.12.87	NELSON RNSETT
Williams, Darrell Anthony	LT(SD)	E	WE	13.06.86	DGSS BRISTOL
Williams, David Clifford , BSc	LT(SL)	I		01.09.91	EXCELLENT
Williams, David Hugh , LLB	LT CDR	S		16.03.86	OSPREY
Williams, David Ian	LT CDR	X	PWO(A)	29.05.92	EXCHANGE CANADA
Williams, David Spencer , BEng	LT CDR	X	PWO(U)	01.09.95	BATTLEAXE
Williams, Helen Diane , MB, BA, BCh	SURG LT	-		04.02.93	ENDURANCE
Williams, Ivan , BSc	LT	X		01.06.95	LONDON
Williams, Ian Richard , psc	CDR	X	H CH	30.06.94	ROEBUCK
Williams, Julian Llewelyn , BA, MIPM, jsdc	CAPT	S		30.06.94	MOD (BATH)
Williams, James Phillip	LT	X	FC	01.06.92	ORKNEY
Williams, Keith (Act Lt Cdr)	LT(SD)	E	AE(M)	14.10.88	SULTAN
Williams, Leo Douglas (Loc Maj)	CAPT RM	RM	MLDR	01.08.78	CTCRM
Williams, Mark , BEng	LT	E	MESM	01.06.93	VIGILANT(PORT)
Williams, Mark Adrian	LT(SL)	X	O	01.06.90	702 SQN OSPREY
Williams, Mark Henry , pce, pce(sm)	LT CDR	X	SM	01.10.91	VANGUARD(STBD)
Williams, Martyn Jon	LT CDR	E	WESM	01.11.95	2SL/CNH FOTR
Williams, Mervyn John , BSc	LT	X		01.12.93	BRAVE
Williams, Michael Richard , pce	LT CDR	X	PWO(U)	01.11.80	LOAN DRA PRTSDWN
Williams, Malcolm Stephen , BA, pce	CAPT	X	PWO(N)	30.06.94	HQRM
Williams, Mark Stuart , BSc	LT	S		29.09.88	BOXER
Williams, Nigel David Blackstone , BSc, jsdc, pce	CDR	X	PWO(U)	31.12.91	HERON

Name	Rank	Spec	Sub-spec	Seniority	Where serving
Williams, Nigel Lamplough , BSc, CEng, MIMarE, I(2)Ge	CDR	E	ME	30.06.91	BRITANNIA
Williams, Peter Charles	LT(SD)	E	ME	18.02.88	MOD (BATH)
Williams, Peter Mark , BEng	LT(SL)	I		01.01.91	INVINCIBLE
Williams, Roderick Charles , BSc	LT CDR	E	ME	01.10.89	MOD (BATH)
Williams, Robert Evan , LLB (Barrister)	CDR	S	BAR	30.06.93	2SL/CNH
Williams, Richard Ivor	LT(SL)	X	P	16.05.92	846 SQN
Williams, Roger John , psc	LT COL	RM	MTO	31.12.91	RM POOLE
Williams, Robert John Stirling	SLT(SL)	X		01.01.94	INVINCIBLE
Williams, Robert Michael , pce, psc (Commodore)	CAPT	X	AWO(A)	30.06.89	PJHQ
Williams, Richard Peter , MBE, jsdc, psc, rcds (Loc Lt Col)	MAJ	RM		31.05.84	RCDS
Williams, Simon Christopher , BSc	LT(SL)	I		16.07.90	40 CDO RM
Williams, Stephen John , BSc	LT CDR	E	AE(P)	18.10.85	RNFSAIC
Williams, Stephen Martin , BSc, CEng, FIMechE, jsdc	CAPT	E	ME	30.06.92	RCDS
Williams, Simon Paul , BSc, pce	LT CDR	X	PWO(C)	01.01.92	FOST SEA
Williams, Simon Thomas , BSc, pce, pce(sm)	CDR	X	SM	30.06.93	FOSM NWOOD OPS
Williams, Stephen Wayne Leonard	LT(SL)	S		01.04.89	CAMBRIDGE
Williams, Thomas Alun	CDR	X	PWO(C)	31.12.90	MOD (LONDON)
Williams, Timothy Nicholas Edward , BSc, pce, pcea, psc	CDR	X	P	31.12.89	MCM1 SEA
Williamson, Stephen John , BSc	LT(SL)	X	P	01.03.89	815 SQN HQ
Williamson, Stephen Michael	LT	X	MCD	01.11.94	CHIDDINGFOLD
Williamson, Tobias Justin Lubbock , BEng, pcea	LT CDR	X	O	01.10.94	MOD (LONDON)
Willing, Nigel Phillip , BSc	LT(SL)	X	P	01.03.94	702 SQN OSPREY
Willis, Alistair James	LT CDR	S		01.12.95	CUMBERLAND
Willis, Andrew Stephen	SLT	E	AE	01.09.95	DARTMOUTH BRNC
Willis, Martyn Stephen	LT	S	CAT	01.07.89	TEMERAIRE
Willis, Richard Michael Vernon , MSc, psc (Commodore)	CAPT	I	METOC	31.12.89	MOD (LONDON)
Willis, Simon Anthony , BSc	LT(SL)	X	P	01.06.89	845 SQN
Willmett, Andrew Malcolm , BSc, pce, psc	CAPT	X	AWO(A)	31.12.93	ARFPS
Wills, Andrew George , MSc	LT CDR	E	MESM	05.08.91	NEPTUNE NT
Wills, John Robert , BSc, CEng, MIMarE	CDR	E	ME	30.06.88	NELSON
Wills, Michael John Charles (Act Lt Cdr)	LT(SD)	X	EW	17.12.93	ELANT/NAVNW
Wills, Michael Vincent (Loc Maj)	CAPT RM	RM		01.09.89	RMR BRISTOL
Wills, Philip , BSc	LT(SL)	X	O	01.01.93	814 SQN
Willson, Neil Julian (Act Capt Rm)	LT RM	RM		01.09.89	RM SCHOOL MUSIC
Wilman, David Mark , BA	LT	S		01.02.94	2SL/CNH
Wilsey, Robert Patrick , jsdc, psc(m)	LT COL	RM	PH	31.12.93	UNOMIG
Wilson, Alexander Charles , MA, psc	MAJ	RM	LC	01.10.95	LOAN KUWAIT
Wilson, Adrian Clive	LT RM(SD)	RM		01.01.95	42 CDO RM
Wilson, Allan John	SLT	X		01.05.95	ARUN
Wilson, Andrew Stott	SLT(SL)	X	P	01.01.93	814 SQN
Wilson, Charles Dominick , BSc, pce	CDR	X	MCD	30.06.95	JSDC GREENWICH
Wilson, Christopher Gordon Talbot , pce, pcea	LT CDR	X	P	01.08.85	LOAN TURKS & C
Wilson, Christopher John , BEng	LT	E	MESM	01.12.88	MOD (BATH)
Wilson, Christopher Ward , BEng	LT	E	WESM	01.08.94	DG SHIPS PTLAND
Wilson, David , OBE, psc(m)	COL	RM		30.06.96	HQRM
Wilson, D M M(David Malcolm Mcgregor) , MBE	LT CDR	X	PWO	01.01.79	SEA CADET CORPS
Wilson, David Robert , n	LT	X		01.05.92	MARLBOROUGH
Wilson, David Timothy	LT(SD)	E	WE	10.06.88	DG SHIPS CAM HSE
Wilson, David William Howard	CAPT RM	RM		25.04.96	BDS WASHINGTON
Wilson, Graham John	LT(SD)	X	MCD	27.07.95	ATHERSTONE
Wilson, Gary Leonard	LT CDR	X	SM	01.04.92	MWC GOSPORT
Wilson, Gavin Scott	LT CDR(SD)	X	C	01.04.87	DRAKE CBP
Wilson, John , BA, BEng	SLT(SL)	X	P U/T	01.01.95	DARTMOUTH BRNC
Wilson, James Andrew	LT(SD)	E	ME	15.06.95	SULTAN
Wilson, Julian	2LT(UCE)	RM		01.09.93	CTCRM LYMPSTONE
Wilson, James Robert , psc (Loc Lt Col)	MAJ	RM	MLDR	30.06.87	MOD (LONDON)
Wilson, Kevin Paul , BSc, CEng, MIEE, AMIEE	LT CDR	E	WESM	01.03.90	NEPTUNE SM1
Wilson, Lindsay Ian , BTech	LT(SD)	E	WE	24.02.95	EXCHANGE RAF UK
Wilson, Marcus Alaric	LT(SL)	X	O	16.07.87	LOAN DTEO BSC DN
Wilson, Philip Anthony , psc (Loc Lt Col)	MAJ	RM	HW	30.06.88	SHAPE BELGIUM
Wilson, Peter Neil	LT(SL)	X	P	15.10.89	899 SQN OEU
Wilson, Peter Sanders , BSc, MIMechE	CAPT	E	ME	31.12.90	DRAKE CFM

Name	Rank	Spec	Sub-spec	Seniority	Where serving
Wilson, Robert	LT CDR	X	H CH	01.07.83	MOD (LONDON)
Wilson, Robert	LT	X		01.09.92	EXCHANGE FRANCE
Wilson, Robert Paul	LT CDR(SD)	X	O	01.10.95	849 SQN HQ
Wilson, Stephen Gordon , MNI, pce, psc	CDR	X	PWO(A)	31.12.91	MOD (LONDON)
Wilson, Stephen Richard , psc	MAJ	RM		30.06.94	539 ASLT SQN RM
Wilson-Chalon, Louis Michael , BSc	LT	X	P	01.04.89	702 SQN OSPREY
Wiltcher, Ross Alexander , BA	LT CDR	S		01.08.93	MONTROSE
Wiltshire, Graham John , MA, MSc, CEng, MIEE, nadc, psc	CAPT	E	WESM	31.12.93	MOD (LONDON)
Wimpenny, Michael Geoffrey , BSc, psc(m) (Loc Lt Col)	MAJ	RM		31.12.84	CTCRM
Winch, Emma , BDS	SG LT(D)	-		24.01.94	DRAKE CBP
Winchurch, Michael Roy Glen , psc, n	LT CDR	X	H CH	16.11.83	2SL/CNH
Windebank, Stephen John	LT(SL)	X	P	01.10.91	SEAHAWK
Window, Stephen Harvey	LT CDR	X	MCD	01.09.95	DRYAD
Windsar, Paul Andrew , BEng	LT(SL)	E	WESM	01.06.94	NEPTUNE SM1
Windsor, Mark , BSc, MA, MIMechE, psc	CDR	I	METOC	30.06.96	CINCFLEET
Wines, David Anthony , MCFA, psc	CAPT	S		31.12.93	MOD (LONDON)
Wingfield, Melissa	SG SLT(D)	-		01.10.94	DARTMOUTH BRNC
Wingfield, Michael James , BEng	LT(SL)	X	O	01.11.94	SEAHAWK
Wingrove, Keir Harvey	LT(SL)	X	SM	01.07.93	NEPTUNE BASE OPS
Winkle, Sean James , BA	LT	I	O	04.10.87	SULTAN
Winn, David	LT CDR	S	SM	16.09.84	EXCELLENT
Winstanley, Keith , MBE, pce	CDR	X	PWO(N)	30.06.94	SOUTHAMPTON
Winston, Lionel Angelo , MBE	LT(SD)	E	ME	23.02.90	SULTAN
Winter, Richard Jason , BEng	LT	E	WE	01.08.93	MANCHESTER
Winter, Timothy McMahon	LT	E	ME	01.05.90	EXETER
Wintle, Geoffrey Lawrence	LT	S	SM	01.02.89	TORBAY
Wise, Graham John , BEng	LT CDR	E	WE	01.04.96	DG SHIPS PTSMTH
Wise, Simon David , BSc	LT CDR	E	WE	01.06.92	HQ DFTS
Wiseman, Ian Carl	LT	X		01.02.95	CATTISTOCK
Wiseman, Jane Elizabeth , BA	LT(SL)	I	PI	01.09.89	NELSON (PAY)
Wiseman, Neil Christopher	SLT(SL)	X	O	01.01.93	814 SQN
Wiseman, Wayne Theodore , BSc, CEng, MIEE, jsdc, I(2)Ge	CDR	E	WE	30.06.84	SA COPENHAGEN
Wishart, Michael Leslie , DipTh	CHAPLAIN	CE		12.02.85	OSPREY
Withers, James Warren , BEng	LT CDR	E	WE	01.04.96	COLLINGWOOD
Witte, Richard Hugh , LLB	SLT(SL)	X		01.01.95	DARTMOUTH BRNC
Wittich, Thomas Steven , OBE, MSc, CEng, MIEE, gw	CAPT	E	WE	30.06.91	MOD (LONDON)
Witton, James William , pce	LT CDR	X	PWO(U)	01.06.93	CAPT F2(SEA)
Wolfe, David Edward , pce, pcea, fsc, I(1)Sp	CDR	X	O	30.06.96	CINCFLEET
Wolsey, Mark Andrew Ronald , BA, psc(m) (Loc Maj)	CAPT RM	RM		30.11.89	HQ ITC
Wolstencroft, Philip John , MB, BCh, ChB	SURG LTCDR	-		01.08.95	RH HASLAR
Wolstenholme, David Peter	LT CDR(SL)	X	P	01.10.93	819 SQN
Wombwell, John Frederick , MA, MSc, CGIA	LT CDR	E	WE	19.02.88	DGSS BRISTOL
Wood, Allan Cawsey MacDonald , BSc	CDR	I	METOC	31.12.86	2SL/CNH FOTR
Wood, Andrew , BEng	SLT(SL)	E	ME	01.01.95	DARTMOUTH BRNC
Wood, Craig , n	LT	X		01.08.93	GRAFTON
Wood, Charles Andrew	LT CDR	X	PWO(U)	09.01.88	MOD (LONDON)
Wood, Christopher Richard	SLT	X		01.09.94	DARTMOUTH BRNC
Wood, David John , BSc, CEng, FRAeS, MBIM, nadc, psc(m)	RADM	-	AE	21.02.95	MOD (BATH)
Wood, Frank Douglas	LT(SL)	X	AV	15.12.89	RNAS YEOVILTON
Wood, Gregory , MB, BS	SURG LTCDR	-	GMPP	01.08.94	RNAS PORTLAND
Wood, Giles Timothy , BA	LT RM	RM		29.04.93	42 CDO RM
Wood, Ian Derrick , IEng, AMIMarE	LT(SD)	E	ME	23.02.90	MOD (BATH)
Wood, Joseph Albert	SLT(SD)	X	PT	03.04.95	LIVERPOOL
Wood, John Lindsay , MSc, MCGI	LT CDR	E	ME	01.03.94	CHATHAM
Wood, Julia Margaret	LT(SL)	S	S	05.10.91	CINCFLEET
Wood, Justin Noel Alexander , BSc, MBIM, MNI, MRAeS, AMNI, pce, pcea, psc	CDR	X	P	30.06.96	FOST DPORT SHORE
Wood, Michael George , CBE, BSc, CEng, MIMechE, rcds, jsdc	CAPT	E	ME	31.12.90	MOD (LONDON)
Wood, Michael Leslie , BSc	SLT(UCE)	X		01.09.93	LEEDS CASTLE
Wood, Paul Roger	LT CDR	X	PWO(U)	01.01.90	DRYAD
Wood, Robert	LT	S		01.09.90	2SL/CNH
Wood, Stephen Graham	LT(SD)	X	O	11.12.92	819 SQN

Name	Rank	Spec	Sub-spec	Seniority	Where serving
Wood, Susan Louise , BSc	LT(SL)	X		01.05.92	JARIC
Wood, Uvedale George Singleton	LT	X	P	01.04.91	801 SQN
Woodall, Jeremy Bryson	LT RM	RM		01.09.95	42 CDO RM
Woodard, Jolyon , BSc	LT(SL)	X	P	01.11.92	845 SQN
Woodard, Neil , BSc	SLT(SL)	S		14.09.93	DARTMOUTH BRNC
Woodard, Steven George	LT CDR(SL)	S		01.10.95	PJHQ
Woodbridge, Graham Francis , psc	LT CDR	X	PWO(U)	01.11.82	DRYAD
Woodbridge, Richard George , BEng	LT(SL)	E	ME	01.08.92	DNPS
Woodcock, Nicholas	CHAPLAIN	CE		31.03.92	SULTAN
Woodcock, Simon Jonathan , BSc, CEng, MIMechE	LT CDR	E	ME	01.10.92	YORK
Woodford, Brian Steen , BA	SLT(SL)	X		01.01.95	DARTMOUTH BRNC
Woodford, Geoffrey Ian , BEng	LT	E	WESM	01.09.88	COLLINGWOOD
Woodham, Robert Henry , BSc	LT(SL)	I	METOC	01.01.91	RFANSU
Woodhouse, Paul , BDS	SG LT(D)	-		08.08.95	SULTAN
Wooding, GrahamAllen	LT(SD)	E	WE	19.02.93	MOD (LONDON)
Woodley, David , BA, I(1)Ru	LT(SL)	I		01.09.88	RNU CHELTENHAM
Woodman, Clive Andrew , BA, psc	LT CDR	I		01.09.87	RALEIGH
Woodroof, Gerard Martin Fenwick , MB, BS, MSc, LRCP, FFOM, MFOM, MRCS, AFOM	SURG CDR	-	CO/M	30.06.90	DRAKE CBS
Woodrow, Kevin	LT(SD)	X	SM	13.12.95	MOD (LONDON)
Woodruff, Anthony Desmond	LT(SD)	X	PWO(U)	11.12.92	DRYAD
Woodruff, Dean Aaron , BEng	LT	E	ME	01.12.91	SULTAN
Woods, Alice Caroline , BSc	LT(SL)	I	METOC	25.04.89	HERALD
Woods, Jeremy Billing	LT	X	PWO(A)	01.07.89	NORTHUMBERLAND
Woods, John Calvin	LT RM(SD)	RM	PH	01.01.89	HQ CDO AVN
Woods, Roland Philip , pce	LT CDR	X	PWO(A)	01.02.91	LANCASTER
Woods, Timothy Christopher , BA	LT(SL)	I		01.02.93	DOLPHIN SM SCHL
Woodward, Darroch John , BA, BSc	LT CDR	X	MCD	01.07.95	DRYAD
Wookey, Mark	LT(SL)	X	O	01.02.96	814 SQN
Woolhead, Andrew Lyndon , BA	LT(SL)	X		01.10.94	PLOVER
Woollcombe-Gosson, David James	LT	X	PWO(A)	01.06.89	MONTROSE
Wooller, Mark Adrian Hudson , BA	LT(SL)	S		01.10.92	ELANT/NAVNW
Woolley, David	LT(SL)	E	MESM	01.06.91	REPULSE(PORT)
Woolley, Michael Broderick , psc(a) (Loc Lt Col)	MAJ	RM		31.12.89	CENTURION
Woolley, Martin James	LT CDR	X	MCD	01.01.93	LOAN OMAN
Woolliams, Michael Frank , MNI, psc	LT CDR	X		01.12.84	RALEIGH
Woollven, Andrew Howard	LT	X	MCD	01.08.89	DRYAD
Woolman, Adam Lloyd	LT(SL)	X	MCD	01.09.95	LEDBURY
Woolman, Tudor Lloyd , MBE (Act Capt Rm)	LT RM(SD)	RM	MTO	01.01.92	RM DIV ASMT
Woolsey, Kevin Edward Keith	LT(SL)	X	ATC	16.05.95	RNAS CULDROSE
Woolston, Anthony John , pce, psc(m)	LT CDR	X	PWO(N)	16.07.81	MOD (LONDON)
Wootton, Timothy Mark	LT(SL)	I		01.05.87	RALEIGH
Worley, Ian Geoffrey	LT(SL)	X	P	16.05.94	819 SQN
Wormald, Robert Edward , MSc, psc	CDR	E	MESM	31.12.92	CAPTAIN SM2
Worman, Robin , BSc	LT(SL)	X	P	16.02.88	EXCHANGE RAF UK
Worrall, Michael William , BSc, MIEE, psc(m)	CDR	I	SM	31.12.87	SULTAN
Worsley, William , BSc, pce, pce(sm)	LT CDR	X	SM	01.10.90	PEACOCK
Wort, Roland	CHAPLAIN	SF		27.07.93	SULTAN
Worth, Hugo Francis , BSc	LT RM	RM		01.09.94	45 CDO RM
Worthington, Jonathan Michael Francis (Act Lt Cdr)	LT(SL)	I		01.07.87	ELANT/NAVNW
Wotherspoon, Steven Robert , psc	MAJ	RM		30.06.94	AST(N)
Wotton, John Charles Lawson , BSc, jsdc, pce	CDR	X	FC	30.06.91	MOD (BATH)
Woznicki, Stanley James	LT CDR	X	PWO(A)	16.06.88	FOST SEA
Wraith, Neil	LT RM	RM	LC	01.09.93	45 CDO RM
Wraith, Nicholas John Paul , pce(sm) (Act Cdr)	LT CDR	X	SM	09.08.82	FOSM NWOOD OPS
Wraith, Richard Somerton ,CBE, FIMgt, pce, psc	CAPT	X	SM	31.12.88	DRAKE NBC(CNH)
Wray, Arthur Douglas	LT(SD)	E	WESM	05.06.92	SOVEREIGN
Wray, Adrian David , MPhil, rcds, psc(m), osc, hcsc (Brigadier)	COL	RM	PH	31.12.91	HQRM
Wren, Ian	LT(QM)	Q		20.08.90	RNDHU DERRIFORD
Wrenn, Michael Reader William , MIEEIE	LT(SD)	E	WE	18.02.94	COLLINGWOOD
Wright, Antony John	LT(SL)	X	O	16.02.89	815 OEU OSPREY
Wright, Adam John , BA	LT	E	WE	01.12.92	SHEFFIELD

Name	Rank	Spec	Sub-spec	Seniority	Where serving
Wright, Bradley Lee , BEng, AMIEE	LT	E	WE	01.06.91	CAPT IST STAFF
Wright, David Anthony	LT(SD)	X	MCD	29.07.94	HURWORTH
Wright, David , BEng	SLT	E	WE	01.01.94	COLLINGWOOD
Wright, David , BSc	LT(SL)	X	P	16.01.92	810 SQN SEAHAWK
Wright, Geoffrey Neil , MBE, BSc	CDR	E	MESM	30.06.93	DG SHIPS DEVONPT
Wright, John , BSc	LT CDR(SL)	I		01.10.90	COLLINGWOOD
Wright, John Vincent , CEng, MIMechE	CAPT	E	ME	30.06.93	NBC PORTSMOUTH
Wright, John William Talbot , BA, pce, pcea	CDR	X	O	30.06.87	CINCIBERLANT
Wright, Michael John , MBE	LT CDR(SL)	X		01.09.85	SEA CADET CORPS
Wright, Nicholas Peter , LVO, jsdc	CDR	S		31.12.89	MOD (LONDON)
Wright, Nigel Seymour	LT	E	ME	01.02.91	SULTAN
Wright, Stuart Hugh	LT	S	BAR	16.01.90	2SL/CNH
Wrighton, Christopher Russell , pce, psc	LT CDR	X	P	16.09.80	RNAS PORTLAND
Wrightson, Hugh Mawson , BSc, MIEE	LT CDR	E	ME	01.06.89	MOD (BATH)
Wrightson, Ian Harry	LT(SD)	X	AV	02.04.93	RFANSU
Wrigley, Peter James	LT CDR	X		16.10.88	NAVSOUTH ITALY
Wroblewski, Jefferey Andre	LT(SD)	E	MESM	16.10.92	DRAKE CBS
Wuidart-Gray, Spencer Richard	LT(SL)	X		01.12.93	DRYAD
Wunderle, Charles Albert	LT CDR(SD)	S	W	01.10.93	NORFOLK
Wunderle, Ruth , BA	LT(SL)	W	X	08.04.87	DRAKE CBP
Wyatt, Christopher	LT(SD)	S	S	17.12.93	FONA
Wyatt, David James	LT CDR	X	H1	01.11.93	FOST MPV(SEA)
Wyatt, Julian Michael , BSc, CEng, MIMarE, MIMechE	LT CDR	E	MESM	01.10.90	TRENCHANT
Wyatt, James Martin , BA	2LT(GRAD)	RM		01.09.95	CTCRM LYMPSTONE
Wyatt, Steven Patrick , BSc	CDR	E	WESM	31.12.95	MOD (LONDON)
Wykeham-Martin, Peter Charles (Commodore)	CAPT	S		30.06.91	BDLS AUSTRALIA
Wykes-Sneyd, Ralph John Stuart , AFC, pce, pcea , psc	CDR	X	P	31.12.83	SA LISBON
Wyld, Anthony Wallace	LT(SD)	E	WE	18.02.94	DRAKE CFM
Wylie, Ian Charles Henfrey , BEng, AMIEE	LT	E	WESM	01.11.92	SPARTAN
Wylie, Robert Daryll Stewart , MB, BCh, ChB	SURG LTCDR	-	GMPP	01.08.90	UKSU IBERLANT
Wyness, Roger Simon	SLT(SL)	X	P	01.03.93	815 FLT 217
Wyness, Sharon	SLT(SL)	X	ATC	01.03.93	RNAS CULDROSE
Wynn, Richard James	LT	X		01.11.94	EXCHANGE BELGIUM
Wynn, Simon Christopher	SLT(SL)	X		01.01.95	DRYAD
Wynn, Simon Raymond , BSc, MEng	LT(SL)	I	METOC	01.09.89	CAPT F1(SEA)
Wyper, James Robert , BSc	LT	X	SM	01.09.92	DOLPHIN SM SCHL

Y

Name	Rank	Spec	Sub-spec	Seniority	Where serving
Yardley, Andrew Philip	LT(SL)	I	METOC	01.05.90	SEAHAWK
Yarker, Daniel Lawrence	LT(SD)	X	PWO(A)	27.07.90	YORK
Yarnall, Nicholas John , MB, BCh	SURG LT	-		01.08.92	RH HASLAR
Yates, Andrew , MB, BS, FFARCS	SURG CDR	-	CA	31.12.86	RH HASLAR
Yates, David Andrew , BSc, BEng, AMIEE	LT CDR	E	MESM	01.06.78	DRAKE CBS
Yates, David Hugh Nation , FBIM, MIMS, psc	CDR	X	P	31.12.82	FONA
Yates, Michael Leslie , MHCIMA	T/LT(SDT)	S	CA	18.06.90	HERON
Yates, Neal Peter , pce, pcea, psc	LT CDR	X	O	01.06.89	702 SQN OSPREY
Yearwood, Konrad , BSc	LT(SL)	I		01.09.89	MOD (LONDON)
Yelland, Christopher Brian	LT(SL)	X	O	16.05.87	702 SQN OSPREY
Yeomans, Paul Andrew	LT(SL)	X		01.09.93	MARLBOROUGH
York, Christopher Bruce , pce, psc (Commodore)	CAPT	X	PWO	30.06.89	MOD (BATH)
York, Gideon	SLT	E	MESM	01.09.93	DARTMOUTH BRNC
York His Royal HIGHNESS The Duke Of , CVO, ADC, pce, pcea, psc(m)	LT CDR	X	P	01.02.92	815 SQN HQ
Young, Andrew , BSc, CEng, MIMechE	CDR	E	ME	31.12.90	MOD (BATH)
Young, Angus , n	LT	X		01.06.91	GLASGOW
Young, Andrew Park , BSc	LT CDR	S		16.06.95	NEPTUNE
Young, Christopher John	LT(SL)	I		18.06.92	DOLPHIN SM SCHL
Young, Colin Patrick , jsdc, pcea	CDR	X	P	31.12.82	FONA
Young, Gavin Lee	LT	X		01.01.90	DRYAD
Young, Ian James , BSc, AMIEE, I(2)Fr (Act Cdr)	LT CDR	E	WE	16.12.80	PAAMS PARIS
Young, Jonathan Howard , psc	CAPT RM(SD)	RM		01.10.88	RMB STONEHOUSE
Young, John Nicholas	SLT(SD)	X	AV	24.07.94	RFANSU

Name	Rank	Spec	Sub-spec	Seniority	Where serving
Young, Keith Hunter	LT(SD)	E	ME	23.02.90	539 ASLT SQN RM
Young, Lawrence George Douglas , MBE, IEng, MIEEIE	LT CDR(SD)	E	WE	01.10.93	SAUDI AFPS SAUDI
Young, Mark James	LT(SL)	X	O	16.09.91	815 FLT 212
Young, Michael Stephen , BSc	LT(SL)	I		01.09.88	EXCELLENT
Young, Philip Charles , MB, BS	SURG LTCDR	-	SM	01.08.91	RH HASLAR
Young, Peter John	LT CDR(SD)	X	PR	01.04.86	NAVAL DRAFTING
Young, Robin	LT(SD)	E	ME	13.02.92	FOSTSEA NBCDPSMH
Young, Rachel , BA	LT(SL)	X		01.12.94	SOMERSET
Young, Richard Arthur Sinclair , BSc, CEng, MIEE, CDipAF	CDR	E	WESM	30.06.89	MOD DGSW PTSMTH
Young, Steven Atkinson	LT CDR	X		01.03.92	DRYAD
Young, Stephen Andrew , BEng	LT	E	WESM	01.02.92	VICTORIOUS(STBD)
Young, Stuart Sheldon , MEng, MSc, CEng, MIMechE, jsdc	CDR	E	ME	30.06.95	BDS WASHINGTON
Young, Stephen William	LT(SD)	S	W	16.12.94	RALEIGH
Young, Timothy Morris	LT CDR(SD)	E	WE	01.10.91	CNSA PORTSDOWN
Young, William David , BA	LT(SL)	S		01.10.92	COCHRANE
Youseman, Nicholas James , pce	CDR	X	PWO(U)	31.12.93	BALTAP
Yuill, Ian Alexander , BSc, adp	LT CDR(SL)	I		01.09.84	MOD (LONDON)

Z

Name	Rank	Spec	Sub-spec	Seniority	Where serving
Zambellas, George Michael , BSc, pce, pcea, psc	CDR	X	P	30.06.94	ARGYLL
Ziegler, Sally Anne	SLT	Q		18.08.93	RH HASLAR

RFA OFFICERS

COMMODORE

N. D. SQUIRE

COMMODORE (ENGINEERS)

P. GOODMAN

Captains

J.R.J. Carew, OBE	D.M. Pitt	J.M.M.Wilkins
J.B. Dickinson, CBE	G.D. Pursall	G.D. Wilson
C.J. Fell	S. Redmond, OBE	D.N.L. Yeomans
I.F. Heslop	A.T.Roach	L. Coupland
S.F. Hodgson psc	P.J.G. Roberts, DSO	N. A. Jones
F.M. Johnson	P.A. Robinson	J. Stones
C.R. Knapp	C.O. Smith	D. Worthington
P.J. Lannin jsdc	J. Summers	M. T. Jarvis
C.A. Mitchell psc	B.P. Tarr, OBE	W. Walworth
P.L. Nelson	P.A. Taylor, OBE	R. L. Williams
S.G. Pearce, OBE,RD*	J.P. Thompson	D. M. Gerrard
A.F. Pitt,DSC	B.J. Waters, OBE	F. Brady

Captain (Engineers)

T. Adam	I.E. Hall	R. Settle
G.R. Axworthy	K. Holder	A.D. Silcock
N.K. Ball	H.R. Hurley	K. Smeaton
D.E. Bass	C. Johnson	C.S. Smith
P.J. Beer, MBE	R. Kirk	D.C. Smith
D.W. Birkett	R.W. Langton	R.J. Smith
R.J. Brewer	J.W. Leach	N.C. Springer
P.C.M. Daniels	S.J. Mathews	A.D. Wills
J. Davis	M. Mission	A. Wilson
R.W. Donkin	K. Nicholls	M. D. Norfolk
A. Edworthy	G.W. Norcott	E. M. Quigley
M. Ellam	V.P. Nugent	G. T. Turner
I. Finlayson	W. Pearce	K. R. C. Moore
J.R. Gerring	J.A. Pearson	
B.B. Hall	D. Phasey	

GENERAL LIST

ADMIRALS OF THE FLEET
(This rank is now being held in abeyance (1996)

Edinburgh, *His Royal Highness The Prince* Philip, *Duke of,* KG, KT, OM, GBE, AC, QSO	15 Jan 53
Hill-Norton, The Lord, GCB	12 Mar 71
Pollock, *Sir* Michael, (Patrick), *GCB, LVO, DSC, psc*	1 Mar 74
Ashmore, *Sir* Edward (Beckwith), *GCB, DSC, IRs. jssc, psc*	9 Feb 77
Lewin, The Lord, *KG, GCB, LVO, DSC, idc, psc*	6 Jul 79
Leach, *Sir* Henry (Conyers), *GCB, psc*	1 Dec 82
Staveley, *Sir* William (Doveton Minet), *GCB, DL, rcds, psc*	25 May 89
Oswald, *Sir* (John) Julian (Robertson), *GCB, rcds,psc*	2 Mar 92
Bathurst, *Sir* (David) Benjamin , *GCB, rcds*	10 Jul 95

ADMIRALS

Slater, *Sir Jock*(John Cunningham Kirkwood) , *GCB, LVO, ADC, rcds, pce* (CHIEF OF NAVAL STAFF AND FIRST SEA LORD JUL 95)	29 Jan 91
White, *Sir* Hugo (Moresby) , *GCB, CBE, pce* (GOVERNOR & CINC GIB DEC 95)	15 Dec 92
Boyce, *Sir* Michael (Cecil) , *KCB, OBE, ADC, rcds, psc* (SECOND SEA LORD AND CINCNAVHOME MAY 95)	25 May 95
Abbott, *Sir* Peter (Charles) , *KCB, MA, rcds, pce* (COMMANDER-IN-CHIEF FLEET-CINCEASTLANT/ OCT 95)	03 Oct 95

VICE ADMIRALS

Frere, *Sir* Toby (Richard Tobias) , *KCB, rcds, odc(Aus), jssc* (CHIEF OF FLEET SUPPORT APR 94)	11 Dec 92
Moore, Michael Anthony Claes , *LVO, pce, psc, I(1)Sw* (COS TO CDR ALLIED NAVAL FORCES S.EUROPE OCT 94)	26 Jan 94
Tod, Jonathan James Richard ,*KCB, CBE, rcds* (DEPUTY COMMANDER FLEET AUG 94)	28 Jun 94
Gretton, Michael Peter , *MA, rcds, pce, psc* (SACLANTREPEUR DEC 94)	10 Dec 94
Dunt, John Hugh , *BSc, CEng, FIEE, rcds, psc* (DEP CHIEF OF DEFENCE STAFF(SYSTEMS) MAR 95)	21 Mar 95
Brigstocke, John Richard , *rcds, pce, psc* (FLAG OFFICER SURFACE FLOTILLA APR 95)	19 Apr 95
Garnett, Ian David Graham , *psc* (DEPUTY SACLANT AUG 95)	24 Aug 95

REAR ADMIRALS

Wilkinson, Nicholas John , *CB, FBIM, rcds, nadc, psc(m), I(2)Fr* (COMMANDANT JOINT SERVICE DEFENCE COLLEGE MAY 94)	02 Jan 91
Tolhurst, John Gordon , *CB* (FOSNNI NBC Clyde APR 96)	29 Sep 92

Blackham, Jeremy Joe , *BA, rcds, pce, psc, I(2)Sp* . . . . 18 May 93
    (ASSISTANT CHIEF OF THE NAVAL STAFF MAR 95)

Essenhigh, Nigel Richard , *rcds, pce, psc* . . . . 15 Feb 94
    (ASST CHIEF OF DEF. STAFF(PROGRAMMES)(1) MAR 96)

Haddacks, Paul Kenneth , *rcds, pce, psc* . . . . 20 Feb 94
    (ACOS.POLICY & REQUIREMENTS SHAPE JUN 94)

West, Alan William John , *DSC, rcds, pce, psc, hcsc* . . . . 22 Feb 94
    (COMUKTG/CASWSF FEB 96)

Trewby, John Allan , *MA, CEng, FIEE, rcds, psc* . . . . 01 Mar 94
    (DIRECTOR GENERAL NAVAL BASES & SUPPLY OCT 96)

Clarke, John Patrick ,*CB, LVO, MBE, pce* . . . . 14 Mar 94
    (HYDROGRAPHER OF THE NAVY & CHIEF EXECUTIVE JAN 96)

Blackburn, David Anthony James , *LVO, pce, psc(a)* . . . . 16 Mar 94
    (HEAD OF BRITISH DEFENCE STAFF WASHINGTON FEB 95)

Scourse, Frederick Peter , *MBE, MA, CEng, FIEE, ndc* . . . . 18 Apr 94
    (ACTING CONTROLLER OF THE NAVY/DIRECTOR GENERAL SURFACE SHIPS
    APR 94)

Franklyn, Peter Michael , *MVO, rcds, pce* . . . . 14 Nov 94
    (FLAG OFFICER SEA TRAINING APR 96)

Perowne, James Francis , *OBE, pce(sm)* . . . . 04 Jan 95
    (FLAG OFFICER SUBMARINES & COMSUBEASTLANT FEB 96)

Wood, David John , *BSc, CEng, FRAeS, MBIM, nadc, psc(m)* . . . . 21 Feb 95
    (DIRECTOR GENERAL AIRCRAFT (NAVY) FEB 95)

Lees, Rodney Burnett(Barrister) . . . . 21 Feb 95
    (CHIEF OF STAFF TO SECOND SEA LORD AND CINCNAVHOME FEB 95)

Spencer, Peter , *MA, MSc, jsdc* . . . . 16 Mar 95
    (DG FLEET SUPPORT(OPERATIONS & PLANS) MAR 95)

Loughran, Terence William , *pcea, psc, ocds(Can)* . . . . 01 Jun 95
    (FLAG OFFICER NAVAL AVIATION JUN 95)

Thomas, Paul Anthony Moseley , *MSc, CEng, FIMechE, MIMechE* . . . . 13 Sep 95
    (CHIEF STRATEGIC SYSTEMS EXECUTIVE DEC 95)

Armstrong, John Herbert Arthur James , *MA, rcds* (Barrister) . . . . 03 Jan 96
    (SENIOR NAVAL MEMBER DIRECTING STAFF RCDS JAN 96)

McAnally, John Henry Stuart , *LVO, MNI, MRIN, rcds, pce, psc, hcsc* . . . . 11 Jan 96
    (FLAG OFFICER TRAINING & RECRUITING FEB 96)

Malbon, Fabian Michael , *rcds, pce, psc* . . . . 15 Jan 96
    (NAVAL SECRETARY/DIRECTOR GENERAL NAVAL MANNING JAN 96)

Phillips Richard Thomas Ryder, MNI, pce, odc (AUS) . . . . 21 May 96
    (ASST CHIEF OF DEF STAFF OPERATIONAL REQUIREMENTS (SEA SYSTEM)

Ross Alastair Boyd, CBE, rcds, pce, pcea, psc (WEF Aug 96) . . . . 02 Aug 96
    (ASST DIR OPERATIONS DIVISION IMS (WEF Aug 96)

CAPTAINS

1983		1987				X	Rotheram, M.	. . . 31 Dec
X	Burns, B. . . . . 30 Jun	S	Slater, A.E. . . . . 30 Jun	X	Canter, P.C.B. . . . 31 Dec
		E	Kirby, N.B. . . . . 31 Dec	X	Elliott, T.D. . . . . 31 Dec
1986		X	Bannister, A.J. . . . 31 Dec	X	Howard, J.J. . . . 31 Dec
X	Hutchison, W.K. . . . 30 Jun	E	Ferguson, A.D. . . . 31 Dec	E	Read, K.F. . . . . 31 Dec
		S	Somervaille, I.P. . . 31 Dec	X	Branscombe, P. . . 31 Dec
		E	Parker, R.M. . . . . 31 Dec	X	Pearson, J.J. . . . 31 Dec

X	Perowne, B.B. . . .	31 Dec

1988

W	Simpson, J.B. . . .	01 Apr
E	Bass, J.D.	30 Jun
X	Sloane, C.M.	30 Jun
X	Harding, R.	30 Jun
X	Morrow, A.J.C. . . .	30 Jun
I	Murray, D.C.	30 Jun
E	Beynon, J.A.	30 Jun
X	Gregory, A.M. . . .	30 Jun
E	Rowley, R.A. . . .	30 Jun
X	Gough, A.B.	30 Jun
S	Dunt, P.A.	30 Jun
E	Kerr, R.G.	30 Jun
X	Cartwright, J.R. . .	30 Jun
X	Band, J.	30 Jun
X	Lippiett, R.J.	12 Dec
E	Toft, B.P.	31 Dec
E	Hirst, R.A.	31 Dec
X	MacPherson, M.D. .	31 Dec
X	Wraith, R.S.	31 Dec
X	Robinson, G.D.B. . .	31 Dec
E	Masterton-Smith, . .	31 Dec
	A.P.	
E	Bailey, K.R.G. . . .	31 Dec
I	Hart, J.W.S.	31 Dec
E	Burbridge, A.J.H. . .	31 Dec
X	Saunders, S.E. . . .	31 Dec
X	Moore, S.	31 Dec
E	Mungo, F.B.	31 Dec

1989

E	Burch, J.A.	30 Jun
X	Brice, D.J.	30 Jun
E	Newsom, S.J.B. . .	30 Jun
S	Shorland Ball, T.D. .	30 Jun
E	Gozzard, J.	30 Jun
X	York, C.B.	30 Jun
S	Lewis, D.R.S. . . .	30 Jun
X	McLees, J.	30 Jun
E	Shirley, M.C.	30 Jun
I	Leavey, B.M.	30 Jun
E	Hughes, D.B.R. . .	30 Jun
X	Melson, P.J.	30 Jun
E	Lamb-Hughes, G. . .	30 Jun
X	Stevens, R.P. . . .	30 Jun
I	Rickard, H.W. . . .	30 Jun
X	Forbes, I.A.	30 Jun
E	Ward, R.G.J. . . .	30 Jun
X	Williams, R.M. . . .	30 Jun
X	Howell, R.	31 Dec
E	Burns, D.J.	31 Dec
E	Denes, C.M.	31 Dec
E	Hibbert, R.J.N. . . .	31 Dec
X	Fish, P.A.	31 Dec
S	Brecknell, J.J. . . .	31 Dec
E	Netherclift, A.W. . .	31 Dec
X	Bradshaw, R.J. . . .	31 Dec
X	Stone, P.D.	31 Dec
X	Billson, G.K.	31 Dec
I	Willis, R.M.V. . . .	31 Dec
S	Leighton, B.	31 Dec
X	Henderson, I.R. . .	31 Dec

E	Chadwick, J. . . .	31 Dec
E	Morgan, B.S. . . .	31 Dec
X	Meyer, S.R.	31 Dec

1990

E	Organ, P.J.	30 Jun
E	Tempest, R.J. . . .	30 Jun
X	Lyddon, A.C. . . .	30 Jun
E	Tamblyn, J.T. . . .	30 Jun
X	Hime, I.M.	30 Jun
X	Taylor, A.J.S. . . .	30 Jun
E	Sadler, J.B.	30 Jun
S	Hart, J.J.	30 Jun
X	Beagley, C.R. . . .	30 Jun
X	Lane, G.B.D.	30 Jun
E	Luard, J.R.	30 Jun
X	Lockyer, R.W. . . .	30 Jun
E	Parkinson, J.M. . .	30 Jun
E	Lashbrooke, D.P. . .	30 Jun
X	Stanford, C.D. . . .	30 Jun
X	de Halpert, J.M. . .	30 Jun
X	Burnell-Nugent, . .	30 Jun
	J.M.	
E	Critchley, H.J. . . .	31 Dec
X	Conley, D.	31 Dec
S	Martin, T.K.	31 Dec
E	Wilson, P.S.	31 Dec
X	Courtenay, K.A. . .	31 Dec
S	Hore, P.G.	31 Dec
I	Kelly, W.H.	31 Dec
E	Johns, R.F.	31 Dec
X	Hance, J.R.	31 Dec
E	Thompson, F.G. . .	31 Dec
X	Turner, R.M.	31 Dec
X	Backus, A.K.	31 Dec
X	Cotton, R.A.	31 Dec
E	Guild, N.C.F.	31 Dec
S	Tribe, P.J.	31 Dec
X	Harris, J.W.R. . . .	31 Dec
E	Wood, M.G.	31 Dec
X	Clare, R.A.G. . . .	31 Dec

1991

W	Duncan, P.E. . . .	01 Apr
X	Thompson, D.J. . .	30 Jun
E	Morrison, K.W.J. . .	30 Jun
E	Wittich, T.S.	30 Jun
X	Tuffley, C.R.	30 Jun
X	Robertson, N.D.V. .	30 Jun
E	Day, K.J.C.	30 Jun
X	Thornewill, S.C. . .	30 Jun
S	Wykeham-Martin, . .	30 Jun
	P.C.	
X	Hamilton, C.F.B. . .	30 Jun
X	Guy, R.L.	30 Jun
X	Hopkins, L.C. . . .	30 Jun
E	Reeve, J.	30 Jun
X	Anthony, D.J. . . .	30 Jun
E	Cooper, A.	30 Jun
X	Hogg, A.J.M. . . .	30 Jun
X	Stanhope, M. . . .	30 Jun
E	Clayden, J.W.A. . .	31 Dec
E	Hall, D.A.	31 Dec
X	Bishop, R.ST.J.S. . .	31 Dec

E	Page, C.L.W. . . .	31 Dec
X	Edwardes, G.H. . .	31 Dec
E	Graham, S.W. . . .	31 Dec
X	Morrison, C.J.N. . .	31 Dec
X	Chilton, A.L.	31 Dec
X	Strange, R.F.	31 Dec
X	Johnson, M.A. . . .	31 Dec
E	Pacey, P.J.	31 Dec
S	Lockwood, R.G. . .	31 Dec
X	Morton, T.	31 Dec
X	Dymock, A.K. . . .	31 Dec
E	Harries, J.M.H. . . .	31 Dec
X	Hiscock, F.H.	31 Dec
E	Greenish, P.D. . . .	31 Dec

1992

S	Humphrey, D.R. . .	30 Jun
E	Robotham, T.	30 Jun
X	Lyall, A.J.	30 Jun
X	Ellison, C.V.	30 Jun
E	Harris, W.B.	30 Jun
X	Goldman, B.A.L. . .	30 Jun
S	Merrick, L.C.P. . . .	30 Jun
X	Poulter, A.M.	30 Jun
X	Herington, P.W. . .	30 Jun
X	Ellis, P.J.	30 Jun
X	Jeffery, P.H.	30 Jun
E	Lord, R.J.	30 Jun
E	Williams, S.M. . . .	30 Jun
X	Kilgour, N.S.R. . . .	30 Jun
X	McLean, R.A.I. . . .	30 Jun
E	Challands, G.D. . .	30 Jun
X	McClement, T.P. . .	30 Jun
X	Bryant, B.W.	08 Dec
E	Brougham, M.J.D. .	09 Dec
X	Atkinson, E.C. . . .	31 Dec
X	Thomas, N.W. . . .	31 Dec
E	Watterson, K. . . .	31 Dec
X	Du Port, A.N. . . .	31 Dec
X	Rimington, J.A. . . .	31 Dec
S	Smith, D.A.H.M. . .	31 Dec
E	Broadhurst, M.J. . .	31 Dec
X	May, H.P.	31 Dec
X	Rodley, J.F.	31 Dec
E	Meryon, R.J.K. . . .	31 Dec
E	Sanderson, P.C. . .	31 Dec
S	Munns, A.	31 Dec
X	Rapp, J.C.	31 Dec
E	Brooks, B.P.S. . . .	31 Dec
I	Tyrrell, P.J.	31 Dec
X	Lidbetter, S.	31 Dec

1993

E	Locke, S.A.	30 Jun
X	Benbow, W.K. . . .	30 Jun
S	Musters, J.B.A. . .	30 Jun
X	Morgan, J.H.	30 Jun
E	Wright, J.V.	30 Jun
X	Owen, N.R.	30 Jun
E	Davies, P.R.	30 Jun
E	Hare, T.W.	30 Jun
X	Harvey, J.B.	30 Jun
X	Swan, P.W.H. . . .	30 Jun
X	Phillips, D.A.	30 Jun

E	Cheadle, R.F. . . .	30 Jun
X	Lewis, D.A.	30 Jun
X	Style, C.R.	30 Jun
X	Mowlam, D.J.M. . . .	31 Dec
X	Jackson, P. . . .	31 Dec
S	Wines, D.A. . . .	31 Dec
X	Milnes, J.L. . . .	31 Dec
E	Cheesman, P.M. .	31 Dec
E	Pelly, R.C.	31 Dec
E	McClintock, D.V.P.	31 Dec
X	Walker, P.J. . . .	31 Dec
X	Massie-Taylor, C.G.	31 Dec
I	Goodall, S.R.J. . .	31 Dec
X	Hewitt, I.R.	31 Dec
E	Kidner, P.J. . . .	31 Dec
X	Edleston, H.A.H.G.	31 Dec
X	Willmett, A.M. . .	31 Dec
X	Kerr, M.W.G. . . .	31 Dec
E	Wiltshire, G.J. . .	31 Dec
X	Russell, D.J. . . .	31 Dec

1994

X	Cosby, R.A.DE.S. . .	30 Jun
S	Ridland, K.	30 Jun
X	Cust, D.R.	30 Jun
E	Holmes, M.J.	30 Jun
E	Pearson, N.J.	30 Jun
X	Keay, H.	30 Jun
X	Barton, T.J.	30 Jun
X	Williams, M.S. . . .	30 Jun
X	Snelson, D.G. . . .	30 Jun
I	Brokenshire, L.P. . .	30 Jun
E	Warnett, D.L.	30 Jun

1978

X	Pearson, G.S. . .	31 Dec

1979

X	Gough, G.L.D.W. . .	30 Jun
E	Simpson, R.H.C. . .	30 Jun
X	Wheen, P.A.C. . .	31 Dec
E	Glancy, M.P. . . .	31 Dec

1980

I	Lovett, R.F.	30 Jun
X	Law, A.N.	30 Jun
X	Ambrose, P.D. . . .	30 Jun
X	Edmonds, R.F. . . .	30 Jun
I	Hartley, J.	31 Dec
E	Parrish, C.A.M. . .	31 Dec
E	Marks, M.R. . . .	31 Dec
X	Gilbert, M.P. . . .	31 Dec

1981

X	Grattan-Cooper, A.C.	30 Jun
X	Seymour, R.P. . . .	30 Jun
E	Stone, R.B.	30 Jun
E	Dore, R.T.	30 Jun
X	Laverty, R.E.	30 Jun
X	Griffin, W.F.G. . . .	30 Jun

S	Williams, J.L. . . .	30 Jun
E	MacLean, D.J. . . .	30 Jun
X	Somerville, A.J.D. . .	30 Jun
X	Boissier, R.P. . . .	30 Jun
X	Thorpe, I.	31 Dec
E	Hurford, P.G.	31 Dec
X	Tall, D.M.	31 Dec
X	Barton, R.P.	31 Dec
X	Ainsley, R.S.	31 Dec
I	Spires, T.A.	31 Dec
X	Parker, J.W.	31 Dec
E	Chittenden, T.C. . .	31 Dec
X	Littleboy, M.N. . . .	31 Dec
S	Preston-Jones, N.C. .	31 Dec
E	Clark, A.I.H.	31 Dec
X	Johns, A.J.	31 Dec
E	Finlayson, R.D. . . .	31 Dec
X	Miller, A.J.G.	31 Dec

1995

X	Booth, M.D.	30 Jun
X	Bray, N.G.H.	30 Jun
E	Fitzgerald, M.P. . . .	30 Jun
X	Waite, C.W.	30 Jun
X	Harris, N.H.L. . . .	30 Jun
E	Raby, N.J.F.	30 Jun
S	Savage, N.D.	30 Jun
X	Clapp, R.J.	30 Jun
I	Auty, S.J.	30 Jun
E	Fairbairn, W.D.M. . .	30 Jun
X	Laurence, T.J.H. . .	30 Jun
X	Wilcocks, P.L. . . .	30 Jun
E	Turner, R.B.	30 Jun

COMMANDERS

I	Linstead-Smith, P.J.	31 Dec
X	Steed, B.E.	31 Dec
E	Blott, R.J.	31 Dec
X	Green, C.R.	31 Dec
X	Welland, C.P.B. . .	31 Dec

1982

E	Lingard, D.M.H. . .	30 Jun
E	Harvey, R.C.	30 Jun
E	Clapham, I.	30 Jun
X	Howat, W.K.	30 Jun
X	Titmus, G.D.	30 Jun
X	Syer, P.G.	31 Dec
X	Gedge, T.J.H. . . .	31 Dec
X	Young, C.P.	31 Dec
X	Crews, N.J.K. . . .	31 Dec
X	Frisken, W.D. . . .	31 Dec
E	Blakeley, T.	31 Dec
X	Yates, D.H.N. . . .	31 Dec
X	Bardolf-Smith, J.L. .	31 Dec

1983

X	Booth, P.S.	30 Jun
X	Unwin, P.J.	30 Jun
X	Higgins, P.	30 Jun
X	Farrow, M.J.D. . . .	30 Jun

E	Searle, E.F.	31 Dec
X	Manning, M.G.B. . . .	31 Dec
X	Tighe, J.G.H.	31 Dec
S	Whitaker, H.R. . . .	31 Dec
E	Kirkpatrick, J. . . .	31 Dec
X	Batho, W.N.P. . . .	31 Dec
I	Stevenson, C.B.H. .	31 Dec
E	Dawson, E.W. . . .	31 Dec
E	Richardson, I.J.W. .	31 Dec
X	Welch, J.	31 Dec
X	Clayton, C.H.T. . . .	31 Dec
S	Lane, M.G.	31 Dec
X	Cooke, D.J.	31 Dec
E	Melly, R.G.	31 Dec
X	Silcock, C.A.J. . . .	31 Dec
E	Borley, K.J.	31 Dec
X	Wilkinson, P.J. . . .	31 Dec

1996

E	Whatmough, D.E. .	30 Jun
X	Fifield, D.J.	30 Jun
X	Watson, P.H. . . .	30 Jun
X	Fanshawe, J.R. . .	30 Jun
X	Barritt, M.K.	30 Jun
E	Heselton, B.L. . . .	30 Jun
X	Boyd, J.A.	30 Jun
X	Dickson, A.P. . . .	30 Jun
S	Sinclair, A.H. . . .	30 Jun
X	Massey, A.M. . . .	30 Jun
X	Lambert, P.	30 Jun
W	Picton, A.M.	30 Jun
E	Latham, N.D. . . .	30 Jun

E	Collicutt, B.F. . . .	30 Jun
E	Fulford, N.J.D. . . .	30 Jun
X	MacKenzie, K.D. . .	30 Jun
E	Fenwick, J.	30 Jun
X	Redford, K.M. . . .	30 Jun
X	Jones, R.L.P. . . .	31 Dec
X	Inskip, I.	31 Dec
S	MacFarlane, I.S. . .	31 Dec
S	Wilkinson, S.R. . . .	31 Dec
X	Fensome, R.G. . . .	31 Dec
E	Sherwin, C.P. . . .	31 Dec
X	Clay, C.J.	31 Dec
X	Hulme, L.S.G. . . .	31 Dec
X	Wykes-Sneyd, R.J.S.	31 Dec
I	Bittles, D.J.	31 Dec
X	Auld, A.D.	31 Dec
E	De Burgh, C.D. . .	31 Dec
E	MacDonald Watson, A.I.	31 Dec
X	O'Connor, R.C. . .	31 Dec
X	Clark, H.S.	31 Dec
E	Darch, B.N.	31 Dec

1984

E	Dutta, M.	30 Jun
X	Knapp, M.G.A. . . .	30 Jun
E	Prichard, J.L.L. . . .	30 Jun

X Meazza, V.M.	. . .	30 Jun
E Blake, R.M.	. . . .	30 Jun
I Hadden, P.G.	. . .	30 Jun
E Crouch, R.T.	. . . .	30 Jun
X Parkes, R.J.	. . . .	30 Jun
E Mattick, D.J.	. . . .	30 Jun
S Abbott, C.P.G.	. . .	30 Jun
E Evans, J.R.	. . . . .	30 Jun
X Money, R.I.	. . . . .	30 Jun
E Hillier, N.J.	. . . . .	30 Jun
E Phelps, M.A.	. . . .	30 Jun
E Wiseman, W.T.	. . .	30 Jun
X Tatman, A.K.	. . .	30 Jun
E Dent, A.R.	. . . . .	30 Jun
X Richardson, D.J.	. .	30 Jun
E Beard, G.S.	. . . .	30 Jun
E Carter, D.A.P.	. . .	31 Dec
X Gale, P.J.	. . . . .	31 Dec
E Douglas, I.K.W.	. .	31 Dec
E Broadbent, J.H.	. .	31 Dec
X Morgan, D.R.	. . .	31 Dec
X de Halpert, S.D.	. .	31 Dec
E Curran, M.G.S.	. . .	31 Dec
X James, M.A.	. . . .	31 Dec
X Talbot, R.J.	. . . .	31 Dec
X McLellan, J.B.	. . .	31 Dec
E Jenkins, W.R.S.	. .	31 Dec
E Hamilton, R.W.	. . .	31 Dec
S Davis, N.H.	. . . .	31 Dec
X Plummer, J.D.	. . .	31 Dec
E Hill, C.A.J.	. . . . .	31 Dec

1985

E Watts, P.	. . . . .	30 Jun
X House, R.E.D.	. . .	30 Jun
X Fisher, A.D.	. . . .	30 Jun
E Phillips, M.F.	. . . .	30 Jun
E Crothers, D.M.	. . .	30 Jun
E Cumming, G.G.A.	. .	30 Jun
X Sanderson, R.D.	. .	30 Jun
X Smith, D.J.	. . . .	30 Jun
E Aldred, I.S.	. . . .	30 Jun
X Hunt, G.C.	. . . .	30 Jun
X Seaward, R.C.	. . .	30 Jun
S Vosper, I.A.	. . . .	30 Jun
E Jeffrey, I.	. . . . .	30 Jun
X Gordon-Lennox, A.C.		30 Jun
X Burne, T.G.L.	. . .	31 Dec
X Mullane, M.J.	. . .	31 Dec
S Bates, M.G.	. . . .	31 Dec
X Behets, B.T.J.	. . .	31 Dec
X Reeves, B.V.C.	. . .	31 Dec
E Harry, N.J.F.V.	. . .	31 Dec
I Prosser, A.J.	. . . .	31 Dec
X Laird, C.R.	. . . .	31 Dec
E Fogden, D.R.	. . .	31 Dec
I Thomas, C.D.	. . .	31 Dec
S Jones, W.E.P.	. . .	31 Dec
E Prynn, R.M.	. . . .	31 Dec
X Cartlidge, D.	. . . .	31 Dec
X Rogers, A.G.	. . . .	31 Dec
S Evans, M.J.	. . . .	31 Dec
X Harris, P.N.	. . . .	31 Dec

1986

S Johnson, A.D.	. . .	30 Jun
X Hildesley, T.I.	. . .	30 Jun
E Dalrymple-Smith, R.		30 Jun
E Goodfellow, R.F.	. .	30 Jun
I Le Manquais, T.W.D.		30 Jun
X Madgwick, J.E.V.	. .	30 Jun
I Jones, K.	. . . . .	30 Jun
E Knox, N.O.G.	. . .	30 Jun
X MacKay, S.V.	. . .	30 Jun
S Guyatt, A.E.	. . . .	30 Jun
E Russell, T.J.	. . . .	30 Jun
E Howells, D.L.	. . .	30 Jun
X Stanley, I.	. . . . .	30 Jun
X Piggott, G.D.	. . .	30 Jun
E Malley, D.S.	. . . .	30 Jun
E Dobson, J.K.	. . .	30 Jun
X Mannering, P.D.	. .	31 Dec
I Wood, A.C.M.	. . .	31 Dec
E Barltrop, J.A.	. . .	31 Dec
I Rennison, W.R.	. .	31 Dec
X James, C.F.	. . . .	31 Dec
X Taylor, A.F.M.	. . .	31 Dec
E Cocks, M.K.F.	. . .	31 Dec
X Lake, R.V.	. . . .	31 Dec
E Wheeler, B.	. . . .	31 Dec
E Graham, W.S.	. . .	31 Dec
E Jay, K.G.	. . . . .	31 Dec
S Endersby, R.J.S.	. .	31 Dec
X Bateman, G.	. . . .	31 Dec
I Gregory, P.C.	. . .	31 Dec
E Duffy, M.J.	. . . .	31 Dec
X Bennett, S.H.G.	. .	31 Dec
X Goddard, R.A.	. . .	31 Dec
X Fyfe, P.M.	. . . .	31 Dec
X Perfect, D.M.	. . .	31 Dec
X Galloway, P.	. . . .	31 Dec
X Davies, R.S.B.	. . .	31 Dec

1987

S Farquhar, J.W.	. . .	30 Jun
S Eaglestone, P.S.	. .	30 Jun
E McKenzie, K.J.	. . .	30 Jun
X Nicoll, A.J.K.	. . .	30 Jun
X Priestley, M.J.	. . .	30 Jun
X Acland, D.J.D.	. . .	30 Jun
E Dennis-Jones, M.	. .	30 Jun
E Sladden, R.D.	. . .	30 Jun
S Hamilton, A.G.	. . .	30 Jun
E Welch, B.C.	. . . .	30 Jun
I Mizen, A.	. . . . .	30 Jun
E Westwood, S.P.C.	.	30 Jun
E Moir, S.	. . . . .	30 Jun
E Soutter, L.D.L.	. . .	30 Jun
X Baudains, D.P.	. . .	30 Jun
X Howick, S.W.	. . .	30 Jun
X Albery, R.J.	. . . .	30 Jun
E Binns, J.B.	. . . .	30 Jun
E Norton, A.J.	. . . .	30 Jun
E Samborne, M.D.P.	.	30 Jun
E Hunt, A.J.	. . . . .	30 Jun
I Edwards, I.	. . . .	30 Jun
X Wright, J.W.T.	. . .	30 Jun
E Fairhurst, G.M.	. .	30 Jun

S Barge, M.A.	. . . .	30 Jun
X Johnson, G.R.	. . .	30 Jun
E Ridley, W.K.	. . .	30 Jun
S Pennefather, W.J.R.		30 Jun
E Eastley, B.R.	. . . .	30 Jun
X Daglish, H.B.	. . . .	30 Jun
X Pott, C.D.	. . . . .	31 Dec
I Worrall, M.W.	. . . .	31 Dec
E Jackson, N.C.	. . .	31 Dec
I Marley, P.S.	. . . .	31 Dec
X Edmonds, G.J.L.	. .	31 Dec
X Richards, I.S.H.	. .	31 Dec
E Carter, B.G.	. . . .	31 Dec
E McFadyen, H.	. . .	31 Dec
E Garland, J.M.R.	. .	31 Dec
E Waters, C.D.	. . . .	31 Dec
S Cordner, K.	. . . .	31 Dec
X Harrison, R.G.	. . .	31 Dec
X Aiken, J.S.	. . . .	31 Dec
X Forsyth, A.W.	. . .	31 Dec
X Robinson, C.P.	. . .	31 Dec
X Hughes, P.J.	. . . .	31 Dec
X McKenzie, I.S.	. . .	31 Dec
X Eberle, P.J.F.	. . .	31 Dec
E Harding, R.A.	. . .	31 Dec
X Moodie, G.R.	. . .	31 Dec
E Bailie, D.J.	. . . .	31 Dec

1988

W Martin, K.M.	. . .	01 Apr
I Thorn, R.G.	. . . .	30 Jun
X Merrett, G.J.	. . .	30 Jun
E Underdown, M.S.	.	30 Jun
X Prime, J.R.M.	. . .	30 Jun
E Cirin, W.R.J.	. . .	30 Jun
E Barnacle, C.A.	. . .	30 Jun
E Smith, A.	. . . . .	30 Jun
X Stenning, M.W.	. .	30 Jun
X Pegg, S.M.	. . . .	30 Jun
E Browne, G.W.	. . .	30 Jun
I Stanesby, D.L.	. . .	30 Jun
X Peach, C.C.	. . . .	30 Jun
E Lindley, R.A.	. . .	30 Jun
X Gale, H.N.	. . . .	30 Jun
X Banting, Q.C.L.	. .	30 Jun
E English, C.R.	. . .	30 Jun
X Gordon, J.H.	. . .	30 Jun
X Teer, D.R.	. . . .	30 Jun
X Goddard, I.K.	. . .	30 Jun
S Godwin, P.E.	. . .	30 Jun
E Jarvis, I.L.	. . . .	30 Jun
X Baxter, G.F.	. . .	30 Jun
E Wills, J.R.	. . . .	30 Jun
X Manning, G.A.	. . .	31 Dec
S Sharp, C.C.G.	. . .	31 Dec
E Harbroe-Bush, R.D.		31 Dec
X Paton, J.	. . . . .	31 Dec
X Butler, R.J.	. . . .	31 Dec
S Cole, C.M.	. . . .	31 Dec
E Egerton, P.M.	. . .	31 Dec
E Hunt, P.V.	. . . .	31 Dec
I Kennaugh, A.J.	. .	31 Dec
X Mitchell, R.H.	. . .	31 Dec
E Madge, R.	. . . .	31 Dec

E	Bernier, N.L.P.	31 Dec	E	Meaken, J.	31 Dec	S	Rayner, B.N.	30 Jun
X	Sayer, D.J.	31 Dec	E	Hayward, L.R.	31 Dec	I	Rees, J.B.M.	30 Jun
X	Welch, A.T.	31 Dec	X	Goodwin, G.	31 Dec	X	Gass, C.J.	30 Jun
S	Gill, M.	31 Dec	S	Stringer, M.C.	31 Dec	X	Avery, M.B.	30 Jun
E	Townsend, J.R.	31 Dec	X	Cowley, N.J.	31 Dec	X	Fisher, P.	30 Jun
X	Lister, J.A.	31 Dec	E	Bray, J.D.	31 Dec	X	Ledingham, H.J.	30 Jun
X	Forster, T.J.A.	31 Dec	X	O'Neill, R.K.	31 Dec	E	Doney, K.R.	30 Jun
X	Meatyard, C.G.B.	31 Dec	I	Potter, M.J.	31 Dec	X	Scorer, S.J.	30 Jun
E	Warne, R.L.	31 Dec	E	Douglas, F.R.	31 Dec	X	Bennett, A.R.C.	30 Jun
X	Steele, R.P.	31 Dec	E	Passingham, R.E.	31 Dec	E	Tibbitt, I.P.G.	30 Jun
E	Hoskins, A.B.	31 Dec	X	Larmour, D.R.	31 Dec	E	Issitt, D.J.	30 Jun
X	Adair, A.A.S.	31 Dec	E	Antcliffe, G.A.	31 Dec	X	Jermy, S.C.	30 Jun
S	Tatham, P.H.	31 Dec	X	Hockin, W.R.J.	31 Dec	E	Love, R.T.	30 Jun
X	Fergusson, D.C.M.	31 Dec	E	Carnt, S.P.	31 Dec	X	Mark, R.A.	30 Jun
E	Binns, J.B.H.	31 Dec	E	Bell, A.D.	31 Dec	E	Geddes, W.B.	30 Jun
X	Parris, K.J.	31 Dec	S	Wellesley-Harding,	31 Dec	X	Hobson, P.	31 Dec
X	Martin, S.C.	31 Dec		I.R.		E	Payne-Hanlon, P.N.	31 Dec
			S	Wright, N.P.	31 Dec	X	Lamb, R.	31 Dec
	1989		X	Greenop, J.P.S.	31 Dec	E	Smith, A.B.	31 Dec
W	Stellingworth, J.P.	01 Apr	X	Smith, N.P.	31 Dec	X	Stockman, C.D.	31 Dec
E	Harris, M.	30 Jun	I	Miklinski, A.S.	31 Dec	E	Whales, N.C.F.	31 Dec
X	Gregory, I.S.	30 Jun	X	Dean, R.	31 Dec	E	Stanton, R.T.	31 Dec
E	Davidson, K.J.	30 Jun	E	Dawson, J.E.	31 Dec	E	Craig, D.M.	31 Dec
E	Higham, A.	30 Jun	X	Docherty, P.T.	31 Dec	X	McCready, G.A.R.	31 Dec
X	Ewins, G.P.	30 Jun	S	Knight, D.J.	31 Dec	X	Dodds, M.	31 Dec
E	Boggust, D.I.	30 Jun	X	Forbes, D.M.	31 Dec	E	Jaynes, P.R.W.	31 Dec
E	Young, R.A.S.	30 Jun	X	Kidd, J.C.	31 Dec	X	Williams, T.A.	31 Dec
X	Skinner, J.R.	30 Jun	X	Munns, C.R.	31 Dec	S	Backhouse, A.W.	31 Dec
X	Lightfoot, C.M.	30 Jun	S	Noble, G.D.	31 Dec	E	Steel, R.J.	31 Dec
I	Jellyman, P.A.	30 Jun	X	Scoles, J.C.	31 Dec	E	Milton, G.J.G.	31 Dec
X	Chapman-Andrews,	30 Jun	X	Knowles, J.M.	31 Dec	S	Hadden, C.S.	31 Dec
	P.C.		X	Williams, T.N.E.	31 Dec	S	Prescott, J.A.	31 Dec
E	Doxsey, R.A.	30 Jun	E	Harrison, R.A.	31 Dec	X	Overington, N.	31 Dec
E	Magill, W.J.	30 Jun	X	Cameron, A.J.B.	31 Dec	E	Young, A.	31 Dec
E	Kongialis, J.A.	30 Jun	X	White, D.S.H.	31 Dec	I	Morris, P.N.	31 Dec
S	Ainslie, A.A.	30 Jun	X	Nance, A.R.	31 Dec	E	Hodgson, R.E.	31 Dec
S	Head, R.R.D'E.	30 Jun	E	Marks, N.	31 Dec	X	Sewell, I.T.T.	31 Dec
X	Bailey, J.	30 Jun				X	Dedman, N.J.K.	31 Dec
X	Matthews, P.	30 Jun		**1990**		X	Hibbert, P.N.	31 Dec
E	Bruce, J.	30 Jun	S	Philpott, G.R.	30 Jun	X	Bearne, J.P.	31 Dec
X	Jones, P.H.	30 Jun	S	Bamborough, M.J.	30 Jun	E	Horrell, M.I.	31 Dec
X	Ford, D.	30 Jun	X	Rich, A.A.	30 Jun	S	Leatherby, J.H.	31 Dec
S	Prior, M.F.	30 Jun	E	Banks, R.G.	30 Jun	I	Parker, G.P.	31 Dec
X	Goodall, D.C.	30 Jun	E	Broad, R.O.	30 Jun	X	Ibbotson, R.J.	31 Dec
E	Western, W.J.H.	30 Jun	E	Podmore, C.F.	30 Jun	X	Twitchen, R.C.	31 Dec
X	Covington, W.M.	30 Jun	X	Craig, R.W.W.	30 Jun	S	Davis, B.J.	31 Dec
S	Hemsworth, M.K.	30 Jun	I	Rogers, M.S.	30 Jun	X	Bryning, C.J.	31 Dec
E	Thatcher, R.P.	30 Jun	X	Skinns, G.M.	30 Jun	X	Simmonds, R.M.	31 Dec
E	Jenkins, I.F.	30 Jun	E	Arthur, J.C.W.	30 Jun	X	Montgomery, C.P.R.	31 Dec
I	Patrick, J.	30 Jun	X	Habershon, D.B.	30 Jun	E	Storey, M.	31 Dec
E	Hollidge, J.H.	30 Jun	E	Murch, J.D.	30 Jun	X	Crabtree, I.M.	31 Dec
X	Lucey, R.N.	30 Jun	X	Morris, R.R.	30 Jun	E	Firth, S.K.	31 Dec
X	Charlton, D.R.	30 Jun	X	Freeman, D.A.K.	30 Jun	S	Kimmons, M.	31 Dec
E	Green, J.A.	30 Jun	E	Coles, G.W.G.	30 Jun	S	Vaughan, D.M.	31 Dec
E	Hodge, C.G.	30 Jun	X	Eltringham, T.J.	30 Jun	E	Cunnison, J.B.	31 Dec
X	Parry, C.J.	30 Jun	E	Legg, M.R.	30 Jun	X	Harris, T.R.	31 Dec
E	Horsted, P.J.	30 Jun	E	Morgan, D.	30 Jun	E	Jarvis, D.J.	31 Dec
X	Kirby, S.R.	30 Jun	X	Sim, D.L.W.	30 Jun			
W	Cole, M.W.	01 Oct	E	Little, R.M.	30 Jun		**1991**	
X	Watkins, C.F.F.	31 Dec	E	Menzies, A.	30 Jun	E	Walton, A.F.	30 Jun
S	Carter, S.F.	31 Dec	E	Cariss, P.	30 Jun	X	Clark, T.H.V.	30 Jun
E	Hill, M.N.	31 Dec	X	Nixon, M.C.	30 Jun	E	Timms, S.J.	30 Jun
X	Webster, G.	31 Dec	E	Palmer, R.A.N.	30 Jun	E	Smith, N.S.	30 Jun
E	Lansdell, R.J.	31 Dec	X	Turner, S.M.	30 Jun	E	Hyldon, C.J.	30 Jun

E	Hutchinson, T.J.	30 Jun
X	Ewing, A.D.	30 Jun
E	Duke, R.L.	30 Jun
X	Wotton, J.C.L.	30 Jun
E	Williams, N.L.	30 Jun
X	Chambers, N.M.C.	30 Jun
X	Foster, G.R.N.	30 Jun
X	Morris, D.S.	30 Jun
E	Ellins, S.J.	30 Jun
X	Boxall-Hunt, B.P.	30 Jun
X	Searle, R.J.	30 Jun
E	Dodd, J.S.C.	30 Jun
S	Quinn, P.A.	30 Jun
E	John, M.L.	30 Jun
E	Moberly, N.G.H.	30 Jun
X	Butcher, M.W.	30 Jun
X	Harland, N.J.G.	30 Jun
X	Steel, P.ST.C.	30 Jun
X	Wardley, P.M.	30 Jun
X	Ferguson, J.N.	30 Jun
E	Leeming, R.J.	30 Jun
X	Ramm, S.C.	30 Jun
X	Palmer, C.L.	30 Jun
I	Pond, D.W.	30 Jun
X	Butler, N.A.M.	30 Jun
E	Graves, M.E.L.	30 Jun
S	Blackett, J.	30 Jun
X	MacDonald, D.H.L.	30 Jun
E	Bowker, M.A.	30 Jun
X	Hudson, N.G.	30 Jun
X	Leaman, R.D.	30 Jun
S	Ross, A.A.	30 Jun
X	Harbun, D.G.	30 Jun
E	Rankin, I.G.	30 Jun
E	Thwaites, G.J.	30 Jun
X	Mansergh, R.J.	30 Jun
E	Hyslop, D.R.	30 Jun
E	Swainson, D.J.	31 Dec
E	Holgate, C.J.	31 Dec
X	Underwood, A.G.H.	31 Dec
X	Wilson, S.G.	31 Dec
X	Bishop, R.J.	31 Dec
E	Sayles, S.	31 Dec
E	Bowker, E.A.	31 Dec
X	Mervik, C.F.	31 Dec
S	Jackson, A.R.	31 Dec
E	Reeder, R.	31 Dec
E	Hume, C.B.	31 Dec
S	Day, N.R.	31 Dec
X	Williams, N.D.B.	31 Dec
E	Van Beek, L.	31 Dec
E	Pancott, B.M.	31 Dec
X	De Sa, P.J.	31 Dec
I	Wilkinson, R.M.	31 Dec
X	Stoneman, T.J.	31 Dec
X	Swain, D.M.	31 Dec
E	Knowling, P.J.	31 Dec
X	Bramley, S.	31 Dec
E	Stefanie, N.B.	31 Dec
X	Croke, A.	31 Dec
I	Fortescue, P.W.	31 Dec
X	Armstrong, C.A.	31 Dec
S	Jones, A.	31 Dec
X	Johnson, G.P.	31 Dec
X	Turner, I.	31 Dec
X	Robinson, P.H.	31 Dec
E	Bailey, J.W.	31 Dec
S	McCarthy, P.J.	31 Dec
S	Pearce, J.K.C.	31 Dec
X	Walpole, P.K.	31 Dec
E	Gibb, R.W.	31 Dec
W	Thorburn, S.A.	31 Dec
E	King, A.M.	31 Dec
X	Lombard, D.	31 Dec
X	Soar, T.A.	31 Dec
E	Henley, S.M.	31 Dec
E	Hart, J.	31 Dec
X	Cooling, R.G.	31 Dec

1992

X	Burston, R.	30 Jun
X	Govan, R.T.	30 Jun
E	Phillips, T.J.	30 Jun
S	Lane, D.F.	30 Jun
E	Jeram-Croft, L.M.	30 Jun
X	Shepherd, I.	30 Jun
X	Ingham, P.C.	30 Jun
I	Ratcliffe, J.P.	30 Jun
I	Stanley, P.	30 Jun
X	Ramsay, G.P.	30 Jun
E	Matters, A.C.	30 Jun
X	Gregan, D.C.	30 Jun
E	Adams, R.A.S.	30 Jun
E	Robb, M.C.	30 Jun
X	Davies, P.N.M.	30 Jun
X	Smee, N.L.	30 Jun
E	Munro, I.R.	30 Jun
E	Lankester, T.J.	30 Jun
E	Dyer, S.J.	30 Jun
X	Durston, D.H.	30 Jun
X	Lankester, P.	30 Jun
X	Donaldson, J.	30 Jun
X	Armitage, M.ST.C.	30 Jun
E	Smith, C.S.	30 Jun
S	Hosker, T.J.	30 Jun
S	MacDonald, G.E.	30 Jun
E	Wadham, J.	30 Jun
X	Hawkins, R.C.	30 Jun
X	Sloan, M.U.	30 Jun
X	Moncrieff, I.	30 Jun
E	Hockley, G.P.	30 Jun
X	Herman, T.R.	30 Jun
S	Cornberg, M.A.	30 Jun
X	Thoburn, R.	30 Jun
E	Jackman, R.W.	30 Jun
S	Martin, T.F.W.	30 Jun
W	Stait, C.J.	30 Jun
E	Rymer, A.R.	30 Jun
X	Rix, A.J.	30 Jun
E	Mathews, A.D.H.	30 Jun
X	Beadnell, N.	30 Jun
E	Alabaster, M.B.	30 Jun
X	Johnstone-Burt, C.A.	30 Jun
X	Pepper, M.R.	31 Dec
X	Maughan, J.M.C.	31 Dec
E	Usborne, A.C.	31 Dec
X	Arrow, J.W.	31 Dec

E	Ayers, R.P.B.	31 Dec
I	Aitken, F.J.	31 Dec
X	Marshall, R.A.	31 Dec
E	Cooper, J.A.	31 Dec
S	Peilow, B.F.	31 Dec
E	Thorpe, C.R.	31 Dec
S	Mizen, M.W.	31 Dec
X	Lye, D.J.	31 Dec
W	Robbins, M.J.	31 Dec
X	Spalton, G.M.S.	31 Dec
X	Brooks, A.S.	31 Dec
E	Arnold, B.W.H.	31 Dec
E	Sherlock, F.C.E.	31 Dec
X	Brocklebank, G.P.	31 Dec
X	Bartholomew, I.M.	31 Dec
X	Tottenham, J.G.	31 Dec
X	Welborn, C.G.	31 Dec
E	Pritchard, T.G.	31 Dec
S	Fraser, R.W.	31 Dec
X	Gibson, I.A.	31 Dec
E	Wormald, R.E.	31 Dec
E	Watts, R.F.	31 Dec
X	Powis, J.	31 Dec
X	Anderson, M.	31 Dec
E	Tate, A.J.	31 Dec
X	Howard, S.C.	31 Dec
E	Hall, J.W.M.	31 Dec
X	Dickens, D.J.R.	31 Dec
X	Steel, C.M.H.	31 Dec
X	Collins, P.N.	31 Dec
E	Branch-Evans, S.J.	31 Dec
X	Morisetti, N.	31 Dec
E	Hussain, A.M.	31 Dec
E	Hughes, R.I.	31 Dec
X	Mathias, P.B.	31 Dec

1993

E	Parsons, G.	30 Jun
E	Febbrarro, N.R.	30 Jun
E	Lineker, R.J.	30 Jun
S	Williams, R.E.	30 Jun
X	Dale, M.J.	30 Jun
X	Andrew, W.G.	30 Jun
E	Bateman, R.D.	30 Jun
X	Grant, A.K.	30 Jun
X	Guy, T.J.	30 Jun
X	Bell-Davies, R.W.	30 Jun
E	McFarlane, A.L.	30 Jun
S	Coupe, R.D.	30 Jun
X	Mason, M.M.D.	30 Jun
X	Chambers, W.J.	30 Jun
E	Stratton, J.D.	30 Jun
X	Upright, S.W.	30 Jun
I	Sutherland, W.M.	30 Jun
E	Bishop, P.R.	30 Jun
X	Snow, M.C.P.	30 Jun
X	Holihead, P.W.	30 Jun
X	Slowe, K.D.J.	30 Jun
E	Wright, G.N.	30 Jun
I	Haines, S.W.	30 Jun
X	Cowdrey, M.C.	30 Jun
X	Hennessey, T.P.D.	30 Jun
X	Tarr, M.D.	30 Jun
X	Williams, S.T.	30 Jun

X Harvey, K. . . . . . 30 Jun	X Horton, R.I. . . . . 30 Jun	E Brough, G.A. . . . 31 Dec
E Mason, R.W. . . . . 30 Jun	E Whitehorn, I.J. . . . 30 Jun	E White, A.R. . . . . 31 Dec
E Cox, P.W.S. . . . . 30 Jun	X Hinchliffe, P.B. . . . 30 Jun	S Airey, S.E. . . . . 31 Dec
X Snow, C.A. . . . . 30 Jun	E Hart, D.J. . . . . . 30 Jun	E Couch, P.J. . . . . 31 Dec
E Dannatt, T.M. . . . 30 Jun	X Wallace, G.W.A. . . 30 Jun	X Moll, A.G. . . . . . 31 Dec
X Greenlees, I.W. . . . 30 Jun	S Nelson, D.T. . . . . 30 Jun	X Karsten, T.M. . . . 31 Dec
E Langbridge, D.C. . . 30 Jun	X Drummond, J.R.G. . 30 Jun	E Jess, I.M. . . . . . 31 Dec
X Williams, B.N.B. . . . 30 Jun	X Cutt, J.J.D. . . . . 30 Jun	S Steel, D.G. . . . . 31 Dec
S Albon, R. . . . . . 30 Jun	E Molyneaux, D.G. . . 30 Jun	
X Gillespie, S.M. . . . 30 Jun	X Reid, M. . . . . . . 30 Jun	**1995**
E Hockley, C.J. . . . . 30 Jun	E Dowle, S.W. . . . . 30 Jun	X Carter, K. . . . . . 30 Jun
X Bateman, S.J.F. . . . 30 Jun	E Sealey, N.P. . . . . 30 Jun	E Loneragan, M.J. . . 30 Jun
X Haill, S.J.J. . . . 31 Dec	E Whyntie, A. . . . . 30 Jun	E Podger, K.G.R. . . . 30 Jun
E Gubbins, V.R. . . 31 Dec	X Humphreys, J.I. . . . 30 Jun	S Mullen, A.J. . . . . 30 Jun
X Turner, S.E. . . . 31 Dec	X Westwood, N.S. . . . 30 Jun	X Stamp, G. . . . . . 30 Jun
E Coombes, D. . . . 31 Dec	I Christie, C.S. . . . . 30 Jun	X Phillips, D.G. . . . . 30 Jun
X Goodwin, D.R. . . 31 Dec	X Ross, A.K. . . . . . 30 Jun	E Apps, J.G. . . . . . 30 Jun
X Thomas, S.A. . . . 31 Dec	X Rothwell, M.K. . . . 30 Jun	X Mather, S. . . . . . 30 Jun
E Jeffcoat, S.M. . . . 31 Dec	E Rowell, G.E. . . . . 30 Jun	X McNair, E.A. . . . . 30 Jun
I Bevan, S. . . . . 31 Dec	S Chelton, S.R.L. . . . 30 Jun	S Crick, R.J. . . . . . 30 Jun
X Youseman, N.J. . . 31 Dec	X Arthur, I.D. . . . . 30 Jun	E Longbottom, C.J. . . 30 Jun
E George, S.A. . . . 31 Dec	X Clarke, G.K. . . . . 30 Jun	X Wilson, C.D. . . . . 30 Jun
X Pothecary, R.E. . . 31 Dec	E Lloyd, S.J. . . . . . 30 Jun	X Shrives, M.P. . . . . 30 Jun
E Stenhouse, N.J. . . 31 Dec	X Finney, M.E. . . . . 30 Jun	X Norris, R.J. . . . . 30 Jun
E Menlove-Platt, C.J. 31 Dec	X Mansergh, M.P. . . 30 Jun	E Evans, D.J. . . . . 30 Jun
S Harbour, J.R.M. . . 31 Dec	X Williams, I.R. . . . . 30 Jun	X Thomas, R.P. . . . . 30 Jun
E Lunn, J.F.C. . . . 31 Dec	X Archibald, B.R. . . . 30 Jun	X Westwood, M.W. . . 30 Jun
X Curd, T.A. . . . 31 Dec	E Gosden, S.R. . . . 30 Jun	X Gasson, N.S.C. . . . 30 Jun
I Allwood, C. . . . 31 Dec	X Zambellas, G.M. . . 30 Jun	X Thomas, G.C. . . . 30 Jun
I Trevithick, A.R. . . 31 Dec	E Baldwin, S.F. . . . 30 Jun	E Kenward, P.D. . . . 30 Jun
X Bosshardt, R.G. . . 31 Dec	E Gower, J.H.J. . . . 30 Jun	E Pendle, M.E.J. . . . 30 Jun
E Coulthard, J.K. . . 31 Dec	E Shaw, M.W.B. . . . 30 Jun	X Cunningham, T.A. . 30 Jun
X Churchill, T.C. . . 31 Dec	X Winstanley, K. . . . 30 Jun	S Walker, C.S. . . . . 30 Jun
E Parker, I.R. . . . 31 Dec	X Brown, M.K. . . . . 20 Sep	I Burrell, P.M. . . . . 30 Jun
X Cleary, S.P. . . . 31 Dec	X Gillanders, F.G.R. . . 08 Nov	X Stanley, N.P. . . . . 30 Jun
X Humphrys, J.A. . . 31 Dec	E Lea, J.H.A. . . . . 31 Dec	I Price, F.E.F. . . . . 30 Jun
X Edgell, J.N. . . . 31 Dec	X James, D.R. . . . . 31 Dec	E Young, S.S. . . . . 30 Jun
I Woodworth, G.P. . 31 Dec	X Brown, R.A.M. . . . 31 Dec	X Lander, M.C. . . . . 30 Jun
E Parry, R.W. . . . 31 Dec	I Wakeling, J.L. . . . 31 Dec	X Richards, C.M. . . . 30 Jun
E Hore, R.C. . . . . 31 Dec	S Whalley, S.D. . . . 31 Dec	E Rusbridger, R.C. . . 30 Jun
X Humphrey, D.A. . . 31 Dec	X Hosking, D.B. . . . 31 Dec	X Charlier, S.B. . . . . 30 Jun
S Marsh, D.J. . . . 31 Dec	W Salt, J.E. . . . . . 31 Dec	X Clarke, C.M.L. . . . 30 Jun
E Coverdale, A. . . . 31 Dec	E Parry, N.T. . . . . 31 Dec	E Jagger, P.R.A. . . . 30 Jun
E Costello, G.T. . . . 31 Dec	X Murgatroyd, A.C. . . 31 Dec	E Ham, D.W. . . . . 30 Jun
X Riley, M.J. . . . . 31 Dec	E Faulconbridge, D. . . 31 Dec	X Wallace, M.R.B. . . 30 Jun
S Crabtree, P.D. . . 31 Dec	X Sykes, S.J. . . . . 31 Dec	E Thompson, R.J. . . 30 Jun
X Richards, A.D. . . 31 Dec	X Hodson, W.M. . . . 31 Dec	X Westbrook, J.S. . . 30 Jun
X Weberstadt, R.R. . 31 Dec	S Dingle, J.C. . . . . 31 Dec	E Peach, G.L. . . . . 30 Jun
E Lister, S.R. . . . 31 Dec	X Fletcher, N.E. . . . 31 Dec	E Herridge, P.G. . . . 28 Nov
X Corder, I.F. . . . 31 Dec	X Davies, A.R. . . . . 31 Dec	W Muxworthy, A.M.B. . 31 Dec
E Keegan, W.J. . . . 31 Dec	E McElwaine, R.I. . . . 31 Dec	X Wain, R.N. . . . . . 31 Dec
X Jones, P.A. . . . 31 Dec	X Horne, T.K. . . . . 31 Dec	X Bourne, R.L. . . . . 31 Dec
	X Fraser, E. . . . . . 31 Dec	X Holmes, R. . . . . . 31 Dec
1994	X Evans, M.C. . . . . 31 Dec	E Cummin, M.A. . . . 31 Dec
X Long, P.J. . . . . . 30 Jun	E Powell, R.N. . . . . 31 Dec	E Smith, M.A. . . . . 31 Dec
S Cooper, S.N. . . . . 30 Jun	X Stallion, I.M. . . . . 31 Dec	E Spicer, C.G. . . . . 31 Dec
S Hatchard, P.J. . . . 30 Jun	E Peckham, D.R. . . . 31 Dec	X Doyne-Ditmas, P.S. . 31 Dec
E Fisher, M.A.L. . . . 30 Jun	X Ward, J.E. . . . . . 31 Dec	S Ireland, R.C. . . . . 31 Dec
X Stanley, C.E. . . . . 30 Jun	X Clark, K.I.M. . . . . 31 Dec	I Rodgers, N.P. . . . . 31 Dec
E Fox, K.A. . . . . . 30 Jun	X Wellesley, R.C.R. . . 31 Dec	E Sewry, M.R. . . . . 31 Dec
E Brockwell, P.E.N. . . 30 Jun	E Holberry, A.P. . . . 31 Dec	X Stonor, P.F.A. . . . 31 Dec
X Evans, D.M. . . . . 30 Jun	E Neave, C.B. . . . . 31 Dec	X Seatherton, E.F.K. . 31 Dec
E Usborne, C.M. . . . 30 Jun	X Stanford, J.H. . . . 31 Dec	E Penny, A.D. . . . . 31 Dec
S Forsyth, A.R. . . . . 30 Jun	X Burrows, M.J. . . . 31 Dec	I Burton, D.S. . . . . 31 Dec

X	Beaumont, I.H.	31 Dec	X	Keble, K.W.L.	31 Dec	X	Furness, S.B.	30 Jun
X	Harrap, N.R.E.	31 Dec	S	Bullock, M.P.	31 Dec	X	Halliday, D.A.	30 Jun
S	Storrs-Fox, R.N.	31 Dec	E	Watts, G.M.	31 Dec	E	Haley, T.J.	30 Jun
X	Davis-Marks, M.L.	31 Dec	X	Hudson, P.D.	31 Dec	S	Smith, M.	30 Jun
X	Douglas, C.F.	31 Dec	E	Johns, T.	31 Dec	X	Robinson, M.E.	30 Jun
X	Sillars, M.C.	31 Dec	X	Lowe, T.M.	31 Dec	X	Rycroft, A.E.	30 Jun
E	Powell, D.C.	31 Dec				X	Warren, B.H.	30 Jun
X	Best, R.R.	31 Dec		**1996**		E	Gourlay, J.S.	30 Jun
S	Keefe, P.C.	31 Dec	X	Nicholson, S.C.L.	30 Jun	X	Perkins, M.J.	30 Jun
E	Anderson, R.G.	31 Dec	E	Nixon, P.W.	30 Jun	X	Corrigan, N.R.	30 Jun
E	Forsey, C.R.	31 Dec	E	Farrington, S.P.	30 Jun	E	Da Gama, J.A.J.	30 Jun
X	O'Reilly, S.A.	31 Dec	E	Heritage, L.J.	30 Jun	S	Finlayson, A.G.	30 Jun
X	Harding, R.G.	31 Dec	X	Betteridge, J.T.	30 Jun	E	Taylor, J.J.	30 Jun
E	Holloway, J.T.	31 Dec	E	Ratcliffe, K.F.	30 Jun	X	Chick, S.J.	30 Jun
X	Murphie, J.D.D.	31 Dec	X	Langhorn, N.	30 Jun	X	Farrington, R.	30 Jun
E	Brunton, S.B.	31 Dec	X	Funnell, N.C.	30 Jun	E	Erskine, P.A.	30 Jun
E	Wyatt, S.P.	31 Dec	S	Hawkins, N.S.	30 Jun	S	King, C.E.W.	30 Jun
E	Fulford, J.P.H.	31 Dec	E	Price, J.P.	30 Jun	E	Beverstock, M.A.	30 Jun
X	Lambert, N.R.	31 Dec	X	Sibbit, N.T.	30 Jun			
X	Pegg, R.M.	31 Dec	E	Drake, E.D.	30 Jun			

LIEUTENANT COMMANDERS

	1972		X	Hadley, M.A.	01 May	S	Turton, T.M.H.	16 Nov
I	Davis, R.D.	09 Sep	X	Monkcom, K.M.	01 May	X	Peacock, A.S.	19 Nov
			X	Tremelling, A.J.	01 Jun	X	Grimsey, R.	05 Dec
	1974		E	Yates, D.A.	01 Jun			
E	Hewitt, I.K.	01 Mar	X	Roberts, D.C.K.	16 Jun		**1980**	
E	Lovelock, R.F.	01 Sep	X	Raine, P.A.W.	01 Sep	I	Anderson, B.	07 Jan
I	Foulger, R.J.	18 Sep	X	Willcocks, L.A.	16 Oct	I	Moult, R.M.	09 Jan
			X	Carleton, C.M.	01 Nov	E	Rampton, W.G.	17 Feb
	1975		X	Tibbits, C.S.	16 Nov	X	Fitzgerald, E.	01 Mar
I	Harbour, R.L.	16 Sep				X	Holloway, M.C.G.	01 Mar
I	Hosking, D.L.	18 Sep		**1979**		E	Allan, L.J.W.	16 Apr
			X	Benham, R.L.	01 Jan	E	Bumby, K.J.	16 Apr
	1976		X	Metcalf, H.N.	01 Jan	S	Potter, A.M.	16 Apr
E	Steinhausen, J.L.P	01 Mar	X	Wilson, D.M.MCG.	01 Jan	X	Pell, G.C.	01 May
I	Simm, G.W.G.	01 May	X	Jackson, S.	01 Jan	E	Stagg, K.A.	01 May
I	Stevenson, G.A.	01 May	X	Molyneux, S.D.	01 Feb	X	Hooker, C.J.	16 May
S	Fletcher, T.R.	01 May	E	Vale, P.D.	01 Mar	E	Stephenson, F.	16 May
E	Eitzen, R.P.	01 Nov	X	Harris, N.G.T.	01 Mar	X	Jones, R.B.	16 Jun
E	Sayer, P.W.	16 Dec	X	Hind, P.	01 Mar	X	Seward, D.R.	16 Jun
			S	Smith, J.	01 Mar	X	Robinson, J.O.	01 Jul
	1977		X	Hearnden, G.E.	01 Apr	X	Pharoah, R.J.	01 Aug
I	Elliott, M.P.	04 Jan	E	Crawford, J.V.	01 May	E	Sanders, A.W.T.	01 Aug
X	Hatton, H.F.	22 Feb	X	Foster, D.M.	01 May	X	Ives, D.M.	13 Aug
X	Scott, D.B.	01 Apr	X	Howse, R.D.	01 May	X	Churton, G.	01 Sep
X	Cockfield, F.B.	01 May	X	Hoyle, G.R.	01 May	X	Wrighton, C.R.	16 Sep
X	Hobbs, D.A.	01 Jul	X	Moodie, J.P.M.	01 May	X	O'Shaughnessy,	08 Oct
E	Jones, A.W.	01 Jul	E	Stanton, R.F.	01 May		F.W.G.	
X	Devine, J.G.	01 Jul	X	Rowell, M.F.	01 Jun	X	Hawkyard, N.J.K.	01 Nov
S	Napier, K.M.	01 Aug	S	Mulligan, I.D.	01 Jun	X	Williams, M.R.	01 Nov
S	Naish, A.J.W.	16 Aug	X	Spencer, M.	16 Jun	X	Black, A.G.C.	01 Nov
			X	Lynch, D.J.M.	01 Jul	X	Brimley, K.S.	01 Dec
	1978		X	Durnford, C.J.	01 Jul	E	Young, I.J.	16 Dec
X	de la Perrelle,	01 Jan	E	Milne, D.M.F.	16 Aug	X	Budd, P.R.	16 Dec
	J.P.		X	Cullen-Jones, H.	01 Sep			
E	Morley-Smith, N.H.	01 Feb	X	Bishop-Bailey, M.	16 Oct		**1981**	
E	Webb, R.E.	01 Feb	X	Hayes, N.H.	01 Nov	E	Bottomley, R.J.	01 Jan
X	Humphrys, N.B.	16 Feb	E	Buggy, M.W.	01 Nov	E	Kelly, D.B.	01 Jan
X	Carter, J.J.	01 Mar	E	Mitchell, B.A.	01 Nov	X	Brady, M.R.	16 Jan
X	Tennant, M.S.	01 Mar	E	Simmons, R.J.	01 Nov	X	Balfour, P.J.	16 Jan
X	Frazer, G.W.	01 Apr	E	Stephens, P.M.	16 Nov	X	Engeham, P.R.	16 Jan

X	Harper, S.A.	01 Feb
E	Pegden, C.	16 Feb
E	Ball, D.K.L.	01 Mar
X	Niven, G.D.	01 Mar
X	Cuming, B.H.D.	16 Mar
X	Rees, A.	19 Mar
X	Shipman, S.A.C.	01 Apr
X	Gent, R.M.	15 Apr
X	Barneby, V.J.	16 Apr
X	Langrishe, J.H.	16 Apr
E	Millard, C.G.	16 Apr
X	Milner, H.J.R.	16 Apr
I	Daly, J.E.	01 May
X	Towl, P.B.	01 May
X	Symonds, P.H.	16 May
X	McKellar, R.A.	01 Jun
X	Cheshire, M.	27 Jun
X	Richardson, J.B.	16 Jul
X	Thompson, C.R.	16 Jul
X	Woolston, A.J.	16 Jul
S	Screech, M.C.	01 Aug
S	Clinton, P.R.	11 Aug
X	Speller, R.A.	01 Sep
X	Read, R.H.	01 Sep
X	Rainbow, J.	14 Sep
E	Barber, T.A.	16 Sep
X	Evans, R.F.	16 Sep
X	Flynn, P.J.	31 Oct
X	Baker, P.C.M.	01 Nov
E	Budge, R.G.	01 Nov
S	Maguire, A.P.D.	01 Nov
X	Jones, B.S.	16 Nov
X	Beavis, J.W.	18 Nov
E	Howe, D.L.	23 Nov
E	Broadbent, A.	29 Nov
E	Moores, L.	01 Dec
X	Wheatley, P.L.	01 Dec
X	Rydiard, D.M.	01 Dec
E	Wain, K.D.	01 Dec
X	Archer, J.C.	08 Dec
E	White, G.L.	16 Dec

1982

X	Edwards, V.	01 Jan
X	Todd, D.	01 Jan
E	Murray, R.H.	01 Jan
S	Pearce, M.J.	01 Feb
X	Murphy, B.J.	16 Feb
E	Williams, C.C.	04 Mar
X	Iles, T.D.S.	16 Mar
E	Chadwick, G.E.	01 Apr
X	Bryce, D.C.	01 Apr
X	Dickinson, P.N.	01 May
X	Carter, T.L.	16 May
X	Riches, K.M.	01 Jun
E	Newling, N.F.L.	01 Jun
E	Warren, K.L.	01 Jun
E	Helby, P.F.H.	16 Jul
E	Ager, R.G.	01 Aug
X	Wraith, N.J.P.	09 Aug
X	Farmer, J.R.	16 Aug
X	Gwilliam, A.C.	01 Sep
I	Moore, G.J.	01 Sep
X	Baker, R.S.	10 Sep

E	Huggins, G.E.	15 Sep
E	Debenham, L.A.	20 Oct
X	Woodbridge, G.F.	01 Nov
X	Bent, G.R.	01 Nov
E	Shand, C.M.	01 Nov
X	Faulks, R.C.	16 Nov
X	Davis, F.J.	28 Nov
E	Kidd, C.J.C.	01 Dec
E	Fernihough, M.R.	08 Dec
S	Austin, S.J.	16 Dec

1983

S	Marshall, J.P.	01 Jan
E	Flockhart, D.N.	01 Jan
X	Toms, R.J.	16 Jan
X	Oakey, J.D.	30 Jan
S	Hepburn, J.	01 Feb
E	Sharp, C.E.F.	01 Feb
X	Long, D.R.	17 Feb
X	Luker, G.P.	01 Mar
S	Stuart, C.W.M.	01 Mar
X	Leyshon, B.S.	16 Mar
W	Rouse, J.R.D.	01 Apr
X	Port, L.A.	15 Apr
X	Jagger, C.E.	16 Apr
X	Sheldrake, T.W.	29 Apr
X	Gooder, S.P.	01 May
X	Felgate, H.	01 May
X	Brindley, K.	04 May
S	Livett, M.W.	16 May
E	Trott, P.A.	19 May
E	Prescott, J.	01 Jun
X	Nelson, T.B.	16 Jun
X	Wilson, R.	01 Jul
S	Hutchinson, T.S.	01 Jul
X	Cook, H.C.	10 Aug
X	Davies, I.H.	16 Oct
I	Melrose, J.	27 Oct
S	Johnson, P.R.	01 Nov
S	Mason, C.E.	16 Nov
X	Winchurch, M.R.G.	16 Nov

1984

X	Squibb, C.J.	16 Jan
X	Sinclair, A.B.	01 Feb
X	Thornton, C.E.	01 Feb
E	Robinson, D.I.	01 Feb
X	Thornton, M.C.	08 Feb
E	Noye, C.L.	21 Feb
X	Manchanda, K.S.	01 Mar
E	Robbins, J.G.	01 Mar
S	Redfearn, G.	01 Mar
X	Scruton, N.	16 Mar
E	Smith, A.C.	16 Mar
E	Aubrey-Rees, A.W.	16 Apr
X	Coley, K.	16 Apr
E	Lockwood, R.J.S.	19 Apr
X	Buckley, P.	01 May
S	Scott, R.M.	01 May
E	McDonald, J.J.B.	01 May
X	Will, A.W.	01 Jun
E	Dixon, R.F.	08 Jun
X	Fraser, D.K.	01 Jul
S	Petrie, M.J.	16 Jul

I	Jackson, M.A.	25 Jul
X	Fewtrell, M.	01 Sep
X	Walton, D.	01 Sep
X	Walton-Waters, L.D.	01 Sep
E	Lemon, R.G.A.	01 Sep
X	Partington, J.	01 Sep
X	Skelding, R.H.	01 Sep
X	Pilley, M.A.	16 Sep
S	Winn, D.	16 Sep
X	Cantello, D.J.	01 Nov
X	Easton, R.N.	16 Nov
E	Kelly, T.D.	16 Nov
S	Lister, J.S.	16 Nov
X	Woolliams, M.F.	01 Dec
X	King, N.A.	01 Dec
X	Jolly, J.E.I.	16 Dec

1985

S	Bryson, P.R.	16 Jan
X	Spens-Black, G.P.	16 Jan
X	Sharman, T.	16 Feb
X	Cook, W.J.	01 Mar
X	Ward, F.S.	01 Mar
X	Archdale, P.M.	16 Mar
X	Brown, P.R.	16 Mar
X	Wainwright, P.A.	16 Mar
X	Munday, I.V.	01 Apr
X	Brown, D.J.	01 Apr
S	Kelly, M.D.R.	01 Apr
X	Bebbington, S.P.	01 May
I	Gray, D.M.	01 May
X	Stone, C.R.M.	01 May
X	Bourn, K.E.	09 May
X	Buckley, M.J.	16 May
X	Jarrett, O.	22 May
E	Pilsworth, D.S.	01 Jun
S	Edwards, C.C.	01 Jul
S	Gopsill, B.R.	01 Jul
S	Jones, P.W.	01 Jul
X	Tidbury, N.	05 Jul
I	Parsons, P.K.C.	29 Jul
X	Wilson, C.G.T.	01 Aug
X	Edmonds, G.	02 Aug
X	McKay, P.A.	16 Aug
I	Hammond, N.J.	01 Sep
S	Craven, J.A.G.	01 Sep
E	Williams, S.J.	18 Oct
E	Lawton, A.C.R.	01 Nov
X	Butcher, M.C.	16 Nov
E	Robison, W.J.	25 Nov
E	Thomas, O.R.	01 Dec
E	Franks, J.P.	01 Dec
X	Barber, P.A.	01 Dec
I	Coulson, J.R.	08 Dec

1986

E	Nolton, J.R.	01 Feb
E	Davies, S.J.R.	01 Feb
X	Simmonds, D.C.	11 Feb
X	Alexander, G.E.	15 Feb
E	Carr, G.	06 Mar
S	Williams, D.H.	16 Mar
X	Gell, B.C.	01 Apr
S	Hayward, P.J.	01 Apr

S	Fishlock, G.N.	16 Apr	X	Hedgley, D.N.	01 Nov	X	Hirst, R.T.	01 Sep
E	Elsworth, R.K.	24 Apr	X	Gaskin, S.E.	01 Nov	X	Pretty, D.	16 Sep
X	Blair, S.R.	01 May	X	Allen, M.J.	01 Dec	X	Nail, V.A.	16 Sep
X	Waters, C.M.	01 May	X	Holmes, G.	01 Dec	X	Watt, S.	29 Sep
X	Evans, J.W.	06 May	X	Franks, K.B.	01 Dec	I	Dinham, A.C.	01 Oct
X	Watson, C.C.	16 May	E	Grafton, M.N.	01 Dec	E	Blake, M.J.	01 Oct
E	Carter, J.D.	01 Jun	E	Trotter, S.	01 Dec	E	Holt, A.F.	01 Oct
X	Kerry, J.T.	01 Jun				X	Brown, A.G.	01 Oct
X	Hudson, M.J.	14 Jun		**1988**		X	Wrigley, P.J.	16 Oct
X	Field, S.N.C.	01 Sep	X	Dismore, O.M.C.	01 Jan	S	Seddon, J.S.M.	16 Oct
X	Daykin, P.M.	09 Sep	E	Pask, R.G.	07 Jan	X	Broom, R.J.	16 Oct
X	Browning, M.L.C.	21 Sep	X	Wood, C.A.	09 Jan	E	Mullin, P.N.	01 Nov
W	Aitkenhead, G.G.	01 Oct	E	Leggett, S.E.	13 Jan	X	Lambert, K.J.	16 Nov
E	Livingstone, C.E.	01 Oct	E	Baker, G.R.	15 Jan	X	Smith, K.M.	16 Nov
E	Lewis, P.R.	21 Nov	E	Thompson, G.N.	25 Jan	E	Lofthouse, I.	01 Dec
X	Wells, D.A.H.	29 Nov	S	Billington, N.S.	01 Feb	E	Quine, N.J.	01 Dec
X	Forrester, T.R.	01 Dec	E	Edwards, A.D.P.	01 Feb	E	Gabriel, C.J.	01 Dec
S	Erskine, R.N.	16 Dec	X	Sharpe, G.J.	01 Feb	E	Gillam, R.L.	01 Dec
X	Wilkinson, A.J.	16 Dec	X	Prince, A.C.V.	16 Feb			
			E	Wombwell, J.F.	19 Feb		**1989**	
	1987		X	Pamphilon, M.J.	01 Mar	I	Windsor, M.	01 Jan
X	Chandler, S.A.	01 Jan	E	Honey, J.P.	01 Mar	X	Thomas, M.N.	01 Jan
X	Lewis, S.B.	01 Jan	X	McLaren, I.	16 Mar	S	Dwane, C.M.R.	01 Jan
X	Staveley, J.R.	01 Jan	X	Spencer, W.M.	01 Apr	X	Newlands, G.A.	01 Feb
X	Dobson, M.F.	01 Jan	X	Cross, M.G.	01 Apr	E	Tweed, C.J.	01 Feb
X	Smith, J.C.	06 Jan	X	Flower, R.W.	01 Apr	X	Gibbs, P.N.C.	01 Feb
E	Fiander, P.J.	01 Feb	E	Hudson, R.P.M.	01 Apr	E	Gill, P.F.	01 Feb
X	Dickens, M.G.C.	01 Feb	X	Nelson, D.E.	01 Apr	X	Searle, D.M.	01 Feb
S	Hattersley, J.P.G.	01 Feb	I	Sullivan, C.	01 Apr	E	Denison, A.R.V.T.	01 Feb
X	White, P.	01 Feb	E	Terry, J.M.	01 Apr	E	Jackson, S.M.	09 Feb
X	Taylor, N.F.	16 Feb	X	Horne, T.G.	01 Apr	S	Cass, P.S.	11 Feb
S	Painter, C.J.	23 Feb	E	Marsh, T.V.	01 Apr	E	Sexton, M.J.	19 Feb
I	Pye, M.F.	01 Mar	X	Malin, M.J.	01 Apr	X	Snook, R.E.	01 Mar
X	Davenport, G.M.	01 Mar	I	O'Brien, P.C.	23 Apr	X	Jefferis, I.M.	01 Mar
E	Maidment, K.C.	01 Mar	S	Nairn, R.	25 Apr	X	Ayres, C.P.	01 Mar
X	Gibson, T.A.	16 Mar	X	MacKett, D.G.	01 May	S	Charlton, C.R.A.M.	01 Mar
E	Brook, J.G.	21 Mar	I	Ridley Jones, B.D.	01 May	E	Daniels, T.C.	01 Mar
X	Harrison, R.F.	22 Mar	X	Johnson, B.	01 May	E	Van Beek, D.	01 Mar
W	Fletcher, P.J.	01 Apr	X	Speller, N.S.F.	01 May	X	Balston, D.C.W.	08 Mar
X	Creates, K.I.	01 Apr	I	Robinson, A.	06 May	E	Enticknap, K.	10 Mar
X	Reynolds, C.H.	01 Apr	I	Evans, M.A.	17 May	X	O'riordan, M.P.	01 Apr
X	Jenks, A.W.J.	16 Apr	X	Evans, R.D.	01 Jun	E	Boreham, N.E.	01 Apr
X	Field, J.D.	16 Apr	E	Hartley, P.T.	01 Jun	E	Cartwright, R.A.	01 Apr
X	Sandover, R.J.	20 Apr	X	Little, N.R.	01 Jun	X	Pollitt, D.N.A.	01 Apr
X	MacNaughton, F.G.	01 May	E	Nurse, M.T.	01 Jun	X	Baudains, T.J.	01 Apr
X	Durbin, C.J.	01 May	X	Lambert, B.	02 Jun	E	Johnstone, I.S.	01 Apr
E	Brooking, S.J.	11 May	E	Mawson, A.J.	02 Jun	E	Spalding, R.E.H.	01 Apr
X	Martin, N.D.	01 Jun	E	Appleyard, T.P.	05 Jun	X	Taylor, C.D.	01 Apr
E	Kirk, T.L.	01 Jun	X	Woznicki, S.J.	16 Jun	X	Taylor, N.G.	01 Apr
X	Brown, S.J.J.	16 Jun	X	Low, I.A.D.	01 Jul	E	Walters, S.G.	01 Apr
E	Edmonds, A.J.	01 Jul	E	Waterman, J.H.	01 Jul	E	Whitaker, M.J.	01 Apr
E	Hunter, K.P.	01 Aug	S	Clark, R.W.	01 Jul	X	Foale, S.J.	01 Apr
X	Lee, D.J.	01 Aug	X	Davis, M.P.	01 Jul	X	Hutchings, P.W.	01 Apr
X	Peters, A.J.U.	01 Aug	I	Ash, J.S.	15 Jul	E	Lovett, M.J.	01 Apr
E	Fyfe, N.H.	11 Aug	S	Stobie, I.C.A.	28 Jul	X	Hamp, C.J.	16 Apr
X	Chapman, L.A.	01 Sep	X	Jennings, P.J.	01 Aug	S	Cushen, A.E.	16 Apr
I	Stillwell, A.J.	01 Sep	E	Braithwaite, A.C.G.	01 Aug	S	Ramsey, J.S.	16 Apr
I	Woodman, C.A.	01 Sep	E	Middlemas, S.R.	01 Aug	E	Cooper, P.F.	21 Apr
E	Butler, B.P.	01 Sep	X	Adams, R.J.	01 Aug	I	Newman, P.H.	01 May
E	Newton, M.R.	22 Sep	E	Boyes, N.	11 Aug	E	Vallis, R.W.	01 May
X	Goddard, D.J.S.	01 Oct	I	Ewers, A.M.	20 Aug	E	Carver, A.G.	01 May
E	Palmer, J.E.	01 Oct	I	Kirkwood, N.C.	01 Sep	E	Greenwood, S.	01 May
W	Melville-Brown, P.G.	01 Oct	I	Nelms, M.J.	01 Sep	X	Joyner, A.	01 May
			X	Scott, P.H.	01 Sep	X	Page, S.P.	01 May

X	Kent, M.D.	01 May
X	Yates, N.P.	01 Jun
E	Davey, P.J.	01 Jun
E	Wrightson, H.M.	01 Jun
E	Marshall, J.N.	01 Jun
S	Burton, N.J.	16 Jun
S	Almond, D.E.M.	01 Jul
E	Holmes-Mackie, N.W.	01 Jul
X	Trundle, N.R.E.	01 Jul
E	Jackson, S.H.	01 Jul
X	Palmer, P.A.	01 Jul
X	Thomas, C.C.	01 Jul
X	Phillips, J.R.	09 Jul
E	Hawkins, I.	12 Jul
E	Harman, D.J.	18 Jul
E	Hall, S.M.	01 Aug
E	Clark, D.K.	01 Aug
E	Derrick, G.G.J.	01 Aug
E	Faulkner, R.I.	01 Aug
E	Torvell, M.D.B.	01 Aug
X	Watson, R.J.	01 Aug
X	Boast, M.T.	01 Sep
I	Bridger, D.W.	01 Sep
I	Straughan, H.	01 Sep
S	Lewis, G.D.	01 Sep
X	Moores, J.K.	01 Sep
E	Penniston, J.R.	01 Sep
E	Watson, R.P.	01 Sep
X	Wainwright, B.G.	01 Sep
X	Jardine, G.A.	16 Sep
E	Sherwin, S.A.	01 Oct
E	Williams, R.C.	01 Oct
E	Mant, J.N.	01 Oct
X	Carroll, P.W.M.	01 Oct
E	Dodgson, S.J.	03 Oct
E	Parsonage, R.J.	07 Oct
X	Grimley, D.M.J.	01 Nov
X	Turner, N.J.	01 Nov
X	Ross, B.J.	16 Nov
X	Baileff, R.I.	01 Dec
E	Davies, T.G.	01 Dec
X	Handley, J.M.	01 Dec
X	Lambourn, P.N.	01 Dec
X	Livingstone, D.L.H.	01 Dec
E	Watson, D.R.	01 Dec
S	Church, A.D.	28 Dec

1990

I	Foster, M.A.	01 Jan
X	Lade, C.J.	01 Jan
X	Wood, P.R.	01 Jan
E	McLennan, R.G.	01 Jan
E	Fincham, B.E.	01 Jan
X	Steeds, S.M.	01 Jan
X	Wade, N.C.	01 Jan
E	Merriman, P.O.	01 Jan
S	Large, J.L.	17 Jan
X	Croome-Carroll, M.P.J.	27 Jan
X	Knight, A.W.	01 Feb
X	Stewart, R.G.	01 Feb
E	Whiteley, N.S.	01 Feb
E	Duffield, G.G.	01 Feb
X	Pomfrett, N.J.	01 Feb

X	Sadler, C.J.	01 Feb
X	Little, C.S.A.	01 Feb
E	Hadfield, D.	14 Feb
X	Beats, K.A.	16 Feb
S	Lewis, S.	16 Feb
S	Rees, J.H.	16 Feb
S	Fleming, A.M.	24 Feb
X	Leaney, M.J.	01 Mar
X	Drewett, R.E.	01 Mar
E	Peck, I.J.	01 Mar
E	Wilson, K.P.	01 Mar
X	Wood, J.N.A.	01 Mar
S	Spiller, M.F.	01 Mar
X	Kerr, W.M.M.	09 Mar
X	Edney, A.R.	01 Apr
X	Kirkwood, J.A.D.	01 Apr
X	Rimmer, M.	01 Apr
X	Currie, D.W.	01 Apr
X	Britton, N.J.	01 Apr
E	Fowler, P.J.S.	01 Apr
E	Graham, G.R.	01 Apr
E	Page, D.M.	01 Apr
X	Thompson, P.W.	01 Apr
X	Cochrane, M.C.N.	01 Apr
E	Dickinson, R.J.	01 Apr
X	Griffiths, D.T.	01 Apr
X	Boraston, P.J.	01 Apr
X	Harrison, P.M.	16 Apr
S	Gorsuch, P.G.	16 Apr
E	Philebrown, S.R.	23 Apr
E	Lewis, D.M.J.	26 Apr
I	Chapple, C.P.	01 May
E	Menzies, A.J.	01 May
X	Barker, N.J.	01 May
X	Brooksbank, R.J.	01 May
X	Hall, C.N.	01 May
X	Chapman, N.J.	01 May
X	Labone, R.D.	01 May
I	Rudman, C.J.	15 May
S	Cropper, M.A.K.	16 May
E	O'Reilly, T.M.	27 May
X	Clegg, M.L.	01 Jun
X	Howarth, D.W.	01 Jun
E	Perry-Evans, S.P.A.	01 Jun
S	Bruce, J.F.	01 Jun
X	Newton, D.J.	01 Jun
X	Chapple, J.C.B.	01 Jun
E	Baker, A.P.	01 Jul
E	Jackman, A.W.	01 Jul
X	White, M.W.	01 Jul
E	Blake, G.E.	01 Jul
E	Howard, K.A.	01 Jul
E	Tindall-Jones, L.D.	01 Jul
E	Hunter, B.J.	01 Jul
X	Chatwin, N.J.	01 Jul
X	Haley, C.W.	01 Jul
E	Orridge, S.K.	01 Jul
E	Plant, I.R.	01 Jul
X	Pringle, A.	01 Jul
E	Selwyn, P.D.	01 Jul
X	Lightfoot, C.D.	01 Jul
X	Pearey, M.S.	01 Jul
X	Thicknesse, P.J.	01 Jul
X	Finnemore, R.A.	09 Jul

X	Gaunt, N.R.	16 Jul
X	Bruggenwirth, S.J.A.	01 Aug
X	Buckland, R.J.F.	01 Aug
E	Jolliffe, G.E.	01 Aug
X	Wass, M.J.	01 Aug
X	Morgan, P.T.	01 Aug
X	Morton, C.P.	01 Aug
X	Mayhew, N.M.	16 Aug
X	Percharde, M.R.	16 Aug
E	Russell, S.J.	22 Aug
I	Mason, N.H.	28 Aug
I	Davies, C.S.	01 Sep
X	Spence, N.A.	01 Sep
X	Mathias-Jones, P.D.	01 Sep
E	Carpenter, C.J.	01 Sep
E	Curnow, M.D.	01 Sep
X	Hughes, N.J.	01 Sep
X	Murphy, N.	01 Sep
S	Bostock, C.E.	09 Sep
I	Dawson, S.L.	12 Sep
E	Johnson, W.C.	30 Sep
X	Riches, I.C.	01 Oct
X	Chichester, M.A.R.	01 Oct
X	Clayton, R.J.	01 Oct
E	Dearden, S.R.	01 Oct
E	Main, E.S.	01 Oct
E	Robertson, D.C.	01 Oct
X	Robinson, J.S.	01 Oct
S	Tinsley, G.N.	01 Oct
X	Bell, R.P.W.	01 Oct
E	Ellis, R.W.	01 Oct
E	Slawson, J.M.	01 Oct
E	Wyatt, J.M.	01 Oct
X	Worsley, W.	01 Oct
E	Hogan, D.	19 Oct
E	McKenzie, D.	31 Oct
X	Roper, M.	01 Nov
E	Perry, R.	01 Nov
E	Gray, A.J.	01 Nov
X	Taylor, K.A.	01 Nov
X	Stewart, A.C.	01 Dec
X	Straughan, C.J.	01 Dec
E	Moreland, M.J.	01 Dec
X	Corner, G.C.	01 Dec
X	Evans, G.R.	01 Dec
E	Fear, R.K.	01 Dec
E	Maw, M.J.	01 Dec
X	Snowball, S.J.	01 Dec
E	Walton, J.C.	01 Dec
E	Starks, M.R.	01 Dec
S	Owen, E.B.	10 Dec
X	Ferguson, R.G.	12 Dec

1991

W	Hawes, G.E.	01 Jan
X	Ewence, M.W.	01 Jan
X	Neil, S.J.	01 Jan
X	Alexander, R.S.	01 Jan
X	Ovens, J.J.	01 Jan
E	MacDonald, A.I.	01 Jan
E	Kerchey, S.J.V.	20 Jan
E	Edmondson, J.C.	27 Jan
X	Belgeonne, D.P.J.	01 Feb

E	Ranson, C.D.	01 Feb	X	Gomm, K.	01 Jun	X	Minns, P.F.	01 Nov
S	Graham, J.E.	01 Feb	X	Hartley, D.	01 Jun	X	Lovell, D.J.	16 Nov
S	Kingsbury, J.A.T.	01 Feb	E	James, C.	01 Jun	X	Hugo, I.D.	01 Dec
I	Taylor, S.A.	01 Feb	E	Jones, D.C.	01 Jun	I	Body, H.J.	01 Dec
X	Tighe, G.	01 Feb	E	Maltby, M.R.J.	01 Jun	X	Metcalfe, A.P.W.	01 Dec
X	Tilley, D.S.J.	01 Feb	X	Malcolm, S.R.	01 Jun	X	Barker, R.D.J.	01 Dec
E	White, P.J.	01 Feb	X	Potts, D.L.	01 Jun	X	Brand, S.M.	01 Dec
X	Woods, R.P.	01 Feb	X	Turner, D.	03 Jun	S	Cunningham, P.	01 Dec
X	Marchant, T.A.C.	01 Feb	E	Gibson, A.	08 Jun	X	Garrett, S.W.	01 Dec
X	MacKay, G.A.	01 Feb	S	Isaac, P.	10 Jun	E	Mason, A.H.	01 Dec
S	Radcliffe, N.	16 Feb	E	Plant, M.G.	13 Jun	X	McHale, G.J.	01 Dec
E	Holdsworth, H.W.	17 Feb	I	Lacey, I.N.	16 Jun	S	Redstone, C.	12 Dec
E	Amor, B.J.	01 Mar	X	Wolfe, D.E.	16 Jun			
X	Clark, A.W.C.	01 Mar	I	Sephton, J.R.	17 Jun		**1992**	
E	Welburn, R.S.	01 Mar	E	Jones, M.R.	01 Jul	I	Basson, A.P.	01 Jan
E	Darwent, A.	01 Mar	E	Stewart, R.W.	01 Jul	I	Greene, M.J.	01 Jan
S	Faulks, D.J.	01 Mar	E	Crossley, C.C.	01 Jul	I	Masters, R.H.	01 Jan
E	Newell, J.M.	01 Mar	X	Robertson, K.F.	01 Jul	X	Morse, A.C.	01 Jan
S	Pike, M.S.	01 Mar	X	Smith, N.P.	01 Jul	I	Price, T.W.	01 Jan
X	Scarth, W.	01 Mar	X	Lilley, D.J.	01 Jul	X	Whitby, S.	01 Jan
E	Schmidt, J.F.K.	01 Mar	X	McBarnet, T.F.	01 Jul	X	Williams, S.P.	01 Jan
E	Thistlethwaite, M.H.	01 Mar	X	Faulkner, J.J.	05 Jul	X	Broadley, K.J.	01 Jan
E	Treanor, M.A.	01 Mar	S	Richardson, M.P.	16 Jul	X	Hadnett, E.R.	01 Jan
X	Backhouse, J.R.	01 Mar	S	Tulley, J.R.	16 Jul	X	Tuppen, R.M.	01 Jan
X	Eedle, R.J.	01 Mar	X	Clarke, N.J.	28 Jul	E	Atkinson, S.R.	01 Jan
E	Parker, M.N.	01 Mar	E	Davies, J.L.	01 Aug	I	Gordon, D.	09 Jan
S	White, S.N.	16 Mar	S	Grindell, M.J.	01 Aug	X	The Duke Of York,	01 Feb
S	Lynch, M.	24 Mar	E	Van Berkel, J.G.	01 Aug		H.R.H.	
X	Crowther, K.W.	29 Mar	E	Wills, A.G.	05 Aug			
X	Henderson, T.M.P.	01 Apr	E	Cochrane, M.D.	09 Aug	X	Drylie, A.J.	01 Feb
X	Dobson, R.A.	01 Apr	X	Hodgkiss, L.	11 Aug	X	Potts, K.M.	01 Feb
X	Cassar, A.P.F.	01 Apr	X	Donaldson, S.B.	01 Sep	X	Smith, S.L.	01 Feb
X	Dunlop, P.F.	01 Apr	I	Greenwood, M.J.	01 Sep	E	Argent-Hall, D.	01 Feb
E	Ellin, A.D.S.	01 Apr	X	Lawson, S.J.	01 Sep	E	Bisson, I.J.P.	01 Feb
E	Gascoyne, D.J.	01 Apr	X	Leaning, M.V.	01 Sep	X	Flanagan, M.E.A.	01 Feb
S	Moxey, D.E.	01 Apr	I	MacKay, C.R.	01 Sep	E	Jenkin, A.M.H.	01 Feb
X	Newton, G.A.	01 Apr	X	Millward, J.	01 Sep	X	Johnson, A.S.	01 Feb
X	Roberts, D.H.W.	01 Apr	I	Stidston, I.J.	01 Sep	X	Pickthall, D.N.	01 Feb
E	Sunderland, J.D.	01 Apr	E	Canty, N.R.	01 Sep	X	Tarrant, R.K.	01 Feb
X	Buckley, P.J.A.	01 Apr	E	Ball, M.P.	01 Sep	X	Trathen, N.C.	01 Feb
E	Stanley-Whyte, B.J.	01 Apr	S	Lloyd, D.P.J.	01 Sep	E	Vandome, A.M.	01 Feb
X	Kelly, R.	03 Apr	E	Clark, A.N.	01 Sep	S	Emerton, M.S.	01 Feb
S	Barnwell, K.L.	23 Apr	E	Paley, I.D.	01 Sep	E	Baker, P.G.	01 Feb
I	Edwards, P.J.	01 May	E	Dumbell, P.	01 Sep	E	Dolton, A.	01 Feb
I	Trewhella, G.G.	01 May	E	Shaw, I.B.	15 Sep	I	Morgan, A.K.G.	06 Feb
X	Naismith, D.H.	01 May	X	Radmore, K.V.	23 Sep	E	White, P.A.	16 Feb
I	Newton, B.J.	01 May	I	Harper, R.J.	25 Sep	X	Moss, P.	18 Feb
X	Stenhouse, R.C.	01 May	X	Carrington-Wood,	01 Oct	X	Layland, S.	01 Mar
E	Barclay, J.H.B.	01 May		C.G.		X	Young, S.A.	01 Mar
X	Baum, S.R.	01 May	X	Graham, D.E.	01 Oct	X	Blakey, A.L.	01 Mar
S	Beard, G.T.C.	01 May	I	Corbett, W.R.	01 Oct	X	Connolly, C.J.	01 Mar
E	Long, N.A.	01 May	X	Williams, M.H.	01 Oct	E	Downing, C.W.	01 Mar
X	MacDonald, G.D.	01 May	X	Chalmers, D.P.	01 Oct	E	Dullage, B.	01 Mar
S	Pattinson, I.H.	01 May	X	Holman, G.C.	01 Oct	E	Parsons, C.G.	01 Mar
X	Pickles, I.S.	01 May	X	Matthews, D.N.	01 Oct	E	Short, G.C.	01 Mar
E	Quaye, D.T.G.	01 May	E	Moss, A.D.	06 Oct	X	Wilson, G.L.	01 Mar
E	Quick, N.H.	01 May	E	Birchall, S.J.	21 Oct	S	Watt, G.N.D.	01 Apr
X	Richmond, I.J.M.	01 May	E	Haworth, J.	25 Oct	X	Abraham, P.	01 Apr
E	Fry, J.M.S.	01 May	I	Lewis, N.M.	27 Oct	X	Hatch, G.W.H.	01 Apr
I	Pett, J.G.	03 May	X	Bean, M.S.	27 Oct	X	Knight, D.A.	01 Apr
S	Pearce, M.L.	16 May	X	Burden, J.C.	01 Nov	E	Mundin, A.J.	01 Apr
E	Stott, J.A.	26 May	X	Cunningham, R.A.	01 Nov	E	Parsons, S.C.	01 Apr
E	Griffiths, D.M.	01 Jun	X	Key, D.F.	01 Nov	X	Pugsley, D.A.	01 Apr
E	Gibson, D.T.	01 Jun	X	Bernau, J.C.	01 Nov	E	Tigwell, N.K.	01 Apr
						S	Blain, R.G.	01 Apr

X McDonnell, P.W. . . 01 Apr	X Ameye, C.R. . . . . 01 Aug	X Walker, N.L. . . . . 01 Feb
E Wiles, S.J. . . . . . 01 Apr	E Snoxall, P.J. . . . . 01 Aug	X Ancona, S.J. . . . . 01 Feb
I Townshend, J.J. . . 03 Apr	E Kirby, S.C. . . . . . 01 Aug	E Cargen, M.R. . . . 01 Feb
X Powell, S. . . . . . 16 Apr	E Randall, R.D. . . . 01 Aug	X Chesterman, G.J. . . 01 Feb
X Brigden, K.W. . . . 16 Apr	E Sennitt, J.W. . . . . 01 Aug	E Parsons, B.R. . . . 01 Feb
I Reynolds, T.E. . . 01 May	E Calvert, G. . . . . . 01 Aug	X Reid, C.I. . . . . . 01 Feb
I Davis, B.C. . . . 01 May	X West, M.W. . . . . 05 Aug	E Strick, C.G. . . . . 01 Feb
S Crook, A.S. . . . 01 May	E Michie, A.R. . . . . 26 Aug	E Upton, I.D. . . . . 01 Feb
I Spencer, E.A. . . 01 May	E Blowers, M.D. . . . 01 Sep	E Hornby, W.F. . . . 03 Feb
E Marmont, K.L. . . 01 May	X Doyle, G.L. . . . . 01 Sep	S Laws, P.E.A. . . . 16 Feb
X Jenkin, J.R.S.L. . . 01 May	I Warden, J.M. . . . . 01 Sep	E Claxton, M.G. . . . 18 Feb
E Deaney, M.N. . . 01 May	E Chidley, T.J. . . . . 01 Sep	E Dustan, A.J. . . . . 19 Feb
X Deighton, D.S. . . 01 May	E John, G.D. . . . . . 01 Sep	S Fergusson, H.J. . . 01 Mar
E Dorey, P.H. . . . 01 May	E Morris, N.J. . . . . 01 Sep	X Hall, N.J. . . . . . 01 Mar
X Evans, K.N.M. . . 01 May	E Naden, A.C.K. . . . 01 Sep	X Muir, K. . . . . . . 01 Mar
S Hughes, G.L. . . . 01 May	E King, P.C. . . . . . 01 Sep	X Wakefield, G.M. . . 01 Mar
E Kennedy, N.H. . . 01 May	E Thompson, S.J. . . 01 Sep	X Fortescue, R.C. . . 01 Mar
X Lloyd, P.R. . . . . 01 May	X Mardon, K.F. . . . 02 Sep	E Ryan, D.G. . . . . 01 Mar
E O'Neill, P.J. . . . 01 May	S Thomas, F.S. . . . 12 Sep	E Jones, A.R.T. . . . 01 Mar
E Plant, J.N.M. . . . 01 May	X King, R.W. . . . . 16 Sep	S Chilman, P.W.H. . . 01 Mar
X Roberts, D.A. . . . 01 May	I Pope, C.M. . . . . 16 Sep	X Hall, A.P. . . . . . 01 Mar
X Giles, K.D.L. . . . 01 May	X Greenfield, D.P. . . 21 Sep	E Harvey, C.A. . . . . 01 Mar
E Green, A.R. . . . . 01 May	I Risley, J. . . . . . . 01 Oct	X Lemkes, P.D. . . . 01 Mar
E Shipperley, I. . . . 01 May	I Suddes, L.A. . . . . 01 Oct	E Loring, A. . . . . . 01 Mar
E Bone, C.J. . . . . 01 May	S Davies, J.P. . . . . 01 Oct	E Pratt, I.H. . . . . . 01 Mar
E Martin, M.T. . . . 12 May	X Harriman, M. . . . . 01 Oct	E Thomas, D.G. . . . 01 Mar
E Abbey, M.K. . . . 16 May	E Woodcock, S.J. . . 01 Oct	X West, G.R. . . . . . 01 Mar
X Bromige, T.R.J. . . 19 May	X Parr, M.J. . . . . . 01 Oct	E Jones, R.W. . . . . 01 Mar
E Clarke, R.D. . . . 27 May	E Braham, S.W. . . . 01 Oct	X Mair, B. . . . . . . 05 Mar
X Williams, D.I. . . . 29 May	X Blunden, J.J.F. . . . 01 Oct	S Murdoch, S.J. . . . 16 Mar
X Ingram, R.G. . . . 01 Jun	I Farrage, M.E. . . . 01 Nov	S Cooter, M.P. . . . . 16 Mar
E Lambert, J.E.H. . . 01 Jun	X Garratt, M.D. . . . 01 Nov	E Cadogan, B.H. . . . 30 Mar
X Abbott, S.S.C. . . . 01 Jun	E Grieve, S.H. . . . . 01 Nov	X Middlebrook, M.S. . 30 Mar
E Burdett, R.W. . . . 01 Jun	X Powell, R.L. . . . . 01 Nov	X Goodall, A.M. . . . 01 Apr
E Peacock, S. . . . . 01 Jun	E Steel, A.J. . . . . . 03 Nov	X Race, N.J. . . . . . 01 Apr
E Wise, S.D. . . . . 01 Jun	X Taylor, L.G. . . . . 15 Nov	E Crago, P.T. . . . . 01 Apr
E Barratt, J.D.B. . . . 01 Jun	E Sykes, M. . . . . . 16 Nov	E Curnow, I.F. . . . . 01 Apr
E Bridger, R.J. . . . 01 Jun	S O'Grady, M.J. . . . 16 Nov	X Hobbs, A.R. . . . . 01 Apr
X Emmerson, G.J. . . 01 Jun	X Hardy, L.C. . . . . 01 Dec	S Lister, S.R. . . . . 01 Apr
S Murphy, J. . . . . 01 Jun	X Carden, P.D. . . . . 01 Dec	X Osbourn, S.E.J. . . 01 Apr
X Blazeby, N.J. . . . 01 Jun	X Hodgkins, J.M. . . . 01 Dec	X Price, D.J. . . . . . 01 Apr
X Bell, A.S. . . . . . 01 Jun	X Howorth, K. . . . . 01 Dec	E Simmons, N.D. . . . 01 Apr
E Morris, P.J. . . . . 10 Jun	S Tothill, N.M. . . . . 01 Dec	E Tulloch, F.M. . . . 01 Apr
X Thomas, W.G. . . . 16 Jun	X Alcock, C. . . . . . 16 Dec	E Fogg, D.S. . . . . 01 Apr
X Martin, C.J. . . . . 16 Jun	X Harris, A.I. . . . . . 16 Dec	X Ireland, A.R. . . . . 01 Apr
X Knibbs, M. . . . . . 19 Jun		X Fraser, T.P. . . . . 01 Apr
E Cheesman, C.J. . . 28 Jun	**1993**	E Hodgson, T.C. . . . 01 Apr
X Petheram, M.J. . . 29 Jun	X Bilson, J.M.F. . . . 01 Jan	E Payne, R.C. . . . . 16 Apr
X Jervis, N.D. . . . . 01 Jul	I Howells, J. . . . . . 01 Jan	S Drabble, R.C. . . . 16 Apr
X Shaw, P.A.G. . . . 01 Jul	X Northwood, G.R. . . 01 Jan	X Greenwood, P. . . . 29 Apr
X Sheehan, M.A. . . . 01 Jul	X Hawthorne, M.J. . . 01 Jan	I Pearce, K. . . . . . 01 May
X Jones, L. . . . . . 01 Jul	S Gray, R.S. . . . . . 01 Jan	S Bond, N.D. . . . . 01 May
X Jones, P. . . . . . 01 Jul	E Ramshaw, G.W.L. . 01 Jan	X Fitter, I.S.T. . . . . 01 May
X Phillips, M.J. . . . . 01 Jul	X Smart, I. . . . . . . 01 Jan	X McCartain, M.B.W. . 01 May
E Tarr, B.S. . . . . . 01 Jul	X Woolley, M.J. . . . . 01 Jan	X Warlow, M.R.N. . . 01 May
X Cree, M.C. . . . . 01 Jul	E Raybould, A.G. . . . 01 Jan	X Dodds, R.S. . . . . 01 May
X McKendrick, A.M. . 01 Jul	X Kings, S.J.N. . . . . 01 Jan	E Green, S.N. . . . . 01 May
X Davey, P.F. . . . . 04 Jul	X Morse, J.A. . . . . 01 Jan	X Horn, P.B. . . . . . 01 May
S Lockwood, I.T. . . 08 Jul	S Teasdale, R.M. . . . 16 Jan	X Smith, R.W.R. . . . 01 May
X Barnes-Yallowley, . 16 Jul	X Roberts, I.T. . . . . 18 Jan	E Westlake, A.J. . . . 01 May
J.J.H.	E Baker, S.V. . . . . 21 Jan	E Carter, A.F.R. . . . 01 May
X Leedham, H.N. . . 16 Jul	X Scott, R.J. . . . . . 26 Jan	X Hall, R.L. . . . . . 01 May
S Flanagan, J. . . . . 16 Jul	X Baines, M.D. . . . . 01 Feb	E Elford, D.G. . . . . 01 May
S Giles, A.R. . . . . . 21 Jul	X Langley, E.S. . . . 01 Feb	X Lacey, S.P. . . . . . 16 May

X	McNeile, R.H.	16 May
S	Mellor, B.J.	16 May
X	Durkin, M.T.G.	01 Jun
E	Hay, J.D.	01 Jun
E	Tarran, M.R.M.	01 Jun
X	Witton, J.W.	01 Jun
E	Sutton, G.D.	01 Jun
X	Collier, A.S.	01 Jun
X	Hayes, S.J.	01 Jun
E	King, E.M.	01 Jun
S	Simpson, I.H.	01 Jun
E	Murdoch, A.W.	01 Jun
I	Sneyd, E.P.B.	20 Jun
X	Bennett, G.L.N.	01 Jul
X	Brown, H.S.	01 Jul
E	Giles, D.W.	01 Jul
E	Grantham, S.M.	01 Jul
X	Hopper, S.O.	01 Jul
E	Martyn, A.W.	01 Jul
S	Morton, N.P.B.	01 Jul
X	Russell, T.	01 Jul
X	Aiken, S.R.	01 Jul
X	McNaughton, J.A.	01 Jul
E	Gray, A.J.	01 Jul
X	Shield, S.J.	01 Jul
E	Smithson, P.E.	01 Jul
X	King, J.N.G.	01 Jul
E	Whittaker, N.J.	01 Jul
X	French, K.L.	09 Jul
X	Hussey, S.J.	15 Jul
X	Harris, S.L.	16 Jul
S	Litchfield, J.F.	16 Jul
E	Walter, P.G.	23 Jul
X	Acton, J.S.	01 Aug
X	Ashcroft, C.	01 Aug
X	Cook, P.R.	01 Aug
E	Nottley, N.R.	01 Aug
X	Robinson, C.E.T.	01 Aug
X	Surgey, I.C.	01 Aug
X	Tarrant, D.C.	01 Aug
S	Wiltcher, R.A.	01 Aug
E	Burnip, J.M.	01 Aug
E	Tarr, R.N.V.	01 Aug
E	Morris, A.J.	01 Aug
E	Oakley, N.G.	01 Aug
X	McMichael-Phillips, S.J.	01 Aug
E	Gulley, T.J.	01 Aug
X	Green, D.P.	13 Aug
S	Atherton, M.J.	20 Aug
I	Davies, J.H.	01 Sep
X	Godfrey, K.R.	01 Sep
I	Smith, M.R.K.	01 Sep
I	Stewart, J.N.	01 Sep
S	Hayden, S.C.	01 Sep
E	Knight, P.R.	01 Sep
E	Vanderpump, D.J.	01 Sep
X	Landrock, G.J.	01 Sep
X	Sutton, G.B.	01 Sep
E	McCormick, J.P.	20 Sep
I	Mills, T.C.	01 Oct
I	Franks, P.D.	01 Oct
X	Davies, C.J.	01 Oct
X	Jones, M.C.	01 Oct
X	Watts, A.P.	01 Oct
X	Acland, D.D.	01 Oct
E	Hooley, R.G.	01 Oct
X	Moore, C.I.	01 Oct
E	Shirley, W.P.	12 Oct
X	Mitchell, H.G.M.	16 Oct
S	Walker, C.L.	16 Oct
X	James, C.W.	27 Oct
S	Batty, M.J.	01 Nov
X	Chapman, D.B.J.	01 Nov
X	Cobb, D.R.	01 Nov
X	Conway, J.J.	01 Nov
S	Taylor, S.M.	01 Nov
X	Williams, A.P.	01 Nov
E	Moffatt, N.R.	01 Nov
X	Raisbeck, P.T.	01 Nov
X	Wyatt, D.J.	01 Nov
S	Flynn, M.T.	01 Nov
X	Kelbie, E.	01 Nov
X	Howell, S.B.	01 Nov
E	Lewis, J.K.	01 Nov
X	Peel, G.R.	01 Nov
X	Elvin, A.J.	06 Nov
E	Godber, S.	24 Nov
X	Cooper, S.J.	01 Dec
X	Gladwell, T.J.	01 Dec
X	Kenny, S.J.	01 Dec
E	Danbury, I.G.	01 Dec
X	Cunningham, J.G.	01 Dec
X	Entwistle, S.C.	01 Dec
S	Forer, T.J.	01 Dec
S	Skidmore, C.M.	01 Dec
X	Smallman, L.D.	01 Dec
S	Spence, A.B.	16 Dec

1994

I	Adams, P.	01 Jan
X	McGrenary, A.	01 Jan
X	Pettitt, G.W.	01 Jan
X	Ventura, D.C.	01 Jan
S	Watts, A.D.	01 Jan
X	Brown, W.C.	01 Jan
X	Axten, B.A.	01 Jan
E	Glennie, A.M.G.	01 Jan
E	Barton, P.G.	01 Jan
E	Blackman, N.T.	01 Jan
E	Denovan, P.A.	01 Jan
S	Gardner, C.R.S.	01 Jan
E	Horton, P.A.	01 Jan
X	Humphreys, R.J.	01 Jan
X	Hunter, N.M.	01 Jan
X	Turnbull, S.J.L.	01 Jan
X	Hare, N.J.	01 Jan
E	Harrison, M.S.	01 Jan
E	Parker, H.H.	01 Jan
S	Buchan-Steele, M.A.	05 Jan
S	Merchant, I.C.	05 Jan
I	Brads, W.	14 Jan
S	Rigby, J.C.	16 Jan
X	Randall, D.F.	16 Jan
E	Johnson, J.C.	23 Jan
X	Gordon, S.R.	01 Feb
E	Corry, S.M.	01 Feb
X	Barrand, S.M.	01 Feb
E	Charlesworth, G.K.	01 Feb
E	Clarke, A.	01 Feb
X	Green, S.M.	01 Feb
E	Shaw, K.N.G.	01 Feb
E	Stokes, R.	01 Feb
S	Webber, S.J.A.M.	01 Feb
X	Doolan, M.	01 Feb
E	Salter, J.A.	10 Feb
X	Neve, P.C.	11 Feb
X	Saxby, K.A.	24 Feb
I	Kirkup, J.P.	01 Mar
X	Titterton, P.J.	01 Mar
X	Willcox, I.	01 Mar
E	Wood, J.L.	01 Mar
X	Moorey, C.G.	01 Mar
X	Harrison, C.A.	01 Mar
X	Adams, A.J.	01 Mar
E	Beckett, K.A.	01 Mar
E	Cattroll, I.M.	01 Mar
X	Deller, M.G.	01 Mar
E	Jones, H.A.	01 Mar
E	Sharman, D.J.T.	01 Mar
E	Whitehouse, M.J.	01 Mar
E	Gething, J.B.	06 Mar
I	Stanley, A.G.	17 Mar
E	Archer, G.W.	01 Apr
X	Falk, B.H.G.	01 Apr
X	Turnbull, G.D.	01 Apr
S	Crozier, S.R.M.	01 Apr
E	Depledge, I.G.	01 Apr
X	Meredith, N.	01 Apr
X	Poole, J.L.	01 Apr
X	Robertson, M.G.	01 Apr
E	Blount, D.R.	01 Apr
X	Crispin, T.A.B.	01 Apr
X	Greaves, M.J.	01 Apr
X	Skeer, M.R.	04 Apr
E	Gilbert, S.A.	29 Apr
X	Stockings, T.M.	01 May
X	Carter, I.P.	01 May
X	Green, T.J.	01 May
E	Waddington, J.	01 May
E	Float, R.A.	01 May
X	Bennett, P.M.	01 May
E	Foster, S.D.	01 May
E	French, S.A.	10 May
X	Chivers, P.A.	16 May
X	Hailstone, J.H.S.	16 May
I	Eaton, P.G.	01 Jun
E	Bolam, A.G.	01 Jun
X	Andrews, P.N.	01 Jun
E	Duncan, I.S.	01 Jun
X	Fields, D.G.	01 Jun
X	Lunn, A.C.	01 Jun
E	Daws, R.P.A.	01 Jun
X	Hardacre, P.V.	01 Jun
X	Haycock, T.P.	01 Jun
X	Towler, P.J.B.	01 Jun
E	Wareham, M.P.	01 Jun
E	Weedon, K.D.	19 Jun
X	Horsley, A.M.R.	01 Jul
E	Pryde, C.S.	01 Jul
X	Birdman, P.M.	01 Jul
X	Houghton, P.J.	01 Jul

X	Allen, R.M.	01 Jul	X	Pollock, D.J.	01 Jan	E	Leigh, A.M.	01 Jun
E	Borland, S.A.	01 Jul	X	Pritchard, G.S.	01 Jan	X	Matthews, S.G.	01 Jun
E	Dabell, G.L.	01 Jul	S	Trundle, D.J.W.	01 Jan	E	Streeten, C.M.	01 Jun
X	Darlington, M.R.	01 Jul	X	Milburn, P.K.	01 Jan	S	Brown, N.L.	16 Jun
X	Seabrooke-Spencer, D.J.	01 Jul	X	George, A.P.	16 Jan	S	Young, A.P.	16 Jun
			X	Hutchison, G.B.	01 Feb	X	Lawson, R.I.	01 Jul
S	Smerdon, C.D.E.	01 Jul	E	Campbell, R.D.H.	01 Feb	E	Pickstone, P.C.	01 Jul
X	Stuttard, M.C.	01 Jul	X	Ovenden, N.S.P.	01 Feb	X	Woodward, D.J.	01 Jul
E	Walker, N.J.	01 Jul	X	Pearson, S.J.	01 Feb	X	Cornish, M.C.	01 Jul
E	Hammond, P.A.	01 Jul	X	Sanguinetti, H.R.	01 Feb	X	Foster, D.G.S.	01 Jul
E	Westwood, M.R.T.	01 Jul	I	Hunt, J.S.P.	05 Feb	E	Gibbs, N.D.	01 Jul
I	Griffiths, A.J.	26 Jul	X	Lewis, T.J.	05 Feb	E	Rhodes, A.G.	01 Jul
E	Walker, M.	31 Jul	X	Cokayne, D.A.	06 Feb	X	Foreman, J.L.R.	01 Jul
X	Horner, P.A.	01 Aug	X	Baldwin, C.M.	01 Mar	X	Lochrane, A.E.R.	01 Jul
E	Dowell, P.H.N.	01 Aug	X	Fulton, C.R.	01 Mar	X	Pollock, M.P.	01 Jul
X	McAlpine, P.A.	01 Aug	S	Hubbard, P.A.	01 Mar	X	Allibon, M.C.	01 Jul
X	McQuaker, S.R.	01 Aug	X	Jones, M.	01 Mar	X	Nisbet, J.H.T.	01 Jul
E	Morritt, D.C.	01 Aug	E	Magan, M.J.C.	01 Mar	E	Roberts, T.J.	01 Jul
X	Denholm, I.G.	13 Aug	S	Shaw, S.M.	01 Mar	X	Smith, M.R.	14 Jul
E	Baldwin, P.I.	30 Aug	E	Boyd, N.	01 Mar	X	Coomber, M.A.	18 Jul
I	Cropley, A.	01 Sep	E	Dathan, T.J.	01 Mar	X	Greenaway, N.M.	01 Aug
I	Grindel, D.J.	01 Sep	E	Jessop, P.E.	01 Mar	E	Rawlings, D.P.	01 Aug
I	Podmore, A.	01 Sep	E	Pillar, C.D.	01 Mar	E	Kennedy, I.J.A.	01 Aug
I	Saunders, T.M.	01 Sep	X	Firth, N.R.	01 Mar	S	Rance, M.G.W.	16 Aug
X	Glass, J.E.	01 Sep	E	Roberts, N.S.	01 Mar	S	Renwick, J.	23 Aug
X	Robin, C.C.E.	01 Sep	X	Stangroom, A.	24 Mar	E	Collins, P.R.	01 Sep
X	Thompson, B.D.	01 Sep	X	Law, J.	27 Mar	X	Evans, M.J.	01 Sep
X	Welton, W.B.D.	01 Sep	E	Gray, D.K.	01 Apr	X	Harper, C.H.	01 Sep
X	Porter, S.P.	01 Sep	X	Miller, D.S.	01 Apr	X	Hill, R.A.	01 Sep
X	Clink, J.R.H.	01 Sep	X	Reed, J.H.	01 Apr	E	Jenkins, G.W.	01 Sep
X	Fleming, S.A.	30 Sep	E	Munro, K.	01 Apr	I	Jones, A.P.	01 Sep
X	Broughton, M.G.	01 Oct	X	Egeland, F.A.	01 Apr	X	Nadin, R.B.	01 Sep
X	Hamilton, G.R.	01 Oct	E	Gill, M.R.	01 Apr	X	Beardall, M.J.D.	01 Sep
E	Snow, P.F.	01 Oct	E	Gillan, G.M.	01 Apr	X	Burke, M.C.	01 Sep
S	De La Mare, R.M.	01 Oct	E	Hayes, J.V.B.	01 Apr	X	Williams, D.S.	01 Sep
X	Disney, P.W.	01 Oct	E	Holmes, R.W.	01 Apr	X	Window, S.H.	01 Sep
X	Reed, A.W.	01 Oct	E	Smith, K.A.	01 Apr	X	Fitzsimmons, M.B.	01 Sep
E	Gilbert, L.G.	01 Oct	X	Turner, D.B.	01 Apr	E	Lobley, R.A.	01 Sep
X	Williamson, T.J.L.	01 Oct	X	Trevor, M.G.	01 Apr	X	Martin, R.G.	01 Sep
S	David, S.E.J.	16 Oct	X	Greenland, M.R.	16 Apr	E	Murphy, P.W.	01 Sep
X	Evans, W.Q.F.	20 Oct	X	Birley, J.H.	01 May	X	Burton, A.J.	01 Sep
I	Gunn, W.J.S.	01 Nov	X	Schnadhorst, J.C.	01 May	X	Bone, D.N.	01 Sep
E	Heley, J.M.	01 Nov	X	Amphlett, N.G.	01 May	E	Clifford, T.J.	01 Oct
X	Hurry, A.P.	01 Nov	E	Harding, D.M.	01 May	X	Fincher, K.J.	01 Oct
E	Stewart, J.C.	01 Nov	E	Hawkins, M.A.J.	01 May	X	Haywood, G.	01 Oct
E	Clark, K.C.	01 Nov	X	Marshall, R.G.C.	01 May	X	Bate, D.I.G.	01 Oct
X	Thomas, P.G.	01 Nov	E	Mills, A.	01 May	X	Welch, A.	13 Oct
E	Bull, G.C.	01 Nov	E	Law, P.R.	01 May	X	MacKenzie, M.D.	01 Nov
E	Saxby, C.J.	01 Nov	E	Mills, S.D.	01 May	X	Vickery, T.K.	01 Nov
E	Clark, I.D.	01 Nov	X	Goldsmith, S.V.W.	01 May	S	Garland, N.	01 Nov
S	Jameson, A.C.	01 Nov	E	Morshead, C.H.	01 May	E	Lipscomb, P.	01 Nov
E	Toy, M.J.	01 Nov	X	Webb, A.J.	01 May	E	Burlington, B.L.	01 Nov
X	Hills, A.A.	01 Dec	X	Walliker, M.J.D.	01 May	X	Hutton, S.J.	01 Nov
E	Harding, G.A.	01 Dec	E	Green, D.P.S.	01 May	E	Allen, D.R.	01 Nov
X	Ashcroft, A.C.	01 Dec	S	Lavery, J.P.	16 May	S	Bath, M.A.W.	01 Nov
X	Swarbrick, R.J.	01 Dec	X	Gurmin, S.J.A.	18 May	E	Williams, M.J.	01 Nov
X	Hart, M.A.	01 Dec	X	Hewitt, A.	01 Jun	X	Shepherd, D.	09 Nov
X	Johnstone, C.C.C.	01 Dec	X	Mannion, R.V.	01 Jun	S	Lines, J.M.	16 Nov
X	Sutcliffe, J.	21 Dec	E	McInnes, J.G.K.	01 Jun	E	Stephenson, D.	22 Nov
			X	Williams, A.J.	01 Jun	S	Willis, A.J.	01 Dec
	1995		E	Cornish, A.M.	01 Jun	E	St Aubyn, J.D.E.	01 Dec
X	Heley, D.N.	01 Jan	E	Brown, P.ST.J.	01 Jun	E	Jordan, P.D.	01 Dec
X	Lydiate, G.	01 Jan	E	Grenfell-Shaw, M.C.	01 Jun	X	Aspden, A.M.	01 Dec
X	Weale, J.S.	01 Jan	X	Johnston, T.A.	01 Jun	X	Waddington, A.K.	01 Dec

X	Wallace, A.	01 Dec
X	Carson, M.J.	01 Dec
X	Pentreath, J.P.	01 Dec
X	Cunningham, D.A.	15 Dec
X	Boddington, J.D.L.	16 Dec
X	Meeds, K.	16 Dec

1996

X	Cramp, A.M.	01 Jan
E	Tate, S.J.	01 Jan
E	Frankham, P.J.	01 Jan
E	Rogers, I.A.	01 Jan
X	Sherriff, D.A.	01 Jan
E	Munns, A.R.	01 Jan
E	Little, G.T.	01 Jan
E	Metcalfe, P.G.	01 Feb
X	Craig, P.D.	01 Feb
X	Dyke, C.L.	01 Feb
X	Atkinson, M.	01 Feb
S	Carter, S.N.	01 Feb
E	Casson, P.R.	01 Feb
X	Tindal, N.H.C.	01 Feb
S	Wade, G.A.	01 Feb
X	Salisbury, D.P.	01 Feb
E	Mace, S.B.	01 Feb
X	Entwisle, W.N.	01 Feb
S	Walmsley, E.A.	08 Feb
X	Bankier, S.	19 Feb
X	Draper, S.P.	26 Feb
X	Barker, D.C.K.	28 Feb
X	Furlong, K.	01 Mar
S	Sutton-Scott-Tucker, J.J.	01 Mar
X	Burke, P.D.	01 Mar
E	Chance, D.M.R.	01 Mar
E	Fieldsend, M.A.	01 Mar
E	Phenna, A.	01 Mar
E	Toft, M.D.	01 Mar
S	Notley, L.P.	01 Mar
E	Gilbert, P.D.	01 Mar
X	Talbot, R.P.	01 Mar
S	Straw, A.N.	16 Mar
S	Smith, C.J.	16 Mar
X	Chrishop, T.I.	01 Apr
X	Warwick, P.D.	01 Apr
E	Wise, G.J.	01 Apr
X	Harry, A.D.	01 Apr
S	Hayle, J.K.	01 Apr
E	Jackson, I.A.	01 Apr
X	Lindsay, I.G.	01 Apr
X	Smith, K.B.A.	01 Apr
E	Withers, J.W.	01 Apr
X	Kilby, S.E.	01 Apr
E	Kingsbury, S.H.	01 Apr
E	Pear, I.K.	01 Apr
E	Scott, N.L.J.	01 Apr
E	Dyer, M.D.J.	01 Apr
X	Key, B.J.	01 Apr
X	Collins, G.J.S.	07 Apr
X	Mahony, C.D.C.	12 Apr
X	Mahony, D.G.	16 Apr
S	Marston, P.A.	16 Apr
S	Taylor, S.J.	16 Apr
X	Wallis, A.J.	16 Apr
X	Waters, N.R.	16 Apr
S	McConochie, A.D.	16 Apr
X	Hine, N.W.	01 May
X	Kingwell, J.M.L.	01 May

LIEUTENANTS

1988

X	Cooper, M.A.	01 Apr
X	Burden, F.W.E.	01 Apr
E	Fitzjohn, D.	01 May
E	Merritt, J.J.	01 May
E	Harrop, I.	01 May
X	Masters, J.C.	01 May
E	Scott, J.B.	01 May
E	Shepherd, R.G.	01 May
E	Childs, D.G.	01 May
X	Maher, M.P.	16 May
E	Carter, J.M.	01 Jun
X	Gazzard, J.H.	01 Jun
X	Moore, P.H.G.	01 Jun
X	Thomas, R.K.	01 Jun
E	Hill, P.J.	01 Jun
X	Solleveld, S.R.	01 Jun
X	Corbett, A.S.	01 Jun
X	Freeman, D.R.	01 Jun
X	Hayward, C.E.W.	01 Jun
E	Hutchins, T.P.	01 Jun
E	Short, J.J.	01 Jun
X	Hill, M.R.	22 Jun
X	Taylor, A.J.	23 Jun
S	Andrews, S.G.	01 Jul
X	Bath, E.G.	01 Jul
X	Bucknell, D.I.	01 Jul
X	French, J.T.	01 Jul
X	Green, P.J.	01 Jul
E	Haines, P.R.	01 Jul
X	McDonough, A.G.	01 Jul
X	Simpson, M.J.	01 Jul
E	Thompson, A.	01 Jul
X	Thomson, D.	01 Jul
X	Tyler, P.L.	01 Jul
S	Taylor, B.D.	01 Jul
X	Bellfield, R.J.A.	01 Jul
E	Buckle, I.L.	01 Jul
E	Chubb, J.J.	01 Jul
E	Gracey, P.P.	01 Jul
X	Reindorp, D.P.	01 Jul
X	Tetlow, H.S.G.	01 Jul
S	Jewitt, C.J.B.	01 Jul
X	McCall, I.R.	01 Jul
E	Pooley, S.W.	01 Jul
X	Power, M.D.	01 Jul
X	Tattersall, P.D.	01 Jul
X	Fancy, R.	01 Aug
E	Geary, T.W.	01 Aug
E	Turner, J.A.E.	01 Aug
E	Adams, A.M.	01 Aug
E	Berryman, C.B.	01 Aug
X	Coles, A.L.	01 Aug
X	Secretan, S.J.	01 Aug
X	Howard, P.M.	16 Aug
X	Bark, J.S.	01 Sep
X	Benton, A.M.	01 Sep
X	Brady, S.E.	01 Sep
E	Geddis, R.D.	01 Sep
E	Enright, K.D.	01 Sep
E	Woodford, G.I.	01 Sep
S	Williams, M.S.	29 Sep
X	Hodkinson, C.B.	01 Oct
E	Lovegrove, R.A.	01 Oct
X	Newland, M.I.	01 Oct
E	Foster, G.J.	01 Oct
X	Seymour, K.W.	01 Oct
E	Leitch, I.R.	01 Oct
E	Myerscough, A.P.	01 Oct
E	Watson, P.G.C.	25 Oct
X	Bowen, N.T.	01 Nov
E	Burwin, H.L.	01 Nov
S	Toomey, N.J.	01 Nov
X	Trubshaw, C.	01 Nov
X	Gale, S.P.	01 Nov
E	Prescott, S.	01 Nov
E	Stirzaker, M.	01 Nov
X	Briers, M.P.	01 Nov
X	Gill, A.R.	01 Nov
X	Hardern, S.P.	01 Nov
E	Leahy, T.P.	01 Nov
E	Robinson, M.P.	01 Nov
E	Wilson, C.J.	01 Dec
S	Blackwell, R.E.	01 Dec
E	Cran, B.C.	01 Dec
S	Hollins, R.P.	01 Dec
X	Barnbrook, J.C.	16 Dec
S	Kyte, A.J.	16 Dec

1989

X	Lister, M.	01 Jan
X	Shepherd, C.S.	01 Jan
X	Adam, I.K.	01 Jan
X	Carson, N.D.E.	01 Jan
X	Dunlop, M.W.S.	01 Jan
E	Jackson, A.S.	01 Jan
E	Stace, I.S.	01 Jan
X	Noyce, N.R.	15 Jan
X	Davies, M.B.	24 Jan
X	Blount, K.E.	01 Feb
E	Thompson, R.C.	01 Feb
S	Wintle, G.L.	01 Feb
X	Abernethy, J.R.G.	01 Feb
X	Drysdale, S.R.	01 Feb
E	Gillies, R.R.	01 Feb
E	Hughes, R.D.	01 Feb
E	Parvin, P.S.	01 Feb
E	Stewart, P.C.	01 Feb
S	Hill, R.K.J.	16 Feb
S	Stanton, P.C.M.	16 Feb
X	Bell, R.D.	01 Mar

X Dunn, R.P. . . . . 01 Mar	E Stevenson, P.M. . . 01 Jul	E Kitchen, S.A. . . . 01 Jan
X Hulme, T.M. . . . 01 Mar	X Swift, R.D. . . . . . 01 Jul	E MacDonald, J.R. . . 01 Jan
X Ireland, P.C. . . . 01 Mar	X Wainhouse, M.J. . . 01 Jul	E Matthews, D.W. . . 01 Jan
E Coles, C.J. . . . . 01 Mar	S Willis, M.S. . . . . 01 Jul	X Proctor, S.J.L. . . . 01 Jan
E Bartlett, D.S.G. . . 01 Mar	X Woods, J.B. . . . . 01 Jul	X Romney, P.D. . . . 01 Jan
X Chandler, N.J. . . . 01 Mar	X Breckenridge, I.G. . . 01 Jul	X Smith, G.C.S. . . . 01 Jan
S Chapell, A. . . . . 01 Mar	E Harper, A.C. . . . . 01 Jul	X Thompson, M.O. . . 01 Jan
X Cummings, A.T. . . 01 Mar	X Irons, P.A. . . . . . 01 Jul	X Young, G.L. . . . . 01 Jan
X Hogg, C.W. . . . 01 Mar	E Matthews, R.J. . . . 01 Jul	S Trump, N.W. . . . 16 Jan
X Pitcher, S.J. . . . 01 Mar	E Rowse, M.L. . . . . 01 Jul	S Hood, K.C. . . . . 16 Jan
E Mallinson, R. . . . 01 Mar	E Reason, I.M. . . . . 01 Jul	S Wright, S.H. . . . 16 Jan
S Murrison, R.A. . . 01 Mar	X Spiller, V.J. . . . . 28 Jul	X Allen, A.D. . . . . 01 Feb
X Swain, A.V. . . . 05 Mar	X Kent, M.A. . . . . . 01 Aug	X Bence, D.E. . . . . 01 Feb
X Cowley, R.M. . . . . 01 Apr	X Stannard, M.P. . . . 01 Aug	X Vitali, R.C. . . . . 01 Feb
X Rich, D.C. . . . . 01 Apr	E Pearson, N. . . . . 01 Aug	E Williams, A.J. . . . 01 Feb
X Toothill, J.S. . . . . 01 Apr	X Woollven, A.H. . . . 01 Aug	X Beadsmoore, J.E. . 01 Feb
E New, C.M. . . . . . 01 Apr	E Graham, D.W.S. . . 01 Aug	X Carroll, B.J. . . . . 01 Feb
X Scott, J.A. . . . . . 01 Apr	S Horswill, M.N. . . . 01 Aug	E Hughesdon, M.D. . . 01 Feb
X Morris, R.J. . . . . 01 Apr	X Bourne, C.M. . . . 16 Aug	X Kyd, J.P. . . . . . 01 Feb
E Hollis, C. . . . . . 01 Apr	S Evans, E.M. . . . 16 Aug	X MacIver, G. . . . . 01 Feb
X Barker, P.T. . . . . 01 Apr	E Holden, S.D. . . . . 24 Aug	X Mugridge, D.R. . . . 01 Feb
X Bowbrick, R.C. . . . 01 Apr	I Page, S.P. . . . . . 01 Sep	E Petitt, S.R. . . . . 01 Feb
X Bower, N.S. . . . . 01 Apr	E Petheram, A.J. . . . 01 Sep	E Reynolds, A.G. . . . 01 Feb
X Elliott, R. . . . . . 01 Apr	X Tebbet, P.N. . . . . 01 Sep	E Rogers, A.G. . . . . 01 Feb
E Foster, G.J.H. . . . 01 Apr	E Bull, C.M.S. . . . . 01 Sep	E Russell, P.R. . . . . 01 Feb
X Holt, S. . . . . . . 01 Apr	E Gaitley, I. . . . . . 01 Sep	X Seakins, P.E. . . . . 01 Feb
X Keyworth, A.J. . . . 01 Apr	X Harvey, R.M.M.J. . . 01 Sep	E Thomas, J.H. . . . . 01 Feb
X Kissane, R.E.T. . . . 01 Apr	X Hutchinson, O.J.P. . . 01 Sep	X Titcomb, M.R. . . . 01 Feb
X Lane, R.N. . . . . . 01 Apr	X Bazley, J.C. . . . . 28 Sep	E Wellington, S. . . . 01 Feb
X Lowson, R.M. . . . 01 Apr	E Davies, T.M. . . . . 01 Oct	E Course, A.J. . . . . 01 Feb
E Dailey, P.G.J. . . . 01 Apr	S Watts, D.J. . . . . 01 Oct	E Franks, C.S. . . . . 01 Feb
X Ryan, R.M. . . . . 01 Apr	X Tabeart, G.W. . . . 01 Nov	X Hatcher, R.S. . . . 01 Mar
X Wilson-Chalon, L.M. . 01 Apr	E Taylor, K. . . . . . 01 Nov	X Perks, J.LE'S. . . . 01 Mar
X Davison, J.E. . . . . 06 Apr	X Hibberd, N.J. . . . . 01 Nov	E Blackburn, S.A. . . 01 Mar
S Nicholson, H. . . . 06 Apr	X Jones, A.D. . . . . 01 Nov	X Goodman, A.T. . . . 01 Mar
S Tew, J.P. . . . . 16 Apr	E Kershaw, S. . . . . 01 Nov	X Martin, D.H. . . . . 01 Mar
E Fairbrass, J.E. . . . 28 Apr	X Radakin, A.D. . . . 01 Nov	X Mules, A.J. . . . . 01 Mar
E Finch, R.L. . . . . 01 May	X Randall, N.J. . . . . 01 Nov	E Powell, M.A. . . . . 01 Mar
E Feeney, M.L. . . . 01 May	X Robinson, G.A. . . . 01 Nov	X Spring, A.R.J. . . . 01 Mar
E Clark, S.R. . . . . 01 May	E Hope, G.R. . . . . 01 Nov	E Ward, S.D. . . . . 01 Mar
E Annett, I.G. . . . . 01 May	S Gibson, A.D. . . . 16 Nov	E Miller, R.H. . . . . 01 Mar
E Knight, P.J. . . . 01 May	X Rolph, A.P.M. . . . 16 Nov	E MacTaggart, A.J.L. . 01 Mar
X Pethybridge, R.A. . 01 May	S Asbridge, J.I. . . . 16 Nov	X Scott, R.J. . . . . 02 Mar
S Philpott, N.E. . . . 01 May	X Barber, A.S. . . . . 01 Dec	S Da Gama, D.D. . . 01 Apr
E Carrick, R.J. . . . 01 May	X Allen, S.M. . . . . 01 Dec	E Gibbs, E.M. . . . . 01 Apr
E King, N.W. . . . . 01 May	E Baker, G.C. . . . . 01 Dec	E Hamilton, A.J.B. . . 01 Apr
E Martin, B.A. . . . 01 May	E Morgan, F.S. . . . . 01 Dec	X Lane, A.W.S. . . . 01 Apr
S Mearns, C.M. . . . 01 May	X Dale-Smith, G. . . . 01 Dec	E Lynn, S.R. . . . . 01 Apr
E Clough, C.R. . . . 01 May	E Graham, J. . . . . 01 Dec	X Miller, J.M. . . . . 01 Apr
X Dible, J.H. . . . . 16 May	X Ince, D.P. . . . . . 01 Dec	X Petherick, J.S. . . . 01 Apr
E Read, J.M. . . . . 23 May	X Montgomery, M.H. . 01 Dec	E Roberts, S.D. . . . 01 Apr
X Reddish, C.A. . . . 01 Jun	S Noyes, D.J. . . . . 01 Dec	X Robinson, N.U.S. . . 01 Apr
X Robertson, D.C. . . 01 Jun	S Venables, A.N. . . . 01 Dec	E Rook, G.I. . . . . . 01 Apr
E Titcomb, A.C. . . . 01 Jun	S Walker, A. . . . . 14 Dec	X Smith, A.P. . . . . 01 Apr
X Dutton, D. . . . . 01 Jun	S Anderson, H.A. . . . 16 Dec	X Stowell, P.I.M. . . . 01 Apr
X Woollcombe-Gosson, 01 Jun	X Prentice, D.C. . . . 22 Dec	X Chapman, S.J. . . . 01 Apr
D.J.		E Hood, K.M. . . . . 01 Apr
S Edge, J.H. . . . . 01 Jun	**1990**	E Mitchell, C.W. . . . 01 Apr
E Gardiner, D.A. . . . 01 Jul	S Burningham, M.R. . . 01 Jan	I Blackaller, W.J. . . 04 Apr
X Kelk, S.J. . . . . 01 Jul	X Lea, J. . . . . . . 01 Jan	X Blackmore, M.S. . . 01 May
X McGhie, I.A. . . . 01 Jul	X Peacock, T.J. . . . 01 Jan	X Royston, S.J. . . . 01 May
S Parton, S.L. . . . 01 Jul	E Corderoy, J.R. . . . 01 Jan	X Welch, A.J. . . . . 01 May
E Prior, G.M. . . . . 01 Jul	E Bartlett, I.D. . . . . 01 Jan	X Merewether, H.A.H. . 01 May
X Smith, C.P. . . . . 01 Jul	X Bellingham, D.B. . . 01 Jan	E Doherty, K.P. . . . 01 May

X	Goodacre, I.R.	01 May	E	Manson, T.E.	01 Oct	X	Waller, S.A.	01 Mar
E	Helliwell, M.A.	01 May	X	Strathern, R.J.	01 Oct	X	Bingham, D.S.	01 Mar
E	Short, A.S.J.	01 May	X	Ward, S.I.	01 Oct	E	Hill, D.	01 Mar
E	Winter, T.M.	01 May	E	McCue, D.	01 Oct	X	Cook, R.G.N.	01 Mar
X	Burns, D.I.	01 May	S	Oliphant, W.	01 Oct	E	Currass, T.D.	01 Mar
E	Dunn, G.R.	01 May	X	Fisher, C.R.A.	06 Oct	E	Douglass, M.C.M.	01 Mar
E	Bowley, J.J.	01 May	X	Davison, J.C.	01 Nov	X	Gray, R.	01 Mar
E	McCartney, C.	01 May	X	Dawson, W.	01 Nov	E	Groom, I.S.	01 Mar
X	Long, A.D.	16 May	X	Olive, P.N.	01 Nov	E	Henderson, S.P.	01 Mar
S	Evans, M.D.	16 May	X	White, J.A.P.	01 Nov	E	Mackie, D.F.S.	01 Mar
X	Deacon, S.	01 Jun	X	Brothwood, M.K.	01 Nov	X	Middleton, D.J.	01 Mar
X	Green, J.	01 Jun	X	Fletcher, N.	01 Nov	E	Rawlinson, S.J.	01 Mar
E	Philo, J.Q.	01 Jun	S	McNally, N.J.	01 Nov	X	Dainton, S.	01 Mar
S	Ryan, J.B.	01 Jun	E	Palmer, R.J.	01 Nov	X	Moss, R.A.	01 Mar
E	Murray, G.M.	01 Jun	E	Reidy, P.A.	01 Nov	X	O'Flaherty, C.P.J.	01 Mar
E	Baker, M.J.	01 Jun	X	Anstey, R.J.	01 Nov	X	Stevens, R.M.	10 Mar
E	Bosustow, A.M.	01 Jun	E	Hall, B.J.	01 Nov	X	Collighan, G.T.	01 Apr
X	Davidson, A.M.	01 Jun	X	Houlberg, K.M.T.	01 Nov	S	Turner, J.S.H.	01 Apr
E	Evans, G.	01 Jun	E	Smith, M.M.	01 Nov	X	Brooks, G.L.	01 Apr
X	Halton, P.V.	01 Jun	E	Stewart, A.M.	01 Nov	X	Beck, S.K.	01 Apr
X	Payne, J.D.	01 Jun	X	Taylor, A.R.	01 Nov	E	Biggs, W.P.L.	01 Apr
E	Shutts, D.	01 Jun	E	Vickers, J.	01 Nov	X	Dodd, K.M.	01 Apr
E	Hanson, N.A.	01 Jun	X	Redman, C.J.R.	23 Nov	E	Goldman, P.H.L.	01 Apr
E	Tipper, M.R.	01 Jun	X	Gilmour, C.J.M.	01 Dec	S	Mardlin, S.A.	01 Apr
X	Abernethy, L.J.F.	01 Jul	X	Tribe, P.D.	01 Dec	E	Marriott, M.N.	01 Apr
E	Folwell, M.W.	01 Jul	X	Curtis, R.S.	01 Dec	E	Maxwell-Heron, G.D.	01 Apr
E	Harrison, P.G.	01 Jul	X	Davies, I.E.	01 Dec	X	McGinty, M.J.	01 Apr
E	Mather, G.P.	01 Jul	E	MacKay, P.	01 Dec	X	Mimpriss, G.D.	01 Apr
X	Ovens, M.J.	01 Jul	S	Clark, S.M.	01 Dec	E	Roscoe, R.D.	01 Apr
S	Porrett, J.A.	01 Jul	E	Coulson, P.	01 Dec	S	Dodd, N.C.	01 Apr
X	Powell, S.R.	01 Jul	X	Powell, W.G.	16 Dec	E	Ferris, D.P.S.	01 Apr
S	Shaw, P.J.	01 Jul	E	Makepeace, P.A.	24 Dec	E	Foster, S.J.H.	01 Apr
X	Bewick, D.J.	01 Jul				X	Harris, K.J.	01 Apr
E	Hutchison, P.G.	01 Jul		**1991**		X	Wood, U.G.S.	01 Apr
X	Price, T.A.	01 Jul	S	Dudley, S.M.T.	01 Jan	X	Garratt, J.K.	01 May
E	Traynor, D.F.	01 Jul	X	Millard, A.R.	01 Jan	X	Ingham, I.M.	01 May
X	Warn, C.J.	01 Jul	X	Hancock, A.P.	01 Jan	X	Pemble, M.W.A.	01 May
S	Donlan, M.S.	01 Jul	X	Manfield, M.D.	01 Jan	E	Bowhay, S.	01 May
E	Hill, G.F.	01 Jul	X	Myres, P.J.L.	01 Jan	E	Scott, M.	01 May
X	Axon, D.B.	01 Jul	S	Cooper, K.S.	01 Jan	E	Bravery, M.A.E.	01 May
X	Bird, R.A.J.	01 Jul	E	Greatwood, I.M.	01 Jan	E	Cooper, S.S.	01 May
E	O'Shea, E.P.	01 Jul	E	Warrington, P.T.	01 Jan	X	Davey, G.S.	01 May
X	Badrock, B.	05 Jul	X	Ward, T.J.	11 Jan	X	Duffy, H.	01 May
E	Hall, A.J.	01 Aug	X	Lees, E.C.	01 Feb	X	Mackey, M.C.	01 Jun
X	Cryar, T.M.C.	01 Aug	X	Southorn, M.D.	01 Feb	X	Young, A.	01 Jun
E	George, P.	01 Aug	X	Clarke, P.J.	01 Feb	E	Hall, S.	01 Jun
X	Ford, M.J.	05 Aug	X	Osborn, R.M.	01 Feb	X	Golden, D.S.C.	01 Jun
X	Hawkins, J.S.	16 Aug	X	Staley, S.P.L.	01 Feb	X	Bush, A.J.T.	01 Jun
X	McGuire, M.J.	31 Aug	E	Copeland, S.N.	01 Feb	E	Graham, M.W.	01 Jun
E	Band, J.W.	01 Sep	X	Godwin, C.A.	01 Feb	X	Allen, P.L.	01 Jun
X	Cartwright, D.	01 Sep	X	Goodsell, C.D.	01 Feb	S	Ferns, T.D.	01 Jun
E	Drummond, C.J.	01 Sep	E	Hancox, M.J.	01 Feb	S	Sparkes, P.J.	01 Jun
X	Murphy, S.R.A.	01 Sep	E	Jackson, P.N.	01 Feb	X	Whitley, I.D.B.	01 Jun
E	Choules, B.	01 Sep	X	Jones, N.P.	01 Feb	E	Wright, B.L.	01 Jun
X	Savage, M.R.	01 Sep	X	Kerslake, R.W.	01 Feb	X	Rogers, T.H.G.	04 Jun
X	May, N.P.	01 Sep	X	Nairn, A.B.	01 Feb	S	Rees, J.P.	29 Jun
X	Thomas, R.A.A.	01 Sep	E	Osmond, J.B.	01 Feb	S	Percival, M.C.	01 Jul
S	Wood, R.	01 Sep	E	Smith, A.G.	01 Feb	X	Lamont, N.J.	01 Jul
S	Leyshon, T.D.	16 Sep	X	Taylor, M.A.	01 Feb	X	McDonald, A.J.	01 Jul
S	Lustman, A.M.	25 Sep	E	Welford, R.C.	01 Feb	X	Hurrell, P.R.	01 Jul
X	Haslam, P.J.	01 Oct	X	Wright, N.S.	01 Feb	E	Jones, D.B.	01 Jul
E	Tritschler, E.L.	01 Oct	X	Betton, A.	01 Feb	E	Parkin, M.I.	01 Jul
X	Arnold, S.	01 Oct	E	Fergusson, N.A.	01 Feb	S	Powell, M.J.	01 Jul
E	MacGillivray, I.	01 Oct	X	Graham, I.E.	01 Feb	S	Perry, A.J.	16 Jul

X	Churcher, J.E.	01 Aug	E	Young, S.A.	01 Feb	X	Hempsell, R.I.	01 Jun
E	Richardson, P.S.M.	01 Aug	X	Barnes, J.R.	01 Feb	E	Nicklas, C.J.	01 Jun
E	Lee, P.A.	01 Aug	S	Challinor, R.A.	01 Feb	E	Saunders, P.W.	01 Jun
E	Collis, M.J.	01 Aug	E	Crofts, D.J.	01 Feb	X	Wilkinson, D.H.	01 Jun
E	Currie, S.M.	01 Aug	E	Gale, M.A.	01 Feb	X	Williams, J.P.	01 Jun
E	Owens, D.T.	01 Aug	E	Martin, S.J.	01 Feb	E	Bond, A.J.	09 Jun
E	Quekett, I.P.S.	01 Aug	E	O'Brien, K.J.	01 Feb	X	Gardner, J.E.	01 Jul
X	Verney, P.S.	01 Aug	S	Rae, S.G.	01 Feb	X	Campbell, L.M.	01 Jul
X	Wickenden, A.R.	01 Aug	E	Dinsdale, A.M.	01 Feb	E	Barton, M.A.	01 Jul
X	Brown, P.A.E.	01 Aug	E	Markham, P.M.	01 Feb	E	Bunn, E.M.	01 Jul
E	Lowe, J.C.	01 Aug	S	Ashman, R.G.	28 Feb	E	Crundell, R.J.	01 Jul
X	Paterson, F.J.B.	01 Aug	S	Sparke, P.R.W.	01 Mar	X	Diggle, W.N.N.	01 Jul
S	Dathan, J.H.M.	16 Aug	E	Cotterill, B.M.	01 Mar	E	Lunn, M.H.B.	01 Jul
E	Bolton, J.P.	01 Sep	E	Nickolls, K.P.	01 Mar	E	Panther, A.M.	01 Jul
X	Cameron, I.	01 Sep	E	Balhetchet, A.S.	01 Mar	E	Lauchlan, R.A.	01 Aug
X	Goode, A.N.	01 Sep	X	Dominy, D.J.D.	01 Mar	S	Goodier, R.M.	01 Aug
X	Ward, N.J.	01 Sep	E	Greenwood, N.J.	01 Mar	X	Dando, J.N.	01 Aug
X	Beard, H.D.	01 Sep	E	Halliwell, D.C.	01 Mar	X	Ley, J.A.	01 Aug
E	Bywater, R.L.	01 Sep	X	Hogben, A.L.	01 Mar	X	Morley, J.D.	01 Aug
E	Greener, C.	01 Sep	X	Lamb, C.F.	01 Mar	E	Ross, I.	01 Aug
E	Taylor, R.	01 Sep	X	Marley, E.C.P.	01 Mar	E	Bolton, M.T.W.	01 Aug
X	Blythe, P.C.	01 Oct	S	Murphy, P.A.	01 Mar	X	Gillespie, C.D.	01 Aug
X	Groves, C.K.	01 Oct	E	Pallot, M.L.A.	01 Mar	X	Wilson, R.	01 Sep
E	Appelquist, P.	01 Oct	E	Reece, N.D.	01 Mar	E	Richter, A.S.B.	01 Sep
E	Bougourd, M.A.	01 Oct	E	Teideman, I.C.	01 Mar	X	Duff, A.P.	01 Sep
X	Chalmers, P.	01 Oct	E	Whitehead, S.J.	01 Mar	X	Oulds, K.A.	01 Sep
X	Lower, I.S.	01 Oct	X	Jackson, D.J.	01 Mar	E	Walton, C.P.	01 Sep
E	McDermott, O.D.	01 Oct	X	Johnson, L.S.	01 Mar	E	Wheal, A.J.	01 Sep
X	Huntington, S.P.	01 Oct	E	Whitfield, K.D.	01 Mar	X	Wyper, J.R.	01 Sep
E	Gazard, P.N.	01 Oct	S	Fletcher, R.J.	16 Mar	E	Rose, M.F.	01 Sep
S	Aplin, A.T.	01 Nov	X	Bruford, R.M.C.	01 Apr	E	Dyke, K.A.	01 Oct
X	Jones, C.A.	01 Nov	E	Bedding, S.W.E.	01 Apr	S	Adlam, G.M.	01 Oct
E	Melton, C.	01 Nov	E	Bignell, S.	01 Apr	X	Horton, S.W.	01 Oct
X	Necker, C.D.	01 Nov	X	Buck, J.E.	01 Apr	E	Childs, D.	01 Nov
X	Baker, A.P.	01 Nov	E	Burgess, G.T.M.	01 Apr	E	Norris, J.G.	01 Nov
X	Bark, A.M.	01 Nov	X	Glaister, M.E.M.	01 Apr	X	Ramsey, R.T.	01 Nov
X	Joyce, T.J.	01 Nov	E	Long, A.M.	01 Apr	E	O'Byrne, P.B.M.	01 Nov
X	Cocker, M.J.	01 Dec	X	Platt, T.S.	01 Apr	E	Shaw, G.R.	01 Nov
X	Tennuci, R.G.	01 Dec	X	Gurr, A.W.G.	01 May	E	Wylie, I.C.H.	01 Nov
E	Clarke, J.J.	01 Dec	E	Hardiman, N.A.	01 May	S	Hally, P.J.	01 Nov
E	Easterbrook, K.I.E.	01 Dec	E	Greenway, S.A.	01 May	E	Lowe, S.M.	01 Dec
E	McRae, P.C.	01 Dec	X	Guy, T.J.	01 May	E	Ballard, M.L.	01 Dec
E	Price, G.P.	01 Dec	X	Parry, J.D.F.	01 May	X	Reeves, C.J.	01 Dec
X	Ryan, J.P.	01 Dec	E	Russell, B.	01 May	X	Broadhurst, M.R.	01 Dec
S	Shrubsole, S.J.	01 Dec	E	Strutt, J.F.	01 May	E	Gayfer, M.E.	01 Dec
E	Woodruff, D.A.	01 Dec	X	Vallis, J.H.	01 May	E	Gregory, A.S.	01 Dec
X	Boynton, S.J.	01 Dec	X	Watt, A.J.L.	01 May	E	Joyce, D.A.	01 Dec
X	McEvoy, G.E.B.	01 Dec	X	Wilson, D.R.	01 May	S	Romney, E.V.	01 Dec
			S	Ackland, H.K.	01 May	S	Talbott, A.H.	01 Dec
	1992		E	Bye, M.D.	01 May	X	Whyte, A.P.	13 Dec
E	Gregory, M.	01 Jan	E	Chambers, I.R.	01 May			
X	Atkinson, E.J.	01 Jan	E	Lison, A.C.	01 May		**1993**	
E	Baxter, I.M.	01 Jan	E	Methven, P.	01 May	S	Cole, A.C.	01 Jan
X	Bryan, R.J.L.	01 Jan	X	Warrender, W.J.	01 May	E	Malley, M.P.	01 Jan
E	Parkinson, R.I.	01 Jan	E	Prinsep, T.J.	01 Jun	E	McKenzie, H.W.	01 Jan
E	Parsons, A.D.	01 Jan	X	Gray, J.A.	01 Jun	E	Thomas, S.M.	01 Jan
E	Roberts, K.E.	01 Jan	E	Bradley, P.M.	01 Jun	E	Atkins, I.	01 Jan
E	Rowland, P.N.	01 Jan	E	Helps, A.R.	01 Jun	X	Brown, M.R.W.	01 Jan
X	Walker, N.M.	01 Jan	E	Howard, N.H.	01 Jun	X	Burton, C.J.	01 Jan
X	Washer, N.B.J.	01 Jan	X	Hunkin, D.J.	01 Jun	S	Donovan, R.J.	09 Jan
X	Meeking, C.G.	09 Jan	E	Reah, S.	01 Jun	E	Ewen, J.P.	01 Jan
X	Connell, M.J.	16 Jan	E	Rogers, C.M.	01 Jun	X	Hayter, E.G.B.	01 Jan
X	Crosbie, D.E.F.	01 Feb	S	Burns, R.C.	01 Jun	E	Higham, J.G.	01 Jan
X	Pierce, A.K.M.	01 Feb	E	Fleisher, S.M.	01 Jun	X	Hughes, M.A.S.	01 Jan

X	MacKinnon, D.J.	01 Jan	E	Love, T.S.N.	01 Jul	E	Barnett, A.C.	01 Feb
X	Varley, I.G.	01 Jan	X	Norgan, D.J.	01 Jul	X	Brent, R.C.	01 Feb
E	MacLeod, J.N.	01 Jan	X	Watts, R.	01 Jul	E	Game, P.G.	01 Feb
X	Brown, S.H.	15 Jan	X	Lett, J.D.	01 Jul	S	Higgs, T.A.	01 Feb
E	Sellers, G.D.	01 Feb	E	Metcalfe, P.I.	01 Jul	X	Johns, J.A.	01 Feb
X	Stanton-Brown, P.J.	01 Feb	E	Prince, M.E.	01 Jul	E	MacLeod, M.S.	01 Feb
E	Whight, R.A.	01 Feb	S	Richardson, G.N.	01 Jul	E	Rodwell, T.R.J.	01 Feb
X	Black, J.J.M.	01 Feb	S	Warne, E.J.	01 Jul	S	Wilman, D.M.	01 Feb
X	Colley, C.J.B.	01 Feb	X	McQueen, J.B.	01 Jul	X	Farmer, J.L.V.	01 Mar
X	Goodrich, S.G.	01 Feb	X	Bower, A.J.	01 Aug	E	Carroll, P.C.	01 Mar
X	Greenacre, J.F.	01 Feb	X	Morgon, R.H.	01 Aug	E	Clarke, R.W.	01 Mar
E	Harrison, A.	01 Feb	X	O'Sullivan, M.L.J.	01 Aug	E	Finn, I.R.	01 Mar
X	Hopper, S.M.	01 Feb	E	Broadbent, A.C.	01 Aug	E	Goddard, A.S.N.	01 Mar
X	Jennings, P.S.	01 Feb	X	Coyle, G.J.	01 Aug	E	Jose, S.	01 Mar
X	Leigh, M.A.	01 Feb	E	Graham, A.N.S.	01 Aug	X	Ketteringham, M.J.	01 Mar
X	Miller, P.D.	01 Feb	X	Matthews, Q.S.	01 Aug	E	Mason, C.M.	01 Mar
X	Thomson, C.D.	01 Feb	S	Preece, D.G.	01 Aug	E	Proctor, W.J.G.	01 Mar
X	Tredray, T.P.	01 Feb	E	Winter, R.J.	01 Aug	X	Stephen, B.M.	01 Mar
X	Walters, R.J.	01 Feb	X	Wood, C.	01 Aug	E	Cunnane, K.J.	01 Mar
X	Chaston, S.P.	01 Mar	X	Markey, A.P.	01 Aug	X	Hocking, C.B.	01 Mar
X	Cox, R.J.	01 Mar	S	Samuel, K.L.H.	01 Aug	E	Derby, B.D.	01 Apr
S	Hallett, S.J.	01 Mar	E	Laing, I.	01 Sep	X	Teague, F.M.	01 Apr
X	Howgill, M.C.	01 Mar	S	Fegan, P.	01 Sep	X	Kohler, A.P.	01 Apr
X	Loosley, D.P.	01 Mar	S	Finch, B.A.	01 Sep	E	Cubbage, J.	01 Apr
X	Mann, B.L.	01 Mar	E	Head, S.A.	01 Sep	S	Goudge, S.D.P.	01 Apr
X	Mann, S.A.	01 Mar	E	Wright, A.J.	01 Sep	E	Johnson, C.C.B.	01 Apr
E	Marshall, P.	01 Mar	X	Corney, A.D.	01 Sep	X	Offord, M.R.	01 Apr
X	Nelson, C.S.	01 Mar	X	Dowsett, P.G.	01 Sep	E	Swan, C.P.	01 Apr
X	Pearson, M.F.	01 Mar	X	Hayles, M.A.	01 Sep	X	Tomlyn, M.T.H.	01 Apr
S	Scott, W.M.	01 Mar	X	Jordan, A.A.	01 Sep	X	Dineen, J.M.G.	01 Apr
X	Bristowe, P.A.	01 Mar	E	Chapman, P.	01 Sep	X	Green, T.C.	01 Apr
X	Giles, R.K.	01 Mar	X	Downes, C.H.	01 Sep	E	Hawley, S.C.	01 Apr
E	Adams, G.H.	01 Apr	X	Beattie, P.S.	01 Oct	X	Paice, S.D.	01 Apr
X	Butterworth, N.G.	01 Apr	X	Dennis, M.J.	01 Oct	E	Wheater, K.J.	01 Apr
E	Parnell, A.D.	01 Apr	S	Knock, G.P.	01 Oct	E	Ford, J.D.	01 May
X	Ryan, S.J.	01 Apr	X	Minter, J.H.H.	01 Oct	X	Hygate, A.M.	01 May
E	Walton, C.P.	01 Apr	X	Reed, M.T.	01 Oct	X	Maxwell, R.	01 May
X	Burns, A.P.	01 Apr	X	Robertson, J.T.	01 Oct	X	Horton, A.S.J.	01 May
E	Drywood, T.	01 Apr	X	Houston, D.J.M.	01 Oct	E	Kelly, H.C.	01 May
E	Reid, J.C.J.	01 Apr	S	Joll, S.M.	01 Oct	X	Howe, J.P.	01 May
E	Daly-Rayner, A.	01 May	X	Sargent, L.M.	01 Oct	E	Noakes, K.M.	01 May
E	Kerr, A.N.	01 May	X	Cooke, G.S.	01 Oct	X	Clark, J.L.	01 Jun
E	Rand, M.J.	01 May	S	Pheasant, J.C.S.	01 Oct	X	Osborn, C.G.	01 Jun
X	Russell, P.	01 May	X	Richards, G.B.	01 Nov	E	Cox, D.J.	01 Jun
X	Utley, M.K.	01 May	X	Noyce, V.R.A.	01 Nov	X	Hempsell, A.M.	01 Jun
X	Forbes, A.R.	01 May	E	Palmer, M.E.	01 Nov	X	Hurley, C.	01 Jun
X	Furlong, C.A.	01 May	X	Curry, R.E.	01 Nov	X	McGlory, S.J.	01 Jun
E	Shaw, M.L.	01 May	X	Chamberlain, N.R.L.	01 Nov	X	Moss, J.R.	01 Jun
E	Aniyi, C.B.J.	01 Jun	X	Buckingham, G.	01 Dec	X	Robinson, S.	01 Jun
X	Bessell, D.A.	01 Jun	X	Lovegrove, T.E.	01 Dec	X	Waterfield, S.J.	01 Jun
X	Douglas, P.J.	01 Jun	E	Rowan, N.A.	01 Dec	E	Doran, S.E.	01 Jul
X	Durham, P.C.L.	01 Jun	E	Edey, M.J.	01 Dec	E	O'Nyons, Y.I.	01 Jul
X	Paterson, M.P.	01 Jun	E	Howse, R.J.	01 Dec	X	Raeburn, M.	01 Jul
X	West, R.J.	01 Jun	X	Sweeney, L.C.K.	01 Dec	X	Price, D.W.	01 Jul
X	Williams, C.N.O.	01 Jun	X	Teasdale, D.A.	01 Dec	E	Garland, D.S.	01 Jul
E	Baller, C.R.	01 Jun				X	Gill, M.H.	01 Jul
E	Bonnar, J.A.	01 Jun		**1994**		E	Mincher, D.J.F.	01 Jul
E	Hutchins, R.F.	01 Jun	E	Lewis, D.J.	01 Jan	X	Payne, P.J.	01 Jul
E	Keen, N.	01 Jun	E	Davies, L.	01 Jan	X	Sellars, S.J.	01 Jul
X	Knight, D.W.	01 Jun	E	Onyike, C.E.	01 Jan	X	Murdoch, C.A.	01 Aug
X	Morton, M.C.	01 Jun	X	Pink, S.E.	01 Jan	X	Wilson, C.W.	01 Aug
E	Ralphson, M.D.	01 Jun	E	Farrington, J.L.	01 Jan	E	Bonner, N.	01 Aug
E	Williams, M.	01 Jun	E	Goldsmith, D.T.	01 Jan	E	Combe, G.R.	01 Aug
X	Dunn, P.E.	01 Jul	E	Richardson, D.	01 Jan	X	Goldstone, R.S.	01 Aug

X	Mortimer, R.P. . .	01 Aug
S	Nicholson, K.J. . .	01 Aug
X	Aitken, A.J. . . .	01 Sep
E	MacDonald, A.J. .	01 Sep
X	Williams, M.J. . .	01 Sep
X	Ahlgren, E.G. . . .	01 Sep
X	Millar, S.J.	01 Sep
X	Warneken, A.E. . . .	01 Oct
X	Drodge, A.P.F. . . .	01 Oct
X	Medland, O.J. . . .	01 Oct
X	Dawson, S.H. . . .	01 Oct
X	Lintern, R.D.	01 Oct
E	Richardson, D. . . .	01 Oct
E	Voyce, J.E.	01 Oct
E	Boyle, J.B.	01 Oct
X	Sharpe, T.G.	01 Oct
X	Pitcher, P.P. . . .	01 Nov
X	Williamson, S.M. .	01 Nov
X	Brown, S.D. . . .	01 Nov
E	Cummings, D.J. . .	01 Nov
E	Davidson, M. . . .	01 Nov
E	Bird, M.G.J. . . .	01 Nov
X	Wynn, R.J. . . .	01 Nov
X	Doull, D.J.M. . . .	01 Nov
X	Kirkwood, T.A.H. .	01 Nov
X	Strong, T.C. . . .	01 Nov
S	Nicholson, S.R. . .	22 Nov
X	Lamb, A.G.	01 Dec
X	Sillers, B.	01 Dec
X	Brodie, R.W.J. . .	01 Dec
E	Patterson, D. . . .	01 Dec
E	Burbridge, D.J. . .	01 Dec
X	MacAulay, N.M.A. .	01 Dec
X	Payne, R.W. . . .	01 Dec
X	Sweet, P.	01 Dec
S	Titmuss, J.F.	01 Dec
E	Trott, E.A.	01 Dec

1995

X	Binks, J.P.	01 Jan
X	Jones, A.E.	01 Jan
E	Block, A.W.G. . . .	01 Jan
X	Braithwaite, J.S. . .	01 Jan
X	Lunn, T.R.	01 Jan
S	Porter, T.B.	01 Jan
S	Roberts, S.M. . . .	01 Jan
X	Stacey, A.M.	01 Jan
X	Tapp, R.C.	01 Jan
S	Walker, D.W.A. . .	01 Jan
X	Allfree, J.	01 Jan
E	Bowden, M.T.E. . . .	01 Jan
X	Drake-Wilkes, N.J. . .	01 Jan
E	Highe, P.	01 Jan

X	Hird, R.P.	01 Jan
X	Jones, M.D.	01 Jan
X	Lovell, R.J.	01 Jan
E	McCarthy, S.J. . . .	01 Jan
E	Ronaldson, G.I. . . .	01 Jan
E	Scopes, D.	01 Jan
X	Laverty, R.E.. . . .	01 Feb
E	Boyes, M.R.	01 Feb
E	Coope, P.J.	01 Feb
X	Dunn, C.L.	01 Feb
S	Dutton, A.C.	01 Feb
E	Easton, D.R.W.	01 Feb
X	Franklin, G.D. . . .	01 Feb
E	Gair, S.D.H.	01 Feb
X	Maynard, C.I. . . .	01 Feb
X	Swigciski, D.P. . . .	01 Feb
X	Walker, A.J.	01 Feb
X	Wiseman, I.C. . . .	01 Feb
E	Benn, S.W.	01 Feb
E	Adams, R.J.	01 Mar
X	Bellis, B.M.	01 Mar
X	Foulis, N.D.A. . . .	01 Mar
S	Gennard, A.	01 Mar
E	Burvill, J.P.	01 Mar
E	Eccleston, J.M. . . .	01 Mar
E	Fisher, P.C.	01 Mar
E	Goulding, J.P.	01 Mar
E	Jennings, W.	01 Mar
E	Large, S.A.	01 Mar
X	Little, S.G..	01 Mar
X	Phillips, J.N.	01 Mar
X	Thompson, M.G. . .	01 Mar
S	Wales, B.D.	01 Mar
X	Watson, I.	01 Mar
X	Percival, A.W.	01 Mar
X	Skelley, A.N.M. . . .	01 Mar
E	Bowker, I.C.	01 Apr
X	Foster, T.G.	01 Apr
E	Hall, T.T.	01 Apr
S	Harris, J.R.J.	01 Apr
E	Stagg, A.R.	01 Apr
X	Stones, N.A.	01 Apr
X	Stride, J.C.	01 Apr
X	Ayers, T.P.	01 Apr
E	Carlisle, C.R.	01 May
S	Dickson, J.I.	01 May
X	Flack, A.A.W. . .	01 May
X	Hutchison, N.D.P. . .	01 May
S	Malins, D.J.H. . .	01 May
X	Stewart, A.B. . . .	01 May
S	White, J.E. . . .	01 May
S	Hall, E.L.	01 May
E	Holmes, R.A.G. . .	01 May

X	Whitfield, R.M.P. . . .	01 May
E	Bowman, R.J. . . .	01 May
X	Codling, D.V. . . .	01 May
X	Murison, L.C.	01 May
X	Peppe, A.G.	01 Jun
X	Euden, C.P.	01 Jun
X	Gough, A.C.	01 Jun
X	Jarrett, M.T.J. . . .	01 Jun
X	Miles, S.A.	01 Jun
E	Ryan, N.	01 Jun
X	Williams, I.J.	01 Jun
X	Freeborn, J.O.	30 Jun
S	Cowan, C.J.	01 Jul
E	Edmonds, L.A. . . .	01 Jul
X	Upton, T.C.	01 Jul
X	Gilmour, J.F.	01 Jul
X	Holden, D.M.	01 Jul
X	Beacham, P.R. . . .	01 Jul
E	Edward, G.J.	01 Jul
X	Jasper, M.J.	01 Jul
E	Letts, A.J.	01 Jul
E	Lincoln, K.J.	01 Jul
E	Sharkey, E.R.	01 Jul
E	Sweeney, K.P.M. . .	01 Jul
E	Pitchford, I.C.	01 Aug
S	Allen, C.W.	01 Aug
X	Syrett, M.E.	01 Aug
E	Hickson, M.S.H. . .	01 Aug
E	Veal, A.E.	01 Aug
E	Rawson, S.M. . . .	01 Sep
X	Cheesman, D.J.M. .	01 Sep
S	Dickins, M.D.J. . . .	01 Sep
E	Gorman, P.B. . . .	01 Sep
E	Lovatt, I.W.M. . . .	01 Sep
E	May, S.C.	01 Sep
S	Murdoch, A.P. . . .	01 Sep
E	Sandle, N.D.	01 Sep
E	Storey, C.L.	01 Sep
X	Aspden, M.C.	01 Oct
E	O'Neill, P.J.	01 Oct
X	Bosley, B.D.	01 Oct
X	Roberts, P.S. . . .	01 Oct
X	Skeels-Piggins, . .	01 Oct

T.S.

X	Ley, A.B.	01 Nov
X	Bassett, D.A.	01 Nov
X	Neild, T.	01 Nov

1996

E	Pakes, D.T.	01 Jan
S	Dean, J.R.	01 Jan
E	Stowell, R.B.M. . .	01 Jan
X	Cahill, K.A.	01 Mar

SUB LIEUTENANTS

1992

E	Edwards, A.G. . .	01 May
E	Etchells, S.B. . . .	01 May
X	Lockett, D.J. . . .	01 May
E	Paulson, R.B. . .	01 May
E	Hiscock, S.R.B. . .	01 Sep
X	Peters, W.R. . . .	01 Sep

E	Powles, D.A.	01 Sep
X	Horne, J.R.	01 Dec

1993

X	George, D.M. . . .	01 Jan
X	Hammond, P.J. . . .	01 Jan
E	Hendrickx, C.J. . . .	01 Jan

X	Hesling, G.	01 Jan
X	Jamieson, R.E. . .	01 Jan
X	Johnstone, J.O. . .	01 Jan
X	Lynn, I.H.	01 Jan
E	Mullins, A.D. . .	01 Jan
X	Cook, C.M.	01 May
S	Curry, A.H.	01 May

X	Irons, R.C.S.	01 May
E	Rae, A.L.	01 May
X	Vink, J.D.	01 May
X	Wheeler, N.J.	01 May
S	Barber, R.W.	01 Sep
E	Barnett, M.A.	01 Sep
E	Bell, J.M.	01 Sep
X	Berisford, A.W.	01 Sep
E	Blair, G.J.L.	01 Sep
X	Bratt, A.R.	01 Sep
X	Capes, S.G.	01 Sep
X	Clark, M.H.	01 Sep
X	Clay, J.C.	01 Sep
X	Crawley, J.E.	01 Sep
E	Edwards, S.G.	01 Sep
X	Evans, C.A.	01 Sep
E	Field, C.R.H.	01 Sep
E	Fraser, H.L.	01 Sep
E	Gardner, M.E.F.	01 Sep
X	Goddard, J.C.	01 Sep
S	Green, S.R.	01 Sep
S	Hanson, M.N.	01 Sep
X	Harper, P.R.	01 Sep
E	Hope, M.R.	01 Sep
E	Hughes, N.D.	01 Sep
X	Ingram, G.J.	01 Sep
X	Johnston, J.A.	01 Sep
E	Jones, D.M.	01 Sep
X	Kidd, J.C.	01 Sep
E	Leach, S.J.	01 Sep
E	Ling, C.	01 Sep
S	MacKay, A.C.	01 Sep
E	McCombe, J.	01 Sep
E	McNamara, I.M.	01 Sep
X	Miller, N.W.H.	01 Sep
X	Parrott, J.P.	01 Sep
E	Parry, M.R.R.	01 Sep
E	Pearce, A.G.E.	01 Sep
E	Perkins, R.J.	01 Sep
X	Philpott, A.M.	01 Sep
E	Purvis, D.M.	01 Sep
X	Rae, D.G.	01 Sep
E	Read, M.R.	01 Sep
X	Readwin, R.R.	01 Sep
X	Redford, D.E.M.	01 Sep
S	Rees, R.T.	01 Sep
X	Reid, W.A.	01 Sep
X	Rimington, A.K.	01 Sep
X	Scandling, P.	01 Sep
E	Screaton, R.M.	01 Sep
X	Shepherd, M.P.	01 Sep
E	Smith, M.J.	01 Sep
E	Stiven, T.D.	01 Sep
X	Stride, J.A.	01 Sep
X	Stroude, P.A.	01 Sep
E	Thompson, M.J.	01 Sep
E	Ubhi, W.G.	01 Sep
E	York, G.R.J.	01 Sep

1994

X	Anderson, R.E.R.	01 Jan
X	Backus, R.I.K.	01 Jan
E	Bailey, J.J.	01 Jan
X	Balletta, R.J.	01 Jan
X	Barry, J.P.	01 Jan
X	Battrick, R.R.	01 Jan
E	Boyes, G.A.	01 Jan
X	Byrne, T.F.	01 Jan
X	Edge, K.L.	01 Jan
E	Fitzsimmons, S.M.	01 Jan
E	Flynn, A.	01 Jan
E	Foreman, S.M.	01 Jan
X	Greasley, M.J.	01 Jan
X	Habgood, S.S.	01 Jan
E	Haddow, T.R.	01 Jan
X	Hains, J.	01 Jan
E	Hambly, M.R.	01 Jan
S	Harding, D.J.	01 Jan
E	Hedgecox, D.C.	01 Jan
E	Kimball-Smith, P.R.G.	01 Jan
X	Laughton, P.	01 Jan
E	Lyons, M.J.	01 Jan
X	May, C.	01 Jan
X	McBratney, J.A.G.	01 Jan
X	Mitchell, C.D.	01 Jan
X	Monk, C.R.	01 Jan
X	Mowatt, P.	01 Jan
E	Murphy, S.M.	01 Jan
X	Parker, R.J.	01 Jan
X	Parr, M.J.E.	01 Jan
X	Patterson, J.D.	01 Jan
E	Robertshaw, I.W.	01 Jan
E	Rowlands, A.R.	01 Jan
E	Schreier, P.J.R.	01 Jan
E	Spooner, R.S.	01 Jan
X	Steadman, R.P.	01 Jan
X	Sutcliffe, M.R.	01 Jan
X	Tabberer, I.C.	01 Jan
E	Thorp, B.T.	01 Jan
X	Turner, C.L.	01 Jan
X	Tyler, J.C.	01 Jan
X	Walsh, K.M.	01 Jan
E	Wright, D.I.	01 Jan
E	Ankah, G.K.E.	01 May
E	Haworth, J.H.T.	01 May
X	Hopper, I.M.	01 May
E	Jefferson, T.S.	01 May
E	Marr, J.	01 May
S	Percival, F.	01 May
E	Puxley, M.E.	01 May
X	Smith, K.M.L.	01 May
X	Spinks, D.W.	01 May
X	Walton, S.D.	01 May
X	Welch, D.A.	01 May
X	Arden, V.G.	01 Sep
X	Birkett, C.L.	01 Sep
X	Black, S.A.	01 Sep
X	Bone, J.	01 Sep
X	Boxall, P.	01 Sep
X	Brooks, G.C.G.	01 Sep
E	Brown, A.M.	01 Sep
X	Butterworth, P.G.	01 Sep
X	Cutler, A.R.	01 Sep
X	Daveney, D.A.	01 Sep
X	Davies, L.E.	01 Sep
X	Davies, S.R.	01 Sep
X	Day, S.N.	01 Sep
S	Dow, C.S.	01 Sep
X	Essenhigh, A.N.P.	01 Sep
S	Exworthy, D.A.G.	01 Sep
X	Fitzpatrick, J.A.J.	01 Sep
X	Gatenby, C.D.	01 Sep
E	Goodale, H.J.	01 Sep
X	Hibberd, K.M.	01 Sep
X	Hounsom, T.R.	01 Sep
E	Kendrick, A.M.	01 Sep
E	Lee, W.	01 Sep
X	Lewis, A.J.	01 Sep
S	Lewis, S.J.	01 Sep
X	Lumsden, P.I.	01 Sep
E	McCallum, N.R.	01 Sep
E	McHugh, R.H.	01 Sep
E	Mealing, D.W.	01 Sep
X	Miles, R.L.	01 Sep
E	Miller, M.C.	01 Sep
X	Nathanson, H.	01 Sep
E	Nicoll, A.J.	01 Sep
X	Northover, A.F.	01 Sep
E	O'Toole, M.C.	01 Sep
X	Oakley, S.E.	01 Sep
X	Ottewell, P.S.	01 Sep
E	Quade, N.A.C.	01 Sep
S	Reed, D.K.	01 Sep
X	Roberts, S.J.	01 Sep
X	Robertson Gopffarth, A.A.J.	01 Sep
X	Rushworth, B.J.	01 Sep
E	Russell, A.	01 Sep
X	Sowerby, A.B.	01 Sep
E	Spiller, S.N.	01 Sep
E	Thorne, D.J.	01 Sep
X	Tilden, P.J.E.	01 Sep
X	Webb, M.D.	01 Sep
S	Wells, M.P.	01 Sep
E	Whitehouse, N.R.	01 Sep
X	Wood, C.R.	01 Sep

1995

X	Babbington, K.L.M.	01 Jan
X	Borbone, N.	01 Jan
X	Brockington, G.C.	01 Jan
E	Burley, M.R.	01 Jan
E	Burns, J.E.	01 Jan
X	Charlton, N.	01 Jan
X	Coles, S.C.	01 Jan
X	Crookes, W.A.	01 Jan
X	Ellison, T.G.	01 Jan
E	Harvey, B.	01 Jan
E	Kennedy, I.	01 Jan
E	Kirk, A.C.	01 Jan
E	Murchie, A.D.	01 Jan
E	O'Shaughnessy, D.J.	01 Jan
E	Patterson, S.D.	01 Jan
E	Richards, J.I.H.	01 Jan
X	Saunders, C.E.M.	01 Jan
E	Selway, M.A.	01 Jan
X	Shaughnessy, T.E.	01 Jan
X	Simcock, J.L.	01 Jan
E	Skidmore, P.J.	01 Jan
E	Skittrall, S.D.	01 Jan
E	Spedding, H.G.W.	01 Jan

X	Steer, A.D.	01 Jan	E	Bartlett, M.J.	01 Sep	E Willis, A.S. . . . . 01 Sep
S	Stowe, E.J.	01 Jan	E	Benstead, N.W.J. . .	01 Sep	
S	Vogel, L.D.	01 Jan	S	Carrigan, J.A. . . .	01 Sep	**1996**
X	Ward, S.	01 Jan	E	Cartwright, J.A. . . .	01 Sep	X Clarke, D. . . . . . 01 Jan
X	Tappenden, E.J. .	01 May	S	Dancer, A.I.	01 Sep	X Gould, J.D. . . . . 01 Jan
X	Wilson, A.J. . . .	01 May	E	Hay, M.	01 Sep	X Hutchins, I.D.M. . . 01 Jan
E	Ablett, S.D. . . .	01 Sep	X	Johns, A.W.	01 Sep	X Pretty, D.L. . . . . 01 Jan
X	Allison, G.J. . . .	01 Sep	X	Mattock, D.B. . . .	01 Sep	X Williams, A.S. . . . 01 Jan
E	Bamforth, C.J.M. .	01 Sep	S	Vollentine, L.	01 Sep	

SUB LIEUTENANTS (UCE)

	1993			**1995**		X	Gillett, D.A.	01 Sep
X	Wood, M.L. . . .	01 Sep	X	Brotton, P.J.	01 Sep	E	Hoather, M.S. . . .	01 Sep
			X	Bussey, E.L.	01 Sep	X	Johnson, M.R.E. . .	01 Sep
	1994		E	Chestnutt, J.M. . . .	01 Sep	X	Jordan, A.F.	01 Sep
E	Griffiths, L.	01 Sep	E	Cross, A.L.	01 Sep	E	Midgley, J.T.J. . . .	01 Sep
X	Wakeford, I.F. . .	01 Sep	X	Dodds, M.L.	01 Sep	E	Mountford, P.C. . .	01 Sep
			X	Gates, D.A.	01 Sep	X	Shorland-Ball, T.J. .	01 Sep

MIDSHIPMEN

	1994			**1995**		X	Knight, D.S.	01 Sep
E	Greig, J.A.	01 May	X	Clark, R.A.	01 Jan	E	Resheph, A.A. . . .	01 Sep
X	Bewley, N.J. . . .	01 Sep	X	Crowe, D.M.	01 Jan	X	Thatcher, L.F.V. . .	01 Sep
E	Corderoy, R.I. . .	01 Sep	E	Gillard, V.A.	01 Jan			
E	Hughes, W.P.M. .	01 Sep	E	Harrington, L.B. . .	01 May		**1996**	
X	James, A.W. . . .	01 Sep	E	Pipkin, P.J. . . .	01 May	S	Hooper, J.	01 Jan
E	McClement, D.L. .	01 Sep	E	Russell, C.M.L. . .	01 May			
X	Sigley, A.D.M. . .	01 Sep	X	Feeney, M.B. . . .	01 Sep			
E	Stafford, B.R. . . .	01 Sep	X	Griffiths, T.G. . . .	01 Sep			

MEDICAL OFFICERS

SURGEON VICE ADMIRAL

Revell, Anthony Leslie , *QHS, MB, ChB, FFARCS, DA, rcds, ndc* . . . . 16 Aug 94
    (SURGEON GENERAL AUG 94)

SURGEON REAR ADMIRALS

Craig, Alexander , *QHP, MB, BCh, ChB, ndc* . . . . 27 Apr 93
    (MEDICAL DIRECTOR GENERAL(NAVAL) AUG 94)

SURGEON CAPTAINS

(Full Career Commission)

1985		1990		- Carne, J.R.C. . . . 30 Jun
- Harland, R. . . . . 31 Dec		- Soul, J.O. . . . . . 31 Dec		- O'Connell, M.R. . . 31 Dec
1986		**1991**		**1994**
- Swain, D.L. . . . . 30 Jun		- Lambert, B.E. . . . 31 Dec		- Cunningham, D.A. . 30 Jun
				- Howard, O.M. . . . 31 Dec
1987		**1992**		
- Marsh, A.R. . . . . 30 Jun		- Curr, R.D. . . . . 30 Jun		**1995**
		- Haydon, J.R. . . . 30 Jun		- Tolley, P.F.R. . . . 31 Dec
1988		- Baldock, N.E. . . . 31 Dec		
- Paine, M.P.W.H. . . 31 Dec		- McMillan, G.H.G. . . 31 Dec		**1996**
- Jenkins, I.L. . . . . 31 Dec				- Edmondstone, W.M. 30 Jun
		1993		
1989		- Farquharson- . . . 30 Jun		
- Evans, C.W. . . . . 30 Jun		Roberts, M.A.		

SURGEON COMMANDERS

(Full Career & Medium Career Commission)

1975	1987	1991
- Warlow, C.N. . . . 31 Dec	- Bevan, N.S. . . . . 30 Jun	- Lunn, D.V. . . . . 30 Jun
	- Gabb, J.H. . . . . 31 Dec	- Cahill, C.J. . . . . 30 Jun
1983	- Johnston, C.G. . . 31 Dec	- Allison, A.S.C. . . . 30 Jun
- Holt, D.C.B. . . . . 31 Dec		- Walker, A.J. . . . . 30 Jun
	1988	- Brown, D.C. . . . 31 Dec
1984	- Taylor, R.H. . . . . 31 Dec	- Stoot, C.J. . . . . 31 Dec
- Doyle, E.H.M.B. . . 30 Jun	- Francis, T.J.R. . . . 31 Dec	- Dale, R.F. . . . . . 31 Dec
- Mugridge, A.R. . . . 30 Jun	- Clark, R.J. . . . . 31 Dec	
- Churcher-Brown, . . 30 Jun		**1992**
C.J.	**1989**	- Campbell, J.K. . . 30 Jun
- Sykes, J.J.W. . . . 31 Dec	- Glover, S.D. . . . . 30 Jun	- Smith, R.W. . . . . 30 Jun
- Douglas-Riley, T.R. . 31 Dec	- Cowley, M.L. . . . 30 Jun	- McArthur, C.J.G. . . 30 Jun
	- Barker, C.P.G. . . . 31 Dec	- Butterfield, N.P. . . 31 Dec
1985	- Ridout, S.S. . . . . 31 Dec	- Broome, J.R. . . . 31 Dec
- Kershaw, C.R. . . . 30 Jun		- Evans, G.H. . . . 31 Dec
- Runchman, P.C. . . 30 Jun	**1990**	
- Ashton, R.E. . . . . 31 Dec	- Ryder, S.J. . . . . 30 Jun	**1993**
	- Jarvis, L.J. . . . . 30 Jun	- Evans, S.D. . . . . 30 Jun
1986	- Waugh, P.J. . . . . 30 Jun	- Dean, M.R. . . . . 30 Jun
- Yates, A. . . . . . 31 Dec	- Woodroof, G.M.F. . 30 Jun	- Cox, H.J. . . . . 30 Jun
- Morgan, N.V. . . . 31 Dec	- Raffaelli, P.I. . . . 31 Dec	- Balmer, A.V. . . . 31 Dec
	- Tulloch, D.N. . . . 31 Dec	- Benton, P.J. . . . 31 Dec
		- Scott, M.M. . . . . 31 Dec

- Hett, D.A.	31 Dec	- Greer, J.P.	31 Dec	**1996**	
		- Gillen, C.D.	31 Dec	- Burgess, A.J.	30 Jun
1994		- Cripps, N.P.J.	31 Dec	- Neal, A.J.D.	30 Jun
- Nicol, P.J.S.	30 Jun			- McNeill Love,	30 Jun
- Baker, A.B.	30 Jun	**1995**		R.M.C.	
- Hodkinson, S.L.	30 Jun	- Sheard, S.C.	30 Jun		
- Pipkin, C.	30 Jun	- Hughes, A.S.	31 Dec		
- Spalding, T.J.W.	30 Jun	- Buxton, P.J.	31 Dec		

SURGEON LIEUTENANT COMMANDERS

(Full Career Commission)

1987		- Wylie, R.D.S.	01 Aug	**1993**	
- Slavin, D.E.	02 Feb	- Loxdale, P.H.	01 Aug	- Glover, M.A.	01 Aug
- Hulland, N.W.	16 Aug	- Midwinter, M.J.	10 Sep	- Bree, S.E.P.	01 Aug
- Haddon, R.W.J.	19 Oct	- Risdall, J.E.	10 Sep	- Preece, R.M.	01 Aug
				- Summerton, D.J.	01 Aug
1988		**1991**		- Stewart, M.D.	03 Aug
- Hague, S.	01 Jul	- Dryden, P.W.	22 Jan	- Price, D.J.A.	09 Aug
- Hedger, N.A.	01 Aug	- Hughes, P.A.	01 Aug	- Guy, R.J.	15 Aug
		- Young, P.C.	01 Aug	- Foster, C.R.M.	19 Sep
1989		- Lambert, A.W.	01 Aug		
- Roberts, A.P.	01 Feb	- Low, C.D.T.	01 Aug	**1994**	
- Pearson, C.R.	15 May	- Ross, R.A.	01 Aug	- McKeating, J.B.	01 Feb
- Howell, G.E.D.	01 Aug	- Hill, G.A.	01 Aug	- Cooke, S.S.	01 Aug
- Johnston, R.P.	01 Aug	- Lygo, M.H.	28 Aug	- Parker, S.J.	01 Aug
- Newson-Smith, M.S.	01 Aug			- Dashfield, A.K.	01 Aug
- Scott, R.C.	01 Aug	**1992**		- Hambling, S.P.	08 Aug
- Crawford, P.I.	01 Aug	- Gent, R.P.ST.J.	01 Aug	- Birt, D.J.	25 Aug
		- Nicholson, G.	01 Aug		
1990		- Turnbull, P.S.	01 Aug	**1995**	
- Campbell, D.J.	01 May	- Howell, M.A.	01 Aug	- Hand, C.J.	04 Jan
- Edwards, C.J.A.	01 Aug	- Murray, S.J.	01 Aug		
- Perry, J.N.	01 Aug	- Groom, M.R.	01 Aug	**1996**	
- Murrison, A.W.	01 Aug			- Sharpley, J.G.	08 Feb

SURGEON LIEUTENANT COMMANDERS

(Short Career Commission)

1988		**1994**		- Loxdale, S.J.	01 Aug
- Ashworth, A.J.	03 Jun	- Wood, G.	01 Aug	- Wolstencroft, P.J.	01 Aug
				- Jarvis, D.H.	01 Aug
1989		**1995**		- Stapley, S.A.	01 Aug
- MacLennan, I.R.	01 Jul	- Dunn, R.L.R.	19 Feb	- Edwards, P.D.	21 Dec
		- Dewhurst, A.T.	01 Jul		
1993		- Farrar, M.W.	01 Aug	**1996**	
- MacLeod, D.B.	01 Feb	- Smith, S.R.C.	01 Aug	- Ogden, G.H.	01 Feb
		- Evershed, M.C.	01 Aug		

SURGEON LIEUTENANTS

(Full Career Commission)

1991		- Tellam, S.M.	01 Aug
- Millar, S.W.S.	01 Aug		

SURGEON LIEUTENANTS

(Short Career Commission)

1991		- Tant, M.C.O.	01 Aug	- Miles, R.	01 Aug
- Billingsley, P.	01 Aug	- Howden, P.E.	01 Aug	- Turner, M.S.	01 Aug

- Tanser, S.J.	01 Aug	- Dowdeswell, K.A.	01 Aug	- Tamayo, B.C.C.	01 Aug
- Leigh-Smith, S.J.	01 Aug	- Ronaldson, T.E.	01 Aug	- Houlberg, K.A.N.	01 Aug
- Nichols, E.A.	01 Aug	- Broadley, A.J.M.	01 Aug	- Wallis, L.A.	01 Aug
- Johnson, G.A.H.	01 Aug	- Craner, M.J.	01 Aug	- Gibson, A.R.	01 Aug
- Mellor, A.J.	06 Sep	- Stenton, M.J.	01 Aug	- Hughes, D.J.	01 Aug
		- Matthews, G.A.	01 Aug	- Clarke, M.D.	04 Aug
1992		- Brunton, L.M.	01 Aug	- Parry, C.A.	12 Aug
- Badham, D.P.	11 Jan	- Streets, C.G.	01 Aug		
- Palmer, A.C.	01 Mar	- Shaw, C.E.	01 Aug	**1995**	
- Whittaker, M.A.	01 Aug	- Reid, C.J.	01 Aug	- Coltman, T.P.	01 Aug
- Blair, D.G.S.	01 Aug	- Smith, J.E.	01 Aug	- Ahling-Smith,	01 Aug
- Yarnall, N.J.	01 Aug	- Rickard, R.F.	03 Aug	H.E.M.	
- Cannon, L.B.	01 Aug	- Freshwater, D.A.	09 Aug	- McCabe, S.E.T.	01 Aug
- Rose, J.D.	01 Aug	- Lewis, C.A.	31 Aug	- Sowden, L.M.	02 Aug
- Kerr, D.J.	01 Aug			- Dickson, S.J.	02 Aug
- Fisher, N.G.	01 Aug	**1994**		- Mercer, S.J.	03 Aug
- Connor, D.J.	01 Aug	- Bowie, A.	11 Mar	- Ayers, D.E.B.	03 Aug
- Thomas, R.C.	05 Aug	- Lawson, L.L.	01 Aug	- McLachlan, J.K.	17 Aug
- Randall, L.S.	14 Aug	- Dekker, B.J.	01 Aug	- Lew-Gor, S.T.W.	05 Sep
		- Greenberg, N.	01 Aug	- Tennant, M.I.	14 Sep
1993		- Heames, R.M.	01 Aug		
- Rawal, K.M.	31 Jan	- Counter, P.R.	01 Aug	**1996**	
- Every, M.	03 Feb	- Heath, C.W.	01 Aug	- Webber, R.J.	01 Feb
- Williams, H.D.	04 Feb	- Snowden, M.B.S.	01 Aug		
- Brinsden, M.D.	15 Jul	- Potiphar, D.W.	01 Aug		

ACTING SURGEON LIEUTENANTS

1995		- Bland, S.A.	05 Jul	- Mather, R.H.	12 Jul
- Nicholl, S.	07 Jan	- Porter, S.	05 Jul	- Mackie, S.J.	15 Jul
- Marshall, F.T.	30 Jun	- Smith, J.J.	10 Jul	- Milner, R.A.	15 Jul
- Anstis, P.A.	03 Jul	- Reston, S.C.	11 Jul	- Davies, S.R.	17 Jul
- Clarkson, S.J.	03 Jul	- Birch, R.J.	12 Jul	- Armstrong, E.M.	21 Dec
- Matthews, J.J.	03 Jul	- Denholm, J.L.	12 Jul		

MEDICAL CADETS SURGEON SUB LIEUTENANTS RN

1993		- Norris, W.D.	01 Jul	- Allsop, A.R.L.	20 Jan
- Stevenson, V.J.	10 Sep	- Payne, D.E.	01 Jul	- Christopher, A.S.	01 Jul
- Prior, K.R.E.J.	15 Sep	- Whybourn, L.A.	01 Jul	- Prendergast, M.P.	01 Jul
- Fisher, M.A.	27 Sep	- Gay, D.A.T.	06 Jul	- Evans, G.C.	07 Jul
- Hutchings, S.D.	18 Oct	- Gallagher, A.J.	27 Jul	- Cormack, A.J.R.	09 Jul
- Beadsmoore, E.J.	01 Nov	- Pearce, L.A.	27 Jul	- Nelstrop, A.M.	07 Aug
- Henry, M.F.	01 Nov	- Rahman, J.	04 Aug	- Price, V.J.	29 Aug
		- Welch, J.F.	03 Oct	- Miller, A.D.	24 Sep
1994		- Brims, F.J.H.	13 Oct	- Barton, S.J.	04 Oct
- Dow, W.A.M.	01 Feb	- McIntosh, J.D.	15 Oct	- Kershaw, D.J.E.	27 Oct
- McAllister, D.R.	01 Feb	- Knight, E.M.	31 Oct		
- Shaw, S.L.	01 Feb			**1996**	
- Rees, P.S.C.	10 Jun	**1995**		- Martin, N.P.	01 Jan
- Carty, J.	01 Jul	- Weldon, D.P.	10 Jan		

DENTAL OFFICERS

SURGEON CAPTAINS(D)

(Full Career Commission)

1987		1991		1995	
- Grant, E.J.	30 Jun	- Hargraves, J. . . .	31 Dec	- Lambert-Humble, S. .	31 Dec
1988		1993			
- Hambly, R.S. . . .	31 Dec	- Holland, J.V.	30 Jun		
1990		1994			
- Rudge, G.H.A. . . .	30 Jun	- Myers, G.W.	31 Dec		

SURGEON COMMANDERS(D)

(Full Career Commission)

1979		1986		1991	
- Harkness, N. . . .	31 Dec	- Morrison, G.L. . . .	30 Jun	- Victor, J.D.	30 Jun
1981		1987		1994	
- Roberts, M.N.D. . . .	30 Jun	- Thomas, D.L. . . .	30 Jun	- Priestland, C.R. . .	30 Jun
1983		1988		1995	
- Lock, W.R.	30 Jun	- Weston, M.W. . . .	31 Dec	- Gall, M.R.C.	30 Jun
1984		1989		- Sidoli, G.E.	31 Dec
- Griffiths, B.J. . . .	31 Dec	- Sanderson, R.C. . .	30 Jun	1996	
1985		1990		- Norris, R.E.	30 Jun
- Iles, J.G.	30 Jun	- Stevenson, R.M. . .	31 Dec		

SURGEON LIEUTENANT COMMANDERS(D)

(Full Career & Medium Career Commission)

1987		1990		1992	
- Culwick, P.F.	01 Jan	- Riden, D.K.	01 Aug	- Hall, D.J.	04 Feb
- Maxwell, A.B.C. . . .	13 Jul	- Jordan, A.M.	07 Dec	1993	
1988		- Aston, M.W.	19 Dec	- Redman, C.D.J. . .	19 Jul
- Howe, S.E.	27 Jan	1991		1994	
1989		- McJarrow, D.J. . . .	01 Jan	- Elmer, T.B.	16 Jan
- Liggins, S.J. . . .	01 Mar				

SURGEON LIEUTENANT COMMANDERS(D)

(Short Career Commission)

1993		- Jameson, B.G.L. . .	20 Dec	1996	
- Smith, B.S. . . .	13 Sep	1995		- Badami, A.A. . . .	01 Jan
1994		- Lamb, K.G.	18 Jan	- Brandon, J.	13 Jan
- Pearson, B.J.	05 Jan	- Fenwick, J.C. . . .	03 Sep	- Featherstone, K.J. .	25 Apr
				- McCorkindale, P.R. .	13 Jun

SURGEON LIEUTENANTS(D)

(Full Career & Medium Career Commission)

1991		1992	
- Murray, C.A. . . . . 23 Sep		- Turnbull, N.R. . . . . 02 Jan	

SURGEON LIEUTENANTS(D)

(Short Career Commission)

1991	1993	
- Marney, J.J. . . . . 12 Jul	- Denny, A.M. . . . . 05 Jan	- James, I. . . . . . 09 Jan
	- Wallace, K.N. . . . 31 Jan	- Leyshon, R.J. . . . 09 Jan
1992	- Gordon, K.A. . . . 31 Aug	- Tsoi, A.C.M. . . . 09 Jan
- Davies, J.G. . . . . 01 Jan	- Purdie, C.F.A. . . . 26 Sep	- Wells, A.J. . . . . 09 Jan
- Kelly, M. . . . . . 01 Jan	- Harris, M.E. . . . . 10 Dec	- Winch, E.J. . . . . 24 Jan
- Davenport, N.J. . . 14 Feb	- Moore, P.G. . . . . 31 Dec	
- Lodge, S.G. . . . . 29 Mar		**1995**
	1994	- Nurton, K.E. . . . 08 Aug
	- Francis, J.M. . . . 09 Jan	- Woodhouse, P.D. . 08 Aug

SURGEON SUB LIEUTENANTS(D)

(Short Career Commission)

1994		1995
- Madgwick, E.C.C. . . 01 Jan	- Wingfield, M.H. . . 01 Oct	- Chittick, W.B.O. . . 01 Apr
- Stevenson, L.A. . . 01 Jan		- Taylor, K.H. . . . . 01 Apr

CHAPLAINS

CHAPLAIN OF THE FLEET

Bucks, *The Ven* Michael William , *QHC, BD, AKC* . . . . 18 Nov 69
(DIRECTOR GENERAL NAVAL CHAPLAINCY SERVICE APR 94)

CHAPLAINS

(Full Career Commission)

1970	1977	
CE Hempenstall, J.A. . 06 May	CE Golding, S.J. . . . 03 May	CE Buckley, R.F. . . . 04 Sep
	CE Hammett, B.K. . . . 11 Jul	CE Harman, M.J. . . . 20 Sep
1971	CE Nurton, R. . . . . . 27 Sep	1980
CE Weldon, W.E. . . . . 14 Apr		CE Hilliard, R.G. . . . . 01 Aug
	1978	
1975	CE Jones, E.W. . . . . 02 Feb	1981
CE Ames, J.P. . . . . . 19 Jun	CE Barlow, D. . . . . . 04 Apr	CE Clarke, B.R. . . . . 30 Jun
1976	1979	
CE French, C.A. . . . 28 Sep	CE Metters, A.J.F. . . . 27 Feb	

CHAPLAINS

(Medium Career Commission)

1980	1985	CE Lewis, T.J. . . . . 28 Nov
CE Stephens, S.E. . . 02 Sep	CE Wishart, M.L. . . . . 12 Feb	
		1990
1982	1986	CE Pyne, R.L. . . . . 23 Jan
CE Howard, C.W.W. . 28 Sep	CE Naylor, I.F. . . . . 16 Sep	CE Callon, A.M. . . . . 05 Jun
	CE Elmore, G.M. . . . . 30 Sep	CE Poll, M.G. . . . . . 14 Jun
1983		
CE Jackson, M.H. . . . 19 Apr	1987	1991
CE Baxendale, R.D. . . 14 Jul	CE Luckraft, C.J. . . . . 05 Aug	CE Green, J. . . . . . 04 Jun
		CE Scott, P.J.D.S. . . . 03 Sep
1984	1988	CE Springett, S.P. . . . 10 Sep
CE Renfrey, E.D.J-B. . 02 Feb	CE Thomas, D.W.W. . . 18 Oct	
CE Brotherton, M. . . 04 Sep		1992
	1989	CE Kelly, N.J. . . . . . 26 May
	CE Franklin, W.H. . . . 10 Jan	

CHAPLAINS

(Short Career Commission)

1987	1992	1994
CE Eglin, I. . . . . . . 27 Jan	CE Woodcock, N.E. . . 31 Mar	CE Hill, J. . . . . . . 17 Jan
	CE Swabey, B.F. . . . 14 Jul	
1988	CE Bromage, K.C. . . . 02 Aug	1995
CE Goodburn, D.H. . . 13 Sep	CE Morris, J.O. . . . . 06 Oct	CE Coates, R. . . . . 06 Jun
1991	1993	1996
CE Cutler, R.C. . . . 28 Jan	CE Beveridge, S.A.R. . . 28 Apr	CE Petzer, G.S. . . . . 09 Jan
CE Fairbank, B.D.S. . 03 Sep	CE Smith, G.J. . . . 25 May	

PRINCIPAL CHAPLAIN CHURCH OF SCOTLAND

Stewart, *Rev* Charles Edward , *QHC, BSc, BD, PhD* . . . . 29 Feb 76
(DIRECTOR NAVAL CHAPLAINCY SERVICES(MANNING) JAN 96)

CHAPLAINS

(Full Career Commission)

1973		1979		1981	
SF Watson, J.K. . . . . 28 Nov		SF Maze, A.T. . . . . . 11 Sep		SF Rae, S.M. . . . . 02 Feb	

CHAPLAINS

(Medium Career Commission)

1980		1982	
SF McCall, M.J. . . . . 27 Aug		SF Robinson, M.W. . . 01 Nov	
1981		1984	
SF Craig, G.W. . . . . 05 May		SF Keith, D. . . . . . 15 May	

CHAPLAINS

(Short Career Commission)

1990		1993		1995	
SF Livingstone, I. . . . 13 Aug		SF Brown, S.J. . . . . 20 Apr		SF Beadle, J.T. . . . . 30 Mar	
1991		SF Shackleton, S.J.S. . 20 Apr			
SF Matthews, W.J.J. . . 12 Aug		SF Wort, R.S. . . . . 27 Jul			

PRINCIPAL ROMAN CATHOLIC CHAPLAIN

Mullin, *The Rt Rev Monsignor* John Raymond Noel , *QHC* . . . . 04 Sep 78
    (DIRECTOR NAVAL CHAPLAINCY SERVICES APR 94)

CHAPLAINS

(Medium Career Commission)

1979		1984		RC Madders, B.R. . . . 09 Sep	
RC Clancy, R.J. . . . . 02 Jul		RC Docherty, V. . . . . 03 Sep			
1981		1985		1990	
RC Lacy, D.A. . . . . . 04 Aug		RC Donovan, P.A. . . . 22 Apr		RC Sharkey, M. . . . . 01 Oct	

CHAPLAINS

(Short Career Commission)

1991		1992		1994	
RC McBride, P.J. . . . 15 Aug		RC Couch, P.H.R.B. . . 05 May		RC Burns, T.M. . . . . 04 Jan	
		RC Geddes, C. . . . . 15 Sep		RC Forster, S. . . . . 08 Aug	

SPECIAL DUTIES LIST

COMMANDERS (SD)

1987		
MS Shone, D.E. . . . . 01 Oct	MS Marshall, G. . . . . 01 Oct	**1994**
X Palmer, D.L. . . . . 01 Oct	E Howell, K. . . . . . 01 Oct	X O'Brien, J.D. . . . . 01 Oct
	E Lane, G.T. . . . . . 01 Oct	E Smith-Jaynes, E.R. . 01 Oct
1988		E Freeston, G. . . . . 01 Oct
X Colmer, A.A. . . . . 01 Oct	**1992**	S Holder, R.J. . . . . 01 Oct
	X Street, R.W. . . . . 01 Oct	X Gregory, A.M. . . . 01 Oct
1989	X Root, W.R. . . . . 01 Oct	E Baker, M.A. . . . . 01 Oct
X Mundy, J.C. . . . . 01 Oct	E Parker, B.C. . . . . 01 Oct	
		1995
1990	**1993**	S Stonham, B.V. . . . 01 Oct
E McAleese, G. . . . . 01 Oct	MS Reed, F. . . . . . 01 Oct	E Wearmouth, P.W.A. . 01 Oct
X Morris, F. . . . . . 01 Oct	S Howden, N. . . . . 01 Oct	X Hilton, D. . . . . . 01 Oct
	E Alexander, S.J. . . . 01 Oct	MS Bootland, E.G. . . . 01 Oct
1991	X Connell, J.A. . . . . 01 Oct	E Kirk, J. . . . . . . 01 Oct
X Bee, M.J. . . . . . 01 Oct		

LIEUTENANT COMMANDERS (SD)

1983	1989	1991
E Palmer, M.R. . . . . 01 Apr	E Aydon, C.G. . . . . 01 Oct	E James, T.C. . . . . 01 Oct
	S Pearson, M.E. . . . 01 Oct	S Turner, D.J. . . . . 01 Oct
1984	E Pile, I. . . . . . . 01 Oct	E Pile, K.J. . . . . . 01 Oct
X Lennon, J. . . . . . 01 Apr	S Burton, C.J. . . . . 01 Oct	E Pittard, P.M. . . . . 01 Oct
X Brawn, A.J. . . . . 01 Oct	E Miller, R.J. . . . . 01 Oct	E Young, T.M. . . . . 01 Oct
	X Dunkley, R.C. . . . 01 Oct	X Jordan, C.W. . . . . 01 Oct
1985	MS Pullyblank, R.J. . . . 01 Oct	E Whetton, A.G. . . . 01 Oct
X Muggeridge, M.A.D. . 01 Apr	S Lynn, R.A. . . . . . 01 Oct	X Aspinall, R. . . . . 01 Oct
X Trotter, H.L. . . . . 01 Oct	E Rawlings, D.M. . . . 01 Oct	X Buchanan, J.R. . . . 01 Oct
E Bailey, P. . . . . . 01 Oct	E Whittleton, J.A. . . . 01 Oct	MS Newcombe, P.J. . . 01 Oct
	MS Golding, D.J. . . . . 01 Oct	X Swaine, R. . . . . . 01 Oct
1986	E Leggett, C.C. . . . . 01 Oct	S Harry, P.N. . . . . . 01 Oct
X Young, P.J. . . . . 01 Apr	X Carlton, I.P. . . . . 01 Oct	S Laycock, P.J. . . . 01 Oct
S Jarrett, M.H. . . . . 01 Apr		E Jones, J.K.P. . . . . 01 Oct
E Churchill, W.J. . . . 01 Oct	**1990**	E Hambrook, D.E. . . . 01 Oct
	X Mattless, T.W. . . . 01 Oct	E Hanslip, M.R. . . . 01 Oct
1987	E Hannaford, W.C. . . 01 Oct	E Wilkinson, A. . . . . 01 Oct
X Appleyard, G.S. . . . 01 Apr	X Davies, E.R. . . . . 01 Oct	X Cronin, A.R. . . . . 01 Oct
E Fowler, J. . . . . . 01 Apr	X Easton, R.W. . . . . 01 Oct	E Bamforth, B.R. . . . 01 Oct
E Lycett, B.L. . . . . 01 Oct	E Northcott, M.R. . . . 01 Oct	E Howard, R.G. . . . . 01 Oct
E Laurie, J.R. . . . . 01 Oct	E Heath, G.R. . . . . 01 Oct	S Brown, B.M. . . . . 01 Oct
X West, R.J. . . . . . 01 Oct	X Simons, A.S. . . . . 01 Oct	E Ballantyne, M.C. . . 01 Oct
E Burgess, B.C. . . . 01 Oct	E Lambert, P.B. . . . . 01 Oct	E Malcolmson, A.D. . . 01 Oct
E Shinn, D.E. . . . . 01 Oct	E Picken, J.D. . . . . 01 Oct	E Pritchard, D.G. . . . 01 Oct
X Jacklin, J.P. . . . . 01 Oct	E Southern, P.J. . . . 01 Oct	E Reid, D. . . . . . . 01 Oct
E Prideaux, D.M. . . . 01 Oct	MS Hayes, D.J. . . . . 01 Oct	E Vamplew, D. . . . . 01 Oct
	E Barber, A.M. . . . . 01 Oct	X Bowen, G.P. . . . . 01 Oct
1988	E Coles, G.J.V. . . . . 01 Oct	MS Harrington, A. . . . 01 Oct
X Fawcett, E.N. . . . . 01 Oct	E Concannon, J.L. . . . 01 Oct	MS Baker, K. . . . . . 01 Oct
X Lawler, J.D. . . . . 01 Oct	E Godwin, J.C. . . . . 01 Oct	S Keeling, F.G. . . . 01 Oct
MS Chandler, M. . . . . 01 Oct	E Martin, V.G. . . . . 01 Oct	X Stockton, J.P. . . . 01 Oct
X Cringle, D.J. . . . . 01 Oct	MS Dalgleish, J.R. . . . 01 Oct	E Brown, M.E. . . . . 01 Oct
E Cooke, R.G. . . . . 01 Oct	X Jones, E.T. . . . . . 01 Oct	E Hyde, C.D. . . . . . 01 Oct
E Collins, A.C. . . . . 01 Oct	S Radcliffe, F.G. . . . 01 Oct	E Crosbie, D.W. . . . 01 Oct
X Palmer, G.D. . . . . 01 Oct	E Elliott, T.F. . . . . 01 Oct	MS Edwards, R.A. . . . 01 Oct
E Jones, D.M. . . . . 01 Oct	X Beardall, J. . . . . 01 Oct	X Slade, R.J.L. . . . . 01 Oct
S Anderson, M.J. . . . 01 Oct		X Haywood, P. . . . . 01 Oct

E	Watson, M.	01 Oct
E	Foster, S.	01 Oct

1992

E	Gordon, R.M.	01 Oct
S	Miles, S.D.	01 Oct
X	Richford, T.F.	01 Oct
E	Kite, R.G.H.	01 Oct
X	Quinnell, K.R.A.	01 Oct
E	Broad, R.A.	01 Oct
E	Brunink, J.W.	01 Oct
E	Jones, A.J.	01 Oct
E	Lynch, P.A.	01 Oct
S	Haley, T.	01 Oct
E	O'Connell-Davidson, J.B.	01 Oct
X	Cooke, D.M.	01 Oct
X	Edwards, E.G.	01 Oct
MS	Noble, P.P.	01 Oct
S	Webb, J.R.	01 Oct
E	Hobbs, W.G.	01 Oct
E	Nurser, J.A.	01 Oct
E	Skinner, N.P.F.	01 Oct
E	Toon, J.R.	01 Oct
S	Chapman, N.P.	01 Oct
X	Kenealy, T.M.	01 Oct
X	Naylor, K.E.E.	01 Oct
X	Millington, J.H.	01 Oct
E	Milne, J.W.	01 Oct
E	Shepherd, A.	01 Oct
X	Shapiro, P.	01 Oct
X	Vasey, S.G.	01 Oct
E	Morrison, K.W.	01 Oct
E	Collins, R.J.	01 Oct
E	Coppin, P.D.	01 Oct
E	Raffle, A.J.	01 Oct
E	Tate, D.A.	01 Oct
E	Hart, W.C.	01 Oct
X	O'Sullivan, A.M.	01 Oct
E	Dalton, D.J.	01 Oct
E	McLean, C.J.R.	01 Oct
X	Kerslake, S.C.	01 Oct

1993

E	Barker, K.A.	05 Mar
E	Young, L.G.D.	01 Oct
X	Bate, C.	01 Oct
S	Smith, R.S.	01 Oct
E	Brazier, F.W.T.	01 Oct
E	Mansfield, R.A.G.	01 Oct
E	Todd, K.	01 Oct
X	Drury, M.H.	01 Oct
X	Stephens, D.R.	01 Oct

E	Cooper, D.	01 Oct
E	Ford, N.P.	01 Oct
E	Hollis, A.	01 Oct
E	Russan, W.R.	01 Oct
E	Tougher, R.	01 Oct
X	Cooper, K.A.H.	01 Oct
E	Burrows, J.A.	01 Oct
E	Pitcher, J.	01 Oct
X	Roberts, A.L.	01 Oct
E	Dickinson, B.	01 Oct
E	Sweeny, B.D.	01 Oct
X	Biggs, P.	01 Oct
X	Croft, M.	01 Oct
E	Goodrich, D.L.	01 Oct
E	Muscroft, P.J.V.	01 Oct
E	Stubbings, P.R.	01 Oct
S	Miles, T.M.	01 Oct
S	Wunderle, C.A.	01 Oct
E	Digweed, K.B.	01 Oct
X	Kelly, T.J.	01 Oct
MS	Jackson, S.K.	01 Oct
MS	Holyer, R.J.	01 Oct
X	Hinch, N.E.	01 Oct
E	Gray, N.	01 Oct
E	Greenfield, K.	01 Oct
MS	McKinlay, S.	01 Oct
S	Burt, P.R.	01 Oct
S	Howell, M.	01 Oct
E	Martin, M.P.	01 Oct
X	Nowosielski, F.	01 Oct

1994

E	Alison, L.A.	01 Oct
E	Brecken, D.G.	01 Oct
E	Haskell, E.T.	01 Oct
E	Mawby, P.J.	01 Oct
S	Lowe, S.A.	01 Oct
X	Piercy, P.A.H.	01 Oct
E	Holden, J.T.	01 Oct
E	Ryder, S.M.	01 Oct
E	Arthur, R.J.	01 Oct
MS	Walker, M.W.	01 Oct
X	Oakes, R.L.	01 Oct
E	Smyth, M.J.	01 Oct
E	McIntosh, K.D.	01 Oct
E	Poole, D.	01 Oct
E	Thomas, P.S.	01 Oct
X	Stephens, R.P.W.	01 Oct
X	Madge, A.W.J.	01 Oct
MS	Mugridge, T.J.G.	01 Oct
E	Hart, R.	01 Oct
X	Suddes, T.	01 Oct
E	Titcumb, R.S.B.	01 Oct

E	Barnden, M.J.	01 Oct
E	Hyde, T.	01 Oct
MS	White, M.A.	01 Oct
X	Denham, N.J.	01 Oct
E	Webb, P.V.	01 Oct
X	Healy, A.J.	01 Oct
X	Hoper, P.S.	01 Oct
S	Marsh, D.T.	01 Oct
E	Nethercott, L.R.	01 Oct
X	Blake, K.B.	01 Oct
E	Harwood, D.B.	01 Oct
E	Sumner, M.D.	01 Oct
X	Bryant, D.J.	01 Oct
S	Price, G.	01 Oct
E	De Jonghe, P.T.	01 Oct
E	Haywood, S.A.	01 Oct
X	Francis, J.	01 Oct

1995

E	MacAulay, N.	01 Oct
E	Morrison, G.R.	01 Oct
X	Skrzypczak, P.R.	01 Oct
E	Goble, I.J.	01 Oct
X	Wilson, R.P.	01 Oct
E	Day, T.S.	01 Oct
E	Edwards, R.A.	01 Oct
X	Thompson, G.	01 Oct
E	Nelson, A.	01 Oct
S	Bonsey, B.J.M.	01 Oct
X	Cox, J.P.	01 Oct
E	Andrews, I.	01 Oct
E	Roberts, E.W.	01 Oct
X	Sutton, R.W.	01 Oct
X	Goldie, K.W.	01 Oct
E	Pickbourne, M.	01 Oct
E	Peerman, S.J.	01 Oct
S	Morris, A.P.	01 Oct
E	Brazendale, C.	01 Oct
E	Kemp, M.S.	01 Oct
S	Dobson, B.J.	01 Oct
E	Dorricott, A.J.	01 Oct
E	Nailor, A.	01 Oct
E	Maidment, P.C.	01 Oct
X	Daniel, A.G.	01 Oct
X	Jenrick, M.F.	01 Oct
S	Llewelyn, B.	01 Oct
X	Nolan, A.L.	01 Oct
E	Baxter, K.C.	01 Oct
E	Hobbs, R.	01 Oct
E	Moore, M.N.	01 Oct
X	Morland, R.M.	01 Oct

LIEUTENANTS (SD)

1978

X	Howe, M.J.	06 Jan

1981

X	Fryer, P.J.	02 Jan
X	Morton, I.	02 Jan
E	Badger, A.J.	30 Oct

E	Sticklee, A.C.	30 Oct

1982

S	Stephenson, E.K.	17 Sep
S	Tough, R.S.	17 Sep
E	Durrant, P.	29 Oct
E	Heather, C.V.S.	29 Oct

E	Moore, M.R.	29 Oct
E	Rowles, H.A.	29 Oct

1983

S	Rodrigues, M.T.	07 Jan
E	Bonnett, N.J.	18 Feb
E	Plumridge, P.	18 Feb

	Name	Date
E	Rodgers, D.H.	18 Feb
S	Heath, C.	02 May
E	Goodings, G.J.	18 Oct
E	Arnold, M.E.	03 Nov
E	Dorset, W.	03 Nov
E	Moughton, J.R.	03 Nov

1984

	Name	Date
E	Maskell, J.M.	16 Feb
X	Smith, G.S.	04 May
E	Gamble, J.	02 Nov
E	Thornback, J.G.	02 Nov

1985

	Name	Date
X	Northcote, K.H.	04 Jan
E	Bryant, P.	15 Feb
X	Hartley, B.H.	03 May
X	Bentley, D.A.	06 Sep
X	Gorrod, P.C.A.	06 Sep
E	Curtis, P.A.	18 Oct
E	Dyche, T.	18 Oct
E	Gratton, S.W.	18 Oct
E	Halls, B.C.	18 Oct
E	Ranger, J.L.	18 Oct
E	Schillemore, P.C.	18 Oct

1986

	Name	Date
X	Cooper, N.J.	03 Jan
E	Reeve, J.M.	14 Feb
E	Anderson, J.J.	13 Jun
E	Davison, T.J.	13 Jun
E	Longstaff, M.	13 Jun
E	Williams, D.A.	13 Jun
E	Evans, B.R.	10 Sep
E	Granger, C.R.	17 Oct
E	Miller, J.C.	17 Oct

1987

	Name	Date
S	Bridgeman, J.W.T.	09 Jan
X	Salley, R.K.	09 Jan
E	Scott, M.A.G.	27 Feb
E	Foubister, R.	18 Jun
E	Richardson, S.F.	18 Jun
S	Rawlings, F.D.	03 Sep
E	Spooner, P.D.	15 Oct

1988

	Name	Date
X	Jones, E.J.	07 Jan
X	Mickleburgh, A.	07 Jan
X	Murray, D.	07 Jan
E	Chamberlain, T.I.	18 Feb
E	Cooper, N.P.	18 Feb
E	Lane, R.M.	18 Feb
E	Williams, P.C.	18 Feb
E	Ashton, R.D.	10 Jun
E	Bracher, H.	10 Jun
E	Carr, M.P.	10 Jun
E	Fisher, R.	10 Jun
E	Gamble, R.	10 Jun
E	Hogg, S.J.	10 Jun
E	Morgan, S.A.	10 Jun
E	Nicholson, P.J.	10 Jun
E	Rook, D.J.	10 Jun
E	White, S.P.	10 Jun

	Name	Date
E	Wilson, D.T.	10 Jun
X	Dearling, P.C.	29 Jul
MS	Murphy, A.	29 Jul
X	Richmond, L.	29 Jul
X	Hudson, P.T.	01 Aug
MS	Lloyd, C.J.	02 Aug
E	Langmead, M.A.	14 Oct
E	Merriman, M.R.	14 Oct
E	Peacock, M.R.	14 Oct
E	Swanney, I.N.	14 Oct
E	Weeks, R.R.	14 Oct
E	Williams, K.	14 Oct
E	Biggs, C.R.	14 Oct
X	Brooks, M.L.	16 Dec
X	Ford, G.H.	16 Dec
X	Fraser, J.A.	16 Dec
X	Haynes, J.W.	16 Dec
X	Silva, A.R.	16 Dec

1989

	Name	Date
E	Cooper, G.C.	17 Feb
E	Davies, L.J.	17 Feb
E	Lawrence, S.R.	17 Feb
E	Thomas, M.G.	17 Feb
E	Sergeant, N.R.	09 Jun
E	Barrett, S.J.	09 Jun
E	Buxton, M.J.	09 Jun
E	Darling, J.I.	09 Jun
E	Dobbin, V.W.	09 Jun
E	Griffiths, A.R.	09 Jun
E	Lindsay, G.	09 Jun
E	Mills, G.W.	09 Jun
E	Price, T.P.	09 Jun
E	Templeton, T.A.M.	09 Jun
X	Braisher, J.L.	28 Jul
MS	Coulton, I.C.	28 Jul
X	Evans, D.J.	28 Jul
X	Hill, N.G.	28 Jul
MS	Steel, D.G.	28 Jul
X	Swann, J.I.	28 Jul
S	Sidebotham, M.J.	28 Jul
E	Bourne, D.S.	13 Oct
E	James, P.E.	13 Oct
E	Lusted, R.P.	13 Oct
E	Wiffin, A.F.	13 Oct
X	Bushell, G.R.	15 Dec
X	Cooke, G.J.	15 Dec
X	Hogan, T.	15 Dec
X	Jackson, G.K.	15 Dec
X	Saynor, R.M.	15 Dec
X	Tomlin, P.D.	15 Dec
X	Wood, F.D.	15 Dec

1990

	Name	Date
E	Smart, S.J.	23 Feb
E	Stevenson, A.	23 Feb
E	Winston, L.A.	23 Feb
E	Wood, I.D.	23 Feb
E	Young, K.H.	23 Feb
E	Ford, A.	23 Feb
E	Allen, D.P.	15 Jun
E	Bremner, D.A.	15 Jun
E	Cole, S.P.	15 Jun
E	Dolby, M.J.	15 Jun

	Name	Date
E	Downie, A.J.	15 Jun
E	Galvin, D.	15 Jun
E	Hill, G.A.	15 Jun
E	Kellow, S.J.	15 Jun
E	Lord, M.	15 Jun
E	O'Shaughnessy, P.J.	15 Jun
E	Picksley, M.R.	15 Jun
E	Rodgers, S.	15 Jun
E	Sheppard, D.G.	15 Jun
E	Sutcliffe, R.W.	15 Jun
E	Teasdale, D.	15 Jun
S	Aitken, K.M.	27 Jul
X	Barrick, P.V.	27 Jul
S	Brier, C.A.C.	27 Jul
S	Dann, A.S.	27 Jul
S	Gilbert, S.K.	27 Jul
X	Harper, J.A.	27 Jul
X	Higgs, R.J.	27 Jul
MS	Holder, S.R.	27 Jul
MS	Kenney, R.P.	27 Jul
X	Mitchinson, L.	27 Jul
X	Thorburn, A.	27 Jul
X	Van-Den-Bergh, W.L.	27 Jul
X	Yarker, D.L.	27 Jul
X	Stuttard, S.E.	27 Jul
S	Walker, N.A.	27 Jul
E	Barrs, H.A.	19 Oct
E	Forward, D.J.	19 Oct
E	Hamilton, J.	19 Oct
E	Mason, M.	19 Oct
E	Mockford, J.A.	19 Oct
E	Robertson, M.N.	19 Oct
E	Simmonds, G.F.	19 Oct
E	Tapping, K.	19 Oct
S	Bennett, A.J.	14 Dec
X	Cowie, K.M.	14 Dec
S	Ewen, R.J.	14 Dec
S	Finch, T.S.A.	14 Dec
X	Imrie, P.B.	14 Dec
X	Morris, P.J.	14 Dec
S	Price, D.W.	14 Dec
S	Tupper, R.W.	14 Dec
E	Gutteridge, J.D.J.	20 Dec

1991

	Name	Date
E	Bennett, M.J.	15 Feb
E	Burnett, G.A.	15 Feb
E	Graham, R.	15 Feb
E	Lake, P.H.	15 Feb
E	Maxwell-Cox, M.J.	15 Feb
E	Moss, T.E.	15 Feb
E	Wheeldon, T.B.	15 Feb
X	Clucas, P.R.	04 Apr
X	May-Clingo, M.S.	04 Apr
MS	McAuslin, T.M.	04 Apr
MS	Simpson, P.	04 Apr
MS	Derby, P.J.	04 Apr
E	Clarke, J.	13 Jun
E	Cooper, K.P.	13 Jun
E	Fraser, W.C.	13 Jun
E	Gilliland, S.S.	13 Jun
E	Grace, T.P.	13 Jun
E	Gunther, P.T.	13 Jun
E	Hellyn, D.R.	13 Jun

E	Horwell, B.B.	13 Jun
E	Jordan, N.S.	13 Jun
E	Low, M.E.	13 Jun
E	McKeown, F.E.	13 Jun
E	Moss, P.J.	13 Jun
E	Nicholls, G.A.	13 Jun
E	Smith, M.J.	13 Jun
E	Richman, P.J.	13 Jun
X	Bennett, W.D.	25 Jul
X	Cottingham, N.P.S.	25 Jul
X	Garlick, E.C.	25 Jul
S	Godfrey, M.C.	25 Jul
S	Kerwood, R.J.	25 Jul
S	McGarel, D.F.	25 Jul
X	McIntyre, A.W.	25 Jul
S	Moore, D.D.V.	25 Jul
X	Thomas, J.E.	25 Jul
X	Morrell, A.J.	25 Jul
X	Green, T.A.	01 Oct
E	Bissett, I.M.	17 Oct
E	Bissett, P.K.	17 Oct
E	Bissett, R.W.	17 Oct
E	Hoyle, J.J.	17 Oct
E	McHale, K.	17 Oct
E	Mee, G.	17 Oct
X	Haggart, P.D.	01 Dec
S	Bryant, G.D.	12 Dec
X	Dunn, P.E.	12 Dec
S	Gill, S.C.	12 Dec
X	Hewitt, D.L.	12 Dec
S	Plaice, G.C.	12 Dec
X	Roberts, S.	12 Dec
X	Talbot, C.M.	12 Dec
X	Ward, D.S.	12 Dec

1992

X	Stephen, J.A.	25 Jan
E	Ball, S.J.	13 Feb
E	Morrison, R.W.	13 Feb
E	Payne, D.	13 Feb
E	Young, R.	13 Feb
X	Gough, S.R.	03 Apr
X	Griffiths, A.	03 Apr
MS	O'Callaghan, S.T.	03 Apr
X	Parry, D.R.	03 Apr
MS	Rich, K.J.N.C.	03 Apr
X	Rogers, A.	03 Apr
MS	Trasler, M.F.	03 Apr
X	Meadows, B.	03 Apr
X	Reilly, T.G.	03 Jun
E	Atherton, G.	05 Jun
E	Birbeck, K.	05 Jun
E	Craib, A.G.	05 Jun
E	Davies, S.P.	05 Jun
E	Dutton, P.J.	05 Jun
E	Dyer, G.R.	05 Jun
E	Glennie, B.W.	05 Jun
E	Hunt, P.E.R.D.	05 Jun
E	Lowes, C.	05 Jun
E	Mitchell, P.	05 Jun
E	Mountjoy, B.J.	05 Jun
E	Pearson, J.R.	05 Jun
E	Porter, A.J.	05 Jun
E	Radbourne, N.I.	05 Jun

E	Rimmer, R.	05 Jun
E	Skelton, R.A.	05 Jun
E	Stokes, A.W.	05 Jun
E	Sutherland, G.M.	05 Jun
E	Walker, R.D.	05 Jun
E	White, R.F.	05 Jun
E	Wray, A.D.	05 Jun
E	Arnell, S.J.	05 Jun
X	Davies, M.J.	24 Jul
S	Freegard, I.P.	24 Jul
MS	Griffiths, D.A.	24 Jul
S	Knill, R.L.	24 Jul
S	Knowles, M.M.	24 Jul
X	Price, T.M.	24 Jul
X	Reid, P.F.	24 Jul
S	Williams, D.	24 Jul
E	Allan, D.J.	16 Oct
E	Cheseldine, D.	16 Oct
E	Cooke, M.J.	16 Oct
E	Dunn, A.J.P.	16 Oct
E	Ferguson, G.H.	16 Oct
E	Goodman, T.M.	16 Oct
E	Gwilliam, D.M.	16 Oct
E	Hutchings, J.S.	16 Oct
E	Maude, D.H.	16 Oct
E	McCaffery, G.F.	16 Oct
E	Pace, S.	16 Oct
E	Parrett, J.W.	16 Oct
E	Parry, R.J.	16 Oct
E	Stobie, P.L.	16 Oct
E	Wroblewski, J.A.	16 Oct
X	Curtis, R.J.	19 Oct
S	Case, P.	11 Dec
X	Edwards, R.	11 Dec
X	Forsyth, D.C.	11 Dec
X	Gunn, C.P.	11 Dec
S	Laggan, P.J.	11 Dec
S	MacAskill, C.H.	11 Dec
X	McTear, N.J.	11 Dec
X	Mitchell, M.	11 Dec
S	Pye, P.M.	11 Dec
X	Snoddon, R.	11 Dec
X	Spayne, N.J.	11 Dec
X	Steele, T.G.	11 Dec
S	Turner, R.F.	11 Dec
S	Twist, D.C.	11 Dec
S	West, A.W.	11 Dec
X	Wood, S.G.	11 Dec
X	Woodruff, A.D.	11 Dec

1993

E	Bannister, A.N.	19 Feb
E	Bassett, N.E.	19 Feb
E	Batten, A.J.	19 Feb
E	Bedelle, S.J.	19 Feb
E	Burge, R.G.	19 Feb
E	Gisborne, W.C.	19 Feb
E	Hatcher, T.R.	19 Feb
E	Johnson, M.J.	19 Feb
E	MacDougall, S.J.	19 Feb
E	McCabe, D.S.	19 Feb
E	Rowe, A.J.	19 Feb
E	Rundle, A.L.	19 Feb
E	Seaman, P.J.	19 Feb

E	Styles, S.B.	19 Feb
E	Tomkins, A.B.	19 Feb
E	Warr, R.F.	19 Feb
E	Wooding, G.A.	19 Feb
X	Barron, P.J.	02 Apr
X	Billington, T.J.	02 Apr
MS	Chilcott, P.L.H.	02 Apr
X	Clements, S.J.	02 Apr
MS	Durning, W.M.	02 Apr
S	Hall, D.A.	02 Apr
X	Hughes, G.G.H.	02 Apr
S	Johnson, M.D.	02 Apr
X	Moreby, M.F.	02 Apr
X	Roberts, S.P.	02 Apr
X	Thomas, L.	02 Apr
X	Wrightson, I.H.	02 Apr
X	Stephens, R.P.	18 Apr
E	Byrne, A.C.	18 Jun
E	Jordan, L.	18 Jun
E	McLachlan, M.P.	18 Jun
E	McLewee, C.J.	18 Jun
E	Pomeroy, M.A.	18 Jun
E	Smith, G.H.	18 Jun
X	Crascall, S.J.	23 Jul
MS	Dell, I.M.	23 Jul
X	Harper, I.L.	23 Jul
X	Hawkes, J.D.	23 Jul
X	Horrocks, C.C.	23 Jul
X	Massey, P.	23 Jul
X	McDonald, W.J.	23 Jul
MS	Richards, B.R.	23 Jul
MS	Ryder, T.J.	23 Jul
MS	Skinner, A.J.	23 Jul
X	Thomas, N.R.	23 Jul
X	Pounder, M.	23 Jul
E	Barrett, D.L.	15 Oct
E	Bell, D.P.J.	15 Oct
E	Bowness, P.	15 Oct
E	Burrows, J.C.	15 Oct
E	Butler, L.P.	15 Oct
E	Ireland, J.M.	15 Oct
E	Jones, D.A.	15 Oct
E	Leaning, D.J.	15 Oct
E	Madders, R.M.	15 Oct
E	Murray, S.	15 Oct
E	Ovenden, K.	15 Oct
E	Phesse, J.P.L.	15 Oct
E	Preece, D.W.	15 Oct
E	Watson, J.	15 Oct
E	Crawford, L.	05 Dec
S	Arnold, A.S.	17 Dec
X	Beaton, E.J.	17 Dec
X	Coyne, J.D.	17 Dec
X	Doyle, N.P.	17 Dec
X	Helliwell, M.G.	17 Dec
S	Johnson, M.D.	17 Dec
X	Kerr, J.	17 Dec
X	Knights, R.	17 Dec
X	Miller, G.	17 Dec
S	Stillwell-Cox,	17 Dec

A.D.R.

S	Tucker, R.S.	17 Dec
X	Walker, E.G.	17 Dec
X	Wardle, M.	17 Dec

X	Wills, M.J.C.	17 Dec	X	Wright, D.A.	29 Jul	E	Wilson, J.A.	15 Jun
S	Wyatt, C.	17 Dec	E	Bryce, N.A.	14 Oct	X	Bishop, G.C.	27 Jul
X	Horne, A.	17 Dec	E	Ford, G.R.	14 Oct	X	Cunningham, N.J.W.	27 Jul
			E	Furnish, K.S.	14 Oct	X	Elsom, G.K.	27 Jul
	1994		E	Midmore, M.J.	14 Oct	I	Estall, J.M.	27 Jul
E	Bradshaw, K.T.	18 Feb	E	Selby, R.C.	14 Oct	X	May, P.J.	27 Jul
E	Brothers, A.H.G.	18 Feb	E	Walton, S.P.	14 Oct	X	McKernan, J.	27 Jul
E	Buckeridge, V.W.	18 Feb	E	White, R.L.	14 Oct	X	Tomlinson, J.H.	27 Jul
E	Chambers, P.	18 Feb	X	Beaumont, S.J.	16 Dec	X	Wilson, G.J.	27 Jul
E	Dewsnap, M.D.	18 Feb	X	Hardy, L.B.	16 Dec	E	Brown, P.A.	07 Sep
E	Dymond, N.R.J.	18 Feb	X	Jaggers, G.G.	16 Dec	E	Holden, P.A.	07 Sep
E	Haworth, S.	18 Feb	X	Kelly, T.	16 Dec	E	Phillips, A.R.	07 Sep
E	Hobson, I.S.	18 Feb	X	Pledger, D.	16 Dec	E	Reed, J.C.	07 Sep
E	Hooper, G.P.	18 Feb	S	Taylor, I.K.	16 Dec	E	Walsh, D.G.	07 Sep
E	Norman, P.D.	18 Feb	X	Whitlam, J.	16 Dec	X	Baxter, J.C.	27 Sep
E	Penfold, M.J.	18 Feb	S	Young, S.W.	16 Dec	X	Byrne, T.M.	13 Dec
E	Sugden, S.R.	18 Feb				S	Fearnley, A.T.	13 Dec
E	Taylor, K.J.	18 Feb		**1995**		S	Jackson, P.A.	13 Dec
E	Wells, B.C.	18 Feb	E	Abbott, D.A.	24 Feb	X	Kirby, C.J.	13 Dec
E	Wrenn, M.R.W.	18 Feb	E	Baird, S.	24 Feb	X	Knight, J.D.	13 Dec
E	Wyld, A.W.	18 Feb	E	Dawson, A.J.	24 Feb	X	Lawson, G.J.	13 Dec
S	Austen, R.M.	08 Apr	E	Eddie, A.G.W.	24 Feb	X	Marsh, M.P.A.	13 Dec
MS	Gerrell, F.J.	08 Apr	E	Evans, S.	24 Feb	X	Morrison, P.	13 Dec
S	Grocott, P.C.	08 Apr	E	Fallowfield, J.P.	24 Feb	X	Woodrow, K.J.	13 Dec
S	Harris, M.T.	08 Apr	E	Harrison, D.	24 Feb			
S	Holland, N.R.	08 Apr	E	Harwood, C.G.	24 Feb		**1996**	
X	Honnoraty, M.R.	08 Apr	E	Henderson, P.P.	24 Feb	S	Trinder, S.J.	30 Jan
S	Lewins, G.	08 Apr	E	Jones, D.L.	24 Feb	E	Edson, M.A.	22 Feb
X	Lister, S.	08 Apr	E	Knight, K.J.	24 Feb	E	Eland, D.A.	22 Feb
MS	McLaughlan, C.J.	08 Apr	E	Obrien, I.P.	24 Feb	E	Gillham, P.R.	22 Feb
S	Melville-Brown, M.G.	08 Apr	E	Watson, C.R.	24 Feb	E	Hyland, R.A.	22 Feb
X	Pugh, M.R.	08 Apr	E	Wilson, L.I.	24 Feb	E	King, D.S.	22 Feb
E	Christian, D.	10 Jun	S	Bunt, K.J.	06 Apr	E	McClarty, M.	22 Feb
E	Cowper, I.R.	10 Jun	X	Gold, J.W.	06 Apr	E	Stubbs, M.A.	22 Feb
E	Dunningham, S.	10 Jun	S	Goldthorpe, M.	06 Apr	E	Watson, C.R.	22 Feb
E	Metcalf, R.	10 Jun	X	Kerr, A.T.F.	06 Apr	MS	Blocke, A.D.	04 Apr
E	Page, T.A.	10 Jun	X	Seward, S.A.	06 Apr	MS	Bradford, T.H.C.	04 Apr
E	Waterman, D.L.	10 Jun	MS	Stead, R.A.	06 Apr	X	Brailey, I.S.	04 Apr
X	Carter, K.S.	29 Jul	S	Walsh, M.A.	06 Apr	S	Brenchley, N.G.	04 Apr
X	Ellwood, P.G.	29 Jul	MS	Wagstaff, N.	10 Apr	S	Carter, S.P.	04 Apr
MS	Howells, M.J.	29 Jul	E	Berry, P.	15 Jun	X	Easton, D.W.	04 Apr
X	Millen, I.S.	29 Jul	E	Dunsby, N.B.	15 Jun	X	Ford, A.J.	04 Apr
X	Nugent, C.J.	29 Jul	E	Green, A.M.	15 Jun	X	Walker, M.J.	04 Apr
MS	Phillips, I.M.	29 Jul	E	Keeley, S.P.	15 Jun	MS	Walton, A.P.	04 Apr
X	Taylor, M.R.	29 Jul	E	Knight, R.H.	15 Jun	X	Welburn, R.C.	04 Apr
X	West, A.B.	29 Jul	E	Mitchell, S.D.	15 Jun	X	Wilkinson, J.	04 Apr
			E	Southern, P.J.	15 Jun			

SUB LIEUTENANTS

	1993		MS	Miller, D.E.	25 Jul	E	Eardley, J.M.	07 Feb
E	Grant, D.J.	14 Jun	X	Parrett, A.D.	25 Jul	E	Fulford, R.N.	07 Feb
E	Harvey, G.	14 Jun	X	Richards, F.C.	25 Jul	E	Humphrey, I.J.	07 Feb
E	Hutchinson, P.	14 Jun	X	Smith, N.J.	25 Jul	E	McTaggart, D.A.	07 Feb
E	Jones, R.V.	14 Jun	E	Bottomley, S.	06 Sep	E	Ridge, M.H.	07 Feb
E	King, G.C.	14 Jun	E	Juckes, M.A.	06 Sep	E	Sheldon, M.L.	07 Feb
E	Rendell, D.J.	14 Jun	E	Napier, G.A.	06 Sep	E	Sullivan, M.	07 Feb
E	Riley, G.A.	14 Jun	E	Stanham, C.M.	06 Sep	S	Barratt, S.M.	03 Apr
X	Brember, P.B.	25 Jul				X	Bennetts, N.	03 Apr
X	Clifford, C.T.	25 Jul		**1994**		S	Buckingham, P.	03 Apr
X	Dale, N.R.	25 Jul	X	Santrian, K.	01 Jan	X	Clark, A.S.	03 Apr
X	Holmes, J.D.	25 Jul	E	Cain, C.W.	07 Feb	X	Conway, M.J.	03 Apr
X	Metcalfe, M.P.	25 Jul	E	Collins, S.A.	07 Feb	S	Darlow, P.R.	03 Apr

X	Dunne, M.G.	03 Apr	X	Potter, D.J.	24 Jul	X	Beale, M.D. . . . . . 23 Jul
MS	Finn, D.W.	03 Apr	X	Rowan, M.E.	24 Jul	S	Brock, R.F. . . . . . 23 Jul
X	Guiver, P.	03 Apr	X	Southwell, N.P.	24 Jul	X	Clelland, G. . . . . . 23 Jul
X	Lewis, K.A.	03 Apr	S	Strudwick, R.	24 Jul	X	Deam, P.A.V. . . . . 23 Jul
X	McGrane, R.J.	03 Apr	X	Taylor, J.P.	24 Jul	MS	Follington, D.C. . . . 23 Jul
MS	McGunigall, R.J.	03 Apr	X	Vowles, M.J.	24 Jul	X	Johns, L.E. . . . . . 23 Jul
MS	Meechan, W.	03 Apr	X	Whild, D.J.	24 Jul	X	Louden, C.A. . . . . 23 Jul
S	Moores, J.	03 Apr	X	Young, J.N.	24 Jul	S	Noon, D. . . . . . . 23 Jul
X	Norford, M.A.	03 Apr	E	Butler, I.A.	12 Sep	X	Parkinson, A.P. . . . 23 Jul
X	Stretton, D.G.	03 Apr	E	Fitzgerald, C.	12 Sep	X	Salmon, R.D. . . . . 23 Jul
S	Teasdale, K.S.	03 Apr	E	Sargent, K.S.	12 Sep	S	Stephenson, P.G. . . 23 Jul
S	Thornton, B.P.	03 Apr				S	Watson, S.B.C. . . . 23 Jul
X	Tomlinson, D.C.	03 Apr		**1995**		E	Brodier, M.I. . . . . 04 Sep
E	Cattroll, D.	13 Jun	S	Goodwin, L.B.	03 Apr	E	Bugg, K.J. . . . . . 04 Sep
E	Finnie, H.M.	13 Jun	X	Hayes, B.J.	03 Apr	E	Connor, M. . . . . . 04 Sep
E	Peace, R.W.	13 Jun	S	Hewitt, L.R.	03 Apr	E	Curtis, D. . . . . . 04 Sep
E	Shuttleworth, S.	13 Jun	X	Peak, M.	03 Apr	E	Henderson, R.J. . . 04 Sep
E	Spofforth-Jones, M.A.	13 Jun	S	Platt, N.	03 Apr	E	Marson, G.M. . . . 04 Sep
			X	Wells, B.I.	03 Apr	E	Metcalfe, R.J. . . . 04 Sep
E	Turle, P.J.	13 Jun	X	White, I.F.	03 Apr	E	Mould, T.P. . . . . 04 Sep
E	Weaver, N.	13 Jun	X	Wood, J.A.	03 Apr	E	Raynor, S.D. . . . . 04 Sep
X	Barraclough, C.D.	24 Jul	S	Magrath, A.R.	01 May	X	Beard, R.G. . . . . 10 Dec
X	Bellingham, I.K.	24 Jul	S	Robb, B.D.	01 May	X	Egerton, S.B. . . . 10 Dec
S	Bower, J.W.	24 Jul	E	Austin, C.J.	19 Jun	S	Jones, M.A. . . . . 10 Dec
X	Collins, M.C.	24 Jul	E	Jones, R.K.	19 Jun	X	Martin, A.J. . . . . 10 Dec
X	Collins, P.W.	24 Jul	E	Morgan, P.	19 Jun	X	Routledge, W.D. . . 10 Dec
X	Corkett, K.S.	24 Jul	E	Norgate, P.R.E.	19 Jun	X	Singleton, M.D. . . . 10 Dec
X	Magill, T.E.	24 Jul	E	Paton, A.J.M.	19 Jun	X	Smith, R.E. . . . . 10 Dec
X	McDermott, P.A.	24 Jul	E	Rankine, I.M.	19 Jun	X	South, D.J. . . . . 10 Dec
X	McEvoy, L.P.	24 Jul	E	Stone, R.J.	19 Jun	S	Thomas, D.J. . . . 10 Dec
S	Morris, K.I.	24 Jul	E	Towell, P.J.	19 Jun		

TEMPORARY LIEUTENANTS

	1990		E	Breeds, F.J.	18 Jun	X	Mayall, C.S. . . . 10 Jun
S	Yates, M.L.	18 Jun	X	Leavey, J.W.	18 Jun	X	Payne, M.S. . . . 10 Jun
	1991		S	Martin, J.H.	18 Jun	E	Stamp, D.W. . . . 10 Jun
X	Mitchell, P.	18 Apr	X	Potter, R.N.	18 Jun	X	Turnbull, J.J. . . . 10 Jun
S	Smalley, G.T.	18 Apr		**1994**		S	Potter, D.G. . . . . 02 Sep
	1993		E	Allen, M.J.	10 Jun		
X	Austin, I.	18 Jun	E	Grant, B.G.	10 Jun		
			X	Lynch, G.P.	10 Jun		

SUPPLEMENTARY LIST

COMMANDERS

(Extended Medium Career Commission)

1986		
I Channon, M.J. . .	01 Sep	

1989		
X Sandiford, D.B. . . .	01 Oct	
X Shaw, P.A.	01 Oct	

1990		
I Munro, S.R.	01 Oct	
X Boag, R.D.	01 Oct	
X Burrows, R.G. . . .	01 Oct	

1991		
X Pallister, R.J.T. . . .	01 Oct	
X Hughes, D.J.	01 Oct	
X MacMahon, T.J. . .	01 Oct	

1992		
I Pickering, M.J. . . .	01 Oct	
X Mansbridge, B.J. . .	01 Oct	
X Arnall-Culliford, N.D. .	01 Oct	

1993		
X Goss, P.G.	01 Oct	
X Pounder, A.G.P. . .	01 Oct	

1994		
X Bennett, N.K. . . .	01 Oct	
X Ward, N.J.	01 Oct	

1995		
X Salter, M.D.	01 Oct	
X Bull, A.J.	01 Oct	

COMMANDERS

(Medium and Short Career Commission)

1989		
E Fisher, C.E.	01 Oct	

LIEUTENANT COMMANDERS

(Extended Medium Career Commission)

1974		
I Chapman, R.W.T. .	16 Sep	

1978		
I Durbin, C.P.J. . . .	03 Jan	
E Jury, J.A.	01 Mar	
X Hails, P.W.	01 Sep	

1979		
X Belding, P.S. . . .	01 Mar	
X Smith, A.R. . . .	01 Mar	
X Phillips, S.B. . . .	01 Mar	
X Lawrence, M.J. . .	01 Sep	
X George, D.R. . . .	01 Sep	
I Hookway, B.C. . .	12 Sep	
I Tovey, P.F.	12 Sep	
I Hay, B.W.	14 Sep	

1980		
X Bates, J.W. . . .	01 Mar	
X Hennell, N.J. . . .	01 Mar	
X Gobey, S.J. . . .	01 Sep	
X Sams, C.	01 Sep	
X Coryton, G.R.A. . .	01 Sep	

1981		
I Willett, R.J.	04 Jan	
E Pearce, B.S. . . .	01 Mar	
X Boland, M.	01 Mar	
X Bridges, S.V. . . .	01 Mar	
I Speat, L.W. . . .	01 Mar	
I Stubbs, P.N. . . .	01 May	

X Dobinson, E.J. . . .	01 Sep
X Boulton, T.J.	01 Sep
X Fogden, P.J.	01 Sep

1982	
I Sutton, B.	07 Jan
X Blight, C.J.	01 Mar
X Skiera, A.P.	01 Mar
X Smith, S.F.	01 Sep
X Roberts, N.L.	01 Sep
X Rothwell, J.F. . . .	01 Sep

1983	
I Marshall, P.E. . . .	01 Jan
E Grindley, R.J. . . .	01 Mar
E Kennedy, D.J. . . .	01 Mar
X Ballance, T.B. . . .	01 Mar
X Tinkley, N.R.	01 Mar
X Jolliffe, J.G.	01 Sep
X Rice, P.L.	01 Sep
X Mathews, L.	01 Sep
X McAllister, I.F. . . .	01 Sep

1984	
I Dyson, P.K.	01 Jan
X Doggett, R.A. . . .	01 Mar
X Eagles, A.J.	01 Mar
X Hoole, R.J.	01 Mar
X Halford, P.	01 Sep
X Deuxberry, H.P.J. . .	01 Sep
I Gardiner, F.K.J. . .	01 Sep
I Yuill, I.A.	01 Sep

1985	
X Wells, M.D.	01 Mar
X Murnane, P.M. . . .	01 Mar
X Pittaway, C.W. . . .	01 Mar
X North, N.J.	01 Mar
X Terrill, K.W.	01 Mar
X Harrall, P.A.R. . . .	03 Mar
I Fergusson, R.R. . .	01 May
X Blaydes, M.H. . . .	01 Sep
X Henry, P.	01 Sep
X Collier, S.R.	01 Sep
E Froggatt, J.R. . . .	01 Sep
X Wright, M.J.	01 Sep
I Rowlands, G.A. . .	01 Sep

1986	
X Evans, M.J.G. . . .	01 Mar
X Grandison, J.A.S. . .	01 Mar
X Davies, G.I.	01 Mar
X Robinson, A.R. . . .	01 Mar
X Robertson, F.W. . .	01 Mar
E Burgess, W.C. . . .	01 Mar
S Edwards, J.M. . . .	01 Apr
X Lord, D.A.	01 Sep
X Mannion, T.S. . . .	01 Sep
X Osman, M.R. . . .	01 Sep

1987	
I Tunnicliffe, P.A. . .	01 Mar
X Richings, P.C. . . .	01 Mar
X Saunders, J.N. . . .	01 Mar
X Stephenson, G.T. . .	01 Mar

X	Smithson, J.W.	01 Sep
X	Crudgington, P.	01 Sep
X	Taylor, J.W.	01 Sep
X	Ball, R.J.	01 Sep
X	Brown, C.D.	01 Sep
S	Hayles, N.C.	01 Sep
X	McHugh, M.J.	01 Sep
X	Raggett, A.	01 Sep
	1988	
X	Bristow, G.D.	01 Oct
X	Schwarz, P.M.G.	01 Oct
X	Clark, M.A.S.	01 Oct
W	Hoath, M.E.J.	01 Oct
X	White, M.E.	01 Oct
X	Tozer, C.V.	01 Oct
X	Balchin, D.J.	01 Oct
X	Cooper, J.A.	01 Oct
X	Gilbert, C.M.L.	01 Oct
X	Daniels, S.A.	01 Oct
X	Abbey, M.P.	01 Oct
X	Chambers, T.G.	01 Oct
	1989	
X	Millward, J.P.	07 Apr
X	Milton, G.B.M.	01 Oct
E	Clement, C.J.	01 Oct
X	Jennings, M.P.	01 Oct
X	McManus, P.	01 Oct
I	Morley, A.D.	01 Oct
X	Howden, A.J.	01 Oct
X	Murray, S.J.	01 Oct
X	Rich, J.G.	01 Oct
X	Booker, G.R.	01 Oct
X	McKie, A.	01 Oct
X	Carr, D.L.	01 Oct
X	Dawson, P.J.	01 Oct
X	Wild, S.	01 Oct
	1990	
X	Hall, D.W.	01 Oct

X	Burgess, S.	01 Oct
X	Ormshaw, R.J.	01 Oct
X	Saunders, J.N.	01 Oct
X	Buckett, E.J.	01 Oct
X	Toms, T.M.	01 Oct
X	Baylis, C.W.	01 Oct
X	Slade, C.	01 Oct
E	Squire, P.A.	01 Oct
	1991	
I	Martin, E.J.	01 Apr
X	Jones, B.A.	01 Oct
X	Connell, J.D.	01 Oct
X	Lee, M.M.	01 Oct
X	Owen, P.C.	01 Oct
X	Harvey, P.A.	01 Oct
X	Hawkins, R.H.	01 Oct
X	Stanton, D.V.	01 Oct
X	Bunn, M.E.	01 Oct
X	Shawcross, P.K.	01 Oct
X	Sigournay, D.S.	01 Oct
X	de Winton, M.R.	01 Oct
	1992	
X	Humphries, J.E.	01 Oct
X	Murton, W.M.	01 Oct
X	Shepherd, P.R.	01 Oct
X	Austin, J.D.	01 Oct
W	Price, T.L.	01 Oct
X	Rogerson, C.S.J.	01 Oct
X	Fox, R.G.	01 Oct
X	Nelson, D.L.	01 Oct
X	Watson, I.	01 Oct
X	Spence, J.A.J.	01 Oct
X	Needham, P.D.	01 Oct
X	Whitehead, D.	01 Oct
X	Marsh, R.J.L.	01 Oct
	1993	
X	Anderson, F.B.	01 Oct
X	MacBean, C.C.	01 Oct

X	Burgess, J.D.A.	01 Oct
X	Thornton, P.J.	01 Oct
X	Doherty, K.	01 Oct
X	Lawrence, S.P.	01 Oct
X	Dukes, N.P.	01 Oct
X	MacKay, D.H.	01 Oct
X	Bradburn, S.J.	01 Oct
X	Stacey, H.A.	01 Oct
X	Owen, P.D.	01 Oct
X	Bowker, G.N.	01 Oct
X	Bird, D.E.	01 Oct
X	Clark, P.M.C.	01 Oct
W	Silver, C.K.	01 Oct
X	Snowball, J.C.	01 Oct
E	Janaway, P.	01 Oct
S	McKnight, N.W.	01 Oct
	1994	
X	Rawson, C.	01 Oct
X	Hands, A.P.	01 Oct
X	Taylor, L.	01 Oct
X	Sewed, M.A.	01 Oct
X	Porter, C.W.	01 Oct
X	Dowdell, R.E.J.	01 Oct
E	Suckling, P.M.	01 Oct
X	Lloyd, P.S.	01 Oct
X	Watson, L.J.	01 Oct
X	Marr, D.C.W.	01 Oct
S	Franks, D.I.	01 Oct
X	Davis, P.B.	01 Oct
X	Burrows, M.J.	01 Oct
X	Thompson, N.J.	01 Oct
X	Savage, S.	01 Oct
X	Elliman, S.M.	01 Oct
	1995	
X	Moffatt, R.	01 Oct
X	Clifford, M.R.	01 Oct
X	Smith, K.J.	01 Oct
X	Brundle, P.R.	01 Oct

LIEUTENANT COMMANDERS

(Medium and Short Career Commission)

	1979	
X	Sewell, D.E.	19 Jul
	1986	
I	Waterhouse, W.M.	01 Mar
I	Bates, S.J.	01 Mar
X	Hayes, F.A.M.	01 Sep
I	Talbot, G.K.	01 Sep
I	Sidebotham, R.S.	01 Sep
	1987	
I	Huxtable, N.	01 Sep
I	Lord, A.S.	01 Sep
I	Wallbank, P.D.	01 Sep
I	Barber, S.	01 Sep
	1988	
I	Ellis, P.A.	01 Oct

I	Sauze, M.J.	01 Oct
I	Grimsley, K.P.	01 Oct
I	Livesey, P.	01 Oct
I	Houghton, A.W.	01 Oct
	1989	
I	Lages, A.E.	01 Oct
I	Rawlings, G.C.	01 Oct
I	Taylor, A.J.	01 Oct
I	Eastaugh, A.C.	01 Oct
I	Hipsey, S.J.	01 Oct
I	Pattison, K.	01 Oct
I	Trelease, F.M.	01 Oct
I	Gill, C.M.	01 Oct
	1990	
I	Pearce, A.W.	22 Sep
I	Monaghan, M.	22 Sep

I	Peacock, J.G.	22 Sep
I	Wright, J.	01 Oct
I	Howells, G.R.	01 Oct
I	Weaver, K.N.	01 Oct
I	Ball, S.G.	01 Oct
	1991	
W	Smith, T.D.	01 Apr
I	James, R.M.	21 Sep
I	Rose, M.S.	01 Oct
I	Gray, S.M.	01 Oct
I	Rogers, R.J.	01 Oct
X	Nicholas, T.W.	01 Oct
W	Kirkpatrick, A.J.	01 Oct
X	Trevarthen, A.G.	01 Oct
I	Cowton, E.N.	01 Oct
I	Murphy, P.J.	01 Oct
X	Townsend, C.N.	01 Oct

1992
W	Keefe, S-A.	30 Apr
I	Thomas, K.I.	01 Oct
I	Moore, M.J.	01 Oct
I	Taylor, P.J.	01 Oct
E	Roberts, M.	01 Oct
X	Baddams, D.T.	01 Oct
X	Dunn, N.G.	01 Oct
X	Maude, C.P.	01 Oct
I	Bright, D.A.	01 Oct
S	Martinson, I.J.A.	01 Oct
E	Beveridge, R.C.	01 Oct
W	Crumplin, C.A.	01 Oct

1993
I	Warren, I.F.	01 Oct
I	Talbot, N.A.	01 Oct
X	Eales, M.J.	01 Oct
I	Smith, G.K.	01 Oct
I	Williams, A.B.	01 Oct
I	Hamilton, R.A.	01 Oct
X	Robertson, D.M.	01 Oct
X	Cheyne, S.	01 Oct
X	Wolstenholme, D.P.	01 Oct
X	Healy, A.M.C.	01 Oct
I	Robinson, B.D.	01 Oct
X	Eastaugh, T.C.	01 Oct
W	Gray, S.K.	01 Oct
X	Powell, S.J.	01 Oct
E	Kempsell, I.D.	01 Oct

1994
X	Davis, A.R.	01 Oct
I	Day, T.M.	01 Oct
X	Spencer, G.J.	01 Oct
I	Bryce, C.G.	01 Oct
I	Monger, P.D.	01 Oct
I	Scott-Dickins, C.A.	01 Oct
I	Davison, A.P.	01 Oct
I	Hicking, N.	01 Oct
X	Sealy, D.E.	01 Oct
X	Eaton, C.R.	01 Oct
X	Walker, M.C.	01 Oct
X	Stidston, D.B.	01 Oct
X	Swales, S.M.	01 Oct
I	Hammersley, J.M.	01 Oct
I	Naden, J.R.	01 Oct
I	Read, A.	01 Oct
X	France, S.J.	01 Oct
X	Chaloner, R.P.	01 Oct
X	Fraser, P.T.	01 Oct
W	Fortescue, J.E.	01 Oct
E	Sugden, M.R.	01 Oct
X	Lee, J.C.	01 Oct
I	Elliott, A.J.	01 Oct
X	Dane, R.M.H.	01 Oct

1995
W	Shawcross, J.M.	03 Jan
X	Ahern, D.J.	01 Oct
X	Dunn, C.J.	01 Oct
X	Evans, A.W.	01 Oct

X	Gobey, C.G.	01 Oct
I	Oldfield, P.H.	01 Oct
X	Stone, R.P.	01 Oct
X	Greaves, C.J.	01 Oct
X	Frost, J.W.G.	01 Oct
X	Dean, W.M.H.	01 Oct
X	Daniels, I.J.R.	01 Oct
I	Nunn, G.E.	01 Oct
X	Holley, A.J.	01 Oct
I	Chapman, G.J.D.	01 Oct
X	Fulford, M.K.	01 Oct
X	Carter, R.I.	01 Oct
W	Buchanan, A.J.	01 Oct
X	Callister, D.R.	01 Oct
I	Cunningham, C.	01 Oct
I	Hassall, H.	01 Oct
X	Pipkin, S.C.	01 Oct
X	Lawler, J.A.	01 Oct
S	Hughes, P.C.	01 Oct
X	Mathieson, K.R.	01 Oct
X	Warnock, G.	01 Oct
X	Lort, T.E.	01 Oct
S	Woodard, S.G.	01 Oct
X	Carretta, M.V.	01 Oct
I	Collins, D.A.	01 Oct
W	Davis, S.B.	01 Oct
X	Daniell, C.J.	01 Oct
I	Rippingale, S.N.	01 Oct

1996
I	Warren, M.K.	01 Jan

LIEUTENANTS

(Extended Medium Career Commission)

1985
X	Corbett, G.J.	16 Jan
X	Hibbert, M.C.	01 Jun
X	Creech, R.D.	16 Jul

1986
X	Webb, C.M.	16 Dec

1987
X	Stringer, R.A.	01 Jun

X	Armstrong, N.P.B.	01 Jul

1989
E	Leonard, M.	01 Sep

LIEUTENANTS

(Medium and Short Career Commission)

1981
X	Kemp, B.I.	01 Sep

1982
X	Newall, J.A.	01 Mar
X	London, M.R.	01 May
X	Dale, D.G.	01 Nov

1983
X	Reid, A.B.	01 Jan
X	Norman, S.J.	16 Jun
X	Shaw, P.A.	01 Nov

1984
X	Ellett, K.G.	01 Jun
X	Kerridge, T.P.	16 Aug
I	Hope, K.	01 Sep
X	Read, A.J.	01 Sep

X	Coles, D.A.	16 Sep

1985
X	Rendle, I.	01 Feb
X	Conway, T.A.	16 Mar
X	Lee, N.F.	01 Apr
X	Meakin, B.R.	01 Apr
I	Evans, M.	01 May
X	Clay, S.C.	01 Jun
X	Bishop, K.A.	16 Jun
X	Sutcliffe, M.J.	16 Jun
X	Hughes, D.P.	16 Jul
X	Ellis, N.M.	18 Jul
W	Ireland, D.M.	27 Jul
I	Monk, C.E.	01 Aug
X	Von Hoven, A.C.	01 Aug
X	Brown, C.	16 Aug
I	England, S.J.	28 Aug

I	Croker, R.W.	01 Sep
I	Hare, J.H.	01 Sep
I	Richardson, M.A.	01 Sep
X	Jefferson, P.M.	16 Oct
X	Llewelyn, K.	16 Oct
X	Smith, D.	01 Nov
I	Walker, P.R.	27 Nov

1986
I	Hartley, S.W.	01 Jan
I	Hunter, P.A.	01 Jan
E	Darbin, M.R.	01 Jan
X	Carroll, P.J.	01 Jan
X	Matthews, G.G.	01 Mar
X	Haseldine, S.G.	01 Mar
X	Bickerton, R.E.	01 Apr
I	Webber, C.J.	03 Apr
W	Burgoine, P.A.	05 Apr

W	Gent, S.J.	05 Apr
I	Evans, S.J.	06 Apr
X	Dundon, J.M.	16 Apr
I	Hill, R.V.S.	01 May
X	Lewis, R.	01 May
S	Hendrick, J.	01 Jun
I	Mann, G.D.	01 Jul
W	Straughan, K.E.	26 Jul
I	Marston, S.A.B.	27 Jul
X	Henty, I.	01 Aug
X	Thomas, A.P.W.	01 Aug
X	Sykes, R.A.	16 Aug
I	Dickson, J.P.E.	01 Sep
S	Werrin, L.R.	01 Sep
X	Munro-Lott, P.R.J.	16 Sep
X	Walters, J.	16 Sep
I	Bowden, M.N.	01 Oct
X	Hoper, P.R.	01 Nov
X	Kessler, M.L.	01 Nov
I	Ruglys, M.P.	16 Nov
I	Boulton, N.A.	20 Nov
X	Biggs, D.M.	16 Dec

1987

I	Briggs, S.L.	01 Jan
I	Clarke, T.J.	01 Jan
I	O'Brien, P.M.C.	01 Jan
I	Swift, I.D.	01 Jan
E	Hill, B.L.	01 Jan
X	Hamilton-Bing, S.P.E.	01 Jan
X	Alwyn, J.S.	09 Jan
X	Broster, P.T.	16 Jan
X	Wilkinson, P.M.	16 Feb
X	Attrill, A.A.	16 Feb
I	Ashton Jones, G.	01 Mar
X	Edwards, J.P.T.	01 Mar
I	Evans, P.G.	01 Mar
I	Forer, D.A.	01 Mar
I	Lauste, W.E.	01 Mar
I	Murphy, P.T.	01 Mar
I	Norris, A.M.	01 Mar
I	Wallace, D.J.	01 Mar
X	Nettleton, P.J.	24 Mar
E	Currie, I.	01 Apr
X	McKinlay, S.	01 Apr
W	Wunderle, R.	08 Apr
X	Green, P.L.	01 May
I	Hart, P.A.	01 May
I	Moore, C.R.	01 May
I	Reynolds, T.P.	01 May
I	Wootton, T.M.	01 May
X	Goram, M.	01 May
I	Harley, L.D.	01 May
W	Spanner, H.M.	02 May
X	Carne, R.J.P.	16 May
X	Walsh, A.S.J.	16 May
X	Yelland, C.B.	16 May
I	Cooper, C.J.	01 Jun
X	Stretton, P.M.	16 Jun
I	Worthington, J.M.F.	01 Jul
X	Wilson, M.A.	16 Jul
I	Dyer, J.D.T.	01 Sep
I	Gamble, M.E.D.	01 Sep

I	Heneghan, J.F.	01 Sep
X	Webster, P.M.	01 Sep
X	Judd, S.A.	01 Sep
I	Tooley, J.E.H.	01 Sep
X	Schwab, R.A.	02 Oct
I	Winkle, S.J.	04 Oct
X	Daw, S.J.	16 Oct
X	McKee, R.L.	16 Oct
X	Tribe, J.D.	16 Oct
W	Whetton, J.B.D.	12 Nov
I	Clarke, R.	01 Dec
W	Brigham, J.M.	10 Dec
W	Cobb, J.E.	10 Dec
W	Markowski, I.M.	10 Dec
W	Springett, J.K.	10 Dec
X	Hubble, R.S.E.	16 Dec
I	Hayle, E.A.	16 Dec
I	Williams, D.	16 Dec

1988

I	Campbell, M.A.	01 Jan
I	Duncan, K.R.	01 Jan
I	Manson, C.R.	01 Jan
I	Reed, M.	01 Jan
I	Routh, N.G.	01 Jan
I	Waldock, M.I.	01 Jan
X	Lambourne, D.J.	01 Feb
E	Swain, T.G.	01 Feb
X	Worman, R.	16 Feb
X	Player, R.C.	16 Feb
I	Potts, J.M.	01 Mar
X	Clucas, M.R.	01 Apr
E	Jarvis, L.R.	01 Apr
X	Kingston, I.J.	01 Apr
I	Black, H.E.	07 Apr
X	Firth, R.J.G.	08 Apr
X	Slocombe, C.A.	16 Apr
I	Collins, S.J.	01 May
I	Copeland-Davis, T.W.	01 May
E	Lias, C.D.	01 May
E	White, D.R.	01 May
E	Morris, S.T.	01 May
X	Richardson, N.M.	01 May
X	Whitworth, R.M.	01 May
X	Salmon, M.A.	01 May
X	Atkinson, E.J.	16 May
X	Reid, I.C.	01 Jun
X	James, A.J.	01 Jun
I	Pellow, A.J.	01 Jul
X	Luscombe, M.D.	16 Jul
S	Richards, N.J.	29 Jul
I	Colvin, A.P.	01 Sep
I	Hutchinson, C.J.	01 Sep
I	Moys, A.J.	01 Sep
I	Philip, M.W.	01 Sep
I	Swannick, D.J.	01 Sep
I	Tench, M.	01 Sep
I	Woodley, D.	01 Sep
I	Young, M.S.	01 Sep
I	Todd, C.F.J.	01 Sep
S	Olliver, A.J.	16 Sep
I	Roberts, C.A.	29 Sep
X	Roberts, M.	01 Oct

I	Skuce, J.L.	01 Oct
I	Tait, J.S.	09 Oct
I	Bone, R.C.	13 Oct
S	Pocock, D.	16 Oct
X	Fedorowicz, R.	16 Oct
I	Condy, S.L.	25 Oct
I	Smith, R.B.W.	26 Oct
I	Evans, C.H.	01 Nov
X	Fleming, K.P.	01 Nov
X	Johns, M.G.	01 Nov
X	King, R.J.	01 Nov
I	Owen, W.A.	01 Nov
I	Green, A.J.	01 Nov
X	Marsh, B.H.	01 Dec
S	Hall, E.C.	15 Dec

1989

I	Cogdell, P.C.	01 Jan
I	Hutchinson, A.J.	01 Jan
I	Rogers, P.M.	01 Jan
I	Bratby, A.M.H.	01 Jan
X	Hartley, J.L.	01 Feb
X	Monk, C.D.	01 Feb
X	Bance, N.D.	16 Feb
X	Brown, P.J.	16 Feb
X	Wright, A.J.	16 Feb
X	Dawkins, M.W.	01 Mar
X	Williamson, S.J.	01 Mar
X	Cook, D.J.	01 Mar
X	Loughran, D.W.	01 Mar
X	Coupland, M.B.	01 Mar
X	Boyes, R.A.	01 Mar
X	Callaghan, P.F.	01 Apr
X	Hickson, C.J.	01 Apr
E	Lang, A.J.N.	01 Apr
S	Williams, S.W.L.	01 Apr
X	Holden, N.	01 Apr
X	Payling, R.S.	16 Apr
X	Ramsdale, T.J.	16 Apr
X	Rowley, M.C.	16 Apr
I	Woods, A.C.	25 Apr
I	Channer, D.I.	01 May
I	Hayde, P.J.	01 May
I	Heir, J.S.	01 May
I	Holland, S.M.W.	01 May
I	Tailor, S.	01 May
I	Grace, J.P.	01 May
I	Henry, D.E.M.	15 May
X	Stone, P.C.J.	16 May
E	Coffey, S.J.	01 Jun
I	Krosnar-Clarke, S.M.	01 Jun
I	Morris, P.	01 Jun
I	Seekings, A.L.	01 Jun
X	Willis, S.A.	01 Jun
E	MacKay, R.	01 Jun
E	Norman, S.L.	01 Jun
X	Howard, D.G.	01 Jun
E	Taylor, S.J.	01 Jun
X	Colquhoun, R.T.	01 Jun
X	Kistruck, D.J.	01 Jun
X	Tyack, T.J.	01 Jun
X	Rae, A.J.W.	16 Jun
X	Nicholson, D.J.	16 Jun

I	Smith, P.C.	16 Jun
X	Barling, N.R.	01 Jul
X	Abernethy, G.	01 Jul
X	Cornick, R.M.	01 Jul
I	Ellis, D.F.	09 Jul
I	Edgley, A.D.	16 Jul
X	Harmer, J.N.J.	16 Jul
X	Bramble, K.R.	16 Jul
W	Whittingham, D.J.	28 Jul
X	McHugh, T.P.	01 Aug
E	Shirley, A.J.	01 Aug
X	Eatwell, R.A.	01 Aug
X	Neave, A.M.	01 Aug
X	Thompson, R.A.	01 Aug
E	Drewer, C.D.	01 Aug
X	Linscott, P.A.	16 Aug
X	Goldsmith, D.	16 Aug
I	Campbell, J.C.	01 Sep
I	Cree, A.M.	01 Sep
I	Hunt, C.J.	01 Sep
I	Jenkins, S.S.	01 Sep
I	Prescott-Pickup, M.L.	01 Sep
I	Spencer, C.R.	01 Sep
I	Taylor, A.	01 Sep
I	Tulloch, A.M.	01 Sep
I	Wynn, S.R.	01 Sep
I	Yearwood, K.	01 Sep
X	Brightling, C.	01 Sep
X	Hargreaves, N.	01 Sep
X	Rowbottom, C.	01 Sep
X	Anderson, S.C.	01 Sep
I	Wiseman, J.E.	01 Sep
I	Fawcett, F.P.	01 Sep
I	Howe, V.H.	01 Sep
I	Palfrey, L.J.	01 Sep
I	Rowe, P.E.	02 Sep
W	Campbell, K.L.	12 Sep
X	Watkins, T.C.	16 Sep
S	Jack, P.J.	16 Sep
X	Cook, G.E.	16 Sep
I	Evison, T.	19 Sep
X	Bennett, S.R.	01 Oct
X	Wilson, P.N.	15 Oct
X	Wilkinson, R.N.	16 Oct
X	Lauretani, A.S.D.	16 Oct
I	Bulcock, L.C.	01 Nov
X	Shallcroft, J.E.	01 Nov
E	George, J.M.	01 Nov
X	Bithell, I.S.	01 Nov
X	Greenfield, D.C.	16 Nov
X	Castle, A.S.	01 Dec
W	Blackett, K.J.	14 Dec
X	Edge, P.A.	14 Dec
W	Mayne, A.	14 Dec
X	Currie, D.G.	16 Dec

1990

I	Browning, R.S.	01 Jan
I	Casson, N.P.	01 Jan
E	Dawson, S.N.	01 Jan
I	Robinson, I.A.L.	01 Jan
X	Smith, P.G.	01 Jan
I	Wilkes, D.J.	01 Jan

X	Maidwell, N.C.	01 Jan
E	Preston, M.R.	01 Jan
X	McDermott, M.	01 Jan
X	Beddoe, A.G.T.	01 Jan
X	Hanrahan, M.W.	08 Jan
X	Wakefield, A.G.	16 Jan
X	Brown, A.A.	16 Jan
X	Holden, R.J.	16 Jan
E	Whild, A.A.	01 Feb
X	Ffrench, D.J.	01 Feb
X	McCreesh, P.M.	01 Feb
S	Parry, A.K.I.	01 Feb
E	Weir, S.D.	01 Feb
X	Goodenough, N.J.	16 Feb
S	Cunane, J.R.	16 Feb
I	Prendergast, S.A.	26 Feb
E	Howard, N.	01 Mar
I	Kendrick, R.S.	01 Mar
X	Liggins, M.P.	01 Mar
X	Russell, R.M.J.	01 Mar
X	Elwood, C.P.	16 Mar
X	Ritchie, D.M.	16 Mar
X	Chapman, D.A.	16 Mar
X	Flavill, S.M.	01 Apr
X	Thorne, S.M.	01 Apr
X	McArdell, S.J.R.	01 Apr
X	Ritchie, J.N.	01 Apr
W	Hodgson, J.L.	04 Apr
W	Simpson, E.J.	04 Apr
X	Lynch, R.D.F.	16 Apr
X	Brotherton, J.D.	16 Apr
X	Franklin, B.J.	16 Apr
X	Reid, J.G.	16 Apr
I	Hepworth, A.W.D.	22 Apr
I	Coulthard, A.J.	01 May
I	Crouch, J.G.	01 May
X	Deeney, S.J.	01 May
I	Flint, H.A.	01 May
I	Mandley, P.J.	01 May
I	Yardley, P.	01 May
E	Smith, S.B.	01 May
X	Tayler, J.R.N.	01 May
X	Tillion, A.M.	01 May
X	Colyer, M.A.J.	01 May
X	Nicholas, B.J.	16 May
X	Anderson, A.R.	16 May
X	Clarke, A.P.	16 May
X	Cobbett, J.F.	16 May
I	Summers, J.A.E.	24 May
I	Lensh, R.M.	01 Jun
X	Robinson, M.A.	01 Jun
X	Wheaton, B.J.S.	01 Jun
X	Williams, M.A.	01 Jun
E	Mitchell, A.J.	01 Jun
X	Terry, A.J.	01 Jun
X	Bhattacharya, D.	16 Jun
X	Lightfoot, R.A.	16 Jun
X	Booker, S.R.	16 Jun
X	Ford, J.A.	01 Jul
X	Kimberley, R.	01 Jul
X	Lowther, J.M.	01 Jul
X	Russell, T.J.	01 Jul
X	Beech, C.M.	01 Jul
X	Lewis, D.J.	01 Jul

I	Williams, S.C.	16 Jul
W	Ellman-Brown, A.C.	27 Jul
X	Davies, A.J.A.	01 Aug
E	Roots, S.	01 Aug
X	Barrett, M.G.	01 Aug
X	Farrant, P.R.	16 Aug
X	Suckling, R.L.	16 Aug
X	Oddy, D.M.	16 Aug
X	D'Arcy, P.A.	16 Aug
I	Albon, M.	01 Sep
I	Critchley, M.S.	01 Sep
X	Crockatt, S.R.J.	01 Sep
I	Ellender, T.J.	01 Sep
I	Foster, J.S.	01 Sep
I	Galbraith, D.S.	01 Sep
I	Gregory, E.	01 Sep
I	Hutton, K.D.	01 Sep
I	Lloyd, S.J.	01 Sep
I	Marratt, R.J.	01 Sep
I	Munroe, J.A.	01 Sep
I	Stephens, R.J.	01 Sep
I	Stewart, K.C.	01 Sep
I	Toor, J.J.S.	01 Sep
I	Turner, K.A.	01 Sep
I	Vincent, A.	01 Sep
I	Walker, R.A.	01 Sep
X	Wells, D.G.	01 Sep
X	Farrell, S.M.	01 Sep
X	Gardiner, P.F.D.	01 Sep
S	Church, C.R.	01 Sep
I	Elcock, C.J.	01 Sep
X	Sopinski, G.F.	16 Sep
X	Barker, J.W.	16 Sep
X	Phillis, I.R.	16 Sep
X	MacMillan, G.	16 Sep
X	Rostron, A.F.	19 Sep
I	Sodhi, M.P.T.	23 Sep
X	Deverson, R.T.M.	01 Oct
X	Harrison, P.D.	01 Oct
X	Graham, M.A.	01 Oct
X	Sant, P.Q.	01 Oct
S	MacDougall, G.R.	01 Oct
I	Nowell, J.S.	01 Oct
X	Knight, A.R.	01 Oct
X	Redfern, T.A.	01 Oct
X	Brunswick, R.E.	16 Oct
X	Hunt, S.N.	16 Oct
I	Adams, I.	01 Nov
I	Kelly, A.B.	01 Nov
X	Pegrum, T.A.	01 Nov
X	Robertson, P.N.	01 Nov
S	Clark, M.T.	01 Nov
S	O'Sullivan, B.O.	16 Nov
S	Cottis, M.C.	16 Nov
X	Grogono, J.G.B.	01 Dec
S	Speake, J.	01 Dec
X	Randell, G.	01 Dec
X	Morrison, B.	01 Dec
I	Foster, B.M.T.	07 Dec
S	Reeve, M.W.	12 Dec

1991

X	Diver, P.H.	01 Jan
I	Faircloth, M.	01 Jan

I	Frost, M.A.	01 Jan	I	Oliver, G.	01 May
I	Gainford, P.	01 Jan	I	Orton, D.M.	01 May
I	Hussain, S.	01 Jan	I	Robertson, K.R.	01 May
I	Leech, K.P.H.	01 Jan	I	Steer, M.A.	01 May
I	Linderman, I.R.	01 Jan	I	Taylor, A.L.	01 May
I	Matthews, P.B.	01 Jan	I	Tippey, M.A.	01 May
I	Pears, I.J.	01 Jan	X	Foster, D.H.	01 May
I	Thomas, A.L.	01 Jan	X	McDonald, I.G.	01 May
I	Twine, J.H.	01 Jan	X	Burstow, R.S.	01 May
I	Walker, M.J.	01 Jan	X	Allen, P.M.	01 May
I	Williams, P.M.	01 Jan	X	Simmonds-Short, M.R.	01 May
I	Woodham, R.H.	01 Jan	I	Bonnett, J.M.	01 May
X	Sage, D.I.	01 Jan	X	Adams, B.M.	16 May
X	Baillie, A.R.	01 Jan	X	Miller, C.R.	16 May
I	Comrie, A.A.C.	01 Jan	X	Banks, I.E.	01 Jun
I	Burns, R.D.J.	06 Jan	X	Bucklow, S.P.	01 Jun
E	Udensi, E.A.A.A.	06 Jan	E	Taylor, N.R.	01 Jun
X	Grindon, M.G.	16 Jan	X	Beirne, S.	01 Jun
X	Hannigan, P.F.	16 Jan	X	Hardy, S.	01 Jun
X	Orchard, A.P.	16 Jan	E	Woolley, D.	01 Jun
I	McDonnell, D.S.	24 Jan	X	Abson, I.T.	01 Jun
I	McGinley, M.P.	25 Jan	X	Brunskill, J.E.T.	01 Jun
X	Massey, S.	01 Feb	X	Conway, C.E.	01 Jun
E	Rossiter, M.A.	01 Feb	E	Green, C.M.	01 Jun
X	Scivier, J.S.	01 Feb	X	Evans, C.	01 Jun
E	Bosustow, B.F.	01 Feb	S	Hunt, E.L.	01 Jun
X	Avison, M.J.	01 Feb	X	Perry, G.A.	16 Jun
X	Gilchrist, K.W.	16 Feb	X	Whitfield, J.A.	16 Jun
S	Powell, J.	24 Feb	X	Smith, D.T.	16 Jun
X	Bowers, J.P.	01 Mar	I	Logan, R.W.	21 Jun
X	Crimmen, D.J.	01 Mar	I	Davies, G.C.	01 Jul
X	Phillips, J.P.	01 Mar	X	Duffy, J.B.	01 Jul
I	Fulcher, J.L.	01 Mar	X	Gladston, S.A.	01 Jul
X	Rogers, J.C.E.	01 Mar	X	Leaver, C.E.L.	01 Jul
X	Burlow, G.	01 Mar	I	Savage, A.P.	01 Jul
E	Roberts, S.C.	01 Mar	X	Tetley, M.	01 Jul
X	Colwell, M.A.	16 Mar	X	Dale, A.	01 Jul
X	Seabrook, I.	16 Mar	X	Johnson, R.W.	01 Jul
X	Murray, A.S.	16 Mar	X	McKnight, D.J.S.	01 Jul
X	Davison, G.J.	01 Apr	X	Hinch, D.G.W.	01 Jul
X	Eldridge, T.J.	01 Apr	X	Tattersall, R.B.	01 Jul
X	Falconer, A.J.	01 Apr	X	Hart, T.G.D.B.	01 Jul
X	Herriman, J.A.	01 Apr	X	Ponsford, P.K.	01 Jul
X	Ridd, D.A.	01 Apr	X	Ash, T.C.V.	08 Jul
S	Atkinson, I.N.	01 Apr	X	Hayward, G.	16 Jul
X	Duncan, J.	01 Apr	W	Mayoh, C.	24 Jul
E	Panteli, J.M.	01 Apr	W	Swannick, C.M.	24 Jul
E	Higgins, G.N.	01 Apr	W	Leigh, S.	25 Jul
X	Davidson, N.R.	01 Apr	S	Shields, C.T.	25 Jul
E	Thomson, I.R.	01 Apr	W	Swift, J.A.	25 Jul
X	Cornes, J.R.	01 Apr	I	Hart, D.R.	01 Aug
I	Waring, J.R.	01 Apr	S	Tucker, K.M.	01 Aug
W	Graham, P.J.	03 Apr	X	Newton, M.J.	01 Aug
W	Maynard, L.	03 Apr	X	Garland, M.J.	01 Aug
W	Stredwick, C.A.	03 Apr	X	Dreelan, M.J.	01 Aug
W	Tant, Z.M.	03 Apr	X	Gray, P.R.	01 Aug
W	Ambler, K.K.	04 Apr	X	Lynch, S.	01 Aug
S	Norsworthy, C.V.	04 Apr	X	Richardson, G.L.	01 Aug
W	Pearce, S.E.	04 Apr	X	Christmas, S.P.	16 Aug
I	Fielder, D.A.	10 Apr	X	Bullen, M.P.	16 Aug
X	Forster, R.A.	16 Apr	X	Westley, D.R.	16 Aug
X	Smith, R.C.V.	16 Apr	I	Dawson, N.J.F.	01 Sep
I	Blackburn Jones, M.	01 May	I	Ellis, J.P.	01 Sep
I	Cook, C.B.	01 May			

I	Grears, J.	01 Sep
I	Jones, G.D.	01 Sep
I	McLarnon, C.P.C.	01 Sep
I	Sloan, D.J.	01 Sep
I	Tatham, S.A.	01 Sep
I	Williams, D.C.	01 Sep
X	Lambie, T.J.	01 Sep
I	Jones, A.F.	01 Sep
X	Anderson, R.G.	01 Sep
X	Carnell, G.J.	01 Sep
X	Kearney, J.R.	01 Sep
E	Moores, C.P.	01 Sep
X	Lancaster, A.N.	01 Sep
X	Powell, J.N.	01 Sep
X	Lindsay, D.J.	01 Sep
X	Young, M.J.	16 Sep
X	Milne, P.B.	16 Sep
I	Howell, H.R.G.	25 Sep
E	Milsom, J.	01 Oct
X	Morrison, G.W.	01 Oct
X	Logan, J.M.	01 Oct
X	Hilson, S.M.	01 Oct
X	Lee, R.	01 Oct
X	Abbott, J.W.	01 Oct
E	Roberts, I.G.	01 Oct
X	Thomas, G.R.	01 Oct
X	Windebank, S.J.	01 Oct
S	Wood, J.M.	05 Oct
X	Armstrong, I.G.	16 Oct
X	Cain, N.E.	17 Oct
X	Walsh, S.C.	01 Nov
X	Lea, S.A.P.	01 Nov
E	Murphy, F.D.	01 Nov
X	Noblett, P.G.A.	01 Nov
E	Donovan, P.	01 Nov
E	Hayhoe, R.D.	01 Nov
X	Slocombe, N.R.	01 Nov
X	Hill, S.J.M.	01 Nov
X	Hutton, G.	01 Nov
X	Adamson, D.	16 Nov
X	Finch, C.R.	16 Nov
X	Hamilton, I.J.	16 Nov
I	Hawker-Cole, R.C.	01 Dec
X	Smith, B.J.	01 Dec
X	Szemerenyi, P.N.	01 Dec
E	Wilkinson, C.H.	01 Dec
W	Easton, C.E.	12 Dec
S	Hill, E.C.A.	12 Dec
W	Hutton, K.L.	12 Dec

1992

I	Arnold, C.J.	01 Jan
I	Baines, D.M.L.	01 Jan
I	Bartlett, P.A.	01 Jan
I	Beadnell, R.M.	01 Jan
I	Harcourt, R.J.	01 Jan
I	Millman, D.J.	01 Jan
I	Ritsperis, A.	01 Jan
I	Stamper, J.C.H.	01 Jan
E	Morgan-Hosey, J.N.	01 Jan
E	Rostron, D.W.	01 Jan
X	O'Leary, S.R.	01 Jan
X	Moulton, S.J.	01 Jan
X	Cranmer, A.J.A.	01 Jan

W	Bolt, J.C.	04 Jan
W	Bullock, S.M.	04 Jan
W	Dible, S.E.	04 Jan
S	Dunthorne, J.A.	04 Jan
W	Laughton, F.A.	04 Jan
W	Pitcher, C.D.	04 Jan
X	Richardson, P.	16 Jan
X	Chan-A-Sue, S.S.	16 Jan
X	Neal, S.M.	16 Jan
X	Poole, T.J.	16 Jan
X	Wright, D.W.	16 Jan
S	Quinn, M.E.	01 Feb
X	Thompson, A.R.	01 Feb
X	Brown, A.P.	01 Feb
X	MacArthur, M.J.	01 Feb
X	Atkinson, G.C.	01 Feb
E	Kelly, J.A.	01 Feb
X	Tidball, I.C.	01 Feb
E	Irwin, M.A.	01 Mar
X	Ellis, C.T.	01 Mar
X	King, A.R.	01 Mar
E	Punton, I.M.	01 Mar
X	Rowlands, K.	01 Mar
X	Canning, C.P.	01 Mar
X	Light, A.J.	16 Mar
E	Cameron, M.J.	01 Apr
X	Sparkes, S.N.	01 Apr
E	Curlewis, A.J.	01 Apr
X	Leach, S.D.	01 Apr
E	Lloyd, G.W.	01 Apr
X	Murphy, D.A.	01 Apr
X	Shrimpton, M.W.	01 Apr
X	Richardson, G.A.	01 Apr
W	Daws, P.D.	03 Apr
X	Milligan, R.J.C.	16 Apr
S	Goodwin, A.L.	25 Apr
W	Oakey, K.F.	25 Apr
W	Spurgeon, N.A.	25 Apr
X	Vincent, C.E.	25 Apr
I	Birse, G.J.	01 May
I	Edmonds, R.M.	01 May
I	Evans, M.	01 May
I	Plackett, A.J.	01 May
I	Smith, N.P.	01 May
X	Watts, P.S.	01 May
X	Hamilton, S.W.T.	01 May
E	Harris, A.G.	01 May
I	Turner, R.B.	01 May
X	Bird, J.M.	01 May
X	Brind, V.J.	01 May
X	Aylott, P.R.F.D.	01 May
X	Wood, S.L.	01 May
X	Quinn, S.A.	16 May
X	Brunsden-Brown, S.E.	16 May
X	Lawrance, G.M.	16 May
X	McCulloch, A.M.B.	16 May
X	Read, C.T.	16 May
X	Williams, R.I.	16 May
I	Solly, M.M.	22 May
I	Rae, P.A.	01 Jun
X	Poole, A.J.	01 Jun
E	Wilkins, R.R.	01 Jun
X	Radford, A.J.	01 Jun
X	Roll, K.S.	01 Jun
X	Abbott, J.J.	01 Jun
S	Barton, A.J.	01 Jun
S	Coyne, C.J.	01 Jun
S	Fletcher, B.R.	01 Jun
X	Moore, M.	01 Jun
E	Mulvaney, P.A.	01 Jun
X	Terry-Brown, P.C.	01 Jun
X	Sneddon, R.N.	16 Jun
X	King, S.J.	16 Jun
I	Young, C.J.	18 Jun
E	Elliott, S.	01 Jul
X	Rasor, A.M.	01 Jul
E	Sansford, A.J.	01 Jul
S	Steele, K.S.	01 Jul
X	Finn, G.J.	01 Jul
E	Moody, D.C.	01 Jul
W	Mayell, J.A.	14 Jul
S	Gray, M.E.	24 Jul
E	Donovan, M.C.	01 Aug
E	Goodbourn, R.N.	01 Aug
E	Mills, I.	01 Aug
X	Wallis, J.S.	01 Aug
X	Brian, N.	01 Aug
E	Hemsworth, K.J.	01 Aug
E	Paul, T.J.	01 Aug
E	Woodbridge, R.G.	01 Aug
X	Lambert, A.	09 Aug
X	Howell, L.C.	16 Aug
X	Jaques, D.A.	16 Aug
I	Baggaley, J.A.L.	01 Sep
I	Bee, M.T.	01 Sep
I	Harding, C.S.	01 Sep
I	Langrill, M.P.	01 Sep
I	Procter, J.E.	01 Sep
X	Skidmore, R.P.	01 Sep
S	Vowles, T.J.	01 Sep
W	Clark, A.C.	01 Sep
I	Wharrie, E.K.B.	01 Sep
X	Flynn, L.P.	01 Sep
X	Mitchell, C.R.	01 Sep
S	Mitton, A.L.	01 Sep
X	Morgan, L.A.	16 Sep
E	Carr, R.G.	01 Oct
S	Bell, M.	01 Oct
X	Langrish, G.J.	01 Oct
E	MacLean, C.L.	01 Oct
X	Wooller, M.A.H.	01 Oct
S	Young, W.D.	01 Oct
X	Allen, L.B.	01 Oct
X	Boorman, J.K.P.	01 Oct
X	Gibbons, N.P.	01 Oct
I	Arnold, K.J.	21 Oct
W	Hood, C.K.	23 Oct
E	Dickens, D.S.	01 Nov
X	Gordon, N.L.	01 Nov
X	Simmons, A.L.P.	01 Nov
S	Fogell, A.D.	01 Nov
X	Reen, S.C.	01 Nov
X	Woodard, J.R.A.	01 Nov
X	Julian, T.M.	16 Nov
X	Fitzgerald, N.J.	01 Dec
X	Clinton, L.A.	01 Dec
X	Godfrey, S.P.	01 Dec
X	Haigh, A.J.	01 Dec
X	Lilburn, L.K.	01 Dec
X	Sargent, P.M.	01 Dec
W	Elborn, T.K.	11 Dec
W	Fairgrieve, L.	11 Dec
W	Green, J.L.	11 Dec
W	McBain, M.S.	11 Dec
W	McLean, H.M.	11 Dec
W	Mules, S.A.	11 Dec
W	Treharne, A.J.	11 Dec
W	Walsh, J.S.	11 Dec
X	Phillips, G.P.	16 Dec
S	Beresford-Green, P.M.	16 Dec

1993

I	Boston, J.	01 Jan
I	Citrine, J.	01 Jan
I	Lewis, S.J.	01 Jan
I	McMullan, N.L.	01 Jan
I	Thompson, A.J.	01 Jan
X	Forester-Bennett, R.M.W.	01 Jan
X	Lawton, G.S.	01 Jan
X	Rowe, K.C.	01 Jan
X	Brothwell, S.E.	01 Jan
I	Ellis, D.R.	01 Jan
I	Peachment, B.L.	01 Jan
I	Schofield, M.K.	01 Jan
I	Swinden, M.B.	01 Jan
I	Walmsley, P.A.	01 Jan
X	Hambly, P.T.	01 Jan
X	Owen, G.	01 Jan
X	Smith, G.D.J.	01 Jan
X	Wills, P.J.	01 Jan
W	Wilkinson, J.M.	04 Jan
X	Jameson, R.M.	16 Jan
X	Mercer, D.C.	16 Jan
I	Lodge, C.N.	01 Feb
I	Woods, T.C.	01 Feb
I	Binstead, K.N.	01 Feb
E	Rollings, H.E.	01 Feb
X	Steil, C.W.R.	01 Feb
X	Crombie, N.G.M.	01 Feb
X	Grose, M.W.	01 Feb
X	Knott, M.B.	01 Feb
X	Trott, C.M.J.	01 Feb
I	McCaughey, V.J.	01 Mar
X	MacNeil, S.W.	01 Mar
X	Simpson, C.C.	01 Mar
X	Whitelock, M.A.	01 Mar
X	Calkin, D.A.	01 Mar
X	Darwent, S.A.	01 Mar
X	Duthie, R.M.M.	01 Mar
X	Griffin, N.R.	01 Mar
X	Evans, R.J.	01 Mar
X	Cogan, R.E.C.	16 Mar
X	Patterson, A.J.	16 Mar
X	Gates, N.S.	16 Mar
E	Donnelly, J.S.	01 Apr
S	Waterhouse, P.	01 Apr
I	Whyte, I.P.	01 Apr
X	Bramwell, J.G.	01 Apr
X	Millen, S.C.W.	01 Apr

E	Waterworth, S.N.	01 Apr	E	Hinks, K.J.	01 Oct	X	Froude, N.W.	01 Apr
S	Whalley, R.J.	01 Apr	X	Larkins, P.D.	01 Oct	X	MacFarlane, I.S.D.	01 Apr
X	McKenzie, M.	16 Apr	X	Bolton, S.J.	16 Oct	X	Rutherford, K.J.	01 Apr
X	Soar, G.	16 Apr	X	Perry, R.J.	01 Nov	X	Willing, N.P.	01 Apr
X	Mason, H.O.D.	16 Apr	X	Gamble, N.	01 Nov	E	Hindson, C.L.	01 Apr
W	Gale, S.L.	25 Apr	E	Lewis, G.D.	01 Nov	E	Nicholas, S.P.	01 Apr
S	Manser, C.T.	25 Apr	E	Stevenson, J.P.	01 Nov	X	Tooze, L.V.	01 Apr
X	Milton, G.P.	01 May	X	Maginn, F.G.	01 Nov	X	Manser, D.N.	01 Apr
E	Guy, M.A.	01 May	X	Baitson, J.A.	01 Nov	X	Childs, J.R.	01 Apr
X	Harlow, S.R.	01 May	X	Moore, S.K.	01 Nov	X	Page, L.	01 Apr
E	Paris, W.	01 May	X	Simpson, D.K.	16 Nov	X	Mailes, I.R.A.	16 Apr
E	Spring, J.M.	01 May	E	Payne, T.	01 Dec	X	Stembridge, D.P.T.	16 Apr
I	Ellis, M.P.	01 May	E	Davies, J.W.	01 Dec	X	Manson, P.D.	01 May
E	Bowyer, P.J.	01 May	X	Long, W.G.H.	01 Dec	X	Townsend, G.P.	01 May
X	Mould, P.	01 May	X	Blackburn, P.R.	01 Dec	E	Wicking, G.S.	01 May
X	Payne, M.J.	01 May	E	Mehta, R.P.	01 Dec	X	Foreman, T.P.	01 May
X	Stock, C.M.	01 May	X	Sherriff, J.	01 Dec	S	Hart, N.L.W.	01 May
X	Crossley, G.A.	16 May	X	Wuidart-Gray, S.R.	01 Dec	X	Hoare, P.J.E.	01 May
E	Cleminson, M.D.	16 May	X	Schunmann, C.P.I.	01 Dec	E	Proud, A.D.	01 May
X	West, P.J.	16 May	X	Wall, D.K.	01 Dec	X	Blackburn, S.J.	01 May
E	Millar, G.C.	01 Jun	X	Scott, M.R.	16 Dec	X	Jones, R.M.	01 May
X	Grace, D.J.	01 Jun				X	Polding, M.	01 May
E	Goodrich, K.A.	01 Jun		**1994**		X	Robinson, M.S.	01 May
X	Harriman, C.	01 Jun	E	Oflaherty, J.S.	01 Jan	X	Smith, D.J.	01 May
X	Loane, M.M.	01 Jun	X	Sharp, G.C.	01 Jan	E	James, T.E.	01 May
X	Newell, P.R.	01 Jun	X	Campbell, P.R.	01 Jan	X	Bradley, M.T.	01 May
X	Robinson, L.C.	01 Jun	I	Kies, L.N.	01 Jan	X	Craig, J.A.	01 May
X	Jacques, N.A.	01 Jun	X	Rodgers, D.	01 Jan	X	Stephenson, K.J.M.	01 May
X	Sutton, R.M.J.	01 Jun	X	Bouch, S.K.	01 Jan	X	McLintock, M.W.	01 May
X	Richards, S.T.	16 Jun	X	Hitchings, D.L.	01 Jan	X	Worley, I.G.	16 May
X	White, S.H.W.	16 Jun	S	Naidoo, D.J.	01 Jan	X	Matthews, J.	16 May
X	Lister, A.R.	16 Jun	X	Nelson, M.C.	01 Jan	X	Douglas, P.G.	01 Jun
E	Elliott, S.	01 Jul	I	Bailey, T.S.	01 Jan	X	Smallwood, R.I.	01 Jun
X	Morris, A.M.	01 Jul	E	Evans, A.J.	01 Feb	X	Pitt, J.M.	01 Jun
S	Stoffell, D.P.	01 Jul	X	Bissell, A.D.	01 Feb	E	Windsar, P.A.	01 Jun
X	Edmunds, D.W.	01 Jul	X	Buckley, D.D.G.	01 Feb	X	Finch, P.A.	01 Jun
X	Walker, G.	01 Jul	X	Jelbart, K.	01 Feb	X	Fuller, J.P.	01 Jun
E	Weaver, A.L.	01 Jul	X	Tite, A.D.	01 Feb	S	Park, B.C.	01 Jun
X	Wingrove, K.H.	01 Jul	X	Phipps, T.A.	01 Feb	X	Rees, M.S.	01 Jun
E	Miles, G.J.	01 Jul	E	Thirkettle, J.A.	01 Feb	X	Collicutt, J.M.	16 Jun
E	Mudge, A.M.	01 Jul	E	Cheshire, T.E.	01 Feb	X	Naylor, A.J.	16 Jun
X	Geary, M.D.	01 Jul	X	Fryer, A.C.	01 Feb	X	Oakes, I.J.	16 Jun
X	Brosnan, M.A.	16 Jul	X	Kerr, S.V.	01 Feb	X	Hunt, S.C.	01 Jul
X	Norris, G.P.	16 Jul	X	Lamb, S.K.	01 Feb	X	Allen, R.	01 Jul
E	Faulkner, D.W.	01 Aug	E	Craggs, S.	01 Feb	E	Campbell-Balcombe,	01 Jul
X	Jones, S.M.	01 Aug	X	Weightman, N.E.	16 Feb		A.A.	
E	Pearson, C.P.B.	01 Aug	X	Taylor, R.J.	16 Feb	X	Forman, R.R.	01 Jul
E	West, G.G.	01 Aug	X	Stockton, K.G.	01 Mar	X	Coley, S.J.	01 Jul
X	Richards, G.	01 Aug	X	Paddock, L.D.	01 Mar	X	Balmain, S.S.	01 Jul
E	Downer, M.J.	01 Aug	X	Duncan, C.J.	01 Mar	X	Haywood, P.J.	01 Jul
X	Cox, S.A.J.	16 Aug	X	Berey, I.D.	01 Mar	X	Jacques, M.J.	01 Jul
X	Choat, J.H.	16 Aug	X	Chadfield, L.J.	01 Mar	X	Carr, A.G.	01 Jul
X	Lavin, G.J.	01 Sep	X	Bryson, S.A.	01 Mar	X	Chaloner, A.C.	01 Jul
E	Rutherford, T.J.	01 Sep	E	Meek, C.S.	01 Mar	E	Hamilton, S.M.	01 Jul
X	Salt, H.S.	01 Sep	X	Money, C.M.	01 Mar	X	Muntz, H.A.J.	01 Jul
E	Steel, R.A.	01 Sep	X	Shellard, G.I.	01 Mar	E	Skelton, J.S.	01 Jul
E	Yeomans, P.A.	01 Sep	X	Stratton-Brown, R.	01 Mar	X	Hopkins, S.D.	16 Jul
X	Davies, E.J.	01 Sep	X	Wallace, S.J.	01 Mar	X	Sheils, D.E.T.	16 Jul
X	Henry, T.M.	01 Sep	X	Clarke, D.	16 Mar	X	Oatley, T.P.	16 Jul
I	Lees, S.N.	02 Sep	X	Aitchison, I.J.	16 Mar	X	Simmonds, R.C.K.	16 Jul
X	Elwell-Deighton,	16 Sep	X	Bailey, H.J.	01 Apr	X	Clarke, P.A.	01 Aug
	D.C.		X	Corbett, T.J.	01 Apr	X	Moran, S.D.	01 Aug
X	Stanley, N.J.	16 Sep	E	Roberts, D.	01 Apr	X	Penrice, I.W.	01 Aug
X	Hunter, P.R.	01 Oct	X	Barnes, P.A.L.	01 Apr	X	Allen, D.J.K.	01 Aug

X	Bing, N.A.	01 Aug	X	Ripley, B.E.	01 Nov	E	Blacow, C.	01 May
X	Bunney, G.J.	01 Aug	X	Allison, G.	16 Nov	X	Cooke-Priest,	01 May
X	Carpenter, P.J.	01 Aug	X	Rowley, S.A.C.	16 Nov		N.C.R.	
X	Garner, S.M.	01 Aug	X	Roster, S.P.	16 Nov	X	Gardner, B.R.J.	01 May
X	Hedworth, A.J.	01 Aug	X	Price, J.S.	16 Nov	S	Norman-Walker, B.S.	01 May
X	Knight, A.C.F.	01 Aug	X	Bratby, S.P.	16 Nov	X	White, P.D.C.	01 May
X	Marquis, A.C.	01 Aug	X	Shears, N.M.R.	18 Nov	X	Inge, D.J.	01 May
X	Puffett, N.W.	01 Aug	X	Russell, N.A.D.	01 Dec	X	Byron, J.D.	01 May
X	Spence, R.G.	01 Aug	S	Artingstall, B.L.	01 Dec	X	Woolsey, K.E.K.	16 May
X	Dobson, A.B.	01 Aug	S	Griffin, H.E.	01 Dec	X	Lindsey, R.J.	01 Jun
E	Scott, R.A.	01 Aug	X	Kurth, R.P.E.	01 Dec	X	McCafferty, M.J.	01 Jun
X	Knight, M.S.	08 Aug	X	Clink, A.D.	01 Dec	X	Noyce, R.G.	01 Jun
X	Kirkham, S.P.	16 Aug	X	Hacon, P.E.	01 Dec	E	Philpot, D.J.	01 Jun
I	Sexton, N.C.	01 Sep	X	Young, R.	01 Dec	X	Monk, S.R.	01 Jun
X	Cottee, B.R.J.	01 Sep	X	Pardoe, E.R.	01 Dec	E	Abbott, L.	01 Jun
E	Hartley, A.P.	01 Sep	E	Cragg, R.D.	01 Dec	X	Asquith, S.P.	01 Jun
E	Hendy, L.S.	01 Sep				E	Spooner, S.L.	01 Jun
E	Hodge, C.M.	01 Sep		1995		X	Turner, D.N.	01 Jun
X	Jones, P.I.	01 Sep	X	Farrell, N.M.B.	01 Jan	X	Ward, A.J.	01 Jun
X	McDonald, N.	01 Sep	S	Gale, C.V.	01 Jan	X	Coulton, J.R.S.	16 Jun
E	Reeves, K.	01 Sep	X	Hughes, J.G.	01 Jan	X	Hynett, W.A.	16 Jun
E	Beautyman, A.J.	01 Sep	X	MacKay, W.J.C.	01 Jan	X	McCowan, D.J.	16 Jun
X	Bourchier, S.A.	01 Sep	X	Mollard, M.J.	01 Jan	X	Maddison, S.	01 Jul
I	Cockshott, C.	01 Sep	X	Mills, S.D.G.	01 Jan	X	May, J.W.	01 Jul
X	Gotke, C.T.	01 Sep	X	Ware, S.A.	01 Jan	X	Dembrey, M.N.S.	01 Jul
X	Hinchcliffe, A.	01 Sep	X	Bishop, D.J.	01 Jan	X	Soul, N.J.	01 Jul
X	Mutch, J.R.	01 Sep	E	Manton, L.M.	01 Jan	X	Parrock, N.G.	01 Jul
E	Ajala, A.A.	01 Sep	X	De Salaberry	16 Jan	X	Clarke, I.B.	01 Jul
E	Balcombe, J.S.	01 Sep		Lewis, J.H.		E	Dalton, F.J.	01 Jul
X	Marandola, S.J.	01 Sep	X	Duncan, G.S.	16 Jan	X	Deavin, M.J.	01 Jul
S	Goldsworthy, P.J.	01 Sep	X	Shalders, M.J.	01 Feb	X	Doran, I.A.G.	01 Jul
X	Downing, I.M.	16 Sep	X	Tate, G.A.	01 Feb	E	Malkin, S.L.	01 Jul
X	Birmingham, T.C.	16 Sep	E	Kellett, A.	01 Feb	X	Pullan, K.J.	01 Jul
X	Grunwell, A.J.	16 Sep	X	Satterthwaite, B.J.	01 Feb	X	Ruddock, G.W.D.	01 Jul
X	Stubbs, G.A.	16 Sep	X	Gray, Y.M.	01 Feb	X	Russell, R.M.	01 Jul
X	Ogilvie, M.A.	01 Oct	X	Webber, J.P.	01 Feb	X	Tate, C.N.	01 Jul
E	Pugh, J.	01 Oct	X	Langrill, T.J.	01 Feb	E	Bagwell, P.	01 Aug
X	Kennington, L.A.	01 Oct	X	McCutcheon, G.	01 Feb	E	McArdle, R.A.	01 Aug
X	Kent, A.J.	01 Oct	X	Pike, S.B.	16 Feb	X	Harris, M.J.	01 Aug
X	Lee, P.M.	01 Oct	X	Johnson, A.R.	16 Feb	S	Goldsworthy, E.T.	01 Aug
X	Mullen, J.J.	01 Oct	X	Bennion, P.B.	01 Mar	X	Higgins, A.J.	01 Aug
X	Penprase, J.M.	01 Oct	X	Hoyle, S.A.	01 Mar	E	Harrington, J.B.	01 Aug
E	Snelling, P.D.	01 Oct	E	Thrippleton, M.G.	01 Mar	X	Hastilow, N.H.	01 Aug
S	Bryant, D.J.G.	01 Oct	X	Laycock, A.	01 Mar	X	Jones, M.D.	01 Aug
S	Goodman, P.R.	01 Oct	X	Peachey, R.M.	01 Mar	X	Larmuth, J.D.D.	01 Aug
X	Lord, R.J.	01 Oct	X	Reese, D.M.	01 Mar	E	Barrows, D.M.	01 Aug
X	Morgan, D.H.	01 Oct	X	Tanner, R.C.	01 Mar	E	Cole, J.	01 Aug
X	Vartan, M.R.	01 Oct	X	Bainbridge, S.D.	01 Mar	X	Flemwell, H.	01 Aug
X	Woolhead, A.L.	01 Oct	X	Harms, J.G.	01 Mar	X	Lucocq, N.J.	01 Aug
X	Mercer, K.R.	16 Oct	X	Rawlinson, D.	16 Mar	S	Redman, H.S.	01 Aug
X	Brayson, M.	16 Oct	X	Alexander, S.J.	01 Apr	X	Brooman, M.J.	16 Aug
X	Ellerton, P.	16 Oct	X	Gray, J.N.S.	01 Apr	X	Armstrong, S.T.	16 Aug
X	Roberts, J.L.	16 Oct	X	Marten, A.D.	01 Apr	X	Brennan, A.J.	01 Sep
X	Webb, I.F.R.	01 Nov	X	Ogden, B.P.	01 Apr	E	Foster, P.J.	01 Sep
X	Waite, T.J.	01 Nov	X	Humphries, J.E.	01 Apr	E	Hancock, R.T.A.	01 Sep
E	Chapman, C.L.	01 Nov	E	Cooper, A.	01 Apr	X	Rhodes, M.J.	01 Sep
X	Temple, M.	01 Nov	X	Ling, J.W.L.	01 Apr	E	Riddle, I.D.	01 Sep
X	Roberts, M.A.	01 Nov	X	Stratford, P.J.	01 Apr	S	Moore, S.B.	01 Sep
X	Billcliff, N.	01 Nov	S	Critchley, H.	01 Apr	X	Reid, G.	01 Sep
X	Hall, C.S.	01 Nov	X	Lovatt, G.J.	01 Apr	I	Tatlow, J.M.	01 Sep
X	Long, S.G.	01 Nov	X	Reid, M.R.	01 Apr	S	Watts, A.J.	01 Sep
X	Webster, A.P.	01 Nov	X	Atkinson, C.P.	01 Apr	X	Cullen, N.L.	01 Sep
X	Wingfield, M.J.	01 Nov	X	Kelynack, M.T.	16 Apr	X	Lanni, M.N.	01 Sep
E	Earl, N.J.C.	01 Nov	S	Armes, C.J.	28 Apr	X	Woolman, A.L.	01 Sep

X	Boag, K.I.	01 Sep	X	Marriott, N.K.	01 Dec	X	Segebarth, R.A.	16 Feb
X	Newton, J.L.	16 Sep	X	Mitchell, J.R.	01 Dec	X	Smith, D.L.	01 Mar
X	Brown, S.J.	01 Oct	X	Pass, D.J.R.	01 Dec	X	Emmerson, S.C.	01 Mar
X	Moore, S.P.	01 Oct	X	Phelps, G.R.	01 Dec	X	Hunt, F.B.G.	01 Mar
X	McLennan, A.	01 Oct	X	Richards, A.S.	01 Dec	X	Packham, C.N.R.	01 Mar
X	O'Leary, A.M.	01 Oct	X	Tacey, R.H.	01 Dec	X	McWilliams, J.E.	01 Mar
X	Smith, A.	01 Oct	X	Watson, A.H.	01 Dec	X	Pickering, I.J.	01 Mar
X	Stubbs, I.	01 Oct	X	Evans, D.A.	20 Dec	X	Hogg, A.	16 Mar
X	Barber, C.J.H.	01 Oct				X	Lawson, R.K.	16 Mar
X	Hendry, P.A.	01 Oct		**1996**		X	Simms, D.M.	16 Mar
X	Nice, P.R.A.	01 Oct	E	Lee, S.Y.L.	01 Jan	X	Long, M.S.	01 Apr
S	Matthews, P.K.	01 Oct	S	Bollen, J.M.	01 Jan	X	Mercer, P.J.	01 Apr
E	Hambly, B.J.	01 Nov	E	Bulcock, M.	01 Jan	E	Clarke, A.R.	01 Apr
X	Jardine, D.S.	01 Nov	X	Okukenu, D.	01 Jan	X	Tregunna, G.A.	01 Apr
X	Jones, P.D.	01 Nov	X	Batchelor, N.J.	01 Jan	X	Carr, M.C.	01 Apr
I	Parker, T.S.	01 Nov	E	Mallen, D.J.	01 Jan	X	Hanneman, M.N.	01 Apr
X	Chick, N.S.	16 Nov	X	Walker, S.P.	01 Jan	X	Harrison, R.S.	01 Apr
E	Gunn, H.I.	01 Dec	X	Whitmee, M.J.C.	01 Jan	X	Mazdon, T.J.	01 Apr
W	Swan, W.	01 Dec	E	Deeks, P.J.	01 Jan	X	Nash, P.D.	01 Apr
W	Watts, S.F.	01 Dec	S	Stewart, G.S.	01 Jan	X	Phillips, M.	01 Apr
E	Sitton, J.B.	01 Dec	X	West, D.C.	01 Jan	X	Squire, E.J.C.	01 Apr
S	Cross, I.	01 Dec	X	Banks, W.L.	16 Jan	X	Donnan, H.M.	01 Apr
X	Head, A.M.	01 Dec	X	Officer, R.L.	01 Feb	X	Harry, M.A.	01 Apr
X	Canning, S.J.	01 Dec	S	Hart, C.L.	01 Feb	X	Ralph, A.P.	01 Apr
X	Day, M.K.	01 Dec	X	Wookey, M.	01 Feb	E	Thomson, R.H.L.	01 Apr
X	Fletcher, K.J.	01 Dec	E	Taylor, H.J.	01 Feb	X	Campbell, I.A.	16 Apr
X	Hodgson, B.C.	01 Dec	X	Smith, M.D.	01 Feb	X	Fraser, I.E.	16 Apr

SUB LIEUTENANTS

(Medium and Short Career Commission)

	1992		X	Wiseman, N.C.	01 Jan	X	Hollis, S.P.	01 Sep
X	MacColl, A.A.J.	01 May	X	Abel, N.P.	01 Mar	X	Hooton, D.A.S.H.	01 Sep
E	Marjoram, G.K.	01 May	X	Brown, A.P.S.	01 Mar	E	Howells, S.L.	01 Sep
W	Shaw, R.	01 May	X	Clarke, R.J.	01 Mar	X	Hurford, E.G.	01 Sep
W	Dobie, F.E.	01 Sep	X	Francis, S.D.H.	01 Mar	X	Moorhouse, S.M.R.	01 Sep
X	Harvey, J.S.	01 Sep	X	Griffiths, R.H.	01 Mar	E	Punch, G.K.	01 Sep
X	Hockenhull, S.I.	01 Sep	X	Hall, D.	01 Mar	X	Rackham, A.D.H.	01 Sep
X	Morris, D.A.J.	01 Sep	X	Spillane, P.W.	01 Mar	X	Snaith, D.R.	01 Sep
X	Simpson, J.H.B.	01 Sep	X	Wyness, S.M.	01 Mar	X	Thomas, S.M.	01 Sep
X	Sturdy, C.C.M.	01 Sep	E	Adams, G.	01 May	E	Townsend, D.J.	01 Sep
X	Robley, W.F.	01 Nov	X	Cooke, J.E.	01 May	X	Watts, J.N.	01 Sep
X	Smith, A.B.D.	01 Nov	E	Cropper, F.B.N.	01 May	S	Wildin, V.	01 Sep
			E	Davis, S.R.	01 May	S	Woodard, N.A.	14 Sep
	1993		E	Gothard, A.M.	01 May	X	Bryant, K.G.	01 Nov
X	Adams, P.N.E.	01 Jan	X	Lambert, I.R.	01 May	X	Criddle, G.D.J.	01 Nov
X	Caldicott-Barr,	01 Jan	X	Lawson, S.	01 May	X	Davies, H.G.A.	01 Nov
	V.A.		X	Ollerton, J.C.	01 May	X	Fisher, R.J.	01 Nov
X	Church, S.C.	01 Jan	E	Potts, G.	01 May	X	Flintham, J.E.	01 Nov
X	Cotton, S.M.	01 Jan	E	Russell Clark, C.	01 May	X	Gilmore, M.P.	01 Nov
X	Fox, T.M.	01 Jan	E	Sanderson, L.D.	01 May			
E	Fraser, P.	01 Jan	S	Simpson, A.M.	01 May		**1994**	
X	Hourigan, M.P.	01 Jan	X	Smith, R.D.	01 May	X	Adshead, C.R.	01 Jan
X	Johnson, S.R.D.	01 Jan	X	King, C.J.	01 Jun	X	Armstrong, N.S.	01 Jan
X	MacKay, C.A.	01 Jan	X	Wilkinson, M.F.	01 Jul	X	Barlow, M.J.	01 Jan
X	McGuire, J.	01 Jan	X	Terry, N.P.	01 Aug	X	Burke, D.E.	01 Jan
E	Nimmons, P.	01 Jan	X	Atkinson, R.J.	01 Sep	S	Burns, A.C.	01 Jan
X	Partridge, C.S.	01 Jan	E	Briggs, M.D.	01 Sep	X	Crabb, A.J.	01 Jan
X	Riggall, A.D.	01 Jan	X	Brown, C.L.	01 Sep	X	Crutchfield, A.J.	01 Jan
S	Scandling, R.J.	01 Jan	X	Crossley, K.M.	01 Sep	E	Cumming, R.A.	01 Jan
X	Strathie, G.S.	01 Jan	X	Donovan, S.J.	01 Sep	E	Davies, B.	01 Jan
X	Tregaskis, N.S.	01 Jan	X	Gibson, J.B.	01 Sep	E	Dollin, A.J.	01 Jan
X	Wilson, A.S.	01 Jan	S	Gulzar, N.A.	01 Sep	X	Donworth, D.M.J.	01 Jan

E	Edwards, J.	01 Jan	S	Pearce, R.A.	01 May	X	Beale, T.D.	01 Jan
X	Enever, S.A.	01 Jan	S	Pring, S.J.	01 May	E	Brutton, J.H.	01 Jan
S	Fisher, T.C.	01 Jan	X	Raeburn, C.	01 May	S	Burnham, J.A.I.	01 Jan
E	Haggerty, S.M.	01 Jan	X	Roberts, N.D.	01 May	X	Clarke, J.C.	01 Jan
X	Hutchins, T.S.	01 Jan	X	Rogers, J.W.	01 May	X	Clemson, A.J.	01 Jan
X	Jaini, A.	01 Jan	X	Sheldrake, J.P.	01 May	X	Cole, D.J.	01 Jan
X	Jones, G.R.	01 Jan	X	Smith, R.J.	01 May	X	Davies, G.W.T.	01 Jan
X	McAvoy, S.P.	01 Jan	X	Stirling, D.J.	01 May	X	Doyle, G.B.	01 Jan
E	McCloskey, I.M.	01 Jan	E	Strange, S.P.	01 May	E	Duesbury, C.L.	01 Jan
X	McCulloch, I.D.	01 Jan	X	Sutherland, S.A.M.	01 May	X	Frean, J.P.	01 Jan
S	McDougall, D.W.	01 Jan	S	Taylor, C.R.	01 May	X	Fuller, C.E.	01 Jan
X	McEwan, A.M.	01 Jan	X	Thom, D.S.	01 May	X	Gamble, S.B.	01 Jan
E	McLaughlin, D.P.	01 Jan	E	Tracey, A.D.	01 May	S	Haigh, J.	01 Jan
X	Ogle, N.S.	01 Jan	X	Welsh, A.	01 May	X	Holder, J.M.	01 Jan
E	Ord, M.	01 Jan	X	White, J.C.E.	01 May	X	Hooton, D.R.	01 Jan
X	Pengelly, S.A.B.	01 Jan	E	White, K.F.	01 May	X	Hughes, S.M.	01 Jan
X	Platt, J.H.	01 Jan	X	Whitlum, A.C.	01 May	X	Humphries, S.M.	01 Jan
X	Powell, E.J.	01 Jan	E	Auld, D.M.	01 Sep	X	Jones, J.	01 Jan
E	Read, P.S.	01 Jan	X	Bernard, A.R.	01 Sep	X	Keith, J.A.	01 Jan
X	Robinson, J.P.	01 Jan	X	Bull, M.A.J.	01 Sep	X	Leighton, M.R.	01 Jan
X	Sewell, M.A.P.	01 Jan	S	Chiles, J.M.	01 Sep	X	Lewis, B.C.	01 Jan
X	Straughan, S.R.	01 Jan	X	Clague, J.J.	01 Sep	X	Lomax, D.	01 Jan
E	Thompson, D.W.	01 Jan	X	Dickins, B.R.	01 Sep	X	McKee, H.M.	01 Jan
X	Vorley, S.W.	01 Jan	S	Dobbins, S.J.	01 Sep	X	McWilliams, A.R.	01 Jan
X	Webber, K.J.	01 Jan	S	Edgar, J.A.	01 Sep	X	Morley, D.S.	01 Jan
E	Wildin, A.	01 Jan	X	Foster, N.P.	01 Sep	X	Normanshire, D.J.	01 Jan
X	Williams, R.J.S.	01 Jan	X	Green, I.A.	01 Sep	X	Obrien, P.T.	01 Jan
E	Pannett, L.W.	01 Feb	X	Grieve, L.H.	01 Sep	X	Osbaldestin, R.A.	01 Jan
X	Bridge, B.L.	01 Mar	S	Gullett, H.R.	01 Sep	E	Palmer, J.	01 Jan
X	Forbes, P.T.	01 Mar	E	Harding, H.R.	01 Sep	X	Pavey, E.L.	01 Jan
X	Mills, A.S.	01 Mar	E	Hassall, I.	01 Sep	X	Pedler, M.D.	01 Jan
X	Pike, R.D.	01 Mar	E	Head, S.G.	01 Sep	S	Porter, D.L.	01 Jan
X	Stevens, A.M.R.	01 Mar	X	Hefford, C.J.	01 Sep	E	Saward, J.R.E.	01 Jan
X	Alexander, O.D.D.	01 May	X	Heil, C.	01 Sep	E	Small, R.J.	01 Jan
E	Ashby, K.J.	01 May	X	Hunwicks, S.E.	01 Sep	X	Studley, S.A.	01 Jan
S	Ashby, M.K.	01 May	X	Jackson, I.	01 Sep	X	Swailes, S.P.	01 Jan
X	Beesting, A.	01 May	X	Jappy, G.W.G.	01 Sep	X	Taylor, S.J.	01 Jan
X	Bradley, R.L.	01 May	S	Kennedy, A.	01 Sep	X	Thomson, K.M.	01 Jan
X	Campbell, M.A.M.	01 May	E	Kingdom, M.A.	01 Sep	X	Toshney, R.J.	01 Jan
X	Chawira, D.N.	01 May	X	Lee, N.D.	01 Sep	E	Tumelty, G.C.	01 Jan
X	Clark, J.M.	01 May	X	Mason, D.J.	01 Sep	X	Wilson, J.	01 Jan
S	Coaker, S.A.	01 May	X	Owen, G.	01 Sep	X	Witte, R.H.	01 Jan
X	Codd, J.S.	01 May	X	Parr, N.K.	01 Sep	E	Wood, A.G.	01 Jan
X	Coutts, W.A.	01 May	X	Philip, A.D.	01 Sep	X	Woodford, B.S.	01 Jan
X	Dennis, P.E.	01 May	S	Quantrill, S.W.	01 Sep	X	Wynn, S.C.	01 Jan
X	Donegan, C.L.	01 May	E	Sayer, J.M.	01 Sep	X	Lindsay, I.B.	21 Jan
E	Evans, M.E.	01 May	S	Stockbridge, A.J.	01 Sep	X	Chippindale, N.	01 May
X	Fairhead, S.	01 May	X	Stringer, K.D.P.	01 Sep	X	Davies, W.G.	01 May
X	Field, J.S.	01 May	X	Stuart, E.E.A.	01 Sep	X	Dingwall, M.	01 May
X	Greetham, C.E.	01 May	E	Sullivan, M.N.	01 Sep	S	Hardwick, M.J.	01 May
E	Griffiths, D.P.	01 May	X	Symington, Z.M.A.	01 Sep	S	Hendy, R.	01 May
S	Harris, R.P.	01 May	X	Thomsen, L.L.	01 Sep	X	Hills, I.E.	01 May
S	Hawkins, K.A.	01 May	X	Tilney, D.E.	01 Sep	X	James, J.S.H.	01 May
E	Hawkins, S.R.	01 May	E	Watkins, K.J.	01 Sep	E	Love, R.J.	01 May
X	Hayden, T.W.	01 May	X	Weeks, C.J.	01 Sep	E	Lyons, A.G.	01 May
X	Hayward, A.L.	01 May	X	West, S.	01 Sep	E	Northcott, M.K.	01 May
X	Heaney, M.J.	01 May	X	Full, R.J.	01 Nov	E	Simm, C.W.	01 May
X	Hill, A.J.	01 May	X	Livesey, J.E.	01 Dec	E	Taylor, K.M.	01 May
X	Hindmarch, S.A.	01 May				X	Whitehead, P.J.	01 May
X	Holloway, S.A.	01 May		**1995**		X	Wilken, A.M.	01 May
X	Jones, D.J.	01 May	X	Ambrose, R.E.F.	01 Jan	X	Blackwell, J.M.	01 Sep
X	Lancaster, N.	01 May	X	Baines, A.R.	01 Jan	X	Kinsey, S.L.	01 Sep
E	McCleary, S.P.	01 May	X	Ball, A.D.	01 Jan	X	White, S.M.	01 Sep
X	Moules, M.A.J.	01 May	E	Banham, A.W.D.B.	01 Jan	X	Roberts, G.M.F.	01 Nov

X Smith, N.J.D. . . . 01 Nov	X Denham, D.J. . . . 01 Jan	X Rawles, J.R. . . . 01 Jan
	X Nimmo, G.S. . . . 01 Jan	X Sharrocks, I.J. . . . 01 Jan
1996	X Noon, P.J. . . . . 01 Jan	X Steel, S.A. . . . . 01 Jan
X Dempsey, S.P. . . . 01 Jan	X Pressdee, S.J. . . . 01 Jan	

SUB LIEUTENANTS (UCE)

(Medium and Short Career Commission)

1995	X Maley, C.E. . . . . 01 Sep
X Knight, S.D. . . . . 01 Sep	

MIDSHIPMEN

(Medium and Short Career Commission)

X Tighe, S.	X Stait, B.G. . . . . 01 May	X Nelson, M.R. . . . 01 May
	S Gibbs, A.M. . . . . 01 Jun	E Newman, D.J. . . . 01 May
1994	X Alsop, S.H. . . . 01 Jul	X Page, M.R. . . . . 01 May
X Aldridge, M.J. . . . 01 May	S Astle, D.S. . . . . 01 Sep	X Elward, M.J. . . . 01 Sep
X Burbidge, K. . . . . 01 May	X Corden, M. . . . . 01 Sep	X Gare, C.J. . . . . 01 Sep
E Chambers, P.D. . . 01 May	S Finn, E.J. . . . . 01 Sep	E Gilmore, S.J. . . . 01 Sep
E Chilton, J. . . . . . 01 May		X Harwood, L.B. . . . 01 Sep
X Clements, E.J. . . . 01 May	**1995**	X Tomes, A.C. . . . 01 Sep
S Cox, M.B. . . . . . 01 May	X Ackerley, R.S.J. . . 01 Jan	
E Goodship, M.T. . . . 01 May	X Daly, P. . . . . . 01 Jan	**1996**
S Haines, R.J. . . . . 01 May	X Finch, I.R. . . . . 01 Jan	X Beeby, M.J. . . . . 01 Jan
E Harrison, M.A. . . . 01 May	S Kerr, J.L. . . . . 01 Jan	X Cossins, E.S. . . . 01 Jan
X Krykunivsky, N.V. . . 01 May	X Moran, R.J. . . . . 01 Jan	X Hember, M.J.C. . . 01 Jan
E McCoy, M.J. . . . . 01 May	X Thomas, D.H. . . . 01 Jan	X Mercer, I.S. . . . . 01 Jan
E Sargent, N.M. . . . 01 May	X Greenwood, P.A. . . 01 Apr	X Mount, J.B. . . . . 01 Jan
	E Mealing, S.P. . . . 01 May	X Simmonite, G.I. . . 01 Jan

CAREERS SERVICE OFFICERS (RN)

LIEUTENANTS

1985		1989			Morley, J. . . . . . 17 Feb
- Jones, J.A. . . . . 12 Aug	- Beaton, F.D.S. . . . 16 Apr	- Finnemore, E. . . . 24 Apr
- Wilks, G.R.D. . . . 19 Nov	- Bennetts, M. . . . . 16 Apr	- Bond, D.R. . . . . . 13 Oct
	- MacGregor, P.C. . 08 May	
1987		1992
- Ferrand, B.D. . . . 22 Feb	1990	- Rosewell, W.A. . . . 05 Jan
- Swan, R.T. . . . . . 18 Oct	- Breslin, M.J. . . . . 07 Jan	
	- Rigby, R.E. . . . . 07 Jan	1993
1988	- Firth, A.F. . . . . . 29 Apr	- Barker, J.M. . . . . 03 Jan
- Weston, P. . . . . 22 Feb	- Moore, A.J. . . . . 17 Jun	- Saxby, D.G. . . . . 25 Apr
- Evans, N.G. . . . 13 Sep		- Waterworth, T.J. . . 05 Sep
- Ruane, J. . . . . . 04 Oct	1991	
- Duncan, A.J. . . . . 16 Oct	- Kirkbright, K.L.M. . . 17 Feb	
- Armstrong, P.W. . 13 Dec	- Leeder, R.J. . . . . 17 Feb	

ACTING LIEUTENANTS

1994
- McDonald, J. . . .   06 Feb

ROYAL MARINES

CREST.- The Globe surrounded by a Laurel wreath and surmounted by the Crowned Lion and Crown with 'Gibraltar' on a scroll. The Fouled Anchor imposed on the wreath below the Globe. *Motto* - 'Per Mare Per Terram'.

THE QUEEN'S COLOUR. - The Union. In the centre the Fouled Anchor with the Royal Cypher interlaced ensigned with the St Edward's Crown and 'Gibraltar' above; in base the Globe surrounded by a Laurel wreath. *Motto* - 'Per Mare Per Terram'. In the case of Royal Marines Commando units the distinguishing colour of the units is interwoven in the gold cords and tassles.

THE REGIMENTAL COLOUR. - Blue. In the centre the Fouled Anchor interlaced with the Royal Cypher 'G.R.IV' ensigned with the St Edward's Crown and 'Gibraltar' above, in base the Globe surrounded by a Laurel wreath. *Motto* -'Per Mare Per Terram'. In the dexter canton the Union in the remaining three corners the Royal Cypher. In the case of Royal Marines Commando units the numerical designation of the unit is shown immediately below the insignia. The distinguishing colour of the unit is interwoven in the gold cords and tassles.

ROYAL MARINES SECRETARY. - Whale Island, Portsmouth Hants PO2 8ER.

CORPS JOURNAL.- 'The Globe and Laurel,' Whale Island Portsmouth, Hants PO2 8ER

ROYAL MARINES ASSOCIATION. - General Secretary, Royal Marines, Eastney, Southsea, Hants.

ROYAL MARINES MUSEUM. - Royal Marines, Eastney, Southsea, Hants.

THE ROYAL MARINES

MAJOR GENERALS

Pack, Simon James , *CBE, psc(m)* . . . . 04 Dec 94
(CBF GIBRALTAR DEC 94)

Pennefather, David Anthony Somerset , *CB, OBE, rcds, psc(m), hcsc* . . . . 07 Jul 95
(CGRM MAR 96)

COLONELS

1991		1993		1995	
- Meardon, M.J.	13 Dec	- Dunlop, C.G.H.	30 Jun	- Nicholls, D.V.	30 Jun
- Thomson, J.J.	31 Dec			- Milton, A.A.	31 Dec
- Wray, A.D.	31 Dec	**1994**			
		- Mason, A.M.	30 Jun	**1996**	
1992		- Hill, S.P.	31 Dec	- Fulton, R.H.G.	30 Jun
- Dillon, R.E.	31 Dec			- Wilson, D.	30 Jun

LIEUTENANT COLONELS

1988		1992			
- Hall, N.M.	31 Dec	- Davis, J.Q.	30 Jun	- Sturman, M.	31 Dec
		- McNeill, I.	31 Dec	- Dutton, J.B.	31 Dec
1989					
- Robinson, N.M.	30 Jun	**1993**		**1995**	
- Bancroft, P.L.	31 Dec	- Gardiner, I.R.	30 Jun	- Lane, R.G.T.	30 Jun
		- Pillar, A.R.	30 Jun	- McDermott, W.M.	31 Dec
1990		- Fry, R.A.	30 Jun	- MacCormick, A.W.	31 Dec
- Atter, J.R.	31 Dec	- Downton, J.G.M.	31 Dec		
		- Wilsey, R.P.W.	31 Dec	**1996**	
1991				- Gregory, T.M.	30 Jun
- Williams, R.J.	31 Dec	**1994**		- Heaver, D.G.V.	30 Jun
		- Pounds, N.E.	30 Jun	- Rose, J.G.	30 Jun

MAJORS

1980		- Berry, A.J.	30 Jun	1989	
- Whittaker, P.A.	31 Dec	- Chibnall, A.C.S.	30 Jun	- George, P.D.	30 Jun
		- Ballantyne, I.	31 Dec	- Lear, J.J.B.	30 Jun
1982				- Ebbutt, G.J.	30 Jun
- Ward, P.N.	31 Dec	**1986**		- Reynolds, P.A.	31 Dec
		- Babbington, P.M.	30 Jun	- Elliott, S.F.	31 Dec
1983		- Lott, J.	30 Jun	- Irvine, P.D.T.	31 Dec
- Haycock, J.E.	30 Jun	- de Val, K.L.	31 Dec	- Woolley, M.B.	31 Dec
- Philpott, T.A.	31 Dec	- Heath, B.C.	31 Dec		
		- Bush, S.J.D.	31 Dec	**1990**	
1984		- Stevens, M.A.	31 Dec	- Grant, R.S.	30 Jun
- Williams, R.P.	31 May			- Hunter, T.C.G.	30 Jun
- Beyts, N.G.B.	30 Jun	**1987**		- Hutchings, R.	30 Jun
- Wheen, D.G.	31 Dec	- Wilson, J.R.	30 Jun	- Tong, D.K.	31 Dec
- Wimpenny, M.G.	31 Dec	- Rundle, R.M.	30 Jun	- Gibson, E.A.	31 Dec
- Noyes, A.J.F.	31 Dec			- Roy, A.C.	31 Dec
- Menheneott, C.J.	31 Dec	**1988**			
		- Wilson, P.A.	30 Jun	**1991**	
1985		- Nunn, C.J.	30 Jun	- Cooke, M.Y.	30 Jun
- Howard-Williams,	01 Jan	- Rowe, V.N.	31 Dec	- Crawford, R.L.	30 Jun
R.B.				- Cox, S.J.	30 Jun

- Grant, I.W. . . . . 30 Jun	**1993**	- Loynes, P.R. . . . 31 Dec
- Bowkett, R.M. . . . 30 Jun	- Crosby, J.P. . . . . 30 Jun	- Heal, J.P.C. . . . . 31 Dec
- Rogers, A.D.F. . . . 30 Jun	- Robison, G.S. . . . 30 Jun	- Noble, M.J.D. . . . 31 Dec
- House, N.P.J. . . . 31 Dec	- Buzza, S.G.L.P. . . . 30 Jun	
- de Jager, H. . . . . 31 Dec	- Canning, W.A. . . . 30 Jun	**1995**
- Hartnell, S.T. . . . 31 Dec	- MacLennan, W.R. . . 30 Jun	- Stewart, D.J. . . . 02 Jan
- Thomas, J.H. . . . 31 Dec	- Gelder, G.A. . . . . 31 Dec	- Guyer, S.T.G. . . . 30 Jun
- Hopley, D.A. . . . . 31 Dec	- Hobson, C.W.P. . . . 31 Dec	- Getgood, J.A. . . . 30 Jun
	- Milne, S.S. . . . . 31 Dec	- Salmon, A. . . . . 30 Jun
1992	- Robbins, J.M.F. . . . 31 Dec	- Wilson, A.C. . . . 01 Oct
- Baxter, J.S. . . . . 30 Jun	- Martin, P.J. . . . . 31 Dec	- Tasker, G. . . . . 31 Dec
- Spicer, M.N. . . . . 30 Jun	- Shadbolt, S.E. . . . 31 Dec	- Chicken, S.T. . . . 31 Dec
- Bibbey, M.W. . . . 30 Jun		- Mason, J.S. . . . . 31 Dec
- Parker, J.V.V. . . . 30 Jun	**1994**	- Heatly, R.J. . . . . 31 Dec
- Balm, S.V. . . . . 30 Jun	- Beadon, C.J.A. . . 30 Jun	
- Parsons, P.H. . . . 31 Dec	- Hughes, S.J. . . . . 30 Jun	**1996**
- McCabe, J. . . . . 31 Dec	- Lovelock, R.B. . . . 30 Jun	- Bruce, S.L. . . . . 30 Jun
- Armstrong, R.I. . . . 31 Dec	- Wilson, S.R. . . . . 30 Jun	- Stearns, R.P. . . . 30 Jun
- Thomson, A.B. . . . 31 Dec	- Wotherspoon, S.R. . . 30 Jun	- Williams, A.D.J. . . 30 Jun
- Haddow, F. . . . . 31 Dec	- Taylor, M.K. . . . . 30 Jun	- McKinney, D.G.D. . 30 Jun
	- Capewell, D.A. . . . 12 Dec	

CAPTAINS

1975	**1985**	**1990**
- Clifford, R.C. . . . . 01 Jul	- Quinlan, P.H. . . . 17 Mar	- Dunham, M.W. . . 27 Apr
- Newing, A.G. . . . 01 Jul	- Clapson, K. . . . . 01 Jul	- Walker, G.S.L. . . . 01 Sep
	- Pritchard, R.C. . . . 01 Aug	- Herring, J.J.A. . . . 01 Sep
1978	- Ellis, M.A.H. . . . . 01 Sep	- Gittoes, M.A.W. . . 01 Sep
- Fanshawe, R.J. . . 01 Jan		- Smith, S.A. . . . . 01 Sep
- Roche, S.M. . . . . 01 Jan	**1986**	- Pearce, T.R. . . . . 01 Sep
- Powell, K.A.T.J. . . 04 Feb	- Walters, D.N. . . . 18 Apr	- Arding, N.M.B. . . . 01 Sep
- Fletcher, R.J. . . . 01 Mar	- Dunn, I.L. . . . . . 01 Sep	- Huntley, I.P. . . . . 01 Sep
- Dow, D.C. . . . . 01 May	- Moyse, R.E. . . . . 01 Sep	- Musto, E.C. . . . . 01 Sep
- Williams, L.D. . . . 01 Aug	- Tyrrell, R.K. . . . . 01 Sep	- Hall, R.M. . . . . . 01 Sep
- Gillson, D.M. . . . . 01 Nov		- Hollington, R.E.C. . 01 Sep
	1987	- Parks, E.P. . . . . 01 Sep
1979	- Conway, S.A. . . . 01 Sep	- Paul, R.W.F. . . . . 01 Sep
- Craven-Phillips, . . 01 Feb	- Mawhood, C.S. . . 01 Sep	- Phillips, S.J. . . . . 01 Sep
T.C.D.	- Ebbens, A.J. . . . . 01 Sep	- Taylor, W.J. . . . . 01 Sep
- Howard, H.C.F. . . 01 Jul		- Westoby, R.M. . . 01 Sep
	1988	- Grixoni, M.R.R. . . 01 Sep
1980	- Whiteley, C.V. . . . 01 May	- Howes, F.H.R. . . . 01 Sep
- Smith, N.D. . . . . 01 Mar	- Underwood, N.J. . . 01 Sep	- Sharland, S.P. . . . 01 Sep
- Wakeford, A. . . . 01 Jul	- Gidney, N. . . . . 01 Sep	
	- Milne, A.R. . . . . 01 Sep	**1991**
1981		- Summerfield, D.E. . 01 May
- Cailes, M.J. . . . . 10 Feb	**1989**	- Denning, P.R. . . . 01 May
- Gordon, J.P.M. . . . 13 Dec	- Stewart, R.M. . . . 01 Mar	- Hutton, J.K. . . . . 01 May
	- Cusack, N.J. . . . 01 Sep	- Webster, T.J.C. . . 01 May
1982	- Ellis, M.P. . . . . . 01 Sep	- Davies, J.R. . . . . 01 May
- Bailey, A.M.S. . . . 01 Aug	- Leigh, J. . . . . . 01 Sep	- Pickup, R.A. . . . . 01 May
- Eales, R.N. . . . . 01 Dec	- Mills, K.P. . . . . . 01 Sep	- Brown, N.P. . . . . 01 Sep
- Stark, T.A. . . . . 01 Dec	- Milner, H.C. . . . . 01 Sep	- Messenger, G.K. . . 01 Sep
	- Mudford, H.C. . . . 01 Sep	- Price, M.J. . . . . 01 Sep
1983	- Wills, M.V. . . . . 01 Sep	- Mansell, P.R. . . . 01 Sep
- Simmonds, P.B. . . 01 Aug	- Sampson, P.H. . . 01 Sep	- Downes, D.P.J. . . . 01 Sep
- Corner, I.L.F. . . . 01 Nov	- Page, M.C. . . . . 01 Sep	- Burnell, J.R.J. . . . 01 Sep
	- Foster, G.R. . . . . 01 Sep	- Walker, R.E. . . . . 01 Sep
1984	- Kelly, J.W. . . . . 01 Sep	
- Rye, J.W. . . . . . 01 Sep	- Wolsey, M.A.R. . . 30 Nov	**1992**
- Haselock, S. . . . . 01 Nov		- Smith, M.L. . . . . 01 May
		- Cook, P.W.J. . . . 01 May

- Barnes, R.W. . . . 01 May	- Watts, R.D. . . . . 07 Jul	- Howe, P.A. . . . . 01 May
- Hook, D.A. . . . . 01 May	- Daniels, T.N. . . . . 01 Sep	- Anthony, N.M.K. . . 01 Sep
- Newing, S.G. . . . 01 May	- Lindley, N.P. . . . . 01 Sep	- Copinger-Symes, . 01 Sep
- Dechow, W.E. . . . 27 Jul	- Evans, M.A. . . . . 01 Sep	R.S.
- Corrin, C.ST.J. . . 01 Sep	- Syvret, M.E.V. . . . 01 Sep	- Forster, R.M. . . . 01 Sep
- Hall, S.J. . . . . 01 Sep	- Hudson, J.D. . . . . 01 Sep	- Proudlock, J.K. . . . 01 Sep
- Bruce-Jones, N.W. 01 Sep	- Cawthorne, M.W.S. . 01 Sep	
- Scott, C.R. . . . . 01 Sep	- Gwillim, V.G. . . . . 01 Sep	**1995**
- Bentham-Green, . 01 Sep	- Spencer, R.A.W. . . 01 Sep	- Salzano, G.M. . . . 30 Apr
N.R.H.	- Allen, R.J. . . . . . 01 Sep	- Marok, J. . . . . . 30 Apr
- Mallalieu, A.J. . . 01 Sep	- Bevis, T.J. . . . . . 01 Sep	- van der Horst, R.E. . 01 Sep
- Davis, E.G.M. . . 01 Sep	- Evans, D.M.M. . . . 01 Sep	- Cameron, P.S. . . . 01 Sep
- Norman, P.G. . . . 01 Sep		- Green, M.G.H. . . . 01 Sep
	1994	- Ross, J.H. . . . . 01 Sep
1993	- Pritchard, S.A. . . . 18 Apr	
- MacDonald, I.R. . . 08 Feb	- Middleton, T.P.W. . 01 May	

LIEUTENANTS

1989	- Palmer, C.B. . . . . 01 Sep	- Ashby, P.J.C. . . . 01 Sep
- Hood, M.J. . . . . . 25 Apr	- McCullough, I.N. . . 01 Sep	- Corn, R.A.F. . . . . 01 Sep
- Pelly, G.R. . . . . . 25 Apr	- Hughes, J-P.H. . . . 01 Sep	- Manson, P.D. . . . 01 Sep
- Taylor, P.G.D. . . 25 Apr	- Magowan, R.A. . . . 01 Sep	- Beach, J.M. . . . . 01 Sep
- Maddick, M.J. . . . 25 Apr	- Cook, T.A. . . . . 01 Sep	- Halls, M.L.S. . . . . 01 Sep
- Manger, G.S.C. . . . 25 Apr	- Kassapian, D.L. . . 01 Sep	- Pierson, M.F. . . . . 01 Sep
- Wilson, D.W.H. . . 25 Apr	- Oliver, K.B. . . . . 01 Sep	- Attwood, P.J. . . . . 01 Sep
- Cullis, C.J. . . . . . 25 Apr	- McKeown, J.R. . . . 23 Sep	- McInerney, A.J. . . . 01 Sep
- Curry, B.R. . . . . . 25 Apr		- Hussey, S.J. . . . . 01 Sep
- Francis, S.J. . . . . 27 Apr	**1991**	
- Ross, A.C.P. . . . . 27 Apr	- Porter, M.E. . . . . 25 Apr	**1993**
- Main, J.R.C. . . . 01 Sep	- Pressly, J.W. . . . . 25 Apr	- Holt, J.S. . . . . . 01 Jan
- Scott, S.J. . . . . 01 Sep	- Joyce, P. . . . . . 25 Apr	- Robertson, N.B. . . 26 Apr
- Freeman, M.E. . . . 01 Sep	- McCormack, C.P. . . 30 Apr	- Hillman, D.R. . . . 26 Apr
- Cundy, R.G. . . . 01 Sep	- Stickland, C.R. . . . 30 Apr	- Mattin, P.R. . . . . 26 Apr
- Webber, S.A. . . . 01 Sep	- Holmes, C.J. . . . . 30 Apr	- Bucknall, R.J.W. . . 26 Apr
- Saddleton, A.D. . . 01 Sep	- Kenworthy, R.A. . . 30 Apr	- Hammond, M.C. . . 26 Apr
- Willson, N.J. . . . 01 Sep	- Mc Laren, J.P. . . . 30 Apr	- Walls, K.F. . . . . 26 Apr
- Moore, C.B. . . . 01 Sep	- Reynolds, S.A. . . . 30 Apr	- May, D.P. . . . . 26 Apr
- James, S.A. . . . 01 Sep	- MacKinlay, G.A. . . 01 Sep	- Chattin, A.P. . . . . 29 Apr
- Bennett, N.M. . . . 01 Sep	- Litster, A. . . . . . 01 Sep	- Congreve, S.C. . . 29 Apr
- Birrell, S.M. . . . 01 Sep	- Morris, J.A.J. . . . . 01 Sep	- Cook, M.F. . . . . 29 Apr
- Holmes, M.J. . . . 01 Sep	- Kemp, P.J. . . . . 01 Sep	- Pearce, D.J. . . . . 29 Apr
- King, D.C.M. . . . 01 Sep	- Sear, J.J. . . . . . 01 Sep	- Dinmore, A.J. . . . 01 Sep
	- Amos, J.H.J. . . . . 01 Sep	- Murchison, E.A. . . 01 Sep
1990	- Thorpe, C.D. . . . . 01 Sep	- Blythe, T.S. . . . . 01 Sep
- Bell, D.W.A. . . . . 26 Apr	- Gilding, D.R. . . . . 01 Sep	- Wraith, N. . . . . 01 Sep
- Coldrick, S.A. . . . 01 May	- Green, G.M. . . . . 01 Sep	- Kern, A.S. . . . . . 01 Sep
- Denning, M.W.P. . 01 May	- Chapman, S. . . . . 01 Sep	- Lemon, R.W.G. . . . 01 Sep
- Gadie, P.A. . . . 01 May	- Jones, M.R. . . . . 01 Sep	- Bakewell, T.D. . . . 01 Sep
- Maybery, J.E. . . . 01 May	- Reed, J.J. . . . . 01 Sep	- Jermyn, N.C. . . . . 01 Sep
- Thurstan, R.W.F. . 01 May		- Hickman, S.M. . . . 01 Sep
- McKinney, M.D. . . 01 May	**1992**	- Shave, A.J. . . . . 01 Sep
- Morris, P.E.M. . . 01 May	- Smith, G.K. . . . . 24 Apr	- Bailey, J.J. . . . . 01 Sep
- Price, A.M. . . . 01 May	- Case, A.C. . . . . 24 Apr	- Brown, L.A. . . . . 01 Sep
- Pulvertaft, R.J. . . 01 May	- Dewar, D.A. . . . . 24 Apr	- Butler, D. . . . . . 01 Sep
- Searight, M.F.C. . 01 May	- Fergusson, A.C. . . 24 Apr	- Davies, H.C.A. . . . 01 Sep
- Slack, J.M. . . . . 01 May	- Cunningham, J.T. . . 24 Apr	
- Stephens, R.J. . . 01 May	- Hills, R.B. . . . . 24 Apr	**1994**
- White, H.J. . . . 01 May	- Kettle, R.A. . . . . 24 Apr	- Geldard, M.A. . . . 25 Apr
- Gray, M.N. . . . . 01 Sep	- Armour, G.A. . . . . 27 Apr	- Bestwick, M.C. . . . 25 Apr
- Livingstone, A.J. . 01 Sep	- Ward, J.G. . . . . 27 Apr	- Bray, M.R. . . . . 25 Apr
- Maynard, A.T.W. . 01 Sep	- Lodge, M.J. . . . . 01 Sep	- Walker, A.J. . . . . 28 Apr
- Davidson, G.D.S. . 01 Sep	- Adcock, B. . . . . 01 Sep	- Spanner, P. . . . . 01 May

- Evans, P.J. . . . . 11 Jul	- Taylor, M.A.B. . . . 01 Sep	- Dresner, R.J. . . . 24 Apr
- Page, D.C.M. . . . 01 Sep	- Fuller, S.R. . . . . 01 Sep	- Everett, E.J. . . . 24 Apr
- Daukes, N.M. . . . 01 Sep	- James, P.M. . . . . 01 Sep	- Moorhouse, E.J. . . 24 Apr
- Dowd, J.W. . . . . 01 Sep	- Coomber, J.M. . . . 01 Sep	- Moncur, J.W. . . . 24 Apr
- Hedges, J.W. . . . 01 Sep	- De Reya, A.L. . . . 01 Sep	- Hardy, D.M. . . . . 24 Apr
- Liddle, S.J. . . . . 01 Sep	- Harris, C.C. . . . . 01 Sep	- Tanner, M.J. . . . 01 Sep
- Murray, W.R.C. . . 01 Sep		- Bailey, D.S. . . . . 01 Sep
- Hermer, J.P. . . . . 01 Sep	**1995**	
- Trickett, C.B. . . . 01 Sep	- Brighouse, N.G. . . 24 Apr	
- Hughes, M.J. . . . 01 Sep	- Coles, W.G. . . . . 24 Apr	

LIEUTENANTS

(Short Career Commission)

1989	- Eyre, K.B. . . . . 26 Apr	- King, R.J. . . . . 28 Apr
- Allison, K.R. . . . . 25 Apr	- Guest, S.J. . . . . 26 Apr	- Lewis, R.J. . . . . 28 Apr
- Andrews, D.W. . . . 27 Apr	- Murray, A.B. . . . . 26 Apr	- Murns, N.P. . . . 28 Apr
	- Finley, R.W. . . . . 29 Apr	- Arnold, N.C. . . . . 01 Sep
1990	- Hough, C.C. . . . . 29 Apr	- Jenkins, G. . . . . 01 Sep
- Chapman, G.L. . . . 01 Sep	- Morrison, C.P. . . . 29 Apr	- Vance, T.O. . . . . 01 Sep
	- Wood, G.T. . . . . 29 Apr	- Morrissey, S.J. . . 01 Sep
1991	- Rowlstone, D.J. . . 11 Jun	- Fraser, G.W. . . . 01 Sep
- Beeson, G.F. . . . 30 Apr	- Turnbull, R.S. . . . 01 Sep	- Franks, J.A. . . . . 01 Sep
- Chandler, M.F.H. . . 30 Apr	- Wallis, A. . . . . . 01 Sep	- Ginnever, M.S.M. . 01 Sep
- Ellis, D.I. . . . . . 30 Apr	- Hale, I.B. . . . . . 01 Sep	- Milliner, C.L. . . . 01 Sep
- Norman, J.R.A. . . . 01 Sep	- Lightbody, C.S. . . 01 Sep	- Kilmartin, S.N. . . . 01 Sep
	- Patterson, S.R. . . 01 Sep	- Pilkington, A.G.H. . 01 Sep
1992	- Stocker, N.J. . . . 01 Sep	- Thomsett, H.F.J. . . 01 Sep
- Hornung, C. . . . . 24 Apr	- Frederick, D.G. . . 01 Sep	- Twist, M.T. . . . . 01 Sep
- Fitzsimmons, J.M. . 24 Apr	- Moorhouse, D. . . . 01 Sep	- Worth, H.F. . . . . 01 Sep
- Baxendale, R.F. . . 01 Sep	- Percey, S.J. . . . . 01 Sep	
- David, T.W. . . . . 01 Sep	- Unsworth, R.N. . . 01 Sep	**1995**
- Goldsmith, A.G. . . 01 Sep		- Balmer, G.A. . . . 24 Apr
- Lunn, R. . . . . . 01 Sep	**1994**	- Sutherland, N. . . . 24 Apr
- Robinson, A.M.E. . . 01 Sep	- Bennett, R.W. . . . 25 Apr	- Harris, T. . . . . . 01 Sep
- Skuse, M. . . . . . 01 Sep	- Carey, A.G. . . . . 25 Apr	- Shetler-Jones, P.R. . 01 Sep
- Stovin-Bradford, M. . 01 Sep	- Chamberlain, H.J. . 28 Apr	- Woodall, J.B. . . . 01 Sep
- Watkinson, N.G. . . 01 Sep	- Craig, K.M. . . . . 28 Apr	- Harker, A.R. . . . 01 Sep
	- Doubleday, ... 28 Apr	- Parr, G.N. . . . . . 01 Sep
1993	I.D.ST.J.	
- Cooper-Simpson, . 26 Apr	- Ethell, D.R. . . . . 28 Apr	
R.J.	- Hall, S.B. . . . . . 28 Apr	

ACTING LIEUTENANTS

1994	- Maltby, R.J. . . . . 29 Apr	**1995**
- Carr, K. . . . . . . 29 Apr	- Morley, A. . . . . 29 Apr	- Burrell, A.M.G. . . 28 Apr
- Gray, J.A. . . . . . 29 Apr	- O'Hara, G.C. . . . 01 Sep	
- Levine, A.J. . . . . 29 Apr		

ACTING LIEUTENANTS

(Short Career Commission)

1994	- Wigham, T.W. . . . 01 Sep	- March, D.R. . . . . 28 Apr
- Rennie, A.B. . . . . 29 Apr	- May, P. . . . . . 01 Sep	- Atherton, J.R. . . . 01 Sep
- Sutton, S.J. . . . . 29 Apr		- Houvenaghel, I.M. . 01 Sep
- O'Neill, S. . . . . . 29 Apr	**1995**	- Hutchinson, P.I. . . 01 Sep
- Jepson, N.H.M. . . 01 Sep	- Friendship, P.G. . . 28 Apr	
- Stear, T.J.F. . . . . 01 Sep	- Collin, M. . . . . . 28 Apr	

SECOND LIEUTENANTS(GRAD)

	1993				Hammond, D.E.	. . 01 Sep			1995	
-	Roylance, J.F.	. . 01 Sep	-	Ballard, S.A.	. . . . 01 Sep	-	Parvin, R.A.	. . . . 01 May
			-	Beeley, W.T.	. . . . 01 Sep	-	Revens, C.A.	. . . 01 May
	1994		-	Board, M.J.	. . . . 01 Sep	-	Muddiman, A.R.	. . 01 Sep
-	Kearney, P.L.	. . . . 27 Apr	-	Bryce, J.F.	. . . . . 01 Sep	-	Raitt, J.E.	. . . . . 01 Sep
-	Hale, J.N.	. . . . . 27 Apr	-	Cunningham, A.N.	. 01 Sep	-	Raynham, M.C.	. . 01 Sep
-	Plewes, A.B.	. . . . 27 Apr	-	Hunter, J.G.	. . . . 01 Sep	-	Whitfield, P.M.	. . . 01 Sep
-	Sibley, G.P.	. . . . 27 Apr	-	Kelly, P.M.	. . . . . 01 Sep	-	Devereux, M.E.	. . 01 Sep
-	Ashton, C.N.	. . . 01 Sep	-	Manning, D.	. . . . 01 Sep	-	Gordon, M.W.	. . . 01 Sep
-	Blanchford, D.	. . 01 Sep	-	McGhee, C.	. . . . 01 Sep	-	Grainger, A.L.	. . . 01 Sep
-	Read, R.J.	. . . . 01 Sep	-	Preston, R.W.	. . . 01 Sep	-	Hazell, M.J.D.	. . . 01 Sep
-	Turner, S.A.	. . . 01 Sep	-	Oherlihy, S.I.	. . . . 01 Sep	-	Janzen, A.N.	. . . 01 Sep

SECOND LIEUTENANTS(GRAD)

(Short Career Commission)

	1994				1995				Clayton, M.J.	. . . 01 Sep
-	Brown, S.M.	. . . . 27 Apr	-	Cole, S.R.	. . . . 01 May	-	Combe, S.A.N.	. . . 01 Sep
-	Lee, S.P.	. . . . . 27 Apr	-	Douglas, A.M.	. . 01 May	-	Cooper, M.C.	. . . 01 Sep
-	Roddy, M.P.	. . . . 27 Apr	-	Greenwood, I.A.	. 01 May	-	Guy, P.S.	. . . . . 01 Sep
-	Stafford, D.B.	. . . . 27 Apr	-	Fenwick, R.J.	. . 01 May	-	Hens, A.R.	. . . . 01 Sep
-	Porter, P.A.	. . . . 27 Apr	-	Raeburn, T.J.	. . 01 May	-	Hughes, D.C.	. . . 01 Sep
-	Parry, J.A.	. . . . . 27 Apr	-	Strain, J.D.R.	. . 01 May	-	Lancashire, A.C.	. . 01 Sep
-	Turner, T.A.S.	. . . 27 Apr	-	Viner, T.R.	. . . . 01 May	-	Lowther, A.D.	. . . 01 Sep
-	Campbell, L.G.	. . 01 Sep	-	Watkins, A.P.L.	. . 01 May	-	McCabe, G.P.	. . . 01 Sep
-	Jackson, M.J.A.	. . 01 Sep	-	Atherton, B.W.	. . . 01 Sep	-	McClay, W.J.	. . . 01 Sep
-	Mayne, C.W.E.	. . 01 Sep	-	Bowra, M.A.	. . . . 01 Sep	-	Rogers, S.J.P.	. . . 01 Sep
-	Paton, C.M.	. . . 01 Sep	-	Brabyn, A.A.B.	. . . 01 Sep	-	Taylor, S.D.	. . . . 01 Sep
-	Pugh, J.R.	. . . . 01 Sep	-	Brady, S.P.	. . . . 01 Sep	-	Wyatt, J.M.	. . . . 01 Sep
-	Lancaster, C.	. . . 01 Sep	-	Chilvers, M.I.	. . . . 01 Sep			

SECOND LIEUTENANTS

	1991				Wilson, J.G.	. . . 01 Sep			1995	
-	Lee, O.A.	. . . . . 28 Oct					-	Read, C.D.	. . . . 01 May
					1994		-	Oura, A.N.	. . . . 01 Sep
	1992		-	Leyden, T.N.	. . . . 01 Sep	-	Turner, A.R.	. . . . 01 Sep
-	Sicker, L.C.J.	. . . . 19 Oct	-	Ordway, C.N.M.P.	. . 01 Sep			
			-	Thompson, D.H.	. . 01 Sep			
	1993		-	Puddicombe, C.A.	. . 01 Sep			
-	Cheesman, D.J.E.	. 01 Sep	-	Nicholson, D.P.	. . . 01 Sep			

SECOND LIEUTENANTS

(Short Career Commission)

	1994				Hopkins, R.M.E.	. . 01 Sep			1995	
-	Moran, J.T.	. . . . 27 Apr	-	Martin, N.A.	. . . . 01 Sep	-	Bowyer, R.J.	. . . . 01 May
-	Blyth, M.	. . . . . 27 Apr	-	Howarth, S.J.	. . . 01 Sep	-	Cole, R.I.	. . . . . 01 May
-	Jenkins, E.J.	. . . . 27 Apr				-	Griffiths, N.A.	. . . 01 May

ROYAL MARINES - SPECIAL DUTIES LIST

MAJORS (SD)

1992		1993		1994	
- Spencer, J.C.V.	. . 04 Sep	- Ketteridge, B.P.	. . 19 Feb	- Barnes, S.M.J.	. . 01 Oct
		- McRae, W.	. . . . 26 Mar		

CAPTAINS (SD)

1988		- Stewart, J.	. . . . 01 Oct	1994	
- Gaze, R.N.G.	. . . 01 Oct	- Chisnall, D.A.	. . . 01 Oct	- Davies, A.	. . . . 01 Oct
- Curtis, B.J.	. . . . 01 Oct			- Wakely, S.A.	. . . 01 Oct
- Young, J.H.	. . . . 01 Oct	1992		- Clark, D.M.J.	. . . 01 Oct
		- Glaze, J.W.	. . . . 01 Oct	- Harradine, P.A.	. . 01 Oct
1989		- Walker, A.J.	. . . . 01 Oct	- Sawyer, T.J.	. . . 01 Oct
- Cook, F.C.	. . . . 01 Oct	- Brown, R.J.	. . . . 01 Oct		
				1995	
1990		1993		- Atkinson, J.C.	. . . 01 Oct
- Euridge, R.E.	. . . 01 Oct	- Fec, Z.M.	. . . . . 01 Oct	- Warren, T.S.E.	. . 01 Oct
- Gorman, C.P.	. . . 01 Oct	- Dyke, R.C.	. . . . 01 Oct	- Gracie, D.L.	. . . . 01 Oct
- Anderson, S.R.	. . . 01 Oct	- Skinner, C.G.	. . . 01 Oct	- Launchbury, S.J.	. . 01 Oct
- March, C.J.	. . . . 01 Oct	- O'Brien, W.C.	. . . 01 Oct	- Matthews, G.	. . . 01 Oct
		- Jones, A.	. . . . . 01 Oct		
1991		- Marino, D.J.	. . . . 01 Oct		
- Brown, R.C.	. . . . 01 Oct				

LIEUTENANTS (SD)

1988		- Corbidge, S.J.	. . . 01 Jan	- Underwood, P.J.	. . 01 Jan
- Cooper, R.T.	. . . . 01 Jan	- Sharpe, G.A.	. . . 01 Jan		
		- Goodridge, T.J.	. . 01 Jan	1994	
1989		- Potter, S.	. . . . . 01 Jan	- Nicoll, S.K.	. . . . 01 Jan
- Disbury, B.N.	. . . 01 Jan	- O'Donnell, I.M.	. . . 01 Jan	- Bourne, P.J.	. . . 01 Jan
- Fitzgerald, B.	. . . 01 Jan			- Ford, D.	. . . . . 01 Jan
- White, J.J.	. . . . 01 Jan	1992		- Green, G.E.	. . . . 01 Jan
- Woods, J.C.	. . . . 01 Jan	- Woolman, T.L.	. . . 01 Jan	- Hannah, W.F.	. . . 01 Jan
		- Wilkie, A.R.	. . . . 01 Jan	- Kelly, A.P.	. . . . 01 Jan
1990		- Bulmer, R.J.	. . . . 01 Jan	- Rearden, R.J.	. . . 01 Jan
- Anderson, S.T.	. . . 01 Jan	- Perry, R.W.	. . . . 01 Jan	- Simcox, P.A.	. . . 01 Jan
- Collins, P.R.	. . . . 01 Jan	- Crouden, S.F.	. . . 01 Jan	- Tyce, D.J.	. . . . 01 Jan
- Greedus, D.A.	. . 01 Jan	- Everritt, R.	. . . . 01 Jan		
- Green, M.R.	. . . . 01 Jan	- Tupman, K.C.	. . . 01 Jan	1995	
- Hembrow, T.	. . . . 01 Jan	- Richards, S.W.	. . . 01 Jan	- Wilson, A.C.	. . . 01 Jan
- Maese, P.A.	. . . . 01 Jan			- Shergold, P.J.	. . . 01 Jan
- Maher, A.M.	. . . . 01 Jan	1993		- Thompson, G.M.	. . 01 Jan
- Ritchie, W.J.	. . . . 01 Jan	- Beazley, P.	. . . . 01 Jan	- Todd, M.A.	. . . . 01 Jan
- Thomas, P.W.	. . . 01 Jan	- Ginn, R.N.	. . . . 01 Jan	- Sellar, T.J.	. . . . 01 Jan
		- Heward, A.F.	. . . 01 Jan	- Jones, G.J.	. . . . 01 Jan
1991		- Nicholls, B.A.	. . . 01 Jan	- Tulloch, S.W.	. . . 01 Jan
- Devlin, H.F.G.	. . . 01 Jan	- Reed, J.W.	. . . 01 Jan	- Clark, P.A.	. . . . 01 Jan
- Cunningham, J.S.	. . 01 Jan	- Richardson, M.C.	. . 01 Jan		
- Bain, D.I.	. . . . . 01 Jan	- Smith, S.F.	. . . . 01 Jan		

ACTING LIEUTENANTS (SD)

1996		- Holloway, N.	. . . 01 Jan	- Scott, S.C.	. . . . 01 Jan
- Best, P.	. . . . . . 01 Jan	- Lugg, J.C.	. . . . 01 Jan	- Ward, C.D.	. . . . 01 Jan
- Cockton, P.G.	. . . 01 Jan	- Maddison, J.D.	. . . 01 Jan	- Watson, R.I.	. . . 01 Jan
- Daniel, I.R.	. . . . 01 Jan	- Merchant, J.M.	. . . 01 Jan		

ROYAL MARINES BAND

MAJORS SD(B)

	1994	
-	Waterer, R.A.	29 Jul

CAPTAINS SD(B)

	1988				1992				1993	
-	Cole, D.C.	01 Oct		-	Rogerson, D.M.J. . .	01 Oct		-	Perkins, J.R.	01 Oct

LIEUTENANTS SD(B)

	1986				1990				1993	
-	Rutterford, P.J. . .	28 Feb		-	Mills, B.	01 Jan		-	Watson, P.F. . . .	01 Jan
								-	Davis, C.J.	01 Jan
	1988				1991					
-	Hillier, J.	01 Jan		-	Henderson, A.D. . .	01 Jan				

CAREERS SERVICE OFFICERS (RM)

LIEUTENANTS (C.S)

	1986				1988				1991	
-	Vickers, K.	04 Mar		-	Patterson, M.C. . . .	17 Apr		-	Ennis, E.C.	13 Oct
				-	Millin, A.J.	12 Jun				
	1987			-	Jones, D.L.	16 Oct				
-	Chambers, D. . . .	18 Oct								
					1990					
				-	Bird, R.V.	18 Feb				

QUEEN ALEXANDRA'S ROYAL NAVAL NURSING SERVICE

PRINCIPAL NURSING OFFICERS

	1990
Taylor, C.M.	09 Jul

CHIEF NURSING OFFICERS

1989	1990	1991
Comrie, G.M. . . . . . 05 Sep	Hambling, P.M. . . . . 09 Jul	Gauld, I.B. . . . . . . 14 Sep

SUPERINTENDING NURSING OFFICERS

1978	1984	Croughan, S. . . . . . 06 Sep
Gill, J.V. . . . . 09 Apr	Brown, J.C. . . . . . 03 Mar	Gibbon, L. . . . . . . 05 Oct
1982	**1986**	**1991**
Cave, P. . . . . 16 Oct	Savage, R. . . . . . . 09 Sep	Onions, J.M. . . . . . 11 Feb
1983	**1988**	
Weall, E.M. . . . . . . 06 Nov	Butcher, L.J. . . . . . 08 Jan	

SUPERINTENDING NURSING OFFICERS

(Medium Career Commission)

1988	1992
Walmsley, D. . . . . . 04 Dec	Smith, B.C. . . . . . . 01 Oct
1991	**1994**
Bowen, M. . . . . . . 01 Oct	Aldwinckle, D.V. . . . . 31 Dec

SENIOR NURSING OFFICERS

(Medium Career Commission)

1985	Broom, N.J. . . . . . 22 Dec	1989
Watts, M.D. . . . . . . 23 Dec	**1987**	McLaughlan, C.L. . . . 21 Aug
1986	Allkins, H.L. . . . . . 08 Feb	**1990**
McKillop, H.E.L. . . . . 14 Feb	Duke, R.M. . . . . . . 24 Apr	Doughty, C.M.A. . . . 16 May
Howes, N.J. . . . . . 28 Mar		

SENIOR NURSING OFFICERS

(Short Career Commission)

1988	1991	1993
Lennon, J.M. . . . . . 24 Nov	Ponting, L. . . . . . . 11 Jan	Coleman, A.A. . . . . 18 Jun
	Hall, C.J. . . . . . . 01 Mar	Mallows, T. . . . . . . 09 Dec
1989	Aldwinckle, T.W. . . . 23 Jun	
Stinton, C.A. . . . . . 09 Nov	Dobson, A. . . . . . . 08 Jul	**1994**
	Spencer, S.J. . . . . . 12 Oct	Knight, D.J. . . . . . 18 Jan
1990		Offen, S.M. . . . . . 18 Jan
Cornell, P. . . . . . . 23 Mar	**1992**	Galvin, C.A. . . . . . 23 Jan
Royle, S.A.E. . . . . . 08 Aug	Esaw, M. . . . . . . 04 Jan	Piper, C.J. . . . . . . 06 Mar
Wren, I. . . . . 20 Aug	Pike, S.A. . . . . . . 13 Apr	Hainsworth, P.M. . . . 30 Mar
Pratt, A.S. . . . . . . 29 Aug		Brett, P.A. . . . . . . 07 May
Jones, L. . . . . 11 Nov		Ryan, D.F. . . . . . . 20 Oct

1995		Griffiths, S.L.	30 May	1996	
Ferguson, V.S.	21 Jan	Charnock, A.S.	01 Sep	Fletcher, S.J.	02 Jan
Mortlock, L.E.	23 May	Piper, N.D.	23 Nov		

NURSING OFFICERS

1993	
Ziegler, S.A.	18 Aug

KEY ROYAL NAVAL PERSONNEL, ATTACHES AND ADVISERS

(See Sec. 1 for Admiralty Board Members and Defence Council Members)

COMMANDERS-IN-CHIEF, FLAG OFFICERS AND OTHER SENIOR OFFICERS

Command or Station	Officers	Ship	Address
NAVAL HOME COMMAND	*Second Sea Lord and Commander in Chief Naval Home Command* Admiral Sir Michael Boyce, KCB, OBE, ADC, rdc, psc	Victory	Victory Building HM Naval Base Portsmouth PO1 3LS
	Cheif of Staff to Second Sea Lord and Commander in Chief Naval Home Command *Rear Admiral* R.B. Lees, (Barrister)	Victory	
FLEET	*Commander-in-Chief Fleet, Commander-in-Chief, Eastern Atlantic Area and Commander Naval Forces North Western Europe* Admiral Sir Peter Abbott, KCB, MA rcds, pce	Warrior	Eastbury Park Northwood Middlesex HA6 3HP
	Deputy Commander Fleet/Chief of Staff Vice Admiral J.J.R. Tod, CBE, rcds	Warrior	
	Commander United Kingdom Task Group and Commander Anti Submarin Warfare Striking Force Rear Admiral A. W. J. West, DSC,rcds, pce, psc, hcsc	—	BFPO 200
	Commodore Amphibious Warfare and Commander UK/NL Amphibious Striking Force Commodore P.C.B. Canter,, CBE	—	RM Barracks Stonehouse Plymouth PL1 3QS
	Commodore Mine Warfare & Patrol Vessels, Diving & Fishery Protection Commodore C. W. Ellison, pce, [sc(a)]	—	HM Naval Base Portsmouth
SURFACE FLOTILLA	*Flag Officer Surface Flotilla* Vice Admiral J.R. Brigstocke,,pce, psc	—	2-6 The Parade HM Naval Base
	Deputy Flag Officer Surface Flotilla Commodore J.R. Cartwright, pce, psc	—	Portsmouth PO1 3NA
NAVAL AVIATION	*Flag Officer Naval Aviation* Rear Admiral T.W. Loughran, pcea, psc, ocds(Can)	Heron	Yeovilton Somerset BA22 8HL
	Chief of Staff (Naval Aviation) Commodore P.A. Fish, pce,psc		

Command or Station	Officers	Ship	Address
SUBMARINES	*Flag Officer, Submarines, Chief of Staff Operations,* *Fleet Commander Submarines, Eastern Atlantic and Commander Submarine Forces North West* Rear Admiral J.F.Perowne, OBE, pce(sm) *Deputy Flag Officer Submarines* Commodore D.J. Anthony, MBE,SDC, pce, pce(sm)	Warrior —	Eastbury Park Northwood Middlesex HA6 3HP
SEA TRAINING AND PORTLAND	*Flag Officer Sea Training and Naval Base* Rear Admiral P. M. Franklyn, MVO,rcds, pce	Osprey	Grenville Block HMS DRAKE Devonport Plymouth PL2 2BG
PORTSMOUTH	*Naval Base Commander* Commodore I. P. Henderson, CBE, ADC, pce, pcea, psc	(Flag flown on shore)	HM Naval Base Portsmouth Hants PO1 3LT
PLYMOUTH	*Naval Base Commander Devonport* Commodore J. A. Burch, CBE, Bsc, CEng, FIMgt, rcds, odc(aus)	(Flag flown on shore)	Mount Wise Devonport Devon PL1 4JH
SCOTLAND NORTHERN ENGLAND AND NORTHERN IRELAND	*Flag Officer Scotland Northern England and Northern Ireland, Commander Northern Sub-Area Eastern Atlantic, Commander Naval Forces North North West and Naval Base Commander Clyde* Rear Admiral J. G. Tolhurst, CB	HMS Cochrane	Office at: HM Naval Base Clyde Helensburgh Dunbartonshire G84 8HL
CLYDE	*Director Naval Base* Commodore F. G. Thompson, MBE, msc, CEng, MIEE, MINucE, JSDC	—	Clyde Submarine Base Faslane Dunbartonshire G84 8HL
GIBRALTAR	*Governor and Commanders in Chief Gibraltar* Admiral Sir Hugo White, GCB, CBE, pce		BFPO 52
GIBRALTAR	*Commander British Forces Gibraltar,* *and COMGIBMED* Major General S.J. Pack, CBE, psc	JHQ Gibraltar	BFPO 52
WASHINGTON	*Head of the British Defence Staff (Washington)* Rear Admiral D.A.J. Blackburn, LVO, pce, psc(a)	Washington	BFPO 2

Command or Station	Officers	Ship	Address
HONG KONG	***Chief of Staff to Commander British Forces Hong Kong*** Captain P.J. Melson, CBE, FNI, jsdc, pce	Tamar	BFPO 162
ROYAL YACHTS	***Commodore Royal Yachts*** Commodore A.J.C. Morrow, ndc, pce	Britannia	BFPO 239
ROYAL MARINES	***Commandant General*** Major General D. A. S. Pennefather CB, OBE, rcds, psc(m), hcsc	—	HQRM West Battery Whale Island PORTSMOUTH PO2 8DX

NATO

Deputy SACLANT	Vice Admiral I.D.G. Garnett psc
UK National Liaison Representative to SACLANT	Commodore A.M. Gregory, OBE,jsdc,pce,pcesm
COMSUBEASTLANT/COMSUBNORWEST ...	Rear Admiral J.F. Perowne OBE, pce(sm)
Assistant Chief of Staff (Policy & Requirements) to the	
Supreme Allied Commander, Europe	Rear Admiral P.K. Haddacks, rcds,pce,psc ...
Chief of Staff to Commander Allied Naval Forces	
Southern Europe	Vice Admiral M.A.C. Moore, LVO,pce,psc,I(1)Sw
COMGIBMED	Major General S.J. Pack, CBE,pcm(m) ... ...
CINCFLEET,CINCEASTLANANT and	Admiral Sir Peter Abbott, KCB, MA, rcds, pce
COMNAVNORWEST	Vice Admiral J.G. Tolhurst, CB ... ...
COMNORELANT and COMNORNORWEST ...	Rear Admiral A.W.J. West, DSC, rcds, pce,psc,hcsc
COMUKTG/COMASWSF	Commodore P. C. B. Canter, CBE,pce,psc ...
COMUKNLPHIBGRU	Vice Admiral M.P. Gretton, MA,MNI,rcds,pce,psc
SACLANTREPEUR	Rear Admiral A.B. Ross, CBE rcds pce pcea psc
Assistant Director Operations Division International	(**WEF Aug 96**) ... ...
Military Staff	

MINISTRY OF DEFENCE (NAVY DEPARTMENT)

Chief of the Naval Staff and First Sea Lord ...	Admiral Sir Jock Slater GCB,LVO ,ADC,rcds
Assistant Chief of Naval Staff	Rear Admiral J.J. Blackham,BA,MNI,rcds,pce,
... ...	psc,I(2)Sp
Second Sea Lord and Commander in Chief ...	
Naval Home Command	Admiral Sir Michael Boyce,
Naval Secretary/Director General Naval Manning	KCB,OBE,ADC,rcds,psc
Chief of Staff to 2SL/CNH	Rear Admiral F.M. Malbon,rcds,pce,psc
Flag Officer Training and Recruitment	Rear Admiral R.B. Lees (Barrister)
... ...	Rear Admiral J.H.S McAnally,
Chief of Fleet Support	LVO,MINI,MRIN,rcds, pce,psc,
Director General Aircraft(Navy)	Vice Admiral Sir Toby Frere, KCB,rcds,jssc
	Rear Admiral D.J. Wood,
Director General Fleet Support (Operations and Plans)	BSc,CEng,FRAes,MBIM,nadc,psc(m)
Director General Ship Refitting	Rear Admiral P Spencer, MA,MSc,jsdc
Hydrographer of the Navy	R.V. Babington,
Acting Controller of the Navy Director General Surface	BSc,MSc,CEng,FRINA,FIMgt,RCNC
Ships	Rear Admiral J.P .CLARKE,LVO,MBE ,pce
... ...	Rear Admiral F.P. Scourse,MBE,MA,CEng,
Chief Strategic Systems Executive	MIEE,MINucE,ndc

Rear Admiral PAM Thomas, Msc, CEng,
FIMechE, MIMechE

HEADS OF SERVICE (ROYAL NAVY)

Medical Director General (N)	*QHP,MB,Bch,ndc*
Director Dental Services(N)	*Surgeon Commodore (D)* E.J. Grant, *QHDS,BDS MSc,DGDP,RCS(UK),LDS RCS(Eng)*
Director Naval Nursing Services & Matron-in-Chief	*Principal Nursing Officer* C. M. Taylor, *ARRC,QHNS*
Director General Naval Chaplaincy Services Surgeon Rear Admiral A. Craig,	*The Venerable M.W. Bucks, QHC,BD,AKC*

FLAG OFFICERS CURRENTLY SERVING IN CENTRALISED MINISTRY OF DEFENCE

Assistant Chief of the Defence Staff,Operational Requirements (Sea Systems)	*Rear Admiral* R.T.R Phillips, MNI, pce, odc (Aus)
Deputy Chief of the Defence Staff (Systems) and Chief Naval Engineer	*Vice Admiral* J.H . Dunt, *Bsc,CEng,MIEE,rcds,psc*
Surgeon General	*Surgeon Vice Admiral* A.L. Revell, *QHS,MB,ChB,FFARCS, DA,rcds,ndc*
Director General Naval Bases and Suppy	*Rear Admiral* J.A. Trewby, MA, CEng, FIEE, rcds, psc

ATTACHES AND ADVISERS

Service Mail   NAVAL ATTACHES IN FOREIGN COUNTRIES

All official service mail is to be forwarded in accordance with the instructions detailed at DCI GEN 177/93

Private Mail
All private mail is to be sent via the GPO. The full address, as shown below, should be given and postage prepaid by the senders.
Where the size of the package is such that 'goods' as opposed to correspondence might be included the appropriate customs form is to be affixed before posting.

Naval Attache
British Embassy

Abidjan
(Defence Attache)
Ivory Coast, is DAdv resident Accra

Abu Dhabi
(Defence Naval & Military Attache)
United Arab Emirates

Amman
(Defence Naval & Military Attache)
Jordan

Ankara
(Naval & Air Attache)
Turkey

Asuncion (Paraguay) Defence Attache is
(Defence Naval Military & Air Attache)
resident Buenos Aires

Athens
(Naval & Air Attache)
Greece

Bangkok
(Defence Attache)
Thailand

Beirut
(Defence Attache)
Lebanon

Belgrade
(Defence Attache)
Former yogoslavia

Berne
(Defence Attache)
Switzerland

Bogota
(Defence Attache)
Colombia

Bonn
(Naval Attache)
Germany

Brasilia
(Naval Attache)
Brazil

Bratislave
(Defence Attache)
Slovakia

Brussels
(Defence Attache)
Belgium
also (Defence Attache)
Luxembourg

Bucharest
(Defence Attache)
Romania

Budapest
(Defence Attache)
Hungary

Buenos Aires
  (Naval & Air Attache)
  Argentina
  also (Defence   Attache)
  (Montevideo)

Cairo
  (Naval & Air Attache)
  Egypt

Caracas
  (Defence Attache)
  Venezuela
  also DA Cuba,Ecuador and Panama

Copenhagen
  (Defence Attache)
  Denmark

Dakar
  (Defence Attache)
  Senegal resides Rabat

Damascus
  (Defence Attache)
  Syria

Dublin
  (Defence Attache)
  Irish Republic

Guatemala City
  Defence Attache
  (Guatemala)

Hague, The
  (Defence & Naval Attache)
  Netherlands

Havana
  (Defence Attache)
  Cuba, is
  Defence Attache resident Caracas

Islamabad
  (Naval & Air Adviser)
  Pakistan

Jakarta
  (Defence Attache)
  Indonesia

Katmandu
  (Defence Attache)
  Nepal

Kiev
  (Defence Attache)
  Ukraine

Kuwait City
  (Defence Attache)
  Kuwait

La Paz
  (Defence Attache)
  Bolivia

Lisbon
  (Defence Attache)
  Portugal

Lome
  (Defence Attache)
  Togo, is D Adv resident Accra

Luxembourg
  (Defence Attache)
  Luxembourg is Defence Attache resident Brussels

Madrid
  (Defence & Naval Attache)
  Spain

Managua
  (Defence Attache)
  Nicaragua, is Defence Attache resident Mexico City

Manila
  Defence Attache
  Philippines

Mexico City
  (Defence Attache)
  Mexico, Nicaragua, Belize,
  El Salvador & Honduras

Moscow
  (Naval Attache)
  Commonwealth of Independent States
  (Defence Attache)
  Azerbaijan, Kazakhstan, Turkmeniya & Georgia
  (Assistant Naval Attache)
  Commonwealth of Independent States
  (Assistant Defence Attache)
  Tajikistan, Ijzbekistan, Kirghizia, Moldavia & Latvia

Muscat
  (Naval & Air Attache)
  Oman

Oslo
(Defence & Naval Attache)
Norway

Paramaribo
(Defence Attache)
Suriname is Defence Advisor Kingstown,

Paris
(Naval Attache)
France

Peking
(Naval Attache)
China

Prague
(Defence Attache)
Czech Republic

Rabat
(Defence Attache)
Morocco, also Defence Attache Mauritania

Riga
(Defence Attache)
Latvia, also Defence AttacheTallinn & Villnius

Riyadh
(Naval Attache)
Saudi Arabia, also Naval and Air Attache Yemen

Rome
(Naval Attache)
Italy

Sana'a
(Naval & Air Attache)
Yemen, is Naval Attache Saudi Arabia

San Salvador
(Defence Attache)
El Salvador, is Defence Attache resident Mexico

Santiago
(Defence Naval & Military Attache)
Chile

Seoul
(Naval & Air Attache)
Korea

Sofia
(Defence Attache)
Bulgaria

Stockholm
(Naval & Military Attache)
Sweden

Tegucigalpa
(Defence Attache)
Honduras, is Defence Attache resident Mexico

Tel Aviv
(Naval & Air Attache)
Israel

Tokyo
(Defence & Naval Attache)
Japan

Vienna
(Defence Attache)
Austria also
(Defence Attache)
Slovenia

Warsaw
(Naval & Military Attache)
Poland

Washington
(Naval Attache & ADA Pol)
(Assistant Naval Attache)
United States of America

Zagreb
Defence Attache
Croatia

DEFENCE AND NAVAL ADVISERS IN COMMONWEALTH COUNTRIES

Accra
Ghana, Sierra Leone, Togo & Ivory Coast

Basseterre
(Defence Adviser)
St Christopher & Nevis (St. Kitts)
resides Bridgetown

Bridgetown
(Defence Adviser)
Barbados, also D Adv Basseterre, Castries,
Kingstown, Roseau, St Georges,
St Johns, Cayman, Grand Tusk, Tortola, The Valley,
Plymouth
(Naval Adviser)
Kingston, Port of Spain

Canberra
(Defence & Naval Adviser & Head British
 Defence Liaison Staff)
Australia

Castries
(Defence Adviser)
St. Lucia,
resides Bridgetown

Colombo
(Defence Adviser)
Sri Lanka & Maldive Islands

Dhaka
(Defence Adviser)
Bangladesh

Freetown
(Defence Adviser)
Sierra Leone, resides Accra Ghana

Georgetown
(Defence Adviser)
Guyana,
resides Kingston Jamaica

Harare
(Defence Adviser)
Zimbabwe also Defence Adv Botswana

Kampala
(Defence Adviser)
Uganda also Defence Adv. Tanzenia and Defence
Attache Rwanda and Burundi

Kingston
(Naval Adviser)
Jamaica
resides Bridgetown

Kingstown
(Defence Adviser)
St. Vincent, resides Bridgetown

Kuala Lumpur
(Defence Adviser)
(Assistant Defence Adviser)
Malaysia

Lagos
(Defence Adviser)
Nigeria

Nairobi
(Defence Adviser)
Kenya
also (Defence Adviser)
Ethiopia

New Delhi
(Naval Adviser)
India

Nicosia
(Defence Adviser)
Cyprus

Ottawa
(Naval and Air Adviser)
Canada

Port Moresby
(Defence Adviser)
Papua New Guinea,
resides Canberra

Port of Spain
(Defence Adviser)
Trinidad & Tobago
resides, Kingston

Pretoria
Naval Adviser
South Africa

Roseau
(Assistant Defence Adviser)
Dominica, resides Bridgetown

St.Georges
(Assistant Defence Adviser)
resides Bridgetown

Singapore
(Defence Adviser)
(Assistant Defence Adviser & RNLO)

Suva
(Defence Adviser)
Fiji, resides Wellington N.Z

Wellington
(Defence Adviser & Head of British Defence Liaison Staff)
New Zealand also Defence Attache Fiji

HIGHER DEFENCE HEADQUARTERS AND
COMMAND ORGANISATIONS OF COMMONWEALTH NAVIES

Australia

(Chief of Naval Staff)

(Deputy Chief of Naval Staff)
(Director General Naval Policy and Warfare)
(Director General of Corporate Management)
(Director General Maritime Studies Program)

Department of Defence (Navy Office)
Canberra ACT 2600

(Naval Adviser - London)
Australian High Commission
Strand
LONDON WC2B 4LA

(Assistant Chief of Naval Staff - Personnel)
(Director General of Naval Manpower)
(Director General of Personal Services and Conditions)
(Director General of Naval Health Services)

(Assistant Chief of Naval Staff -Materiel)
(Director General of Naval Production
(Director General of Equipment Production
(Submarine Project Director)
(ANZAC Ship Project Director)
(Director General of Naval Logistics Policy)
(Director General of Naval Engineering Requirements)

Department of Defence (Navy Office)
Canberra ACT 2600

(Maritime Commander Australia)
(Chief of Staff to Maritime Commander)
(Commodore Flotillas)
(Director of Naval Warfare)

Maritime Headquarters
GARDEN ISLAND NSW 2000

(Hydrographer RAN)

8 Station Street
Wollongong NSW 2500

(Commander Australian Submarine Squadron)

HMAS Striling
PO Box 228
ROCKINGHAM WA 6168

(Commander Australian Minewarfare and Diving Forces

HMAS Waterhen
Balls Head Road
WAVERTON NSW 2060

HMAS Cairns
CAIRNS QLD 4870

(Flag Officer Naval Support Command)
(Chief of Staff to the Naval Support Commander
(Chief of Logistics)

Locked Bag 12
PYRMONT NSW 2009

(Commodore Naval Air Station Nowra)

Naval Air Station
NOWRA NSW 2540

(Commanding Officer HMAS Stirling)

PO Box 228
ROCKINGHAM WA 6168

(Commanding Officer HMAS Cerberus)

HMAS Cerberus
WESTERNPORT VIC 3920

(Flag Officer Naval Training Command

HMAS Cerberus
WESTERNPORT VIC 3920

New Zealand

(Chief of Naval Staff)
  (Deputy Chief of Naval Staff)
  (Chief of Naval Materiel)
  (Chief of Naval Operations, Requirements and Plans)
  (Chief of Naval Personnel)

Headquarters New Zealand Defence Force
Private Bag
Wellington

Maritime Commander

Maritime Headquarters
HMNZ Naval Base
Devonport
Auckland

Chief Executive

HMNZ Dockyard
HMNZ Naval Base
Devonport
Auckland

(Captain Naval Training)
(Captain Fleet Support)

HMNZ Naval Base
Devonport
Auckland

(Hydrographer RNZN)

Hydrographic Office
PO Box 33 - 341
Takapuna

(Head of New Zealand Defence Staff London)

New Zealand High Commission
New Zealand House
Haymarket
London SW1Y 4TQ

India

(Chief of the Naval Staff)
  (Vice Chief of the Naval Staff)
  (Deputy Chief of the Naval Staff)
  (Chief of Personnel)
  (Chief   of   Materiel)(Flag   Officer
  Commanding-in-Chief)

Headquarters Western Naval Command
Bombay - 400 001

(Flag Officer Commanding-in-Chief)

Headquarters Easten Naval Command
Visakhapatnam - 530 014

(Flag Officer Commanding-in-Chief)

Headquarters Southern Naval Command
Cochin - 682 004

Bangladesh

(Chief of the Naval Staff)
  (Assistant Chief of Naval Staff (Operations))
  (Assistant Chief of Naval Staff (Personnel))
  (Assistant Chief of Naval Staff (Materiel))
  (Assistant Chief of Naval Staff (Logistic))

Naval HQ
Banani
 Dhaka 1213

(Naval Administrative Authority Dhaka)

BNS Haji Mohsin
Dhaka Cantonment

(Commodore Commanding Chittagong)

(Commodore Commanding BN Flotilla)

(Commodore Superintendent Dockyard)

New Mooring
Chittagong 4218

(Commodore Commanding Khulna)

Town Khalishpur
Khulna 9000

NAVAL BASE

(BNS Issa Khan)
   (Bangladesh Naval Academy)
   (Naval Stores Depot)
   (Naval Armament Inspection and Supply Depot)

New Mooring
Chittagong - 4218

(BNS Shaheed Moazzam)

Kaptai
Chittagong Hill Tracts

(BNS Haji Mohsin)

Dhaka Cantonment
Dhaka 1206

(BNS Titumir)

Town Khalishpur
Khulna - 9000

Malaysia

(Chief of Navy)
   (Deputy Chief of Navy)
   (Assistant Chief of Navy (Manpower))
   (Assistant Chief of Navy (Supply & Finance))
   (Assistant Chief of Navy (Plans))

Ministry of Defence
Jalan Padang Tembak
50634 Kuala Lumpur
Malaysia

(Fleet Operational Commander)

Naval Base
32200 LUMUT
Perak
Malaysia

(Fleet Operational Commander (FOC RMN)

Naval Base
32100 LUMAT
Perak
Malaysia

(Commander Naval Area 1)

Naval Base
Tanjong Gelang
25990 Kuantan Pahang
Malaysia

(Commander Naval Area 2)

Naval Base
87007 Federal Territory
Labuan
Malaysia

Naval Base
KD Sri Labuan
87007 Federal Territory
Labuan
Sabah
Malaysia

(Director of Maritime Enforcement
   Centre (NSC))
Naval Base
32100 Lumut
Perak
Malaysia

National Maritime Enforcement Centre
Naval Base
32200 Lumut
Perak
Malaysia

INTERPRETERS

OFFICERS WHO ARE NOTED AT THE ADMIRALTY AS HAVING
QUALIFIED AS INTERPRETERS ((1)-*1ST CLASS*; (2)-*2ND CLASS*)

ARABIC

Name	Rank	Standard	Date of Qualifying or re-qualifying
Pearce, J.K.C.	CDR	1	Mar 90
Roberts, S.P.	LT	2	Mar 94
Vosper, I.A.	CDR	1	Feb 73
Wilkinson, N.J., *CB*	RADM	2	Sep 72
Young, I.J.	A/CDR	2	Mar 93

CHINESE

Name	Rank	Standard	Date of Qualifying or re-qualifying
Gopsill, B.R.	LT CDR	1	Sep 84
Lewis, S.	LT CDR	1	Oct 88
Petrie, M.J.	LT CDR	2	Nov 83
Rayner, B.N.	A/CAPT	1	Dec 83
White, S.N.	LT CDR	2	Sep 90

DANISH

Name	Rank	Standard	Date of Qualifying or re-qualifying
Watson, P.H.	CAPT	2	Oct 76

DUTCH

Name	Rank	Standard	Date of Qualifying or re-qualifying
Davies, A.R.	CDR	2	Mar 84
Ewence, M.W.	LT CDR	2	Mar 88
Rickard, H.W., *CBE, ADC*	CDRE	2	Mar 94

FRENCH

Name	Rank	Standard	Date of Qualifying or re-qualifying
Airey, S.E.	CDR	1	Mar 80
Bray, N.G.H.	CAPT	2	Oct 77
Carson, M.J.	LT CDR	2	Mar 89
Cooke, J.G.F., *OBE*	CDRE	2	Mar 92
Craven, J.A.G.	LT CDR	2	Mar 90
De Salaberry Lewis, J.H.	LT	1	Mar 93
Fanshawe, J.R.	CAPT	2	Mar 76
Jeffrey, I.	CDR	2	Sep 72
Keefe, S-A.	LT CDR	2	Mar 89
MacMahon, T.J.	CDR	1	Mar 92
Mansergh, M.P.	CDR	2	Mar 91
Martin, T.K.	CAPT	2	Feb 69
Mulligan, I.D.	LT CDR	2	Feb 73
Murphy, B.J.	LT CDR	2	Mar 91
Newell, J.M.	LT CDR	2	Mar 94
Prichard, J.L.L.	CDR	2	Mar 90
Shirley, M.C.	CDRE	2	Mar 84
Stonor, P.F.A.	CDR	2	Mar 88
Storey, M.	CDR	2	Mar 93
Tribe, P.J.	CAPT	1	Mar 88
Turner, J.S.H.	LT	2	Mar 94

GERMAN

Name	Rank	Standard	Date of Qualifying or re-qualifying
Airey, S.E.	CDR	1	Apr 81
Apps, J.G.	CDR	2	Mar 84
Bishop, R.ST.J.S.	CAPT	2	Mar 79
Black, A.G.C.	LT CDR	2	Mar 75
Dashfield, A.K.	SURG LTCDR	2	Mar 90
Davis, P.B.	LT CDR	2	Mar 92
Durston, D.H.	CDR	2	Mar 83
Eberle, P.J.F.	CDR	1	Mar 77
Hutchison, W.K.	CDRE	2	May 87
Jeffery, P.H.	CAPT	2	Dec 83
Massey, A.M.	CAPT	1	Mar 80
Nurse, M.T.	LT CDR	2	Mar 86
Prynn, R.M.	CDR	2	Apr 78
Sparke, P.R.W.	LT	1	Mar 92
Stanton, R.F.	LT CDR	2	Mar 94
Townsend, C.N.	LT CDR	2	Mar 89
Williams, N.L.	CDR	2	Mar 85
Wiseman, W.T.	CDR	2	May 87

ITALIAN

Name	Rank	Standard	Date of Qualifying or re-qualifying
Cooke, J.G.F., *OBE*	CDRE	2	Sep 60
Musters, J.B.A.	CAPT	2	Mar 89
Rutherford, M.G., *CBE*	VADM	2	Sep 69

JAPANESE

Name	Rank	Standard	Date of Qualifying or re-qualifying
Chelton, S.R.L.	CDR	2	Oct 88

NORWEGIAN

Name	Rank	Standard	Date of Qualifying or re-qualifying
Carter, B.L., *OBE*	COL	2	Mar 83
Lash, W.R.DE.W.	LT COL	1	
Stallion, I.M.	CDR	2	Mar 79
Taylor, W.J.	LOC MAJ	2	Mar 91

POLISH

Name	Rank	Standard	Date of Qualifying or re-qualifying
Fec, Z.M.	LOC MAJ	1	Mar 92

PORTUGESE

Name	Rank	Standard	Date of Qualifying or re-qualifying
Fec, Z.M.	LOC MAJ	1	Apr 85

Name	Rank	Standard	Date of Qualifying or re-qualifying
Harrison, R.A. .... CDR	1	Mar 83
RUSSIAN			
Airey, S.E. .... CDR	2	Mar 94
Connolly, C.J......... LT CDR	2	Mar 89
Davies, A.R.............. CDR	1	Mar 89
Drewett, R.E. .... LT CDR	2	Mar 91
Ellis, P.J............... CAPT	2	Mar 73
Fairbrass, J.E.............. LT	2	Mar 94
Fec, Z.M. .... LOC MAJ	2	Mar 89
Fields, D.G. .... LT CDR	1	Mar 90
Foreman, J.L.R. .... LT CDR	1	Mar 92
Green, T.J. .... LT CDR	2	Mar 89
Hodgson, T.C. .... LT CDR	1	Mar 94
Hoper, P.S., *MBE* ..... LT CDR	2	Mar 92
Hudson, G.F.G. .... LT	2	Mar 92
Jones, L. .... LT CDR	2	Mar 89
Lister, S.R. .... CDR	1	Mar 90
Littleboy, M.N.......... CAPT	2	Mar 75
McCready, G.A.R., *MBE* ... CDR	2	Mar 77
Merrick, L.C.P.......... CAPT	2	Feb 74
Newing, A.G. .... CAPT RM	2	Feb 71
Newton, G.A. .... LT CDR	2	Mar 94
Parrish, C.A.M., *OBE*... A/CAPT	2	Mar 91
Pearce, A.I............ LT CDR	2	Mar 80
Pearce, K............. LT CDR	1	Mar 91
Simpson, E.J. .... LT	2	Mar 91
Stanton, R.F. .... LT CDR	1	Mar 93
Turner, R.B............. CAPT	2	Mar 85
Watson, C.C. .... LT CDR	2	Mar 88
Woodley, D............... LT	1	Mar 92
SPANISH			
Adam, I.K................ LT	2	Mar 91
Blackham, J.J. .... RADM	2	Feb 68
Cumming, G.G.A......... CDR	2	Jul 90
Dedman, N.J.K........... CDR	2	Mar 86
Fec, Z.M. .... LOC MAJ	2	Mar 93
Harrison, C.A. .... LT CDR	1	Mar 89
Hore, P.G. .... CAPT	2	Feb 68
Lynch, R.D.F. .... LT	1	Mar 91
McGlory, S.J.............. LT	1	Mar 94
McLennan, R.G. .... LT CDR	1	Mar 94
Miller, A.J.G............ CAPT	2	Oct 75
O'shaughnessy, F.W.G... LT CDR	2	Mar 93
Sanguinetti, H.R....... LT CDR	1	Mar 90
Wolfe, D.E. .... A/CDR	1	Mar 95
SWEDISH			
Hore, P.G. .... CAPT	2	Sep 70
Moore, M.A.C., *LVO* ..... VADM	1	Mar 80
Noble, G.D.............. CDR	1	Mar 75
Rigby, J.C............ LT CDR	2	Mar 86

BARRISTERS

OFFICERS OF THE SUPPLY AND SECRETARIAT SPECIALISATION QUALIFIED AS BARRISTERS
AND CALLED TO THE BAR

CAPTAI NS

Humphrey, D.R. (Chief Naval Judge Advocate)

COMMANDERS

Davis, B.J.
Blackett, J.
Martin, T.F.W.
Fraser, R.W.
Williams, R.E.
Albon, R.
Crabtree, P.D.
Cooper, S.N.
Dingle, J.C.
Steel, D.G.
Hawkins, N.S.

LIEUTENANT-COMMANDERS

Hattersley, J.P.G.Melville-Brown,
P.G.Kingsbury, J.A.T.
Emerton, M.S.
Blain, R.G.
Flanagan, J.
Gray, R.S.
Forer, T.J.
Spence, A.B.
Crozier, S.R.M.
Jameson, A.C.
Brown, N.L.

LIEUTENANTS

Hollins, R.P.
Tew, J.P.
Walker, A.
Wright, S.H.
Cooper, K.S.

THE ADMIRALTY AND COMMERCIAL COURT OF ENGLAND AND WALES

AND LEGAL ADVISERS TO THE ADMIRALTY BOARD

HIGH COURT OF JUSTICE
QUEEN'S BENCH DIVISION, ENGLAND

The Admiralty and Commercial Court (and Prize Court)

Royal Courts of Justice

Judges
The Hon. Mr Justice May
The Hon. Mr Justice Lewis
The Hon. Mr Justice Bowsher
The Hon. Mr Justice Loyd
The Hon. Mr Justice Hicks
The Hon. Mr Justice Havery
The Hon. Mr Justice Lloyd
The Hon. Mr Justice Newman
The Hon. Mr Justice Thornton

Admiralty and Commercial Registrar and
Marshal's Office (Admiralty and Prize Courts)

Royal Courts of Justice, East Wing

Registrar - P M Miller
Marshal and Chief Clerk - A Ferrigno

Judge Advocate of the Fleet -
His Honour Judge J L Sessions
Address:- Law Courts
Baker Road, Maidstone, Kent.

Chief Naval Judge Advocate -
Captain D R Humphrey RN
Address:- Royal Naval College,
Greenwich, SE10 9NN

Legal Adviser
To The Admiralty Board

Solicitor - The Treasury Solicitor, Sir Gerald Hosker KCB. QC.
Address -: Queen Annes Chambers,
28 Broadway, London SW1H 9JS

Standing Council to the Crown in Admiralty matters -
T Brenton

Scotland

Solicitor in Scotland to the Admiralty Board -
S J Hall, W S Robson McLean W S
Address:- 28 Abercomby Place
Edinburgh EH3 6QF

Solicitor in Scotland to the Admiralty Board
(Collisions at Sea)
Robert Knox, Henderson, Boyd & Jackson W S
Address:- 19 Ainslie Place, Edinburgh, E3 6AU.

Junior Council in Scotland to the Admiralty Board-
I M Duguid
Address: Advocates Library
Parliament House, Edinburgh

Northern Ireland

Solicitor - The Crown Solicitor, G N T P Roberts
Address: Royal Courts of Justice (Ulster)
PO Box 410
Belfast, BT1 3JY

Law Agents to the Treasury

Solicitor for Admiralty Purposes

United Kingdom

Belfast and Londonderry - Messrs McKinty and Wright
Cardiff - Messrs Cartwrights
Chatham and Rochester - Messrs Bassett and Boucher
Deal and Walmer - Messrs Hardman and Watson
Devonport and Plymouth - Messrs Foot and Bowden
Dover - Bradley and Messrs Mowll & Mowll

Harwich - Messrs Hanslip Ward & Co
Hull - Messrs Andres M Jackson & Co
Liverpool - Messrs Alsop, Stevens, Batesons & Co
Newcastle - Messrs Eversheves
Portsmouth - Messrs Brutton
Sheerness - John Copland and Son
Weymouth and Portland - Messrs Wickham and Lloyd
Edwards

Overseas

Bahamas - D B McKinney Nassau Bahamas
Cyprus - The HON Sir Panayotis L Cacoyannis Kt,LLB
PO Box 122 Limassol Cyprus
Gibraltar - HM Attorney-General
Hong Kong - C Munro and Claypole
Sincere Insurance Building 5/F 4 - 6 Hennessy Road
Hong Kong Clyde and Co Admiralty Centre Tower on
(10th Floor) Harecourt Road Hong Kong
Kenya - Messrs Hamiltin Harrison & Mathews Nairobi
Malaysia - Messrs Presgrave & MathewsPO Box 81 Penang
Malta -_Riccardo Farrugia Esq. BA, LLD
Singapore - Messrs Drew & Napier Chartered Bank
Chambers

RULES FOR APPOINTMENT AS
NAUTICAL ASSESSORS

Appointments as Nautical Assessors will be made under the following rules:

(Under Section 111 of the Supreme Court of Judicature Act 1891)

(1)   To be retired Naval Officers of the rank of Admiral or Captain who have had at least 3 years' service in command of one of HM Ships at sea.

(2)   The number will be limited to 6

(3)   The age limit is 65

(4)   Appointments will be for a limited period of 3 years at the first instance, and extension beyond that period will be specially considered before the term of the appointment expires. No appointment will exceed six years.

COURT OF APPEAL

(Under Section 98 of the Supreme Court of Judicature (Consolidation) Act 1925)

1   To be Naval Officers retired from the Commanders', Captains' or Flag Officers' Lists.

2   The number will be limited to 2

3   The appointment will be 3 years in the first instance. Any extension beyond that period will be specially considered before the term of the appointment expires. No appointment will exceed six years.

CLASS 111. ASSESSORS

(Under the Merchant Shipping Act 1892)

1   To be retired Officers of the rank of Admiral or Captain who have had 3 years' sevice in command of one of HM Ships at sea, Commanders or Lieutenant Commanders who are qualified Navigation Officers with more than three years' service since qualifying in the Advanced Navigation Course are also eligible for appointment.

2   The number wiil be limited to 2

3   The age limit is 70

4   The appointment will be for 3 years in the first instance.

Application for appointment as Assessors to the House of Lords or Court of Appeal should be made to the Ministry of Defence (Naval Secretary)

Applications for appointment as Class 111 Assessor should be addressed to the Home Office.

SHIPS' AGENTS - NAVAL AGENCY AND DISTRIBUTION ACT 1864

The persons named below are prepared to undertake the duties of Ships' Agents:

M G Hattom Esq., C/O The Royal Bank of Scotland Plc Holts Branch Kirkland House Whitehall SW1A 2EB
J D Simmonds Esq., C/O Lloyds Bank Plc (Cox's & King's Branch) Pall Mall SW1Y 5NH
J M Matthews Esq., C/O National Westminster Bank Plc (Stillwell & Sons) 26 Haymarket SW1Y 4ER

Appointment of Ships' Agents under the Naval Agency and Distribution Act 1864 are made by Commanding Officer. Solicitors and persons in the service of the Crown are ineligible for appointment , as incorporated bodies, but partnership bodies not incorporated, individual officials of incorporated bodies in person capacity, or any other individuals may be nominated if otherwise eligible under the Act. QRRN Appendix 14 (Form of Appointment) refers.

HM SHORE ESTABLISHMENTS

CAMBRIDGE
HMS CAMBRIDGE
Wembury
nr PLYMOUTH
Devon
PL9 0AZ
CDR X   A T Welch

CENTURION
2SL/CNH
Centurion Building
Grange Road
GOSPORT
Hants
PO13 9XA
CDR X   S B Furness

COCHRANE
HMS COCHRANE
ROSYTH
Fife
Scotland
KY11 2XT
SGCDR(D) . . . .   G E Sidoli

COMMW SHORE
Commodore Minor War Vessels
Minewarfare & Diving
Lancelot Building
PP 29A
HM Naval Base
PORTSMOUTH
PO1 3NH
LT X   J H De Salaberry Lewis

COLLINGWOOD
HMS COLLINGWOOD
Newgate Lane
FAREHAM
Hants
PO14 1AS
CDRE . . . . . .   J Chadwick

DAEDALUS
HMS DAEDALUS
LEE-ON-SOLENT
Hants
PO13 9NY
LT CDR X   G C Pell

DARTMOUTH BRNC
Britannia Royal Naval College
DARTMOUTH
Devon
TQ6 0MJ
CAPT . . . . . . E   A P Masterton-Smith ADC

DOLPHIN
HMS DOLPHIN
GOSPORT
Hants
PO12 2AB
CAPT X   R F Strange

DRAKE

DRYAD
HMS DRYAD
Southwick
FAREHAM
Hants
PO1 7 6EJ
CAPT X   R J Lippiett MBE

FOREST MOOR
HMS FOREST MOOR
Menwith Hill Road
Darley
HARROGATE
HG3 2RE
LT CDR . . . . E   C J Gabriel

GANNET
HMS GANNET
RNAS Prestwick
Greensite
MONKTON
Ayrshire
KA9 2RZ
CDR X   N D Arnall-Culliford AFC

HERON
HMS HERON
RNAS Yeovilton
YEOVIL
Somerset
BA22 8HT
CDRE . . . . . .   S Lidbetter

NELSON
HMS NELSON
PORTSMOUTH
Hants
PO1 3HH
VADM . . . . . .   M G Rutherford CBE

NEPTUNE
HMS NEPTUNE
FASLANE
Dunbartonshire
ScotlandD
G84 8HL
CAPT X   R Harding

OSPREY
HMS OSPREY
PORTLAND
Dorset
DT5 1BL
CAPT X   J B Harvey LVO

RALEIGH
HMS RALEIGH
TORPOINT
Cornwall
PL11 2PD
CDRE . . . . . .   H W Rickard CBE ADC

RNEC MANADON
RNEC Manadon
HMS THUNDERER
Manadon
PLYMOUTH
Devon
PL5 3AQ

SEAHAWK
HMS SEAHAWK
HELSTON
Cornwall
TR12 7RH
CDRE . . . . . .   S C Thornewill DSC

SULTAN
HMS SULTAN
GOSPORT
Hants
PO12 3BY
CDRE . . . . . .   M C Shirley

SULTAN AIB
Admiralty Interview Board
HMS SULTAN
GOSPORT
Hants
PO12 3BY
CAPT . . . . .   E   H J Critchley

TAMAR
HMS TAMAR
BFPO 1
CDR   X   R Thoburn OBE

TEMERAIRE
HMS TEMERAIRE
Burnaby Road
PORTSMOUTH
Hants
PO1 2HB

VICTORY
HMS VICTORY
HM Naval Base
PORTSMOUTH
Hants
PO1 3PZ
LT CDR   X   M Cheshire

WARRIOR
HMS WARRIOR
NORTHWOOD
Middlesex
HA6 3HP
CAPT   X   A M Poulter OBE

HM SHIPS

ALDERNEY (Island)

BFPO 203
LT CDR X   G R Northwood

ANGLESEY (Island)

BFPO 207
LT CDR X   M R Skeer

ARCHER (Attacker)

BFPO 208
LT CDR X   M P Pollock

ARGYLL (Type 23)

BFPO 210
CDR X   G M Zambellas

ARUN (River)

BFPO 214
LT X   A P Hancock

ATHERSTONE (Hunt)

BFPO 215
LT CDR X   P N Lambourn

BATTLEAXE (Type 22)

BFPO 223
CDR X   A A S Adair

BEAGLE (Bulldog)

BFPO 224
LT CDR X   M J Malin

BEAVER (Type 22)

BFPO 225
LT CDR X   D G Mahony

BERKELEY (Hunt)

BFPO 226
LT CDR X   A C Ashcroft

BICESTER (Hunt)

BFPO 227
LT CDR X   S R Malcolm

BIRMINGHAM (Type 42)

BFPO 228
CDR X   M C Evans

BITER (Attacker)

BFPO 229
LT x   A L Hogben

BLACKWATER (River)

BFPO 230
LT X   T H G Rogers

BLAZER (Attacker)

BFPO 231
LT CDR X   M J Buckley

BOXER (Type 22)

BFPO 232
CDR X   E Fraser

BRAVE (Type 22)

BFPO 233
CDR X   C A Johnstone-Burt

BRAZEN (Type 22)

BFPO 234
LT CDR . . . . S   J M Lines

BRECON (Hunt)

BFPO 235
LT CDR X   I D Hugo

BRIDPORT (Sandown)

BFPO 236
LT CDR X   R L Hall

BRILLIANT (Type 22)

BFPO 237
A/CDR X   D L Potts

BRITANNIA (Royal yacht)

BFPO 239
CDRE . . . . . .   A J C Morrow

BROCKLESBY (Hunt)

BFPO 241
LT CDR X   C C Thomas

BULLDOG (Bulldog)

BFPO 242
LT CDR X   A F Holt

CAMPBELTOWN (Type 22)

BFPO 248
CAPT X   A J Johns

CARDIFF (Type 42)

BFPO 249
CDR X   N A M Butler

CATTISTOCK (Hunt)

BFPO 251
LT CDR X   M P Oriordan

CHARGER (Attacker)

BFPO 252
LT CDR X   T P Haycock

CHATHAM (Type 22)

BFPO 253
CAPT X   C H T Clayton

CHIDDINGFOLD (Hunt)

BFPO 254
LT CDR X   W Scarth

CORNWALL (Type 22)

BFPO 256
CAPT X   G K Billson

COTTESMORE (Hunt)

BFPO 257
LT CDR X   A R Ireland

COVENTRY (Type 22)

BFPO 259
LT CDR . . . . . S   S A Lowe

CROMER (Sandown)

BFPO 260
LT CDR X   N M Hunter

CUMBERLAND (Type 22)

BFPO 261
CAPT X   T J H Laurence MVO

DASHER (Attacker)

BFPO 271
LT X   J C Davison

DULVERTON (Hunt)

BFPO 273
LT CDR X   S J N Kings

DUMBARTON CASTLE (Castle)

BFPO 274
LT X   C P Atkinson

EDINBURGH (Type 42)

BFPO 277
CDR X   P Fisher

ENDURANCE (Ice patrol)

BFPO 279
CAPT X   B W Bryant

EXAMPLE (Attacker)

BFPO 281
LT CDR X   M J Buckley

EXETER (Type 42)

BFPO 278
CAPT X   P W Herington

EXPLOIT (Attacker)

BFPO
LT X   M K Utley

EXPLORER (Attacker)

BFPO
LT CDR X   S R Gordon

EXPRESS (Attacker)

BFPO
LT CDR X   B J Carroll

FEARLESS (Fearless)

BFPO 283
CAPT X   R A I McLean OBE

GLASGOW (Type 42)

BFPO 287
CDR X   A J Rix

GLEANER (Gleaner)

BFPO 288
LT X   I E Davies

GLOUCESTER (Type 42)

BFPO 289
CDR X   T A Cunningham

GUERNSEY (Island)

BFPO 290
LT CDR X   M R Greenland

HECLA (Hecla)

BFPO 293
CDR X   D J Lye

HERALD (Hecla)

BFPO 296
CDR X   I M Bartholomew

HURWORTH (Hunt)

BFPO 300
LT CDR X   S J Neil

ILLUSTRIOUS (Invincible)

BFPO 305
CAPT X   J Band ADC

INVERNESS (Sandown)

BFPO 307
LT CDR X   A P F Cassar

INVINCIBLE (Invincible)

BFPO 308
CAPT X   I A Forbes CBE

IRON DUKE (Type 23)

BFPO 309
CDR X   C J Bryning

ITCHEN (River)

BFPO 310
LT X   M R Titcomb

IXWORTH (Diving tndr)

BFPO 200

LANCASTER (Type 23)

BFPO 323
CDR X   N J G Harland

LEDBURY (Hunt)

BFPO 324
LT CDR X   M R Percharde

LEEDS CASTLE (Castle)

BFPO 325
LT CDR X   P J Thicknesse

LINDISFARNE (Island)

BFPO 326
LT CDR X   N Murphy

LIVERPOOL (Type 42)

BFPO 327
CAPT X   R S Ainsley

LONDON (Type 22)

BFPO 328
CDR X   A S Brooks MBE

LOYAL CHANCELLOR (Attacker)

BFPO
LT CDR X   R H McNelle

LOYAL WATCHER (Attacker)

BFPO
LT CDR X   M D Mackenzie

MANCHESTER (Type 42)

BFPO 331
CDR X   S C Howard

MARLBOROUGH (Type 23)

BFPO 333
CAPT X   J F Rodley

MIDDLETON (Hunt)

BFPO 335
LT CDR X   D J S Goddard

MONMOUTH (Type 23)

BFPO 338
LT CDR . . . . S   J P Lavery

MONTROSE (Type 23)

BFPO 339
CAPT X   N S R Kilgour

NEWCASTLE (Type 42)

BFPO 343
LT CDR . . . . E   I J Goble

NORFOLK (Type 23)

BFPO 344
CDR X   J P S Greenop OBE

NORTHUMBERLAND (Type 23)

BFPO 345
LT CDR . . . . S   L P Notley

NOTTINGHAM (Type 42)

BFPO 346
CDR X   P T Docherty

ORKNEY (Island)

BFPO 354
LT CDR X   I S Pickles

ORWELL (River)

BFPO 355
LT X   P R Hurrell

PEACOCK (Peacock)

BFPO 359
LT CDR X   W Worsley

PLOVER (Peacock)

BFPO 360
LT CDR X   G B Sutton

PUNCHER (Attacker)

BFPO 362
LT CDR X   J G Cunniningham

PURSUER (Attacker)

BFPO 363
LT X   I E Graham

QUORN (Hunt)

BFPO 366
LT X   S Dainton

RANGER (Attacker)

BFPO 369

RENOWN(PORT) (Resolution)

BFPO 371
LT CDR . . . . E   P G Walter

REPULSE(PORT) (Resolution)

BFPO 372
LT CDR X   N R Firth

RESOLUTION(PORT) (Resolution)

BFPO 373
LT CDR . . . . E   R N V Tarr

RICHMOND (Type 23)

BFPO 375
CDR X   A G H Underwood

ROEBUCK (Bulldog)

BFPO 376
CDR X   I R Williams

SANDOWN (Sandown)

BFPO 379
LT CDR X   M J Petheram

SCEPTRE (Swiftsure)

BFPO 380
CDR X   M E Finney

SHEFFIELD (Type 22)

BFPO 383
CDR X   T M Karsten

SHETLAND (Island)

BFPO 385
LT CDR X   D N Matthews

SMITER (Attacker)

BFPO 387
LT X   R P Dunn

SOMERSET (Type 23)

BFPO 395
CDR X   M W Westwood

SOUTHAMPTON (Type 42)

BFPO 389
CDR X   K Winstanley MBE

SOVEREIGN (Swiftsure)

BFPO 390
CDR X   D M Vaughan

SPARTAN (Swiftsure)

BFPO 391
CDR X   P B Hinchliffe

SPEY (River)

BFPO 392
LT X   R M Stevens

SPLENDID (Swiftsure)

BFPO 393
CDR X   K I M Clark

STARLING (Peacock)

BFPO 394
LT CDR X   A W C Clark

SUPERB (Swiftsure)

BFPO 396
LT CDR . . . . . E   D B Harwood MBE

TALENT (Trafalger)

BFPO 401
CDR X   J S Westbrook MBE

TIRELESS (Trafalger)

BFPO 402
LT CDR . . . . . E   N R Moffatt

TORBAY (Trafalger)

BFPO 403
CDR X   G C Thomas

TRAFALGAR (Trafalger)

BFPO 404
CDR X   J H J Gower

TRENCHANT (Trafalger)

BFPO 405
CDR X   D M Forbes

TRIUMPH (Trafalger)

BFPO 406
CDR X   J J D Cutt

TRUMPETER (Attacker)

BFPO 407
LT X   R J Morris

TURBULENT (Trafalger)

BFPO 408
LT CDR . . . . . E   P C Pickstone

UPHLDER TRG TEAM (Upholder)

LT CDR . . . . . E   N L J Scott

VALIANT (Valiant)

LT CDR . . . . E   J K P Jones MBE BEM

VANGUARD(PORT) (Trident)

BFPO 418
CDR X   I D Arthur

VANGUARD(STBD) (Trident)

BFPO 418
CDR X   I M Stallion

VICTORIOUS(PORT) (Trident)

BFPO 419
CDR X   J H Gordon

VICTORIOUS(STBD) (Trident)

BFPO 419
CDR X   J Powis

VIGILANT(PORT) (Trident)

BFPO 420
CDR X   J G Tottenham

WALNEY (Sandown)

BFPO 423
LT X   S P Hardern

WESTMINSTER (Type 23)

BFPO 426
CDR X   A J B Cameron

YORK (Type 42)

BFPO 430
CDR X   A G Moll

RN FISHERY PROTECTION & MINE COUNTERMEASURES SQNS

FIRST MCM SQN
CDR X   T N E Williams

SECOND MCM SQN
CDR X   A E Rycroft

THIRD MCM SQN
CDR X   R M Simmonds

FISHERY PROTECTION SQN
CDR X   C M Lightfoot

ROYAL NAVY & ROYAL MARINE AIR SQUADRONS

HQ CDO AVN (Gazelle)

CDR X   G R N Foster

700 SQN LOFTU ()

702 SQN OSPREY

LT CDR X   N P Yates

705 SQN SEAHAWK

LT CDR X   M R Osman

706 SQN SEAHAWK

LT CDR X   S M Steeds

707 SQN HERON

750 SQN OBS SCH

LT CDR X   K W Terrill

771 SK5 SAR

LT CDR X   G B M Milton

772 SK4 SAR

800 SQN (Sea harrier)

BFPO 200
LT CDR X   J P Millward

801 SQN (Sea harrier)

BFPO 200
LT CDR X   C W Baylis

810 SQN SEAHAWK

LT CDR X   C J Hamp

814 SQN (Sea king mk6)

BFPO 200
LT CDR X   R E Drewett

815 SQN OSPREY

819 SQN (Sea king mk5)

LT CDR X   D M Searle

820 SQN (Sea king mk6)

BFPO 200
LT CDR X   A McKie

826 SQN (Sea king mk5)

829 SQN OSPREY

845 SQN (Sea king mk4)

LT CDR X   M P Abbey

846 SQN (Sea king mk4)

LT CDR X   F W Robertson

849 SQN A FLT (Sea king aew)

BFPO 200
LT CDR X   K Muir

849 SQN B FLT (Sea king aew)

BFPO 200
LT CDR X   J G Rich

849 SQN HQ

LT CDR X   J N Saunders MBE

899 SQN HERON

LT CDR X   M T Boast

ROYAL NAVAL RESERVE UNITS

CALLIOPE RNR
HMS CALLIOPE
South Shore Road
GATESHEAD
Tyne & Wear
NE8 2BE

CAMBRIA RNR
HMS CAMBRIA
Hayes Point
Sully
PENARTH
CF6 2XU

CAROLINE RNR
HMS CAROLINE
BFPO 806

DALRIADA RNR
HMS DALRIADA (MOB)
Navy Buildings
Eldon Street
GREENOCK
PA16 7SL

EAGLET RNR
HMS EAGLET
Princes Dock
LIVERPOOL
L3 0AA

FLYING FOX RNR
HMS FLYING FOX
Winterstoke Road
BRISTOL
BS3 2NS

FORWARD RNR
HMS FORWARD
Trafalgar House
10/20 Sampson Road North
BIRMINGHAM
B11 1BL

NORTHWOOD RNR
HMS NORTHWOOD
Brackenhill House
The Woods
NORTHWOOD
HA6 3EX

PRESIDENT RNR
HMS PRESIDENT
72 St Katherine's Way
LONDON
E1 9UQ

SCOTIA RNR
HMS SCOTIA
Pitreavie
DUNFERMLINE
KY11 5QE

SHERWOOD RNR
HMS SHERWOOD
Chalfont Drive
NOTTINGHAM
NG8 3LT

VIVID RNR
HMS VIVID
Mount Wise
DEVONPORT
PL1 4JH

ROYAL MARINE ESTABLISHMENTS AND COMMANDO UNITS

CDO LOG REGT RM
Commando Logistic Regiment
Royal Marines
Royal Marine Barracks
Chivenor
BARNSTABLE
Devon
E X31 4AZ
LT COL . . . . RM   N E Pounds

HQ 3 CDO BDE RM
RM Barracks
Stonehouse
PLYMOUTH
Devon
P L1 3QS
BRIG . . . . . RM   A A Milton OBE

WKSP SQN DET
Workshop Squadron Detachment
RM CONDOR
ARBROATH
Angus
SCOTLAND
DD11 3SJ

40 CDO RM
Norton Manor Camp
TAUNTON
Somerset
TA2 6PF
LT COL . . . . . RM   I R Gardiner

42 CDO RM
Bickleigh Barracks
Shaugh Prior
nr PLYMOUTH
Devon
PL6 7AJ
LT COL . . . . . RM   R G T Lane OBE

45 CDO RM
RM CONDOR
ARBROATH
Angus
Scotland
DD1 1 3SJ
LT COL . . . . . RM   R A Fry MBE

539 ASLT SQN RM
539 ASRM
RM Turnchapel
Barton Road
Turnchapel
PLYMOUTH
PL9 9XD
MAJ . . . . . . RM   S R Wilson

ROYAL MARINE RESERVE UNITS

RMR BRISTOL
Dorset House
Litfield Place
BRISTOL
BS8 3NA

RMR LONDON
2 Old Jamaica Place
Bermondsey
LONDON
SE16 4AN

RMR MERSEYSIDE
South Atlantic Building
Vittoria Dock
BIRKENHEAD
Merseyside
L41 1EQ

RMR SCOTLAND
37-51 Birkmyre Road
Govan
GLASGOW
G51 3JH

RMR TYNE
Anzio House
Quayside
NEWCASTLE UPON TYNE
NE6 1BU

ROYAL FLEET AUXILIARY SERVICE

ARGUS, Aviation Training Ship
BAYLEAF, Auxiliary Oiler Transport
BLACK ROVER, Auxiliary Oiler Light
BRAMBLELEAF, Auxiliary Oiler Transport
DILIGENCE, Forward Repair Ship
FORT AUSTIN, Armaments/Food
FORT GRANGE, Armaments/Food
FORT VICTORIA, Auxiliary Oiler Replenisher
FORT GEORGE, Auxiliary Oiler Replenisher
GOLD ROVER, Auxiliary Oiler Light
GREY ROVER, Auxiliary Oiler Light

OAKLEAF, Auxiliary Oiler Transport
OLNA, Auxiliary Oiler
OLWEN, Auxiliary Oiler
ORANGELEAF, Auxiliary Oiler Transport
RESOURCE, Armaments/Food
SIR BEDIVERE, Landing Ship Logistics
SIR GALAHAD, Landing Ship Logistics
SIR GERAINT, Landing Ship Logistics
SIR PERCIVALE, Landing Ship Logistics
SIR TRISTRAM, Landing Ship Logistics

DIRECTOR GENERAL OF SUPPLIES AND TRANSPORT (NAVY)

BEITH (RN Armament Depot)
Ayrshire
KA15 1JT

CAMPBELTOWN (Nato Pol Depot) (Administered by
Superintendent Rosyth)
Argyll
PA28 6RD

COPENACRE (RN Store Depot)
Hawthorn
Wilts
SN13 0PW

COULPORT (RN Armament Depot)
PO Box 1
Cove
Helesburgh
Dubartonshire
G84 0PD

DST(W)
HM Naval Base
Devonport
PL1 4SR

DEAN HILL (RN Armament Depot) (Under the
charge of Superintendent Gosport)
Salisbury
Wilts
SP5 1EY

EAGLESCLIFFE (RN Store Depot)
Stockton-on-Tees
Cleveland
TS16 0PH

EXETER (RN Store Depot)
  (Under the charge of Superintendent (NS) Devonport)
Topsham
Exeter
Devon

DST(N)
SSTO Link Building
Clyde Submarine Base
Faslane
G84 8HL

GLEN DOUGLAS (NATO Ammunition Depot)
PO Box 1
Arrochar
Dunbartonshire
G83 7BA

Gosport (RN Armament Depot)
Hants
PO13 0AH

Loch Ewe (NATO POL DEPOT)
Administered by Superintendent Rosyth)
Aultbea
Achnasheen
Ross-shire
IV22 2HU

LOCH STRIVEN (NATO, POL Depot)
(Administered by Superintendent Rosyth
Toward
Argyll
PA23 7UL

PORTLAND (HM Naval Base)
Officer in Charge
HM Naval Base
Portland
Dorset
DT5 1BQ

DST(S)
HM Naval Base
Portsmouth
Hants
PO1 3LU

Superintendent (NS)
HM Naval Base
Rosyth
Fife
KY11 2XU

Singapore (OFD Senko)
RNSTO Singapore
NP1022
BFPO 489
London

KEY ADDRESSES

COMBINED CADET FORCE

Director of Naval Reserves
Victory Building
HM Naval Base
Portsmouth
Hants
PO1 3LS

COMMITTEES

UNITED KINGDOM COMMANDERS IN CHIEF COMMITTEES (UKCICC)

Erskine Barracks
Wilton
Salisbury
Wiltshire.
SP2 0AG
(01722-6222)

COMMONWEALTH LIAISON OFFICES

AUSTRALIA
Australia House
Strand
London.
WC2B 4LA
(0171-379-4334)

BANGLADESH
28 Queens Gate
London.
SW7 5JA
(0171-584-0081/4 & 0171-589-4842/4)

CANADA
1 Grosvenor Square
London.
W1X 0AB
(0171-629 9492)

GHANA
13 Belgrave Square
London.
SW1X 8PR
(0171-235-4142)

INDIA
India House
Aldwych
London.
WC2B 4NA
(0171-836-8484)

KENYA
24/25 New Bond Street
London.
W1Y 9HD
(0171-636 2371/5)

MALAYSIA
45 Belgrave Square
London.
SW1X 8QT
(0171-235 8033)

NEW ZEALAND
New Zealand House
Haymarket
London.
SW1Y 4TQ
(0171-930 8422)

NIGERIA
Nigeria House
9 Northumberland Avenue
London
WC2N 5BX
(0171-839 1244)

DEFENCE RESEARCH AGENCIES

Haslar
Gosport
Hants
PO12 2AG
(01705-822351)

Holton Heath
Poole
Dorset
BH16 6JU
(01202-622711)

Portland
Dorset
DT5 2JS
(01305-820381)

(Includes Admiralty Compass Observatory)
Portsdown
Portsmouth
Hants
PO6 4AA
(01705-379411)

Queens Road
Teddington
Middlesex
TW11 0LN
(0181-977-3231)

(Maritime Division)
Warwick Road
West Drayton
Middlesex
UB7 9BZ
(01895 442204)

DIRECTOR QUALITY ASSURANCE

NORTH
Ministry of Defence (PE)
76 Newton Street
Manchester. M1 1FF
(0161-236-9681)

Deputy Naval Ship Production Overseer
Sheffield
(01742-28671)

WEST
Ministry of Defence (PE)
Ladywood House
45/46 Stephenson Street
Birmingham.
B2 4DY
(0121-632-4311)

EAST
Ministry of Defence
Empress State Building
London.
SW6 1TR
(0171-385-1244)

SOUTH
Ministry of Defence (PE)
Aquila
Golf Road
Bromley
Kent.
BR1 2JB
(0181-467-2600)

EDUCATIONAL ESTABLISHMENTS

ROYAL NAVAL STAFF COLLEGE
Greenwich
London
SE10 9NN
(0181-858-2154

THE ROYAL COLLEGE OF DEFENCE STUDIES
Seaford House
37 Belgrave Square
London
SW1 X8NS
(0171-235 1091)

THE JOINT SERVICE DEFENCE COLLEGE
Greenwich
London
SE10 9NN
(0181-858-2154

BRITANNIA ROYAL NAVAL COLLEGE
Dartmouth
Devon.
TQ6 0HJ
(01803-832141)

ROYAL NAVAL ENGINEERING COLLEGE
Manadon
Plymouth
Devon
PL5 3AQ
(01752-553740)

HM NAVAL BASES

HM NAVAL BASE PORTSMOUTH
Portsmouth
Hants
PO1 3LT

HM NAVAL BASE DEVONPORT
Plymouth
Devon
PL1 4JH

HM NAVAL BASE ROSYTH
Fife
KY11 2YA

HM NAVAL BASE PORTLAND
Dorset
DT5 1BJ

DIRECTORATE OF MARINE
SERVICES (NAVAL)

Chief Executive (Marine Services)
Ministry of Defence
Block E,
Foxhill,
BATH
BA1 5AB
(01225 -88565)

PORTSMOUTH
Marine Services Manager
Kings Stairs
HM Naval Base
PORTSMOUTH
PO1 3LT
(01705 - 822351)

DEVONPORT
Marine Services Manager
Building MO 19
Morice Yard
HM Naval Base
DEVONPORT
PL1 4SG
(01752 -553740)

PEMBROKE DOCK
Marine Services Manager
HM Mooring and Marine
Salvage Depot
Pembroke Dock
SA72 6TB
(01646-683235)

NORTH
Marine Services Manager
Great Harbour
Greenock
PA15 2AR
(01475 -787912)

Officer -in-Charge
NATO Mooring and Support Depot
Fairlie
Ayrshire
KA29 OAS
(01475 - 568411)

Master Ashore
British Underwater Test and
Evaluation Centre
Kyle of Lochalsh
Ross-shire
IV40 8AJ
(01599 -534262)

ROSYTH
Marine Services Manager
HM Naval Base
Rosyth
KY11 2XZ
(01383 -412121)

MEDICAL SERVICES

OPERATIONAL MEDICAL SERVICES
Royal William Yard
Plymouth
Devon
PL1 3RP

Royal Naval Hospital
Haslar
Gosport
Hants
PO12 2AA

Royal Naval Hospital Derriford Hospital Unit
Derriford Hospital
Plymouth
Devon
PL6 8DH

Royal Naval Hospital
Gibraltar
BFPO 52

NAVAL MEDICINE AND TRAINING, DEAN OF NAVAL MEDICINE AND DEFENCE RADIOLOGICAL PROTECTION SERVICE

Institute of Naval Medicine
Alverstoke
Gosport
Hants
PO12 2DL

MINISTRY OF DEFENCE POLICE HEADQUARTERS

Ministry of Defence
Empress State Building
London
SW6 1TR
0171-385-1244

NAVY, ARMY AND AIR FORCE INSTITUTES

NAAFI HQ
London Road
Amesbury
Wiltshire
SP4 7EN
0198 627000

NATO HEADQUARTERS-MILITARY COMMITTEE (UKMILREP)

UKMILREP
NATO Headquarters

BFPO49

SUPREME ALLIED COMMANDER ATLANTIC(SACLANT)

HEADQUARTERS,ALLIED COMMAND ATLANTIC
(SACLANT)
Naval Party 1964
(Saclant)
BFPO Ships

ISLAND COMMANDER BERMUDA
HQ ISCOMBERMUDA
HMS Malabar
BFPO 162

IBERIAN ATLANTIC COMMAND (CINCIBERLANT)
NATO HQ of CINCIBERLANT
BFPO 6

CENTRAL SUB-AREA (CENTLANT)
Mountwise
Plymouth
Devon

NORTHERN SUB-AREA (NORLANT)
MHQ
Pitreavie
Dunfermline
Fife

SUBMARINE FORCES EASTERN ATLANTIC
(SUBEASTLANT)
Eastbury Park
Northwood
Middlesex
HA6 3HP

ANTI-SUBMARINE WARFARE STRIKING FORCE
Fort Southwick
Fareham
Hants
PO17 6AR

SACLANT UNDERSEA RESEARCH CENTRE
Viale San Bartolomeo 400
I-19026 San Bartolomeo (SP)
Italy

SUPREME ALLIED COMMANDER EUROPE (SACEUR)

SUPREME HEADQUARTERS ALLIED POWERS
EUROPE (SHAPE)
BFPO 26

NATO SCHOOL (SHAPE)
Oberammergau
Box 2003
BFPO 105

ALLIED FORCES SOUTHERN EUROPE (AF SOUTH)
HQ Allied Forces Southern Europe
BFPO 8

COMSTRIKFORSOUTH
COMSUBMED
U.K. NATIONAL SUPPORT UNIT HQ AFSOUTH

ALLIED NAVAL FORCES SOUTHERN EUROPE
(NAVSOUTH)
HQ COMNAVSOUTH
BFPO 8

NAVAL COMMAND SOUTH REPRESENTATIVE,IZMIR
(NAVSOUTHREP IZMIR)
Office of COMNAVSOUTHREP
HQ 6 ATAF
Sirinyer
Izmir
Turkey

NORTH-EAST MEDITERRANEAN (MEDNOREAST)
C/O British Embassy
Ankara
Turkey

EASTERN MEDITERRANEAN (MEDEAST)
Papagos Camp
Holargos
Athens
Greece

FRENCH COMMANDER-IN-CHIEF MEDITERRANEAN
(CECMED)
Prefecture Maritime
83800 Toulon Naval
France

CENTRAL MEDITERRANEAN (MEDCENT)
BFPO 8

GIBRALTAR MEDITERRANEAN (GIBMED)
BFPO 163

ALLIED FORCES CENTRAL EUROPE (AFCENT)
BPFO 28

ALLIED FORCES NORTHERN EUROPE (AFNORTH)
HQ AF NORTH
BFPO 50

HQ ALLIED FORCES BALTIC APPROACHES
(HQ NAVBALTAP)

(a) (BFPO) Naval Party 1004
BFPO Ships

(b) (Danish) 7470 Karup
Jutland
Denmark

HQ ALLIED LAND FORCES SCHLESWIG-HOLSTEIN
AND JUTLAND (HQ LANDJUT)

(a) (BFPO) HQ LANDJUT
BFPO 27

(b) (Germany) Post Box 921
Rendsburgh
Germany

ALLIED COMMANDER-IN-CHIEF CHANNEL AND EASTERN ATLANTIC AREA (CINCHAN AND CINCEASTLANT)

ALLIED COMMAND CHANNEL AND EASTERN
ATLANTIC AREA (ACCHAN) AND (EASTLANT)
Eastbury Park
Northwood
Middlesex
HA6 3HP

NORE SUB-AREA CHANNEL AND NORTH ATLANTIC
AREA (NORECHAN) AND (NORLANT)
MHQ
Pitreavie
Dunfermline
Fife

PLYMOUTH SUB-AREA CHANNEL AND CENTRAL
ATLANTIC AREA (PLYMCHAN) AND (CENTLANT)
M.H.Q.
Plymouth
Devon

NAVAL PERSONAL AND FAMILY SERVICES

Area Office Family Services (Eastern)
HMS Nelson
Portsmouth
Hants
PO1 3HH

Area Office Family Services (Western)
HMS Drake
Plymouth
Devon
PL2 2BJ

Area Office Family Service (Northern)
HMS Cochrane
Rosyth
Fife
KY11 2XT

NAVAL REGIONAL OFFICES

SCOTLAND & NORTHERN IRELAND REGIONS

Maritime HQ
Pitreavie
Dunfermline
KY11 5QE
(01383-412161 Ext. 4297)

Sub-Office
Naval Regional Office
Kentigern House
65 Brown Street
Glasgow
G2 8EX
(0141-224- 059)

NORTHERN ENGLAND REGION

The Port of Liverpool Building
Pier Head
Liverpool
L3 1BY
(0151-236-8056)

Sub-Office
Naval Regional Office
HMS Calliope
South Shore Road
Gateshead
Tyne and Wear
NE8 2BE
(0191-477-8607)

WALES & WESTERN REGIONS

HMS FLYING FOX
Winterstoke Road
Bristol
BS3 2NS
(01272-530-996)

EASTERN ENGLAND REGION

HMS PRESIDENT
72 St Katherines Way
London
E1 9UO
(0171-480-7219)

ORDNANCE BOARD

Empress State Building
Lillie Road
London
SW6 1TR
(0171-385-1244)

REGULAR FORCES EMPLOYMENT ASSOCIATION

(NATIONAL ASSOCIATION FOR EMPLOYMENT OF REGULAR SAILORS SOLDIERS AND AIRMEN)
25 Bloomsbury Square
London
WC1A 2LN
(0171-637 3918)

ABERDEEN
46A Union Street
Aberdeen
AB1 1BD

BEDFORD
28 Bedford Road
Kempston
Beds.
MK42 8AJ

BELFAST
Northern Ireland War Memorial Building
5 Waring Street
Belfast
BT1 2DW

BIRMINGHAM
Room 2A
City Gate
12 Digbeth
Birmingham
BS 6BH

BRIGHTON
5 Air Street
Brighton
BN1 3FB

BRISTOL
Esso Building
35 Colston Avenue
Bristol
BS1 4TY

BURY ST. EDMUNDS
31 Abbeygate Street
Bury St. Edmunds
IP33 1LW

CARDIFF
Maindy Barracks
Cardiff
CF4 3YE

CARLISLE
40 Aglionby Street
Carlisle
CA1 1JP

CHATHAM
7 Railway Street
Chatham
ME4 4HU

CHELMSFORD
T.A.V.R. Centre
Victoria Road South
Chelmsford
CM1 1LN

CHELTENHAM
3rd Floor
Belgrave House
Imperial Square
Cheltenham
Glos.
GL50 1QB

CHESTER
Room 4
Napier House
The Castle
Chester
CH1 2DN

DARLINGTON
Office 119
Imperial Centre
Grange Road
Darlington
DL1 5QN

DERBY
19/20 Corn Market
Derby
DE1 1QH

DUNDEE
68 Murraygate
Dundee
DD1 2BB

EDINBURGH
New Haig House
Logie
Green Road
Edinburgh
EH7 4HQ

EXETER
Higher Barracks
Howell Road
Exeter
EX4 4NB

GLASGOW
20 Renfrew Street
Glasgow
G2 3BW

HULL
Wenlock Barracks
Anlaby Road
HULL
HU3 6PB

LEEDS
West Bar Chambers
38A Boar Lane
Leeds
LS1 5DB

LINCOLN
9 West Parade
Lincoln
LN1 1NL

LIVERPOOL
Room 74
'D' Building
The Temple
24 Dale Street
Liverpool
L2 5RU

LONDON (CENTRAL, S.W., S.E. and EAST)
25 Bloomsbury Square
London
WC1A 2LN

(NORTH, WEST and N.W.)
Room 5E
Government Building
Bromyard Avenue
London
W3 7HZ

MANCHESTER
T.A.V.R. Centre
Belle Vue Street
Manchester
M12 5PW

NEWCASTLE-ON-TYNE
MEA House
Ellison Place
Newcastle-on-Tyne
NE1 8XS

NORTHAMPTON
T.A. Centre
Clare Street
Northampton
NN1 3J

NORWICH
Britannia Barracks
Norwich
NR1 4HJ

NOTTINGHAM
59A Derby Road
Nottingham
NG1 5BA

PLYMOUTH
The Naval Recreation Ground
Saltash Road
Keyham
Plymouth
PL2 1QL

PORTSMOUTH
2B Tipner Road
Stamshaw
Portsmouth
PO2 8QS

PRESTON
17 Winckley Square
Preston
PR1 3JJ

READING
Watlington House
Watlington Street
Reading
RG1 4RJ

SALISBURY
Avon House
Avon Approach
Salisbury
SP1 3SN

SHEFFIELD
41 Church Street
Sheffield
S1 2GL

SHREWSBURY
1 Dogpole
Shrewsbury
SY1 1EN

STOKE-ON-TRENT
Room 8
Bethesda Buildings
Bethesda Street
Hanley
Stoke-on-Trent
ST1 3DE

SWANSEA
T.A.Centre
The Grange
West Cross
Swansea
SA3 5LB

WOLVERHAMPTON
34 Berry Street
Wolverhampton
WV1 1HA

RESEARCH AND DEVELOPMENT ESTABLISHMENTS PRINCIPAL RESEARCH ESTABLISHMENTS

AEROPLANE AND ARMAMENT EXPERIMENTAL ESTABLISHMENT
Boscombe Down
Salisbury
Wilts.
SP4 0JF
(01980-623331)

ATOMIC WEAPONS RESEARCH ESTABLISHMENT
Aldermaston
Reading
Berkshire
RG7 4PR
(01734-814111)

CHEMICAL AND BIOLOGICAL DEFENCE ESTABLISHMENT
Porton Down
Salisbury
Wilts
SP4 0JQ
(01980-613000)

DOCKYARD LABORATORY
HM Naval Base
Portsmouth
Hants

HM Naval Base
Portland
Dorset

EXPERIMENTAL DIVING UNIT
HMS Nelson (Gunwharf)
Portsmouth
Hants

Glen Fruin
Helensburgh
Dunbartonshire

Haslar
Gosport
Hants

Douglas Pier
Loch Goil
Argyl

MILITARY VEHICLES AND ENGINEERING ESTABLISHMENT
Chobham Lane
Chertsey
Surrey
KT16 0EE
(01990-23366)

NAVAL AIRCRAFT MATERIALS LABORATORY
Fleetlands
Gosport
Hants

DEFENCE RESEARCH AGENCIES
Bedford
Bedfordshire
MK41 6AE
(01234 270077)

Farnborough
Hants
GU14 6TD
(01252-24461)

Pyestock
Farnborough
Hants
GU14 0LS
(01252-44411)

ROYAL ARMAMENTS RESEARCH AND DEVELOPMENT ESTABLISHMENT

Halstead
Sevenoaks
Kent
TN14 7BP
(01959-32222)

ROYAL SIGNALS AND RADAR ESTABLISHMENT

Malvern
Worcestershire
WR14 3PS
(016845-2733)

VULCAN NAVAL REACTOR TEST ESTABLISHMENT

Dounreay
Thurso
Caithness
Scotland

RN AIRCRAFT YARDS

Fleetlands
Gosport
Hants
PO13 0AW
(01705-22351)

Wroughton
Swindon
Wilts
SN4 0QY
(01793-812291)

RN Aircraft Workshop
Almondbank
Perth
(01738 -83301)

RN, RM, QARNNS, REGIONAL HEADQUARTERS AND CAREERS INFORMATION OFFICES

NORTH REGION

Headquarters
Orchardhead
Castle Road
Rosyth
KY11 2AS
(01383-419031)

63 Belmont Street
Aberdeen
AB1 1JS
(01224-639999)

Palace Barracks
Belfast
BT18 9RA
(01232-427040)

9 - 13 Scotch Street
Carlisle
CA3 8QD
(01228-23958)

29/31 Bank Street
Dundee
DD1 1RW
(01382-27198)

49 Lothian Road
Edinburgh
EH1 2DN
(0131-229-4268/9)

Charlotte House
78 Queen Street
Glasgow
G1 3DN
(0141-221-6110/6119)

21 Raby Road
Hartlepool
TS24 8AX
(01429-274040)

3 Bridge Street
Inverness
IV1 1HG
(01463-233668)

Gunner House
Neville Street
Newcastle upon Tyne
NE1 5HD
(0191-2327048)

CENTRAL REGION
Headquarters
Ladywood House
45/46 Stephenson Street
Birmingham
B2 4DY
(0121-631-609/3/4/5)

46 The Pallasades
Birmingham
B2 4XD
(0121-633-4995/8150/3)

8th Floor
Southgate House
Wood Street
Cardiff
CF1 1GR

1st Floor
Broadgate House
Upper Precinct
Coventry
CV1 1NU
(01203-226513)

Graeme House
Derby Square
Liverpool
L2 7SD
(0151-227-1764)

Townbury House
Blackfriars Street
Salford
Manchester
M3 5AF
(0161-835-2923)

83A Fishergate
Preston
PR1 2NJ
(01772-555675)

7/8 St Mary's Street
Shrewsbury
SY1 1EB
(01743-232541)

36/38 Old Hall Street
Hanley
Stoke
ST1 3ZY
(01782-214688)

17/19 Castle Street
Swansea
SA1 1TE
(01792-642516/654208)

44 Forgate Street
Worcester
WR1 1EE
(01905-723677)

21 Rhosddu Road
Wrexham
LL11 1NF
(01978-263334)

35/36 Castlefields
Main Centre
Derby
DE1 2PE
(01332-48120)

Town Centre House
82/85 Prospect Street
Hull
HU2 8PF
(01482-25902)

36 Wellington Street
Leeds
LS1 2DL
(01532-458195)

Rutland Centre
Yeoman Street
Leicester
LE1 1UT
(01533-620284)

Sibthorpe House
350/352 High Street
Lincoln
LN5 7BN
(01522-525661)

70 Milton Street
Victoria Centre
Nottingham
NG1 3QX
(01602-419503)

Castle Market
Sheffield
S1 1FZ
(01742-721476)

SOUTH REGION
Esso Buildings
35 Colston Avenue
Bristol
BS1 4TY
(01272-260233)

Georgian House
Trinity Street
Dorchester
DT1 1UD
(01305-264664)

Fountain House
Western Way
Exeter
EX1 2DQ
(01392-74040)

105 Mayflower Street
Plymouth
PL1 1SD
(01752-266487)

41 Arundel Street
Portsmouth
P01 1ND
(01705-826536)

151 High Street
Southampton
SO9 4PB
(01703-223464)

18 Milton Road
Swindon
SN1 5JN
(01793-534750)

Eagle Star House
74/75 Lemon Street
Truro
TR1 2NP
(01872-73788)

9 Lee Road
Blackheath
London
SE3 9RQ
(0181-852-7988)

83 Queens Road
Brighton
BN1 3XE
(01273-325386)

17 St Peter's Street
Canterbury
CT1 2BG
(01227-760738)

1 Dock Road
Chatham
ME4 4JR
(01634-826206)

1-3 Dorset House
Duke Street
Chelmsford
CM1 1HS
(01245-355134)

18 Park Street
Croydon
CR0 1YE
(0181-688-0489)

20 Chertsey Street
Guildford
GU1 4HF
(01483-571465)

180A Cranbrook Road
Ilford
IF1 4LX
(0181-518-4565)

58 Princes Street
Ipswich
IP1 1BJ
(01473-254450)

453/454 Strand
London
WC2R 0RG
(0171-839-4643)

Dunstable House
Dunstable Road
Luton
LU1 1EA
(01582-21501)

13 Derngate
Northampton
NN1 1TY
(01604-37518)

45 Prince of Wales Road
Norwich
NR1 1BL
(01603-620033)

35 St Giles
Oxford
OX1 3LJ
(01865-53431)

23 Hereward Centre
Peterborough
PE1 1TB
(01733-68833)

71/73 Market Street
Watford
WD1 7AR
(01923-244055/223786)

SENIOR CAREERS LIAISON OFFICES
EAST
1A Iverna Gardens
Kensington
London
W8 6TN
(0171-938-4646)

WEST
HMS Flying Fox
Winterstoke Road
Bristol
BS3 2NS
(01272-635251)

CENTRAL
46 The Pallasades
Birmingham
B2 4XD
(0121-643-8670)

NORTH
Orchardhead
Castle Road
Rosyth
KY11 2AS
(01383-414224)

ROYAL NAVAL FILM CORPORATION

Registered Office
HM Naval Base (PP23)
PORTSMOUTH PO1 3LL

SEA CADET CORPS

HEADQUARTERS
202 Lambeth Road
London
SE1 7JF
(0171-928-8978)

NORTHERN AREA
HMS Cochrane Annexe
Rosyth
Fife
KY11 2XT
(013834-16300)

NORTH WEST AREA
HMS Eaglet
Princes Dock
Liverpool
L3 0AA
(0151-236-7377)

SOUTH WEST AREA
Ministry of Defence
Room 88
A Block
Ensleigh
Bath
Avon
BA1 5AD
(01225-67748/67572)

EASTERN AREA
RAF Swinderby
Lincoln
LN6 9QE
(0152-286-477)

LONDON AREA
Ministry of Defence
Room 1928
Empress State Building
Lillie Road
London
SW6 1TR
(0171-385-1244 Ext 3164/65/66)

SOUTHERN AREA
HMS Nelson
Portsmouth
Hants
PO1 3HH
(01705-822351 Ext 24263)

SHIPPING POLICY DIVISION (SEA TRANSPORT)

Department of Transport
2 Marsham Street
London
SW1P 3EB

SHIPYARD OVERSEEING SERVICE

CLYDE
c/o Yarrow Shipbuilders Ltd.
Glasgow
(0141-954-9241)

SOUTHAMPTON
c/o Vosper Thornycroft (UK) Ltd.
Victoria Road
Woolston
Southampton
SO9 5GR
(01703-444853)

BARROW
c/o Vickers Shipbuilding & Engineering Ltd.
Barrow-in-Furness
(01229-825601)

OFFICERS OF THE ACTIVE LIST OF THE ROYAL NAVAL RESERVE, ROYAL MARINES RESERVE, QUEEN ALEXANDRA'S ROYAL NAVAL NURSING RESERVE, SEA CADET CORPS AND COMBINED CADET FORCE

ROYAL NAVAL RESERVE

Name	Rank	Branch	Unit	Seniority
A				
Abrahams, Louise Marie	ASl		Flying Fox	19.11.94
Ackland, Simon Robert	Slt	MW	Cambria	10.12.88
Adams, A C, RD	Cdr	AW	President	30.09.89
Ainsworth, Jeffery	Lt	AIR	RNR Air Br VI	16.11.85
Alcock, Charles Edward Hayes	Lt	SEA	President	01.09.90
Alcock, David John, RD	Lt Cdr	MWHQ	King Alfred	18.02.87
Alcock, Maria Luisa	Slt	INTR	Ferret (RNR)	14.01.91
Allan, Richard Michael	Lt	SEA	Flying Fox	20.05.94
Allan, William Alexander, RD	Lt Cdr	HQ	Scotia	02.09.88
Allen, James Ian	Lt	MWHQ	Caroline	16.05.89
Anders, Richard	Lt Cdr	AIR	RNR Air Br VI	23.06.87
Anderson, John Christopher	Slt	MW	President	07.12.90
Anderson, Kerry McGowan, BSC	Lt	HQ	Caroline	10.02.90
Andrews, Mark David	ASl		Flying Fox	29.02.92
Andriessen, Kevin John	Lt	NCS	Vivid	17.05.92
Arthurs, Cedric James, RD, JP	Cdr	NA	Eaglet	30.09.95
Ashpole, Richard David	Sg Ltcdr		Calliope	01.08.90
Aspinell, Charles Jonathan, RD	Lt Cdr	NCS	King Alfred	20.09.87
Aspinell, Pamela Ann	Lt	Q	King Alfred	01.03.87
Aston, Dora Ann	ASl		King Alfred	19.03.94
Aston, Susan Helen	Lt	Q	Forward	27.02.87
Atkin, Keith	Lt Cdr	AIR	RNR Air Br VI	01.10.80
Austin, David Timothy	Lt	SEA	King Alfred	09.06.92
Austin, Jane	Lt	NCS	Vivid	15.09.88
Austin, Kevin	Lt	AW	Sherwood	18.03.89
Avery, Philip	Lt	AIR	RNR Air Br VI	29.08.94
Avis, Robert Graeme, RD	Lt Cdr	AW	King Alfred	10.12.87
Awenat, William	Lt Cdr	AIR	RNR Air Br VI	31.03.95
B				
Babbington, Katharine Louise	ASl		King Alfred	17.12.93

Name	Rank	Branch	Unit	Seniority
Baird, Andrew Wilson	Lt	HQ	Caroline	07.08.90
Baird, Elaine Harper	Lt	Q	King Alfred	19.07.87
Baker, John	Lt Cdr	AIR	RNR Air Br VI	01.09.83
Baker, Kevin James	Lt Cdr	NCS	President	31.03.93
Baker, Nicholas	Lt Cdr	AIR	RNR Air Br VI	18.12.91
Baker, Peter Alan	Lt Cdr	NCS	President	31.03.94
Baldwin, Brian	Lt Cdr	AIR	RNR Air Br VI	01.09.85
Balston, Carole Elizabeth Madeleine	Lt	INTR	Ferret (RNR)	10.04.88
Bancroft, David Gideon	Psl	AW	Calliope	19.11.94
Bankhead, Maurice	Lt Cdr	NCS	Caroline	31.03.95
Barclay, Neil Howard	Palt	AW	Vivid	18.09.93
Barfield, Kevin Lloyd	Lt	COMM	Forward	09.04.88
Barnwell, Andrew	Lt Cdr	AIR	RNR Air Br VI	11.11.90
Barrett, William	Lt Cdr	AIR	RNR Air Br VI	17.03.93
Barton, Christopher James, RD	Lt Cdr	HQ	Cambria	30.09.87
Bassett, Nigel Peter	Lt	AW	Flying Fox	14.11.86
Bassett, Stephen Charles, RD	Lt Cdr	SM	Northwood	15.08.92
Bathgate, Charles	Lt	AW	Scotia	12.11.87
Baughan, Pj(Philip John), RD	Lt Cdr	HQ	Sherwood	01.11.89
Baxter, Ross John	Lt	NCS	Sherwood	01.09.91
Bean, Christopher	Lt Cdr	AIR	RNR Air Br VI	01.10.89
Beattie, Jane Elizabeth	Lt Cdr	Q	Northwood	31.03.93
Beaumont, Andrew John	Lt	MWHQ	Eaglet	31.07.95
Becket, Noel Stephen	Lt	AW	King Alfred	14.10.88
Beech, Eric Edward	Lt	DIS	Ferret (RNR)	03.06.87
Beedall, Richard Anthony	Lt	HQ	Sherwood	24.03.95
Belfield, David John, RD	Cdr	HQ	King Alfred	30.09.94
Bell, Andrew Robert	Lt	SEA	King Alfred	02.10.90
Bell, Patrick Martin, RD*	Lt Cdr	AW	Eaglet	01.01.80
Benn, Peter Quentin	Slt	MW	Northwood	17.07.92
Bennett, Nicholas James, MBE	Lt Cdr	PA	Vivid	19.03.88
Bennett, Simon Patrick, RD	Lt Cdr	AW	Flying Fox	22.06.92
Bereznyckyj, Susan Dorothy	Lt Cdr	Q	Sherwood	31.03.94
Bernard, David Maurice, RD	Cdr	AWNIS	Vivid	30.09.84
Berry, Ian Graham	Lt	MWHQ	Scotia	12.09.88
Bevins, Philip	Lt	AIR	RNR Air Br VI	01.11.86
Bewley, Geoffrey	Lt	MWHQ	King Alfred	15.11.88
Bicknell, Richard Anthony	ALt	MW	Eaglet	14.07.90
Biggerstaff, Adam Graham, RD	Lt Cdr	HQ	Dalriada	03.04.85
Biggs, Nigel	Lt	SEA	President	31.07.95
Birch, Anthony	Lt	AIR	RNR Air Br VI	03.09.87
Bird, Stephen Peter Glover	Sg Ltcdr		Scotia	01.08.90
Bishop, Jonathan	Lt	AIR	RNR Air Br VI	27.12.86
Black, Lorna Elizabeth, BSC	Lt	COMM	Scotia	20.07.88
Black, Simon Mitchell	Lt Cdr	HQ	Scotia	30.06.83
Blacker, Christopher William	ALt	AW	King Alfred	11.05.91
Bloy, Michael William	Lt	COMM	Northwood	20.07.88
Bloy, Rosemary Claire	Lt	AWNIS	Northwood	12.11.89
Blyth, Anne Scotland	Sg Ltcdr		Dalriada	14.08.83
Blythe, Wendy Elizabeth	Slt	LOGS	King Alfred	11.03.90
Boal, Michael Alexander	Slt	MW	Caroline	25.09.91
Bonning, Michael John	Lt	SEA	Eaglet	17.07.88
Boughton, John, QGM	Lt Cdr	AIR	RNR Air Br VI	07.04.92
Boulton, Jeremy Charles	Lt	SM	President	14.12.90
Bourne, Robin John	Lt Cdr	PA	Northwood	08.06.91
Bowey, Russell	Lt Cdr	AIR	RNR Air Br VI	31.03.93
Bowles, William Francis	Lt	MW	Scotia	06.10.88
Bown, Anthony Mark	Lt Cdr	HQ	Cambria	08.03.91
Boyd, Edward Russell	Slt	AWNIS	King Alfred	12.12.90
Boyd, Frances Ann, RD	Cdr	NCS	Dalriada	01.10.94
Boyden, Tobert	Lt	AIR	RNR Air Br VI	23.03.88

Name	Rank	Branch	Unit	Seniority
Brabner, Susan Ann	Lt Cdr	DIS	Northwood	31.03.94
Bradford, Christine Mary Patricia	Lt Cdr	NCS	Eaglet	31.03.93
Bradford, Nigel Stuart	Lt	SM	Eaglet	18.12.87
Bradshaw, Francis John C, LVO	Cdr	MWHQ	Eaglet	01.02.82
Braine, David	Lt	AIR	RNR Air Br VI	12.12.86
Brampton, Susan	Slt	Q	President	14.05.90
Branyan, Lawrence Ode	Lt	SEA	Eaglet	06.09.89
Brayfield, Rosalind Marion	Lt Cdr	PA	Northwood	26.12.84
Breyley, Nigel	Lt	AIR	RNR Air Br VI	16.05.87
Bridgen, Andrew Urquhart	Lt	INTR	Ferret (RNR)	23.07.92
Bridges, Stuart McGow	Lt	LOGS	Scotia	04.06.90
Broadhurst, Audrey	ASI		Northwood	15.11.92
Brockie, Brian	ALt Cdr	MS	Scotia	01.03.95
Bromley, Debra Julie	Lt	Q	Forward	06.07.87
Brookes, Charles Richard, RD	Lt Cdr	NCS	President	03.04.89
Brooks, Christopher Scott	Lt Cdr	PA	President	04.11.87
Brooks, William George	Cdr	MWHQ	Vivid	30.09.90
Brown, Andrew	Lt Cdr	AIR	RNR Air Br VI	01.10.90
Brown, Charles David	Lt	X	U/A	
Brown, Edwin	Lt Cdr	AIR	RNR Air Br VI	24.09.92
Brown, John Erskine	Lt	AWNIS	Forward	01.10.88
Brown, Katherine Jane	Lt Cdr	PA	Northwood	12.03.86
Brown, Karl	Lt	AIR	RNR Air Br VI	24.06.88
Brown, Malcolm Stuart, RD	Lt Cdr	AW	Scotia	02.07.84
Brown, Timothy	Lt Cdr	AIR	RNR Air Br VI	19.03.93
Bryant, Ian	Lt Cdr	AIR	RNR Air Br VI	01.10.91
Bryce, Fiona Lorraine Stirling	Slt	COMM	Scotia	24.02.90
Bryce, Richard Paul	Sg Ltcdr		Northwood	24.09.89
Bryson, Elizabeth Mary, RD*	Cdr	NA	Calliope	05.04.88
Buckley, Jonathan Mark	Slt	MW	Cambria	08.08.89
Bucknell, Aw(Alan), MBE	Lt Cdr	AIR	RNR Air Br VI	09.12.85
Bugler, Martin	Lt	AIR	RNR Air Br VI	12.07.88
Burne, Penelope Jane, RD	Lt Cdr	INTR	Ferret (RNR)	30.09.91
Burton, Grahame Anthony, RD*	Cdr	AW	Flying Fox	30.09.90
Burton-Hall, John Robert, RD*	Cdr	AW	King Alfred	30.06.78

C

Name	Rank	Branch	Unit	Seniority
Cade, Arnold Nigel	Sg Ltcdr		Vivid	10.05.80
Cambridge, Aaron Russell	Lt Cdr	PA	King Alfred	20.02.89
Cameron, Anne Louise	Lt	NCS	King Alfred	28.10.91
Campbell, Charles Lennox	Lt	HQ	Scotia	27.12.91
Campbell, William	Lt Cdr	AIR	RNR Air Br VI	01.04.92
Canham, Wendy Jacqueline	Lt	COMM	Sherwood	08.10.89
Cannock, Robert	Lt	HQ	Flying Fox	28.04.91
Carpenter, D A(David Iain), RD	Lt Cdr	PA	Scotia	05.06.85
Carr, Anthony Matthew	Lt	MW	Calliope	20.07.90
Carr, David Arthur, RD**	Capt	AW	King Alfred	30.09.88
Carslaw, D C H	Lt	LOGS	Dalriada	16.08.87
Carss, George Alexander	Sg Ltcdr		King Alfred	09.12.81
Carver, Andrew	Lt	AIR	RNR Air Br VI	01.05.88
Casey, Graham Peter	Lt	DIS	Ferret (RNR)	10.02.90
Casey, Neil	Lt	AIR	RNR Air Br VI	23.12.90
Caskie, Iain Neil	Lt Cdr	SM	Dalriada	16.05.92
Casson, Hilary Patricia	Lt	HQ	Vivid	08.02.89
Chadwick, Jillian	Lt	LOGS	Calliope	15.01.93
Chalmers, Amalia Lourdes, RD	Lt Cdr	MWHQ	Vivid	31.03.95
Chapman, Anthony	Lt	MW	President	31.07.95
Chapman, David Ralph	ALt	AW	Calliope	05.12.87
Chapman, Graham Philip	ALt	AW	President	14.11.92
Chapman, David Quentin	Lt Cdr	X	RNR Air Br VI	01.10.90
Charlwood, Rachel Diana	Slt	SEA	Vivid	03.10.93

Name	Rank	Branch	Unit	Seniority
Chatterton, Robert Martin	Lt Cdr	AW	President	31.03.95
Chauvelin, David Coulson Wyllie	Slt	MW	Scotia	13.07.90
Chiodetto, Sarah Emilia, BSC	Lt	NCS	Scotia	16.05.89
Chitty, David Austen	Lt	MWHQ	President	08.01.88
Church, Elizabeth Ann, RD	Lt	SM	President	16.11.88
Churchley, Richard	Lt	AIR	RNR Air Br VI	06.02.83
Clark, Suzanne	Lt	AIR	RNR Air Br VI	07.02.89
Clarke, Peter	Lt Cdr	AIR	RNR Air Br VI	01.10.90
Clarke, Roger Derek	Lt	NCS	Vivid	17.01.87
Clarke, Steven David	Lt	AW	Calliope	09.06.90
Clarke, William Stephen	Lt	MWHQ	Caroline	12.07.89
Cleary, Deidre Ann Miles	Lt	PA	President	31.01.91
Coad, Ivan Harry, RD	Lt Cdr	AW	Flying Fox	13.03.88
Cobbold, Andrew Reginald, MA	Lt	INTR	Ferret (RNR)	12.11.95
Cochrane-Dyet, Fiona Elizabeth	Lt	NCS	Scotia	17.11.88
Cockburn, Frank W	Lt Cdr	PA	Calliope	01.10.89
Cockcroft, John Paul	Lt	SM	King Alfred	14.09.89
Cohen, James Seymour Lionel, BSC, RD	Lt	HQ	President	09.02.88
Colborne, Raymond	Lt Cdr	AIR	RNR Air Br VI	01.01.89
Cole, James	Lt Cdr	AIR	RNR Air Br VI	01.09.84
Coleman, Colin	Lt Cdr	AIR	RNR Air Br VI	28.02.83
Colley, Derek Peter	Lt Cdr	AW	Forward	01.04.94
Collin, John	Lt Cdr	AWNIS	King Alfred	22.07.77
Collingwood, Nigel John, RD	Lt Cdr	AW	President	01.07.79
Collins, Steven Mark	Lt Cdr	SEA	Forward	31.03.94
Colquhoun-Flannery, William	Pasg Lt		King Alfred	02.04.90
Colton, Ian	Lt Cdr	AIR	RNR Air Br VI	22.11.92
Combe, Gerald Peter Donovan, RD	Lt Cdr	AW	King Alfred	02.06.80
Conway, Keith Alexander	Lt	MWHQ	Scotia	21.03.89
Cook, David, RD	Lt Cdr	AW	Flying Fox	31.03.93
Cook, Peter Andrew	Lt	DIS	Ferret (RNR)	10.08.86
Cook, Simon Hugh Home	ASI		Flying Fox	24.05.95
Coombes, Stewart	Lt Cdr	AIR	RNR Air Br VI	31.03.95
Cooper, David John	Lt	HQ	President	18.09.88
Cooper, Graham Peter Harrison	Lt Cdr	DIS	Ferret (RNR)	17.09.75
Cooper, Susan, BSC	Lt	HQ	President	21.07.91
Cooper, Susan Carol	Lt	Q	King Alfred	22.03.87
Cottam, Simon Roscoe	Lt	AWNIS	Flying Fox	17.01.87
Cowan, Andrew Stuart	Lt	MWHQ	Dalriada	08.05.88
Cox, Rhoderick	Lt Cdr	AIR	RNR Air Br VI	01.12.88
Craig, John Terence, RD	Cdr	NA	President	30.09.95
Crawford, Andrew John	Lt Cdr	AW	Vivid	01.06.91
Critchley, Julian Arthur John Hall	Sg Ltcdr		Scotia	07.08.83
Crockett, Victor Andrew, RD	Lt Cdr	DIS	Ferret (RNR)	31.03.95
Crombie-Smith, Harry John Christopher	Sg Ltcdr		Scotia	04.09.78
Crone, David James Edward, RD	Lt Cdr	MWHQ	Caroline	26.02.90
Crooks, Louis Warden, RD	Lt Cdr	NCS	Flying Fox	31.03.93
Crump, Peter Charles, RD	Lt Cdr	AW	King Alfred	26.09.86
Culver, Peter Charles Leonard	Lt	SEA	President	08.08.89
Cunnah, David	Lt Cdr	AIR	RNR Air Br VI	31.03.94
Curley, Ronald Robertson	Lt	MW	King Alfred	17.10.90
Curran, John Thomas Anthony, BSC	Lt	HQ	Vivid	14.09.89
Curran, Peter Michael Thomas	Lt Cdr	AW	King Alfred	01.01.90

D

Dace, Katherine Elizabeth	Lt Cdr	DIS	Ferret (RNR)	31.03.95
Dalton, Neil Jarvis	Lt	NCS	Northwood	02.06.92
Daly, Paul	Lt Cdr	AIR	RNR Air Br VI	31.03.95
Dalziel, Simon Anthony Cannon	Lt Cdr	PA	Northwood	16.02.89
Daniels, J W R	Lt Cdr	AW	President	18.08.90
Darkins, Colin Richard	ASI		Flying Fox	23.06.94

Name	Rank	Branch	Unit	Seniority
Davies, Anita Claire, RD	Lt	INTR	Ferret (RNR)	14.05.90
Davies, Dennis James	Lt	AWNIS	President	05.09.87
Davies, Paul Richard, RD	Cdr	AW	King Alfred	30.06.80
Davies, Robert Michael	Lt	SEA	Forward	17.11.90
Davies, Simon Lovat	Lt	MWHQ	King Alfred	15.09.95
De La Fosse, Timothy	Lt	AIR	RNR Air Br VI	08.05.86
De Maine, Michael John	Lt Cdr	NCS	Scotia	08.03.91
Derbyshire, Neil David James	Sg Ltcdr		Forward	01.08.90
Derrick, Malcom	Lt Cdr	AIR	RNR Air Br VI	10.12.91
Devall, Clive Andrew, RD*	Sg Cdr		Eaglet	30.09.85
Devereaux, James	Lt	AIR	RNR Air Br VI	04.08.88
Devitt, Katherine Rose	Lt	INTR	Ferret (RNR)	22.06.85
Dilks, Paul David Peter, RD	Lt Cdr	AW	King Alfred	05.04.87
Dorins, Hugh Lawrence	Slt	MW	Eaglet	15.12.87
Dorman, Nicholas Roger Vause	Lt	MW	Scotia	29.05.88
Douglas, Norman	Slt	SEA	Calliope	22.09.87
Downie, Anne Louise, RD	Lt	SEA	cotia	01.12.95
Downing, Angela Margaret, RD	Lt Cdr	NCS	Flying Fox	30.09.85
Downing, Neil Edmond	Lt	MW	Caroline	25.09.91
Drake, Roderick Allan	Lt	NCS	Flying Fox	04.10.89
Duff, Heather Janine Rosemarie	Slt	MW	Scotia	08.04.90
Duggua, Rodney, RD	Lt Cdr	COMM	King Alfred	31.03.93
Duncan, Barbara Mary	Lt	MW	Eaglet	14.03.91
Duncan, Keith Julian	Lt Cdr	AW	Eaglet	31.03.94
Dunkley, Ian Max, RD	Lt Cdr	AW	President	01.10.88
Dunne, Lawrence John	Slt	SEA	Forward	18.11.89
Dunster-Price, Paul Lewis, RD	Lt Cdr	AWNIS	President	01.11.85
Durham, Marion Ruth	Lt	AWNIS	Scotia	11.03.90
Duthie, David	Lt Cdr	AIR	RNR Air Br VI	01.10.89
Duthie, David James Ralph	Sg Ltcdr		President	31.03.95
Dutt, Trevor Peter	Sg Cdr		President	30.09.89

E

Name	Rank	Branch	Unit	Seniority
Eagles, Susan Jane	Cdr	PA	Flying Fox	30.09.89
Easterling, Katrina Lauraine	Slt	SEA	Flying Fox	20.09.88
Eastham, Allan Michael, BSC	Lt Cdr	NCS	Forward	01.04.94
Edwards, Michael Steven De La Warr	Psg Lt		Flying Fox	19.02.94
Elliott, Fiona Barbara	ASI		Scotia	09.05.92
Ellis, John Anthony	Cdr	MWHQ	Flying Fox	30.09.87
Ellis, Richard Allyn	Lt	HQ	President	18.08.90
Emsley, Richard John Paul	Slt	MW	Sherwood	04.06.87
England, Robert Frederick Charles	Slt	QM Q	King Alfred	27.07.86
English, Martin William	Sg Ltcdr		Forward	01.08.92
Esfahani, Sharokh	Slt	HQ	Northwood	26.09.90
Evans, Ann, RD	Lt Cdr	DIS	Vivid	31.03.94
Evans, Alex	Lt	AIR	RNR Air Br VI	09.05.88
Evans, Huntley William Sylvester	Lt Cdr	MW	Flying Fox	24.05.91
Evans, Kevan David	Lt	MWHQ	Scotia	04.04.90
Evans, Richard	Lt Cdr	AIR	RNR Air Br VI	01.11.87
Ewing, Simon	Lt Cdr	AIR	RNR Air Br VI	31.03.93

F

Name	Rank	Branch	Unit	Seniority
Fairlamb, Jane Laura Catherine	ASI		President	19.08.93
Farmer, Gary Gordon	Lt	HQ	Dalriada	28.06.92
Farrand, Rachel, RD	Lt Cdr	NCS	Sherwood	30.09.89
Farrant, Crispin Victor, RD	Lt Cdr	AW	King Alfred	01.04.81
Faulkner, Keith Michael	Lt Cdr	LOGS	Flying Fox	26.05.90
Fearnley, David George, B.ED	Lt Cdr	MWHQ	Eaglet	31.03.93
Ferguson, Neil	Lt	HQ	Caroline	20.08.89
Ferguson, Nicholas Alistair Malcolm	Lt	HQ	Vivid	22.12.88
Figg, Keith Anthony	Lt Cdr	DIS	Ferret (RNR)	11.12.92

Name	Rank	Branch	Unit	Seniority
Filce, Susannah Caroline	ASI		Scotia	23.10.95
Filtness, Rosemary Jane, RD	Lt Cdr	DIS	Ferret (RNR)	31.03.93
Finan, Peter	Lt Cdr	AIR	RNR Air Br VI	27.11.89
Findlay, Alan	Lt	AIR	RNR Air Br VI	28.10.88
Fitch, Steven R	ASI		Northwood	16.11.95
Fleming, Samuel Andrew	Lt	HQ	Sherwood	20.01.92
Foster, Stephen Edward	Lt Cdr	NCS	Forward	31.03.95
Fowler, Alan	Lt Cdr	AIR	RNR Air Br VI	01.06.78
Fraser, Ian David	Slt	HQ	Flying Fox	14.11.91
Fry, Christopher Wesley	Lt	HQ	Forward	28.07.95
Fry, Stephen Michael	Lt	NCS	Cambria	15.06.95

G

Name	Rank	Branch	Unit	Seniority
Galway, Ian, QCVSA	Lt Cdr	AIR	RNR Air Br VI	11.10.89
Gammie, Richard	Lt Cdr	AW	King Alfred	01.05.90
Gannon, John Patrick	Psg Lt		Eaglet	08.07.92
Gardiner, George David	Sg Lt		Caroline	01.08.89
Garner, Philip	Lt	AIR	RNR Air Br VI	01.07.87
Gausden, Christine	Lt	SM	President	04.08.89
Gavey, Stephen John	Lt Cdr	HQ	Vivid	01.08.88
Georgeson, Ian	Lt Cdr	AIR	RNR Air Br VI	01.06.91
Geraghty, Ian Martin	Lt Cdr	MWHQ	King Alfred	01.05.92
Gibb, Peter	Lt Cdr	AIR	RNR Air Br VI	31.03.93
Gibson, Stephen	Lt Cdr	AIR	RNR Air Br VI	31.03.94
Gleave, James Alexander	Lt	COMM	Sherwood	15.09.95
Glendinning, Neil	Lt	AW	President	
Glover, John Gordon	Lt Cdr	LOGS	Eaglet	19.03.90
Glover, Martyn Richard Timothy, MA	Lt	NCS	President	04.10.90
Goldthorpe, Sally Louise	Lt Cdr	PA	Eaglet	31.03.95
Goode, Patrick Alfred, RD	Lt Cdr	AW	King Alfred	24.07.77
Goodes, Simon Newbury	Lt	NCS	Northwood	09.07.86
Goodwin, Jonathan Paul Kerr	Lt	SM	Northwood	17.02.87
Gough, Nicholas William	ALt	MW	Eaglet	11.05.90
Gould, Andrew Edward	Lt Cdr	LOGS	Scotia	13.05.86
Gow, Neil Henry Keefe	Lt	SM	Northwood	21.03.94
Graham, Adrian William	Lt	DIS	Ferret (RNR)	19.02.89
Graham, Stephen	Lt Cdr	AIR	RNR Air Br VI	31.03.94
Graves, Malcolm Harold, RD*	Lt Cdr	AW	Cambria	19.07.82
Graveson, Allan	Lt Cdr	AW	King Alfred	09.07.92
Greaves, Jeremy Justin	Lt	PA	Northwood	13.06.95
Greenacre, Richard Paul	Lt	SD	Vivid	09.08.88
Griffiths, Andrew Derek	Lt	AW	Flying Fox	26.02.94
Griffiths, Michael Edward, BSC	Lt	SM	Cambria	03.05.89
Griffiths, Peter	Lt	AIR	RNR Air Br VI	03.07.83
Grimes, Craig Richard	Slt	MW	Dalriada	15.12.90
Guest, Steve	Lt Cdr	AIR	RNR Air Br VI	31.03.94
Guild, Malcolm Donald	Sg Ltcdr		Scotia	12.07.87
Gunn, Debra Ann, RD	Lt Cdr	HQ	Scotia	31.03.94

H

Name	Rank	Branch	Unit	Seniority
Haffenden, Simon, BSC, MIEE, C.ENG	Slt	SM	Flying Fox	05.04.87
Haigh, Julie Ann	Lt	AW	Cambria	13.10.90
Haikin, Peter Harry, BSC	Slt	HQ	Sherwood	23.04.90
Hailwood, Paul Joseph	Palt	AW	Vivid	16.10.93
Halblander, Craig James Michael, BA, LLB	Lt	MW	Scotia	06.05.94
Hall, Euan James Armstrong, RD	Lt Cdr	LOGS	Dalriada	16.11.92
Hall, Suzanne	Lt	HQ	President	05.04.93
Haller, Pauline Mary, RD	Lt Cdr	NCS	Northwood	31.03.93
Halliday, Ian	Lt Cdr	AIR	RNR Air Br VI	01.09.90
Hamilton, Andrew Robert	Sg Ltcdr		Scotia	01.08.86
Hamilton, Ronald	Lt	LOGS	Dalriada	14.10.95

Name	Rank	Branch	Unit	Seniority
Hamlin, Paul Richard	ALt	AW	Calliope	23.02.91
Hancock, Angela Margaret	Lt	PA	Vivid	10.10.90
Handley, Dane	Lt	AIR	RNR Air Br VI	26.04.88
Hands, Carolyn, RD	Lt Cdr	NCS	Flying Fox	30.09.85
Hankey, Mark Harold	Lt	SEA	President	31.07.95
Hansen, Markus Sebastian	Slt	SEA	President	17.04.92
Harding, Janet Elizabeth, RD*	Lt Cdr	HQ	Northwood	31.03.93
Hardinge, Christopher Harold	Lt	SM	Forward	27.12.89
Hargrave, Anthony James	Lt Cdr	SM	Flying Fox	31.03.93
Harper, Robert Simon	Lt	HQ	Caroline	27.01.95
Harper, Richard	Lt Cdr	AIR	RNR Air Br VI	31.03.95
Harrington, Anthony Christopher Robert	Lt	INTR	Ferret (RNR)	26.03.88
Harris, Adrian James	Lt	SM	President	30.07.95
Harris, Raymond Leo, RD	Lt Cdr	ME	U/A	
Harrison, John Frank	Slt	AW	Eaglet	25.06.88
Harrison, Richard William	ASg Lt		Sherwood	17.05.95
Harrower, William	Lt Cdr	AIR	RNR Air Br VI	15.01.88
Hart, Keith	Lt Cdr	AWNIS	Northwood	31.03.93
Hartley, Ann Theresa	Lt Cdr	DIS	Northwood	30.09.87
Hartley, Sheila Ann	Lt	HQ	Vivid	20.01.89
Hartley, Sarah Boyt	Slt	NCS	President	13.01.92
Harwood, Steven	Lt	PA	President	16.10.85
Hathway, Steven	Lt	AIR	RNR Air Br VI	18.09.90
Hawes, Alison Linda	Lt	PA	King Alfred	16.12.88
Hayman, Matthew Robert	ASI		President	18.09.93
Hayward, James Douglas, MA, B.ENG	Lt	LOGS	Forward	08.12.92
Healy, Pamela Joyce, BSC	Lt Cdr	PA	King Alfred	30.09.90
Heathcote, Paul	Lt	AIR	RNR Air Br VI	16.03.84
Helsby, Edward	Lt	AIR	RNR Air Br VI	01.12.82
Henton, Andrew Michael	Slt	HQ	Northwood	15.10.90
Henwood, A, RD	Lt Cdr	AW	President	01.10.86
Heweth, Christopher	Lt Cdr	AIR	RNR Air Br VI	01.10.92
Hewins, Clive William	Lt Cdr	AW	Sherwood	20.05.91
Hewitt, Susan	Sg Ltcdr		Sherwood	26.05.81
Heyd-Smith, Brian John	Lt	SM	Scotia	28.04.85
Hickey, Gurney	Lt	AIR	RNR Air Br VI	16.10.83
Hicks, John David	Lt	HQ	Eaglet	07.02.90
Hicks, Peter John, RD, MA, C.ENG, MIMECHE	Lt Cdr	NCS	King Alfred	01.10.77
Higgins, G E	Lt	AW	Calliope	29.07.85
Higgs-Goodwin, Marilyn Lee, BA, MA	Lt Cdr	NCS	Northwood	31.03.95
Highet, Rhona Frances	Lt	HQ	Northwood	10.10.91
Hill, David Rowland	Lt Cdr	MW	King Alfred	08.05.91
Hill, Matthew Charles	Slt	SEA	Flying Fox	25.01.91
Hill, Paul Terence	Lt	SM	President	20.05.90
Hill, Stuart John	ALt	SM	King Alfred	22.10.90
Hills, Stephen John	Pasl	AW	Vivid	16.11.95
Hinchliffe, Mary-Jane	Lt	COMM	Flying Fox	23.03.90
Hindle, Sean	Lt	SM	Eaglet	18.09.91
Hindmarsh, John Reed	Sg Ltcdr		Calliope	05.10.87
Hines, Barbara Mary	Lt Cdr	PA	King Alfred	30.09.90
Hines, Stephen Frederick, RD	Lt Cdr	AW	King Alfred	01.08.86
Hingley, Peter Dennis	Lt	SM	President	15.03.87
Hinks, David Andrew, RD	Lt Cdr	AW	Eaglet	23.06.88
Hoare, Christopher James Albert, BSc	Lt	SM	Eaglet	07.06.89
Hocking, Muriel Edwina, RD*	Capt	NA	Vivid	30.09.92
Hogan, Francis John, RD	Lt	MWHQ	Eaglet	16.07.88
Hogan, Patrick Felix, RD*	ACdr	NA	Cambria	01.05.92
Hollis, Robert Leslie Graham	Lt	AWNIS	Eaglet	11.07.89
Holloway, Stephen Leslie	Lt	AW	Eaglet	17.09.88
Holmes, David Grindall, RD	Lt Cdr	NCS	Flying Fox	30.12.89
Holmes, Jane Frances, RD	Lt Cdr	NCS	Flying Fox	30.09.86

Name	Rank	Branch	Unit	Seniority
Hooper, Nicholas Robert Joseph, RD	Sg Cdr		Flying Fox	30.09.90
Hope, Nigel Charles Dawson, RD	Lt Cdr	AW	Scotia	06.06.86
Hopkins, Mary	Lt	Q	King Alfred	04.03.85
Hopps, Francis	Lt	AIR	RNR Air Br VI	16.06.88
Horne, Martin	ASI		President	15.05.93
Horner, Ian David	Lt Cdr	DIS	Ferret (RNR)	01.11.83
Horner, Robert Bamford	Lt Cdr	SM	Northwood	02.05.85
Horrell, Stephen Peter	Lt	COMM	Vivid	22.11.91
Horton, Bruce Andrew, BSC	Lt	AWNIS	President	15.04.91
Houghton, Nicholas	Lt	AIR	RNR Air Br VI	01.10.79
Houghton, Philip Arthur, BSC, LBIOL, FCA, RD*	Cdr	LOGS	Eaglet	30.09.86
Houston, Colin James	Lt	AWNIS	Dalriada	06.07.89
Howard, The Hon Alexander	Lt Cdr	AIR	RNR Air Br VI	31.03.94
Howard, David Pelham	Lt	MW	President	31.07.95
Howard, Penny Ann	Lt	HQ	Vivid	29.11.90
Howard, William Jonathon, RD	Cdr	AW	King Alfred	30.09.92
Howell, Colin, AMIMFGE	Lt	HQ	King Alfred	24.01.90
Howes, Simon Tee	Lt Cdr	DIS	Ferret (RNR)	28.03.84
Howling, Rex Andrew	Lt Cdr	SM	President	01.02.92
Hubber, Keith Michael	Lt	SEA	Flying Fox	01.10.86
Hughes, Clare Yvonne, RD	Lt Cdr	COMM	President	30.09.90
Hughes, Jill Elizabeth	Lt Cdr	NCS	Caroline	31.03.95
Hughes, John Fraser	Lt Cdr	PA	King Alfred	14.05.92
Hughes, Kai	Lt Cdr	DIS	Ferret (RNR)	01.05.92
Hughes, Paul James	Sg Cdr		King Alfred	30.09.95
Hulett, Peter, AFC	Lt Cdr	AIR	RNR Air Br VI	26.06.87
Humphreys, Cristine Alison	Lt	HQ	Northwood	24.09.92
Humphreys, John Martyn, PHD, BSc	Lt	MWHQ	Northwood	25.06.90
Hunt, Nigel William	Lt Cdr	AW	King Alfred	01.07.88
Hustwick, Adrian Robert, RD*	Lt Cdr	AWNIS	Sherwood	18.04.87
Hutchinson, Janice Elizabeth	Lt Cdr	NCS	Eaglet	31.03.93
Hutton, Miles	Lt	AIR	RNR Air Br VI	09.07.90

I

Inwood, John Maxwell	Sg Ltcdr		Scotia	01.02.89
Irvine, Gordon Henry	Sg Ltcdr		Flying Fox	23.06.84
Isacke, Stephen	Lt Cdr	AIR	RNR Air Br VI	16.11.86
Iveson, Maureen	Lt	COMM	Calliope	08.04.89

J

Jachnik, Clive Victor	Lt	INTR	Ferret (RNR)	20.07.88
Jackson, Clive	Lt Cdr	AIR	RNR Air Br VI	31.03.93
Jackson, Graham	Lt Cdr	AIR	RNR Air Br VI	01.10.88
Jackson, Trevor	Lt Cdr	AIR	RNR Air Br VI	01.10.94
Jago, Edward Ross, RD	Sg Lt		Eaglet	18.10.88
James, Christopher Henry, RD	Lt Cdr	AW	Flying Fox	01.07.82
James, Peter Wilson, MBE, OSJ, RD*, DL	Cdr	NA	Cambria	30.09.83
James, Roy Arthur, BSC	Lt Cdr	SM	Calliope	01.03.83
Jameson, Susan Catherine	Slt	HQ	Flying Fox	18.01.89
Jardine, Corriene Marie	Lt	AWNIS	President	12.10.93
Jayram, Raveen	Lt	QM Q	Forward	22.02.88
Jeffrey, James Edward	Lt Cdr	HQ	Calliope	11.03.90
Jeffrey, Margaret Claire	Lt	NCS	Vivid	20.08.89
Jenkins, Adele Elizabeth	Lt	HQ	Cambria	14.10.89
Jevons, Matthew Gregory	Lt	AW	President	14.11.83
John, Peter Martin	Lt Cdr	AW	Cambria	11.06.92
Johns, Gavin Haydn	Lt	SEA	Cambria	01.01.93
Johnson, Craig Rothwell	Lt	LOGS	Flying Fox	04.04.89
Johnson, Jill Ena	Lt	Q	Cambria	09.10.88
Johnson, Robin	Lt Cdr	AIR	RNR Air Br VI	01.10.90
Johnstone, Peter Hughes, RD	Lt	LOGS	President	05.01.87

Name	Rank	Branch	Unit	Seniority
Jones, Christopher, RD	Lt Cdr	AW	President	01.05.88
Jones, Charles David, RD	Lt	SM	Dalriada	17.09.90
Jones, Geoffrey Mark	Slt	AW	Eaglet	09.06.90
Jones, Keith Robert	ALt	AW	King Alfred	15.10.88
Jones, Peter Lloyd, RD	Sg Cdr		Cambria	30.09.84
Jones, Pauline Lesley	Lt	LOGS	Calliope	25.12.89
Jones, Sheila Elizabeth	Lt	Q	Cambria	10.01.87
Joyce, Anna Louise	Sg Ltcdr		President	28.09.87

K

Kay, David	Lt	LOGS	Flying Fox	16.05.89
Kay, Ivan CharlesMichael	Lt	AW	King Alfred	12.11.88
Kearney, Melian Jane	Lt	HQ	Vivid	26.06.89
Kelly, Timothy Desmond	Lt Cdr	X	RNR Air Br VI	21.03.88
Kembery, Simon John	ALt	AW	Cambria	11.06.93
Kemp, Simon Michael	Lt	DIS	Ferret (RNR)	19.04.88
Kennedy, Inga Jane	Lt	Q	Scotia	08.04.89
Kenney, Dawn Elizabeth	Lt Cdr	Q	Vivid	31.03.93
Kenny, Phillip, RD	Lt Cdr	AWNIS	Caroline	02.03.81
Kent, Thomas William Henry, RD	Lt Cdr	AW	Sherwood	01.10.90
Kenyon, Christopher Mortiford	Lt Cdr	HQ	President	03.04.82
Kerr, Elizabeth Jane	Lt	PA	King Alfred	17.07.88
Kerr, Harold Leslie	Lt	NCS	Caroline	20.10.89
Kibble, David George, RD	Lt Cdr	SM	Sherwood	10.08.91
Kidd, Nicholas	Lt Cdr	AIR	RNR Air Br VI	01.03.83
King, Andrew Stephen	Lt	MWHQ	King Alfred	28.09.88
King, Charles Guy Hall	Lt	SEA	King Alfred	16.08.92
King, Ian	Slt	HQ	Eaglet	23.03.89
Kinsella, Kevin John, RD	Lt Cdr	MWHQ	King Alfred	16.09.85
Kirk, Joseph	Lt	S	URNU (RNR) Ssx	01.09.93
Kirk, William Walter	Slt	MW	Sherwood	10.12.87
Knight, David	Lt Cdr	AIR	RNR Air Br VI	01.10.88
Knott, Clive	Lt	AIR	RNR Air Br VI	01.05.88
Knowles, Donna Maureen	Lt	SEA	Caroline	28.10.91
Kyle, Timothy, RD	Cdr	AIR	RNR Air Br VI	01.10.95

L

Laidlaw, Kenneth Robert	ASl		President	19.03.94
Laird, James	Lt Cdr	AIR	RNR Air Br VI	30.10.89
Lake, Rosemarie Elizabeth, BEM, RD	Lt Cdr	Q	King Alfred	31.03.95
Lamb, Simon John Francis, RD	Lt Cdr	NCS	Sherwood	19.10.82
Langmead, Clive Francis, RD	Lt Cdr	AW	Forward	01.07.90
Lapage-Norris, Thomas Richard William	ASl		Flying Fox	03.03.92
Largey, Alan Gerald, RD	Lt Cdr	MWHQ	Caroline	25.06.87
Last, Nicholas, AFC	Lt Cdr	AIR	RNR Air Br VI	01.10.91
Lawrence, Stuart James, RD	Capt	AW	King Alfred	30.09.90
Leather, Roger James, RD	Lt Cdr	AW	Eaglet	01.06.87
Ledwidge, Francis Andrew	Slt	COMM	Ferret (RNR)	15.01.92
Lee, David Anthony	Lt	SM	Dalriada	29.08.93
Lee, John	Lt Cdr	NCS	Calliope	31.03.94
Lees, Norman	Lt Cdr	AIR	RNR Air Br VI	05.11.90
Lemon, John	ALt	X	URNU (RNR) Aberd	09.02.88
Leonard, John Francis	Sg Ltcdr		President	14.07.85
Lewis, John Charles	Lt	SM	President	31.07.95
Lewis, Kathryn Elizabeth	Lt	MWHQ	President	31.07.95
Lewis, Simon John	Lt	LOGS	Eaglet	01.02.95
Leyshon, Sally Louise	Lt Cdr	AWNIS	Flying Fox	31.03.93
Lindsley, Michael James	Lt	AW	Calliope	18.03.89
Lippell, Sabrina Rose, BSC	Lt Cdr	PA	President	30.09.89
Littleboy, Alison Helen	Lt Cdr	PA	Northwood	31.03.93
Livingstone, Martin Jeremy	Lt	SEA	Eaglet	26.12.89

Name	Rank	Branch	Unit	Seniority
Lloyd, Conrad Michael Rawlings, RD	Cdr	AW	King Alfred	31.12.79
Lloyd, David Vernon	Lt	AW	King Alfred	07.10.88
Lloyd, Gareth	Lt	HQ	Eaglet	17.05.87
Lloyd, Peter John	Lt	AW	King Alfred	27.11.86
Locock, Victoria Jane, RD	Lt Cdr	NCS	President	30.09.91
Lomas, Hugh, DSC	Lt Cdr	AIR	RNR Air Br VI	01.04.80
Lorton, Jonathan David, RD	Lt Cdr	HQ	Flying Fox	31.03.94
Loughran, Cedric Grenville, RD	Lt Cdr	AW	Eaglet	14.01.90
Ludgate, John MacKay, RD*	Cdr	NA	President	30.09.84
Luke, Warren Munro, RD	Sg Ltcdr		Scotia	03.09.78
Lunt, Dean	Lt Cdr	AIR	RNR Air Br VI	03.12.86
Luscombe, Francis	Sg Ltcdr		Vivid	01.08.86
Lyall, Kenneth Alexander	Lt	HQ	Scotia	09.06.86
Lydon, Michael	Slt	LOGS	Calliope	15.09.88
Lyle, Christopher	Lt Cdr	AIR	RNR Air Br VI	05.01.90
Lynch, Suzanne Marie	ASI		Cambria	31.10.95

M

Name	Rank	Branch	Unit	Seniority
MacDonald, Angus	Lt	AIR	RNR Air Br VI	16.05.89
MacDonald, Donald Gordon, RD*	Capt	NA	Dalriada	30.09.88
Mace, Sharon Barbara	Lt	Q	Calliope	04.03.89
MacFarlan, Martin Duncan	Cdr	HQ	President	31.12.83
Machin, Peter Charles Clive, RD	Lt Cdr	HQ	Cambria	21.12.87
MacKenzie, James Graham, RD	Lt Cdr	MWHQ	Dalriada	14.09.86
MacKenzie-Philps, Linda	Lt	PA	King Alfred	24.11.92
MacLean, Nicholas Peter	Lt	SM	President	24.07.89
Macleod, Alistair David	Sg Ltcdr		Scotia	17.10.78
Macleod, Murdo	Lt Cdr	AIR	RNR Air Br VI	20.08.83
MacTaggart, Alastair Duncan, RD	Lt Cdr	COMM	Dalriada	31.03.94
Maddock, Lesley Ann, RD	Lt Cdr	COMM	Flying Fox	30.09.83
Magnay, Claire Georgina	ASI		Forward	16.07.94
Maitland, John, RD	Sg Capt		President	30.09.95
Mallinson, Stuart Jeffry, MSC	Slt	MWHQ	Flying Fox	18.12.88
Malpas, Peter	Lt	NCS	King Alfred	22.03.92
Maltby, Robert Edmund	Slt	AWNIS	Flying Fox	18.03.89
Manley, John Preston	ASI		Vivid	17.10.95
Manning, Jacquline Vera	Lt	SM	President	11.02.89
Marlow, Stephen, QGM	Lt	AIR	RNR Air Br VI	26.07.86
Marshall, Peter John	Lt	MW	Flying Fox	26.01.86
Martin, Andrew	Slt	MW	President	01.07.92
Martin, David Gordon	Sg Ltcdr		Northwood	18.07.87
Martin, Nicholas John	Lt Cdr	MWHQ	Calliope	31.03.95
Maryon, Karen Anne	Lt	Q	Sherwood	24.12.87
Maryon, Michael Ian	Lt	PA	Sherwood	11.07.88
Mason, Ann Margaret	Lt	LOGS	Flying Fox	26.06.89
Mason, Thomas	Lt Cdr	AIR	RNR Air Br VI	01.10.88
Massey, S A Stj(Simon)	Lt Cdr	AIR	RNR Air Br VI	29.12.91
Maxwell, Andrew Alistair, RD	Lt Cdr	INTR	Ferret (RNR)	05.08.88
McAllister, DonaldD, MCALISTER, MBA, BSC	Lt Cdr	HQ	Sherwood	21.02.90
McAuley, Carrie Jane	Lt Cdr	PA	President	30.09.91
McBride, Maurice, BSC	Lt Cdr	AIR	RNR Air Br VI	02.08.86
McCabe, Jeremy Charles	Slt	AW	Vivid	10.10.87
McClure, Ian Andrew MacDonell	Lt Cdr	INTR	Ferret (RNR)	09.08.81
McCollum, Richard William	Sg Ltcdr		Calliope	16.05.78
McCormack, Patrick, RD	Lt Cdr	NCS	Dalriada	15.07.92
McCreery, Robert George	Lt	SEA	Caroline	20.06.89
McDonald, Roger	Lt Cdr	AIR	RNR Air Br VI	01.09.87
McDowell, Peter Ronald	Lt Cdr	HQ	Eaglet	01.11.88
McGhee, Stephen James	Slt	HQ	Dalriada	16.07.90
McHarg, Andrew, MA	Lt Cdr	AIR	RNR Air Br VI	02.09.91
McIlwee, Anthony Patrick	ASI	QM Q	Forward	18.09.93

Name	Rank	Branch	Unit	Seniority
McKinty, Andrew	Slt	SEA	Caroline	23.07.92
McKnight, Edward	ASl	X	URNU (RNR) Glasg	17.10.90
McLaren, Alastair, QCVSA	Lt Cdr	AIR	RNR Air Br VI	09.03.92
McLaverty, Karen Anne	ASl		Caroline	17.07.93
McMurran, Robert Campbell	Lt	SEA	Caroline	06.10.86
McNaught, Edward William Gordon	Lt	MW	Calliope	17.01.88
McNeill, Patricia Eilish	ASl		Caroline	23.01.93
McPhail, Austar John, RD	Lt Cdr	NCS	President	14.03.85
Meekins, Timothy	Lt Cdr	AIR	RNR Air Br VI	06.12.89
Meharg, Neil	Lt	MW	Caroline	03.10.95
Mendelsohn, Katharine Anne	Lt Cdr	INTR	Ferret (RNR)	31.03.93
Meyerhoff, Peter David	Lt	AW	Eaglet	05.12.87
Middleton, John	Lt Cdr	AIR	RNR Air Br VI	01.10.91
Midgley, David	Lt Cdr	AIR	RNR Air Br VI	09.12.91
Miller, Carol Diane, BA	Slt	HQ	King Alfred	26.09.92
Mills, Mary Kathleen	Lt Cdr	COMM	Flying Fox	31.03.93
Milne, Ian	Lt Cdr	AIR	RNR Air Br VI	01.03.84
Milne-Home, Elizabeth Mary	ASl		Scotia	15.05.93
Milner, Philip Michael, RD	Sg Ltcdr		Eaglet	15.08.84
Minter, Louise I H	Lt Cdr	Q	Dalriada	01.08.83
Miskin, Peter	Lt Cdr	AIR	RNR Air Br VI	31.03.94
Mitchell, Charles Anthony, RD	Cdr	AW	Vivid	30.09.87
Mitchell, Robert	Lt Cdr	AIR	RNR Air Br VI	31.03.93
Moffat, Ian	Lt Cdr	AIR	RNR Air Br VI	11.11.89
Moffat, Linda Winifred	Lt Cdr	INTR	Ferret (RNR)	30.09.88
Monckton, Hugh Francis	Lt Cdr	AW	Scotia	21.07.85
Montgomery, William George	Lt	INTR	Ferret (RNR)	21.05.91
Moore, Adrian David	ASl		Northwood	14.12.95
Moore, Peter Russell, RD*	Lt Cdr	NCS	Sherwood	21.09.77
Moorehead, Peter	Lt Cdr	AIR	RNR Air Br VI	31.03.94
Morbey, Alan Hedley	Lt	AW	King Alfred	28.01.89
Morgan, Charles Edward William	ASl		Scotia	16.10.93
Morgan, Eugene Peter	Lt	MW	President	31.07.95
Morgan, Gareth	Lt	AIR	RNR Air Br VI	08.08.88
Morgan, Gareth William	Lt	LOGS	Cambria	29.06.90
Morgan, Linda Frances	Slt	Q	President	17.06.86
Morley, Dietmar Allen	Slt	MW	Sherwood	17.08.88
Morley, Graham David, RD	Cdr	MWHQ	Northwood	30.09.93
Morley, Jane Mary	Lt Cdr	Q	President	02.09.86
Morris, David John	Lt Cdr	SM	Northwood	02.08.82
Morris, Paul	Lt Cdr	AIR	RNR Air Br VI	01.09.79
Morris, William Alexander	Lt	MW	Scotia	19.07.89
Mortlock, Alison Jane	Slt	SEA	Flying Fox	06.03.92
Mostyn, Andrew Anthony Rowland	Sg Ltcdr		King Alfred	09.12.89
Mowbray, Roger, QCVSA	Lt Cdr	AIR	RNR Air Br VI	01.10.88
Mulhern, Kevin, RD	Lt Cdr	AIR	RNR Air Br VI	14.04.87
Muncer, Anthony Douglas, RD	Lt Cdr	AW	Eaglet	01.12.84
Munson, Eileen Patricia	Lt	Q	Forward	23.09.95
Murphy, Denzil	Lt Cdr	AIR	RNR Air Br VI	01.10.90
Murray, Edward Charles, RD	Lt	HQ	Vivid	25.12.89
Murray, Thomas Leslie Gillespie, RD	Lt	MS	Scotia	12.11.87
Murrison, M P	Lt	AW	President	24.06.89
Myers, Margaret Cynthia, RD	Lt Cdr	COMM	Vivid	31.03.93
Myers, Paul	Lt	AIR	RNR Air Br VI	01.08.84
Myerscough, Janet Margaret, RD	Lt Cdr	HQ	Northwood	31.03.94

N

Neale, Kirsty A	Lt	NCS	Scotia	30.11.94
Neil, Hugh Andrew Wade, RD	Sg Ltcdr		President	01.11.81
Newby Grant, William Robert, RD	Lt Cdr	INTR	Ferret (RNR)	26.03.80
Newton, Ingrid Catherine	Lt	LOGS	Eaglet	23.11.90

Name	Rank	Branch	Unit	Seniority
Nichol, R C F	Lt Cdr	PA	President	18.09.75
Nicholson, Jeremy David, RD	Lt Cdr	AW	Flying Fox	01.10.84
Nicholson, Peter Adrian, RD	Lt Cdr	INTR	Ferret (RNR)	19.02.87
Noakes, David Anthony	Slt	LOGS	Eaglet	18.01.93
Noble, Moira, RD	Lt Cdr	COMM	Scotia	30.09.85
Noble, Robert Howard, BSC	Lt	NCS	Forward	20.07.88
Northcott, John	Lt	LOGS	Calliope	31.03.91
Norwood, Jeffrey Michael	Sg Ltcdr		Forward	16.10.88
Noton, Angela	Slt	HQ	Flying Fox	18.06.88
Nunn, James	Lt	AIR	RNR Air Br VI	01.09.88

O

Name	Rank	Branch	Unit	Seniority
O'Callaghan, Penelope Jane	Lt	Q	King Alfred	16.02.86
O'Connor, Catherine Jayne, RD	Lt Cdr	NCS	Vivid	31.03.93
O'Neill, George Paul	Lt	INTR	Ferret (RNR)	08.08.93
O'Sullivan, Kathryn Winifred	Slt	SEA	Vivid	28.02.90
Oag, Denis Cairns	Lt	MWHQ	Scotia	07.01.90
Oaten, Timothy John	Lt	COMM	Sherwood	03.06.87
Oates, Edward	Lt Cdr	AIR	RNR Air Br VI	16.02.93
Olivant, David Francis	Lt	COMM	Sherwood	25.10.90

P

Name	Rank	Branch	Unit	Seniority
Packman, Robert Steven	Lt	AW	President	21.02.86
Padget, Joanna Louise	ASI		Calliope	10.08.95
Palmer, Alon, RD	Lt Cdr	AW	Scotia	09.05.91
Palmer, Helen	ASI	URNU	URNU (RNR) Manch	01.10.90
Pardoe, Christopher Richard	Lt Cdr	PA	Vivid	13.09.86
Parkinson, Deborah Maria	Slt	HQ	Eaglet	27.12.89
Parris, John Stewart	Lt Cdr	PA	Flying Fox	31.03.93
Parrott, Lorraine, RD	Lt	COMM	Calliope	04.08.89
Parsonage, Neil David, LLB	Lt	NCS	Eaglet	07.01.90
Passmore, Susan Margaret	Lt Cdr	HQ	Flying Fox	30.09.89
Patten, Nicholas William	Lt	NCS	Forward	17.09.90
Pattenden, Neil Schrivener	Lt Cdr	INTR	Ferret (RNR)	01.09.81
Patterson, Jarroo Lee	Lt	PA	President	07.09.91
Payne, Christine Jane Marion	Supt No(R)		Northwood	31.03.94
Payton, Philip John	Lt Cdr	PA	Vivid	24.07.86
Pearce, Stuart Gordon, RD*	Cdr	AW	King Alfred	30.06.80
Pears, Elinor Jane	Lt Cdr	HQ	Vivid	30.09.91
Pethick, Ian Charles	Slt	LOGS	Vivid	27.10.89
Phelps, Richard Douglas Stanley	Lt	SEA	Scotia	20.04.91
Phillips, Nigel John	ASI		Cambria	18.09.93
Pickup, David Julian	Lt Cdr	PA	Northwood	17.09.75
Pike, Christine Margaret	Lt Cdr	DIS	Ferret (RNR)	31.03.95
Pirie, Katherine	Lt	AIR	RNR Air Br VI	15.12.89
Pollard, Colin William	Lt	AW	Northwood	08.12.86
Pollard, James	Lt Cdr	AIR	RNR Air Br VI	29.10.91
Pollock, William	Lt Cdr	AIR	RNR Air Br VI	16.06.78
Porteous, Peter Anthony, RD	Lt Cdr	HQ	Flying Fox	01.01.85
Posnett, Dickon	Lt	AIR	RNR Air Br VI	01.08.88
Poulton, Andrew Ritchie	ASI		Scotia	10.01.96
Powell, Jonathan Charles Boyd	Lt	MWHQ	President	02.07.86
Powell, William	Lt	AIR	RNR Air Br VI	17.10.91
Powley, Simon Owen Maxwell	Lt	INTR	Ferret (RNR)	16.08.92
Pratt, Ian David	Lt	SEA	Vivid	01.05.92
Pressagh, John Patterson, RD	Lt Cdr	INTR	Ferret (RNR)	02.04.78
Preston, Robert George	Slt	MW	Calliope	20.05.88
Price, Christopher	Lt Cdr	AIR	RNR Air Br VI	01.01.92
Price, David Lewis	Slt	AW	Vivid	23.09.89
Price, Susan Elizabeth	Lt	NCS	King Alfred	01.04.89
Prichard, Robert Edward, RD	Lt Cdr	COMM	President	14.10.92

Name	Rank	Branch	Unit	Seniority
Pugh, Hywel Jones	ALt	AW	President	10.06.90
Pugh, Neil	Lt	LOGS	Cambria	15.05.91

Q

Quartly, Christopher Francis	Sg Ltcdr		Northwood	01.02.88
Quick, David	Lt	NCS	Eaglet	28.01.89

R

Raffan, Gordon Innes	Lt	LOGS	Caroline	17.03.87
Rainey, Peter	Lt Cdr	AIR	RNR Air Br VI	01.03.90
Ramsay, Brian P., MA	Lt	SM	Forward	17.08.90
Rankin, John Graham, RD	Cdr	AW	Vivid	30.09.95
Read, David Arthur, BSC	Lt	HQ	President	03.04.87
Redmond, Robert	ALt Cdr	AW	President	04.08.95
Reece, Christopher	Lt	AIR	RNR Air Br VI	01.11.88
Reece, Victor Alan Cyril	Sg Cdr		Calliope	30.09.89
Reed, Martin, RD*	Capt	AW	King Alfred	30.09.94
Reed, Philip	Lt Cdr	AIR	RNR Air Br VI	31.03.95
Reeves, Alexander Christopher	Lt Cdr	DIS	Ferret (RNR)	31.03.95
Reid, Robert Downie	Lt Cdr	HQ	Cambria	28.06.85
Rennell, Ian Joseph	Slt	SEA	Eaglet	26.06.89
Reynolds, Nelson James Elliott, RD	Cdr	MWHQ	Caroline	30.09.94
Reynoldson, Howard	Lt Cdr	AIR	RNR Air Br VI	30.11.90
Richard-Dit-Leschery, Stanley Ernest, RD	Lt Cdr	AW	Vivid	22.11.92
Richards, Derek Paul, RD*	Cdr	AW	President	30.09.84
Richardson, Ian John	Lt Cdr	INTR	Ferret (RNR)	15.01.91
Richardson, Margaret Lynda Maither, RD	Lt	Q	Dalriada	16.11.90
Rickard, Margaret Mary	Lt	MS	King Alfred	14.07.92
Riley, Peter John	Lt	AW	President	24.11.87
Rimell, Katherine Elizabeth Alice	ASI	SEA	Scotia	01.08.95
Robertson, Lorne Thomas	Lt	MW	Dalriada	11.03.88
Robertson, Wendy	Lt	Q	Dalriada	08.12.95
Robinson, Anthony Michael, RD	Lt Cdr	AW	Cambria	16.06.92
Robinson, Ian Michael, RD	Cdr	NCS	Sherwood	30.09.89
Robinson, James Brian	Lt	AW	Calliope	24.02.90
Robinson, Jonathon Charles King	Lt Cdr	AIR	RNR Air Br VI	01.11.91
Robinson, James	Lt Cdr	AIR	RNR Air Br VI	08.07.89
Robinson, Michael	Lt	AIR	RNR Air Br VI	14.07.86
Robinson, Nigel	Lt Cdr	AIR	RNR Air Br VI	31.03.94
Roche, Philip Brynley	Lt Cdr	HQ	President	31.03.93
Rodger, Emma Mary, BA	Lt	SEA	President	14.09.95
Roelich, Alan	Lt Cdr	AIR	RNR Air Br VI	01.03.86
Rollings, David Jonathon, RD	Lt Cdr	HQ	Cambria	30.10.87
Rose, Norman, RD			URNU (RNR) Aberd	23.02.90
Rosindale, Philip Michael	ASI		Vivid	15.05.93
Ross, Jonathan Anthony Duncan	Lt	MW	Dalriada	28.01.90
Ross, Robert John, RD*	Lt Cdr	AW	King Alfred	17.03.79
Rouse, Brendan Donald Michael	ASI		Scotia	16.03.92
Rowe, Susan Margaret	Lt	NCS	Vivid	23.11.91
Rowland, Stuart William	Lt Cdr	AW	Vivid	01.05.88
Rowles, Joanne	Slt	COMM	Cambria	25.01.92
Rule, John Stewart	Lt	MWHQ	President	23.04.90
Russ, Philip John	Lt	MWHQ	Eaglet	03.02.87
Russell, David Robert	Lt Cdr	PA	King Alfred	19.03.89
Russell, Jane Patricia Katherine	Lt Cdr	INTR	Ferret (RNR)	01.10.88
Ryan, Simon John D Arcy	Lt	HQ	Eaglet	07.07.89

S

Sambrook, Mitchell	Lt Cdr	AIR	RNR Air Br VI	31.03.93
San, Howald Kin Hong	Lt	SM	President	15.12.90
Sanderson, Jennifer Patricia	Slt	HQ	King Alfred	12.10.89

Name	Rank	Branch	Unit	Seniority
Sanderson, Peter	Lt Cdr	AIR	RNR Air Br VI	31.03.95
Sarawgi, V K	ALt	AW	Caroline	01.11.89
Sard, Alexandra, RD	Lt Cdr	LOGS	King Alfred	31.03.95
Satchell, Peter James	Lt	MW	Flying Fox	10.03.90
Saunders, David James	Lt Cdr	MWHQ	President	31.03.95
Scott, Edward Martin, RD*	Capt	AW	King Alfred	30.09.91
Scott, J G	Lt	AW	President	11.11.85
Scribbins, Christopher John	Lt Cdr	HQ	Calliope	11.10.91
Searle, Geoffrey Derek	Lt	MW	King Alfred	16.12.90
Seaton, Christopher Shaun Tudor	Lt Cdr	SM	Flying Fox	01.11.91
Seaton, Judith Ann	Pasg Lt		Sherwood	20.06.95
Shakespeare, Martin, B.PHARM	Lt	DIS	Ferret (RNR)	09.07.89
Shanks, Elizabeth Mary, RD	Lt Cdr	SM	Caroline	30.09.87
Shannon, Tom			URNU (RNR) Glasg	01.11.95
Sharp, David	Lt Cdr	AIR	RNR Air Br VI	01.10.88
Sharples, Derek	Lt Cdr	AIR	RNR Air Br VI	01.06.91
Shaw, James Elliot, RD	Lt Cdr	AW	President	01.07.86
Shears, Stephen	Lt	AIR	RNR Air Br VI	05.09.86
Shepherd, Simon John	Lt	DIS	Ferret (RNR)	15.04.90
Shepherd, William James	Lt	AWNIS	Calliope	25.04.95
Sherriff, Robert Stewart	Lt Cdr	SM	Scotia	02.11.92
Shinner, Patrick Anthony	Lt	SM	President	01.10.88
Shinner, Stephanie Katherine Fleur	Lt	NCS	Northwood	26.05.89
Sides, Susan C.	Lt Cdr	HQ	Sherwood	30.09.91
Siebenaller, Mark	Lt	MWHQ	Flying Fox	08.12.89
Sime, John	Lt	AIR	RNR Air Br VI	01.09.87
Simmonds, Timothy Paul	Slt	MW	President	06.03.92
Simpson, Michael David, RD*	Cdr	HQ	Scotia	30.09.92
Simpson, Paul John Caesar, RD	Lt Cdr	COMM	Sherwood	04.07.88
Sims, Richmal Jane	ASI		King Alfred	17.07.93
Skimming, Joseph Thomas	Lt	HQ	Calliope	18.10.91
Skinner, Douglas	Lt Cdr	AIR	RNR Air Br VI	31.03.95
Skinner, Nigel Guy, BSC, M.ENG	Slt	MW	Sherwood	13.09.90
Slade, Hugh	Lt Cdr	AIR	RNR Air Br VI	01.08.81
Sleeman, Robin	Lt Cdr	AIR	RNR Air Br VI	01.09.87
Sloan, Alan Graham, RD*	Cdr	SM	Northwood	30.09.93
Small, Peter Kenneth	Sg Ltcdr		Scotia	01.08.88
Small, Tracy Sharon	ASI		Northwood	17.07.93
Smart, Roy, RD	Lt Cdr	AIR	RNR Air Br VI	30.05.85
Smellie, Catherine Sharpe, BSc	Lt	NCS	Eaglet	11.07.88
Smellie, David Lewis	Lt Cdr	LOGS	Eaglet	31.03.94
Smith, Charles Allan, RD*	Lt Cdr	AW	King Alfred	14.05.84
Smith, Graham Kenneth Cooper, RD*	Cdr	AWNIS	Vivid	30.09.86
Smith, Lesley Gay Isabel, RD	Lt Cdr	LOGS	Vivid	20.09.89
Smith, Neil L, RD*	Lt Cdr	AWNIS	Dalriada	31.03.81
Smyth, Michael Paul	Lt	MW	Caroline	05.06.89
Solleveld, Andrew	Lt	AIR	RNR Air Br VI	19.12.86
Souter, Michael David, RD	Lt Cdr	PA	Northwood	01.01.84
Speake, John Graham	Sg Ltcdr		Vivid	03.07.83
Spencer, Colin Gregory Rowe, RD*	Lt Cdr	AW	King Alfred	01.10.77
Spray, Alison	Lt Cdr	NCS	Vivid	31.03.93
Sprowles, K J	Lt Cdr	NCS	President	04.11.90
Squire, Robert James, RD	Lt Cdr	COMM	Forward	11.05.91
Stafford-Smith, Karen Julie	Lt	SM	King Alfred	03.05.87
Stanley, Dermot Alan	Slt	SEA	Calliope	09.04.87
Starkey, Peter Gordon, RD	Cdr	AW	President	30.09.85
Steer, Colin N	Lt	HQ	Northwood	25.07.90
Stephenson, Richard	Lt Cdr	AIR	RNR Air Br VI	01.03.80
Stewart, David William	Lt Cdr	LOGS	Caroline	31.03.93
Stewart, Iain Alexander, RD	Lt Cdr	LOGS	Scotia	21.03.87
Stickland, Anthony Charles Robert	Lt	SEA	King Alfred	16.03.88

Name	Rank	Branch	Unit	Seniority
Stoy, John George Frederick, RD*	Capt	NA	President	30.09.95
Strachan, Robin Kinnear	Sg Cdr		President	30.09.95
Strudwick, Peggy Barbara	Slt	LOGS	Vivid	18.03.89
Sudbury, Jeanette, RD	Lt Cdr	NCS	Flying Fox	30.09.87
Sudbury, Peter John, RD	Lt Cdr	HQ	Flying Fox	18.09.87
Sutton, Kevin	Lt Cdr	AIR	RNR Air Br VI	16.08.92
Swann, Judith Helen, RD*	Cdr	NCS	Sherwood	03.09.90
Sweenie, John Fraser	Sg Ltcdr		Dalriada	13.02.90
Syme, Allan, RD	Lt Cdr	HQ	Dalriada	11.02.83
Symons, Robert John, RD	Cdr	NCS	Forward	30.09.90

T

Name	Rank	Branch	Unit	Seniority
Tait, Andrew, AFC	Lt Cdr	AIR	RNR Air Br VI	01.09.85
Tallack, Robert Linsey, RD*	Cdr	AW	President	31.03.81
Tapley, Richard	Lt	AIR	RNR Air Br VI	27.07.87
Taylor, David Paul, RD	Lt Cdr	MS	Flying Fox	11.08.89
Taylor, Louise Elizabeth	Lt	NCS	Eaglet	15.12.90
Taylor, Peter John, B.ENG	Slt	NCS	Caroline	28.11.88
Taylor, Patrick	Lt Cdr	AIR	RNR Air Br VI	12.01.81
Taylor, Rupert James	Lt	SEA	King Alfred	21.06.85
Teasdale, John, RD	Cdr	AIR	RNR Air Br VI	01.10.92
Tebbs, Christopher John, RD*	Cdr	COMM	Calliope	30.09.92
Telfer, Alison Averil, RD	Lt Cdr	NCS	Eaglet	30.09.91
Templeton, Susan Marie	Lt	LOGS	Flying Fox	13.12.85
Thain, Julie Christina	Lt	Q	Scotia	25.06.89
Thom, Eleanor Margaret Jeanne	Lt	NCS	Dalriada	21.08.95
Thomas, Emma Margaret	Lt	PA	King Alfred	26.07.86
Thomas, Jeffrey	Lt Cdr	AIR	RNR Air Br VI	01.09.92
Thomas, John	Lt Cdr	AIR	RNR Air Br VI	01.10.90
Thomas, Merion James	Slt	SEA	Dalriada	12.07.88
Thomas, Peter Glyn	Lt	MWHQ	Eaglet	19.07.89
Thomas, Stephen Paul	Slt	MW	Cambria	15.05.92
Thomason, Michael	Slt	LOGS	Eaglet	17.07.93
Thompson, Alison Denise	Lt	NCS	Vivid	27.01.95
Thompson, Andrew John	Lt Cdr	NCS	Vivid	31.03.94
Thompson, Ceri	Sg Ltcdr		Northwood	30.08.86
Thompson, Glenn	Lt	AIR	RNR Air Br VI	23.11.90
Thomson, Patricia Anne Grant, RD	Lt	DIS	Ferret (RNR)	20.06.88
Thomson, Susie Jane	Lt	PA	Flying Fox	07.03.90
Thorne, Brian John, RD	Lt Cdr	COMM	Cambria	17.06.89
Thorne, Lee James	Slt	SEA	King Alfred	29.09.91
Thorne, Stephen Paul, RD	Lt Cdr	COMM	King Alfred	31.03.93
Thwaites, Barbara Ann	Lt	PA	President	17.06.86
Tidd, Michael	Lt Cdr	AIR	RNR Air Br VI	01.10.90
Tindall-Jones, Julia Mary, BA	Lt Cdr	LOGS	Vivid	31.03.94
Todd, Andrew Harry Campbell	Lt	NCS	Scotia	28.07.88
Tonkin, Neil	Lt Cdr	AIR	RNR Air Br VI	01.10.90
Tonks, David John	Slt	MW	Scotia	22.07.88
Topping, Mark	Lt	MWHQ	Cambria	24.05.87
Townsend, John Stafford	Sg Ltcdr		Sherwood	11.02.85
Toy, John Michael, RD	Lt Cdr	NCS	Caroline	19.07.79
Trayhurn, Robert Stephen	Lt Cdr	PA	Dalriada	01.01.84
Trelawny, Christopher Charles	Lt	SEA	President	14.12.89
Treloar, Philip Michael	Lt Cdr	PA	Northwood	16.09.88
Tribe, David	Lt	AIR	RNR Air Br VI	16.07.88
Trimmer, Patrick David Mark	Lt	SEA	Calliope	09.08.85
Tulloch, Alan	Slt	X	URNU (RNR) Aberd	08.04.87
Turner, Jonathan Andrew McMahon, RD	Sg Ltcdr		King Alfred	22.07.76
Tweed, Susan Linda, JP, RD	Lt Cdr	NCS	Forward	30.09.90

Name	Rank	Branch	Unit	Seniority

U

Name	Rank	Branch	Unit	Seniority
Ure, Fiona	Slt	Q	Scotia	23.01.87
Uren, Margaret	Lt	AIR	RNR Air Br VI	15.12.89

V

Name	Rank	Branch	Unit	Seniority
Valentine, Robert Innes	Lt	SEA	Scotia	14.09.90
Van Onselen, Ian	Lt	AIR	RNR Air Br VI	16.08.88
Vandal, Stuart Bertram Alisdair	Slt	HQ	Dalriada	25.09.90
Varley, Peter	Lt Cdr	AIR	RNR Air Br VI	07.09.81
Vernon, Michael Anthony, RD	Lt Cdr	COMM	Vivid	27.08.90
Vote, Richard Malcolm	Lt Cdr	DIS	Ferret (RNR)	06.08.78

W

Name	Rank	Branch	Unit	Seniority
Waddell, Verity Noeline, RD	Lt Cdr	NCS	Calliope	31.03.93
Wake, Thomas Baldwin	Lt	COMM	Sherwood	14.05.89
Walden, Geoffery George	Lt	SM	Eaglet	10.12.90
Wale, Martin Charles Johnson	Lt Cdr	DIS	Ferret (RNR)	01.08.86
Wales, Frederick Anthony	Lt	AW	King Alfred	18.03.88
Walker, David Iain	Lt	LOGS	President	14.09.86
Walker, Josephine Susan, RD	Cdr	NCS	Forward	30.09.91
Walker-Spicer, Ian Edward	Lt Cdr	AW	President	12.11.84
Wall, Susan Frances, B.ED	Slt	HQ	Flying Fox	28.10.89
Wallace, James	Lt Cdr	AIR	RNR Air Br VI	21.10.91
Wallace, Stuart Iain	Psl	AW	President	19.11.94
Waller, Helen Sarah	Lt	NCS	Vivid	20.02.90
Waller, Vincent Francis, RD	Lt Cdr	AW	Calliope	01.09.88
Walmsley, Stephen Graham	ASI		Caroline	15.05.93
Walters, Philip	Lt Cdr	AIR	RNR Air Br VI	26.10.82
Walton, Paul Ronald	Lt	AW	Eaglet	03.12.92
Walworth, William Michael	Cdr	AW	President	30.09.95
Warden, Bradley Martin Spencer	Lt	MWHQ	Eaglet	17.07.87
Wardrope, G J	Lt	HQ	King Alfred	19.11.87
Ware, James Robert	Lt	MW	Caroline	20.08.89
Warren, David	Lt Cdr	AIR	RNR Air Br VI	17.01.92
Warren, Helen Louise	Slt	SEA	President	24.07.89
Watson, Catherine Jennifer	Lt	HQ	Eaglet	07.09.87
Watson, Karen Marie	Lt	INTR	Ferret (RNR)	09.10.88
Waugh, Graham, RD*	Lt Cdr	AW	President	09.11.78
Webber, Michael	Lt Cdr	AIR	RNR Air Br VI	30.04.89
Weldon, Helen Wright	Lt	HQ	Dalriada	16.03.89
Wells, Christopher Michael	Lt Cdr	AW	King Alfred	31.03.94
Welsh, John Christopher	Lt	COMM	Caroline	12.10.95
Wesley, John R	Lt Cdr	HQ	President	12.11.89
West, Nicholas	Lt	AIR	RNR Air Br VI	13.08.87
West, Susan Elizabeth	Sg Ltcdr		President	27.09.84
Westwood, Steve	Lt Cdr	AIR	RNR Air Br VI	01.10.92
Whawell, Peter Gerald Maber	ASI		President	19.02.94
Wheeler, Juliet Claire	Slt	Q	King Alfred	26.02.87
Wheeler, Robert Alec	Sg Ltcdr		King Alfred	18.12.92
Wheeler, Susan Mary	Lt Cdr	PA	President	31.03.94
Whitaker, Gary	Lt	AIR	RNR Air Br VI	01.01.87
Whitby, David John, RD	Cdr	AW	President	30.09.84
Whitby, Philip	Lt Cdr	SM	Northwood	26.12.90
White, Antony	Lt Cdr	AIR	RNR Air Br VI	10.02.86
White, Ian Roy	Lt	SEA	Calliope	18.10.85
Whitehead, Keith Stuart, BSC	Lt	HQ	King Alfred	09.10.89
Witham, Andrew Slater	Lt Cdr	AW	King Alfred	01.10.91
Whitlock, Michael Anthony	Lt	SEA	King Alfred	27.01.92
Whorwood, Julia Margaret	Lt	AWNIS	King Alfred	31.10.89
Wickens, Ian	Lt	AIR	RNR Air Br VI	24.12.91

Name	Rank	Branch	Unit	Seniority
Williams, Mark	Lt	NCS	Eaglet RNR	27.10.92
Williams, Paul David	Lt Cdr	AW	Calliope	05.08.86
Williams, Peter Lunt, RD	Lt Cdr	COMM	Eaglet	11.05.90
Williams, Timothy Paul	Lt	MW	King Alfred	22.09.95
Williamson, Kevin	Lt Cdr	AIR	RNR Air Br VI	01.03.93
Williamson, Nicholas John Bruce	Lt	HQ	Eaglet	14.06.89
Wilson, Gary			U/A	10.10.95
Wilson, Jennifer Maureen	Lt Cdr	Q	Flying Fox	31.03.95
Wilson, James	Lt Cdr	AIR	RNR Air Br VI	22.11.89
Wilson, Karyn Stewart	Lt	NCS	Flying Fox	19.07.90
Wilson, Stephen John	Sg Lt		Forward	01.08.91
Winfield, Adrian	Lt	AIR	RNR Air Br VI	20.06.89
Winstanley, Nichola Ann	Lt Cdr	PA	Vivid	31.03.95
Wood, Gerald Norman, RD*	Capt	NA	Flying Fox	30.09.93
Wood, John	Lt	COMM	Calliope	02.05.92
Woodham, Jeremy	Lt Cdr	AIR	RNR Air Br VI	02.07.92
Woods, Fergus	Lt Cdr	AIR	RNR Air Br VI	01.10.88
Woods, Michael	Lt Cdr	AIR	RNR Air Br VI	31.03.94
Woods, Peter Anthony, RD*	Capt	AW	Eaglet	30.09.88
Woolley, Thomas Richard, RD	Cdr	MWHQ	Scotia	30.09.91
Wordie, Andrew George Lyon	Lt Cdr	COMM	Sherwood	31.03.95
Worsley, Alistair Louis	Lt	PA	Northwood	05.07.87
Wray, Ronald Maurice	Lt	NCS	Caroline	07.05.90
Wreford, Katrine Patricia	Lt Cdr	LOGS	Scotia	31.03.93
Wrigglesworth, Peter John	Sg Ltcdr		Sherwood	02.08.88
Wright, Alan Howard	Lt Cdr	AW	Eaglet	01.11.91
Wright, Gordon, RD	Lt Cdr	AIR	RNR Air Br VI	17.04.86
Wright, Martin Thomas Ian	Lt	MWHQ	Dalriada	19.08.86
Wright, Stephen	Lt	SEA	King Alfred	23.08.89
Wring, Matthew Anthony	Lt	MW	Flying Fox	25.01.95
Wrynn, David James	ASI		Calliope	12.07.95
Wyatt, David Alexander, RD*	Lt Cdr	AW	President	08.12.77
Wyatt, Mark Edward, RD	Lt Cdr	MWHQ	King Alfred	16.09.89
Wyglendacz, Jan Andrew	Lt	LOGS	Cambria	28.01.90
Wynne, Rena Julie	Slt	HQ	Vivid	15.08.89

Y

Name	Rank	Branch	Unit	Seniority
Yates, Steven	Lt	MW	Flying Fox	16.12.90
Yearsley, John	Lt Cdr	AIR	RNR Air Br VI	25.03.87
Yetman, Philip John, RD	Lt Cdr	NCS	King Alfred	13.08.87
Young, Carl	Lt	AIR	RNR Air Br VI	01.12.87
Young, Duncan Alexander	Lt	MW	Calliope	02.11.87
Young, Deborah Joy	ASI		Calliope	15.05.93

ROYAL MARINES RESERVE

Name	Rank	List	Unit	Seniority
A				
Ackroyd, Charles	Maj	M1	BRISTOL	28.09.91
Askins, Stephen	Capt	M1	LONDON	16.04.93
B				
Barnwell, Barry	Maj	M1	SCOTLAND	01.12.90
Bell, Stephen	Capt	M1	BRISTOL	13.09.94
Billington, Edward	Lt	M1	MERSEYSIDE	07.06.92
Brooker Gillespie, Robin	Lt	M1	LONDON	04.01.95
Brown, Roger	Lt	M1	LONDON	15.07.90
Brownhill, Terence	Capt	M1	MERSEYSIDE	27.10.88
Bruce, Rory	Loc Capt	M1	BRISTOL	08.04.90
Burnett, Simon	Capt	M2	BRISTOL	01.08.89
C				
Cadwallader, Barry	Lt	M1	MERSEYSIDE	11.06.93
Campbell, Michael	Lt	M1	TYNE	01.04.95
Campbell, Ross	Act Lt	M1	SCOTLAND	02.11.92
Carpenter, Nicholas	Lt	M1	MERSEYSIDE	16.11.93
Carstairs, Douglas	Capt	M1	SCOTLAND	14.07.89
Coard, John	Lt	M1	SCOTLAND	22.08.88
Cumming, James	Capt	M1	SCOTLAND	01.05.92
D				
Dudley, Andrew	Capt	M2	LONDON	01.05.92
Dugard, Peter	Capt	M1	MERSEYSIDE	08.08.87
F				
Figgins, Phillip	Capt	M1	LONDON	01.04.91
G				
Galley, Christopher	Lt	M1	SCOTLAND	25.05.93
Gibson, Mark	Lt	M1	MERSEYSIDE	20.01.92
Gibson, Richard	Act Lt	M1	BRISTOL	22.10.90
H				
Hatt-Cook, Mark, *RD*, ADC*	Col	M1	LONDON	07.02.92
Hebron, Bryan	Lt	M1	TYNE	22.05.90
Holmyard, Clive	Act Capt	M1	MERSEYSIDE	01.10.91
Holt, Andrew	Maj	M1	MERSEYSIDE	31.12.93
Hough, Brian, *RD*	Maj	M1	MERSEYSIDE	28.07.92
Hoyle, David	Lt	M1	BRISTOL	01.05.87
I				
Ing, John	Capt	M1	SBS POOLE	01.09.94
J				
Jackson, Fraser	Lt	M1	SCOTLAND	01.10.92
Jenkins, Mike	Locltcol	M2	BRISTOL	03.07.89
Jobbins, Paul	Lt Col	M1	BRISTOL	28.01.94
Johnson, Alan	Lt	M1	MERSEYSIDE	09.05.93
K				
Kelly, Anthony, *RD*	Maj	M1	BRISTOL	16.05.93

Name	Rank	List	Unit	Seniority

L

Lang, Tom	Col	M1	BRISTOL	28.02.95
Lindfield, Bary	Capt	M1	MERSEYSIDE	25.10.91
Lyons, Michael	Lt	M1	MERSEYSIDE	15.06.93

M

MacTaggart, Robin	Col	M2	SCOTLAND	01.06.77
Mannion, Stephen	Lt	M1	LONDON	09.05.93
March, Jefreey	Maj	M1	MERSEYSIDE	25.08.92
Mason, Andrew	2lt	M1	BRISTOL	01.01.94
Mather, Nicholas	Lt	M1	LONDON	19.05.90
Maw, Paul	Capt	M1	LONDON	27.11.90
McGinley, Michael	Lt	M1	MERSEYSIDE	11.06.93
McLaughlin, Stephen	Lt	M1	SCOTLAND	18.09.91
McNeil, David	Lt	M1	LONDON	01.06.94
Mirtle, Frank	Act Maj	M1	LONDON	25.07.94

P

Paul, Thomas	Capt	M1	SCOTLAND	01.06.91
Phillips, Andrew	Capt	M1	BRISTOL	01.09.95
Pike, Andrew	2lt	M1	TYNE	31.07.94

R

Reed, Dougal	Lt	M1	TYNE	01.05.92
Richards, Gavin, *RD*	Capt	M1	LONDON	16.09.93
Robinson, David	Act Maj	M1	TYNE	14.11.95
Rowland, Johnny	Lt	M1	BRISTOL	01.04.94
Rowlstone, David John	Lt	M1	MERSEYSIDE	11.06.93

S

Smallwood, Justin	Capt	M1	BRISTOL	11.07.92
Smith, Fraser	Act Lt	M1	LONDON	31.07.90
Smith, John	Act Capt	M1	BRISTOL	01.08.89
Street, Charles	Capt	M1	TYNE	01.08.94

T

Tarnowski, Thomas	Lt	M1	LONDON	12.01.95
Tayler, Harry	Lt	M1	LONDON	01.07.95
Taylor, Robert	Lt	M1	BRISTOL	01.01.90
Terry, Stuart	Capt	M1	BRISTOL	01.02.93
Thomas, Martyn, *RD*	Capt	M1	BRISTOL	25.10.89
Tompkins, Richard	Lt	M1	BRISTOL	24.02.92
Tonner, Raymond	Act Capt	M1	BRISTOL	02.02.93
Travis, Adrian	Lt	M1	LONDON	01.05.88

W

Waddell, Ian	Lt	M1	MERSEYSIDE	01.08.91
Walford, Adrian	Act Lt	M1	LONDON	21.10.92
Watt, David	Act Lt	M1	LONDON	22.01.94
Wilson, Alan	2lt	M1	SBS POOLE	01.05.95

SEA CADET CORPS

Name	Rank	Seniority
A		
Adams, Michael	Lt	5. 2.83
Adams, Thomas	Lt	7. 9.83
Agar, Andrew	Lt	22. 3.91
Alderton, Gerald	Lt	17.11.77
Allam, John	Lt	31. 8.87
Allen, John	Lt	15. 6.95
Allen, John	Slt	17.11.91
Allen, Karen	Lt	8.10.88
Allen, Leslie	Lt	23. 5.85
Allo, David	Lt Cdr	6. 5.72
Anderson, William	Lt	21. 2.84
Andrews, Colin	Lt Cdr	18. 2.77
Annett, Jennifer	Slt	21. 3.94
Anson, Robert	Lt	29.11.94
Appleby, Gary	Slt	15.11.94
Appleby, Keith	Slt	23. 1.93
Archbold, Dennis	Lt	1. 4.69
Archbold, Theresa	Slt	20. 1.95
Archer, Barry	Lt	8. 3.94
Archer, Lynn	Slt	14.11.94
Armstrong-Smith, Helen	Lt	6.12.95
Arrighi, Paul	Slt	6.11.93
Atkins, Doreen	Lt	8. 4.92
Attwood, Anthony	Lt	22. 2.87
Attwood, Robert	Lt	8.11.79
Avill, Susan	Lt	1.11.89
B		
Baddley, Aljeana	Lt	28.11.95
Baddley, Stephen	Lt	28.11.95
Bagley, Bruce	Lt Cdr	1. 7.81
Bailey, John	Lt	8. 4.74
Bailey, Robert	Lt	12. 3.91
Bailey, Terence	Lt	1.12.95

Name	Rank	Seniority
Baillie, Janet	Slt	21. 3.94
Baines, Penelope	Slt	2.12.95
Baker, Michael	Lt RMR	24. 5.95
Baker, Roy	Capt RMR	27. 6.70
Ball, Maurice	Lt Cdr	16. 2.75
Bancroft, David	Slt	6. 5.94
Banks, Michael	Lt Cdr	6. 9.88
Banks, Paul	Slt	5. 6.94
Banner, Peter	Slt	30. 3.92
Barber, Anthony	Lt	12. 3.91
Barker, David	Slt	1.11.95
Barlow, Albert	Slt	1.11.95
Barnard, John	Lt	8. 4.90
Barras, Hugh	Lt	1. 1.94
Barritt, Richard	A/Lt Cdr	5. 3.89
Barron, Edward	Lt RMR	2. 8.70
Barron, Valery	Lt Cdr	1.11.92
Barrow, George	Lt	9.10.90
Barrow, Joan	Slt	5.11.95
Bartlett, Colin	Lt	1.10.76
Bartlett, Jonathan	Slt	21. 9.94
Bartlett, Peter	Lt Cdr	5. 1.78
Bartlweman, Alexander	Lt	25.11.72
Barton, William	Lt Cdr	1.10.78
Bassett, Gary	Slt	16.11.94
Bateman, Wendy	Slt	29.11.95
Baxter, Thomas	Slt	22.11.95
Bayliss, John	Lt Cdr	18. 2.87
Bayliss, Peter	Lt Cdr	1. 8.91
Bayly, Peter	Slt	23. 3.91
Beach, Andrew	Lt	18. 7.84
Beal, Peter	Lt	26. 3.85
Beaumont, Marilyn	Lt	28. 2.95
Beckett, Alan	Lt	8. 3.94
Bedford, Michael	Lt	1. 4.86
Bell, Brian	Slt	31. 8.88

Name	Rank	Seniority	Name	Rank	Seniority
Bell, Frederick	Lt Cdr	21. 7.90	Broadbent, Graham	Lt Cdr	1. 1.88
Bell, John	Lt	25. 7.84	Broadfoot, Robert	Lt Cdr	1. 7.82
Bell, Ruth	Lt	3.11.93	Brockwell, Graham	Lt	21. 9.90
Bell, Veronica	Slt	5. 2.94	Brooks, Henry	Lt Cdr	19. 9.76
Bennions, Margaret	Lt	1. 8.86	Brotherton, Stephen	Slt	4. 6.95
Benton, Ruth	Lt	8.10.91	Brown, Alexander	Lt	22. 9.86
Bereznyckyj, Nicholas	Lt RMR	3.11.93	Brown, Anthony	Lt	4. 2.87
Bilby, Glyn	Lt	20.11.91	Brown, David	Lt Cdr	30. 3.80
Billinghay, Sandra	Lt	1. 7.85	Brown, David	Lt Cdr	2. 6.86
Billingsley, Raymond	Slt	17. 3.95	Brown, Jeffrey	Lt	25. 2.92
Bilverstone, Brian	Lt	24. 3.91	Brown, John	Lt Cdr	4. 7.78
Bingham, Keith	Lt	1. 3.95	Brown, Keith	Lt	26.10.84
Bingham, Maurice	Lt	1. 1.88	Brown, Lawrence	Lt RMR	23. 1.94
Birkwood, Geoffrey	Capt RMR	15.10.87	Brown, Margaret	Lt	28. 8.88
Bishop, Peter	Lt	1.11.95	Brown, Richard	Lt	28. 2.95
Bisson, Keith	Slt	21.10.89	Brown, Richard	Lt	1. 5.91
Black, Magdalene	A/Lt Cdr	1. 1.96	Brown, Sylvia	Lt	1. 9.88
Blackburn, Alan	Slt	3. 3.91	Brown, William	Lt	14. 3.92
Blackwood, Alan	Lt	9. 1.92	Browning, Tony	Slt	19. 5.91
Blakely, Roy	Lt	17.10.85	Broxham, Roy	Lt	21. 9.90
Blaker, Carol	Lt Cdr	1.10.81	Bryant, Charles	Lt	19. 2.87
Blaker, Malcolm	Lt Cdr	3. 1.80	Budd, Anthony	Lt	16. 8.83
Bloor, John	Lt RMR	15. 5.93	Budden, Ralph	Lt	16. 6.93
Board, Brian	Lt	15.11.91	Bullock, Geoffrey	Lt Cdr	1. 7.87
Board, Peter	Lt Cdr	1. 4.88	Burden, John	Lt Cdr	19. 4.78
Boardman, Richard	Lt Cdr	27. 4.86	Burke, William	Capt RMR	25. 5.77
Bodycote, Stephen	Lt	24. 9.91	Burns, Clifford	Lt	1.11.93
Bond, Paul	Lt	1. 4.80	Burns, Desmond	Lt	18. 2.78
Bonfield, Christopher	Slt	6.11.94	Burns, Philip	Lt	27. 6.80
Bonjour, Andre	Lt	27. 5.92	Burr, Peter	Lt	3.11.93
Boorman, Nicholas	Lt	12.11.86	Burrage, Richard	Lt	25. 6.90
Booth, Christina	Lt	3.12.91	Burt, Christopher	Slt	1.10.92
Booth, Kenneth	A/Lt Cdr	1.12.94	Burton, Colin	Lt	7. 3.88
Bosustow, John	Lt	26. 2.82	Bushen, Martyn	Lt	28.11.95
Bott, Frederick	Lt	1.11.87	Butcher, David	Lt	17. 8.94
Bowen, Terrence	Lt	3. 3.82	Butler, Brian	Lt	9. 6.82
Bowman, Thomas	Lt	29. 9.89	Butler, John	Slt	20.11.95
Bowskill, Michael	Lt	10.11.85	Butterworth, John	Lt	23. 3.87
Boxall, Alan	Lt	2. 8.89			
Boxall, Keith	Lt	20. 2.95	**C**		
Boxall, Lisa	Slt	20. 3.94	Cade, John	Lt	27.11.87
Boyes, Stephen	Slt	20.11.95	Cadman, Julie	Lt	7.10.89
Boyle, Alexander	Lt	30. 9.91	Cadman, John	Lt Cdr	29. 4.70
Boylin, Mark Gordon	Lt Cdr	1. 1.92	Calder, Robert	Slt	24.11.95
Boyne, John	Slt	16. 3.94	Calvert, Martin	Lt	19.11.91
Bradbury, David	Lt	1. 1.88	Campbell, Diane	Slt	5. 6.92
Bradford, David	Lt	8.10.85	Campbell, William	Lt	1. 1.88
Bradford, William	Lt	28.12.79	Carney, Robert	Slt	2. 8.95
Bradley, John	Lt	10. 9.91	Carpenter, Michael	Lt Cdr	1.12.83
Bramley, Derek	Lt	3.12.88	Carr, Leonard	Lt Cdr	19. 2.76
Bran, Janette	Slt	1.11.92	Carroll, Paul	Lt	2. 5.86
Bratley, Charles	Lt	9.10.90	Carter, David	Lt	4. 3.92
Brayford, John	Lt Cdr	2. 2.83	Carter, John	Lt Cdr	1. 3.92
Brayshaw, Maurice	Lt	1.11.91	Cartwright, Adrian	Slt	5.11.95
Brazier, Colin	Lt	29. 9.82	Caslaw, Paul	Lt	1. 8.94
Brentnall, Charles	Slt	24. 9.94	Cassidy, Michael	Slt	1.12.80
Bridle, Stephen	Lt	12.11.94	Catterall, Susan	Lt	20. 1.87
Briggs, Donald	Lt	1. 9.77	Catterall, Timothy	Lt	11. 4.78
Brimelow, Michael	Slt	22. 5.95	Cauley, John	Lt Cdr	1. 1.95
Briscoe, Robert	Slt	14.11.94	Cavalier, David	Lt	16. 1.73
Bristow, David	Lt	1. 1.87	Cea, Franklin	Lt	18. 7.92

Name	Rank	Seniority	Name	Rank	Seniority
Chadwick, Daniel	Lt	1. 9.90	Crick, Kenneth	Lt	20.10.92
Chadwick, Heather	Lt	26. 2.93	Crighton, Ian	Lt Cdr	6. 2.90
Chadwick, Peter	Slt	23.11.94	Critchlow, Jonathan	Lt	5. 2.87
Challacombe, Jonathan	Lt Cdr	27. 6.90	Crockett, Robert	Lt	24. 6.82
Chalmers, Janette	Lt	1. 1.91	Crook, Robert	Lt	18. 9.92
Chalmers, John	Lt Cdr	29. 7.92	Cross, Stuart	Slt	5.11.95
Chambers, John	Lt Cdr	1. 1.88	Crossley, Vincent	Lt Cdr	4. 4.77
Chappell, Michael	Lt	1. 6.89	Crowley, Derek	Lt	1. 7.90
Charlton, Adrian	Lt	1. 1.88	Cruse, Malcolm	Lt Cdr	17.10.89
Chesworth, Howard	Lt	3.12.91	Cumming, Peter	Lt	1.10.82
Chinn, John	Lt Cdr	1. 1.83	Cummins, Sheila	Lt	1.11.86
Chittock, Michael	Lt	25. 3.94	Cumper, Alan	Slt	19. 4.95
Chritchlow, Julian	Lt	8. 9.95	Cunningham, Isabella	Lt	1.10.89
Cioma, Antoni	Lt Cdr	1. 7.90	Curran, Paul	Lt	1. 2.88
Clark, Anne	Slt	5.11.95	Curtis, Owen	Lt	25. 6.85
Clark, Ian	Lt Cdr	1. 3.92	Cuss, Melvin	Lt	1.10.85
Clarke, Judith	Lt	6. 7.87			
Clarke, Leonard	Slt	9. 6.94	**D**		
Clarke, Reuben	Lt	30.12.89	D'Henin, John	Lt Cdr	10.10.67
Clay, Joseph	Lt	16. 8.72	Daly, Martin	Lt	19.11.91
Clifford, Ian	Slt	14.11.94	Daniels, Joan	Lt	1.10.85
Clissold, Mark	Lt	1. 4.93	Daniels, Roger	Lt Cdr	14. 1.91
Clunas, William	Lt	3.10.88	Dann, John	Lt	9. 7.95
Coast, Philip	Lt Cdr	9. 7.90	Davies, Bruno	Lt Cdr	15. 4.86
Cockell, Richard	Lt	27. 2.87	Davies, Colin	Slt	18. 9.93
Cole, Christopher	Lt	18.11.76	Davies, Frederick	Slt	24. 4.94
Cole, Ain	Slt	8. 6.95	Davies, Peter	Lt	6. 9.83
Coles, Thomas	Lt Cdr	19.12.87	Davies, Richard	Lt Cdr	7.12.81
Collier, David	A/Lt	1. 9.88	Davies, William	Lt	9. 4.70
Collins, Ann	Lt	25. 1.91	Davis, Brian	Lt Cdr	21. 2.81
Collins, David, *CENG, MRINA*	Lt Cdr	1. 1.88	Davis, Shelagh	Lt	14. 6.95
Collins, Raymond	Slt	31. 8.94	Daw, Clifford	Lt Cdr	1. 1.88
Compton, Paul	Lt Cdr	10.11.65	Dawson, James, *BED(HONS), M1PM,*	Lt Cdr	24.10.87
Constable, David	Lt	1. 3.81	*TENG*		
Cooling, Philip	Lt	4.11.91	Day, Jean Stevenson	Lt	5. 2.91
Coombes, Paul	Lt	25. 1.94	Deegan, Peter	Slt	15.10.95
Cooper, Frederick	Lt	9.10.90	Delin, Roual	A/Lt RMR	1.11.93
Cooper, James	Lt Cdr	24. 1.88	Demellweek, Gilbert	Lt	1. 1.92
Cope, Derek	Lt Cdr	16. 2.82	Desmond, Raymond	Lt Cdr	1. 1.94
Cope, Yvonne	Slt	1. 6.84	Devenish, Ian	Slt	5.11.95
Copeland, Philip	Lt	5. 3.93	Devereux, Edwin	Lt Cdr	31. 7.72
Copelin, Maureen	Lt	5.10.87	Dibben, Michael	Lt	3.11.86
Copelin, Roger	Lt	6. 9.78	Dibben, Nigel	Lt	1. 1.88
Cormack, Raymond	Slt	20.11.95	Dibnah, Robert	Slt	29.10.95
Cornell, Nicholas	Lt	12. 8.74	Dickinson, Keith	Lt	10.11.85
Cornish, Michael	Lt	15. 9.89	Dickson, James	Lt	1. 9.92
Costerd, David Lloyd	Lt	4.11.92	Docking, Keith	Lt	7.11.79
Costin, Raymond	Lt Cdr	3.11.90	Doggart, Norman	Lt	1. 7.88
Cotgrove, David	Lt	16. 7.94	Donovan, Terence	Slt	6.11.94
Cotton, Colin	Lt	21. 1.79	Dorey, Thomas	Lt	28. 2.95
Cowan, Peter	Lt	4. 6.63	Dorricott, Peter	Lt	26.10.85
Cowell, Christopher	Lt RMR	28. 5.87	Dougal, Alexander	Lt	2.10.81
Cowell, Ian	Lt Cdr	1. 1.92	Dowdeswell, Robin	Lt	12. 7.86
Cowell, John	Lt	1. 4.91	Dowding, John	Lt Cdr	23. 3.82
Cowie, Malcolm	Lt	29.10.68	Dowsett, Mark Samuel	Lt	7. 6.90
Crabb, Alan	Lt	15.11.79	Doyle, Ellen	Lt Cdr	31. 3.80
Craig, Neil	Lt	1. 4.86	Dryden, Stephen	Lt	19. 1.81
Craighead, Roderick	Lt	8. 3.93	Duffy, Julia	Lt	23. 4.93
Crawford, Edmund	A/Lt Cdr	11. 1.96	Dulling, Kevin	Lt	24. 7.91
Crawley, Stephen	Lt RMR	4. 6.94	Duncan, Clive	Lt	1.11.91
Creighton, Edward William	Lt	26.11.92	Duncan, Niall	Slt	1. 3.89

Name	Rank	Seniority	Name	Rank	Seniority
Dunkeld, Brian	Slt	4. 6.95	Forster, Thomas	Lt	19. 6.80
Dunn, Simon	Slt	20. 3.94	Foster, Andrew	Lt	19.11.91
Dutton, Martin	Lt Cdr	29. 7.86	Foster, David	Slt	5.11.95
Dyer, Geoffrey	Lt RMR	1. 7.92	Foster, Ian	Lt	5. 8.85
Dyer, Gillian	Lt	21. 6.94	Fowler, Alison	Slt	6.11.94
Dyer, Roger	Slt	7. 6.95	Freeman, Brian	Lt	16. 6.95
Dyer, Trevor	Lt	3.11.93	Freestone, Andrew	Lt	7.11.95
Dymond, Paul	Lt	18.11.94	Frost, Michael	Slt	21. 6.92
Dyster, Ian	Lt Cdr	1. 1.88	Fry, Brian	Lt	25. 9.78
			Fulcher, Diane	Lt	6. 9.94
E			Fulcher, Graham	Slt	24. 4.94
Eagles, Alan	Lt	5. 2.94	Fuller, Keith Duncan	Lt	4. 5.92
Eaton, Trevor	Slt	22. 3.92	Fussell, Christopher	Lt	1.10.90
Edwards, Stuart	Slt	4. 6.95			
Egan, Terence	Lt	1. 1.86	**G**		
Eland, Robert	Lt	1. 7.90	Gale, Ronnie	Lt	1.11.90
Ellicker, Robert	Lt	7. 5.83	Gallacher, David	Lt	1.11.91
Ellis, David	Slt	22. 9.93	Gallagher, Eamon	Lt	23. 6.92
Ellis, Henry	Lt	27.11.94	Gambell, Mark	Slt	14.12.94
Ellis, Wininfred	Lt	21. 4.93	Gardner, Keith	Lt	1. 5.94
Ellison, Michael	Lt Cdr	1. 1.88	Gardner, Robert	Lt	6. 3.82
Ellsmore-Creed, Derek	Lt Cdr	1. 1.85	Garner, James	Lt	4. 6.81
Elson, John	Lt	18. 3.90	Garner, Joshua Paul	Lt Cdr	1. 1.91
English, Michael	Lt Cdr	1. 4.88	Garnsworthy, Derek	Slt	25. 2.90
Erskine, Richard	Slt	27. 9.94	Garrett, John	Lt	7. 5.86
Evans, Janet	Lt Cdr	1. 7.94	Garrett, Robert	Slt	6.11.94
Evans, John Philip	Lt RMR	2. 5.91	Gate, Frederic	Lt	12. 4.79
Evans, Mark	Lt RMR	12. 3.90	Gault, Clements	Lt Cdr	4. 7.88
Evans, Wendy	Lt Cdr	1. 4.90	Gauntlett, Brian	Slt	21. 3.94
Every, Paul David	Lt	17. 4.92	Gearing, Robert	Lt Cdr	1. 9.77
			Gell, Dorothy	Lt	16.10.87
F			Gerrard, David	Lt Cdr	1.12.88
Faldo, David	Lt	21. 4.93	Gerrard, Mary	Lt	20. 5.84
Farrant, Paul	Slt	27. 4.94	Gibson, James	Lt Cdr	25.10.91
Farrell, Martin	Lt	16. 9.85	Gibson, Peter	Lt	22. 5.93
Faulkner, Peter	Lt	1. 4.93	Gilbert, John	Lt Cdr	31.12.75
Feist, Ivor	Lt Cdr	12. 7.80	Gilbert, Robin	Lt RMR	11.11.82
Fenner, Keith	Lt RMR	6.12.89	Gilbert, Susan	Lt	21. 4.90
Fifield, Mark	Slt	14. 6.95	Giles, Roger	Lt Cdr	30. 6.94
Finister, Anthony	Lt RMR	15. 8.94	Gill, Jacqueline	Lt	28. 2.95
Finlay, David	Slt	18. 9.93	Gillard, Terence	Lt Cdr	1. 1.95
Finley, Martin	Lt RMR	27. 4.95	Gillert, Valerie	Lt	19.10.91
Fisher, Barry	Lt	29.10.81	Gilliam, Kevin	Lt	1. 7.93
Fisher, Hazel	Lt	26. 1.92	Glanfield, Mark	Lt	6. 2.82
Fitzgerald, Paul	Slt	15. 6.94	Glanville, Barry	Lt	9. 2.91
Flack, Brian	Slt	4. 9.94	Glendinning-Smith, Elizabeth	Lt	2. 7.92
Flack, Janet	Lt Cdr	1. 5.79	Glenesk, Lindsay	Lt	22. 2.92
Fleet, Gordon	A/Lt RMR	21. 3.94	Godfrey, Paul	Slt	9.11.94
Fleming, Alan	Lt	10. 7.93	Goode, Eric	Slt	13.12.95
Fletcher, Carol	Lt Cdr	1. 4.80	Gooding, Peter	Lt Cdr	1. 1.81
Fletcher, David	Slt	19. 2.95	Goodrich, Marine	Slt	1.12.95
Fletcher, John	Lt Cdr	1. 8.87	Gordon, Andrew	Lt	19. 2.89
Fletcher, Jane	Slt	4. 1.89	Gould, Alan	Lt	17.11.72
Fletcher, Malcolm	Lt	20. 2.84	Govier, Adrian Terry	Lt	1. 2.94
Flett, William	Lt RMR	17.11.94	Grace, Roger	Lt Cdr	13. 7.76
Flynn, John, , *MBE*	Lt Cdr	9.11.75	Graham, Robert	Lt Cdr	1. 2.87
Forbes, John	Lt	18. 9.89	Grant, Malcolm	Lt	28. 2.95
Ford, Stuart	Slt	10.11.93	Gratwick, Geffrey	Lt	29. 3.95
Fordy, Cyril	Lt Cdr	1. 7.79	Gravestock, Denise	Lt Cdr	31. 3.80
Foreman, Waleria	Slt	12. 9.93	Gray, Albert	Capt RMR	23.11.81
Forrester, Michael	Lt	1. 2.79	Gray, Brian	Lt	24.12.87

Name	Rank	Seniority	Name	Rank	Seniority
Gray, Josephine	Lt	7.11.95	Hatrick, James	Lt	29. 7.93
Green, Cecilia	Slt	2.12.87	Havelock, Maureen	Lt	1. 8.88
Green, Malcom	Slt	26. 3.91	Hawes, Sandra	Lt	6.11.95
Green, Paul	Lt	1. 9.86	Hayes, Colin	Slt	3.12.85
Green, Thomas	Lt	4.12.89	Hayes, Debra	*Lt*	*1.10.92*
Greenhalgh, Peter, *ENGTECH, AM*	Lt	30. 4.86	Hayes, Stephen	Lt	30. 5.86
MINSKSCE,			Hayes, Stephen	Slt	1.11.92
Greenhough, St.john	Lt	20.12.87	Hayton, Alan	Lt	20. 7.89
Greenwin, Sheila	Lt	5. 1.91	Hazeldon, Donald	Slt	28. 4.93
Greer, John	Lt Cdr	1. 1.88	Hazzard, Keith	Slt	29.11.95
Gregory, Malcolm	Lt	2. 5.86	Healen, Stephen	Lt	5. 5.82
Greig, Fiona	Lt	15.12.95	Hearl, James	Lt	21.12.89
Grice, Robert	Lt Cdr	5. 7.73	Heathcote, Victoria	Slt	16. 4.95
Griffin, Paul	Lt	24.10.86	Hebbes, Margaret	Slt	5. 6.94
Griffiths, Kenneth	Lt	21.12.93	Hebbes, Peter	Slt	1. 9.91
Griffiths, Meirion	Lt Cdr	4.11.88	Helkin, Margaret	Lt	1. 1.88
Griffiths, Peter	Lt	22. 2.87	Hender, Robert John	Slt	10.12.86
Grimshaw, Thomas	Lt Cdr	1. 6.92	Henderson, David	Lt	15.12.83
Grocott, Alan	Slt	22. 5.95	Henwood, Martin	Lt Cdr	21.10.80
Grogan, Kenneth	Lt	16. 9.78	Herbert, Michael	Lt	13. 6.85
Groombridge, Marlene	Lt	4.11.91	Hercock, Norman	Lt	3.11.93
Groves, Richard	Lt Cdr	11.12.85	Hesselwood, John	Lt	6. 7.87
Grundy, Terence	Lt	15.12.92	Heward, Diana	Lt Cdr	31. 3.80
Guiver, Carl	Capt RMR	1. 1.96	Heward, Paul	Lt	12. 5.86
Gumbrell, Richard	Slt	17. 2.93	Hewitt, Graham	Lt Cdr	7. 4.92
Guppy, Graham	Capt RMR	20. 6.85	Hicks, Barbara	Lt	7.12.83
Gutteridge, Ian	Lt	1. 3.94	Hicks, Ian	Lt	24. 1.94
Guy, Kevin	Lt	3.11.93	Higham, Richard	Lt	4. 3.94
			Higman, Roger	Lt	26. 7.83
H			Hill, Anthony	Slt	26. 6.85
Hackett, Clive	Lt Cdr	12.10.90	Hill, David	Slt	3.11.91
Hadfield, Philip	Lt	9. 4.91	Hill, Ian	A/Lt	15. 3.89
Hagan, George	Slt	29.11.92	Hill, John	Lt	1. 8.75
Hailwood, Paul	Lt Cdr	1.12.92	Hill, Monica	Lt	18.11.93
Haines, Linda	Lt	1.11.89	Hill, Reginald	Lt Cdr	1. 3.88
Hale, Carol	Slt	14. 5.95	Hillier, Christopher	Lt Cdr	11. 5.78
Hale, Ronald	Lt Cdr	23. 2.77	Hinds, Michael	Lt	10.11.95
Hall, Allan	Lt	1. 2.74	Hirst, Simon Richard	Lt	4.11.92
Hall, Derek	Lt	8.10.81	Hiscock, Andrew	Lt	1. 3.83
Hall, Helen	Lt	22. 4.94	Hitchcock, David	Capt RMR	1. 4.90
Halliday, Angela	Lt	1. 9.94	Hithersay, John	Lt	28.10.78
Hamilton, Kerry	Lt	1. 5.92	Hocking, Victoria	Lt	7.11.92
Hanley, David	Lt	18.11.93	Hodgson, Ian	Lt	4. 1.92
Hannay, Alastair	Lt	16. 7.82	Hodierne, John	Slt	4.12.93
Hanson, David	Lt Cdr	26. 7.88	Hoey, David	Lt	10.11.94
Hardick, Roger	Lt	13.10.93	Holden, Terence	Lt	1. 4.88
Hardy, Malcolm	Lt	26.11.86	Holland, Donald	Lt	15. 9.84
Hare, Terence	Lt	17. 7.80	Holliday, Anthony	Lt	21. 4.93
Hargreaves, Andrew	Lt Cdr	1. 8.82	Hollywell, Gary	Lt	26.11.89
Harman, Robert	Lt	4. 8.90	Holman, John	Capt RMR	1. 1.94
Harper, Pamela	Lt	28. 5.87	Holmes, Kevin	Lt	9.11.90
Harries, Mark	Slt	5. 6.94	Holt, Martin	Lt	10. 9.83
Harris, Brian Stanley	Lt	4. 7.92	Hooper, Marion	Lt	20. 9.85
Harris, Stephen	Lt	1.10.91	Hopper, Colin	Slt	20. 9.95
Hart, Kenneth	Lt	20. 6.84	Horne, Allan	Lt	16. 9.89
Hartley, Jacqueline	Lt Cdr	27. 3.87	Horner, John	Lt Cdr	16. 9.92
Hartley, Lorraine	Slt	29.10.95	Horner, Lynda	Slt	7. 8.88
Harvey, Brian	Slt	1.11.94	Hossack, Andrew	Lt	19. 4.72
Haslam, Gordon	Lt	1. 2.86	Houlden, Paul	Lt	1. 9.91
Hatchett, Robin	Lt	27. 9.86	Howcutt, Leonard	Lt Cdr	4. 3.69
Hatley, John	Lt	24. 9.74	Howe, Keith	Capt RMR	4. 2.87

Name	Rank	Seniority	Name	Rank	Seniority
Howe, Margaret	Lt Cdr	1.10.85	Jupe, Paul	Slt	2. 3.86
Howie, Thomas	Lt Cdr	1.11.88	Justice, D R	Lt	7. 2.84
Howieson, John	Slt	27.11.91	**K**		
Hoyle, Keith	Slt	1.10.86			
Huckett, Andrew	Lt	19. 2.91	Kane, Patrick	Slt	14.11.94
Hudson, Christopher	Slt	29.11.95	Kaye, Frances	Slt	26. 7.92
Hudspith, George	Lt	15.12.95	Kaye, Malcolm	Lt	1.11.89
Hughes, Thomas	Lt Cdr	14. 9.83	Kayne, Robert	Slt	22.11.92
Hulbert, Richard	Lt	22.12.93	Kean, Robert	Lt	15. 1.80
Hull, James	Lt	1. 4.88	Keegan, William	Lt Cdr	16. 7.84
Hulonce, Michael, AMS	Lt Cdr	12. 3.82	Keenan, Robert	A/Lt Cdr	1. 4.91
Hunt, Claire	Slt	14. 6.95	Keery, William	Lt Cdr	1. 1.83
Hurst, Paul	Slt	29. 9.93	Kelsall, Alan	Lt Cdr	1. 1.88
Hurst, Thomas	Lt Cdr	12. 7.85	Kemmis Betty, Mark	Lt Cdr	5. 5.87
Hurst, Walter	Lt	30. 9.91	Kemp, David	Lt	23. 9.94
Huttley, Kenneth	Lt	13.11.87	Kempton, Edward	Lt	1. 1.89
Hyde, Peter	Lt	27. 6.86	Kenna, Bryan	Lt Cdr	22.10.84
I			Kennedy, Frederick	Lt RMR	19.11.90
			Kennedy, Ivan	Lt	16. 5.87
Iggo, David	Lt	26. 1.96	Kenrick, Peter	Lt	23.11.94
Ingham, David	Lt	7. 6.85	Kerwin, James	Slt	9. 4.95
Ingram, Thomas	Lt	1. 7.92	Ketch, Roy	Lt	2.11.89
Ivol, Gordon	Lt Cdr	4. 8.93	Killick, Brian	Lt	11. 5.85
J			Killick, Peter	Lt	9.10.85
			King, Paul Anthony	Lt	29. 3.92
Jackson, Graeme	Lt	18. 9.94	Kings, Ralph	Lt	16. 2.90
Jackson, Steves	A/Lt RMR	14.11.94	Kirby, Peter	Slt	1. 8.95
James, George	Lt	22. 8.78	Kirkham, Stephen	Lt	12.12.87
James, Kevin	Lt	6. 9.94	Kirkpatrick, Pauline Ann	Lt	29.10.93
James, Leslie	Slt	12. 7.94	Kissock, Robert Frederick	Slt	4.11.90
James, Robert	Lt Cdr	1. 1.95	Knibbs, Catherine	Slt	10. 3.93
Jardine, Roderick	Lt	5.10.94	Knight, Nicholas	Lt	1.11.91
Jayes, Michael	Lt	18. 1.92	Knill, Colin	Lt	1. 5.89
Jeffcoate, John	Lt	1.11.73	Kohler, Anthony	Lt	23. 4.90
Jeffery, Stephen David	Lt	14. 6.92	Korth, David	Slt	23.11.92
Jeffrey, Andrew	Slt	30. 8.94	Kyle, Raymond	Slt	1.11.90
Jehan, Paula	Slt	19. 5.91	**L**		
Jenkins, Ian	Lt RMR	1. 7.81			
Jenkins, Terence	Slt	6.11.88	Lamb, David	Lt	1. 4.71
Jennings, William	Lt	19.10.84	Lamb, Maureen	A/Lt Cdr	15. 3.95
Jepson, David	Lt	19. 2.91	Lambert, John	Lt Cdr	1. 1.88
Johns, Bevan	Lt Cdr	21. 5.91	Lampert, Brian	Lt Cdr	11. 1.85
Johns, Deirdre	Lt	1.11.88	Lampert, Susan	Lt	1.11.89
Johns, Nicholas	Lt	8. 4.92	Lance, Roderic	A/Lt	1. 1.90
Johnson, Andrew	Lt	17. 2.96	Lane, John	Lt	31. 5.91
Johnson, Laurence	Lt Cdr	2. 8.87	Langley, Peter	Slt	20. 2.94
Johnson-Paul, David	Lt	18. 4.92	Larsen, Colin	Slt	29. 4.95
Johnston, Peter	Lt	2.11.84	Latham, Steven	Slt	12. 9.93
Johnstone, James	Lt	25. 6.87	Lawes, Sonia	Lt	8. 3.94
Jones, Antony	Slt	19. 5.87	Lawrence, Barrie	Lt	4.10.92
Jones, Christopher	Lt	19.11.87	Lawrence, Marion	Slt	20. 3.94
Jones, Dorothy Edwina	Lt	22.10.94	Lawrence, Pail	Lt	1. 6.82
Jones, Lily	Lt	9. 4.91	Lawrence, Trevor	Lt	10. 2.87
Jones, Margaret	Slt	5.11.95	Lawson, Kenneth	Lt RMR	24. 9.91
Jones, Mark	Slt	6.11.94	Lazenby, George	Lt	25. 5.90
Jones, Neil	Lt	24. 3.94	Lazenby, Pauline	Lt	5.12.89
Jones, Peter	Lt	16. 6.89	Leatherbarrow, Ronald	Lt	29. 3.95
Jordan, Robert	A/Lt Cdr	1. 1.95	Ledgeton, Anthony	Lt RMR	15. 1.90
Jordan, Roger	Lt	22. 6.87	Lee, Arthur	Lt	1. 3.87
Jordan, Sheila	Lt	26. 7.90	Lee, David	Lt Cdr	31. 3.79
Jukes, Eric	Lt Cdr	30. 6.83	Lee, Roger	Lt	23.11.94

Name	Rank	Seniority	Name	Rank	Seniority
Lees, Martin	Slt	19. 9.92	MacNeill, Lorna	Lt	9. 6.93
Legg, Philip	Lt RMR	1. 3.92	Madden, Brian	Lt Cdr	1.11.88
Leggatt, David	Lt	5.10.87	Magnall, Edward	Lt Cdr	1. 4.80
Lehan, Thomas	Lt	5. 2.87	Mahoney, Jane	Lt	4.11.93
Leith, Sheena	Slt	9. 8.94	Mahoney, John	Lt Cdr	21. 6.90
Lentle, Robert	Lt	1.11.90	Main, Paul	Lt	12. 3.91
Leslie, Harry	Slt	3. 3.91	Mair, Brian	Lt	27. 9.87
Lewis, Alan	Lt	5. 5.85	Malik, Camron	Slt	31. 1.96
Lewis, Clifford Bruce	Lt	4.11.92	Mannough, John	Lt	14. 5.90
Lewis, Christopher	Lt Cdr	1. 6.78	Mansell, Nicholas	Lt	7.10.92
Lewis, Eleanor	Lt	23.11.94	Marsh, Margaret	Lt	13. 1.92
Lewis, John	Lt	13. 1.69	Marston, Ronald	Lt	1. 6.87
Lewis, John	Lt	30. 3.83	Martell, Terence	Slt	24. 4.94
Lewis, Peter	Lt	31.10.90	Martin, John	Lt Cdr	1. 1.87
Lewis, Robert,	*Lt*	*16. 6.90*	Martin, Kevin	Lt	14. 3.94
Lewis, Walter	Lt	6. 5.79	Martindale, William	Lt Cdr	1. 1.88
Lincoln, David	Lt	1. 1.96	Mason, Edward	Lt Cdr	18.11.69
Lincoln, John	Slt	13. 9.94	Mason, John	Lt Cdr	1.11.91
Lloyd, Terence	Lt	8. 5.87	Masters, Albert	Lt	3.10.77
Lock, Keith	Slt	1.12.92	Mathers, David	Slt	1. 4.94
Locke, David	Lt	10. 9.88	Matson, Christopher	Slt	16.11.94
Login, Brenda	Lt	10.11.89	Mattey, Barry John	Lt Cdr	4. 2.91
Login, Derek	Lt Cdr	12.12.88	Matthews, Christopher	Lt	26. 1.95
Long, Adam	Slt	6.11.94	Matthews, John	Lt	19. 6.95
Long, Trevor	Lt	20. 4.90	Matthews, Philip Kenneth	Lt Cdr	1. 2.89
Lonsdale, Bryan	Lt Cdr	1. 9.90	Matthews, Ronald	Slt	8.10.89
Louden, Elizabeth Jane	Slt	1. 7.90	Mayhew, Anthony	Lt	6.11.95
Lount, Carole	Slt	8. 2.95	Maynard, Robert	Lt Cdr	21. 3.76
Loveland, John	Lt	21. 4.93	Mc Cord, William	Lt	16. 2.91
Loveridge, Anthony	Lt Cdr	1.12.89	Mc Williams, Zoe	Lt	27. 7.93
Low, William	Slt	5. 4.94	McAllister, Josephine	Slt	9.10.86
Lowden, Byron	Lt Cdr	1. 9.73	McAvady, Andrew	Slt	22. 5.95
Lowe, Barry	Lt	1. 1.88	McAvennie, John	Lt	3. 2.90
Lowe, David	Lt	23. 7.77	McAvoy, William	Lt	17.12.79
Lubbock, Peter	Lt	14. 8.58	McClements, George	Capt RMR	1. 1.86
Luckman, Bruce Innes	Lt	1.10.92	McCune, Barry	Lt	4. 6.88
Ludford, Samuel	Lt	1. 2.65	McDonald, Alexander	Slt	1. 9.87
Lumley, Margaret	Slt	14. 6.95	McDonald, Duncan	Lt	15. 5.79
Luxton, Peter	Lt Cdr	20. 5.69	McDonald, Peter	Lt	29. 6.92
Lynch, Paul	Lt	2. 7.77	McDonald, Sandy	Lt	13. 3.81
			McEwan, William	Lt Cdr	1. 9.90
M			McFarlane, Stuart	Slt	28.11.92
Mckeown, Glenda	Slt	24. 4.94	McGarry, George	Lt	3. 9.80
Mclaughlin, Jack	Lt	1. 1.91	McIntyre, Rosamund	Lt Cdr	11. 1.80
Mac Iver, Lynn	Slt	19. 4.94	McKaig, Alexander	Lt	8. 1.87
MacAusland, Craig	Lt	1.11.93	McKee, David	Lt Cdr	1. 4.88
MacAusland, Iain	Lt	25. 3.87	McKenna, Paul	Slt	23.11.92
MacDonald, Peter	Lt	7.11.91	McKone, David	Lt	10. 5.79
MacDonald, William	Lt	9.10.76	McLaren, George	Slt	2.12.95
MacEy, Mark	Lt	13.11.93	McMaster, George	Lt	6.10.88
Machin, Ian	A/Capt RMR	1. 8.86	McMillan, David	Lt	14. 3.84
Mack, Derek	Lt	1. 2.92	McNee, Julia	Lt	4. 8.82
MacKay, David	Lt	1. 7.84	McRobb, Brian	Lt	6. 4.85
MacKay, Norman	Lt Cdr	29.11.72	Mead, Colin	Lt Cdr	16. 5.86
MacKay, Norman	Slt	20.10.93	Meadows, Paul	Slt	28.12.92
MacKinlay, Colin	Lt	8. 4.92	Meldon, Michael	Lt Cdr	1. 3.92
MacKinlay, Sherie	Lt	1. 9.93	Menhams, Angela	Lt	2.12.90
MacKrell, Roger	Lt Cdr	11. 9.87	Meyer, Jonathan	Lt	16.11.90
MacLean, Colin, *M, INST, T, T*	Lt Cdr	14. 8.89	Milby, Stuart	Lt Cdr	27. 7.93
MacLean, Donald	Lt	28. 3.90	Miles, Gail	Lt	26.10.83
Macleod, Kenneth	Lt	1.11.91	Millard, Lesley	Lt	24. 7.94

Name	Rank	Seniority	Name	Rank	Seniority
Millmore, John	Slt	1.12.93			
Millmore, Susan	Slt	18. 6.95	**O**		
Mills, John	Lt	1. 5.93	O Brien, Gary	Lt	30. 1.96
Mills, William	Lt	23. 6.93	O Neill, Dawn	Lt	2.12.94
Milne, John	Lt Cdr	17. 6.73	O'Connor, Brian	Lt	30. 7.85
Milner, Anna	Lt Cdr	1. 3.85	O'Donnell, Adrian	Lt	6.11.90
Mitchell, Dennis	Slt	9.12.82	O'Donnell, Dominic	Lt	1.12.83
Mitchell, Ray	Lt	22. 4.81	O'Hagan, William	Lt	19. 5.86
Mitchell, Tony	Lt	1. 4.91	O'Keefe, Richard	Lt	28. 4.89
Moffitt, Andrew	Lt Cdr	3. 2.88	O'Neill, Terence	Slt	26. 4.95
Moffitt, Joan	Lt	3. 7.90	O'Shaughnessy, Helen	Slt	22. 5.95
Mohammed, John	Lt Cdr	9. 9.87	Oldcorn, Geoffrey	Lt	3.11.93
Moir, Brian	Lt	18. 9.95	Osborne, Brian	Lt	26.10.83
Money, Alan	Lt	25. 3.94	Osborne, Dawn	Lt	20. 4.83
Monkcom, Susan	Slt	14. 6.95	Osborne, James	Lt Cdr	1.10.74
Monks, David Charles	Lt	23. 9.94	Owen, John	Lt	1. 1.84
Mons-White, John Michael	Lt Cdr	15. 8.83	Owen, William	Slt	6. 6.94
Mons-White, Margaret	Lt	1. 9.92	Owens, Brian	Lt	17. 2.88
Moody, Roger	Lt Cdr	1. 4.74	Owens, Christopher	Slt	22. 5.95
Moore, Antony	Lt	7.12.85	Owens, Michael	Lt RMR	18. 6.87
Moore, Robert	Lt	3. 7.90	**P**		
Morgan, John	Lt	10. 2.90			
Morgan, Norman	Lt	1. 1.95	Packwood, Shelagh	Lt Cdr	1.12.86
Morgan, Stephen	Slt	13. 4.94	Page, Helen	Lt	1.10.90
Morley, Michael	Lt	16. 3.88	Paget, Gerald	Lt Cdr	28. 1.83
Morrell, Colin	Lt Cdr	13. 7.83	Painter, Lorretta	Lt	10. 6.92
Morrin, Kevin	Slt	5. 4.95	Painter, Mervyn	Lt	1. 7.90
Morris, David	Lt	14. 4.94	Painter, Siomon	Slt	1. 8.94
Mould, Peter	Lt Cdr	1. 8.78	Painting, Peter	Lt	5.10.71
Moulton, Nicholas	Lt	15.11.79	Paling, John	Lt	29. 4.95
Mountier, Peter	Lt	19.11.90	Palmer, David	Slt	22. 5.95
Moyse, Janet	Lt	5. 6.95	Palmer, Robert	Lt	18.11.93
Muggeridge, Edwin	Lt	6. 5.84	Palmer, Richard	Lt	8.10.88
Mulholland, Ross	Lt Cdr	1. 6.87	Parker, David	Slt	9.11.94
Mullin, Margaret	Lt	1. 6.84	Parker, Derek	A/Lt Cdr	1. 6.90
Mullin, William	Lt	15.11.86	Parker, Ian	Slt	20. 9.95
Munday, Eileen	Lt	20. 2.93	Parker, Simon	Lt	1. 3.90
Mundy, John	Lt	15. 2.93	Parkhurst, John	Lt Cdr	16. 8.78
Munro, Gordon	Slt	20. 3.91	Parks, Edwin	Lt	2.12.95
Murchison, Donald	Lt Cdr	12.12.67	Parr, Geoffrey Lawrence	Lt	28.11.92
Murdock, Gordon	Lt Cdr	11. 2.76	Parr, John	Lt RMR	3.12.89
Murphy, Arthur	Lt	26. 9.93	Parris, Stephen	Lt RMR	5.11.95
Murphy, Richard	Lt	1. 9.89	Parrotte, Gordon	Lt	14. 6.95
Murray, Donald	Lt	1. 5.93	Parry, Michael	Lt	1. 6.84
Musselwhite, Andrew	Lt	14. 7.95	Parry, Robert	Slt	5.11.95
N			Parsons, Frederick	Lt	26. 4.89
			Pascoe, William	Lt	26. 7.84
Nadin, William	Lt	9. 4.91	Patterson, Alexander	Lt Cdr	1.10.83
Neal, David	Lt	30. 5.73	Patterson, Phillip	Slt	6.11.94
Nelson, Harry	Lt	9.10.90	Payne, Carl	Lt	9. 6.95
Newell, Terence	Lt	1.10.92	Payne, Derek	Lt	27.11.86
Newman, Raymond	Lt	24.10.82	Payne, Joseph	Lt	1. 7.90
Nice, David	Lt	1. 1.88	Peachey, Keith	Lt Cdr	1. 6.69
Nicholles, Thomas	Lt	12. 9.94	Pearce, Michael	Slt	31. 1.87
Nicholls, David	Slt	6.11.94	Pearce, Neil	Slt	5.11.95
Nixon, Joseph	Lt	30. 6.84	Pearce, Peter	Slt	22. 1.95
Nolan, James	A/Lt	9.10.88	Pearch, Robert	Lt	5. 4.65
Norman, David	Lt	1. 4.86	Peck, John	Slt	23. 4.94
Norman, John	Lt Cdr	1. 8.87	Peirse, Roy	Lt	11.11.94
Norrris, Norman Terence	Lt	1. 4.92	Pelling, Jane	Lt	11.12.92
			Perchard, Ronald	Lt	4.12.72

Name	Rank	Seniority	Name	Rank	Seniority
Perkins, Jonathon	Slt	14. 8.86	Rees, Susan	Slt	5. 4.95
Perkins, Kevin	Slt	5.11.95	Reeve, John	Lt	19.11.91
Perrin, Daphne	Lt	28. 2.83	Reeve, Michael	Slt	20. 3.94
Perrins, John	Lt Cdr	26.11.86	Reeve, Sydney	Lt Cdr	17.12.81
Perry, Paul	Lt Cdr	4. 2.94	Reeves, Angela	Lt	12. 9.90
Pether, Phillip	Lt	7. 7.65	Regan, Paul	Lt RMR	9.10.88
Pettifer, Frank	Lt Cdr	1. 1.64	Regler, Stanley	Lt	7.12.82
Phelps, Joanne	Slt	4. 4.88	Reynolds, Denis	Lt Cdr	1. 1.88
Phillips, Brian	Lt	1.10.90	Reynolds, Michael	Lt RMR	12. 4.82
Phillips, John	Lt	17. 3.82	Rhind, Robert	Lt	22. 3.90
Phillips, Paul	Lt	19. 9.93	Rich, Linda	Slt	29. 4.95
Phillips, Pamela	Slt	5.11.95	Richards, Mary	Lt	4. 9.91
Pickering, Jean	Lt	3. 7.90	Richards, Norman	*Lt Cdr*	*1. 4.92*
Pickles, Christopher	Lt RMR	7.11.86	Richardson, Michael	Lt Cdr	5. 4.91
Picton, Janet	Lt Cdr	18. 9.87	Ridgway, Paul	Lt	22. 7.88
Piercy, Peter	Lt Cdr	25.10.86	Ridley, Christoher	Lt	14. 6.85
Pietkiewicz, Richard	A/Capt RMR	17. 3.91	Ridsdale, Lorna	Slt	10.11.93
Pike, John	Slt	4. 9.91	Rigby, Peter	Lt	26.11.87
Plummer, Thomas	Lt	1.10.90	Rigden, Anthony	Lt	1. 6.81
Pocock, Stewart	Lt Cdr	1. 7.88	Rimmer, David	Lt	1. 2.80
Pogson, Godfrey	Lt Cdr	11.12.85	Rimmer, Kevin	Lt	30. 3.94
Poke, David	Lt RMR	5.11.93	Roach, Brian	Lt	1. 1.88
Pollard, Colin William	A/Lt	24. 7.90	Robbins, Allan	Lt	17. 6.86
Polson, William	Lt	7. 5.73	Roberts, Ronald	Lt Cdr	6. 1.86
Pool, Adam	Slt	8. 6.94	Robins, William	Lt	1. 9.74
Pope, Darren	Lt	22. 4.93	Robinson, Brian	Lt	23.11.94
Porter, John	Lt	3. 2.84	Robinson, Paul	Slt	20.11.95
Poth, Anthony	Lt Cdr	17. 3.86	Rogers, Sallyanne	Slt	22.11.95
Potter, Maurice	Lt Cdr	1. 1.88	Rolfe, Victor	Lt	2. 8.91
Pountney, David	Lt	9.12.89	Ross, David	Lt	13.10.90
Pow, David John	Lt	6.10.92	Ross, Edward	Lt	3.12.84
Powell, Denise	Lt Cdr	19. 1.94	Ross, Malcolm	Lt	9. 5.95
Preston, Frank	Slt	1. 6.94	Rotherham, Thomas	Slt	10. 1.96
Price, David	Lt RMR	25. 2.90	Rothwell, Jacquelyn	Lt	12. 3.91
Prince, Michael	Lt	22. 1.73	Rowbotham, Alan	Lt Cdr	8. 3.84
Print, Cyril	Lt	9. 8.84	Rowland, Graham Keith	Lt	9.10.90
Pritchard, Carol	Lt	6. 9.94	Rowland, Victor	Lt	19. 1.80
Pritchard, David	A/Lt Cdr	1. 1.95	Rowles, David	Lt Cdr	1. 1.88
Prout, Michael George	Lt Cdr	17.12.90	Rummins, Ann	Lt	1. 1.88
Pugh, Frank	Lt Cdr	28. 4.70	Rundle, Trevor	Lt	5. 4.88
Pugh, Heather	Lt	8. 8.82	Rusiecki, Lawrence Joseph	Lt RMR	4.11.90
Pugh, John	Lt	8. 5.86	Russell, John	Lt	1.11.89
Puxty, Peter	Lt Cdr	1. 1.88	Russett, Terence	Lt	9.10.90
Pyke, Lesley	Lt	1. 1.94	Rutter, Philip	Lt Cdr	1. 9.83
			Rutter, Thomas	Lt	30.10.87
R			Rycroft, Paul	Lt Cdr	8. 9.89
Radcliffe, Brian	Lt Cdr	15. 1.89	Rylance, James	Lt	5. 8.93
Raisborough, Jayne	Lt	3.12.91			
Ramsay, Thomas	Ramsay Cdr	1. 2.89	**S**		
Ramsden, David	Lt	21.11.89	Salisbury, Linda	Slt	19. 2.95
Rattenbury, John	Lt	10.11.94	Salveson, Anthony	Lt Cdr	1. 3.79
Rawcliffe, Michael	Slt	21. 3.94	Saunders, Donald	Lt	28. 8.94
Rawlings, John	Lt Cdr	11. 7.69	Saupe, Peter	Lt	1. 1.88
Rawlinson, Martin	Slt	31. 1.96	Sawford, Michael	Lt	9. 2.85
Rayson, Trevor	Lt	20.10.81	Sayer, Janet	Lt	30. 1.87
Reddecliffe, Phillip	Lt	13. 4.91	Scanlan, John	Lt	31. 3.89
Redmond, Lee	Slt	7.11.93	Scarrott, Peter	Lt	1. 1.95
Reed, Sonia	Lt Cdr	22. 4.90	Schembri, Winifred	Lt	21. 1.87
Rees, Andrew	Lt	14. 7.86	Schofield, George	Slt	1. 4.88
Rees, Clifford	Lt	15. 9.82	Schofield, Julie	Lt	3.12.91
Rees, Celia	Lt Cdr	1. 1.94	Scholes, David	Lt RMR	12. 3.89

Name	Rank	Seniority	Name	Rank	Seniority
Scholes, Walter, *BA*	Lt Cdr	1. 5.66	Soards, Sonia	Lt Cdr	15. 4.93
Schwarzer, Peggy	Slt	5. 4.95	Southcott, Michael	Lt	13.10.95
Scott, Francis	Lt Cdr	1. 4.92	Southernwood, John	Lt	20.11.67
Scott, James	Lt	10. 9.86	Sowerby, Deborah	Lt	20. 1.89
Scourfield, Royston	Lt	1. 6.91	Spear, Michael	Lt	7. 9.83
Scrivens, Stuart	Lt	3.12.91	Speariett, Gail	Lt Cdr	16.11.91
Seabrook, Warren	Lt	24. 5.91	Spencer, Allan	Lt	15.10.93
Seabury, Paul	Slt	30.11.87	Spencer, Edward	Lt	9. 9.76
Seagers, Gavin	Slt	14. 2.96	Spicer, Janice	Lt	10.11.72
Searles, Andrew	Slt	9.11.94	Spindler, William	Capt RMR	30. 4.84
Senior, Allan	Lt RMR	16. 4.88	Spink, James	Lt	1. 9.83
Senior, John	Lt	1. 4.88	Spittal, George	A/Lt Cdr	1. 1.96
Servis, Thomas	Lt	20. 8.85	Spong, Victor	Lt Cdr	20. 7.76
Sewell, Ronald	Lt	5. 9.93	Sprogis, Alfred	Lt	22. 4.94
Sharp, Christine	Lt Cdr	31. 3.80	Squires, John	Lt	6.12.86
Sharp, Terence	Lt Cdr	8. 9.80	Stacey, Stephen	Lt	16. 2.87
Shaw, David	Lt	1. 3.88	Stafford, Albert A	Lt	28. 9.79
Shaw, Geoff	Slt	20.11.95	Stafford, Rita	Lt	21.10.94
Shaw, James	Lt	21. 4.93	Standen, Roy	Lt Cdr	31.12.67
Sheeran, Ceri	Lt	1. 8.84	Stanford, Willaim	Lt	30. 9.93
Sheil, Garry	Lt	18. 3.90	Steele, Thomas	Slt	17.10.94
Shelton, Clive	Lt	1. 8.80	Steggall, Mark	Lt	19.11.91
Sherry, Christine	Lt	1. 1.87	Steggall, Stephen	Lt	19. 5.87
Sherwin, *P W*(Peter), *MBE*	Lt Cdr	1.10.77	Stentiford, Roger	Lt	26. 6.88
Shiels, Robert	Lt Cdr	8. 9.76	Stevenson, Ian	Lt	31. 3.87
Short, Keith	Lt Cdr	6. 4.76	Stevenson, Roy	Lt	19. 6.78
Sickelmore, Barry	Lt	31. 1.87	Steward, Karen	Slt	14. 2.96
Sidney, Gerald	Lt RMR	5. 7.88	Stewart, John	Lt	5. 2.83
Sigley, Dermid	Lt	1. 5.89	Stewart, James	Lt	22. 5.79
Silverthorne, Robert	Lt	31.10.91	Stewart, Patrick	Lt Cdr	27. 7.83
Simister, Alan	Lt	10.11.95	Stewart, Rosaleen	Slt	1.10.90
Simmons, Melvyn	Lt	10. 4.93	Stickland, John, *AMNI*	Lt Cdr	1. 1.88
Simpson, Alfred	Lt Cdr	1. 2.74	Stirrup, William	Lt	18. 6.62
Simpson, Anthea	Slt	4. 6.95	Stobbart, Michael	Lt RMR	1. 9.88
Simpson, Leonard	Slt	1. 5.93	Stone, Terrence	Lt	26. 2.91
Simpson, Timothy	Lt	1. 2.95	Stott, Barry	Slt	20. 4.93
Sinclair, Derek	Slt	3.12.93	Straderick, Barbara	Lt	10.11.95
Sirett, Ian Edward	Lt	1. 8.93	Street, Brenda	Lt	14. 4.77
Skelton, Philip	Lt	4. 5.91	Street, Frederick	Lt	2. 7.71
Slavin, John	Lt	12. 2.94	Streete, Brenda	Lt	17. 5.84
Slaymaker, Robert	Lt Cdr	3.11.87	Stringman, Michael	Slt	22. 5.95
Smales, Geoffrey	Lt	3. 7.90	Strutt, Dupre	Slt	17. 1.85
Smart, Claude	Lt Cdr	26. 4.79	Stubbs, Edward	Lt	18.11.93
Smith, Adrian	Lt	21. 8.92	Summers, Andrew	Lt	22. 5.87
Smith, Alan	Lt Cdr	14. 2.68	Sumner, *P A* (Peter), *MBE, LRAM, ARCM*	Capt RMR	23. 2.81
Smith, Alan	Lt RMR	3.12.91	Sutherland, Shane	Lt	1. 7.94
Smith, Alan	Slt	1. 1.88	Sutton, Alexander	Lt	7. 7.87
Smith, Deborah	Lt	29. 3.95	Sutton, Gerald	Lt	4. 5.88
Smith, Darren	Slt	7.11.93	Svendsen, Peter	Lt	23.11.90
Smith, Ernest	Lt Cdr	5. 9.73	Swan, Gordon	Slt	11. 3.94
Smith, Frank	Lt Cdr	1. 9.82	Sykes, Philip	Lt	11. 4.84
Smith, Graeme	Slt	6. 9.95			
Smith, Graham	Slt	5. 4.95	**T**		
Smith, James	Slt	5.11.95	Tait, Beryl	Lt	18.11.93
Smith, James	Lt	9. 5.94	Tait, Graham	Slt	19. 9.92
Smith, Lorts	Lt	5. 2.88	Tanner, Roland	Lt Cdr	21. 7.87
Smith, Robin	Lt	6. 7.89	Tannock, Andrew	A/Lt RMR	19. 2.95
Smith, Terence	Lt Cdr	1. 1.83	Tapp, Maria	Lt	23.10.95
Smith, Victoria	Lt Cdr	1. 4.80	Tarran, Mark	Lt Cdr	1. 4.76
Smith, William	Lt	10. 2.90	Taylor, Brian	Lt RMR	1. 7.90
Smith-Gosling, Malcolm	Lt	15. 6.95	Taylor, Christopher	Lt	9. 2.79

Name	Rank	Seniority	Name	Rank	Seniority
Taylor, Duncan	Slt	22.11.95	Tyson, Michael	Lt	22. 3.83
Taylor, Nigel	Slt	13. 4.89	**U**		
Taylor, Pauline	Lt Cdr	1. 3.81			
Taylor, William	Lt	1. 4.91	Ulrich, Geoffrey	Lt Cdr	27.11.82
Teare, Glenys	Lt	8. 2.86	**V**		
Tearle, Celilia	Lt Cdr	4. 5.83			
Tearle, Kevin	Lt Cdr	5. 1.92	Vanns, Jonathan	Lt	4. 5.92
Teasdale, Gordon	Lt	7. 5.88	Vaughan, Jeffery	Lt	10.11.95
Tebby, Christine	Lt	5. 9.89	Veres, Stephen	Lt	13. 9.95
Temple, Edward	Lt Cdr	1. 1.88	Voysey, Anthony, *RD*	Lt Cdr	23.10.75
Terry, Peter	Lt	31. 5.75	**W**		
Thackery, Richard	Lt	2. 3.96			
Theobald, Robert	Lt	10.11.87	Waddleton, Michael	Lt	9. 4.79
Theobald, Wendy Margaret	A/Lt Cdr	1. 1.96	Wade, John	Lt	15.10.71
Thomas, Derek	Lt	10.10.94	Wagstaff, Melvin	Slt	21. 6.92
Thomas, Jacqueline	Lt	31. 5.93	Wain, Alan	Lt Cdr	1.10.87
Thomas, Michael	Lt	19. 7.80	Waite, Trevor	Lt	12. 4.75
Thomas, Roderick Leslie	Lt	26.11.92	Wales, David	Lt	12. 2.88
Thomas, Susan	Slt	10. 1.95	Walker, Keith	Lt	5. 2.88
Thomas, Valerie	Slt	20.11.95	Wall, Margaret	Lt	26.10.84
Thomas, William	Lt	1. 1.82	Wallace, Iain	A/Lt Cdr	1. 4.95
Thompson, Brian	Capt RMR	5. 5.90	Wallis, Alexander	Lt	7. 6.95
Thompson, David	Slt	29. 3.95	Walsh, Barry	Slt	1. 3.95
Thompson, Ian	Lt	1. 7.93	Walsh, Edward	Lt Cdr	1. 6.82
Thompson, John	Lt	1. 3.80	Walsh, Maxwell	Lt Cdr	1. 3.91
Thompson, Marjorie	Lt	1. 4.80	Walton, Malcolm	Slt	21. 5.87
Thompson, Michael	Lt Cdr	31.12.83	Ward, John	Lt Cdr	18. 5.82
Thompson, Philip	Lt	26. 7.94	Ward, John	Lt	2. 3.88
Thompson, Peter	Lt Cdr	1.12.74	Ward, Terence	Slt	5. 4.94
Thomson, Andrew	Lt	7. 4.95	Waring, Peter	Slt	14.11.94
Thomson, Robert	Lt	17. 3.71	Waring, Paula	Slt	22. 5.95
Thornber, John	Lt Cdr	27. 7.71	Warner, Peter	Lt RMR	10. 3.95
Thornton, Peter	Lt	24.11.79	Warwick, Stephen	Slt	9. 4.95
Thwaites, Carol	Lt	1. 6.93	Waters, Alan	Lt Cdr	1. 1.81
Thwaites, David	Lt Cdr	1. 1.95	Waters, Scott	Lt	21. 4.94
Tilley, Susanne	Slt	26. 2.86	Watson, Ian	Lt	20. 7.91
Timothy, Emile	Capt RMR	20. 4.92	Watson, Samuel	Lt RMR	2. 4.85
Titley, John	Lt	4. 7.93	Watterson, Jeanette	Lt	26. 4.82
Totty, Paul	Lt RMR	5.10.95	Watts, Reginald	Lt Cdr	27.10.91
Touhey, Martin	Lt	15. 7.87	Waugh, John	Lt	6. 9.78
Townley, Frederick	Lt Cdr	4. 9.89	Webb, Colin	Lt	17.11.95
Townsend, Graham	Slt	20.11.95	Webb, John	Lt Cdr	9.11.85
Trahair, David	Lt Cdr	8. 5.78	Webb, John	Lt	14. 1.90
Trahair, Estelle	Slt	24. 4.94	Webb, Martin	Slt	14. 6.93
Tranter, Gary	Lt Cdr	1. 3.87	Webling, Ann	Slt	15.12.93
Treverton, Mary	Slt	21. 3.94	Webster, John	Lt Cdr	14.12.90
Trott, Peter	Lt Cdr	2. 6.83	Weightman, Eric	Lt	22. 5.85
Truelove, Gary	Lt	20.11.89	Welford, Alan	Lt	26.10.91
Truscott, Gary	Lt Cdr	1. 1.96	Welsh, John	Lt	7.11.93
Tubman, Vernon	Slt	18.10.91	Welsh, Michelle	Lt	7.11.95
Tucker, Neil	Lt	3.11.95	Weobley, Malcolm	Capt RMR	28. 8.86
Turnbull, Kenneth	Lt	28. 2.89	Wesley-Rogers, David	Lt Cdr	1. 4.85
Turnbull, Peter	Lt	16. 2.76	Weston, Mark	Lt	7.11.95
Turnell, Terence	Slt	19. 4.95	Westover, Robert	Lt	1. 4.74
Turner, Ian	Slt	5.11.95	Wheatley, Noel	Lt Cdr	1. 1.95
Turner, John	Lt Cdr	6. 2.68	Wheatley, Paul	Lt	1. 3.91
Turner, Philip	Lt	18. 1.91	Wheeler, Michael	Lt	22. 3.75
Turner, Sharon	Slt	22. 5.95	Whitaker, Ginty	Slt	20. 3.94
Tuson, Denise	Slt	30. 3.94	White, Christopher	Lt	19. 3.87
Tweed, Alan Campbell	Lt	6. 1.93	White, David	Slt	2.12.95
Tyrrell, Richard	Lt Cdr	19. 6.91	White, Frederick James	Lt	3. 9.92

Name	Rank	Seniority	Name	Rank	Seniority
White, Suzanne	Lt	4.11.92	Windle, John	Lt	13. 7.90
White, Susan	Slt	28.11.92	Winterton, Martin	Lt	22. 2.87
Whitehouse, Alan	Lt	16. 2.90	Wood, Christopher	Lt	27.10.92
Whiteman, Mark	Lt	1. 1.88	Wood, Mclhael	Lt	1. 6.84
Whiteman, Paul	Lt Cdr	27. 3.90	Wood, Norman	Lt Cdr	1. 3.90
Whitley, Glenda	Lt	8. 5.85	Woodage, Alan	Lt	21.10.89
Whitworth, Duncan	A/Lt Cdr	1. 9.94	Woodcock, Anthony	Lt Cdr	8. 9.70
Whyte, Lawrence	Lt	1. 7.91	Woodrow, Clive	Slt	6. 9.92
Wickenden, Frances	Slt	1.11.95	Woods, Edward Arthur	Lt	4.11.92
Wilde, James	Slt	1. 3.93	Woodward, Stewart	Lt Cdr	14.11.84
Wilkinson, Christopher	Slt	5.11.95	Wooldridge, Donald	Lt	3. 2.94
Willett, Marion	Lt	21.12.86	Woolgar, Victor	Lt Cdr	1. 1.88
Williams, Alan	Lt Cdr	1. 5.84	Woolley, Paul	Lt Cdr	18. 1.90
Williams, Derek	Lt RMR	13.12.88	Worrall, Ian	A/Lt RMR	14.11.94
Williams, Deborah Karen	Lt	4.11.92	Wright, Clifford	Lt	13. 7.90
Williams, George	Lt	1. 6.74	Wright, Eugene	Lt	18. 2.88
Williams, Peter John	Lt	16.11.92	Wright, James Brian	Lt	31.10.92
Williams, Suzanne	Lt	1. 3.80	Wright, Thomas	Lt	1. 4.87
Williamson, William	Lt Cdr	21. 4.72	Wrin, Jane Frances	Lt	26.11.92
Wilson, Brian	Slt	21. 9.94	Wylie, Mary	Lt	20. 8.88
Wilson, Edward	Slt	8. 5.89	Wylie, William	Lt Cdr	5.12.83
Wilson, Ethel	Slt	29.10.95	Wynne, David	Lt	21. 4.93
Wilson, George	Slt	5. 6.94	Wythe, Jay	Lt	20.11.92
Wilson, George	Lt	1.11.95			
Wilson, Ian	Lt	21. 2.82	**Y**		
Wilson, Ian	Lt RMR	24. 3.89	Yeomans, Roy	Slt	5. 6.94
Wilson, Paul	Lt	8.10.91	Yorke, Barrie	Lt	1. 7.87
Wilson, Perry	Lt	29.11.91	Young, Jean	Slt	8. 8.88
Wilson, William	Lt	4.11.85	Young, Steven	Lt	5. 5.95
Wilton, Christopher	Lt	2.10.92			

COMBINED CADET FORCE

Name	Rank	School/College	Name	Rank	School/College
A			Bowles M G	LT	Brentwood
			Brazier R E	S/LT	HQCCF
Adams T R C	LT	Cheltenham	Bridgeman K G	LT	MTS Northwood
Agutter N A	S/LT	St Bartholomews	Brittain N A	LT	Oundle
Aldridge M I	S/LT	St Dunstans	Brook M E	A/S/LT	Arnold
Alexander E	A/S/LT	Kings Taunton Col	Brooks J P	LCDR	St Peters C of E
Allen B W	S/LT	Elizabeth	Brown A D	S/LT	Royal Hospital
Allison P G	LT RMR	Charterhouse	Brown A G	LCDR	Malvern
Andrew J (W)	S/LT	Dundee High Sch	Brown A J	S/LT	Sevenoaks
Ansell L A	S/LT	Alleyns	Brown S G	S/LT	Shiplake Col
Arliss J (W)	S/LT	Re-call	Brown S J	S/LT	Milton Abbey
Armstrong I B	S/LT	Campbell	Buckerfield R P	S/LT	Woodroffe
Asquith A	LT	Re-call	Burden R D	A/LT RMR	Harrow
Aston P R	A/S/LT	Loretto Sch	Burgess C B	LT	Bradfield Col
B			Burns D A	LT RMR	Wellington Col
			Burns J A F	LT	Re-call
Bailey R J	LT	Bradfield Col	Burring L M (W)	LT	Hele's
Bailey S J	LT RMR	Winchester Col	Burrowes C J	LT	Churchers
Baker P G H	LT	Victoria Jersey			
Baker W J	S/LT	Hele's	**C**		
Barker J E (W)	S/LT	Re-call	Callow M A	LT RMR	Royal Hospital
Barker S R	LT	RGS High Wycombe	Calverley M	A/S/LT	St Dunstans
Barlass S	A/S/LT	Radley Col	Cardwell A	LT	Bangor
Barton R M (W)	LT	Sevenoaks	Carless B	LT	Re-call
Barton W E	LCDR	SCC HMS RALEIGH	Carley J D F	LT	Shiplake Col
Bearman D J	LT	Taunton	Carpenter B H (W)	A/S/LT	Bedford Mod
Belcher J H	LT	Solihull	Carter I S	A/S/LT	Cheltenham
Benson D H	CDR	King Edwards	Carter M J	LT	Kelly
Benson R	S/LT	Nottingham High	Carter N C	LT	Newcastle High
Berry D A	LT RMR	Bedford Mod	Carter S P	LCDR	Downside
Bevington M J	LCDR	Stowe Sch	Cartwright R I	LCDR	Re-call
Bieneman P J	LT	Harrow	Chapman K J	S/LT	Stamford
Bird T L	LT	Kelly	Charlton T R	LT	Dulwich
Borking G	S/LT	Queen Victoria	Chetwood J W	S/LT	Portsmouth
Boucher B C	A/S/LT	Merchiston	Clarke R F	LT	Re-call
Boughton C D	S/LT	Royal Hospital	Cochrane R F	LT	Dundee High Sch

Name	Rank	School/College	Name	Rank	School/College
Collier A J	S/LT	Hereford Cath	Giblin J R	LT	Wellington Col
Collins J W (W)	S/LT	RGS Newcastle	Gilson A	S/LT	Victoria Jersey
Collins M J	S/LT	Magdalen	Glasbey M J	S/LT	Ryde
Collins W L (W)	LT	Alleyns	Glasspoole P J	LCDR	Hele's
Corbould L	A/S/LT	Nottingham High	Glimm K O F	CAPT RMR	Strathallan
Couch P Q	A/S/LT	St Lawrence	Glover W	S/LT	Bournemouth
Crabtree J M	LCDR	Kings Taunton Col	Goodwin M K	S/LT	Reading Blue Coat
Creasey P E	S/LT	Royal Hospital	Goude M (W)	S/LT	Fettes
Crees D R J F	CDR	Allhallows	Green G M	CDR	Brighton
Crooks T J	LT	St Johns	Green J N	LT	Perse
Cuthbertson J	S/LT	Kelvinside	Guise L J	S/LT	Bedford Sch
Curtis B J	LT	Epsom			

D

			H		
			Hall A C L	LT	Dulwich
Dalton A	A/S/LT	Stowe Sch	Hamilton I R W	LCDR	Re-call
Daniel M E	S/LT	Ryde	Hamilton K	LCDR	Liverpool
Davies P H J	S/LT	Ellesmere	Hamilton L A	S/LT	Liverpool
Dawson C J	LCDR	Dover	Hamon C G B	A/S/LT	Sherborne
Deighton Gibson A J	S/LT	Blundells	Harding S	LT CDR	Kelly
Delpech D R	LT	Haberdashers Askes	Hardman T B W	S/LT	Haberdashers
Dore K F	S/LT	Stowe Sch	Hardy D E	LT	Radley Col
Dubbins K J	LT	Ryde	Harris D	CAPT RMR	Pangbourne
Dunn A	CDR	HQCCF(SailingG)	Harris R E	LCDR	Portsmouth
Dunn N	LT	Rossall	Harris S J	LT	Exeter
Durrans H K D	S/LT	Bridlington Sch	Harrison A R	LT	Sandbach
Durrant R C	CDR	Ruthin	Hart T K W	LT RMR	Kings Taunton Col
			Hartley G A	S/LT	Ruthin
E			Harvey P D	LT	Kings Rochester Sch
Egglesfield J M	S/LT	Berkhamsted	Haughton M	S/LT	RGS Lancaster
Eames A K	LT COL RM	Hereford Cathedral	Hawkins K S	LCDR	Birkenhead
Elbourne N J	LCDR	Wellingborough	Heale R E	A/LT RMR	Sherborne
Elkington H D H	CDR	Wellington Sch	Henderson J L (W)	S/LT	RGS High Wycombe
Ellis T J	LT	Hereford Cath	Hendry A	S/LT	Reigate Sch
Ettinger D J	LT	Prior Park	Henry T J	LT	George Heriots
Evans S D	LT	Edinburgh Academy	Hewett M	LT	Re-call
Everest D C	LT	King Edwards	Hewitt R N	LT	Durham
Exley G	LT	Royal Hospital	Hey R L	S/LT	Dulwich
Eyles R H	S/LT	MTS Northwood	Hobb A R	A/LT	Canford
			Hocking J W	S/LT	Plymouth
F			Hodgkiss T	CDR	Alleyns
Field M	LT	Downside	Holmes N P	LT	Haberdashers Askes
Finn M	LT/CDR	HQCCF(ATO)	Holmstrom W F	S/LT	Oundle
Fletcher R P J	LT	Calday Grange	Hudson J W	S/LT	Kings Taunton Col
Foster S M	S/LT	Rugby	Hughes S P M	LT	Harrow
Foulger T R	S/LT	Edinburgh Academy	Hutchinson J J	LCDR	Wellington Col
Fox S A A	LT	Shrewsbury			
Francis P R	LT	Canford	**I**		
Francis-Jones A R	S/LT	Kings Taunton Col	Ibbetson-Price W C R	LCDR	Oratory
Fraser P T	A/LT RMR	Bradfield Col	Ing J L	LT RMR	Harrow
Freedman S J	LT	MTS Crosby	Iredale J F (W)	S/LT	Taunton
Freeman C	S/LT	Prior Park			
Friend D J	S/LT	Kings Bruton Sch	**J**		
Frost R A	CDR	Exeter	Jackson H G	LT	Worksop Col
Fudge K E (W)	LT	Langley	Jackson P J	LCDR	Harrow
Fulton-Peebles P K	LT	Fettes	Jago J P	A/S/LT	RGS Lancaster
Funston B W	LT	Campbell	James F B W	LT	Scarborough
			Jeans-Jakobsson M R	LT	St Bartholomews
G			Jelley R G	LT	Wellingborough
Gale J M	CAPT RMR	Kelly	Jenkins D A	LCDR	Bedford Mod
Gardner C H	S/LT	Cheltenham	Jervis-Dykes A	LT	Victoria Jersey
Georgiakakis N S	LT	Charterhouse	Johnson M D B	S/LT	Exeter

Name	Rank	School/College	Name	Rank	School/College
Jolliff T	S/LT	Loughborough	Morgan B J D	LT	Brentwood
			Moss-Gibbons D F	LCDR	Bradfield Col
K			Mundill R R	LT	Christs Hospital
Kay A E	S/LT	Re-call			
Kermode E J	S/LT	King Williams IOM	**N**		
Killgren C V	S/LT	Stamford	Newton J	LT	Allhallows
King R A	LT	Haileybury	Newton REI	LT CDR	Re-call
Kingsland J D (W)	LT	Bradfield Col	Nicholson J C	LT	Ipswich
Kirwin C J	CDR	Kelly	Nicholson R P L	LCDR	Milton Abbey
			Norbron S J (W)	S/LT	Gordons Sch
L			Norman M D G E	LCDR	Maidstone
Lankester R A	LT RMR	Uppingham	Norton R L	LT	Batley
Larby J	LT CDR	Kelly	Nurton M D	LT RMR	Sherborne
Law B	S/LT	Bedford			
Lawson D J	LT	RGS Newcastle	**O**		
Lee D	LT	Malvern	OConnor K T (W)	S/LT	Oratory
Lee J P	LT	Ruthin	Ogilvie F D G	A/LT RMR	Giggleswick
Lemieux S	LT	Portsmouth	Oldbury D J	CDR	Kings Rochester Sch
Lewis A R	S/LT	Christs Hospital			
Limrick J C	S/LT	Haileybury	**P**		
Little J E	LCDR	Eastbourne	Packer T A	LTCDR	Re-Call
Loader M	LT	Kelly	Parker A P (W)	S/LT	St Bartholomews
Loudon I	S/LT	Rossall	Parkinson K	LT	Re-Call
Lovell K J	S/LT	Re-call	Paton G A J	LCDR	Ipswich
Lovell S	S/LT	RHS	Payne A C	LT	Loughborough
Lowles I R	S/LT	Clifton Col	Pearce D C R	LT CDR	HQCCF(Sailing)
Lucas I N	LT	Sevenoaks	Peckham A F	S/LT	Fettes
Lyon D	A/S/LT	MTS Crosby	Pidoux H	S/LT	Maidstone
			Pilbeam J G	LT	Blundells
M			Platts-Martin P	S/LT	Kings Bruton Sch
MacDonald C M	S/LT	Bangor	Pointing A N	S/LT	Durham
MacDonald F S	LT	Trinity	Pollard E P J	CDR	HQCCF(NCFBO)
Mackie A J	LT	Bangor	Powell A	LT	Reigate Sch
Magor B S	CDR	Calday Grange	Powell J R	A/S/LT	Pangbourne
Manners D R G	LT	Woodroffe	Prescott J C	LCDR	Taunton
Marks M J	LT	Christs Col Brecon	Prior A M	LT	Milton Abbey
Marsh L D (W)	LCDR	Hereford Cath	Prior S J	S/LT	West Buckland
Martin S	LT	Kelly	Prosser N M H	LCDR	Tonbridge
Matthews C J	LT	Churchers			
Maw J E	LCDR	Re-call	**R**		
McConnell S M (W)	LT	Kings Canterbury Sch	Raines D F	LT	Elizabeth
McConnell W R	LT	Kings Canterbury Sch	Reade T	S/LT	King Williams IoM
McCormick I	LT	Liverpool	Reed W	LT	RGS Worcester
McDermott R G	LT RMR	Kelly	Refell D W	S/LT	Ellesmere
McGuff N	A/S/LT	Wellington Sch	Rennison C	A/LT RMR	Royal Hospital
McKee D M	S/LT	Campbell	Renold P N	S/LT	Batley
McLeod-Jones S E	S/LT	Oratory	Reynolds C M	LT	Bournemouth
Melville J G	S/LT	Birkenhead	Rhodes T E	S/LT	Kimbolton
Mercer L K L (W)	S/LT	Prior Park	Richard P D	LT	Rugby
Merrett N S	S/LT	Uppingham	Richards P G	LT	HQCCF(AATO Scotland)
Middleton P	LT	St Edwards	Ridley-Thomas M S	LT	Calday Grange
Millard M J	A/S/LT	Victoria Jersey	Riley N S	S/LT	Arnold
Mills A (W)	S/LT	Monkton Combe	Ripley M P	LT	Sedbergh
Mills S P	A/S/LT	Sandbach	Roberts D	LT	Brighton
Minto N V	S/LT	Re-Call	Roberts M	LT	Re-Call
Mitchell I C E	S/LT	Wellington Col	Roby R	CDR	Re-Call
Mitchell R J	LCDR	Kings Wimbledon Col Sch	Rooms L P	LCDR	Oundle
Montgomery P S	S/LT	Dean Close	Rothwell G W S	LT CDR	HQCCF(Sailing)
Moody S M M (W)	LT CDR	St Dunstans	Rowse I H	LT	Wellingborough
Moore D J	LT	Lancing	Rowse S A	S/LT	Charterhouse
Moore T M (W)	S/LT	Re-Call	Roy K E	S/LT	Kings Rochester Sch

Name	Rank	School/College	Name	Rank	School/College
Rule P H	LCDR	Trinity	Thomas C D	LT	St Bartholomews
Russell J A O	LT RMR	Malvern	Thompson D	2LT	Pangbourne
			Tidey R D	LT CDR	Re-call
S			Tinker C G	LCDR	Sedbergh
Salt G R	S/LT	Kings Wimbledon Col Sch	Todd M K	LCDR	HQCCF(Diving Officer)
Sanders B J	CDR	Bournemouth	Tolhurst A J	LCDR	City Of London
Sanders R W	S/LT	Oratory	Trelawny G N	S/LT	Exeter
Savidge J M	LT	Solihull	Trundle S F	LT	RGS Worcester
Scorgie H M (W)	S/LT	Clifton Col	Tudor C M L (W)	S/LT	King Edwards
Scorgie S J	LT	Clifton Col	Turnbull A	LT	Batley
Shannon T M	LT	Queen Victoria	Tyas K J	S/LT	Arnold
Sharman D J (W)	LCDR	West Buckland			
Shorrocks J M	LT	RGS Worcester	**V**		
Sibley P C	LCDR	Monkton Combe	Van Der Werff T (W)	S/LT	Reading Blue Coat
Simpson	S/LT	Ellesmere	Varnham J M	S/LT	Maidstone
Sissons S	S/LT	HQCCF	Vickery D J	LT	Monkton Combe
Slade A J	S/LT	Mill Hill	Vigers R A (W)	LT	Sherborne
Smallcombe B P	S/LT	Framlingham	Vince A E	A/S/LT	Mill Hill
Smith G (W)	S/LT	Royal Hospital	Vine R L	LT	City Of London
Smith R D	S/LT	Kelvinside			
Solly R J	LCDR	St Lawrence	**W**		
Spence D	A/S/LT	Campbell	Wake A D	S/LT	George Heriots
Spence R	S/LT	Campbell	Wakelin F E	CDR	HQCCF
Spike N T	LT	Glasgow Academy	Walker C N	CAPT	Strathallan
Stacey M	A/S/LT	Gordons Sch	Walters D P	S/LT	Uppingham
Stacey W	A/S/LT	Gordons Sch	Ward D A T	LT	Kimbolton
Stansbury W	A/S/LT	MTS Northwood	Waugh P B	A/S/LT	Wellingborough
Stevens L	LT	St Bartholomews	Whale A C	LT	Pangbourne
Stevens P R	CDR	Plymouth	Wheater L E (W)	S/LT	Berkhamsted
Stilwell V (W)	S/LT	Epsom	Whitfield J	LT	West Buckland
Stocker P	S/LT	Uppingham	Whitmill D	S/LT	Oundle
Stokes I W	LT	Kimbolton	Whittaker D J	CDR	Haberdashers Askes
Strickland G C	LCDR	Plymouth	Whittel P A	LT	Birkenhead
Stringer C A	LT RMR	Malvern	Wigley G	LT	Framlingham
Strong G M	S/LT	Wellingborough	Wilkins P C E	LT	St Peters C of E
Stubbs M E	S/LT	Canford	Williams R M I	LT	Glasgow Academy
			Williams S H L	S/LT	Kings Wimbledon Col Sch
T			Witney J C	A/S/LT	Mill Hill
Tate N S (W)	S/LT	Oundle	Woodward C J	A/LT RM	Bedford Modern
Taylor A R	LT RMR	Wellington Col	Wright N P	LT	Kelly
Taylor L N	LT RMR	Winchester Col	Wylie J P	LT	Radley
Tennant D H	LT	Tonbridge			

OBITUARY

ROYAL NAVAL SERVICE

Commander

Hourigan, P R . . . . 01.08.95. |

Lieutenant Commander

Auckland, M F . . . . 23.02.96. | McClenaghan, D B . . . . 12.03.96 .
Green, R C . . . . 17.12.95. |

Lieutenant

Pym, A M F . . . . 10.10.95. | Gay, T J . . . . 05.10.95 .

Sub Lieutenant

Chapman, G D . . . . 05.10.95. |

ROYAL NAVAL RESERVE

Lieutenant Commander

Wallace, R . . . . 08.05.95. |

ABBREVIATIONS OF RANKS AND LISTS

A	Acting
A/	Acting
ACT	Acting
ADM	Admiral
ADM OF FLEET	Admiral of the Fleet
ASL	Acting Sub-Lieutenant
AT	Acting Temporary
BRIG	Brigadier
CAND	Candidate
CAPT	Captain
CDT	Cadet
CHAPLAIN-FLT	Chaplain of the Fleet
CDR	Commander
CDRE	Commodore
CNO	Chief Nursing Officer
COL	Colonel
COMDT	Commandant
(CS)	Careers Service
(D)	Dental
E	Engineering
(FS)	Family Service
GEN	General
(GRAD)	Graduate
HON	Honorary
I	Instructor
LOC	Local
LT	Lieutenant
LCDR	Lieutenant-Commander
LT CDR	Lieutenant-Commander
LT COL	Lieutenant-Colonel
LT GEN	Lieutenant-General
MAJ	Major
MAJ GEN	Major-General
MID	Midshipman
(NE)	New Entry
NO	Nursing Officer
OFF	Officer
OFFR	Officer
P/	Probationary
PNO	Principal Nursing Officer
PR	Principal
RADM	Rear-Admiral
REV	Reverend
RM	Royal Marines
S	Supply & Secretariat

(SD)	Special Duties List
(SDT)	Special Duties List Temporary
SG	Surgeon
SURG	Surgeon
(SL)	Supplementary List
SLT	Sub-Lieutenant
SNO	Senior Nursing Officer
SUPT NO	Superintendent Nursing Officer
T	Temporary
T/	Temporary
TLT	Temporary Lieutenant
TSLT	Temporary Sub-Lieutenant
(UCE)	University Cadet Entrant
VADM	Vice-Admiral
X	Seaman
2LT	Second Lieutenant, Royal Marines

ABBREVIATIONS OF QUALIFICATIONS

(Eur Ing)	European Engineer
(A)	Specialist in Anaesthetics
(A/E)	Specialist in Accident/Emergency
A/TK	Heavy Weapons Anti-Tank
AC	Aircraft Controller
ACC/EM	Accident and Emergency
ACGI	Associate, City and Guilds London Institute
ACIS	Associate of The Institute of Chartered Secretaries and Administrators
ACMA	Associate, Institute of Cost & Management Accountants
(AD)	Medical and Dental Administration
ADIPM	Associate, Institute of Data Processing Management
adp	Passed Advanced Adp Course Dadptc
AE	Air Engineering
AE(L)	Air Engineering (Electrical)
AE(M)	Air Engineering (Mechanical)
AE(O)	Air Engineering (Observer)
AE(P)	Air Engineering (Pilot)
(AE)	Assault Engineer
AFIMA	Associate Fellow, Institute Mathematics & Its Applications
AFOM	Associate, Faculty of Occupational Medicine
AGSM	Associate of The Guildhall School of Music and Drama
AIL	Associate, Institute of Linguists
AIM	Associate, Institute of Metallurgists
AIMgt	Associate of The Institute of Management
AInstP	Associate, Institute of Physics
AKC	Associate, King's College London
ALCD	Associate, London College of Divinity
AMASEE	Associate Member, Association of Electrical Engineers
AMBCS	Associate Member, British Computing Society

AMBIM . . . . Associate Member, British Institute of Management
AMHCIMA . . . . Associate Member, Hotel Catering & Institutional Management Association
AMIAM . . . . Associate Member, Institute of Administrative Management
AMICE . . . . Associate Member, Institute of Civil Engineers
AMIEE . . . . Associate Member, Institute of Electrical Engineers
AMIERE . . . . Associate Member, Institution of Electronic and Radio Engineers
AMIIE . . . . Associate Member, Institute of Industrial Engineers
AMIMarE . . . . Associate Member, Institute of Marine Engineers
AMIMechE . . . . Associate Member, Institute of Mechanical Engineers
AMInstP . . . . Associate Member, Institute of Physics
AMINucE . . . . Associate Member, Institution of Nuclear Engineers
AMIPIE . . . . Associate Member, Institution of Plant Engineers
AMNI . . . . Associate Member, Nautical Institute
AMRAeS . . . . Associate Member, Royal Aeronautical Society
AMRINA . . . . Associate Member. Royal Institution of Naval Architects
ARAM . . . . Associate, Royal Academy of Music
ARCM . . . . Associate, Royal College of Music
ARCS . . . . Associate, Royal College of Science
ARCST . . . . Associate, Royal College of Science and Technology (Glasgow)
ARIC . . . . Associate, Royal Institute of Chemistry
ARICS . . . . Professional Asssociate, Royal Institution of Chartered Surveyors
ATC . . . . Air Traffic Control Officer
ATCU/T . . . . Air Traffic Control Officer Under Training
AV . . . . Aviation
AWO(A) . . . . Advanced Warfare Officer(Above Water)
AWO(C) . . . . Advanced Warfare Officer(Communications)
AWO(U) . . . . Advanced Warfare Officer(Underwater)
aws . . . . Qualified Air Warfare College
BA . . . . Bachelor of Arts
BA(OU) . . . . Bachelor of Arts, Open University
BAO . . . . Bachelor of Art of Obstetrics
BAR . . . . Barrister
BCh . . . . Bachelor of Surgery
BChD . . . . Bachelor of Dentistry
BChir . . . . Bachelor of Surgery
BComm . . . . Bachelor of Commerce
BD . . . . Bachelor of Divinity
BDS . . . . Bachelor of Dental Surgery
BEd . . . . Bachelor of Education
BEng . . . . Bachelor of Engineering
BM . . . . Bachelor of Medicine
BMedSc . . . . Bachelor of Medical Science
BMus . . . . Bachelor of Music
BPh . . . . Bachelor of Philosophy
BPharm . . . . Bachelor of Pharmacy
BS . . . . Bachelor of Surgery
BSc . . . . Bachelor of Science
BSc(Eng) . . . . Bachelor of Science (Engineering)
BTech . . . . Bachelor of Technology
BURNS . . . . Burns

C	Communications
C/T	Clinical Teacher
CA	Caterer
(CA)	Consultant in Anaesthetics
(CA/E)	Consultant in Accident/Emergency
(CA/P)	Consultant in Applied Physiology
(CAT)	Caterer
CC	Coronary Care
(CC)	Consultant in Paediatrics
CD	Clearance Diver
CDipAF	The Certified Diploma in Accounting and Finance
(CDO)	Commando Trained
CE	Communications (Wrns)
(CE)	Consultant in Otorhinolaryngology
CEng	Chartered Engineer
Cert Ed	Certificate of Education
(CG)	Consultant in Obstetrics and Gynaecology
CGIA	Insignia Award of The City & Guilds of London Insitute
(CGS)	Consultant in General Surgery
ChB	Bachelor of Surgery
(CK)	Consultant in Dermatology
(CL)	Consultant in Pathology
(CM)	Consultant in General Medicine
CMA	Management Accountant
(CN)	Consulant in Nuclear Medicine
(CN/P)	Consultant in Neuro-Psychiatry
(CO)	Consultant in Opthalmology
(CO/M)	Consultant in Occupational Medicine
(CO/S)	Consultant in Orthopaedic Surgery
(COSM)	Consultant in Oral Surgery/Oral Medicine
(CP/M)	Consultant in Rheumatology and Rehabilitation
CPN	Community Psychiatric Nurse
CQSW	Certificate of Qualification in Social Work
(CU)	Consultant in Urology
(CX)	Consultant in Radiology
D	Direction Officer
DA	Diploma in Anaesthesia
DAppDy	Diploma in Applied Dynamics
DCH	Diploma in Child Health
DCL	Doctor of Civil Law
DCP	Diploma in Clinical Pathology
DD	Doctor of Divinity
DDPH	Diploma in Public Dental Health
DEH	Diploma in Environmental Health
df	Qualified Defence Fellowship
DGDP RCS(UK)	Diploma in General Dental Practice Rcs (Uk)
DGDPRCS(Eng)	Diploma General Dental Practice Rcs(Eng)
DHMSA	Diploma in The History of Medicine (Society of Apothecaries)
DIC	Diploma of The Imperial College
DIH	Diploma in Industrial Health

Dip FFP . . . . Diploma of The Facalty of Family Planning
DipAvMed . . . . Diploma in Aviation Medicine
DipEd . . . . Diploma in Education
DipIMC RCSED . . . . Diploma in Immmediate Medical Care of Royal College Surgeons (Edinburgh)
DipTh . . . . Diploma in Theology
DLitt . . . . Doctor of Letters
DLO . . . . Diploma in Laryngology and Otology
DM . . . . Doctor of Medicine
DMRD . . . . Diploma in Medical Radiological Diagnosis
DO . . . . Diploma in Ophthalmology
DObstRCOG . . . . Diploma Royal College of Obstetricians and Gynaecologists
DOrth . . . . Diploma in Orthodontics
DPH . . . . Diploma in Public Health
DPhil . . . . Doctor of Philosophy
DPhysMed . . . . Diploma in Physical Medicine
DPM . . . . Diploma in Psychological Medicine
DRD . . . . Diploma in Restorative Dentistry
DSc . . . . Doctor of Science
DTM&H . . . . Diploma in Tropical Medicine and Hygiene
E . . . . Engineer
Eur Eng . . . . European Engineer
EW . . . . Electronic Warfare
F . . . . Pilot and Observer
FA . . . . Fleet Analyst
FBCS . . . . Fellow, British Computer Society
FBIM . . . . Fellow, British Institute of Management
FC . . . . Fighter Controller
FCIS . . . . Fellow, Institute Chartered Secretaries & Administrators
FCMA . . . . Fellow, Chartered Institute of Management Accountants
FDS . . . . Fellow in Dental Surgery
FDS RCPSGlas . . . . Fellow in Dental Surgery Royal College of Physicians & Surgeons (Glasgow)
FDS RCS(Eng) . . . . Fellow in Dental Surgery, Royal College of Surgeons of England
FDS RCS(Irl) . . . . Fellow in Dental Surgery Royal College of Surgeons in Ireland
FDS RCSEdin . . . . Fellow in Dental Surgery Royal College of Surgeons of Edinburgh
FDS(RCS) . . . . Fellow in Dental Surgery, Royal College of Surgeons of England
FFA . . . . Fellow, Institute of Financial Accountants
FFARCS . . . . Fellow, Faculty of Anaesthetists, Royal College of Surgeons of England
FFARCSI . . . . Fellow, Faculty of Anaesthetists, Royal College of Surgeons in Ireland
FFOM . . . . Fellow, Faculty of Occupational Medicine
FHCIMA . . . . Fellow of The Hotel and Catering Management Association
FIAA . . . . Fellow, Institute of Actuaries of Australia
FIEE . . . . Fellow, Institute of Electrical Engineers
FIEIE . . . . Fellow, Institute of Electrical and Electronic Incorporated Engineers
FIERE . . . . Fellow, Institution of Electronic and Radio Engineers
FIL . . . . Fellow, Institute of Linguists
FIM . . . . Fellow of The Institute of Metals
FIMA . . . . Fellow, Institute of Mathematics and Its Applications
FIMarE . . . . Fellow, Institute of Marine Engineers
FIMechE . . . . Fellow, Institution of Mechanical Engineers
FIMgt . . . . Fellow of The Institute of Management

FIMS	Fellow, Institute of Management Specialists or Mathematical Statistics
FInstAM	Fellow Institute of Administrative Management
FINucE	Fellow, Institute of Nuclear Engineers
FIPM	Fellow of The Institute of Personnel Management
FITE	Fellow, Institution Electrical & Electronics Technician Engineers
FNI	Fellow, Nautical Institute
FP	Family Planning
FRAeS	Fellow, Royal Aeronautical Society
FRAM	Fellow, Royal Academy of Music
FRC.Psych	Fellow of The Royal College of Psychiatrists
FRCOG	Fellow, Royal College of Obstetricians and Gynaecologists
FRCP	Fellow, Royal College of Physicians, London
FRCPath	Fellow, Royal College of Pathologists
FRCPEd	Fellow, Royal College of Physicians, Edinburgh
FRCPGlas	Fellow, Royal College of Physicians and Surgeons of Glasgow
FRCR	Fellow, Royal College of Radioligists
FRCS	Fellow, Royal College of Surgeons of England
FRCS(ORTH)	Fellow Royal College Surgeons (Orthopaedics)
FRCSEd	Fellow, Royal College of Surgeons of Edinburgh
FRCSGlas	Fellow, Royal College of Physicians and Surgeons of Glasgow
FRGS	Fellow, Royal Geographical Society
FRHistS	Fellow Royal Historical Society
FRICS	Fellow Royal Institute Chartered Surveyors
FRIN	Fellow, Royal Institute of Navigation
FRINA	Fellow, Royal Institute of Naval Architects
FRMS	Fellow, Royal Meteorological Society
FRSA	Fellow, Royal Society of Arts
fsc	Qualified Foreign Staff College
G	Gunnery
#	Gunnery (Mortar Course)
GASTRO	Gastroenterological Nursing
GCIS	Graduate of The Institute of Chartered Secretaries and Administrators
GISVA	Graduate Institute of Surveyors, Valuers and Auctioneers
GMPP	General Medical Practitioner
GradIMA	Graduate Member, Institute of Mathematics and Its Applications
GradIMS	Graduate Institute of Management Specialists
GradInstPS	Graduate Institute of Purchasing and Supply
(GS)	Specialist in General Surgery
GU	Genito Urinary
gw	Guided Weapons Systems Course RMCS Shrivenham
H CH	Hydrographer (Charge)
HCH	Hydrographer (Charge)
hcsc	Higher Command & Staff College
HNC	Higher National Certificate
HND	Higher National Diploma
(HP)	Health Physicist
HULL	Hull Engineering
HV	Health Visitor
HW	Heavy Weapons
H1	Hydrographer (First Class)

H2	Hydrographer (Second Class)
I	Instructor
I(1)Ab	Interpreter 1st Class Arabic
I(1)Ch	Interpreter 1st Class Chinese
I(1)Da	Interpreter 1st Class Danish
I(1)Du	Interpreter 1st Class Dutch
I(1)Fi	Interpreter 1st Class Finnish
I(1)Fr	Interpreter 1st Class French
I(1)Ge	Interpreter 1st Class German
I(1)Id	Interpreter 1st Class Indonesian
I(1)It	Interpreter 1st Class Italian
I(1)Ja	Interpreter 1st Class Japanese
I(1)Ma	Interpreter 1st Class Malayan
I(1)No	Interpreter 1st Class Norwegian
I(1)Pl	Interpreter 1st Class Polish
I(1)Po	Interpreter 1st Class Portugese
I(1)Ru	Interpreter 1st Class Russian
I(1)Sh	Interpreter 1st Class Swahili
I(1)Sp	Interpreter 1st Class Spanish
I(1)Sw	Interpreter 1st Class Swedish
I(1)Tu	Interpreter 1st Class Turkish
I(1)Ur	Interpreter 1st Class Urdu
I(2)Ab	Interpreter 2nd Class Arabic
I(2)Ch	Interpreter 2nd Class Chinese
I(2)Da	Interpreter 2nd Class Danish
I(2)Du	Interpreter 2nd Class Dutch
I(2)Fi	Interpreter 2nd Class Finnish
I(2)Fr	Interpreter 2nd Class French
I(2)Ge	Interpreter 2nd Class German
I(2)Id	Interpreter 2nd Class Indonesian
I(2)It	Interpreter 2nd Class Italian
I(2)Ja	Interpreter 2nd Class Japanese
I(2)Ma	Interpreter 2nd Class Malayan
I(2)No	Interpreter 2nd Class Norwegian
I(2)Pl	Interpreter 2nd Class Polish
I(2)Po	Interpreter 2nd Class Portugese
I(2)Ru	Interpreter 2nd Class Russian
I(2)Sh	Interpreter 2nd Class Swahili
I(2)Sp	Interpreter 2nd Class Spanish
I(2)Sw	Interpreter 2nd Class Swedish
I(2)Tu	Interpreter 2nd Class Turkish
I(2)Ur	Interpreter 2nd Class Urdu
IC	Intensive Care
ICNN	Intensive Care Neonates
idc	Qualified Imperial Defence College
IEng	Incorporated Engineer
ifp	Qualified, International Fellows Programme
INFCON	Infection Control
JCPTGP	Certificate of Prescribed Experience in General Practice
jsdc	Joint Service Defence College

jssc . . . . Joint Services Staff College
LC . . . . Landing Craft
LDS . . . . Licentiate in Dental Surgery
LDS RCPSGlas . . . . . Licenciate in Dental Surgery Royal College of Physicians & Surgeons (Glasgow)
LDS RCS(Eng) . . . . Licentiate in Dental Surgery, Royal College of Surgeons of England
LDS RCS(Irl) . . . . Licenciate in Dental Surgery Royal College of Surgeons in Ireland
LDS RCSEdin . . . . Licenciate in Dental Surgery Royal College of Surgeons of Edinburgh
LGSM . . . . Licentiate, Guildhall School of Music and Drama
LHCIMA . . . . Licentiate Hotel, Catering and Institutional Management Assn
LIEE . . . . Licentiate, Institute Electrical Engineers
LIMA . . . . Licentiate Institute Mathematics & Its Applications
LLB . . . . Bachelor of Law
LLD . . . . Doctor of Laws
LMCC . . . . Licentiate, Medical Council of Canada
LMHCIMA . . . . Licentiate Member of Hotel,Catering and Institutional Management Assn
LMSSA . . . . Licentiate in Medicine & Surgery, Society of Apothecaries
LRAM . . . . Licentiate, Royal Academy of Music
LRCP . . . . Licentiate, Royal College of Physicians, London
LRCPSGlas . . . . Licentiate, Royal College of Physicians and Surgeons of Glasgow
LRCS . . . . Licentiate, Royal College of Surgeons of England
LRPS . . . . Licentiate, Royal Photographic Society
(LT) . . . . Laboratory Technician
LTh . . . . Licentiate in Theology
M.Univ . . . . Master of The University (Ou)
(M) . . . . Specialist in General Medicine
MA . . . . Master of Arts
MA(Ed) . . . . Master of Arts in Education
MAPM . . . . Member of The Association of Project Managers
MB . . . . Bachelor of Medicine
MBA . . . . Master of Business Administration
MBCS . . . . Member, British Computer Society
MBIM . . . . Member, British Institute of Management
MCD . . . . Mine Warfare Clearance Diver
MCD/MW . . . . Mine Clearance Diving & Mine Warfare
MCDPWO . . . . Mine Warfare Clearance Diver & Principal Warfare Officer
MCFA . . . . Member of The Catering and Food Association
MCGI . . . . Member of City and Guilds Institiute
MCh . . . . Master in Surgery
MChOrth . . . . Master of Orthopaedic Surgery
MCIT . . . . Member, Institute of Training Officers
MD . . . . Doctor of Medicine
MDA . . . . Master of Defence Administration
MDSc . . . . Master of Dental Science
mdtc . . . . Maritime Defence Technology Course
ME . . . . Marine Engineering
ME(L) . . . . Marine Engineering (Electrical)
MEng . . . . Master of Engineering
MESM . . . . Marine Engineering (Submarine)
MET . . . . Meteorology
METOC . . . . Meteorology & Oceanography

MFCM	Member, Faculty of Community Medicine
MFOM	Member, Faculty of Occupational Medicine
MGDS RCS	Member in General Dental Surgery, Royal College of Surgeons of England
MGDS RCSEd	Member in General Dental Surgery, Royal College of Surgeons of Edinburgh
MHCIMA	Member, Hotel Catering & Institutional Management Association
MHSM	Member of The Institute of Health Services Mamagement
MICE	Member, Institution Civil Engineers
MIDPM	Member Institute of Data Processing Management
MIEE	Member, Insitution of Electrical Engineers
MIEEE	Member of The Institution of Electrical and Electronic Engineers
MIEEIE	Member of The Institute of Electrical and Electronic Incorporated Engineers
MIERE	Member, Institution of Electrical & Radio Engineers
MIExpE	Member, Institute of Explosives Engineers
MIL	Member, Institute of Linguists
MILDM	Member of The Institute of Logistics and Distribution Management
MIM	Member, Institute of Metals
MIMarA	Member, Institute of Marine Architects
MIMarE	Member, Institute of Marine Engineers
MIMechE	Member, Institution of Mechanical Engineers
MIMechIE	Member of The Institute of Mechanical Incorporayed Engineers
MIMgt	Member of The Institute of Management
MIMS	Member, Institute of Management Specialists
MInsD	Member of The Institute of Directors
MInstAM	Member, Institute of Administrative Management
MInstFM	Member, Institute of Facilities/Resources Management
MInstP	Member, Institute of Physics
MInstPS	Member, Institute of Purchasing and Supply
MINucE	Member, Institute of Nuclear Engineers
MIOSH	Member, Institute of Occupational Safety and Health
MIPlantE	Member, Plant Engineers
MIPM	Member, Institute of Personnel Management
MIProdE	Member, Institute of Production Engineers
MISecM	Member of The Institute of Security Management
MITD	Member Institute of Training and Development
MITE	Member, Institute of Technical Engineers
MLDR	Mountain Leader
MLITT	Master of Letters
ML2	Mountain Leader 2 (Rm)
MNI	Member, Nautical Institute
MNZIS	Member of The New Zealand Institute of Surveyors
MOR	Heavy Weapons Mortar Course
MOrth	Master of Orthodontics
MPH	Master of Public Health
MPhil	Master of Philosophy
MPS	Member, Pharmaceutical Society
MRAeS	Member, Royal Aeronautical Society
MRCGP	Member, Royal College of General Practitioners
MRCOG	Member, Royal College Obstetricians & Gynaecologists
MRCP	Member, Royal College of Physicians, London
MRCP(UK)	Member, Royal College of Physicians

MRCPath	Member, Royal College of Pathologists
MRCPE	Member, Royal College of Physicians, Edinburgh
MRCPGlas	Member, Royal College of Physicians and Surgeons of Glasgow
MRCPI	Member, Royal College of Physicians of Ireland
MRCPsych	Member, Royal College of Phsyciatrists
MRCS	Member, Royal College of Surgeons of England
MRIC	Member, Royal Institute of Chemistry
MRIN	Member, Royal Institute of Navigation
MRINA	Member, Royal Institute of Naval Architects
MS	Master of Surgery
MSc	Master of Science
MScD	Master of Dental Science
MSE	Member, Society of Engineers
MSRP	Member of The Society For Radiological Protection
MTO	Motor Transport Officer
MW	Mine Warfare
n	Frigate Navigating Officer's Course
N	Navigation
(N)	Specialist in Nuclear Medicine
nadc	Nato Defence College Course Over 12 Months
ndc	National Defence College
NInstC	Nuclear Instrument Calibration Course
nrf	Qualified, Nato Research Fellowship
O	Observer
O U/T	Observer Under Training
(O/M)	Specialist in Occupational Medicine
ocds(Can)	Qualified Canadian National Defence College
ocds(Ind)	Qualified Indian National Defence College
ocds(No)	Qualified, Norwegian Defence College
ocds(Pak)	Qualified Pakistan National Defence College
ocds(US)	Qualified TheUnited States National War College
ocds(USN)	Qualified, United States Naval War College
odc(Aus)	Qualified Australia Joint Services Staff College
odc(Fr)	Qualified French Cours Superieur Interarmees
odc(US)	Qualified United States Armed Forces Staff College
OHNC	Occupational Health Nursing Certificate
ONC	Orthopaedic Nursing
OPHTH	Opthalmic
osc	Qualified Overseas Staff College
osc(Nig)	Qualified Nigerian Command & Staff College
osc(us)	Qualified, Usmc Command & Staff College
(OSM)	Specialist in Oral Surgery/Oral Medicine
OTSPEC	Operating Theatre Specialist
P	Pilot
P U/T	Pilot Under Training
(P)	Physiotherapist
PADJT	Parade Adjutant
pce	Passed Command Examinations
pce(sm)	Passed Command Examinations (Sm)
pcea	Passed Command Examinations (Air)

(PD)	Pharmacy Dispenser
pdm	Principal Director of Music
PGCE	Post Graduate Certificate of Education
PH	Helicopter Pilot
PhD	Doctor of Philosophy
PHOT	Photography
PI	Photographic Interpreter
PR	Plotting & Radar
psc	Passed Staff Course
psc(a)	Passed Staff Course (Raf)
psc(m)	Passed Staff Course (Army)
PT	Physical Training
ptsc	Completed Technical Staff Course at The Rmsc Shrivenham
PWO	Principal Warfare Officer
PWO A3	Pwo A 3rd Job
PWO(A)	Principal Warfare Officer Above Water
PWO(C)	Principal Warfare Officer Communications
PWO(N)	Principal Warfare Officer Navigation
PWO(U)	Principal Warfare Officer Underwater
(RAD)	Radiographer
rcds	Royal College of Defence Studies
RCPS(Glas)	Royal College of Phsicians and Surgeons of Glasgow
RCS	Royal College of Surgeons of England
RCSEd	Royal College of Surgeons of Edinburgh
REG	Regulating
REGM	Registered Midwife
(RGN)	Registered General Nurse
RL	Reconnaissance Leader
RMN	Registered Mental Nurse
RMP1	Pilot 1
RMP2	Pilot 2
RNT	Registered Nurse Tutor
RSCNO	Registered Sick Childrens Nurse
S	Supply and Secretariat
(S)	Stores
(SA)	Senior Specialist in Anaesthetics
(SA/E)	Senior Specialist in Accident/Emergency
SBS	Special Boat Squadron
SCM	State Certified Midwife
SEC	Secretarial
(SGS)	Senior Specialist in General Surgery
SM	Sm Qualified
SM(G)	Submarine (Gunnery)
SM(N)	Submarine (Navigation)
(SM)	Senior Specialist in General Medicine
SMTAS	Submarine Torpedo Anti-Submarine
(SO)	Senior Specialist in Opthalmology
(SO/M)	Senior Specialist in Occupational Medicine
(SO/S)	Senior Specialist in Orthopaedic Surgery
(SOSM)	Senior Specialist in Oral Surgery/Oral Medicine

sowc	Senior Officer's War Course
(SP/M)	Senior Specialist in Rheumatology and Rehabilitation
sq	Rm Major Staff Qualified After Holding Two Specified Staff Appointments
(SX)	Senior Specialist in Radiology
tacsc	Territorial Army Command and Staff Course
TAS	Torpedo Anti-Submarine
AS#	Torpedo Anti-Submarine Basic
TEng	Certificate of Technical Engineering
tp	Qualified Test Pilots Course
(W)	Writer
(X)	Specialist in Radiology
WE	Weapons Engineering
WESM	Weapon Engineering (Submarine)
WTO	Weapon Training Officer
X	Executive

ABBREVIATIONS OF PLACE WHERE OFFICER IS SERVING

WHEN NOT SERVING AT SEA

AACC MID WALLOP	Army Air Corps Centre Middle Wallop
ACDS OR (SEA)	Assistant Chief of Defence Staff Operational Requirement (Sea Systems)
ACDS OR(AIR)	OR34a (Air)
ACDS OR(LAND)	Assistant Chief of the Defence Staff Operational Requirements (Land Sytems)
ACDS(LOGISTICS)	Assistant Chief of Defence Staff (Logistics)
ACDS(O/SEAS)	Assistant Chief of Defence Staff (Overseas)
ACDS(OPS/SY)	Assistant Chief of Defence Staff (Operations & Security)
ACDS(PERS/RES)	Assistant Chief of the Defence Staff (Personnel and Reserves)
ACDS(POL&NUC)	Assistant Chief of Defence Staff (Policy and Nuclear)
ACDS(POL&NUC)BPN	Assistant Chief of Defence Staff (Policy & Nuclear) Brampton
ACDS(POL&NUC)USA	Assistant Chief of Defence Staff (Policy and Nuclear) USA
ACDS(PROGRAMME)	Assistant Chief of Defence Staff (Programmes)
ACE CENTRAL RGN	Allied Forces Central Europe
ACE SRGN GIBLTAR	Allied Forces Southern Europe (Gibraltar)
ACE SRGN GREECE	Allied Forces Southern Europe (Greece)
ACE SRGN ITALY	Allied Forces Southern Europe (Italy)
ACE SRGN TURKEY	Allied Forces Southern Europe (Turkey)
ADMIN SUP GRP(B)	Administration Support Group (B)
AFNORTHWEST FWD	Headquarters Allied Forces North West Europe (Forward)
ARFPS	Ace Reaction Forces Planning Staff
ASC CAMBERLEY	Army Staff College Camberley
ATTURM	Amphibious Training & Trials Unit Royal Marines
AUS SP POL	Assistant Under Secretary Service Personnel Policy
AUS(IL)	Assistant Under Secretary of State (Infrastructure and Logistics)
AUS(SCT)	Assistant Under Secretary of State (Security and Counter Terrorism)
BALTAP	Baltic Approaches
BDLS AUSTRALIA	British Defence Liaison Staff Australia

BDLS CANADA	British Defence Liaison Staff Canada
BDLS INDIA	British Defence Liaison Staff India
BDS WASHINGTON	British Defence Staff Washington
BF GIBRALTAR(NE)	British Forces Gibraltar (Naval Element)
BMATT S AFRICA	British Military Advisory and Training Team
BRNC RNSU SOTON	Royal Naval Support Unit - University of Southampton
C OF N	Controller of the Navy
CABINET OFFICE	Cabinet Office
CALLIOPE	Royal Naval Reserve Tyne (RN Staff)
CAMBRIA	Royal Naval Reserve South Wales (RN Staff)
CAPT(H) DEVPT	Captain (Hydrographic) Devonport
CAPTAIN RNP TEAM	The Captain Royal Naval Presentation Team
CAPTAIN SM1	Captain First Submarine Squadron
CAPTAIN SM2	Captain Second Submarine Squadron
CAPTPORT CLYDE	Captain of the Port Clyde
CAPTPORT PTSMTH	Captain of the Port Portsmouth
CDO LOG REGT RM	Commando Logistics Regiment Royal Marines
CDP OFFICE	Chief of Defence Procurement's Office
CDRPORT PORTLAND	Commander of the Port (Portland)
CDS/VCDS/COSSEC	Chief of Defence Staff and Vice Chief of Defence Staff
CENTURION	2SL/CNH Centurion
CFLEET OSISOSEAS	CINCFLEET Ocean Surveillance Information System (O/Seas)
CFLT COMMAND SEC	Commander-in-Chief Fleet Command Secretary's Division
CFM ROSYTH	Captain Fleet Maintenance (Rosyth)
CFP SHORE	Captain Fishery Protection Squadron Shore
CFS BATH	Chief of Fleet Support
CINCFLEET CBDE	CINCFLEET Chemical Biological Defence Establishment
CINCFLEET FMS	Commander-in-Chief Fleet (Fleet Management Services)
CINCFLEET MWDC	Maritime Warfare Development Centre
CINCFLEET	Commander-in-Chief Fleet
CINCIBERLANT	Commander in Chief Iberian Atlantic Area
CLYDE MIXMAN2	Clyde Mixed Manning 2
CMDFP	Captain Mine Warfare Diving and Fishery Protection
CNATS	Controller of National Air Traffic Services
CNOCS GROUP	Captain Naval Operational Combat Systems Group
CNS/ACNS	Chief of Naval Staff and Assistant Chief of Naval Staff
CNSA BATH	Commodore Naval Ship Acceptance
CNSA PORTLAND	Commodore Naval Ship Acceptance (Portland)
CNSA PORTSDOWN	Commodore Naval Ship Acceptance (Portsdown)
COM/NBC CLYDE	Commodore and Naval Base Commander
COMACCHIO GP RM	Comacchio Group Royal Marines
COMAW	Commodore Amphibious Warfare
COMBINED ARMS TC	Combined Arms Training Centre
COMCEN SOUTHWICK	Communications Centre Fort Southwick
COMMW NWOOD	Commodore Minor War Vessels and Minewarfare (Northwood)
COMMW SHORE	Commodore Minor War Vessels and Minewarfare (Shore)
COMSTRIKFORSTH	Commander Strike Force South
CON DCN	Controller Defence Communications Network
COPIT PORTLAND	Closure of Portland Implementation team
CSSE LONDON	Chief Strategic Systems Executive

CSSE USA	MOD Chief Strategic Systems Executive (USA)
CSST SHORE DEVPT	Captain Sea & Shore Submarine Training (DEVONPORT)
CSST SHORE FSLN	Captain Sea & Shore Submarine Training
CTCRM BAND	Band of HM Royal Marines Commando Training Centre Royal Marines
CTCRM	Commando Training Centre Royal Marines
CWTA PTSMTH	Captain Weapon Trials and Assessment (Portsmouth)
D DEF SYSTEMS	Directorate of Defence Systems
D PERS	Director of Personnel
D RAD PROT SVCE	Defence Radiological Protection Service
D REL	Director Reliablity
D WORKS (SS)	Director of Works (Strategic Systems)
DA BRIDGETOWN	Defence Attache Bridgetown
DA KIEV	Defence Attache KIEV
DA PEKING	Defence Attache Peking
DA SINGAPORE	Defence Attache Singapore
DADPTC SHRIVNHAM	Defence ADP Training Centre Shrivenham
DARTMOUTH BRNC	Britannia Royal Naval College Dartmouth
DCDS(C)	Deputy Chief of Defence Staff (Commitments)
DCDS(P&P)	Deputy Chief of Defence Staff (Programmes and Personnel)
DCDS(S)	Deputy Chief of Defence Staff (Systems)
DCIS(N)	Directorate of Communication & Information Systems (Navy)
DCTA	Directorate of Clothing & Textiles
DEF DIVING SCHL	Defence Diving School
DEF EX SVCS	Defence Export Services
DEF EXP ORD SCHL	Defence Ordnance Disposal School
DEF NBC CENTRE	Defence Nuclear Biological Chemical Centre
DEF SCH OF LANG	Defence School of Languages
DEFENCE MAT POL	Defence Material Policy
DEVON & DORSETS	1st Battalion Devon and Dorsetshire Regiment
DFCT	Ministry of Defence - Directorate of Foreign and Commonwealth Training
DFP(N) BATH	The Director Future Projects (Naval)
DFS(CIS) BTH	MoD Directorate of Fleet Support(Communications & Information Systems)Bath
DFS(CIS) GOS	Directorate of Fleet Support(Communications & Information Systems)Gosport
DGA(N) ASE SHAWK	Director General Aircraft (Navy) Aircraft Support Executive (Seahawk)
DGA(N) ASE	Director General Aircraft (Navy) Aircraft Support Executive
DGA(N) NAML	DGA (N) Support Executive Naval Aircraft Materials Laboratory
DGA(N) SU LN	Director General Aircraft (Navy) Strategy Unit
DGA(N)ASE MASU	Mobile Aircraft Support Unit
DGA(N)RNHSMP	Director General Aircraft(Navy) RN Helicopter Special Maintenance Party
DGA(N)SU BATH	Director General Aircraft (Navy) Strategy Unit, Bath
DGFS(ES) BATH	Director General Fleet Support (Equipment and Systems) Bath
DGFS(ES) CAM HSE	Director General Fleet Support (Equipment & Systems)
DGFS(ES) PTLAND	Director General Fleet Support (Equipment & Systems) (Portland)
DGFS(ES) PTSMTH	Director General Fleet Support (Equipment ans Systems) Portsmouth
DGFS(S) ILS(N)	Director General Fleet Support (Ships) Bath Integrated Logistic Support (N)
DGFS(SHIPS)BATH	Director General Fleet Support (Ships)
DGFS(SHIPS)DEVPT	Director General Fleet Support Ships (Ships) Devonport
DGFS(SHIPS)PTMTH	Director General Fleet Support (Ships) Portsmouth
DGFS(SHIPS)ROSYH	Director General Fleet Support (Ships) Rosyth
DGICS	Director General Information and Communication Services

DGMA . . . . Director General Manpower Audit
DGNBS . . . . Director General Naval Bases and Supply
DGSM DERBY . . . . Director General Submarines (Derby)
DGSM DNREAY . . . . MOD Director General Submarines (Dounreay)
DGSM LONDON . . . . Director General Submarines (London)
DGSM PTLAND . . . . Director General Submarines (Portland)
DGSS BATH . . . . Director General Surface Ships
DGSS PTSMTH . . . . MOD Director General Surface Ships (Portsmouth)
DGST(N)BR31D . . . . Director General of Supplies & Transport (Naval) Branch.31D
DGST(N)DSFMO . . . . Directorate Services Food Management Organisation
DGSW PARIS . . . . FAMS Project - PARIS
DGSW PTSMTH . . . . Director General Surface Weapons (Portsmouth)
DGSW(N)DVPT . . . . Director General Surface Weapons (Naval) Devonport
DGSWS BARROW . . . . Director General Strategic Weapons Systems (Barrow)
DGSWS BATH . . . . MOD Director General Strategic Weapons Systems (Bath)
DGSWS LONDON . . . . Director General Strategic Weapons Systems
DGUW PTLAND . . . . Director General Underwater Weapons
DHSA . . . . MOD Defence Helicopter Support Authority
DIO . . . . MOD - NATO and European Directorate
DIS RES SHIP ORG . . . . Disposal & Reserve Ships Organisation
DIS . . . . Defence Intelligence Staff
DISS ASHFORD . . . . Defence Intelligence & Security School
DMCS . . . . Directorate of Manpower Consultancy Services
DMEDLUDGERSHALL . . . . Defence Medical Equipment Depot Ludgershall
DMO . . . . Director of MIlitary Operations
DMSD . . . . Defence Medical Services Directorate
DNA BATH . . . . Director Naval Architect (Surface Ships)
DNES . . . . Directorate of Naval Environment and Safety
DNLSD BATH . . . . Directorate of Naval Logistic Staff Duties (BATH)
DNLSD LONDON . . . . Directorate of Naval Logistics Staff Duties (LONDON)
DNO . . . . Director Naval Operations
DNPS . . . . Directorate of Naval Personnel Systems
DNR OUTPORTS . . . . Department of Naval Recruiting (Outports)
DNSD . . . . Director Naval Staff Duties
DNSOM . . . . The Director of Naval Surveying Oceanography and Meteorology
DNST . . . . Director of Naval Shore Telecommunications
DNSY . . . . Directorate of Naval Security
DOR(JS) . . . . Directorate of Operational Requirements (Joint Systems)
DPR STAFF . . . . Defence Public Relations Staff
DRAKE BSO(W) . . . . DRAKE BSO (Waterfront)
DRFC . . . . Director Reserve Forces & Cadets
DSF HEADQUARTERS . . . . Directorate of Special Forces Headquarters
DSSC BATH . . . . Director Surface Ships C (Bath)
DSSC GLASGOW . . . . Director Surface Ships C (Glasgow)
DSSC PTSMTH . . . . Director Surface Ships C (Portsmouth)
DTR BARROW . . . . Director Trident
DTR BATH . . . . MOD Director Trident - Bath
DTR PORTLAND . . . . MOD Director Trident - Portland
EAGLET . . . . Royal Naval Reserve Mersey (RN Staff)
ELANT/NAVNW . . . . CinC Eastern Atlantic Area and Commander Naval Forces Northwest Europe

EXCH ARMY SC(G)	Exchange British Army On the Rhine
EXCHANGE ARMY UK	Exchange UK Army Units
EXCHANGE AUSTLIA	Exchange Service Australian Navy
EXCHANGE BELGIUM	Exchange Service Belgium
EXCHANGE BRAZIL	Exchange Service Brazilian Navy
EXCHANGE CANADA	Exchange Service Canadian Armed Forces
EXCHANGE DENMARK	Exchange Service Denmark
EXCHANGE FRANCE	Exchange Service France
EXCHANGE GERMANY	Exchange Service German Navy
EXCHANGE NLANDS	Exchange Service Netherlands Forces
EXCHANGE NORWAY	Exchange Service Norway
EXCHANGE RAF GER	Exchange Royal Air Force Germany
EXCHANGE RAF UK	Service With the Royal Air Force
EXCHANGE USA	Exchange Service United States
FAAIT MAN ORG VL	Fleet Air Arm Information Technology Management Organisation (Yeovilton)
FIELD GUN FAA	Fleet Air Arm Field Gun Crew
FLT TGT GRP	Fleet Target Group
FLYING FOX	Royal Naval Reserve Severn (RN Staff)
FMDU W DOWN	Royal Army Pay Corps
FO PLYMOUTH COMS	Flag Officer Plymouth (Communications)
FO PLYMOUTH OPS	Flag Officer Plymouth (Operations)
FO PLYMOUTH	Flag Officer Plymouth
FO PORTSMOUTH	Flag Officer Portsmouth
FONA COLLINGWOOD	Flag Officer Naval Aviation (HMS COLLINGWOOD)
FONA CRANWELL	Flag Officer Naval Aviation (Cranwell)
FONA DAEDALUS	Flag Officer Naval Aviation (HMS DAEDALUS)
FONA DARTMOUTH	Flag Officer Naval Aviation (BRNC Dartmouth)
FONA HERON	Flag Officer Naval Aviation (HMS HERON)
FONA LINTON/OUSE	Flag Officer Naval Aviation (Linton On Ouse)
FONA NORTHWOOD	Flag Officer Naval Aviation (Northwood)
FONA OSPREY	Flag Officer Naval Aviation (HMS OSPREY)
FONA SEAHAWK	Flag Officer Naval Aviation (HMS SEAHAWK)
FONA VALLEY	Flag Officer Naval Aviation (Valley)
FONA	Flag Officer Naval Aviation
FORWARD	RNR Communications Training Centre (Birmingham) (RN Staff)
FOSF ENG DEVPT	Surface Flotilla Engineering Staff (Devonport)
FOSF NORTHWOOD	Flag Officer Surface Flotilla (Northwood)
FOSF PHOT UNIT	Flag Officer Surface Flotilla (Photographic Unit)
FOSF ROSYTH	Flag Officer Surface Flotilla (Rosyth)
FOSF	Flag Officer Surface Flotilla
FOSM FASLANE	Flag Officer Submarines (Faslane)
FOSM NORTHWOOD	Flag Officer Submarines (Northwood)
FOSNNI COMMS	Flag Officer Scotland,Northern England and Northern Ireland (Communications)
FOSNNI OPS	Flag Officer Scotland, Northern England and Northern Ireland (Operations)
FOSNNI	Flag Officer Scotland, Northern England and Northern Ireland
FOST COMMS	Flag Officer Sea Training (Communications)
FOST DPORT SHORE	Flag Officer Sea Training
FOST FMG	Flag Officer Sea Training Fleet Maintenance Group
FOST	Flag Officer Sea Training
FS SEC	MOD Fleet Support Secretariat

HERON FLIGHT . . . . HERON Flight
HONG KONG DENTAL . . . . No 10 Dental Group - Royal Army Dental Corps
HOUSING TASK FCE . . . . Housing Task Force Secretariat
HQ ARRC . . . . HQ Ace Rapid Reaction Corps
HQ BF HK . . . . Combined Forces and Joint Service Units Hong Kong
HQ DFTS . . . . HQ Defence Fixed Telecommunications System
HQ DSF . . . . Headquarters Training Special Forces
HQ FIRE SVCS . . . . Headquarters MOD Fire Services
HQ NORTH . . . . Headquarters North
HQ 3 CDO BDE RM . . . . 3 Commando Brigade Royal Marines
HQAFNORTHWEST . . . . Headquarters Allied Forces North West Europe
HQBF CYPRUS . . . . Headquarters British Forces Cyprus
HQBF GIBRALTAR . . . . Headquarters British Forces GIBRALTAR
HQMATO UXBRIDGE . . . . Headquarters Military Air Traffic Operations Uxbridge
HQRM . . . . Headquarters Royal Marines
HYDROG TAUNTON . . . . Hydrographer Taunton
IMS BRUSSELS . . . . International Military Staff, Brussels
INM ALVERSTOKE . . . . Institute of Naval Medicine
JACIG . . . . Joint Arms Control Implementation Group
JARIC . . . . Joint Air Reconnaissance and Intelligence Centre
JATEBRIZENORTON . . . . Joint Air Transport Establishment, RAF Brize Norton
JFOS WILTON . . . . Joint Forces Operating Staff (Wilton)
JMOTS TURNHOUSE . . . . Joint Maritime Operational Training Staff (Turnhouse)
JS PHOT SCHOOL . . . . Joint Services Photographic School
JS SCH OF P I . . . . Joint Services School Of Photographic Interpretation
JS SUB AQUA DC . . . . Joint Services Sub Aqua Diving Centre
JSCSCPT . . . . Joint Service Command and Staff College Project Team
JSDC GREENWICH . . . . Joint Service Defence College Greenwich
JSIO ASHFORD . . . . Joint Service Interrogation Organisation
JSMU HK . . . . Joint Service Medical Unit Hong Kong
JT PLAN STAFF . . . . Joint Planning Staff
JWS POOLE . . . . Joint Warfare Staff, Poole
LANG TRNG(UK) . . . . Language Training (UK)
LOAN ABU DHABI . . . . Loan Abu Dhabi
LOAN BRUNEI . . . . Loan Brunei
LOAN BVI . . . . Loan British Virgin Islands
LOAN CDA ADAC . . . . Centre for Defence Analysis Farnborough
LOAN CDA HLS . . . . Centre for Defence Analysis HLS
LOAN CDA NAG . . . . Loan Centre for Defence Analysis Naval Analysis Group
LOAN CDA OSA . . . . Loan CDA OSA
LOAN CDA OSN . . . . Loan CDA OSN
LOAN DRA BEDFORD . . . . Defence Research Establishment Bedford
LOAN DRA FARN . . . . Defence Research Agency Farnborough
LOAN DRA FRT HAL . . . . Defence Research Agency Fort Halstead
LOAN DRA HASLAR . . . . Defence Research Agency Haslar
LOAN DRA MALVERN . . . . Defence Research Agency Malvern
LOAN DRA PRTSDWN . . . . Defence Research Agency Portsdown
LOAN DRA WNFRITH . . . . Defence Research Agency Winfrith
LOAN DRA WT DRAY . . . . Defence Research Agency West Drayton
LOAN DTEO ABRPTH . . . . Defence Test & Evaluation Organisation Aberporth

LOAN DTEO BSC DN	Defence Test & Evaluation Organisation Boscombe Down
LOAN DTEO CHRTSY	Defence Test & Evaluation Organisation Chertsey
LOAN DTEO KYLE	Defence Test & Evaluation Organisation Kyle
LOAN DTEO PNDINE	Defence Test & Evaluation Organisation Pendine
LOAN DTEO PTSMTH	Defence Test & Evaluation Organisation Portsmouth
LOAN DTEO PYSTCK	Defence Test & Evaluation Organisation Pyestock
LOAN NEW ZEALAND	Loan New Zealand
LOAN OMAN	Loan Oman
LOAN PORTUGAL	Loan Portugal
LOAN RSS BMATT	British Military Advisory Training Team. Barbados
LOAN SAUDI ARAB	Loan Saudi Arabia
LOAN TURKS & C	Loan Turks & Caicos
LOAN UK IND-GEC	Loan UK Industry - GEC
MAS BRUSSELS	Military Agency For Standardisation Brussels
MCTC	Military Corrective Training Centre
MINISTERSOFFICES	Office of the Secretary of State for Defence
MTS	Market Testing Service
NAAFI HQ & REPS	NAAFI Headquarters And Representatives
NACISA	NATO CIS Agency-NACISA
NAIC NORTHOLT	Naval Aeronautical Information Cell
NATO DEF COL	Nato Defence College
NATO MEWSG VL	NATO Multi-Service Electronic Warfare Support Group Yeovilton
NAVAL DRAFTING	Captain Naval Drafting
NAVSOUTH ITALY	Allied Naval Forces Southern Europe (Italy)
NBC PORTSMOUTH	Naval Base Commander
NBC ROSYTH	Naval Base Commander Rosyth
NELSON DTS	Nelson Dental Training School
NELSON RNSETT	The Royal Naval School of Educational and Training Technology (RNSETT)
NEPTUNE SM1	Captain First Submarine Squadron HMS NEPTUNE
NP 1002 DIEGOGA	Naval Party 1002 Diego Garcia
NP 1061	Naval Party 1061 - Royal Naval Liaison Officer -Split
NP 1062	Naval Party 1062 - Royal Naval Liaison Officer -Bari
NP1044	Naval Party 1044 - JHQ Salisbury -Op Hamden
NP1607(BROADSWD)	Royal Naval Advisory & Training Team, Naval Party NP1607(Broadsword)
NRO EE	Naval Regional Officer Eastern England
NS OBERAMMERGAU	United States Army School Oberammergau
NTP 31 FBR	Defence Research Agency (Maritime Division)
NWOOD CIS	Northwood Communications Information Systems
ORDNANCE BOARD	Ordnance Board
PACS	Director Proliferation & Arms Control Secretariat
PARA REGT	Parachute Regiment
PE ASC	MOD Procurement Executive Air Systems Controllerate
PJHQIT	Permanent Joint Headquarters Implementation Team
PORTSMOUTH ACDU	Portsmouth Area Clearance Diving Unit
PORTSMOUTH FMRO	Portsmouth Fleet Maintenance and Repair Organisation
PRESIDENT	Royal Naval Reserve London (RN Staff)
PRESTWICK	Royal Naval Air Station PRESTWICK
PROJECT BOWMAN	Arms Cis Group/Bowman Military Team
RAF AWC	Central Tactics and Trial Organisation Boscombe Down
RAF BENTLEY PRIY	Royal Air Force Bentley Priory

RAF BRACKNELL . . . . Royal Air Force Bracknell
RAF CRANWELL EFS . . . . Royal Air Force College Cranwell (Joint Elementary Flying Training School)
RAF HANDLING SQN . . . . Royal Air Force Handling Squadron
RAF LINTON/OUSE . . . . Royal Air Force Linton-on-Ouse
RAF SHAWBURY . . . . Royal Air Force Shawbury
RAF THATCHAM . . . . Royal Air Force Distribution Authority Thatcham
RAF WEST DRAYTON . . . . Royal Air Force West Drayton
RAF WYTON . . . . Royal Air Force Wyton
RCDS . . . . Royal College of Defence Studies
REGION CADET ORG . . . . Sea Cadet Corps/ Combined Cadet Forces
RM BAND PLYMOUTH . . . . Band of HM Royal Marines Plymouth
RM BAND PTSMTH . . . . Band of HM Royal Marines Portsmouth
RM BAND SCOTLAND . . . . Band of HM Royal Marines Scotland
RM DTS LECONFLD . . . . Royal Marines Driver Training School Leconsfield
RM NORTON MANOR . . . . Royal Marines Norton Manor
RM POOLE . . . . Royal Marines Poole
RM SCHL MUSIC . . . . Royal Marines School of Music
RMB STONEHOUSE . . . . Royal Marine Barracks Stonehouse
RMC OF SCIENCE . . . . Royal Military College of Science Shrivenham
RMR BRISTOL . . . . Royal Marines Reserve Bristol
RMR LONDON . . . . Royal Marines Reserve London
RMR MERSEYSIDE . . . . Royal Marines Reserve Merseyside
RMR SCOTLAND . . . . Royal Marines Reserve Scotland
RMR TYNE . . . . Royal Marines Reserve Tyne
RMSM STAFF BAND . . . . Band of HM Royal Marines, Royal Marines School of Music
RN C AMPORT HSE . . . . Royal Naval Chaplains Amport House
RN HYDROG SCHL . . . . Royal Navy Hydrographic School
RN MSS HASLAR . . . . Royal Naval Medical Staff School Haslar
RNAS CULDROSE . . . . Royal Naval Air Station Culdrose
RNAS PORTLAND . . . . Royal Naval Air Station Portland
RNAS YEOVILTON . . . . Royal Naval Air Station Yeovilton
RNAW PERTH . . . . Royal Naval Aircraft Workshop Perth
RNAY FLEETLANDS . . . . Royal Naval Aircraft Yard Fleetlands
RNC CEN SUP STF . . . . Royal Naval College Greenwich, Central Support Staff
RNC DPT NS&TECH . . . . RN College Greenwich, Department of Nuclear Science and Technology
RNDHU DERRIFORD . . . . Royal Naval District Hospital Unit -Derriford
RNEWOSU . . . . Royal Naval Electronic Warfare Support Unit
RNFSAIC . . . . Royal Naval Flight Safety Centre, Yeovilton
RNH GIB . . . . Royal Naval Hospital Gibraltar (ROOKE)
RNH HASLAR . . . . Royal Naval Hospital Haslar
RNH PLYMOUTH . . . . Royal Naval Hospital Plymouth
RNLO GULF . . . . Royal Naval Liaison Officer (GULF)
RNLO JTF4 . . . . Royal Naval Liaison Officer for Commander Joint Task Force 4,USN
RNSC GREENWICH . . . . Royal Naval Staff College, Greenwich
RNSE CALEDONIA . . . . RNSE Caledonia
RNU CHELTENHAM . . . . . . Royal Naval Unit Government Communciations Headquarters Cheltenham
RNU CRANWELL . . . . Royal Naval Unit Royal Air Force College Cranwell
RNU RAF EDZELL . . . . Royal Naval Unit Royal Air Force Edzell
RNU ST MAWGAN . . . . Royal Naval Unit St Mawgan
ROCLANT PORTUGAL . . . . Regional Operating Centre Atlantic

ROCNORTHWEST	Regional Operating Centre North West
ROSYTH SOSM(R)	Senior Officer Submarine Refitting, Rosyth
ROYAL HOUSEHOLD	Royal Household
SA ANKARA	Service Attache Ankara
SA ATHENS	Service Attache Athens
SA BONN	Service Attache Bonn
SA BRAZIL	Service Attache Brazil
SA CAIRO	Service Attache Cairo
SA CARACAS	Service Attache Caracas
SA COPENHAGEN	Service Attache Copenhagen
SA ISLAMABAD	Service Attache Islamabad
SA LISBON	Service Attache Lisbon
SA MADRID	Service Attache Madrid
SA MALAYSIA	Service Attache Malaysia
SA MOSCOW	Service Attache Moscow
SA MUSCAT	Service Attache Muscat
SA OSLO	Service Attache Oslo
SA PARIS	Service Attache Paris
SA PRETORIA	Service Attache Pretoria
SA RIYADH	Service Attache Riyadh
SA ROME	Service Attache Rome
SA SANTIAGO	Service Attache Santiago
SA SEOUL	Service Attache Seoul
SA SRI LANKA	Service Attache Sri Lanka
SA THE HAGUE	Service Attache the Hague
SA TOKYO	Service Attache Tokyo
SACLANT BELGIUM	Supreme Allied Commander Atlantic, Belgium
SACLANT USA	Supreme Allied Commander Atlantic, USA
SAUDI AFPS SAUDI	Saudi Armed Forces Project Sales Saudi
SAUDI AFPS UK	Saudi Armed Forces Project Sales UK
SAUDI AFPS(SEA)	Saudi Armed Forces Project Sales (sea)
SCEA	Service Children's Education Authority
SCH INF N AVON	School of Infantry Netheravon
SCH OF NAVAL SY	School of Naval Security
SCU LEYDENE ACNS	SCU Leydene ACNS
SHAPE BELGIUM	Supreme Headquarters Allied Powers In Europe (Belgium)
SHERWOOD	RNR Communications Training Centre (Nottingham) (RN Staff)
SMDIRECTORS BATH	Submarine Directors Bath
SMOPS NELSON	School of Maritime Operations - Her Majesty's Ship NELSON
SM3 UPKEEP ROS	Captain Third Submarine Squadron Upkeep Group (Rosyth)
SSC DGSM BATH	SSC Director General Submarines (Bath)
SSPAG	Strategic Systems Performance Analysis Group
STMA	Shore Telecommunications Maintenance Agency
SULTAN AIB	Admiralty Interview Board
SUPT OF DIVING	Superintendent of Diving
TRAINTEAM BRUNEI	Training Team Brunei
TSRO ST GEORGECT	TRI-Service Resettlement Organisation
UKMILREP BRUSS	United Kingdom Military Representative Brussels
UKNMR SHAPE	United Kingdom Military Representative SHAPE
UKNSE AFNORTH NY	United Kingdom National Support Element Allied Forces Northern Europe

UKSU AFSOUTH	United Kingdom Support Unit Allied Forces Southern Europe
UKSU IBERLANT	United Kingdom Support Unit Iberlant
UKSU SHAPE	U K Support Unit Supreme Headquarters Allied Powers In Europe
UN NEW YORK	United Nations New York
UNIKOM	United Nations IRAQ KUWAIT Observation Mission
UNTAT WARMINSTER	United Nations Training Advisory Team
URNU ABERDEEN	University Royal Naval Unit (Aberdeen)
URNU BIRMINGHAM	University Royal Naval Unit -Birmingham
URNU BRISTOL	University Royal Naval Unit (Bristol)
URNU CAMBRIDGE	University Royal Naval Unit - Cambridge
URNU CARDIFF	University Royal Naval Unit - Cardiff
URNU GLASGOW	University Royal Naval Unit (Glasgow)
URNU HULL	University Royal Naval Unit - Hull
URNU LIVERPOOL	University Royal Naval Unit (Liverpool)
URNU LONDON	University Royal Naval Unit (London)
URNU MANCHESTER	University Royal Naval Unit (Manchester)
URNU NEWCASTLE	University Royal Naval Unit -Newcastle-upon-Tyne
URNU OXFORD	University Royal Naval UnitOXFORD
URNU SOUTHAMPTON	University Royal Naval Unit (Southampton)
URNU SUSSEX	University Royal Naval Unit (Sussex)
WEU	Western European Union
WWII COMM TEAM	World War II Commemoration Team
2LI PADERBORN	2 LI Paderborn
2SL/CNH ASHFORD	Defence Intelligence and Security School
2SL/CNH	Second Sea Lord/Commander-in-Chief Naval Home Command
3CDO BDE AIR SQN	3 Commando Brigade Air Squadron
32(THE ROYAL)SQN	Royal Air Force Northolt - 32 The(The Royal) Squadron
40 CDO RM	40 Commando Royal Marines
42 CDO RM	42 Commando Royal Marines
45 CDO RM	45 Commando Royal Marines
539 ASLT SQN RM	539 Assault Squadron Royal Marines
702 SQN OSPREY	702 Naval Air Squadron Her Majesty's Ship OSPREY
705 SQN SEAHAWK	705 Naval Air Squadron Her Majesty's Ship SEAHAWK
750 SQN OBS SCH	750 Naval Air Squadron/ Observers School
771 SK5 SAR	771 Naval Air Squadron (Sea King Mk5) Search & Rescue
772 SK4 SAR	772 Naval Air Squadron (Sea King Mk4) Search & Rescue
815 SQN HQ	815 Headquarters Naval Air Squadron, Her Majesty's Ship OSPREY
848 SQN HERON	848 Naval Air Squadron
849 SQN HQ	849 Naval Air Squadron Headquarters
899 SQN HERON	899 Naval Air Squadron Her Majesty's Ship HERON

P
Physicians, Honorary to the Queen 3

Q
Quenn Alexandra's Royal Naval Nursing Service
Seniority List 196

R
Rear Admiral of the United Kingdom 1
Royal Fleet Auxiliary Officers 137
Royal Family,Members of 1
Royal Marines 188
Royal Marines Seniority List 189
Royal Marines Special Duties List 194
Royal Marines Reserves 260
Royal Naval Reserves
Alphabetical Index of Officers 243

S
Sea Cadet Corps 202
Special Duties List 169
Supplementary List 175
Ships Agents - Naval Agency & Distribution
Act 1864 214
Ships Establishments & units of the
Royal Navy
HM Shore Etablishments 215
HM Ships 217
RN Fishery Protection & Mine-
Countermeasures Sqadrons 222
RN/RM Air Squadrons 223
RNR Units 224
RM Estb & Cdo Units 225
RMR Units 226
RFA Service 227
Director General of Supplies and Transport 228
Surgeons Honorary to the Queen 3

V
Vice Admiral of the United Kingdom &
Lieutenant of the Admiralty 1